The Collector's Complete Dictionary
of American Antiques

Books by Frances Phipps

Colonial Kitchens, Their Furnishings and Their Gardens
The Collector's Complete Dictionary of American Antiques

The Collector's Complete Dictionary

of

American Antiques

by Frances Phipps

Doubleday & Company, Inc. / Garden City, New York

1974

ISBN: 0-385-03337-0
Library of Congress Catalog Card Number 72–97257

For

Dorothy L. Shapleigh Taylor and Virginia L. Donaldson

who provided the original incentives

Contents

Key to Abbreviations of Dictionary Sources Cited

(B)   *Dictionarium Britannicum,* Nathaniel Bailey, 1730 and 1775.

(C)   *Cyclopaedia,* Ephraim Chambers, 1751.

(H)   *Dictionary of Archaic and Provincial Words,* J. O. Halliwell, 1847.

(J)   *Dictionary of the English Language,* Samuel Johnson, 1755.

(M)   *New Complete Dictionary of the Arts and Sciences,* Erasmus Middleton, 1778.

(W)   *A Compendious Dictionary of the English Language,* Noah Webster, 1806.

Other sources are listed in full under each item.

From Discovery to Revolution

For many Americans throughout the eighteenth century and the first half of the nineteenth, who lived in settled communities along the Atlantic Coast, it seemed sometimes, as Lucy Larcom wrote of growing up in Beverly, Massachusetts, that "the sea was [our] nearest neighbor. It penetrated to every fireside, claiming close intimacy with every home and heart . . ." In New England towns "men talked about a voyage to Calcutta, or Hong-Kong, or 'up the Straits'—meaning Gibraltar and the Mediterranean—as if it were not much more than going to the next village. It seemed as if neighbors lived over there across the water; we breathed the air of foreign countries, curiously interblended with our own.

"The women of well-to-do families had Canton crape shawls and Smyrna silks and Turk satins, for Sabbath-day wear, which somebody had brought home for them. Mantel-pieces were adorned with nautilus and conchshells, and with branches and fans of coral; and children had foreign curiosities and treasures of the sea for playthings.

"We were accustomed to seeing barrels full of cocoanuts rolled about; and there were jars of preserved tropical fruits, tamarinds, ginger-root, and other spicy appetizers, almost as common as barberries and cranberries, in the cupboards of most housekeepers.

"And we had also many living reminders of strange lands across the sea. Green parrots went scolding and laughing down the thimbleberry hedges that bordered the cornfields, as much at home out of doors as within. Java sparrows and canaries and other tropical song-birds poured their music out of sunny windows into the street, delighting the ears of passing school children long before the robins came. Now and then somebody's pet monkey would escape along the stone walls and shed-roofs, and try to hide from his boy-persecutors by dodging behind a chimney, or by slipping through an open scuttle, to the terror and delight of juveniles whose premises he invaded. [Then] the history of the United States could only tell the story of the American Revolution, of the War of 1812." *A New England Girlhood, Outlined from Memory* (Boston, 1889).

A study of newspaper advertisements of the Colonial and Early Federal periods confirms the fact that many household furnishings used by early Americans were imported from England. It was not simply a matter of choice and taste, but of common sense as well, for until after 1800 numerous articles could be made in

Britain and exported here less expensively than they could be produced here. Perusal of old newspapers and journals reveals also the reason for our two broad classifications of American antiques today: the accomplished work of the expert cabinetmaker and the simple work of the countryman. Until the continent was spanned, the urbane, cosmopolitan sense of which Lucy Larcom wrote could not extend far beyond the settled coastal towns. So long as frontier settlements still were being established there were those who relied only on their own ingenuity, who lived in a lonely world of their own making, almost totally independent of men or markets, just as had those who first sailed here in the early seventeenth century.

Thus, in 1830 Frances Trollope, English traveler and a keen observer then living outside Cincinnati, commenting on the life she saw, said, "We visited one farm [whose inhabitants were entirely dependent] upon their own resources. It was a partial clearing in the very heart of the forest . . . A noble field of Indian corn stretched away on one side . . . Immediately before the house was a small potatoe garden, with a few peach and apple trees. The house was built of logs, and consisted of two rooms, besides a lean-to, that was used as a kitchen. Both rooms were comfortably furnished with good beds, drawers, Ec. The farmer's wife, and a young woman who looked like her sister, were spinning, and three little children were playing about. [She] told me that they spun and wove all the cotton and woollen garments of the family, and knit all the stockings; her husband . . . made all the shoes. She manufactured all the soap and candles they used, and prepared her sugar from the sugar trees on the farm. All she wanted with money, she said, was to buy coffee, tea, and whiskey, and she could get enough any day by sending a batch of butter and chickens to market. I have been minute in the description of this forest farm," Mrs. Trollope continued, "I think it the best specimen I saw of the backwoods independency of which so much is said in America. These people were indeed independent . . . and they eat and drink abundantly, but yet it seemed to me that there was something awful and almost unnatural in their loneliness." *Domestic Manners of the Americans* (London, 1832).

Well-to-do merchant-shippers and landowners had more in common than some of them may have wished to admit with the solitary frontier cabin dweller. Never far from the frontier and an awareness of the wealth that so much still-to-be-developed land represented, seventeenth- and eighteenth-century colonists scarcely envisioned the industrial civilization that would develop in the nineteenth and twentieth centuries. Thus, despite the fact that urban centers were developing steadily all along the Atlantic Coast, emotionally if not pragmatically, many wealthy colonists continued to dream, as did Thomas Jefferson, of a new federation of states that would continue eminently agricultural, at least in its social philosophy.

Jefferson expressed the inherent desires of many well-to-do Americans, North and South, when he wrote near the end of the Revolutionary War period, that although "our commerce has suffered very much from the beginning of the present conflict [importation of furnishings from abroad would be resumed once the war was concluded] such is our attachment to agriculture and such our preference for foreign manufactures, that be it wise or unwise, our people will certainly return as soon as they can, to the raising of raw materials and exchanging them for finer manufactures than they are able to execute themselves.

"The political economists of Europe have established a principle that every state should endeavour to manufacture for itself, [but in Europe] manufacture must be resorted to of necessity, not of choice, to support the surplus of their people. [Here] we have an immensity of land courting the industry of the husbandman. [It is] best then that all our citizens should be employed in its improvement [for] those that labour in the earth are the chosen people of God, if ever he had a chosen people . . . [thus even though] the natural progress and consequences of the arts has sometimes been retarded [by lack of manufacture] while we have land to labour, let us never wish to see our citizens occupied at a work-bench, or twirling a distaff . . . Let our work-shops remain in Europe. It is better to carry provisions and materials to workmen there, than bring them to the provisions and materials, and with them their manners and principles." *Notes on the State of Virginia* (London, 1787; Richmond, 1853).

Jefferson's statement was, of course, more wishful than accurate; it expressed a yearning for an age already swiftly passing, rather than a prophecy of the one to come. The end of the Revolutionary War saw the full blossoming of a new American pride. Colonists had battled for, and won the right to, a separate national identity—to be exemplified not only in a system of government but in the new economy needed to sustain that government.

> *I am always sorry when any language is lost, because languages are the pedigrees of nations.*
> Samuel Johnson, quoted by James Boswell, *Journal of a Tour to the Hebrides* (London, 1785).

In order to encompass as many as possible of the variations in our early styles, to include those articles made at home and by village joiners or smiths, as well as those designed and turned to order by the skilled urban craftsman for well-to-do patrons, the terms given here are those we are familiar with today; their origin and original usage are then clarified and exemplified through extracts from primary sources. Many definitions are from the dictionaries that were used in this country; such attributions are in this book indicated by code letters (see "Key to Abbreviations of Dictionary Sources Cited," page ix).

The newspaper advertisements from Boston, Massachusetts, to Charleston, South Carolina, herein quoted, include advertisements placed by merchants now better known in other roles, as John Hancock, Paul Revere, Benjamin Franklin, and Benedict Arnold, and, of course, also by the men whose names today are synonymous with prized antiques: the Danforths and Boardmans, William Henry Stiegel, Simon Willard, among many others. Other quotations are from estate inventories, invoices, and, of course, the books and magazines read by earlier Americans. These are included to illustrate terms, the use of which has not changed over three centuries, as well as to clarify the many changes in descriptive terms employed by collectors during the last century.

To show the range of styles we now recognize as "antique," the 1,017 illustrations in this book are all of documented furnishings that were made or imported for use in this country between 1640 and 1840, the years from the Pilgrim Century of Discovery and Exploration to the beginning of the Industrial Revolution.

Higganum, Connecticut   F.P.

Illustration Credits

Photographic illustrations are used through the courtesy of the Antiquarian & Landmarks Society, Inc., Hartford, Connecticut, photographers, Louis R. Frohman (interior and exterior settings) Richard Gipstein and Susan Hansen (items)—the Connecticut Historical Society, Inc., Hartford, Connecticut, photographers, Irving Bloomstran and T. R. Harlow—the Henry Francis du Pont Winterthur Museum, Winterthur, Delaware, photographer, Gilbert Ask—Colonial Williamsburg, Williamsburg, Virginia. Items from the author's own collection were photographed by Susan Hansen; various other photographs are by Einar Chindmark, *The Hartford Times,* Hartford, Connecticut, and R. Scudder Smith, *The Newtown Bee,* Newtown, Connecticut. Those lent by individual private collectors are identified in the captions. New drawings for Chapter 5 and Chapter 12, (ARMORIAL BEARINGS) are by Susan Hansen.

Acknowledgments

The author expresses deepest appreciation to all those who have given so generously and unselfishly of time and knowledge to this project, especially Arthur W. Leibundguth, Director, the Antiquarian & Landmarks Society, Inc., of Connecticut, for the use of his research notes on the crafts of eighteenth-century Philadelphia, Charleston, and New York, and to the Society for permission to photograph its collections of furnishings—to Mrs. Nancy Goyne Evans, Registrar, the Henry Francis du Pont Winterthur Museum, Winterthur, Delaware—to Thompson R. Harlow, Director, and Mrs. Joan Friedland, Registrar, of the Connecticut Historical Society, Inc.—to Susan C. Finlay, Administrator, Wethersfield properties, National Society of Colonial Dames in the State of Connecticut—to John F. Page, Director, the New Hampshire State Historical Society, Inc.—to Henry Maynard, former Curator of American Arts, the Wadsworth Atheneum, Hartford, Connecticut—to Tim and Betsy Trace of Peekskill, New York, for supplying "impossible to find" books—to Nat. A. Sestero, Managing Editor, and Einar Chindmark, Chief Photographer, the *Hartford Times*—to those friends and family members at home in Charleston and Higganum who assumed additional responsibilities so that deadlines could be met, Florence Walker Singler, Kathryn Walker Robertson, Elizabeth Forbes, Sarah Sprague Marvin, Florence, Richard, and Mary Hickish—and to the many others who have helped along the way by asking or answering questions about antique houses and furnishings and the way our ancestors lived.

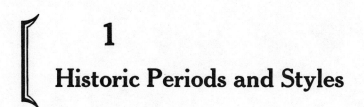

1
Historic Periods and Styles

"The eye is always in search of beauty," the ancient Roman architect, Vitruvius, wrote twenty centuries ago, and man's desire and ability to translate that need first into a design and then into tangible form always have been regarded as direct evidence of the advancement of each society in each age. However, "There are two things to be principally considered, first, the merit of the Design itself, and secondly, the Facility of putting it into Execution," Robert Manwaring, *The Cabinet and Chair-Maker's Real Friend and Companion* (London, 1765).

Thus, while the designer's intuitive genius and innovative skill have provided each generation with patterns reflecting the contemporary understanding of beauty, from the standpoint of the collector of tangible art, the dexterity of the craftsman is of equal importance. Only through the work of the joiner and turner, the carver and decorator, can style be given substance, the stone or wood or metal acquire the special grace of line and the beauty of form that create a pleasing, decorative object as well as a utilitarian piece of house furniture.

The English furniture and furnishings brought or made here during the seventeenth century may be divided into two broad categories of style. During the first half of the century, the solid, rectilinear more-useful-than-elegant styles of the Elizabethan and Jacobean eras continued in use, followed by those of the brief, austere Puritan or Commonwealth period. During the second half of the century our furnishings reflected the more delicate and skillfully contrived designs of the English Restoration period.

With the return to the throne in 1660 of the Stuart King Charles II "all the world [was] in a merry mood," Samuel Pepys declared, and the desire of the new court for luxurious appointments prompted a stylistic rebellion, a drawing away from the massive architectural furniture of the first half of the century. At the court and in the homes of the very wealthy, the old, heavily carved oak pieces were replaced by more lightly proportioned and colorfully decorated furnishings. English craftsmen were influenced by the skilled European cabinetmakers who then were being encouraged to work in London. As a result, English joiners and cabinetmakers were, in John Evelyn's often-quoted critique, happily no longer "very vulgar and pitiful artists [but] are now come to produce works as curious for the fitting, and admirable for their dexterity in contriving, as any we meet with abroad." "An Account of Architects and Architecture," *The Miscellaneous Writings of John Evelyn,* ed., William Upcott (London, 1825). Those fashionable new Restoration styles in walnut, ornamented with handsome veneers and marquetry work could be afforded, of course, only by a relative few; in the average home, whether in England or colonial America, the work of the village joiner continued in favor well into the eighteenth century.

From the early-seventeenth-century settlements through the eighteenth-century establishment of the Republic, the furniture and decorative designs used in America basically were those popular in England, whether pieces were ordered by

The massively carved wainscot or oak great chair of the early seventeenth century, medieval in appearance, was typical of the type used in England and brought here by well-to-do settlers. The example pictured is believed to have been used in New England about 1630–40. (Courtesy, Connecticut Historical Society, Inc.)

An excellent example of the ladder or slat-back mushroom armchair turned by the New England country chairmaker of the early eighteenth century. (Courtesy, Connecticut Historical Society, Inc.)

colonists from English workshops or made here following patterns shown in current London design books. Those who could afford the cost of importing fine furniture ordered it made in the fashionable wood of the time. The less-affluent colonist ordered his home furnishings from his neighbor craftsmen, or made them himself from indigenous woods.

By the end of the Colonial period, well-made American furniture and decorative objects, however much influenced by the style leadership of London and Paris, had acquired a simplicity and refinement of line easily identifiable as our own: politically, philosophically, materially, and artistically, we had proven that, as Adam Smith wrote in *An Inquiry Into the Nature and Causes of the Wealth of Nations* (London, 1776), "The colony of a civilized nation which takes possession either of a waste country, or of one so thinly inhabited that the natives easily give place to the new settlers, advances more rapidly to wealth and greatness than any other human society."

Today, whatever its original shop origin, we recognize each of those now-antique furnishings by its design, and value it according to the extent of the maker's ability to interpret the style requirements of the period.

The broadest classifications of style generally used by collectors today are those designating the principal or most fashionable wood of the period. Obviously, other woods also were used for many pieces of early furniture, decorative objects, and utensils. (See Chapter 4.) The three major "wood categories" preferred by wealthy Englishmen, at home or in the colonies, were oak, walnut, and mahogany. The more definitive style names used within these great ages are noted in the accompanying table and glossary:

The New England or Boston chair of the second quarter of the eighteenth century depended on brass studs and bright leathers in seat and back for richness of appearance. Such chairs were favorites up and down the Atlantic Coast, however, and were ordered by merchants in Philadelphia and Baltimore for their customers in those more southerly cities. (Courtesy, Connecticut Historical Society, Inc.)

Cherry and pine armchair with slip seat; possibly made by Eliphalet Chapin (1741–1807). Superb arms terminate in handsomely carved knuckled and scrolled handholds. The tightly interwoven splat is set above a base shaped as are some Gothic-back chairs. The cross motif is not common in New England, although it is found in some Philadelphia and New York Chippendale-inspired chair designs. (Courtesy, Connecticut Historical Society, Inc.)

The Oak Age, 1540–1660

Historic Periods	*Associated Names*	
1500–60	Elizabethan or Early Tudor	
1560–1600	Late Tudor	
1600–50	Jacobean or Early Stuart	
1650–60	Commonwealth	Puritan
		Cromwellian

The Walnut Age, 1660–1730

1660–90	Restoration; Carolean or Stuart; Late Jacobean
1690–1700	William and Mary
1700–30	Queen Anne; Early Georgian

The Mahogany Age, 1730–1840

1730–1810   Georgian; Classic Revival

1810–30   Regency; Greek Revival; Empire

1830–60   Early Victorian; Gothic Revival

ADAM STYLE

Specifically, the name refers to the work and influence on others' work (such as that of Hepplewhite) of two architects and designers, Robert and James Adam. More than any other individuals they were responsible for the classical revival of the second half of the eighteenth century. These eminently talented brothers provided co-ordinated plans for the furniture and decoration of fine private homes. They provided designs for everything from ceiling moldings, chimney-surrounds, and window frames to drapery and furniture fabrics, and carpeting, as well as for the furniture itself. Their work and name became synonymous with the period's most tasteful adaptations of classic Greek and Roman motifs. Of their work, they wrote, "we have adopted a beautiful variety of light mouldings, gracefully formed, delicately enriched and arranged with propriety and skill. We have introduced a great diversity of ceilings, friezes, and decorated pilasters, and have added grace

Cherry armchair with scarlet morocco seat, was made in 1796 by Lemuel Adams for the new Connecticut State House Senate Chamber and typifies the restrained elegance of the American interpretation of the Neo-Classic period, more commonly called the Federal period in this country. (Courtesy, Connecticut Historical Society, Inc.)

and beauty to the whole, by a mixture of grotesque stucco and painted ornaments . . . We flatter ourselves we have been able to seize, with some degree of success, the beautiful spirit of antiquity, and to transfuse it, with novelty and variety, through all our numerous works." Robert and James Adam, *Works in Architecture* (London, 1773–79, 1822).

This American carved press cupboard of the early seventeenth century was patterned after those remembered from the halls of English homes. Used for the display of plate or pewter on its top board and shelf, the press also provided storage space for other valuables, and was a major piece of furnishing in better halls, parlors, or chambers. (Courtesy, Connecticut Historical Society, Inc.)

This clothes chest-over-drawers, often today called a blanket chest, is typical of seventeenth-century work in the Connecticut Valley. The tulip-and-sunflower motif, however, was common in New York and Pennsylvania as well as Massachusetts and Connecticut. Many believe it should be called a tulip-and-rose design. The applied bosses were painted black to simulate ebony. (Courtesy, Connecticut Historical Society, Inc.)

BAROQUE STYLE

From the French word for curious or bizarre, and the Portuguese *barocco,* for irregularly shaped pearl, this was a general term for the lavish, extravagant elaboration on classical motifs evolved during the seventeenth century just after the Restoration and continuing in fashion during the early years of the eighteenth century.

CAROLEAN

A term designating the years roughly coinciding with the reign of Charles II (1660–85). (See Restoration Style.)

CHIPPENDALE STYLE

Chippendale Period

The collector's broad designations for fine furniture produced from the mid-1750s through the 1780s, based more or less on designs published in Thomas Chippendale's catalogue, *The Gentleman and Cabinet-Maker's Director,* and the style books of his contemporaries. Each of these mirrored Mid-Georgian reaction against the formal classicism of the Early Georgian period. To many today the term Chippendale Style generally and erroneously signifies richly carved mahogany furniture with cabriole legs terminating in ball-and-claw feet. These Queen Anne

A painted clothes chest-over-drawers made at the turn of the eighteenth century, a type used throughout the first quarter of that age, has applied molding, painted in a darker color, and massive ball feet. (Courtesy, Connecticut Historical Society, Inc.)

The high chest on a frame, commonly called a highboy since the early nineteenth century, is a form developed in this country during the William and Mary period: The cherry wood example illustrated has the pad feet and gently curved cabriole legs first developed shortly thereafter in the Queen Anne era. (Courtesy, Connecticut Historical Society, Inc.)

Fine ropelike gadrooning of the skirt joins broadened knee brackets and handsomely curved legs terminating in strongly shaped claw-and-ball feet of this Georgian or Chippendale period case or chest of drawers. The balls of the feet and the front and side gadrooning are gilded. Cherry with pine as the secondary wood. (Courtesy, Connecticut Historical Society, Inc.)

and Early Georgian design elements are more properly associated with the furniture of the first half of the eighteenth century; indeed the ball-and-claw foot is not shown in any drawing included in the popular *Director*. For his own "new pattern chairs" in the Rococo manner, published in the 1754 *Director*, Chippendale showed a preference for a modified, carved cabriole leg terminating in a scroll foot.

Bold three-dimensional rope-turned corners complement the reverse spiral turning on the finials and shaped bracket feet of this mahogany blocked front chest-over-chest or double chest of the late eighteenth century. (Courtesy, Connecticut Historical Society, Inc.)

Although undoubtedly influenced by the work of Mathias Lock and others, Chippendale's *Director,* originally published in 1752, was the first truly comprehensive pattern book of furniture designs. Its popularity in its own time was attested by the need to reprint in 1754 and the further publication in 1762 of an enlarged third edition.

In addition to his designs in the Rococo manner, Chippendale skillfully and gracefully adapted and blended design elements derived from the ancient Gothic and Chinese motifs then popular, giving each a new lightness of line and delicacy of proportion.

CLASSICAL STYLE

A general term for furniture or other furnishings of the last half of the eighteenth century, based on designs derived from the five classical orders of architecture.

The term "order of architecture" means a method or system of design by which the ratio of proportions of vertical and horizontal members to each other can be determined. The term "members" refers to the principal parts of a classic column: the base or pedestal, the column or shaft, the capital, the entablature.

Generally, ornamentation of the five classic orders was based on stylized plant forms, the obvious exceptions being the Greek fret or labyrinth, and the bead-and-reel motif.

The original Greek orders included the Doric, Ionic, and Corinthian, each of which was adapted by the Romans, who added the Tuscan and Composite orders to the list.

Composite Order. A combination of elements of the Ionic and Corinthian orders; "a medly, or an *amasse* of all the precedent *Ornaments,* making a new kind by stealth, and though the most richly tricked, yet the poorest in this, that he is a borrower of all his Beauty." Henry Wotton, *Elements of Architecture* (London, 1624).

Composite Order, drawing from Thomas Chippendale's *The Gentleman and Cabinet-Maker's Director* (London, 1762).

Corinthian Order. This classic third order of Greek architecture, adopted and modified by the Romans, is chiefly identified today by its use of a stylized acanthus leaf and of volutes in the form of scrolls. (See under ACANTHUS in Chapter 3.) The Corinthian column "is an imitation of the slenderness of a maiden, for the outlines and limbs of maidens, being more slender on account of their tender years, admit of prettier effects in the way of adornment." The first century B.C. Roman architect Marcus Vitruvius Pollio, *Ten Books of Architecture,* translated by Morris Hickey Morgan (Harvard University Press, 1914).

Corinthian Order, drawing from Thomas Chippendale's *The Gentleman and Cabinet-Maker's Director* (London, 1762).

Doric Order. The earliest and simplest of the Greek orders of architecture, the Doric column with its massive fluted shaft and almost severely plain capital, was used in the Parthenon. The Roman adaptation of the Greek design, as seen in the Colosseum, was generally of greater slenderness. Of the origin and design of the Doric column, Vitruvius wrote, "wishing to set up columns in a temple (to Panionion Apollo) but not having rules for their symmetry, and being in search of some way by which they could render them fit to bear a load and also of a satisfactory beauty of appearance, they measured the imprint of a man's foot and compared this with his height. On finding that in a man the foot was one sixth of the height, they applied the same principal to the column, and reared the shaft including the capital, to a height six times its thickness at its base. Thus the Doric column [exhibited] the proportion, strength, and beauty of the body of a man." Ibid.

Doric Order, drawing from Thomas Chippendale's *The Gentleman and Cabinet-Maker's Director* (London, 1762).

Ionic Order. The Ionic column was developed in the ancient Ionian colonies of Greece in Asia Minor. It is distinguished by its spreading, scroll-shaped capital and slender shaft carved with twenty-four flutings. The combination of spiral scrolls, egg-and-dart ornamentation, and cyma molding made it especially popular not only during the Renaissance but in each subsequent period.

Ionic Order, drawing from Thomas Chippendale's *The Gentleman and Cabinet-Maker's Director* (London, 1762).

Tuscan Order. In codifying the Roman orders, the Italians of the sixteenth century established the Tuscan order, a simplified form of the Doric in which the column was not fluted and the capital and entablature were left unadorned.

Tuscan Order, drawing from Thomas Chippendale's *The Gentleman and Cabinet-Maker's Director* (London, 1762).

COLONIAL STYLE, COLONIAL GEORGIAN STYLE

General terms sometimes used to designate furniture and other objects made here during the reigns of George I, George II, and George III prior to 1776. These were colonial variations, often greatly simplified, of the English designs predominant in each period.

COMMONWEALTH FURNITURE

Cromwellian Period

The term sometimes used to designate the austere solid furniture produced during the Civil War or Puritan Revolution in England dating from the time when Charles I was beheaded and a Commonwealth form of government was established in 1649. The period was dominated by Oliver Cromwell who in 1653 was named Lord Protector. The Commonwealth parliament remained in power until the restoration of the monarchy and the coronation of Charles II in 1660.

DIRECTOIRE STYLE

Correctly, the term for transitional French furniture designs based on classic Greco-Roman styles, produced between 1793 and 1804, just prior to the Empire

period. The term is also often applied loosely today to English furniture designs based on Sheraton patterns.

EMPIRE STYLE

A general term designating French furnishings with extravagantly gilded or bronze decoration and ornamentation, produced during the first quarter of the nineteenth century. Specifically, the reference is to the period from 1804 when Napoleon crowned himself Emperor until his abdication and exile to St. Helena in 1815.

English Empire. The collector's term for Regency period, or Greek Revival furnishings developed in England during the first years of the nineteenth century and thus concurrent with the French Empire period.

American Empire. An awkward term, sometimes used for that furniture made here during the early nineteenth century from designs influenced by the popular French fashions of the period. Woods used for this fairly heavy furniture were mahogany, rosewood, and black walnut.

FEDERAL STYLE

Federal Period

The collector's general terms for American furniture and other objects produced during the early years of the Republic, from the 1780s through 1820, and especially for those pieces decorated with a spread eagle, figure of Columbia, thirteen stars, crossed cannons, or a shield incorporating stars and bars. The basic designs of the period were based on Adam and Hepplewhite or classic styles. (See also GREEK REVIVAL.)

GEORGIAN STYLE

A general term for the architecture and furnishings developed in England during the reigns of the Hanoverian monarchs:

George I,	1714–27
George II,	1727–60
George III,	1760–1820

These had as their common denominator adherence to design principles based on the conventional proportions and stylized ornamentation of the classical orders of architecture.

This lengthy span is divided by collectors into the Early-Georgian period, from about 1720 to the 1730s; the Mid-Georgian period of the 1740s through the 1760s; the Late-Georgian period running to the end of the eighteenth century.

Some collectors include also the reign of George IV (1820–30) in this broad category.

The Early-Georgian period, England's greatest era of prosperity, is notable for the introduction of mahogany as the most fashionable of furniture woods. Today we are used to the rich time-darkened brown colors of antique mahogany pieces. When new, however, the reddish hues of mahogany were especially popular, so much so that they were imitated by village craftsmen who stained oak and other light woods with ox blood. In the colonies, native cherry and some maple woods were obvious and natural substitutes for the much more expensive mahoganies. The cabriole leg, handsomely carved at the knee, and finished off with a ball-and-claw foot became increasingly popular during the Early-Georgian years, as were the club foot, paw foot, and scroll foot.

GOTHIC REVIVAL

A term used to describe two periods when medieval designs were revived and adapted for contemporary furniture and decoration: The mid-eighteenth-century fad for the "gothick taste" during the 1750s and 1760s, and the early-nineteenth-century years when "old English" motifs were in vogue.

GREEK REVIVAL

Generally, the years of the 1790s through the 1820s, when designers such as Thomas Sheraton adapted classic Greek decorative motifs in contemporary furniture and architecture.

HEPPLEWHITE STYLE

A general term for furniture developed from designs attributed to George Hepplewhite and which were published after his death by his widow, Alice, in *The Cabinet-Maker and Upholsterer's Guide* (London, 1788). Hepplewhite modified and simplified the style ideas of Robert Adam, providing designs more easily worked out by a great number of cabinetmakers. In this country the term is used for furniture produced from the 1770s through 1810, characterized by light, direct lines, gracefully tapered legs, and fine inlay work.

JACOBEAN

Jacobus is the Latin form of James. A general designation for any of the rectilinear, solid style of furniture made during the reign of James I (1603–25).

The term Late Jacobean sometimes is used to describe pieces produced at the close of the Stuart period and thus coinciding roughly with the reign of James II (1685–88).

PILGRIM CENTURY, PILGRIM FURNITURE

The modern collector's terms for the simple furniture made in New England during the seventeenth century but prior to the colonial adaptation of William and Mary or Queen Anne period styles. So-called Pilgrim furniture thus includes regional adaptations of Jacobean, Cromwellian, and Carolean period designs.

PURITAN PERIOD, PURITAN FURNITURE

Somewhat more specific terms than Pilgrim Century and Pilgrim Furniture in that they are used only to describe the plain, little-ornamented furniture made in England and the colonies in the years just prior to and encompassing the Commonwealth or Cromwellian period, or from about 1650 through the early 1660s.

QUEEN ANNE STYLE

A term memorializing the reign of Anne (1702–14) but used generally to designate English furniture designed and produced during the first quarter of the seventeenth century, and for derivative pieces made in this country as late as the 1730s and 1740s. The period was notable for the introduction in English furniture of the cabriole leg terminating in a spade, club, trifid, or pad foot, for the use of richly grained walnut and decorative veneers, and for generally lighter framing and well-defined curves.

REGENCY STYLE

A rather loose term for a derivative of the Greek Revival style. Regency period furniture reflected the fashionable English interest of the time in classical and Egyptian motifs, before and during the years when George, Prince of Wales, was Regent (1811–20). During this period, concurrent with that of the French Empire, rosewood and mahogany were favorite woods. Black japanning was almost equally popular and was often decorated with gilding, and with brass inlays and mounts. Influential design books of the time included *Household Furniture and Decoration* by Thomas Hope (London, 1807), and *A Collection of Designs for Household Furniture and Interior Decoration* by George Smith (London, 1808).

RESTORATION PERIOD

Specifically the years following the end of the Commonwealth and consequent restoration to the throne of Charles II. Collectors thus use the term to designate furniture or other objects produced during the reigns of both Charles II and James II, or from 1660 to 1688. Thus, Restoration, Carolean, and Stuart are synonymous terms for that happily flamboyant period when once again it was popular and proper to indulge a desire for luxurious appointments. The contemporary satirical poem, *A Voyage to Marryland, or, The Ladies' Dressing Room,* believed to have been written by the versatile John Evelyn, included a description of the furnishings of a bed chamber in one wealthy manor:

You furnish her apartment with . . .
A damask bed, or velvet richly embroidered;
Branches, brassero, cassolets,
A cofre-fort, and cabinets,
Vases of silver, porcelain,
Store to set, and range about the floor;
The chimney furniture of plate
(For iron's now quite out of date);
Tea-table, skreens, trunks and stand;
Large looking-glass, richly japann'd;
An hanging shelf, to which belongs Romances, plays and amorous songs,
Repeating clocks the hour to show . . .

Although oak still was favored for numerous cupboards, paneled pieces, and bedsteads, walnut was the predominantly fashionable wood for Restoration furniture and small decorative furnishings. Olive, cedar, laburnum, prince's-wood, coromandel, and ebony also were popular. It was during this period that upholstered "easy" chairs—arm chairs with cheeks or wings—were introduced.

ROCOCO STYLE

The term was coined from a combination of the French words, *rocailles* (rocks) and *coquilles* (shells) to designate lavish, artificial decoration. Although more graceful and restrained than its predecessor, Rococo nevertheless was a resurgence of the Baroque style. First developed in France during the Early Louis XV period, these exuberant curvilinear designs were popular in England during the mid-eighteenth century. The first to popularize a subdued English version of French Rococo was Mathias Lock in his *New Drawing Book of Ornaments, Shields, Compartments, Masks, etc.* (London, 1740). Such English adaptations of "the French taste" incorporated elaborately carved scrolls, flowers, leaves, rocks and shells, and birds. In 1752 Lock printed a second influential design catalogue, *New Book of Ornaments,* in which a combination of French and Chinese motifs was suggested. Perhaps today the best-known Rococo designs are those included by Thomas Chippendale in *The Gentleman and Cabinet-Maker's Director* (London, 1754). Chippendale's English Rococo patterns were graceful and light and much less ornate than those of the French. Nevertheless, his "Three Designs of Chairs with Ribband-Backs" were accompanied by a somewhat defensive explanation: "Several sets have been made, which have given entire Satisfaction. *If any of the small Ornaments should be Thought superfluous,* They may be left out, without spoiling the Design."

SHERATON STYLE

The collector's broad term for a variety of lightly framed fine mahogany, rosewood, satinwood, and painted Classic-Revival furniture designs produced from the late 1790s through the 1820s. Thomas Sheraton was an excellent draughtsman who sometimes supplied designs to other cabinetmakers. He was not so much an innovator as he was an adapter, refiner, and compiler of others' work. The best of his designs were published in *The Cabinet-Maker's and Upholsterer's Drawing-Book* (London, 1791–94), considered by many the most influential design catalogue of its time. Although Sheraton had been a journeyman cabinetmaker, he apparently never owned his own warehouse, nor does it seem he ever was financially able to own the kind of fine furniture he designed. In 1804, while at work on his *Encyclopedia,* he hired Adam Black (who later published the *Encyclopaedia Britannica*) as a kind of general assistant. Of the then ill designer, Black wrote that Sheraton lived "in an obscure street . . . and looked like a wornout Methodist minister, with threadbare black coat . . . My host seemed a good man, with some talent. He had been a cabinetmaker, was now author and publisher, teacher of drawing, and I believe, occasional preacher." *Memoirs of Adam Black,* ed., Alexander Nicholson (London, 1885).

STUART PERIOD

A broad term, confusing to many, for correctly it covers the long period from 1603 to 1688 (broken from 1649 to 1660 by the Commonwealth or Cromwellian or Puritan years). Thus, the term does not refer to one specific style or period but includes the reigns of James I and the Jacobean Style; the Early Stuart period of Charles I; the Carolean period of Charles II, known also as the Restoration or Late Stuart period, each of which see.

VICTORIAN PERIOD

Historically, the term refers to the lengthy reign of Queen Victoria. Collectors divide these years into three periods:

Early Victorian, 1830–60
Mid-Victorian, 1860–80
Late Victorian, 1880–1901

The Early Victorian era marked the decline of individual hand craftsmanship and the general introduction of mass-produced, machine-made furniture and furnishings. During these years of great enthusiasm for the new power-driven tools, the style evolved was an eclectic conglomeration of Elizabethan, Gothic, and Greco-Roman, with overtones of the Baroque.

WILLIAM AND MARY STYLE

William and Mary Period

The terms refer specifically to the reign of William III (1689–1702), but are used more generally to denote those transition years in English furniture design that bridged the close of the seventeenth century and the first decade of the eighteenth. During this period Flemish, Huguenot, Portuguese, and Dutch craftsmen settled in England and greatly influenced the work of British turners and joiners.

Seventeenth-century hall. The walls of the great hall of the authentically restored 1692 Buttolph Williams house, Wethersfield, Connecticut, were painted white to reflect as much sun, fire, and candlelight as possible. The brass dome or lantern clock, forerunner of the tall-case clock, still keeps time. The oak court cupboard is garnished with pewter chargers of the late seventeenth century, the mantel shelf with dated delft wedding-gift plates. A cherry pipe box on the wall and a flat-bottomed rum bottle on the trestle-foot gate-leg table are reminders of New England hospitality of the period. Squabs or cushions covered in velvet and wool added comfort to the carved, crested, and painted oak chairs common in better houses of the late seventeenth and early eighteenth centuries. (Courtesy, Antiquarian and Landmarks Society, Inc.)

Seventeenth-century chamber. The hall chamber of the four-room Buttolph Williams manor house includes the home's best standing bedstead, with its bed furniture of quilted coverlet, red woolen tester, valance, and curtains. The flame-stitch embroidery of the valance is similar to that used on the day bed—an innovation of the William and Mary period—and on the cushion of the massively crested chair. A jewel casket stands between two late-seventeenth-century mid-drip candlesticks on the table at left. The paneled late-seventeenth-century clothes box or chest under the window is decorated with bosses painted to simulate ebony. (Courtesy, Antiquarian and Landmarks Society, Inc.)

Queen Anne parlor. The Queen Anne style, first popular in England early in the eighteenth century, continued longer in favor in the colonies, and thus well into the 1750s. The Readbourne parlor originally was part of a house built near Centreville, Maryland, in 1733, where it was considered the colony's first mansion. As was customary in such Maryland rooms for entertainment, the panelled walls and bolection molding of the fireplace surround were painted a soft gray-white. The chairs and sofa are in Philadelphia manner, with handsomely carved cabriole legs terminating in claw-and-ball, pad and trifid feet. The popularity of decoration in "the Chinese taste" is reflected in the japanned case of the tall clock and the frame of the looking glass. The tea table is set with salt-glazed teapot, cream pot, cups, and saucers painted in imitation of Chinese porcelain. The pair of quillwork sconces are fitted with silver candle arms made by Jacob Hurd of Boston. The Irish silver chandelier originally was made in the early 1740s for a Galway church. (Courtesy, The Henry Francis du Pont Winterthur Museum.)

Queen Anne chamber. Originally
part of an early-eighteenth-century
home in Cecil County, Maryland, this
chamber has blue-painted,
raised-panel walls as background for
basically New England furnishings.
The pad-foot maple bedstead from
Rhode Island is furnished with mid-
eighteenth-century crewel-embroidered
hangings. The floral-and-stropwork-
pattern cover was owned by Thomas
Hancock, Boston merchant-shipper,
and was inherited by his nephew,
John Hancock, signer of the
Declaration of Independence. The
Rhode Island desk was made about
1750, as was the comb-back Newport
corner chair. The walnut side chair
in the left foreground has the notched,
vase-shaped, and horseshoe seat
associated with Queen Anne furniture
made in Newport. The carpet is a
late-seventeenth-century Ushak.
(Courtesy, The Henry Francis du
Pont Winterthur Museum.)

Mid-eighteenth-century Hudson Valley room. The one-story stone house built by Johannes Hardenbergh near Kerkonkson, New York, in the early 1760s included a kitchen, a parlor, and a bedroom. The bedroom, now restored at Winterthur, Delaware, is furnished with pieces typical of the Hudson Valley work of Dutch settlers. Blue-and-white Dutch delft serves as garniture for the top of the massive, carved, grisaille-decorated Kast or paneled two-door cupboard. The wide rush-seat chairs with trumpet-turned legs and pad feet are of a type known as fiddleback chairs throughout the eighteenth century. The swinging cradle in trestle-foot frame is painted green and yellow. The carpet exemplifies late-eighteenth-century continental needlework. The bed hangings are of blue-and-white resist-dyed English cotton. The clock is a Friesland type popular in the homes of Dutch settlers in New York and Long Island. (Courtesy, Henry Francis du Pont Winterthur Museum.)

Parlor with German influence. One of two rooms in the original stone house built by the Kerschner family in Berks County, Pennsylvania, in the mid-1750s, the parlor shows the influence of German Renaissance architectural designs, brought here by settlers. The long walnut sawbuck table frame and board are set with horn cups, pewter tankards, and wooden plates made in Pennsylvania. The massive walnut schrank is dated 1768, and the painted blanket box or dower chest beneath the window, 1774. The tall-case clock was made by Jacob Graff of Lebanon; the walnut-and-gilt looking glass retains the label, printed in both English and German, of Philadelphia craftsman, John Elliott. (Courtesy, The Henry Francis du Pont Winterthur Museum.)

Bed chamber-sitting room. The soft gray-yellow paneling for this chamber came from Patuxent Manor, the plantation home near Lower Marlboro, Maryland, completed for Charles Grahame about 1744. The setting recalls the seventeenth- and eighteenth-century custom of combining sitting-room appointments with those of the bed chamber. Here a Philadelphia tea or breakfast table is set with transfer-printed English porcelain. The leaf-shape plate holds spoons made by William Homes of Boston. The teakettle on the stand is pewter from Connecticut. Card tables, made in Philadelphia, are set at each side of the high mahogany bed, which is furnished with crewel embroidery once owned by the Penn family. Above the table at right is a rare copy of Paul Revere's 1770 engraving, "A View of Part of the Town of Boston in New-England and Brittish Ships of War Landing Their Troops, 1768." The brass chandelier is from England. (Courtesy, The Henry Francis du Pont Winterthur Museum.)

Mid-Georgian parlor. This setting illustrates in detail the elegance of the Rococo style, exemplified in Thomas Chippendale's design book, *The Gentleman and Cabinet-Maker's Director*, as it was interpreted and combined with such classic elements as those of the fireplace wall with its pedimented mantel and Doric pilasters. Between the pair of Philadelphia sofas is an oval stool; beside each sofa is a carved mahogany stand. The high chest, a furniture form developed in this country and now popularly called a highboy, is an excellent example of crisp, handsome Philadelphia carving and cabinetmaking of the 1760s. The mantel shelf is garnished with Chinese Export porcelain bowls and cut-glass candelabra. The glass-and-ormolu chandelier was made in England. The painting is of *American Ships Off Dover* by Dominic Serres, the French artist, who numbered as chief among his English patrons, George III. (Courtesy, The Henry Francis du Pont Winterthur Museum.)

Southern dining parlor. Charleston, South Carolina, was a major seaport of eighteenth-century America and the room setting shown here reflects that city's trade with other colonies of the British Empire. The three-part dining table came from Massachusetts, and is set with English porcelain and glass for the service of a favorite dessert of the day, syllabub and fresh fruit. As was customary at the time, the cloth had been removed prior to the serving of dessert.

The twelve walnut chairs with pierced splats and pad feet are typical of Rhode Island work, and are believed to have been exported from Newport, a town whose cabinetmakers carried on extensive trade with southern and West Indian ports. The fireplace interior is lined with white delft tiles, a treatment favored in Charleston homes where also a coal-burning grate was used rather than logs and andirons. The double portrait above the fireplace is attributed to Thomas McIlworth who worked in New York in the 1760s. The mahogany side table with an imported marble top, however, is believed to have been made in Charleston.

The room paneling originally was made about 1772 for William Burrows, a prominent attorney, judge, and landholder. Carved foliage decorates the mantel frieze and ornamental framing; the pedimented doorways are ornamented with a dentil cornice. (Courtesy, The Henry Francis du Pont Winterthur Museum.)

Philadelphia elegance. Furniture by highly skilled colonial craftsmen working in Philadelphia just prior to the Revolutionary War is shown in this room, which was originally built and decorated for a Pine Street house. The handsome sample chair near the richly carved mahogany side table is attributed to Benjamin Randolph. The white-and-gold looking glass, hanging between the windows, was owned originally by the Cadwalader family. The cut-glass chandelier was imported from Ireland, but the piecrust center table and the boldly curved easy chairs are American. The portrait is attributed to Thomas McIlworth. (Courtesy, The Henry Francis du Pont Winterthur Museum.)

Farmhouse dining parlor. In the same year that much wealthier colonial merchant-shippers could afford to order furniture "in the newest fashion," others living in inland villages and farmhouses continued to use and make home furnishings in the style of an earlier period. This dining room is from the ten-room "new manor house" built by Deacon Richard Hale in 1776 on his 200-acre farm in Coventry, Connecticut. Nathan Hale's boyhood fowling gun hangs above the fireplace of the pine-paneled wall. The long table is set with family plates and tankards of Connecticut pewter. The copper teakettles belonged to Nathan's sister, Joanna, as did the English luster-decorated soft paste in the standing cupboard. (Courtesy, Antiquarian and Landmarks Society, Inc.)

Federal parlor. Oliver Phelps remodeled a 1765 house in Suffield, Connecticut, during those years of the late 1780s and early 1790s, when his land speculations in the Genesee Valley and in the newly opened lands of western New York and Ohio made him the new nation's wealthiest landowner. The paneling with plaster composition ornament and the Etruscan design of the blue French wallpaper complement the pale tan woodwork and terra-cotta ceiling border. The cherry bookcase and desk inlaid with American eagle designs is attributed to Eliphalet Chapin of East Windsor, Connecticut. The lolling chair, now popularly called a Martha Washington chair, and the shield-back chair at the desk also are of Connecticut origin. The Connecticut cherry stand at the right of the fireplace holds a silver-rimmed English coffee urn dated 1802–3; the table at the left is set with Chinese Export porcelain cups. The carpet is a nineteenth-century Persian. (Courtesy, The Henry Francis du Pont Winterthur Museum.)

Federal dining parlor. Above the eight-legged long New York sideboard is a sketch begun in 1782 by Benjamin West for his commemorative painting of the American Commissioners who met in Paris to negotiate peace terms with England. The painting symbolizes the era of political change here and the beginning of the Federal period. Urn-shaped English knife cases stand on the sideboard with a set of six silver tankards made by Paul Revere. The three-part mahogany dining table is set with Chinese Export porcelain including two glaciers for ice cream. The breakfront, made in Massachusetts about 1800, has painted, gilded, and silver glass panels. The mahogany chairs were made in New York for Victor Marie du Pont. (Courtesy, The Henry Francis du Pont Winterthur Museum.)

Duncan Phyfe parlor. Best known today of American cabinetmakers working during the Federal period is Duncan Phyfe of New York City. In 1807 he sold William Bayard this set of mahogany chairs at $12.50 each. The chairs and settee are upholstered in blue-and-yellow lampas, a nineteenth-century French fabric. The sofa table in front of the cane-back settee is the type often used as a writing table. The card tables with tripod bases were made so that two of the feet swing to balance the table when the leaf is opened for use. Silver-plated Argand lamps stand on the card tables beneath cut-glass wall sconces. (Courtesy, The Henry Francis du Pont Winterthur Museum.)

Empire parlor. Influenced by designs first used in France when Napoleon was Emperor, the Empire style, with its repetitions of ancient classic themes, found quick favor in this country, especially for new homes being built in the so-called Greek Revival style. The woodwork used in this room is from the house built for General Rufus King in Albany, New York, about 1839; the plaster is painted a soft mauve. Porcelain pitchers made by William Ellis Tucker in Philadelphia are set on the shelf of the marble-topped side table with marble column legs and gilded paw feet. The mull window curtains are embroidered with silver stars. The round center pillar-base table has a composition top decorated with a painting of "The Capture of the Pirate Ship *La Gloria*" by the *Cornwallis*. The slipcover of the Klesmos side chair is green silk, the carpet, a green-and-gray Aubusson. (Courtesy, The Henry Francis du Pont Winterthur Museum.)

Empire chamber. Chalk-white woodwork and pale blue plaster walls serve as background for the c. 1815 mahogany sleigh bed, a typically bold example of furniture used here in the early nineteenth century. The regal blue silk drapery above the bed is suspended from a mahogany crown, the dressing table is covered in matching figured silk. The small marble-topped stand at the end of the bed holds alabaster candlesticks and a green silk candle screen. The carpet is a French tapestry weave of multicolored flowers on an olive-brown background. (Courtesy, The Henry Francis du Pont Winterthur Museum.)

2
Rooms – Their Placement and Use

For a man's house is his castle,
*et domus sua cuique est
tutissimum refrugium.*

Sir Edward Coke, *Institutes,* III

Of the tall, narrow houses, reminiscent of those of Jacobean England, built here in the seventeenth century, a seventh-generation American, Leonard Withington, wrote; "There is the old mansion, with every story jutting out, contrary to all the rules of modern architecture, wider at the top than at the foundation; there is the tall well-pole, rising towards the sky, with a good quantity of old iron on the farther end, to balance the bucket when full of water; there is the pear-tree, with the huge grindstone under it; there is the meadow, with its maple grove, from whose recesses on some summer evening, I used to hear the Whippowil; the sun-dial, the pasture, the great rock, the barberry bushes, the lilacs, the sprigs of mullen and elecampane, all, all are present to the mental eye, and are seen through the mist of years with a deeper interest than ever. If the reader will step with me into the house, I will show him the *best room,* with its homemade carpet, carefully woven with strips of cloth, in which the red, blue, and yellow, are nicely adjusted to produce the best effect. I will show him the kitchen, with its vast fireplace, an apartment in itself, collected in which the family was wont to huddle on a cold winter evening, to hear stories of olden time. I can show him the red dresser, with its well-scoured platters, made of pewter, but bright as silver, lessening in rows one above the other. I can present him with a family Bible, bound in buff leather, and printed at Oxford by his Majesty's special command. I can show him the old worn hourglass, standing in two leather loops on a shelf above the fireplace, which my grandfather used to turn exactly at eight o'clock in the evening, that we might be sure to go to bed duly at nine." *The Puritan, A Series of Essays* (Boston, 1836).

So it was that in 1778 the Rev. Erasmus Middleton, editor of the *New Complete Dictionary of Arts and Sciences,* would write, describing the handsome Georgian homes then being built by wealthy Englishmen on both sides of the Atlantic, "If we compare the modern with the old way of building we cannot but wonder at the genius of those times. Our fore-fathers were wont to dwell in houses, most of them with a blind stair-case, low ceilings, and dark windows, the rooms, built at random, without any contrivance, and often with steps from one to another; whereas the genius of our times requires light stair-cases, fine sash-windows, and lofty ceilings, with conveniences far superior to those that houses in ancient days afforded against the weather, and in which the offices may be remote from the parlour and rooms of entertainment and yet in the same house."

The writer perhaps would have approved Mt. Vernon, the home of General and Mrs. Washington. Describing that now-restored house, Amariah Frost wrote in his *Diary* for June 26, 1797, that "Mr. Croker introduced me to [the President] as a gentleman from Massachusetts who wished to see the country and pay his respects. He thanked us and desired us to be seated. His lady also came in and conversed with us very familiarly respecting Boston, Cambridge, the officers of the army, etc. We [had] arrived at the President's seat about 1 o'clock [when] the General was out on horseback viewing his labourers at harvest . . . We viewed the garden and walks, which are very elegant, abounding with many curiosities, fig trees, raisins, limes, oranges, etc., large English mulberries, artichokes, etc.

"The situation of Mount Vernon is pleasant, very nigh the Potomac, not on any post road. We passed a number of gates and long tracts of wood before we came to the most cultivated parts of the General's farm. There are large fields of Indian corn under good cultivation, except the number of trees left for shade and for their growth, yet they prevent the corn from coming to maturity. Planting corn, however, prevents the shrubs from growing and well prepairs the ground for wheat and also for grass when seeded.

"There are beautiful groves arranged in proper order back of both the gardens and rows of trees exactly corresponding with each other, between which and the two gardens is the great green and circular walk fronting northerly from the house and seen at a great distance. The southern part of the house fronts the river.

"The house is long but not high, with a cupola in the centre of the roof. The chamber windows are small, being only 12 lights, 8 by 10, or less, to a window. The lower windows are larger. Two wings and other buildings corresponding to each other on either side, also, a large piazza in the front, add much to the beauty of the house.

"About two o'clock, the President desired us to walk into dinner. We then walked into a room where were Mrs. Law, Mrs. Peters, and a young lady, all granddaughters of Mrs. Washington. The President directed us where to sit (no grace was said). Mrs. Washington sat at the head, the President next to her at her right. The dinner was very good, a small roasted pigg, boiled leg of lamb, roasted fowles, beef, peas, lettice, cucumbers, artichokes, etc., puddings [were served]."

Of course, such lighter, more convenient houses as Mt. Vernon could be afforded by relatively few. The majority of Americans continued to live in houses that first had been built as single one-room homes to which the colonist added as time, actual need, and finances allowed. Many rooms in eighteenth-century houses, and many in those begun in the nineteenth century retain connecting "steps from one to another." True, in each generation, about 10 per cent of our houses were fine structures furnished according to the latest fashion—often to the astonishment of travelers from abroad who noted, as did the English amateur botanist John Josselyn in 1673, that some Bostonians "are damnably rich." Nevertheless, as late as 1807, almost two centuries after settlement, another traveler, Edward Augustus

Kendall, reported great contrast in Boston's three thousand houses. They were, he said, of "much variety, many being mean, but many also of a costly, modern, and elegant architecture and finishing. *All new ones, more than ten feet high,* are now [as a safeguard against fire] required by law to be of brick or stone." *Travels Through the Northern Parts of the United States in 1807 and 1808* (New York, 1809).

Obviously, one-story homes of one or two rooms, their low ceilings averaging seven feet or less in height and with lofts not high enough to stand erect in, continued to be built in the old, long-settled Atlantic Coast towns in the early nineteenth century, much as they had been in the early seventeenth century. Similarly, when taxes were levied in New York City just after the Revolution, such small houses were still taken for granted there: "Every log house with two rooms in which there is a stove or fireplace, to pay 2s for each room. On every other dwelling house which shall contain two rooms as aforesaid, 2s on each room; if three rooms 3s in each room, if four rooms 4s on each room." *New York Daily Advertiser,* March 13, 1787.

Usually it was not until the second generation after settlement, whether in the seventeenth century or the nineteenth century, that many houses showed improvement and additions to the finishing and furnishing of the interiors. Hence, of Vermont, mainly settled after 1800, Hosea Beckley wrote:

"Vermonters have made some advances from the rustic in manners towards the civil; and from the civil towards the elegant; and from the elegant towards the urbane and polished. You see evidence of this in the furniture of their dwellings; their wardrobes and their parlor accommodations. The gourd, so to speak, has given place to the brown earthen pitcher; and this to the plain white glazed [faïence and soft paste] and this again to the porcelain and china. In the place of the hemlock floor, has come the spruce and white pine; to the husk foot-brush has been added the rag and homespun carpet; to this the Brussels; and to the Brussels the Turkish. The tripod [stool] has been followed by the splintered and flag bottomed; and these again by the spring cushioned chair and sofa, on which for indolence and apathy to stretch their limbs. The bedstead of curled maple and polished, they have added to the mattress and hammock. Where they might once have been seen dining over a barrel head, a board placed across it; or on a rough four-legged stool; you may find them at a polished cherry, or mahogany, rolling table.

"The circular [corner] cupboard may yet occupy and fill up one corner of their best apartment; but near it stands the splendid side-board furnished with silver spoons and plate, where once were used pewter and wooden dishes, [and] the trencher." *The History of Vermont, with Descriptions, Physical and Topographical* (Brattleboro, 1846).

Because we have been a nation in which frontier communities continued to be established as late as the first quarter of this century, in many areas we retained the same simple "ancient" building methods and type of furnishings common to early-eighteenth-century coastal settlements. As a result, Bishop Morris, reporting in 1846 on the pioneer or "western style of living," wrote that "When a young married couple commenced housekeeping, from thirty to forty years ago, a very small outfit sufficed, not only to render them comfortable, but to place them on an

ATTENTION RIFLE MEN.
124 Dollars and
160 Acres of Land
BOUNTY,

TO all able bodied active young men who are willing to join the RIFLE corps in defence of their country's injured rights, can have an opportunity by applying to Capt. E. BOARDMAN, near the little Bridge, Hartford ; Lieut. J. BOARDMAN, New-Haven, or Lieut. J. ROBINSON, New-London, Con. They will receive the following articles of uniform cloathing—

    1 Cap,
    1 Stock,
    2 Coats,
    1 Rifle Frock,
    1 Great coat,
    4 Shirts,
    2 pr linen Pantaloons,
    2 pr woollen do.
    2 pr. Stockings,
    2 pr. Socks,
    2 pr. Gaters,
    4 pr Short Boots, and
    1 Blanket,

and will serve under those able and distinguished commanders Cols. CLARK and FORSYTH.

E. BOARDMAN, Capt.
U. S. Rifle corps,
Hartford, Con. June 6th, 1814.   62
N. B. A Drummer, Fifer, and Bugleman wanted immediately.

AN ACT

Whereas by an act of Congress passsed on the third day of March, one thousand eight hundred and fifteen, entitled " an act to provide for the accertaining and surveying of the boundary lines fixed by the Treaty with the Creek Indians, and for othe. purposes," the President of the United States is authorized to cause the lands acquired by the said Treaty to be offered for sal when surveyed ; and whereas the lands north of the Tennessee River have been surveyed.

Therefore, I James Monroe, President of the United States, in conformity with the said act, do hereby declare and make known, that public sales, for the disposal (agreeably to law) of the lands in Alabama Territory, north of the River Tennessee, shall be held at Huntsville, in Madison County, in said Territory, viz. on the first Monday in February next, for the lands contained in the ranges numbered, one, two, three, four, five, and six ; and on the first Monday in March next, for the remainder of the aforesaid lands ; each sale shall remain open for three weeks, and no longer ; the sales shall commence with the first section of the lowest numbers of townships and ranges, and proceed in regular numerical order.

Given under my hand at the City of Washington, the twenty-first day of November, one thousand eight hundred and seventeen.

JAMES MONROE.

By the President :
JOSIAH MEIGS,
Commissionnr of the General Land Office.
Printers of newspapers who publish the Laws of the United States will publish the above for six weeks, and send their bilss with receipts to the General Land Office.   6w44

Advertisement of 1814 reflects government offer of 160 acres of land to all who served in the War of 1812 against England.

Advertisement of New Lands offered for public sale by presidential order, *American Mercury* (Hartford, Connecticut), November 21, 1817.

HEZEKIAH BULL,

EXPECTS shortly to leave this State for the State of Ohio, and requests all persons indebted to him to make payment;—He wishes to engage some young enterprising men to go with him, to settle on New Lands, on advantageous terms, House and other carpenters, Black Smiths, good Axe men &c: He wants to purchase 3 yoak of likely working Cattle.

Hartford, Feb. 15.　　　46

Typical advertisement for the help needed to begin a new settlement, *American Mercury* (Hartford, Connecticut), February 15, 1814.

Abraham Lincoln, an attorney and rising young Whig politician in Springfield, Illinois, purchased this two-room log-and-clay house, built about 1840, for his father and stepmother. The house stands in the same rural setting in southeastern Illinois, now a state park near Charleston.

To those disposed to emigrate to the Southern or Western Country.

NOTICE is hereby given to all those desirous of emigrating to the southern or western section of the Union, that several gentlemen of this city, who have determined to emigrate and having duly appreciated the advantages resulting to an association over individuals in the purchase and settlement of new lands, have drafted *a compact or constitution* for the regulation and government of a company that may be formed; one of the articles of the constitution confines the purchase to *navigable or boatable* waters, and contemplates that from 50 to 100 families will avail themselves of this opportunity to better their situation—and when it is considered that a large tract of land can be purchased at a much less rate than a small one, and more especially, when it is considered with what ease and facility a new country may be settled with the introduction of 100 families into it, and the consequent *immediate* rise of the lands—it is presumed that a company like the one contemplated presents an inducement to industry and enterprize, too engaging, and too obvious to need illustration. Besides Farmers, a good opportunity offers itself to a Physician and Surgeon, as well as to the following artizans, to wit, *Carpenters, Joiners, Wheelwrights, Millwrights, Coopers, Blacksmiths, Hatters, Taylors, Clothiers, Shoemakers, Saddle and Harness Makers, Tanners and Courriers, Brick-Layers, Stone-Cutters, Boat-Builders, &c. &c.* From the zeal already manifested by many of our citizens to embark in the enterprize, it is imagined that no difficulty will be found in getting the stock taken up; but in order to give all an opportunity to hear the constitution read and subscribe, it has been thought advisable to give public notice to all who are desirous of becoming interested, to meet at the tavern of Col. UTLEY in this city at 1 o'clock on Tuesday the 11th of February instant; in the interim, such as may wish to learn the particular provisions of the constitution, and more minutely the objects of the association, will be made acquainted therewith on application at the office of

ISAAC PERKINS.

Hartford, Feb. 3.　　　1

Advertisement for emigrants. *American Mercury* (Hartford, Connecticut), February 11, 1817.

Painted wood desk box. (Courtesy, Antiquarian and Landmarks Society, Inc.)

equality with their friends and neighbors. They needed a log cabin, covered with clapboards, and floored with wooden slabs, called puncheons. The openings between the logs [were] closed with billets of wood and crammed with mortar, to keep all warm and dry—all which a man could erect himself, without any mechanical training, with one day's assistance from his neighbors to raise the logs.

"Usually, one room answered for parlor, sitting-room, dining-room, kitchen, and dormitory, while the potato hole under the puncheons, formed, of course, by excavating the earth for mortar, was a good substitute for a cellar.

"As to furniture, they needed a stationary corner cupboard, formed of upright and transverse pieces of boards, arranged so as to contain upper, lower, and middle shelf, to hold the table ware and eatables. In order to comfort and convenience, it was requisite, also, to have the following articles: one poplar slab table, two poplar or oak rail bedsteads, supplied with suitable bedding, and covered with cross-barred counterpanes of homemade, one of which was for the accommodation of visitors; six splint-bottomed chairs, one long bench, and a few three legged stools were amply sufficient for themselves and friends; a half a dozen pewter plates, as many knives and forks, tin cups, and pewter spoons for ordinary use, and the same number of delf plates, cups, and saucers for special occasions; also, one dish, large enough to hold a piece of pork, bear meat, or venison, with the turneps, hommony, or stewed pumpkin.

"All this table ware was kept in the corner cupboard, and so adjusted as to show off to the best advantage, and indicated that the family were well fixed for com-

Countryman's stool and broad ax. (Courtesy, Antiquarian and Landmarks Society, Inc.)

Hand-shaped oblong wooden chopping bowl.

Carved burl cup. (Courtesy, Antiquarian and Landmarks Society, Inc.)

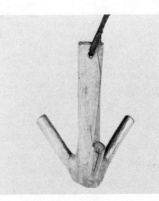

Candle drier whittled from natural tree branch. (Courtesy Antiquarian and Landmarks Society, Inc.)

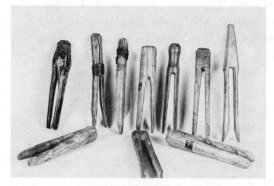

Hickory and maple clothes pins. (Courtesy, Antiquarian and Landmarks Society, Inc.)

Turned lignum vitae table mortar. (Courtesy, Antiquarian and Landmarks Society, Inc.)

Corn shucker made from hickory and leather harness strap.

Large samp or corn mortar. (Courtesy, Antiquarian and Landmarks Society, Inc.)

Cherry and pine worktable. (Courtesy, Antiquarian and Landmarks Society, Inc.)

fortable living. When the weather was too cold to leave the door or the [shutter] window open, sufficient light to answer the purpose came down the broad chimney, and saved the expense of glass lights; and as for andirons, two large stones served as a good substitute. The whole being kept clean and sweet, presented an air of comfort." *The Ladies Repository and Gatherings of the West,* Vol. 6.

Great contrasts in income and location dramatized the diversity of American lives and homes. During the early nineteenth century while frontier families still were building rough new cabins, furnishing them as had the majority of their predecessors two hundred years earlier, Mrs. Trollope wrote of the burgeoning New World metropolis that "In New York City, the dwelling houses of the higher classes are extremely handsome and very richly furnished. Silk or satin furniture is as often, or oftener, seen than chintz; the mirrors are as handsome as in London, the chiffoniers, slabs, and marble tables as elegant; and in addition they have all the pretty tasteful decoration of French porcelaine, and or-molu in much greater abundance, because at a much cheaper rate. Every part of their houses is well carpeted . . . I saw many rooms decorated within, exactly like those of an European *petite maitresse.*

"Little tables, looking and smelling like flower-beds, portfolios, nick-nacks, bronzes, busts, cameos and alabaster vases, illustrated copies of lady-like rhymes bound in silk, and in short, all the pretty coxcomalities of the drawing-room [are] scattered about, with the same profuse and studied negligence as with us." *Domestic Manners of the Americans* (London, 1832).

THE NOMENCLATURE OF ROOMS—
AND OTHER DIVISIONS OF SPACE WITHIN THE HOUSE

AISTRE
The ancient word for house, and more specifically, for the kitchen hearth or main part of the house; the part where the family's living quarters were situated.

ALCOVE
The alcove is "Part of a parlour or chamber separated by pillars, pilasters, or other ornaments, and in which is placed a bed of state or seats for company." (M) "A recess, or part of a chamber, separated by an estrade or partition, and other correspondent ornaments, in which is placed a bed of state, and sometimes seats to entertain company." (J)

ALGATE HOLE
A small recess or niche within a chimney wall, placed at the side, to hold tinder, flints, and small tools, or placed in the back to serve as a kind of warming oven.

ANTI-CHAMBER
"An outer chamber, for strangers to wait in, till the person to be spoken with is at leisure." (M) "The chamber that adds to the chief apartment." (J) "The Anti-Room is an introduction to the drawing-room . . . serving as a place of repose before the general intercourse. Here may be placed a number of sofas of a second order with a piano forte or harp, and other matters of amusement till the company be collected." Thomas Sheraton, *The Cabinet Dictionary* (London, 1803).

APARTMENT
"A portion or part of an house containing the necessary conveniences for a person to reside in it." (M)

Kitchen bedroom as seen through a door of the kitchen of the 1728 Nathaniel Hempsted house, New London, Connecticut. (Courtesy, Antiquarian and Landmarks Society, Inc.)

BEDROOM

In seventeenth- and eighteenth-century America, this was the designation for a small room, usually partitioned off the Kitchen, q.v., or in a back Ell, q.v., and furnished simply with a low post or other plain Bedstead, q.v. Chamber, q.v., designated the larger better-furnished second-floor room now generally called a bedroom.

BUTTERY

The term from *Butta* or *Butt, q.v.,* meaning a large container and hence a storeroom for liquor or casks, and thus, eventually, any room "wherein provisions are laid up." (J) "A room in houses of opulent families appropriated to the use of the butler, and where he deposits table linen, napkins, plate, etc." (M)

CELLAR

The term is from the Latin, *cella,* for "a place underground where stores and liquors are reposited." (J)

CHAMBER

"Any room situated between the lowermost and the uppermost rooms," (M) but generally used to describe the better Bedrooms, q.v., on the second floor of the house. In fine houses, the chamber often was fitted with a Breakfast or Tea Table, Day Bed, qq.v. and comfortable chairs, as well as the Bedstead, q.v., and thus served as a combination of boudoir and Parlor, q.v. "My dinner was noble and enough. I had my house mighty clean and neat; my room below with a good fire in it, my dining room above, and my chamber being made a withdrawing chamber; and [in] my wife's [chamber] a good fire, also." Samuel Pepys, *Diary,* January 13, 1662–63.

CLOSET

"A small private room," (W) such as a home office or room in which to keep records and accounts. "I and my wife up to her closet, to examine her kitchen accounts, and there I took occasion to fall out with her, for her buying a laced handkercher and pinnes without my leave." Samuel Pepys, *Diary,* August 12, 1666. "A small room of privacy and retirement, a private repository of curiousities and valuable things." (J) "I am making up a Bundle of Papers to send you. Put them into my Room . . . I left my best spectacles on the Table. Please to send them to me . . . In my Room on the Folio Shelf between the Clock and our Bedchamber and not far from the Clock, stands a Folio, call'd the *Gardener's Dictionary* by P. Miller. And on the same side of the Room on the Lowest Shelf or lowest but one, near the Middle, and by the side of a little Partition, you will find standing or rather lying on its fore Edge a Quarto Pamphlet, cover'd with blue Paper, call'd a *Treatise of Cyder-Making.* Deliver these two Books to Mr. Parker." (Benjamin Franklin from New York, May 27, 1757, to his wife at Philadelphia.) *Writings of Benjamin Franklin,* ed., A. H. Smyth (New York, 1907).

COCKLOFT

The room or loft at the very top of the house; "the room that is over the garret." (W)

COUNTINGHOUSE

"The room appropriated by traders to their books and accounts." (J)

DAIRY

The word "implies a room where milk is kept, and manufactured into butter and cheese." (M)

DINING ROOM, DINING PARLOR

"The principal apartment of the house; the room where entertainments are made." (J)

    Entertainment: "Conversation; convivial provision; hospitable reception." (J) "Being appropriated for the chief repast, [it] should not be encumbered with any article that would seem to intrude on the accommodation of the guests. The large sideboard, inclosed or surrounded with Ionic pillars, the respectable and substantial looking chairs; the large face glass; the family portraits; the marble fireplaces; and the Wilton carpet, all the furniture that should supply the dining parlour." Thomas Sheraton, *The Cabinet Dictionary* (London, 1803). "After dinner, to hang up my fine pictures in my dining room, which makes it very pretty, and so my wife and I abroad to the King's play-house." Samuel Pepys, *Diary,* August 8, 1664.

DRAWING ROOM

"A room for receiving company." (W) "In [the furniture for] Drawing Rooms, Boudoirs, Anti-Rooms or other dressed apartments, East and West India satin-woods, rose-wood, tulip-wood, and other varieties [of fine woods] Brought from the East, may be used." George Smith, *A Collection of Designs for Household Furniture* (London, 1808).

DRESSING ROOM

"The room in which clothes are put on." (J)

ELL

The word, a corruption of the Latin, *ala,* meaning aisle or wing, was used to describe the one-story lean-to added to the rear of previously completed houses. It generally was built to contain a new or extra kitchen, pantry, storeroom, loom, or other workroom; sometimes a bedroom.

ENTRY

The general term for any "door, gate, passage, Ec. through which we arrive at any place." (M) "A narrow passage, a porch, or small hall." (H)

ESSHOLE

An old term for the ash bin; ess was a colloquialism for ashes, or "the place under the grate to receive them in." (H)

FRONT ROOM

"An apartment in the forepart of the house." (J)

FRUITERY

The name for the "fruit loft [or attic], a repository for [dried] fruit." (J) It should "be inaccessible to any thing of moisture, even to frost." (M)

GALLERY

"A covered place in a house, that is longer than it is broad, which is commonly in the wings of an edifice, where persons may conveniently walk." (M) "Histories, grave stories, and the best works become galleries; where any one may walk, and exercise their

Series of ell rooms, including kitchen, pantry, and other storage areas, connected the 1776 main house with the barn of the Nathan Hale Homestead, Coventry, Connecticut. (Courtesy, Antiquarian and Landmarks Society, Inc.)

Greater elegance of ell-and-wing architecture was achieved in 1794 by Oliver Phelps, then America's largest landowner, when he added the Neo-Classic section at the right to his Suffield, Connecticut home, the original part of which was built in the 1760s. Builder Asher Benjamin charged Phelps $11.00 for the carved capitals of the classic columns of the new entrance. (Courtesty, Antiquarian and Landmarks Society, Inc.)

When Joseph Arnold married Thankful Clark, he purchased the original or first-phase section of this Haddam, Connecticut, gambrel-roof side-hill house in 1794–95. At that time the house included two rooms with a loft, the section from the side door to the main entrance. About 1800 he added the second portion to the right of the chimney stack, and in 1810 bought a 1752 building, moved it up to the 1800 right side, thus economically adding an ell or wing. That same year, the new long kitchen was added along the length of the back of the house to form the salt-box type ell shown to the rear of the photo. (Courtesy, Haddam Historical Society, Inc.)

senses in viewing, examining, and delighting." William Salmon, *Polygraphice* (London, 1675).

GARRET
"The uppermost room," (W) or room "on the highest floor of the house." (J)

GLORY HOLE
"A cupboard at the head of a staircase for brooms, etc." (H)

GREECE, GREEZE, GRISE
"A flight of steps." (W)

GUEST CHAMBER
"A room kept for entertainment." (W)

Entertainment: "A reception, welcome, treat, fare, diversion." (W) Hence, this was a ballroom, best parlor, or dining parlor. "Put cheerful and merry Paintings as Baccus, Centaures, Satyrs, Sirens and the like, but forbearing all obscene Pictures." William Salmon, *Polygraphice* (London, 1675).

HALL
"The first, largest, and finest partition," (M) or room in the house. "A large room." (W) "Let the Hall be adorned with [paintings] of Shepherds, Peasants, Milkmaids, Meat Herds, Flocks of Sheep and the like, in their respective places and proper attendants, as also Fowls, Fish and the like." William Salmon, *Polygraphice* (London, 1675). "Make the hall of such fashion that the parlour be annexed to the head of the hall, and the buttrye and pantrye at the lower end thereof." Andrew Boorde, *Dyetorie* or *Regiment of Healthe* (1547).

KEEPING ROOM
A north British and Scottish colloquialism for sitting room or parlor, the room in which the family's better furnishings were kept and displayed.

KITCHEN
The term from the Saxon, *cycene,* for "the room in a house where the provisions are cooked," (J) chiefly equipped with a hearth or fireplace, a Dresser, *q.v.,* or table; wall shelves, and/or Cupboards, *q.v.,* for the storage of utensils; Chairs or Stools, *qq.v.,* and side tables. "No one can see aught but black ugliness in a modern

This kitchen hearth is in the restored 1692 Buttolph Williams House at Wethersfield, Connecticut. A horn and sheet-iron lantern hangs from the summer beam; clock jack and weights are suspended from the mantel shelf to turn the spit rod. Trammels hold cooking pots above the embers. Mortars and chopping bowls are in the foreground. (Courtesy, Antiquarian and Landmarks Society, Inc.)

Opposite the cooking hearth in "ye greate kitchen," as a 1692 inventory designated this room of the Buttolph Williams House, are the worktables that served also as family dining tables. Wall boxes hold drying herbs and candles. The casement window—in general use before the new-style sash windows of the mid-eighteenth century became common—is hung with red wool curtains. The rear wall shelves hold a complete supply of wood plates, platters, and bowls. On the hutch table in the foreground are a wooden tankard, a large covered sugar bowl, a covered porringer on a plate, small eating bowls, and horn spoons. (Courtesy, Antiquarian and Landmarks Society, Inc.)

kitchen range. How many of us have peeped inside a cottage or farm house and longed to sketch its comfortable chimney corner and ample hearth. And yet there was a time when no difference existed between such appointments of town and country dwellings." Charles L. Eastlake, *Hints on Household Taste* (London, 1850).

LARDER
"A room for provisions; the room where meat is kept or salted." (J) "A place where meat is kept." (W)

LAUNDRY
"A room to wash or iron clothes in." (W)

LAVATORY
"A laundry." (W)

LIBRARY
The "apartment destined for the placing of books." (M)

LIVERY
"A kind of cupboard but sometimes a separate room for safekeeping of plate and linen." (J) (See also LIVERY, Chapter 12.)

LOBBY
"An opening before a room; antichamber." (W)

LOFT
"The highest floor; a convenience." (W)

LUMBER
"Old household stuff; also things useless and of small importance." (B) A term

51

for furnishings not in use at the time, hence lumber room or storage closet; a place to keep household goods.

OFFICES

"The rooms in a large house, appropriated to the use of upper servants; a word applied to menial apartments generally." (H) In the southern colonies, the term referred to Ells, *q.v.,* wings, or separate small buildings. "All their drudgeries of Cookery, Washing, Dairies, Ec. are performed in offices detached from the Dwelling Houses, which by this means are kept more cool and sweet." Robert Beverley, *The History and Present State of Virginia* (London, 1722; Richmond, 1855).

PANTRY

"A small room to put provisions in." (W)

PARLOR

"Commonly it denotes a fair lower room, designed principally for the entertainment of company." (M) "A lower [ground floor] room kept for entertainment." (W)

"In those days [the first half of the eighteenth century] six mahogany chairs in a shut-up parlor were considered magnificent; we never got beyond cherry." *Autobiography of Lyman Beecher,* ed., Charles Beecher (New York, 1866). "The parlor was a large, pleasant room . . . There were half a dozen dark green, wooden chairs, and two rockers to match . . . a large mirror occupied the front pier [between two windows]. There was no carpet, floors had not then become generally covered, and, if carpeted in winter, they were usually bare in summer, carpets being considered hot and dusty." (Description of a Newburyport home c. 1790.) Sarah Anna Emery, *Reminiscences of a Nonagenarian* (Newburyport, Massachusetts, 1879).

PORCH

The room at the front of the house into which the main door opened, and above which a small chamber usually was built.

The front entry room or porch of the restored 1678 Joshua Hempsted house at New London, Connecticut, has a small chamber above. (Courtesy, Antiquarian and Landmarks Society, Inc.)

PRESCENCE CHAMBER
"A room to receive company." (W)

SAFE
"A buttery, a pantry." (J)

SALOON
"A large or spacious hall." (W)

SCULLERY
"A place to wash and keep things in," (W) "as common utensils, or kettles and dishes in the kitchen." (J)

SOLLAR, SOLAR, SOLARIUM
"An upper room; a garret." (J), (W)

STOREHOUSE
"The place in which things are hoarded and reposited against a time of use." (J)

STORY
"A floor; a flight of rooms; to range one under another." (J)

STOWAGE
"A room for laying up." (J)

Tis plate of rare device, and jewels
Of rich and exquisite form; their value's
great;
And I am something curious, being
strange,
To have them in safe stowage.
Shakespeare, *Cymbeline,* I, vi.

WARDROBE
"A closet or a little room adjoining to a bed-chamber, serving to dispose and keep a person's apparel in; or, for a servant to lodge in; to be at hand to wait Ec." (M)

WITHDRAWING ROOM
"A room for retirement." (W) Decorate "the inward or withdrawing chambers with draughts of the life of Persons of Honour, intimate or special friends, and acquaintances." William Salmon, *Polygraphice* (London, 1675).

GARDEN BUILDINGS

GROTTO
"A small artificial edifice made in a garden, in imitation of a natural grotto. The outsides of these grottoes are usually adorned with rustic architecture, and their inside with shell work, coral, Ec." *Encyclopedia Americana* (Philadelphia, 1831).

KIOSK
The term adapted from the Turkish for a "kind of partition introduced from the Turks and Persians into (our) gardens. (It is) a summerhouse, with a tent-shaped roof, open on all sides, and isolated. It is supported by pillars (commonly placed in a square) round the foot of which is a balustrade. It is built of wood, straw, or similar materials, and is chiefly erected to afford a free prospect in the shade but it also serves to embellish a rural or garden view." *Encyclopedia Americana* (Philadelphia, 1831).

PIAZZA
"A portico or covered walk, supported by arches . . . all walks with porticoes around them are piazzas." *Encyclopedia Americana* (Philadelphia, 1831). "A walk under a roof supported by pillars." (J)

PORTICO
The term from the Latin, *porticus,* for a "continued range of columns, covered at top, to serve as a shelter from the weather; also a common name for buildings which had such covered walks supported by pillars." *Encyclopedia Americana* (Philadelphia, 1831).

PRIVY
"A necessary house." (W)

3
Crafts, Trades, and Useful Professions

ALLUMINOR

From the French, *allumer,* to light, this was a synonym for illuminator in the eighteenth century. "One who colours or paints upon paper or parchment, [so-called] because he gives graces, light, and ornament to the letters or figures coloured." (J)

ANTIQUARY

"A person who studies and searches after monuments and the remains of antiquity. There were formerly in the chief cities persons of distinction called antiquaries, who made it their business to explain the ancient inscriptions, and give every assistance in their power to strangers, who were lovers of that kind of learning." (M)

APPRENTICE

"Contracts for apprentices are made before a magistrate, who . . . obliges the master to engage by a written indenture, not only that, during the time of service, the apprentice shall be duly provided with meat, drink, apparel, washing, and lodging, and at its expiration with a complete new suit of clothes, but also, that he shall be taught to read, write, and cast accounts; and that he shall be well instructed in the art or profession of his master, or some other, by which he may afterward gain a livelihood, and be able in his turn to raise a family. . . . This desire among the masters, to have more hands employed in working for them, induces them to pay the pas-

Famed New Haven engraver Amos Doolittle allowed his apprentice son to sign this song sheet. (Courtesy, Connecticut Historical Society, Inc.)

sages of young persons, of both sexes, who, on their arrival, agree to serve . . . those who have already learned a trade, agreeing for a shorter term in proportion to their skill, and the consequent immediate value of their service; and those who have none, agreeing for a longer term, in consideration of being taught an art their poverty would not permit them to acquire in their own country." "Information to Those Who Would Remove to America," *The Works of Dr. Benjamin Franklin* (Hartford, (1845).

APOTHECARY
From the Latin, *apotheca,* for repository, "a man whose employment is to keep medicines for sale." (J)   "Surgeons and mates, or other officers attached to the U. States' or state's service, or all other persons holding hospital supplies of any description whatever, belonging to the U. S. army, are hereby required to report the same without delay to this office, or to either of my assistants at the following stations, viz.: Burlington [Vermont], Williamsville and Brownsville [New York], Boston, New-London, New-York, Philadelphia, Norfolk [Virginia], Charleston [South Carolina], and New-Orleans [Louisiana]. Each article of Medicine, Surgical Instruments, Regimental Medicine and Store Chests, Hospital Stores, Furniture, Bedding, or equipments, not immediately wanted, must be forthwith returned to this department, and placed in either of the above named deposits: receipts will be given for the same, which will exonerate the present possessor from further responsibility and enable him to settle his accounts with the government. Francis Le Baron, U.S. Apothecary General," United States' Apothecary General's Office, Albany, 31st March, 1815.

APRON-MAN
A general term for anyone who did manual labor; apron was the apparel and therefore the emblem of the man. The word was derived, according to Dr. Johnson, from *aforeman,* meaning a cloth hung before to keep the other dress clean, and so, *The nobility think scorn to go in leather apron,* Shakespeare. Hence, "apron-man, a workman or manual artificer," (J) as *The cobler apron'd, and the parson gown'd,* Alexander

Pope. "In the spring of 1828, being about fifteen years of age, I bid my mother, sister and uncle farewell, and left home for Middlebury [Vermont] . . . to learn the cabinet making trade with one Nahum Parker. I put on my apron and went to work, sawing table legs from two-inch planks, making wash-stands, bed steads, etc. . . . I then felt contented and happy and never aspired to any other distinction than that connected with my trade and improvements in the arts . . . [But] I formed a taste for reading, particularly political works . . ." Stephen A. Douglas, *Autobiography,* ed., Frank A. Stevens, Illinois State Historical Society (Springfield, 1913). "Ever and anon the stage stopped before some low shop or dwelling, and a wheelwright or shoemaker appeared in his shirt-sleeves and leather apron . . ." Henry David Thoreau, *Cape Cod* (Cambridge, 1865).

ARKWRIGHT
One who made containers of wedged and pegged boards.

Ark: Any receptacle made of split (not sawn) boards.

ARTIFICER
The name generally given a person "whose employment it is to manufacture any kind of commodity, as in iron, brass, wood, Ec. Such are smiths, weavers, carpenters, Ec." (M)

ART TEACHER
"T[homas] Sheraton, 106 Wardour Street, Soho," advertised in London in 1795 that he "teaches perspective, architecture and ornaments. Makes designs for cabinet makers and sells all kinds of drawing books."

ATTORNEY
"One who acts for another in law." (W)

AUCTIONEER
"The manager of an auction or sale." (W)

Auction: "A kind of publick sales very much in use for household goods, books, plate, etc. By this method of sale the highest bidder is always the buyer." (M) "To be sold by Auction, Household Furniture . . . including Fine Sconce Glasses, large Looking Glasses, Leather Bottom Chairs, sundry Mahogany and other Tables . . . two Silver watches, sundry sorts of good China Ware, Ec. . . ." *Boston News-Letter,* May 17, 1739.

BADGER
"A kind of peddler." (W) That is, one who bought goods at one place and carried them elsewhere to sell, as at a public market or fair. "A hawker or huckster." (M) Hence, the term badgered, from the Badger's practice of calling to passers-by and importuning them to buy.

BAILLIE, BAILIFF, BAILEY
"An officer that arrests, a steward, overseer. One who receives goods in trust." (W) An agent for another such as a landlord or a shipper. Elder William Brewster (c. 1566–1643) of the Plymouth Colony had been postmaster and bailiff at Scrooby, England; later he was a tutor and printer during the Pilgrims' exile in Holland.

BAKER
"A person that bakes for a livelihood." (W) "The subscriber has removed three rods west of his late Stand where he intends to keep every article in the baking line, viz. Crackers, Biscuit, Loaf-Bread, Ec. Ec. made of the best materials the market will afford. Also 4 barrels of Ale for sale cheap. William Stephenson, Mill St." *American Mercury* (Hartford, Connecticut), June 17, 1816.

BARBER
"One that shaves beards, etc." (W) As with many who performed personal services, barbers often emigrated as indentured servants, their passage over thus paid and their livelihood guaranteed by the one who purchased their services or time for a set number of years. Sometimes the purchaser was a wealthy landowner or merchant who wanted a personal servant to work as barber, valet, to keep his wigs and clothing in order. Other purchasers were barbers who had set up their own shops in trade centers and wanted assistants. "The B[eare]r of this Mr. Jones a very honest Mechanic informs me of his intention to purchase of you a Journeyman Barber: Should you think proper to let him have the Ser't I dare believe there would be no Danger of his not being punctual in his payment." Order from James Innis, Williamsburg, February 20, 1774. Frances Mason, *John Norton and Sons, Merchants of London and Virginia* (Richmond, 1935).

BARBER CHIRURGEON
"A man who joins the practice of surgery to the barber's trade; such as were all surgeons formerly, but now it is used only for a low practice of surgery." (J)

BARKER
"A tanner, but also one who barks trees." (W)

BARRISTER
"A pleader at the bar, a lawyer." (W)

BEADLE
"A cryer; messenger; petty officer of a court, parish or college." (W)

BEDDER
A cant term for the "upholsterer." (H)

BED-JOINER
The early colonial term for the craftsman who supplied frames for beds, easy chairs or couches; that is, all those parts generally covered by hangings or upholstery. His work usually was in conjunction with that of the chairmaker, cabinetmaker, and, of course, the upholsterer. As with similar terms, this description seldom was needed after 1830 when mechanical mass production obliterated many specialized crafts.

BELLMAN
"A cryer of goods, a common crier." (W) "He whose business it is to proclaim anything in towns, and to gain attention by ringing his bell."(J)

BLACKSMITH

"A person who works on iron." (W) "For Sale. A Small Farm lying on the turnpike road leading from Middletown to Hadam containing about twenty acres of mowing, pasture and plow land . . . the buildings consist of a convenient dwelling house, barn, horse shed, and blacksmiths shop, and is a good location for a tavern. Rebekah Ford." *American Mercury* (Hartford, Connecticut), February 25, 1812.

Blacksmith, shown in popular c. 1800 print.

TAKE NOTICE.
GEORGE BARNARD,

RESPECTETLLY informs the public. that he carries on the Blacksmith business, in all its various branches. particularly in making edges tools, and horse and cattle shoeing. He flatter himself, from his long experience, and the en couragement he has received from his numer rous friends, that he shall be able to execute his work to the satisfaction of all, who may please to honor him with their custom.
Ten rods east of the little Bridge.
Dec. 30   96

American Mercury (Hartford, Connecticut), December 30, 1816.

BLAZER

"A spreader or publisher of reports." (W)

Blaze: "To publish, to make known, to spread far and wide." (J)

BODGER

"A chair-leg turner." (M)

BONDMAN, BOUNDER

"A bond-servant." (M)

So every bondman in his own hand bears The power to cancel his captivity.

Shakespeare, *Julius Caesar,* I, iii.

BOOKSELLER

"One who trades in books." (W) Also, very often in the seventeenth and eighteenth centuries, the publisher of books, not always with as much attention to copyright regulations as some wished: "July 28, 1642. Now came over a book of Mr. Cotton's sermons upon the seven vials. Mr. Humfrey had gotten the notes from some who had took them by characters [shorthand], and printed them in London, he had 300 copies of it, which was a great wrong to Mr. Cotton, and he was much grieved at it, for it had been fit he should have perused and corrected the copy before it had been printed." John Winthrop, *Journal, History of New England* (Boston, 1825). (See also PAMPHLET, Chapter 12.)

BORSHOLDER

"A petty constable." (W)

BOTCHER

"A mender of old clothes." (W) "The same to a taylor as a cobbler to a shoemaker." (J)

BOWMAN

"An archer," (W) "that shoots with a bow." (J)

BOWYER

"Artificers whose employment is to make bows." (M) Also "one that uses the bow." (J)

BRASS FOUNDER

"A caster of vessels in Metal." (W) "Notice, The Copper Smiths and Brass Foundering Business heretofore carried on by Ward & Bartholomew will in future be carried on by the subscribers who will pay every attention to the business. They have on hand a good supply of the best materials suitable to make Stills or Boilers to any particular pattern that may be wanted. Also for sale, warranted Worms, Copper, Dyers and Hatters kettles. Stoves and Pipes of various descriptions such as Box, Cooking, and Franklin Stoves, Church & Sleigh Bells, Ec. Ec. Ward, Bartholomew & Brainard." *American Mercury* (Hartford, Connecticut), January 25, 1814.

October 1, 1816, they advertised a "new assortment of Goods in their line" including "Brass Kettles, Brass Andirons, Shovel and Tongs, brass Warming Pans, do. Wash Basons, Candlesticks, Knives and Forks, Snuffers and Trays, Tea Trays, Fruit Baskets, Nursing Cases, Copper Tea kettles, Surveyors' Compasses, Pocket do.; Thermometers, Gauging Rods, Crucibles; Sheet and bar copper, etc., church Bells; School, and ship do.; sleigh do., Watch Materials." *American Mercury* (Hartford, Connecticut).

Connecticut Gazette (New Haven), December 12, 1829.

BRAZIER
"A tradesman who makes and sells copper and brass vessels." (M) "Thomas Russell, Brazier, near the Draw Bridge in Boston Makes, Mends and New-Tins all sorts of Braziery ware, viz. Kettles, Skillets, Frying Pans, Kettle Pots, Sauce Pans, Tea Kettles, Warming Pans, Wash Basins, Skimmers, Ladles, Copper Pots, Copper Funnels, Brass Scales, Gun Ladles, Ec. . . . and buys old Brass, Copper, Pewter, Lead and Iron." *Boston News-Letter,* October 30, 1740. (See also COPPERSMITH, BRASS FOUNDER.)

BREWER
Any concocter of malt liquors.

BREWSTER
Originally, "the woman who brews." (W) Later, any brewer.

BRICKLAYER
"A person whose business it is to build houses, walls, Ec., with bricks." (M)

BRICKMAKER
"One who makes or deals in bricks."

Brick: "Clay with sand and water, shaped in a mold." (W) "Just arrived from London in the Ship Borden William Harbert, Commander, a parcel of likely young men Servants consisting of Husband-Men, Joiners, Shoe-Makers, Weavers, Smiths, Brick Makers, Brick Layers, Sawyers, Taylors, Stay-Makers, Butchers, Chair-Makers, and several other trades and are to be sold very reasonable either for ready money, Wheat, Bread, or Flour by Edward Harne in Philadelphia." *American Weekly Mercury* (Philadelphia), November 21, 1728.

Brickmaker, as shown in *The Book of Trades* (London, 1805).

61

BRIGHTSMITH

The manufacturer of tin and tin-plated wares: "Anvils, vices, screw-plates, smith's hammers, bick-irons. Bright smith's and black smith's bellows pipes." *American Mercury* (Hartford, Connecticut), November 4, 1812.

BURNEWIN

"A blacksmith." (M)

BUTLER

"Now generally signifies a servant in the houses of opulent persons to whom the care of the wine, plate, etc. is entrusted." (M)

CABINETMAKER

"One who makes nice things in wood." (W) "To be sold by Auction . . . on Monday, the 24th instant, and the following days. The entire genuine and valuable stock in trade of Mr. Chippendale and his late partner, Mr. Rennie, deceased, Cabinetmakers and Upholsterers, at their house in St. Martin's Lane, consisting of a great variety of fine mahogany and tulip wood, Cabinets, Desks, and Book-Cases, Cloaths Presses, double Chests of Drawers, Commodes, Buroes, fine Library, Writing, Card, Dining, and other Tables, Turkey and other Carpets, fine pattern Chairs, and sundry other pieces of curious cabinet work, a large parcel of fine season'd Feathers; as also the large unwrought Stock consisting of fine mahogany and other woods, in Plank, Board, Vanier [veneer] and Wainscot . . . The Business to be carried on for the future by Mr. Chippendale, on the Premises, on his own Account." *Public Advertiser* (London), March 17, 1766.

CALENDAR

"One who presses, smoothes and gives a gloss to silks, stuffs and linens." (M)

CARDER

"One who cards." (W)

To card: "To comb or work wool." (W) "Nathan Allyn, Ten rods NW of the State House, manufactures and keeps constantly for sale Hand Cards, Steel Teeth, and Cotton filleting made of steel teeth. He will supply on short notice Double and single Carding Machines complete." *American Mercury* (Hartford, Connecticut), March 25, 1816. William White (c. 1592–1621) of the Plymouth Colony, had been a wool carder in England before emigrating.

CARMAN

"One who drives a cart." (W)

CARPENTER

"A worker in wood, a builder." (W) "Hezekiah Bull, expects shortly to leave this state for the state of Ohio . . . He wishes to engage some young enterprising men to go with him, to settle on New Lands, on advantageous terms, House and other Carpenters, Blacksmiths, good Axe men, Ec. He wants to purchase 3 yoak of likely working Cattle." *American Mercury* (Hartford, Connecticut), February 15, 1814. "The trade or art of the carpenter, and artificer in wood; a builder of houses and ships. He is distinguished from joiner, as a carpenter performs larger and stronger work." (J)

CARRIER

"A person who makes it his business to carry goods for other persons, from one place to another, for hire." (M) "A porter, a messenger." (W)

CARTER

"A person who drives a cart." (W)

Cart: "A carriage of two wheels used for burden." (W)

CARTWRIGHT

"A person whose business it is to make carts, wagons, etc." (M)

CARVER

"One who carves wood or stone." (W)

CHAIRMAKER

The joiner or turner who specialized in making chairs. "John I. Wells offers employment for a good workman at Chair

Making—Would give the highest price for long Hair, such as is suitable for Mattrasses." *American Mercury* (Hartford, Connecticut), June 28, 1810.

Connecticut Journal (New Haven), April 19, 1797.

CHAMBERLAIN
"An officer charged with management and direction of a chamber." (M) "The sixth officer of the crown, a steward." (W)

CHANDLER
"A person who deals in candles." (W) "To be sold by Edward Langdon, in Fleet Street, near the old North Meeting House . . . good old candles both Mould and Dipt, fit for Shipping or Families, also Mould Candles of Bayberry wax, all by the box or by Retail." *Boston Gazette,* July 24, 1750.

CHAPMAN
A contraction of cheap, plus man; that is, a vendor of chapbooks or pamphlets and small wares of the type now called notions. "No person shall trade and traffic as a pedlar, hawker, or petty-chapman, in any foreign goods, and which are not the produce or manufacture of the United States, on penalty of forfeiting all such goods . . ." *Connecticut Statutes* (Hartford, 1835).

CHIRURGEON
The polite early colonial title for a surgeon "December, 1645. Mr. Pratt, an experienced chirurgeon, had lived in New England many years, and was one of the first chirurgeons at Cambridge in Mr. Hooker's time, and had a good practice, and wanted [for] nothing, but he had been long discontented because his employment was not so profitable to himself as he desired, and therefore he would needs go back into England (for chirurgeons were then in great request by occasion of the wars)." John Winthrop, *Journal, History of New England* (Boston, 1825). "Instruments for Barbers & chirurgeons, Incision Sheeres, Setts (the bundle) Paices or Tooth drawers, Phillicanes, Trepans" were listed in House of Parliament Rates, 1660, for Imports and Exports—*Statutes of the Realm* (London, 1819).

CLOCKMAKER
"One who makes or sells clocks." (W) "Such gentlemen or ladies as will favor (Simon) Willard with their commands . . . may depend on having their work done in the neatest manner, and may be supplied with Mahogany Cases in the newest taste. Those who live at a distance may have Clock Work sent them, with direction how to manage and set them up without the assistance of the Clock-Maker." *Massachusetts Spy or Worcester Gazette,* March 11, 1784.

CLOTHIER
"One who fulls and scours cloths." (W) "The subscribers having purchased the clothier's works lately owned by Bohan Dewey in the parish of Wintonbury, they intend now to carry on the business in every branch, such as blue-dying, Ec., with punctuality and expedition, they are now ready to receive cloth, and so far as the neatness may entitle them to custom they solicit a

share." Jacob Gillet, Chauncey Goodrich, *American Mercury* (Hartford, Connecticut), August 9, 1814.

COACHMAKER

The craftsman in wood who manufactured all vehicles for public and private transport until forced out of business by the "iron horse" locomotive of the nineteenth century, and the "horseless carriage" of the twentieth century. "James Lawrence, living in the Broad-way, at the Sign of the Riding Chair . . . Makes and Mends all sorts of Carriages, such as Coaches, Chariots, Chaises, Chairs, Kittereens, Four-wheel chaises, Waggons, Carts, Sleds of all sorts, and wheels of all Sorts, likewise Chair-Boxes and Kittereen-Boxes of any form or shape after the best and neatest manner, and newest Fashion . . ." *The New York Gazette and The Weekly Post-Boy,* March 1, 1750. Thomas Prence (1600–73) of Plymouth Colony, had been a carriage or coachmaker in London.

COBBLER

"A mender of shoes; botcher; bungler." (W)

> Thou art a cobbler, art thou?
> Truly, Sir, all that I live by is with the
>   awl . . .
> I am indeed, Sir, a surgeon to old shoes.
> Shakespeare, *Julius Caesar,* I, i.

COLLIER

"A digger or dealer in coals." (W)

CONFECTIONER

"One who sells sweet-meats." (W)

Sweet-meat: "A fruit that is preserved with sugar." (W)

"New Confectionary's Fruit & Toy Store, Main Street, a few rods south of the Episcopal Church, formerly occupied as a Muff and Tippet Factory. Charles Cottu . . . has opened a store where he intends to keep all kinds of Confectionaries, Sweet Meats, Cakes, and fancy articles—Fruit of all kinds dried and in their natural state. He also intends to keep on hand all kinds of Cakes, such as Loaf Cake, Pound do., Sponge do., Tea do., Ec., Ec. Families will find it their advantage to come and look; he will supply them very near as cheap as they can make at home, always fresh or made at a short notice. Loaf cakes ornamented in the best style . . . A large assortment of peppermint drops, Lozenges, all kinds of Candy, Sugar Plums, Non pareils to put on Cakes . . . All orders from the Country received and thankfully attended to. Ice Cream now kept on hand constantly, all kinds of refreshments, Sirup, Cordials, New-York Ale, Bottled Cider, Beer, Ec., Ec." *American Mercury* (Hartford, Connecticut), April 28, 1816.

Confectioner, as shown in *The New Dictionary of Arts and Sciences* (London, 1788).

COOPER

"A maker of barrels." (W) "John Henry Dyer, Cooper, lately arrived from London . . . makes all sorts of cooper's ware, after the best manner, as Rum Hogsheads, Barrels, Caggs, Little Tubs and Trays, as cheap and good as any in the town." *Boston Ga-*

zette, July 30, 1751. "John Alden was hired for a cooper at South-Hampton, when the ship victualed; and being a hopeful young man, was much desired, but left to his own liking to go or stay when he came here; but he stayed, and maryed here." William Bradford, *Of Plimouth Plantation* (Boston, 1856).

COPPERSMITH
"One who works in or sells copper." (W) "William Stephenson Ten Rods east of the Bridge Market has on hand a fine assortment of warranted stills and worms, clothiers' and Hatters' kettles, etc., etc., and also, Repairs old stills & worms and other kinds of Copper and Brass work . . . Cash and the highest price given for Old Copper, Brass, Pewter and Lead. Said Stephenson wants an apprentice to the Coppersmith business, an active young lad of 14 or 15 years of age. One from the country would be preferred." *American Mercury* (Hartford, Connecticut), July 1, 1814. (See also BRAZIER, BRASS FOUNDER.)

CORDINER
"A shoemaker, cordwainer." (W)

CORDWAINER
"From cordwain, a kind of Spanish shoe lether, a shoemaker." (W)

CORK CUTTER
"The cork-cutter's business requires but little ingenuity; the knives used in the operation have a peculiar construction, and they must be exceedingly sharp. The knife is almost the only instrument wanted in the trade. The principal demand for corks is for stopping bottles. These are cut by men and women who receive a certain price per gross for their labour. It is one of the blackiest and dirtiest of all trades and not very profitable." *The Book of Trades* (London, 1805).

CORRECTOR
In printing this was the name given the employee generally called a proofreader today.

"As mistakes will occur, a sheet, which is called a proof, is printed off and given to the corrector of the press, who examines it while a boy reads the copy to him, making the requisite alterations in the margin; which being done, he gives the proof to the compositor to be corrected . . . Another proof, having been read again by the corrector, is sent to the author, who, if he wishes it, writes on it 'revise', which signifies that another proof is to be sent to him to see that all the mistakes marked in the last proof are corrected." *The Book of Trades* (London, 1805).

CRIMP
"An agent for coals or shipping; one hired to procure seamen." (W)

CROCKER
"A potmaker or potter." (M) "China, glass and earthenware, 309 Hogsheads and Crates, now in store and of a superior quality and will be sold as low as can be bought in this city or New York comprising all articles in the crockery line. Offered for sale by Frederick Bange." *American Mercury* (Hartford, Connecticut), December 22, 1818.

Crocker, as shown in a popular c. 1800 print.

CROWDER
"A fiddler." (W)

CUPPER

"One who cups, one who scarifies." (W)
A surgeon or physician's assistant.

CURRIER

"A dresser of leather already tanned." (W)
"Those who dress and color leather." (M)
"They carry on the Tanning and Currying at their works on Tanners St. where they have constantly on hand a general assortment of Boot, Shoe, and Harness Leather, as low as can be purchased in this town for cash. They wish to purchase hides, Calf, and Sheep skin Pelts for which they will pay cash—also, oak and hemlock bark—they have for sale most kinds of curriers tools. E & S Arnold." *American Mercury* (Hartford, Connecticut), March 8, 1814.

DAB, DABSTER

A common term for "an artist," (W) and specifically one who worked in oils or water colors. "Then came to Albany . . . and [wished] to gain some knowledge in painting . . . for all the practice that I had had in miniature was when I was at Charlestown. I been in the habit of painting on paper and a Gentleman says, can't you paint on Ivory? Oh yes, but I am out of Ivory. Very well I have a piece and you may paint my miniature, so for the first time I attempted Ivory painting and went so much beyond my expectations that I thought I soon would be a dabster." *The Travel Diary of James Guild* (itinerant Massachusetts silhouette cutter 1797–1841), Vermont Historical Society Proceedings, New Series, V, (1937).

DANCING MASTER

The instructor in dancing and other helpful social arts. "W. C. Hulet, Dancing Master . . . has offered his Public Dancing School at his House in Broad-Street near the corner of Beaver Street at Three o'clock in the Afternoon, and an Evening School for such Ladies and Gentlemen who cannot attend in Day-Time . . . He teaches the Minuet and Country Dances by the whole, by the month, or quarter; and likewise the Violin, German Flute, and Use of the Small Sword. N.B. The great Advantage that many Gentlemen have over others that have not learned the Hornpipe in Country Dancing, has induced Mr. Hulet to open a private School for such Gentlemen who may choose to attend." *The New York Gazette and The Weekly Post-Boy,* October 15, 1770.

DANCING SCHOOL.
LOUISE GÉRVAIS,

HAS the honor to inform the Ladies and Gentlemen of Hartford, that she intends opening a DANCING SCHOOL at Mr. Ransom's Ball Room, on the first of July next, until the first of October following.—From the encouragement which she has received for several years that she has taught in New York, she hopes to meet the approbation of the inhabitants of Hartford. The terms, days and hours of tuition, will be made known when she arrives. March 8.

American Mercury (Hartford, Connecticut), March 3, 1810.

DAUBER

"A coarse, low painter," (W) as a house painter; one who white-washed or painted interior walls and ceilings.

To daub: "To smear, trim gaudily." (W)

Daubry: "Bad or coarse painting." (W)
Dauber was a colloquialism for an unskilled artist whose work was, of course, called a daub: "All [the museums] I have ever entered in the United States . . . invariably have a large collection of daubs, called portraits of eminent personages, one-half of whom a stranger never heard of—but that is national vanity." Captain Maryat, *Diary of Travels in North America* (Philadelphia, 1839).

DIER, DYER

"One who follows the trade of dying; one who dies clothes." (J)

Die: "To colour, tinge, stain." (J)

DISHER

The turner; a "maker of bowls or dishes." (H)

DRAPER

"A person who sells or deals in cloth." (W)

DRUGGIST

"One who sells physical drugs." (J)

DRUGSTER

"One who sells physical simples." (J) "Wanted. As an Apprentice to a Druggist, an active boy, 14 or 15 years old, of good morals and respectable parentage. Enquire of Joseph Lynde." *American Mercury* (Hartford, Connecticut), September 2, 1816.

ÉBÉNISTE

The French for cabinetmaker, literally one who works in ebony; a term used in the seventeenth and eighteenth centuries to describe anyone who worked with veneers.

EDITOR

"A person of learning, who has the care of an impression of any work." (M)

FACTOR

"An agent for another, a deputy or substitute." (W) The agent or correspondent "residing beyond the seas, commissioned by merchants to buy or sell goods on their account, or assist them in carrying on their trade. A factor receives, in lieu of wages, a commission . . . according to the business he transacts." (M)

   Factory: "A place where a number of factors reside to negotiate for their masters or employers." (M) We might call this an office building today.

FANCYMONGER

"A dealer in tricks of imagination." (W) That is, one who supplied magicians with their tools.

FARMER

One who takes land on lease, the owner who cultivates land, one who takes other things on rent.

   To Farm: "To lease or rent." (W) Until well into the nineteenth century, Americans continued to use Farmer (as today we would say tenant Farmer) as opposed to yeoman. "Wanted, A man that has a small family, (without children would be preferred) to labour at Farming for one year— suitable encouragement will be given to one that can come well recommended, for sobriety, industry, and integrity by Ebenezer Barnard." *American Mercury* (Hartford, Connecticut), February 22, 1814. By 1830, however, farmer more often was used to mean the owner who cultivated his own land.

WANTED.

A MAN, that has a small family, (without children would be prefered,) to labour at Farming for one year—suitable encouragement will be given, to one that can come well recommended, for sobriety, industry and integrity, by
EBENEZER BARNARD.
Hartford, Feb. 22, 1814.   4w47

American Mercury (Hartford, Connecticut), February 22, 1814.

FARRIER

"One whose employment is to shoe horses, and cure them when diseased or lame." (M) "A horse doctor." (W)

FELLMONGER

"A dealer in the skins of sheep." (W)

FENCING MASTER

"A person who teaches fencing." (W) "To all Gentlemen who desire to learn the right Method and true Art of Defense and Pursuit of the Small-Sword in its greatest Perfection, and extraordinary quick and speedy, with all the Guards, Parades, Thrusts and Lessons thereunto belonging . . . and the best Rule for Playing against Artists or others with Blunts or Sharps . . . may be taught by me, Richard Tineall, professor and Master of said Art." *The New York Gazette and The Weekly Post-Boy,* June 22, 1752.

FLETCHER

"One who makes bows and arrows." (W)

FLORIST

An author or botanist "who writes a treatise called Flora, comprehending only the plants and trees to be found growing naturally in any place. In common [language] florist signifies a person well skilled in flowers, their kind and cultivation." (M)

FLOWERER

The name given the craftsman who cut or etched decorations on glass; also used to designate the craftsman who similarly "embellished" metals. (See also GLASS CUTTER.)

Flower: "To adorn." (W)

FOOTMAN

"A man servant in livery." (W)

FOSTER

"A forester." (W)

FOUNDER

"A caster." (W)

Foundery: "A place to cast vessels of metal." (W)

FRANKLIN

Another name for "a steward, a bailiff of land. It signified originally a little gentleman, and is not improperly Englished a gentleman servant." (J)

FULLER

"One who fulls cloth." (W)

Full: "To cleanse and scour cloth, and render it more compact." (W)

GARDENER

"A person who cultivates a garden." (W)

Garden: "A place to raise kitchen plants, flowers and fruits." (W) "Thomas Vallentine . . . has been employed by several of the Nobility and Gentry to lay out their Gardens and Improvements. He also surveys Land . . . draws Designs for Gardens . . . green Houses, forcing Frames, Ec. . . . He is willing to attend any Gentleman's Gardens within ten or twelve Miles of this City, a Day or two in the week . . ." *The New York Gazette and The Weekly Mercury,* August 8, 1768.

> *There is no ancient gentlemen but gardeners, ditchers and grave-makers: they hold up Adam's profession.*

Shakespeare: *Hamlet,* V, i.

GAUGER

"A man who gauges or measures vessels." (W)

GILDER

"One who gilds." (W)

Gilding: "Gold or silver laid on for ornament." (W) "Journeymen and Apprentices wanted. Nathan Ruggles will give good wages to 2 or 3 first rate Gilders, at his *Looking-Glass Factory* in Hartford. Likewise, wanted immediately 3 or 4 Boys, well educated, and from respectable parents, from 14 to 16 years old, as apprentices at said Factory." *American Mercury* (Hartford, Connecticut), January 10, 1811.

GLASS CUTTER

The artisan who decorated glass by cutting on the surface. "American Flint Glass is now made at the Factory in Manheim, in Lancaster County. Equal in quality with any imported from Europe . . . N.B. A Glass Cutter and Flowerer, on application, will meet with good encouragement, at said Manufactory. Henry William Stiegel." *Pennsylvania Gazette* (Philadelphia), June 20, 1771.

GLASS GRINDER

"One who grinds or polishes glass." (W)

GLASSMAN

"One who deals in or sells glass." (W) "This is to acquaint the public and my kind customers that I have lately been at the Glass Factory in Mannheim, in Lancaster County, and contracted with Mr. William Henry Stiegel for a large and complete assortment of his Flint Glass, consisting of quart, pint, half-pint, gill, and half-gill tumblers, wine glasses; vinegar glasses; salt cellars, cream pots, sugar dishes with covers, jelly glasses, syllabub glasses, proof bottles, etc., etc., to be delivered to me immediately at my house in Market Street, next door to the Indian King, where I will sell them as low, or lower and equal in quality with flint glass imported from England. Alexander Bartram." *Pennsylvania Gazette* (Philadelphia), June 27, 1771.

Glassworkers, as shown in *The New Dictionary of Arts and Sciences* (London, 1805).

GLAZIER
"An artificer who works in glass and whose principal business is in fitting panes of glass to sashes, pictures, Ec., and in making lead lights for window frames, and cleaning of sash-windows, Ec." (M) "Thomas and James Barrows in Broad Street, near City Hall cut glass for clock faces, pictures, hall lanthorns, Ec. . . ." *The New-York Gazette and The Weekly Mercury,* January 27, 1777.

GLEEK
A cant term for "a musician." (W)

GLOVER
"One who makes or sells gloves, or covers for the hand and arm." (W)

GOLDBEATER
The artificer who beat or hammered gold into extremely thin sheets or leaves ready for the gilder to use. "GOLD LEAF MANU-FACTORY, T. S. Uffington, Gold-Beater, No. 434, Greenwich St., New York, Informs the venders and consumers of gold Leaf, that he manufactures the same equal to any im-

ported. The advertiser having also a Manufactory in London, will be enabled to supply the market with any quantity required, and render it upon more favorable terms than any other importer. All orders to the above address, or to Robert Henderson, Pocket-Book manufacturer, No. 170 Pearl St., will be immediately attended to." *American Mercury* (Hartford, Connecticut), June 7, 1810.

GOVERNANT, GOVERNESS
"A lady who tutors young girls; an instructress, mistress." (W)

GROCER
"A dealer in teas, sugars, liquors, Ec." (W)

GUNSMITH
"A man who makes or sells guns." (W) "At the Sign of the Sportsman on the Broad Way opposite Hull's Tavern in New York . . . Gilbert Forbes, Gun Maker Makes and sells all sorts of guns . . . has for sale silver and brass mounted pistols, rifle barrel guns, double swivel and double roller gun locks . . . 50 readymade new bayonet guns." *The New York Journal or The General Advertiser,* March 16, 1775.

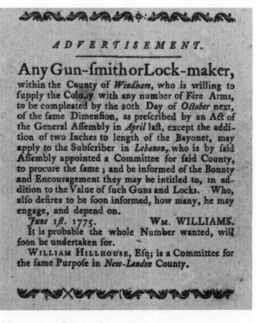

(Courtesy, Connecticut Historical Society, Inc.)

HABERDASHER

"A dealer in small wares." (W) The name was derived from the Icelandic word, *hapertask,* the haversack in which peddlers carried their wares.

HARDWAREMAN

"A maker or seller of hardware; wares made of iron, steel, brass, Ec." (W)

HAWKER

"One who cries goods in the streets." (W)

HAYWARD

The person who "keeps the common herd or cattle of a town . . . to see that the cattle neither break nor crop the hedges . . . to look to the fields, and impound cattle that commit trespass therein." (M)

HIGGLER

"One who hawks provisions by retail." (W)

HORNER

"One who works or deals in horn." (W) "Horner. Cash paid for any quantity of ox and cows Horns by Normand Dexter, New Haven, or by George Burr, opposite the south Meeting-House, Hartford." *American Mercury* (Hartford, Connecticut), January 6, 1817.

HORSE'S MILLINER

"There is a distinct trade called a horse's milliner, who makes roses for bridles, and other articles used in highly ornamented caparisons. This tradesman should have an inventive genius, and a considerable share of taste to set off the furniture belonging to a horse, and decorate it in a neat and elegant style." *The Book of Trades* (London, 1805).

HOSIER

"One who sells stockings." (J) "Silk stockings were first worn by Henry II of France at his sister's wedding in 1559. The art of knitting stockings with needles was introduced into England from Spain in 1561 and Queen Elizabeth is said to have been the first to wear silk stockings. Before this time princes wore cloth hose." Noah Webster, "Chronology" in *The Dictionary* (1806). "The hosier purchases stockings, nightcaps, socks, gloves, Ec. from the manufacturer, and sells them again . . . the business of the hosier consists in being able to properly appreciate the value of the goods in which he deals, an art which is easily acquired." *The Book of Trades* (London, 1805).

HOUSE CARPENTER

Generally, the man who did the heavy framing work but not the "finish" or interior paneling, hanging of doors, etc. "A man wanted. A man with a small family that can come recommended to live on a small Farm. If he is a House Carpenter he will be employed part of his time at that business, and a part farming. Apply 50 rods east of the South Meeting House. Ebenezer Barnard." *American Mercury* (Hartford, Connecticut), May 3, 1816. (See also HOUSE JOINER.)

HOUSE JOINER

The craftsman who did finer carpentry work, such as, mortising and pegging of a frame; and/or interior paneling, molding, window and door framing. "Notice. White and Crocker, want immediately 10,000 feet of timber suitable for brick buildings. They also want three apprentices to the House-Joiner's business, about 16 years of age. They have for sale one good new canvas top chaise with plated harness." *American Mercury* (Hartford, Connecticut), May 3, 1810.

JAPANNER

"One who japans." (W) That is, one who paints furniture with lacquers; also, a contemporary cant term for "a shoe black." (W) "To the Nobility and Gentry, Sebastian Guenbel, just Arrived in this City has for sale a quantity of beautiful furniture elegantly Painted and varnished in the Japan taste; he has some compleat toilets. He also undertakes to paint and varnish coaches and chairs in the same manner

JOINER

"A person who joins wood together." (W) Thus, makers of fine furniture were joiners. "All sorts of Chairs and Joiners work Made and Sold by William Savery at the Sign of the Chair, a little below the Market, in Second Street." Philadelphia. (Furniture label.)

KIDDER

"An engrosser of corn, a huckster." (W)

KNACKER

"A maker of knacks [small items]; a collar-maker." (W)

LAPIDARY

An artificer who cuts precious stones. "The French, though they fell into it but lately, have not withstanding carried this art to a very great perfection, but not in any degree superior to the English." (M)

LATIMER

The term is a corruption of Latiner, the Old Anglo-Saxon Latynere, for an interpreter; that is, anyone who understood and spoke Latin or any other foreign language.

LAUNDRESS

One who collected the laundry, washed and ironed, then returned it to the owner's house.

LAWYER

"A pleader." (W) "Notice. The employment of an Agent or Attorney is not necessary in any claim against the government. It is most generally attended with expense, and sometimes with *actual loss.*" John Quincy Adams, Washington City. *American Mercury* (Hartford, Connecticut), May 27, 1818. (During the Colonial and Early Federal periods many American considered attorneys at best, a "necessary evil.")

LEATHER SELLER

"A person who deals in leather." (W) "Philip Freeman, lately from London,

1780 Bill from laundress to Col. Jeremiah Wadsworth included rare holiday greetings. (Courtesy, Connecticut Historical Society, Inc.)

makes and sells super-fine Leather Breeches and Jackets, not to be discerned from the best super-fine Cloth." *Boston Gazette,* June 21, 1743.

LIMNER

"A painter, a face-painter." (W) "Window-glass and putty, a general assortment of Paints, Linseed oil, Paint Brushes, Limners tools, Gold and Silver Leaf, with a great variety of Camel's Hair Pencils [brushes] cheap for cash, or approved notes. John Vander Pool, Sign Painter, Gilder, No. 75 Pearl-Street." *Weekly Museum* (New York), January 6, 1798.

LISTER

"One who receives and makes return of ratable estate." (W) The estate appraiser for probate courts; the tax collector.

LORIMER, LORINER

The ancient name for the "bridlecutter, who makes the headstall and reins by which the horse is governed." (J)   A harness maker.

MANTUAMAKER

A dressmaker. (See advertisement quoted under MILLINER.)

MARBLE CUTTER

The sculptor who carved tombstones, chimney jambs and shelves, doorsteps and other useful objects from marble. "Anthony Dodane, Marble Cutter . . . also furnishes Slabs, [for table tops] and mends those that are broken, provided they are not in too many Pieces, at a reasonable Price." *The New York Gazette and The Weekly Mercury,* July 4, 1768.

MASON

"A builder with stone." (J)   "Notice is hereby given that Masonry in all its Branches is performed by William Holland, Mason, lately from London, viz., Marble Chimney pieces, gravestones, mortars, Tables, Monuments and Steps, Pavements of all kinds, Hearths, Ec. . . . at his shop in Water Street next door to Mr. Stephen Beezley. N.B. . . . he is now at New York fixing some works for a Gentleman . . . wherefore . . . all Gentlemen and others to apply to Mr. Anthony Wilkinson, ship-carver, until he returns which will be 7 days from the date of this Paper if God permit." *Pennsylvania Gazette* (Philadelphia), November 29, 1739. William Bassett (c. 1590–1655) of the Plymouth Colony, had been a master mason in Middlesex, England.

MECHANIC(K)

"A handicraftsman." (W)

MIDWIFE

"Midwifery is the art of assisting nature in bringing forth a perfect . . . child from the mother. The knowledge of this art depends greatly on an intimate acquaintance with the anatomy in women." (M) "January 30, 1686/87. About 3/4 past eight at night my wife is delivered of a Son. Eliza. Weeder, Midwife. My wife sent not for the Midwife till near 7 at night." Samuel Sewall, *Diary.* During the seventeenth and eighteenth centuries—and in some rural areas well into the twentieth century—it was not considered seemly or necessary for the invariably male physician to attend a woman at childbirth.

MILLER

"One who attends a mill." (W)

To mill: "To grind, beat up, stamp." (W) "An experienced Miller may be obtained the year ensuing, by applying to the subscriber at Capt. Chauncey Barnard's Mills, who wishes for constant employment in a grist mill, either upon wages or shares, as may best suit the owner. Ephraim Warfield." *American Mercury* (Hartford, Connecticut), March 29, 1809.

MILLINER

"One who makes women's caps, Ec." (W)

Milliner-dressmaker, as illustrated in *The Book of Trades* (London, 1805).

Usually, also, a dressmaker: "C. Filley Milliner and Mantuamaker, Begs leave to inform her friends and customers that she is opening at her Chamber in State Street, a few rods east of Bennett's Coffee-House, a new supply of elegant winter Hats and Bonnets, Lace Caps, and Turbans, Crape, Muslin and Leno, Shag of all colors, with Feathers . . . imperial Hats and Bonnets . . . twilled and plain Bonnets. N.B. She invites those Ladies which know the impropriety of a gentleman's fitting a garment to them that she will cut and fit Coats, Habits, Mantles, Silk Pelisses, Gowns, and all kinds of garments in the newest fashion. She informs them who may favor her with their custom that they shall be accommodated with warm rooms . . ." *American Mercury* (Hartford, Connecticut), November 8, 1814.

MUSKETEER
"A soldier whose weapon is his musket." (J) "August, 1643. The commissioners of the United Colonies [New England Confederation] met at Boston, taking into serious consideration that Miantunnomoh should be put to death [because he] was the head and contriver [of the general conspiracy among the Indians] and sent for Oakus [a friendly Sachem] who readily undertook the execution of Miantunnomoh . . . and that the Indians might know the English did approve . . . [we] sent 12 or 14 musketeers home with Oakus to abide a time with him for his defence." John Winthrop, *Journal, History of New England* (Boston, 1825).

NEEDLEMAKER, NEEDLER
"One who makes needles." (W) "John Ernst Juncken, Needle-Maker, living in Second-Street, near the Dutch Vendue House, in Philadelphia . . . makes and hath to sell . . . tent Hooks, Worked over with Pewter, Small Hooks and Eyes fit for Regimentals, Worms for Gunns, Brass and Iron Chairs, and Brushes for Musquets, Chains for squirrels, Cages for Parrots and other Birds . . ." *The New York Gazette and The Weekly Post-Boy,* January 1, 1759.

Needlemaker, as shown in *The Book of Trades* (London, 1805).

NIGHTMAN
"One who empties privies by night." (W)

PACKMAN
"A peddler." (H)

PAINTER
"One who paints or professes painting (colors mixed together)." (W) "Painting done in the best manner by Gustavus Hesselius, from Stockholm, and John Winter, from London, viz. Coats of Arms drawn on Coaches, Chaises, Ec. or any other kind of ornaments, Landskips, Signs, Shewboards, Ship and House Painting, Gilding of all Sorts, Writing in Gold or Colours. Old Pictures clean'd and mended Ec." *Pennsylvania Gazette* (Philadelphia), September 18, 1740.

PALMER

Properly, "a pilgrim who had visited the Holy Land, from the palm or cross he bore as a sign of such visitation, but Chaucer seems to consider all pilgrims to foreign parts as palmers, and the distinction was never much attended to by Englishmen." (H)

PARKER

"The keeper or overseer of a park." (W)

Park: "An enclosed ground for deer, Ec." (W)

PASTOR

"A shepherd." (W)

PATCHER

"One who patches or mends; a botcher." (W)

PEDLAR, PEDDLER

"One who travels to sell goods." (W)

PITCHER

The term for "the man who lifts or pitches corn or hay up on to a waggon. His work is of course called pitchen, his implement a pitchfork." (H)

PITMAN

"A man who works in pits; a sawyer." (W)

Pitsaw: "A large saw used by two men." (W)

PLANTER

"One who cultivates ground in the Colonies." (J)

Plantation: "A colony; the place planted." (J) "The People wherewith you Plant, ought to be Gardeners, Plough-Men, Labourers, Smiths, Carpenters, Joyners, Fisher-Men, Fowlers, with some few Apothecaries, Surgeons, Cookes, and Bakers." Francis Bacon, *Essay XXXIII, of Plantations; The Essayes or Counsels, Civill and Morall* (London, 1625).

"America was not conquered by William the Norman . . . Our ancestors, who migrated hither, were laborers, not lawyers." Thomas Jefferson, pamphlet, Williamsburg, Virginia, 1774.

"As concernes those Common[ers], There is little danger from them, except it be, where they have Great and Potent Heads, Or where you meddle, with the Point of Religion; Or Their Customes, or Meanes of Life." Francis Bacon, *Essay XIX, of Empire; The Essayes or Counsels, Civill and Morall* (London, 1625).

PLATER

Plate: "To cover with plate." (W) "A Journeyman who is a good Plater, may find employment, and good wages, by applying soon at Eli Wadsworth's Factory, in Front Street, Hartford. Likewise, Two boys as apprentices at the Plating business, about 15 years old, are wanted immediately." *American Mercury* (Hartford, Connecticut), January 25, 1814. "Wanted immediately. One or two Journeymen Tin Plate Workers, that are good workmen, to whom the highest wages will be given by Cyrus Woodruff, Main St." *American Mercury* (Hartford, Connecticut), June 18, 1814.

PLOWBOY

"A boy who drives a team in plowing." (W)

PLOWMAN

"A person who holds the plow." (W) One of the tenants or workmen on a farm:

The ploughman near at hand,
Whistles o'er the furrowed land,
And the milkmaid singeth blythe,
And the mower whets his scythe,
And every shepherd tells his tale
Under the hawthorn in the dale.

John Milton, *L'Allegro*

PLUMBER

"A person who works upon lead." (W) "Emery and Newman, from London, Plumbers, Painters, and Glaziers . . . near the Fly-Market, New-York. Sheet Lead cast to any given weight, Lead Cisterns, Ditto pumps, put down any depth, Ditto Wall pipes with elegant ornamented cistern heads . . ." *New-York Gazetteer,* May 31, 1785.

PORTER

"One who has the charge of a gate, a carrier of burdens." (W)

PRENTICE

"One bound to a master for instruction." (W) The same as apprentice.

PRINTER

"One who prints books." (W) "The workmen by whom the art of printing is performed are of two kinds, (1) *Compositors,* who range and dispose the letters into words, lines, pages, and sheets; and (2) *Pressmen,* who apply the ink and take of the impressions." *The Domestic Encyclopedia* (Philadelphia, 1821). Edward Winslow (1595–1655) of the Plymouth Colony had been a printer in Worcestershire, England, and at the Choir Alley Press in Leyden during the years of the Pilgrims' exile in Holland.

Calico printer, as shown in *The Book of Trades* (London, 1805).

Printer, as shown in *The Book of Trades* (London, 1805).

Printing: This is "The art of taking impressions from wooden blocks, types, or plates, upon paper, silk, calico, or any other substance. Printing is that very important art by means of which books are multiplied, and consequently, knowledge diffused among mankind." *The Domestic Encyclopedia* (Philadelphia, 1821).

PUBLICAN

"A man that keeps a house of general entertainment." An innkeeper. "This is to inform the public and my friends in particular, that I still continue to keep a Public House on the Green in New Haven, and further acquaints gentlemen and ladies who have been in the habit of putting up at my house, that I have provided new Hacks, and always ready to convey them down to the Steam Boat, or Packets. Every attention shall be paid to accommodate them, and they may rely on a still house, and beds in the same, except Commencement and during the session of the Assembly. Jacob

Ogden, New Haven, May 22d." *American Mercury* (Hartford, Connecticut), 1815.

REELER
The workman who operates a reel.

To Reel: "To wind [thread] on a reel." (W)   (See also SPINNER.)

REEVE, REVE
"A steward, bailiff, assistant." (W)

ROPEMAKER
"Lately imported in the Brig John a Parcel of very likely Men and Women servants, the men mostly Tradesmen as Smiths, Weavers, Rope-Makers, Joyners, Shoe Makers, and Framers. To be sold by Anthony Peel in Mulberry St. commonly called Arch St. at very reasonable rates or at the Brig lying over against the said street by the master." *American Weekly Mercury* (Philadelphia), September 26, 1734.

Ropemaker, as shown in *The Book of Trades*, (London, 1805).

ROVER
"An archer," (H) so called because rover also was the term to describe the arrows

shot at a target at a specified angle, such as 45 degrees.

SADDLER
The craftsman in leather who made "horse furniture" including saddles, saddle bags, and harness: "This is to inform all Gentlemen, Ladies and others, that James Eltridge, Sadler, in the Broad-way, New York, late from London; Makes and sells all sorts of sadels, bridles, and furniture, as neat as in London, viz. Ladies hunting side saddles, and all other sorts of side saddles, forest saddles without trees, demipacks, hunter's with doe-skin, seats, either welted or plain, portmantures, leather bags, villeases for bedding [covers or cases for blanket rolls]." *The New York Mercury,* August 29, 1763.

Saddler, as shown in *The Book of Trades,* (London, 1805).

SAD(D)LER'S IRONMONGER
One of the several specialists in the manufacture of saddles and harnesses. "The

sadler's ironmonger furnishes the iron or steel stirrup, buckles of all kinds, bits for bridles, and other steel or brass furniture required for the harness of a horse, either for riding or drawing in a carriage." *The Book of Trades* (London, 1805).

SALTER
"One who sells salt." (W) Roger Conant (c. 1592–1679) first governor of the Cape Ann Settlement and a founder in 1636 of Beverly, Massachusetts, was a salter from London.

SCHOOLMASTER, SCHOOLMISTRESS
"One who teaches a school. A master, instructor, tutor." (W) "New Boarding School. Mrs. Value proposes opening a Boarding School for young ladies on the first Monday in January next when she will re-commence teaching those branches of instruction which she formerly taught with success . . . viz. orthography, reading prose and verse, arithmetic, Parsing English grammar, the elements, astronomy on the celestial globe, geography on the terrestrial globe, with a correct knowledge of the atlas and maps, history, Blair's lectures, composition, drawing, painting, plain sewing, needle work on muslin, and embroidery. In addition, Mr. Value will give them a lesson every day (Sundays excepted) in polite manners, dancing, the French language and music. Terms for board and tuition $3 per week—it being understood that each young lady will furnish herself with whatever will be necessary to use in school (the globe, atlas and piano excepted), also her own wood and candles when she is not with the family. According to the former custom in Mrs. Value's School, the young ladies will read once in the bible every day. The number of Boarders shall be limited to twenty, who shall be treated with respect, delicacy and attention, and who, it is presumed, will find the family and accommodations agreeable and satisfactory." *American Mercury* (Hartford, Connecticut), November 29, 1814.

SCOUT
A professional guide, but also a professional or government-paid spy.

Scoutmaster: A chief of intelligence or espionage. George Downing of Salem became Scoutmaster-General of the Commonwealth, later served Cromwell's government in England and finally Charles II during the Restoration, thus earning the epithet "a perfidious rogue." Samuel Pepys, *Diary,* March 12, 1662.

SEAMSTRESS, SEMSTRESS, SEMPSTRESS
All variations of the term for "A woman whose business it is to sew," (J) for others.

SHEARER
"A person that shears sheep or cloth." (W)

Shearman, Sherman: "A man who shears or finishes cloth." (W) "Sheares for Shearmen, for Glovers, for Seamesters, for Taylers," were listed in the House of Parliament rates, 1660, for Imports and Exports —*Statutes of the Realm* (London, 1819).

SHIP'S TAILOR
"The person who shapes and sews together the cloth into sails is a sail-maker, and is denominated a ship's taylor." *The Book of Trades* (London, 1805).

SHIPWRIGHT
The master carpenter-contractor who built ships and often served as captain. "November, 1645. Captain Thomas Hawkins, a shipright of London, who had lived here divers years, had built at Boston a ship of 400 tons and upward, and had set her out with much strength of ordnance, and ornament of carving, painting, etc. and called her the *Seafort*." John Winthrop, *Journal, History of New England* (Boston, 1825). Francis Eaton (1595–1633) of the Plymouth Colony had been a ship's carpenter in Bristol, England.

SHOPKEEPER

"A trader who sells in a shop; not a merchant, who only deals by wholesale." (J)

Shopkeeper, as shown in *The Book of Trades* (London, 1805).

SHOPMAN

"A petty trader." (J)

SICKLEMAN, SICKLER

"One who reaps, a reaper." (W)

Sickleman, as shown in a popular c. 1800 print.

SIGN PAINTER

The man who painted and varnished devices and ornaments used as identifying insignia. "Military Standards, Cap Fronts, Knapsacks, Ec. painted at short notice. Freemasons' carpets and Aprons, done to any patterns. Sign and Ornamental painting done as usual, at the Stand lately occupied by C. & W. Andross, two doors east of the Hartford Bank, William Rice." *American Mercury* (Hartford, Connecticut), April 3, 1820. Colorful old tavern and shop signs are sought by collectors today.

SILK THROWER, SILK THROWSTER

The silk spinner, called "The silk-throwster prepares by means of a mill the raw silk for the use of the weaver; he employs women chiefly. Spinning the raw silk and winding it employ a great number of hands of almost all ages." *The Book of Trades* (London, 1805).

SILVERSMITH

"One that works in silver." (J)

SIMPLER, SIMPLEST

A common term for an Apothecary, *q.v.*, or "one skilled in simples; an herbarist." (J)

Simple: "A single ingredient in a medicine; a drug. It is popularly used for an herb." (J)

SKINKER

"A person that serves drink to others." (W)

SKINNER

"A dealer in skins, a fellmonger." (W)

SLATER

"One who covers houses with slates." (W)

SMITH, SMITHING

"Smithing comprehends all trades which use either the forge or file, from the anchor smith to the watchmaker, they all working by the same rules, though not with equal exactness, and all using the same tools, though of several sizes." Joseph Moxon, *Mechanick Exercises, or The Doctrine of Handy-Works* (London, 1683–84).

SOAP BOILER

"One whose trade is to make soap." (J)

SPICER

"One who deals in spices" (W); a grocer.

SPINNER, SPINSTER

"[The male and female] persons that spin."

To Spin: "To draw out in threads." (W) "Wanted—A spinner and a number of steady boys and girls to work in a Cotton Factory. A few expert Reelers will find good encouragement. Also, two or three large families, the children to work in the Factory. Pardon Brown, Agent, Glastonbury." *American Mercury* (Hartford, Connecticut), August 28, 1815.

SPINNING-WHEEL MAKER
"Wanted two or three steady Lads as Apprentices to learn the trade of a turner and spinning wheel maker. Apply to George Fix in North Second-Street, No. 152, where the said branches of business are carried on. N.B. Lads from the country would be preferred." *Pennsylvania Gazette* (Philadelphia), November 16, 1791.

SPURRIER
"One who makes or deals in spurs." (W)

STAINER
A popular term for "one who stains; a dyer." (J) Thus, specifically, also a calico printer; a paper stainer.

STONECUTTER
"One whose trade is to hew stones." (J) "To be Sold very Cheap, An Elegant Marble Chimney Piece, Inlaid with Egyptian Green Marble; also, several Setts of Obelisks and Vases Made of Derbyshire Spar, for ornaments on mantle pieces. William Stiles, Stone-Cutter." *Pennsylvania Packet* (Philadelphia), August 30, 1787. (See also MARBLE CUTTER.)

SURGEON
The term, corrupted by conversation from Chirurgeon, *q.v.,* for "one who cures by manual operation; one whose duty is to treat external maladies by the direction of the physician." (J)

SURVEYOR
"A county surveyor shall have the power to lay out lands, to renew the bounds of lands already laid out, according to their original grants, to run lines, to survey and measure land . . . provided he produce a certificate . . . that he is duly qualified in point of science, in the art of surveying lands." *Connecticut Statutes* (Hartford, 1835).

SUTLER
"One who sells provisions to soldiers." (W)

SWORD CUTLER
"One who makes or deals in swords." (W) "Those gentlemen who are forming themselves into Companies in Defence of their Liberties, and others that are not provided with swords may be suited therewith by applying to Charles Oliver Bruff in Maiden Lane . . . Small Swords silver-mounted, Cut-and-Thrust and Cutteau De Chase . . . Broad Swords . . . being a collection of the most elegant swords ever made in America . . ." *The New York Gazette and The Weekly Mercury,* June 19, 1775.

TAILOR, TAYLOR
"One who makes men's clothes." (W) Often, as was true of many who provided personal services, tailors were brought over as indentured or bonded servants, their passage paid in return for the promise to serve a set number of years at a stipulated wage. ". . . request you to send to me a Taylor indented to serve me four years at the usual wages of abt £10 or £12 pr. ano. I should be glad he could be sent soon by any ship to York or James River, as I could get him from thence full as easily as a bale of any other wares. I pray that he may not be too old, having seen some that have brought their Spectacles with them and were fitted for a hospital than for the shopboard." Order from William Nelson, September 12, 1766, Yorktown, Virginia. Frances Mason, *John Norton and Sons, Merchants of London and Virginia.* (Richmond, 1935).

"I credit you £20:9:6 for expenses of the Taylor . . . I particularly thank you for the trouble you took to procure the Taylor without the usual Expense of Crimpage. He is young and healthy and seems to know his Business as well as I desire." August 14, 1767. Ibid. *Mayflower* passenger Isaac Allerton had been a tailor in London before emigrating; later he became a merchant at New Haven, Connecticut.

Tailor, as shown in a popular c. 1800 print.

TALLOW CHANDLER

"A maker of tallow candles." (W) "Cyprian Nichols continues to purchase tallow and will pay a high price in cash for the article on delivery at his Soap and Candle Manufactory, 20 rods west of Hudson and Goodwin Printing Office." *American Mercury* (Hartford, Connecticut), December 28, 1814.

TANNER

"One who tans hides for lether." (W) "15 Dollars Reward. Runaway from the subscriber on the 25th inst. an indented apprentice to the Tanning and Shoemaking business named Erastus Waters, nineteen years of age, light complexion, and rather a downcast look—had on a black coat, light colored vest, black woollen trowsers, took with him a pair of tow trowsers, a black great coat, a pair of cotton stockings . . . Zadock Bliss, Windsor parish." *American Mercury* (Hartford, Connecticut), July 5, 1814.

TAVERNER, TAVERNKEEPER, TAVERNMAN

"One who keeps a tavern." (J)

TAWER

"A tanner or dresser of white lether." (W)
   Taw: "To dress white lether." (W)

THATCHER

"One who covers places with straw." (W)

THRASHER

"One who thrashes." (W)
   To Thrash: "To beat grain." (W)

THROWSTER

"One who twists silk, thread, Ec." (W)

TILER, TYLER

"One who tiles; a mason's porter." (W)

TINKER

"A mender of kettles and pans." (W) "A mender of old brass," so called because "their way of proclaiming their trade is to beat a kettle, or because in their work they make a tinkling noise." (J)

TINMAN

"A manufacturer of tin, or iron tinned over." (J)

TIREMAN

The prefix is a contraction of attire and so this term signified "a dealer in dresses and all kinds of ornamental clothing." (H)

TIREWOMAN

"A milliner." (H)

TOBACCONIST

"A. Jeffery, Tobacconist, offers for sale at his factory, head of Ferry-Street, Junk and Pigtail Tobacco, manufactured from best quality Virginia Leaf. Spanish Segars, best quality, all of which he will warrant good and cheap." *American Mercury* (Hartford, Connecticut), January 6, 1817.

TOOTHDRAWER

"One who pulls out carious teeth," (W) and fitted artificial ones, of his own manufacture or that of others. Artificial teeth often were carved of bone, ivory, or hardwood and set in place, secured by jeweler's wire. Others were made of steel, silver, or gold by silversmiths (including Paul Revere). The "mechanick" who did the work often moved from town to town, announcing his arrival in this fashion: "The subscriber wishes to inform the publick that he has taken a convenient room over Mr. S. Whiting's Hardware store, directly opposite the office of the *Connecticut Courant,* where he sets Artificial Teeth, of all descriptions, so as to look as well as the natural ones, and nearly answer the same purpose with little or no pain, fills hollow teeth, so that they nearly answer the same purpose as the sound ones and in many instances prevent the aching . . . He presumes those ladies and gentlemen that wish for his assistance in this line will not be disappointed if they call David Greenleaf." *American Mercury* (Hartford, Connecticut), February 21, 1816. Although the word Dentist was evolved in the second half of the eighteenth century, apparently it was not in common enough use in this country for Webster to include it in his 1806 Dictionary.

TRADER, TRADESMAN
A tradesman is "a shopkeeper. A merchant is called a trader, but not a tradesman; distinguished from a man that labours with his hands." (J)

TREEMAKER
The name given one of the specialized craftsmen in the saddlery trade. "The tree-maker furnishes only the wooden parts of the saddle; this is, however, a very important branch of the business, because upon the saddle-tree the fitting of the saddle depends; and in cases when gentlemen wish to have their saddles fit properly, it is as necessary to measure the horse's back, as for the shoemaker to measure his customer for boots or shoes. The tree-maker requires no great strength or ingenuity." *The Book of Trades* (London, 1805).

TURNER
"One who turns on a lathe." (W) The term used in England since the sixteenth century to describe the craftsman who cuts and shapes wood, or some other hard substance, symmetrically by turning it on a lathe. "Some turners to show their dexterity, turn long and slender pieces of ivory, as small as an hay-stalk." Joseph Moxon, *Mechanick Exercises, or the Doctrine of Handy-works* (London, 1683–84).

Turner, as shown in *The Book of Trades* (London, 1805).

TITHINGMAN, TYTHINGMAN
"An officer who keeps order in church." (W) "Each town shall, at their annual meeting choose two or more tything-men, in each society or congregation, who shall make due presentment of all breaches of [the act] for the due observation of the Sabbath, or Lord's Day, and days of public Fasting and Thanksgiving." *Connecticut Statutes* (Hartford, 1835).

UPHOLSTERER
"One who furnishes houses, beds, etc." (W) with any item made of fabric or paper; including wall hangings of cloth or paper; window curtains and draperies; bed curtains, valances, mattresses, covers, as well as the work of covering and stuffing chairs and sofas. "Thomas Elfe, Cabinet-Maker, having now a good upholsterer from London, does all kinds of upholsterer's work in the best and newest manner and at the most reasonable rates, fiz: tapestry, damask, stuff, chints, or paper hangings for

rooms; beds after the newest fashion and so they may be taken off to be washed without inconvenience or damage; all sorts of festoons and window curtains to draw up; chairs stuff covered, tight or loose cases for ditto." *South Carolina Gazette* (Charleston), January 7, 1751. (The earlier form of the word was upholder.)

WAITING MAID

"An upper servant attending a lady." (W)

WAITS

"Nightly musicians," (W) street singers.

WALKER

"An officer, a forester." (W)

WARDEN

"Head officer; keeper," (W) the superintendent or overseer of an estate.

WARDER

"A keeper, guard." (W)

WATERMAN

"A boatman, ferryman, sailor." (W)

WEATHER CASTER

"The person who computed the weather for the almanacs." (H)

WEATHER SPY

"A stargazer, astrologer, wizard," (W) a weather forecaster.

WEAVER

"One who makes threads into cloth." (W) "Wanted by the subscriber, a Weaver, who is acquainted with the Broad Loom, to he that can come well recommended, good wages and long employ will be given." James Babcock. *American Mercury* (Hartford, Connecticut), March 3, 1814. "The common weaver requires but little ingenuity in carrying on his business, but weavers on flowered silks, damasks, velvets, Ec., ought to be people possessed of a considerable capacity; it is an advantage to them if they are able to draw and design their own patterns. It is a business that requires no great degree of strength, and a lad may be bound apprentice at twelve or thirteen years

Weaver, as shown in *The Book of Trades* (London, 1805).

Stocking weaver, as shown in *The Book of Trades* (London, 1805).

of age. Among weavers are frequently found men of a thoughtful and literary turn. One of the first mathematicians of England was Mr. Thomas Simpson, an industrious weaver at Spitalfields. The broad weaver is employed in stuffs, broad-cloths, woollen goods, Ec.; the narrow weaver in ribbons, tapes, and other such things." *The Book of Trades* (London, 1805).

WEBSTER
"One who weaves cloth, a weaver." (W)

WHEELER, WHEELWRIGHT
"A maker of wheels." (W)

WHETTER
"One who sharpens knives, Ec." (W)

WHITESMITH
Another name for the Brightsmith, *q.v.;* that is, one who generally worked in metals other than iron—but, there were exceptions. "John Martin, Gun and White Smith . . . will carry on his business as usual. All kinds of brands, stamps, and impressions made in copper, iron, brass, steel or wood, from two inches down to the common size of printers types, made in the neatest manner . . ." *New-York Daily Advertiser,* April 24, 1788.

WIDOW
"A woman who has lost her husband. In London, a freeman's widow may exercise her husband's trade, as long as she continues such." (M) The same custom, of course, was followed in the colonies; hence, many advertisements of this type: "Notice is hereby given that the widow of Balthaser Sommers now lives next door to Mr. Taffert's on Pot-Baker's Hill, in Smith Street . . . grinds all sorts of optic Glasses to the greatest Perfection, such as Microscope Glasses, Spying Glasses . . . Spectacles, Reading Glasses, for near-sighted People or others . . ." *The New York Gazette or The Weekly Post-Boy,* May 21, 1753.

WIREDRAWER
"A person who draws out or makes wire," (W) and thus an employee of tinsmiths and pewterers. "Two or three smart young men acquainted with drawing fine Wire can find employ by applying to Henry King." *American Mercury* (Hartford, Connecticut), May 3, 1814.

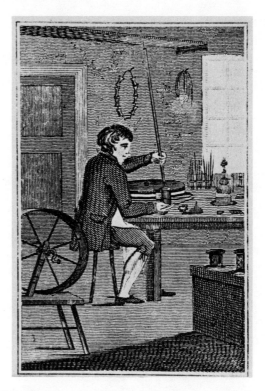

Wiredrawer, as shown in *The Book of Trades* (London, 1805).

WOODMAN
"A hunter, officer, bailiff." (W)

WOODREVE
"A steward or overseer of a wood." (W)

WOOL COMBER
"One who lives by combing wool." (W)

YEOMAN
"A gentleman farmer, freeholder, officer." (W)

4
Weights and Measures

Engraving from *The American Atlas* (Thomas Jeffery, London, 1776) shows Virginia tobacco planter merchants with clerk overseeing the packing and loading of hogsheads bound for London sales agencies. Note merchant checking weight of casks on tall balance scale in center background.

"Our weights and measures are the same as those which are fixed by acts of parliament in England" Jefferson wrote in 1781, adding, "how it has happened that the nominal value of coin was made to differ from what it was in the country we left—and to differ among ourselves, too, I am not able to say with certainty." Thomas Jefferson, *Notes on the State of Virginia* (London, 1787; Richmond, 1853).

Seldom is the contrast in manner and ease of living with our own times better shown than in the descriptions of household needs offered in those small advertisements that crowded the front pages of newspapers published here during the eighteenth and early nineteenth centuries. Consider these notices published in the autumn of 1812, shortly after the beginning of the second war with England, when the average householder purchased many supplies by the keg, cask, barrel, or gallon, enough for a season if not for a year:

"Just received and offered for sale by Frederick Bange & Co. 30 chests Hyson, Young Hyson, Souchong and Bohea Teas, 6 pipes, 6 half pipes & 8 quarter casks Vidonia, Lisbon and Malaga Wines, 4 pipes Bordeaux Brandy, 1 do. Cognac

Apothecary's scales and weights.

Brandy, 1 do. pure Holland Gin, 1 hogshead old Cherry Rum, 8 hogsheads well-flavor'd West Indies Rum, 1 puncheon old Jamaica 4th proof Spirit, 2000 lbs. Coffee, 30 barrels brown Sugar, 15 kegs Ginger, 16 do. warranted Tobacco, 30 puncheons, West India Rum of the best quality, this day received and for sale on accomodating terms by Kimberling & Brace." *American Mercury* (Hartford, Connecticut), October 23, 1812.

"John I. Wells Offers for sale Old Linseed Oil, of an excellent quality, by the barrel or Gallon, and furniture Varnish from one to eight dollars per gal." Ibid.

"New Goods. Justin Campbell Has this day received . . . a quantity of Gun Powder, constantly for sale by one Cask or less quantity." Ibid.

Quart ink bottle from which smaller desk bottles or inkstands were filled.

Glazed earthenware storage jar for oil or other liquid stores.

New England storage jar and pots. (Courtesy, Antiquarian and Landmarks Society, Inc.)

"20 Boxes Soap, 6 bags Pepper and Pimento, 8 bales New Orleans cotton, 20 boxes Spanish Segars, 40 boxes 7 by 9 and 6 by 8 glass, 6 boxes chocolate, 10 barrels Shad, 6 boxes Muscatel Raisins, 2 Ton Bed Cords and white Rope, 20 boxes China Setts, 60 doz. china dining Plates . . ." Ibid., November 18, 1812.

"Molasses, suitable for retailing in Hogsheads, Tierces, and Barrels, For Sale by L. Savage & Co. who exchange Salt for Flax Seed & Beans." Ibid.

The householder who required smaller amounts than those ready to be delivered by the keg or cask, more often than not was expected to supply his own containers. Many of the crocks, jars, jugs, baskets, barrels, and boxes stacked in the cellars, attics, and pantries of old houses were used not only for the storage of home-prepared foods, but were carried to the market to be filled to order by the storekeeper.

Two-gallon size mustard
storage jar.

Splint market basket.

Wicker market basket.

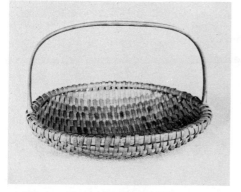

Splint basket often used for bread.

Covered splint storage basket.

Clothes or storage splint basket with alternating
squares painted. (Courtesy, Antiquarian and Landmarks Society, Inc.)

Toy basket. (Courtesy, Antiquarian and Landmarks Society, Inc.)

Eighteenth-century iron brand for stamping owner's or shipper's initial on casks and other wooden containers of exported goods. Wood haft fits into the socket.

"ALE AND BEER MEASURES

2 pints	=	1 quart
4 quarts	=	1 gallon
9 gallons	=	1 firkin
2 firkins	=	18 gallons or 1 kilderkin
2 kilderkins	=	36 gallons or 1 barrel
1½ barrels	=	54 gallons or 1 hogshead
1⅓ hogshead	=	72 gallons or 1 puncheon
1½ puncheon	=	103 gallons or 1 butt

The ale gallon contains 282 cubic inches; the cask of 108 or 110 gallons is called a hogshead or a puncheon." (W)

BARREL
"A wooden vessel." (W) "200 New and well-made Cider Barrels suitable for Brandy or Cider to be sold by E. & H. Averill." *American Mercury* (Hartford, Connecticut), October 7, 1812.

"Barrel Measures:

Wine: The ⅛ part of a tun,
       or ¼ part of a pipe,
       or ½ a hogshead,
each equalling 31½ gallons.

Beer: 36 gallons
Ale: 32 gallons
Soap: 256 pounds
Herring: 32 gallon wine measure or 28 gallons of about 1,000 herrings
Salmon: 42 gallons" (M)

"All barrels and half-barrels containing beef or pork shall be made of good seasoned white oak, rock oak free from sap, or white ash staves and heading, hooped with twelve substantial hoops, well seasoned. Each barrel for pork shall guage not less than twenty-nine gallons; each barrel for beef not less than twenty-eight, and contain two hundred pounds weight." *Connecticut Statutes* (Hartford, 1835).

Wooden hooped flour barrel made in early eighteenth century. (Courtesy, Antiquarian and Landmarks Society, Inc.)

"CLOTH MEASURES:

2¼ inches	=1 nail
4 nails	=1 quarter
4 quarters	=1 yard
3 quarters	=1 ell Flemish
5 quarters	=1 ell English
6 quarters	=1 ell French" (W)

"DRY MEASURES:

8 pints	=1 gallon
2 gallons	=1 peck
4 pecks	=1 bushel
4 bushels	=1 coom
2 cooms	=1 quarter
5 quarters	=1 wey
2 weys	=1 last

The gallon contains 272¾ cubic inches." (W)

"LINEAR MEASUREMENTS:

3 barleycorns	=1 inch
12 inches	=1 foot
3 feet	=1 yard
5½ yards	=1 pole, perch or rod
40 rods or perches	=1 furlong
8 furlongs	=1 mile
4 inches	=1 hand
6 feet	=1 fathom
3 miles	=1 league

The weights and measures of the United States are the same as the standard weights and measures in England." (W)

"SQUARE MEASURES:

9 feet	=1 yard
30¼ yards	=1 pole
40 poles or rods	=1 rood
4 roods	=1 acre

An aker contains 10 square chains, 160 square rods, 4,840 square yards, 100,000 square links [because] the chain for measuring land is 100 links which is 4 rods or perches, 22 yards, or 66 feet." (W)

"WINE MEASURES:

4 gills	=1 pint
2 pints	=1 quart
4 quarts	=1 gallon
42 gallons	=1 tierce
1½ tierce, or 63 gallons	=1 hogshead
1⅓ hogshead or 84 gallons	=1 puncheon
1⅓ puncheon or 126 gallons	=1 pipe
2 pipes	=1 tun
231 cubic inches	=1 gallon
10 gallons	=1 anker (anchor)
18 gallons	=1 runlet
31½ gallons	=1 barrel" (W)

Wicker basket of the type used to carry produce, such as the grapes shown in this c. 1800 print being taken to the wine press.

WOOL

"The dealers in wool in England use the following weights:

The sack	=2 weighs
The weigh	=6½ tods
The tod	=2 stones

The stone   =2 cloves

The clove   =7 pounds

12 sacks make a last or 4,368 pounds

56 pounds of old hay or 6 pounds of new hay makes a truss

36 trusses make a load of hay or straw

14 pounds make a stone

 5 pounds of glass make a stone." (W)

ALMENE
"A weight of two pounds, used in weighing saffron." (M)

AMPHORA
Half an urna.

AROLEC
"A weight equal to twenty five pounds." (M)

AUME
."A wine measure of forty gallons." (M)

ALNAGE, AULNAGE
"The measuring of woolen manufactures with an ell. There are now three officers relating to the alnage, a searcher, a measurer, and alnager all which formerly were comprised in the alnager, until by his own neglect it was thought proper to separate these offices." (M)

BOLE
"A measure of six bushels." (W)

BOLL
"Two bushels." (W)

BUSHEL
"A dry commodity measure containing four pecks or eight gallons or one-eighth of a quarter. Every bushel should have a plain and even bottom, be eighteen-and-a-half inches wide throughout." (M)

BUTT
The term from the Latin *butta* for cask or wine-skin, to describe a "vessel or measure of capacity containing two hogsheads or one hundred twenty six gallons." (M) "May 6, 1646. The court had imposed [a tax of]

A By-Law concerning the measuring of Coal

BE it ordained by the Mayor, Aldermen, Common Council and Freemen of the City of Hartford,—That there shall be provided at the expence of this City, and kept at such places as the inspector of wood shall designate and under his superintendence, ten baskets each of which whenever full shall be of the capacity of three bushels coal measure, which said baskets shall be sealed and kept as aforesaid to be used by the sellers of coal in this City free of expence. And all coal brought into this City and sold to any person in this City shall be measured in some one or more of the said baskets.

2. And be it further ordained,—That if any person shall sell or purchase any coal brought into this City as aforesaid, contrary to the provisions of this By-Law, every person so selling and every person so purchasing shall forfeit and pay the Treasurer of this City for the use of the City a fine of Five dollars for each and every offence.

The foregoing By-Law was made and passed in Court of Common Council on the 16th day of May A. D. 1818. Read and approved in City meeting on the 23d day of May A. D. 1818.   Attest.
        J. BROWN, Clerk.

Ordinance regulating coal measures: ten baskets equals three bushels. *American Mercury* (Hartford, Connecticut), May 30, 1818.

ten shillings upon every butt of sack, etc. to be landed in our jurisdiction, and this spring there came in four ships with sack, and landed about 800 butts, but the merchants being much offended (having no intelligence of it before) after much debate, the court remitted one half." John Winthrop, *Journal, History of New England* (Boston, 1825).

CADE
"A cag, cask, or barrel containing a certain number of some particular commod-

ities. A cade of red herrings is a vessel containing 300; a cade of sprats contains 1000 of those fishes." (M)

CAG
"Or keg of sturgeon, salmon Ec. signifies a barrel containing 4 to 5 gallons." (M)

CASE
"A case of crown glass contains usually twenty-four tables, each table being nearly circular and about three feet six inches diameter." (M)

CHALDRON
"A dry measure of 36 bushels." (M)

CORD OF WOOD
"The dimensions are eight feet long, four feet high and four feet broad." (M)

CRIB
"A measure of 100 square feet of window glass." (W)

CURNOCK
"A measure of corn containing four bushels or half a quarter." (M)

DICKER
"An old term [that] signifies ten, thus a dicker of hides is ten skins, a dicker of gloves implies ten pair, Ec." (M)

FANGOT
"A quantity of wares; as raw silk, Ec., containing from one to two hundred weight three quarters." (J)

FATHOM
"A measure of length containing six foot, or two yards; the space to which a man can extend both arms." (J)

FLAGON
"A two-quart measure of wine." (W)

HAND
"A measure of four inches or of a clenched fist." (M)

HOGSHEAD
"A measure of sixty three gallons." (W) "For Sale on the Green Woods Turnpike Road two miles above Mr. Theodore Cowles's Tavern at E. Wood's Saw Mills, an assortment of Pine Timber, 2 inch plank, 1¼ inch Board, scaling and siding Boards, Clapboards, white and red Oak hogshead Staves and barrels do. E. W. Wood. Barkhamstead." *American Mercury* (Hartford, Connecticut), June 11, 1815. "Provisions sent in the Rebecca . . . A hogshead of oatmeal, two hogsheads of meal, Five casks of peas, Seven barrels of beef, A hogshead of pork, Two kilderkins of butter, put in by Mr. Pierce for Sergeant Willes." (John Winthrop at Boston to his son, Governor John Winthrop, Jr., of Connecticut, June 10, 1636.) *Journal, History of New England* (Boston, 1825).

JACK
"A half or quarter of a pint." (W)

KENTLE
"In trade, a hundredweight." (W)

KILDERKIN
A wooden barrel or cask made to hold 18 gallons. "Sergeant Willes's two kilderkins of B [eef] cost 7.4.4. at 7d the pound. If you have more peas and beef than you need, you may send back some." (John Winthrop at Boston to his son, Governor John Winthrop, Jr., of Connecticut, June 23, 1636.) *Journal, History of New England* (Boston, 1825).

LANDYARD
"Two staves or eighteen feet are a landyard; 160 landyards an acre." (H)

LUG
"Originally a pole measure of sixteen and one-half feet; anciently, of twenty feet." (W)

MEDIN
"A dry measure." (W)

MEER, MERE
A measure or boundary; thus a merestone is a boundary marker. Anciently, meer meant the distance "from bound to bound, or house to house; and was the term also for a measure of 29 to 31 yards." (M)

NIPPERKIN

"A small measure of beer." (H)

NOTT

"A quantity of thread, consisting of 40 rounds of a reel, the 20th of a run, or 80 yards." (W)

PACE

"Usually reckoned two feet and a half." *The Domestic Encyclopedia* (Philadelphia, 1821).

PENNYWEIGHT

"A Troy-weight containing 24 grains, each of which is equal in weight to a grain of wheat gathered out of the middle of the ear, and well dried." *The Domestic Encyclopedia* (Philadelphia, 1821).

POTTLE

"A two quart bottle; a measure of four pints." (W)

PUNCHEON

A wooden cask containing 72 gallons. "RUM. 30 puncheons West India Rum of the best quality this day received and for sale on accommodating terms by Kimberly & Brace." *American Mercury* (Hartford, Connecticut), October 28, 1812.

QUAUTERN

"The fourth part of a pint." (W)

QUINTAL

"A hundred pounds, a kintle." (W)

SACK

"A bag of three bushels." (W)

SELVAGE

"A hank of rope." (W)

SEAM

"A measure of eight bushels." (W)

SEXTARY

"A measure of a pint and one half." (W)

SHAFTMAN, SHAFMET, SHAFTMENT

"The measure of the fist with the thumb set up." Ray, *English Words* (1674).

SKEIN

"Each skein of sewing-silk [shall] consist of twenty threads, each thread of the length of two yards." *Connecticut Statutes* (Hartford, 1835).

STRIKE

"Four pecks, a bushel." (W)

TIERCE

"A third part of a pipe." (W)

TOD

"A weight of twenty-eight pounds." (W)

TUN

"A cask of four hogsheads; twenty hundred weight." (W)

5

Terms Used By Joiners and Cabinetmakers

ABACUS

"The uppermost member of a column, which serves as a sort of crowning both to the capital and the column." (J) "Vitruvius tells us that the Abacus was originally intended to represent a square tile laid over an urn or basket. An Athenian old woman happening to place a basket over the root of an acanthus, that plant shooting up the following spring encompassed the basket all around, till meeting with the tile, it curled back in a kind of scroll. An ingenious sculptor, passing by, took the hint . . . Abacus is also a concave molding on the Tuscan pedestal." (M)

ACANTHUS

Classic Greek and Roman motif based on the leaves of the thistle-like herb; used as a carved decoration on Georgian, Federal, and Empire furniture, accessories, and moldings; architecturally on Corinthian and Composite capitals. "A genus of polyandrious plants called in English bear's-breech [or bear's foot], known when not in flower by its beautiful leaves which are so elegant as to be imitated on carvings." (M)

ACORN

The nut fruit of the oak tree and inspiration for the stylized turned oval decoration used as pendants on William and Mary chest frames, tables, and other furniture; as finials on chair uprights, bed posts, etc., throughout the eighteenth century.

Chair with acorn finials. (Courtesy, **Antiquarian and Landmarks Society, Inc.**)

ACROTERIA

"Small pedestals upon which globes, vases, or statues stand at the ends or middle of pediments [*q.v.*]." (M)

AJOURÉ

Any pierced or open work producing a lace-like effect by carving, modeling, or molding.

ALMOND

"Is also a name given to pieces of rock-crystal which lapidaries use in adorning branch candlesticks, Ec. on account of the resemblance they bear to the fruit of the same name." (M)

AMORINO

The term from the Italian for "little love," generally used in the plural, *amorini*, to describe those small cupids or cherubim represented in carved and gilded ornaments.

ANNULETTED

Decorated with a ring or rings, as that around a column.

ANTHEMION

Stylized, classic Greek honeysuckle flower-and-leaf design favored by Greek Revival architects and as a decoration for Empire, Regency, Louis XV, and Louis XVI furniture, silver, glass, and porcelain. Sometimes referred to as the Greek honeysuckle. Earlier this stylized design was used by Hepplewhite and other late-eighteenth-century designers for chair backs. The name Anthemion-back has been given to these chairs in the twentieth century, although it was not used to describe them when they were made.

APPLIED FACET

Small shaped pieces of wood, such as lozenge or triangle forms, applied to a panel or frame as ornamentation. (See also BOSS.)

APPLIED MOLDING

Any molding added to the surface of a case piece, a frame, or clock case, or to a door to give the appearance of a panel, or to add a heaviness or ornateness to the piece it otherwise would not have.

APPLIED TURNING

Lathe-turned ornaments, such as split spindles or pillars, applied as additional surface decorations to case furniture and clock cases.

APRON

The facing strip beneath the front of a chair seat, or at the base of a chest, or the frieze rail of a table, extending between the legs, and usually shaped, carved, or otherwise decorated.

ARABESQUE

Arabian-like; a general name for fanciful and curving designs of intricately intertwined flowers, fruits, animals, and figures in single groups or combinations, often used in Georgian inlays and marquetry work. Introduced in Hispano-Moresque art.

ARCADING

The use of arches applied as decorative panels on chests, cupboards, beds, and overmantels in the sixteenth and seventeenth centuries; the style was revived in the nineteenth century during the Neo-Gothic period.

ARCHITRAVE

In furniture and interior work, the name for the molded frame used around a door or window.

ARROW-BACK

A nineteenth-century chair or settee back of three or more flat spindles shaped as broad arrows, with the arrowhead just under the top rail.

ASTRAGAL

"A little round moulding in the form of a ring." (M)   (See also BEADING.)

ATLANTES

The masculine equivalent of the Caryatids, *q.v.;* that is, figural supporting columns or pillars used to ornament late-sixteenth-century and seventeenth-century furniture.

AU POCHOIR

Decorated with stencil painting.

BACK BOARD

The wooden board or boards which form the back of a piece of case furniture or of a looking glass.

BAGUETTE

"A small, round moulding, something less than the astragal." (M)

BALL FOOT

The round or ball-shaped foot used on late-seventeenth- and early-eighteenth-century case pieces.

Ball foot.

BALLOON, BALLON

"A large round short-necked ball or globe placed on top of a pillar by way of crowning." (M)

BALUSTER BACK

Split balusters (which Webster in 1806 described as little pillars) with the rounded side to the rear, set vertically beneath the top rail to form chair backs, especially favored by New England joiners in the first half of the eighteenth century.

BALUSTER LEG

The table leg turned in the shape of a baluster, used in the seventeenth century and into the second quarter of the eighteenth century.

BANDING

A thin veneer border; a narrow band of wood inlay at the edge of a drawer front or table rim.

BANDY LEG

(See CABRIOLE.)

BANISTER

"The same as baluster." (W)

BANTAMWORK

"A kind of painted or carved work, resembling that of Japan, only more gaudy." (M) (See also COROMANDEL.)

BARLEY SUGAR TWIST

A decorative turning used for the frames of tables, cupboards, stands, and chairs, dating from the early sixteenth century and so called because it resembled a stick of barley sugar candy, also called double rope or double-twist turning.

BASE

In cabinetmaking, the lowest horizontal part of a case.

BAS RELIEF

The shallow decoration or pattern carved in wood or cast in plaster. Sometimes the Italian term, *basso-rilievo,* is used for this kind of low-relief ornamentation.

BATTEN

"A name workmen give to a scantling of wooden stuff from two to four inches broad and about one inch thick. The length is undetermined." (M) This is the thin strip of wood used to keep two or more larger pieces of wood tightly joined and to prevent warping; thus the horizontal strip(s) or boards(s) on some doors; the strips added beneath or at the edges of table and desk tops.

BEAD AND REEL

A variation of beaded molding where oval beads are alternated with discs.

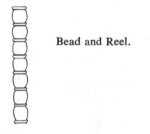

Bead and Reel.

BEADING

Fine half-round molding "commonly made upon the edge, cut or carved in short embossments like beads in a necklace." (M) Also, especially in colonial architecture, and as an edging for drawer fronts, a plain half-round edge made with a molding plane.

BEARER

In furniture, any horizontal part that serves to carry another; thus, a drawer runner is a bearer.

BED BOLT

The nut and bolt that secure the side rails and posts of bedsteads to each other; usually covered with a decorative brass (or other metal) shield.

BENDED BACK

An eighteenth-century name for what in the twentieth century more commonly is called a Fiddleback, *q.v.*

BENDING

"Of timber-boards is effected by means of heat [steam] whereby their fibres are so relaxed that you may bend them into any fiture." (M)

BEVEL

The sloping edge of any flat surface; especially the edge of a piece of glass or metal so finished off. (See also CHAMFER.)

BIRD CAGE

An eighteenth-century device to allow the top of a pedestal or tripod table to be turned and tilted, so called because it was formed of four small pillars enclosing a central pivot. When set between the underside of the table and the top of the pedestal, the device resembled an open cage.

BLANKET RAIL

Sometimes also called a blanket roll, this was the common name for the upper stretcher uniting the foot posts of a bed.

BLOCK FRONT

The eighteenth-century swelled-front design for case pieces, perhaps first developed in this country at Newport and so now associated particularly with Goddard and Townsend designs. A block front is cut to recess the center and thus allow the two side sections to curve forward.

BOLECTION

A decorative multilevel molding used to cover a joint and so project above the surfaces of the two joined parts.

BOLSTER ARM

The nineteenth-century description of the upholstered easy-chair arms that were cylindrical in shape and thus resembled small bolsters or round pillows.

Silas Deane's tip-and-turn table with bird cage, dish-tip-molded rim, carved knee above a modified claw-and-ball foot. (Courtesy, Connecticut Historical Society, Inc.)

Chimney surround with bolection molding, c. 1700. (Courtesy, Antiquarian and Landmarks Society, Inc.)

Ebony painted boss decoration on paneled chest-over-drawer, seventeenth century. (Courtesy, Antiquarian and Landmarks Society, Inc.)

BOMBÉ

From the French for blown-out, swollen, or bulging; the adjective is used to describe a case piece, such as a desk or chest, the sides and front of which are rounded or bulged out toward the base; a design popular in the second half of the eighteenth century. Also referred to as a kettle base or kettle shape.

BONNET TOP

A decorative hood or top used on tall case furniture in the second half of the eighteenth century. (See also PEDIMENT.)

BOSS

A half oval, lozenge, or circle of wood applied to seventeenth-century cupboards, boxes, and chests to simulate the expensive ebony ornaments then fashionable. Usually set within the angle formed at intersections of joined parts, as between a stile and rail of a chest.

BOTTLE TURNING

A term to describe the bottle-shaped, that is, large, round, or ovoid, turnings, often used on late-seventeenth-century chair and table legs, especially those based on Dutch designs of the William and Mary period.

BOW BACK

The term used in this country almost exclusively to describe the curving frame of the back of a type of Windsor chair.

BOULLE OR BUHL

A term applied generally to nineteenth-century marquetry or elaborate inlays of brass, silver, pewter, ivory, horn, or tortoiseshell, used to ornament boxes, screens, table tops, etc., so named for the inlay first devised by André Charles Boulle (1642–1732), an *ébéniste* patronized by Louis XIV.

BOULTINE

This is a "convex moulding of which the convexity is exactly one fourth part of a circle." (M)

BOW-FRONT

The adjective used to describe a case piece, the front of which curves outward in the shape of an archer's bow. Such chests and sideboards were made from the second half of the eighteenth century through the first of the nineteenth.

BRACKET

The triangular-shaped decoration made to brace a shelf, table top, or leg. Hence, bracket foot, when used to describe the base of a chest, means the foot is shaped like a bracket. "Brace, signifies a piece of timber formed with bevil joints to keep the building, etc. from swaggering or swerving either way." (M)

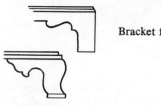

Bracket foot.

BREAK FRONT
The opposite of block front in that the center section projects forward and the two sides thus are recessed. Used in the eighteenth century to describe the "break" in the flat line of a large, wide case piece; today used as a noun to signify a tall, wide cupboard usually topped by a set of shelves with glazed doors.

BULB
The somewhat ovoid, melon-shaped turning used to ornament the columns or upper pillars of sixteenth- and early-seventeenth-century press cupboards, table legs, and bedstead posts.

BUN FOOT
A large ball-shaped foot, flattened top and bottom, so that it resembles a bun; used to support tables, chairs, and chests in the late seventeenth and early eighteenth century.

Bun foot.

BUTTERFLY WEDGE
(See DOVETAIL, DUTCHMAN.)

BUTT JOINT
The square joint formed when two pieces meet end to end.

CABOCHON
From the French for a brass nail (colloquially, a head or pate). A small smooth, round, or oval decoration, convex or concave, carved on furniture in the second half of the eighteenth century, especially on the knees or shoulders of cabriole chair and table legs.

CABRIOLE
From the French for caper or leap. The cabriole leg was used on Chinese stands and tables as early as the fifteenth century. This reverse-curved leg style with convex knee, which becomes concave just above the shaped foot, was popularized in England during the Queen Anne period; it was used throughout the eighteenth century until superseded by the Neo-Classic designs of the Adam brothers and the slim tapered leg shown in Hepplewhite's *Guide*. Cabriole was not used as an adjective, however, until the late nineteenth century; in the eighteenth century and early nineteenth century, cabriole signified a French easy chair or any upholstered piece.

CANT
A chamfer or bevel, each of which see.

CANTED
The term used to describe the legs of a table, chair, or stand, that turn out and away from the top board which they support; for example, the legs of a butterfly table are said to be canted. The more common description today is splayed.

CAPITAL
The head or top of any column.

CAPSTAN
The drum around which an anchor chain is wound. Hence, any concave-sided drum shape, such as a capstan base for a candleholder.

CARCASE
The box, case, or frame for a piece of furniture. (See also CASE FURNITURE.)

CARTOUCHE

From the French for cartridge signifying rolled-up scroll. A decoration in the form of a scroll or shield such as is used on maps to enclose the legend, on porcelain to frame a monogram; any "ornament representing [an open] scroll of paper to receive a motto or inscription," (M) whether carved, etched, inlaid, impressed, painted, stamped, or applied on any ware.

CARVING

In furniture, the art of sculpturing on wood to achieve a decorative three-dimensional effect. "This business which has lately been carried to great perfection, requires much ingenuity, a lively and elegant fancy skill in drawing with great neatness foliages, fruit, flowers, birds, heads, Ec., a good eye, and a steady hand." J. Collyer: *Parent's and Guardian's Directory* (London, 1761).

CARYATID

The classic Greek column or pillar in the form of a female figure, originally an image of a priestess at the Temple of Diana, used to support an entablature; a decorative motif after 1750 during the Classic Revival and in Empire furniture, bowls, urns, lamps, and vases. "Caryatides [are] dressed in long robes after the manner of the Carian people." (M)

CASE FURNITURE

The all-inclusive term for any furniture in which drawers or sections are enclosed in a box or case, such as, chests of drawers, desks, bookcases, cabinets, cupboards.

CASED-SEAT

The eighteenth-century term for the removable Slip Seat, *q.v.,* an upholstered, carved, rushed, or roped frame made to fit within a chair to form the seat.

CASEMENT

The term for the seventeenth- and early-eighteenth-century window that swung out, as opposed to the later rising sash window.

Casement window. (Courtesy, Antiquarian and Landmarks Society, Inc.)

CASTELLATED

The descriptive term for the decorative coping or molding that separates the panel from the frieze, and in form resembles a line of miniature battlements.

CAVETTO

Quarter-round concave molding.

CERTOSINA

The term describing inlay or marquetry of tile or porcelain; alternating squares of geometric patterns of black and white, simulating marble or a combination of ebony and ivory.

CHAMBRANLE

"An ornament of wood or stone surrounding the sides of door windows and chimnies." (M)

CHAMFER (Chamfret)

"An ornament consisting of half a scotia, being a kind of small furrow or gutter on a column. [Chamfering is] cutting the under edge of anything aslope or level." (M) To plane off the sharp right-angled edge of a board or beam.

CHAPLET

"A small ornament [in the form of] round beads, pearls, olives, Ec." (M)

CHEEKS

The late-seventeenth- and eighteenth-century term for the side pieces now called the wings of an easy chair.

CHEVRON

In furniture, the type of inlay made in the shape of an inverted V.

CHIMERA

The fabulous hybrid monster, first used as a carved decoration in ancient Greece and Rome, was revived in the late eighteenth and early nineteenth century as a carved and gilded stylized ornamentation for Neo-Classic furniture. The chimera had the head and body of a lion, the tail of a serpent, and the wings of an eagle. (See also GRIFFIN.)

CHINOISERIE

A general term for western adaptations of Chinese art or decorative motifs first popularized in the seventeenth century in Europe, England, and, hence, the colonies. (See also JAPANNING, Chapter 7.)

CHIP CARVING

Low-relief carving or chipping out of a design on wood.

C. 1800 low stool with chip-and-gouge carving.

CHUMP

"A thick, heavy piece of wood." (J)

CLAPBOARD, CLAP-HOLT

Anciently, these were narrow boards cut of a size to make staves for casks or barrels; later the term meant "A narrow board used to cover buildings." (W) One of the first colonial exports to countries whose woodlands already were depleted: "May, 1643. Here arrived one Mr. Carman, master of a ship of 180 tons. He went from New Haven in December last, laden with clapboards for the Canaries, being earnestly commended to the Lord's protection by the church there." John Winthrop, *Journal, History of New England* (Boston, 1825).

C. 1700 New England oak clapboards.

CLAW-AND-BALL

Favorite eighteenth-century European and, hence, colonial adaptation of the classic Chinese carved-foot design incorporating a dragon's claw holding a pearl. Popularly, but erroneously, associated with Chippendale designs. The 1754 *Director* does not include this type of foot. The claw-and-ball foot was used in England and in this country, notably in Philadelphia, to enhance handsome Georgian chairs, tables, etc.

Claw-and-Ball foot.

COCKED BEAD

A type of semicircular beading that projects beyond the edge; used chiefly on drawer fronts of case pieces, less often on the edges of desk fall-fronts and cupboard doors.

COQUILLAGE

From the French for shell or shellfish, the noun refers to the shell ornament favored in the eighteenth century as a carved decoration on chair crest rails, drawer fronts, etc., and as an inlay in the late eighteenth and early nineteenth centuries.

CORN SAW-WORT Way-Thistle
Serratula arvensis

"Its seeds are enveloped in large downy crowns, which may be advantageously combined with wool, and thus converted into blankets and coarse cloth. [It is] useful for stuffing pillows, bolsters, and mattresses." *The Domestic Encyclopedia* (Philadelphia, 1821).

CORNICE (also spelled Corniche, Cornish)

Decorative molding projecting at the top of a case piece, a column, or a window frame, adapted from the architectural term for the uppermost section of an entablature.

CORNSHUCKS

Twisted and braided, these were used in place of rushes for weaving chair seats, and as stuffing for pillows, mattresses, or other cushions.

CORNUCOPIA

The gilded and/or painted horn of plenty was a favorite decorative motif in the second half of the eighteenth century and the first of the nineteenth. "The Horn of Plenty, among painters and carvers is represented under the figure of a large horn, out of which issues fruits, flowers, Ec. Upon medals, the cornucopiae is given to all deities, genii, and heroes, to mark the felicity and abundance of all the wealth procured by

Eighteenth-century embroidery picture on silk, cornucopia decoration.

the goodness of the former, or the care and valour of the latter." (M)

COROMANDEL (sometimes spelled Caramandel)

In furniture, the reference is to the use of ebony, a black wood with faint stripings, imported from the Coromandel coast of India and especially popular for banding and inlay decorations during the Regency period. In *The Cabinet Directory* (1803) Sheraton wrote that Coromandel was "a foreign wood lately introduced into England, and is much in use for banding. It resembles black rosewood but is intermingled with light stripes." The reference in the seventeenth and eighteenth centuries was to japanning of incised designs, a method also called Bantamwork—named for the Dutch East India trading center from whence lacquer was exported.

CORONA, CROWN, CROWNING

The term for "a large, flat, massive member of the corniche, so-called because it crowns not only the corniche, but the entablature, and the whole." (M)

COVE

Bold concave molding used in ceiling decorations, cornices, window, and fireplace framing.

CREST

"Among carvers, an imagery, or carved work, to adorn the head or top of anything." (M) The carved decoration, somewhat resembling a crest or crown used on the top rail of a chair or settee.

Spanish foot chair, c. 1700, with crested top rail, banister back. (Courtesy, Antiquarian and Landmarks Society, Inc.)

CROCKET

A projecting, carved decoration of curved leaves used on gables and sometimes on furniture of the Gothic and Gothic-Revival styles.

C-SCROLL

An ornament in the shape of the letter C, first used in the early eighteenth century. C-scrolls were carved in the wood, cut separately, and applied; or used, doubled and reversed, as stretchers.

CUP TURNING

The William and Mary design resembling an inverted bowl.

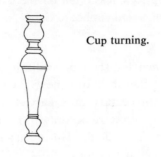

Cup turning.

CYMA

A double curve.

CYMA RECTA

A molding with the upper curve concave.

CYMA REVERSA

A molding with the lower curve concave and the upper curve convex, popularly called ogee.

DAGGIES

The name for bits and pieces, such as "Lethern latchets; and the ends of wool," (W) used for stuffings.

DENTIL

Perhaps a corruption of the French *dentelure* meaning indentation. Spaced rectangular blocks used as an applied decoration to form a kind of molding, especially below cornices, in architecture and on case pieces.

DIAPER

The term, signifying a kind of decoration, originally meant to paint in colors, later to paint decorative geometric patterns in colors. Also, a diamond-shaped textile weave imitated on glass, porcelain, etc. To diaper is to "variegate; to diversify; to flower [or] to draw flowers upon clothes." (J)

DISH-TOP

The description of a table or tray top with a plain raised rim.

DISTRESSED

Used by cabinetmakers to describe wood torn during the cutting of veneers, and of late by novice collectors and dealers to describe any wood damaged or roughened by age, through exposure to the elements, or at the hands of the unknowing and avaricious who believe such damage adds quaintness and value.

DOGBANE *Apocynum*
"The doun of some sorts of these plants are much used in France for stuffing easy chairs, it being extremely light and elastick. It is also used in quilts, which are very warm." (M)

DOME TOP
The name for the unbroken semicircular top piece of a tall-case clock or chest; first used in the eighteenth century. (See also PEDIMENT.)

DOUBLE ROPE
(See BARLEY SUGAR.)

DOUBLE TWIST
(See BARLEY SUGAR.)

DOVETAIL
Any wedge, cleat, hinge, or joint made in the shape of a dove's tail; sometimes now called butterfly, especially in reference to hinges. An ancient method of joining two pieces of wood, such as the front and side of a drawer, at right angles; the dovetails are the cut-out tenons of one board which are fitted into open slots or sockets in the second board, "and therefore cannot fall out." (J)

DROP
In furniture any turned, ornamental pendant.

DROP-FRONT
The fall-front lid of a desk hinged so that it falls forward and out to form a writing surface.

DROPS
The decorative pendants used to ornament furniture, turned or carved in a variety of shapes, including acorn, egg, pear, pineapple, thistle, urn, or vase.

DUTCHMAN
A kind of repair so called because it seemed to resemble the wide pantaloons of the Netherlands. Also called a dovetail or butterfly cleat, a dutchman is used to pull together two pieces of wood, as a table-top board that has warped and split.

EBONIZE
The practice of staining wood to simulate ebony.

EGG-AND-DART
A convex molding incorporating a continuous carved design in which an oval or egg shape is alternated with that of a dart; sometimes called egg-and-tongue.

EMBATTLED
The nineteenth-century term for Castellated, *q.v.*

ESCALLOP, SCALLOP
The term used to describe the carved or incised shell used as a form of decoration or ornament during the eighteenth century.

EPISTYLE
An Architrave, *q.v.*

ESCUTCHEON
The shield or metal plate surrounding and protecting the edges of a keyhole; sometimes made with a metal cap or cover on a pivot.

Escutcheon, c. 1700, brass. (Courtesy, Antiquarian and Landmarks Society, Inc.)

FACET
"A small surface or face." (W)

FACING
"An ornamental covering in front." (W)

FANBACK

The adjective for a type of American Windsor chair, the spindles of the back of which fan out or incline away from either side of the center spindle: "Wells & Flint . . . have on hand . . . an elegant assortment of Gilt, Fancy, Bamboo and Fanback Chairs, to be disposed of on accomodating terms . . ." *Connecticut Courant* (Hartford), September 2, 1807.

FEATHER EDGE

More precisely, feathered edge. A term applied to boards used in sheathing that have been planed thin—feathered out—at the edge, "or sloped on one side." (W)

FESTOON

From the French *festonner,* to scallop. A series of decorative loops or swags carved or painted below cornices, ceiling moldings, the rims of bowls, etc., usually in the form of a garland or rope of flowers, leaves, or fruit.

FIDDLEBACK

A solid splat for a chair back shaped with a concave curve to resemble the outline of the body of a violin.

FILIGRANE OR FILIGREEWORK

"Any piece of gold or silver [lacy] work curiously formed with grains or drops on the filaments or threads." (M)

FILLET

"In architecture [or case pieces] a little square member, ornament or moulding used in divers places but generally as a crowning over a greater moulding. In painting, gilding, Ec. [it] is a little rule or reglet of leaf-gold, drawn over some mouldings or on the edges of frames, pannels, Ec., especially when painted white by way of enrichment." (M)

FINIAL

The turned, carved, cut, or molded decoration that finishes off the top piece or part, as on the uprights of chairs or the tops of clock cases. Favored shapes included acorn, bud, flower, flame, leaf, urn, vase, and birds, such as the phoenix and eagle.

Eighteenth-century American chair with acorn finials, fiddleback.

William and Mary period armchair with Flemish scroll feet, the scroll design repeated on the stretchers, back and crested top rail. (Courtesy, Antiquarian and Landmarks Society, Inc.)

FLAMBEAU

The term from the French for "a lighted torch," (W) and thus the name given to the stylized finial or pediment made in the shape of a flame or torch.

FLEMISH SCROLL

The reverse, elongated, or flattened C- or S-scroll used on stretchers and chair legs in the William and Mary period.

FLEUR-DE-LIS

The stylized garden lily used especially as a decorative motif on French furniture, but also on some made here and in England in the late eighteenth and early nineteenth centuries.

FLUTING

In furniture, the series of parallel half-round channels separated by sharp fillets or ridges and carved into flat wood surfaces, as the stiles of a chest or a table leg. "Notice is hereby given that all Persons may be supplied with all sorts of Joyner's and Cabinet-Maker's Work, as Desk and Book Cases, with Arch'd, Pediment and O.G. Heads, Common Desks of all sorts, Chests of Drawers of all Fashions, fluted or plain . . . by Josiah Claypoole from Philadelphia . . ." *The South Carolina Gazette* (Charleston), March 22, 1740.

FOOT

The termination of a table, chair, stand, or other furniture leg. Various types include ball, bracket, bun, club, French, hoof, leaf scroll, lion's paw, claw and ball, pad, paw, scroll, splayed, web, and whorl.

FRENCH FOOT

A delicate, outward curving bracket foot, used in the late eighteenth and early nineteenth centuries.

FRETWORK

Open, carved trellis or lattice-like crisscross design used to ornament furniture during the second half of the eighteenth century and the first quarter of the nineteenth, particularly in Chinese and Gothic-inspired designs, such as those popularized in Chippendale's *Director*. Frequently used to form the brackets joining legs to a table top, the pediments of tall chests, chair backs, and seat brackets.

FRONTAL

A contemporary colloquialism for "a pediment over a small door or window." (W)

GADROON

Decorative rim in the form of a ruffle or series of curves used on furniture, silver, porcelain, glass.

GALLERY

The decorative open railing rising above a tray or table, or encircling the outer rim of a console, the back and sides of a sideboard, top or sometimes the top board of a desk. Slender brass, silver, or sometimes ivory, rails set in wood or brass supports.

GESSO

From the Italian for plaster. Throughout the eighteenth and nineteenth centuries gesso was chalk or whiting, linseed oil, and sizing made into a paste and used on wood as a base for light carving, painting, or gilding.

GILDING

"The art of spreading or covering thin gold over any substance." Thomas Sheraton, *Cabinet Directory* (London, 1803). Decorating with gold leaf or gold dust was popular for stands, small cabinets, and chairs, first during the reign of Charles II; the fashion was revived in the early eighteenth century, and continued into the nineteenth. (See Chapter 7.)

GORGERIN

The name for a "little frieze between the astragal and annulets of a capital." (W)

GRAINING

Any method of painting or staining wood to simulate the grain, texture, or color of another wood. Thus, pine often was grained to resemble mahogany, walnut, oak, or rosewood. (See Chapter 7.)

GRIFFIN

A mythological creature, the representation of which was used as a decoration, carved and often gilded, at the top of case pieces and looking-glass frames: "The griffin is another fabulous being [whom] the ancient heathen poets . . . represented it partly an eagle, and partly a lion; that is, the lower part of it . . . it was consecrated to the sun, whose chariot was drawn by a number of them. And these, if you please, may be introduced into subjects intended to represent covetousness; or they may be placed over cabinets where treasure is kept." Thomas Sheraton, *The Cabinet-Maker's and Upholsterer's Drawing-Book* (London, 1802).

GUILLOCHE

The French for a classic Greek decorative motif incorporating a continuous series of interlacing circles.

HORN OF PLENTY

Another term for the Cornucopia, *q.v.*

HEART BACK

A contemporary term for Fiddleback, *q.v.*

INLAY

The decoration of a larger surface made by setting or laying into prepared recesses small strips, bands, or variously shaped pieces of contrasting wood, ivory, or bone, sometimes brass, or silver.

IN-THE-WHITE

The cabinetmaker's term for any piece of furniture made of any wood not as yet stained or polished.

IVORY

The "hard, solid, and firm substance of a white colour, capable of a very good polish; the tusk of the elephant. These tusks grow on each side of the elephant's trunk in form of a horn. Each tusk is seven or eight feet in length, and as thick as a man's thigh at the base and almost solid; and both together

sometimes weigh about three hundred and thirty pounds." (M) Esteemed for its beautiful creamy color, "Ivory is used as a material for toys, and as panels for miniature painting . . . Ivory may be stained or dyed [see Chapter 7]." *Encyclopedia Americana* (Philadelphia, 1831).

KNUCKLE ARM

The name for a series of curves carved on the terminals of the arms of a variety of eighteenth-century chairs from Chippendale types to Windsors.

KNULL

(See GADROON.)

LACQUER WORK

(See JAPANNING, Chapter 7.)

LADDER-BACK

The twentieth-century name for an eighteenth-century chair back with horizontal slats or rails.

LATTICE

(See FRETWORK.)

LINENFOLD

A type of paneling made of vertical moldings carved to look as if they were folded at each end, thus resembling folded linen; used on chests, chair backs, and walls.

LOBING

Rim decoration in the form of a series of upright lobes.

LUMBER

The term for timber in general, but chiefly "small timber as boards, staves, hoops, scantling, Ec." (W)

LUNETTE

Little moon; specifically, the half-moon motif often used as a shallow carved decoration on seventeenth- and early-eighteenth-century furniture, such as boxes and chests; also, as an inlay in the early nineteenth century.

MAP DRAWER

The shallow, full-length drawer still set below the writing board of a desk, originally was intended as a repository for property surveys and portfolios of engravings. "The middle Drawer [of the Library Table] goes from front to front for holding Maps, Prints, Ec." Thomas Chippendale, *The Gentleman and Cabinet-Maker's Director* (London, 1762).

MARBLING
Painting wood to simulate marble was a popular method of decoration from the late sixteenth century through the nineteenth; usually used on table tops, consoles, and on the sheathing of chimney surrounds.

MARLBORO LEG
A late-eighteenth-century term for the squared, slightly tapered leg, said to have been named in honor of the fourth Duke of Marlborough.

MARQUETRY
From the French *marquetrie,* meaning inlaid work. A decorative, patterned veneer created by gluing numerous wood, ivory, silver, other metal, or tortoise shell pieces to a ground.

MELON-BULB
The elliptical bulbous turning resembling a vertical oval melon, used during the sixteenth and seventeenth centuries for furniture legs.

MODILLION
Projecting brackets set below a cornice or pediment.

MORTISE-AND-TENON
A method of joining two sections of wood. The end of one piece, called the tenon, is inserted into the mortise or socket cut in the end of the second, the joint thus formed further secured by a pin.

MUNTIN
The uprights between panels; used also to describe the narrow pieces of wood used to separate and hold panes of glass.

NEST-OF-DRAWERS
The seventeenth- and eighteenth-century name for a chest of drawers. Later it meant a set of small drawers affixed to a dressing table or writing table.

NULLING
Alternating concave and convex flutes. (See also GADROON.)

OGEE
(See CYMA REVERSA.)

OGIVE
The same as Ogee.

ORMOLU
Adapted from the French *Or Moulu* for gilt made from ground gold mixed with mercury and used to gild eighteenth-century furniture. Later, a term for an alloy of copper or brass and zinc used to decorate mounts for Empire and Victorian furnishings, and often cast in molds for vases, candlesticks, clock cases, etc.

OVOLO
A convex molding, also called the quarter-round.

PAD FOOT
Perhaps the most common of all terminals

Side chair, Queen Anne period, with pad foot.

for the cabriole leg; somewhat oval in shape and set above a disc.

PANEL
A board fitting into the grooves of surrounding rails and stiles; that is, one surface framed by another. Thus, the panel itself may be either recessed or raised above its frame.

PAPIER-MÂCHÉ
The French for chewed paper and presumably used because it sounded more elegant than the "paper ware" made from linen rags patented in 1772 by Henry Clay of Birmingham, England. In 1836, another Birminghamian, Richard Brindley, was awarded a patent for his "papier mache japan furniture" made from a base of rag pulp. Clay's process resulted in a smooth, strong material, Brindley's was more brittle and more easily cracked and broken. Both types were decorated in gold leaf, with mother-of-pearl shell in the 1820s, with oil colors after the 1830s. Used for small pieces of furniture, such as light stands and screens, trays, picture frames, boxes.

PARGET
To rough-cast a wall; "to plaster the inside of a chimney with mortar made of cow-dung and lime." (H) Parget is "plaster; plaster-stone." (W)

PARGETRY
Ornamental plaster moldings used on ceilings and columns.

PARQUETRY
A mosaic of contrasting woods arranged in geometrical patterns as a base ground and then applied as a decorative veneer; sometimes combined with marquetry. Most popular as a furniture decoration after 1775, although it first was used in the seventeenth century.

PATINA
The natural surface of wood evolved through years of daily use and polishing.

PEDIMENT
The uppermost decoration, the decoration above a cornice, in the form of a triangle. In furniture, the pediment surmounts tall chests, bookcases, and looking glasses. A broken pediment is one lacking the apex of the triangle. A broken, scrolled pediment is also open at the top, with rising "arms" curved or scrolled. The swan or goose neck (broken) pediment has simpler curved arms.

PENNY FEET
The term for flat, circular disc feet so called because their shapes is similar to a large penny; used almost exclusively on metal objects.

Rushlight holder with penny feet.

PIECRUST
Used to describe a circular table or tray top, the edge of which has been carved in scallops and thus resembles a stylized crimped piecrust; a design introduced about 1750.

PIGEONHOLE
The contemporary term for the small recesses or compartments set in the interiors of dressing tables, writing desks, and some commodes to hold accessories: "A Dressing Table for a Lady. The drawer above the Recess hath all the Conveniences for Dressing; on each side is a Cupboard . . . with doors . . . and on the Inside, Drawers, or

Pigeon-Holes . . . Places for combs, Rings, Bottles, Boxes, Ec." Thomas Chippendale, *The Gentleman and Cabinet-Maker's Director* (London, 1762).

PILASTER
In architecture, a pillar projecting slightly outward from the wall of which it is a part. In decoration, the half round or rectangular pillar used as a surface ornament on clock cases, picture frames, at the corners of chests and cabinets.

PILGRIM FURNITURE
A twentieth-century name given to any furniture made in New England in the seventeenth century.

PLASTER-OF-PARIS
"Gypsum or plaister stone when calcined and wrought up with water makes parget or plaister of Paris." (M)

PRETZEL BACK
Late-eighteenth-century term for the undulating chair-back slat with a central open design resembling the shape of a pretzel.

PURITAN FURNITURE
A term applied generally to the simple, austere furniture made in both New England and England just prior to and during the Cromwellian period.

RABBET
Sometimes written rebate, a method of joining two pieces of wood. To rabbet is to chisel a recess in the edge of one board into which the edge of a second board can be fitted.

REEDING
A decoration carved in semicircular relief or parallel beads to resemble stylized reeds. Thus, the opposite of fluting. A favorite decoration for Sheraton-type furniture.

REVERSE OGEE
The *cyma reversa* molding; a double curve that is convex above, concave below.

RIBBAND BACK
This was the contemporary term for chair slats shaped and carved to simulate ribbons. The most intricate and elegant were carved in the form of ribbons tied in bow-knots; the simplest were narrow curving, or undulating slats. As Thomas Chippendale said, "Chairs with Ribband-Backs . . . have been made which give entire Satisfaction. If any of the small ornaments should be thought superfluous, they may be left out, without spoiling the Design." *The Gentleman and Cabinet-Maker's Director* (London, 1762).

Ribband-back chair from Thomas Chippendale's *The Gentleman and Cabinet-Maker's Director* (London, 1762).

ROCAILLE
From the French for rockwork; an asymmetrical decoration using tiny shell and rock motifs, popular, as the name implies, at the height of the Rococo style in England, France, and America.

ROPE TURNING

The popular term for the turning that in form resembles a spiraling or twisted rope, usually added as a decoration to corners, posts, or aprons, and often used as a finial on chest pediments.

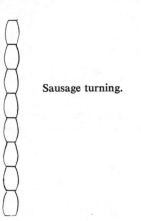

Rope turning.

ROSETTE

A stylized flower usually carved within a circle or square or sometimes an ellipse, used as a decoration on seventeenth- and eighteenth-century columns or posts beneath the cornice of a corner cupboard, on boxes, and on chair crests.

SAUSAGE TURNING

A common term for the turning often used for early chair stretchers and table legs, and so called because it resembles a continuous row of sausage links.

Sausage turning.

SCANTLING

"Timber cut into a small size." (W)   "John I. Wells wants . . . to purchase scantling suitable for Bedsteads . . ." *Connecticut*

Courant (Hartford), February 19, 1798. Branches, saplings, and small trees provided scantling; 2×4 inch or 4×6 inch posts or rails were scantlings.

Seventeenth-century side table with sausage-turned stretchers, scalloped apron and breadboard top. (Courtesy, Antiquarian and Landmarks Society, Inc.)

SCOTIA

A concave molding.

SCRATCH CARVING

The simplest low-relief carving using incised lines to form a pattern.

SERPENTINE FRONT

An undulating front for a case piece, convex in the center and concave at the ends. Used for cabinets, chests, sideboards, chair-seat fronts, and table friezes in the second half of the eighteenth century.

SHIDE

The term from the Old Saxon word for divide to describe "a board, a cutting." (J)

SKIRT, SKIRTING PIECE
(See APRON.)

SLATBACK

A name for a chair, the back of which is made of flat horizontal rails or slats.

SLIPPER FOOT

A more sophisticated version of the pad foot, this is the delicately elongated and pointed terminal introduced during the Queen Anne period.

Slipper foot.

SLIP SEATS

"Richard Magrath, Cabinet and Chair-Maker, in King Street . . . is now making some Hollow-seated Chairs, the seats to take in and out, which have a light, airy Look, and make the sitting easy beyond expression." *South Carolina Gazette* (Charleston), July 9, 1772.

SNAKE FOOT

So called because in profile it resembles a snake's head; used throughout the eighteenth century on tripod-base tables.

Snake foot.

SOCLE

The term for "a flat square member under the bases of pedestals of statues and vases; it serves as a foot or stand." (B)

SPADE FOOT

The foot, used in the late eighteenth century on a tapered leg, cut to resemble a square spade; sometimes called a therm foot.

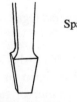

Spade foot.

SPANISH FOOT

The favorite late-seventeenth-century ribbed scroll terminal inspired by Spanish-Portu-

guese motifs introduced following Charles II's marriage to Catherine.

Spanish foot.

SPANISH MOSS   *Tillandsia usneoides*

"On examining Spanish beard, a kind of [wispy] moss, one sees it is a blackish filament similar to horsehair. Most of the mattresses in New Orleans are made of this . . ." Edouard de Montulé, *Voyage en Amérique* . . . (Paris, 1821).

SPINDLE TURNING

So called from the "pin to form thread on." (W)   Such turnings were slender, shaped rods used chiefly for chair backs.

Spindle turning.

Dated 1672 on frieze, sunflower-and-tulip chest with split spindle and boss decorations. (Courtesy, Antiquarian and Landmarks Society, Inc.)

SPLAT (SPLAD)

The center part of the chair back connecting the top rail and the seat.

SPOOL TURNING

The design reminiscent of a continuous row of small, flat bulbs or spools, especially popular during the mid-Victorian era.

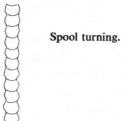
Spool turning.

SPOON BACK

The back of a chair curved and shaped to fit the user more comfortably.

STAND

Any small supporting frame. The name "applied to different small pieces of furniture, as a music-stand, bason stand, table stand, or small pillar and claw table stand, and a tray stand." Thomas Sheraton, *The Cabinet Dictionary* (London, 1803).

STRETCHER, STRETCHER RAIL, STRETCHING RAIL

The stabilizing underbraces or horizontal rails used to connect the legs of stools, chairs, stands, or tables; a decorative as well as a functional addition to such furniture throughout the Colonial period. The stretcher seldom was used after 1800.

STRING AND SHADE

The late-eighteenth-century description of a dark wood inlaid with stringing in a light wood.

STRINGING

The extremely narrow inlay, as thin as a string, of contrasting wood set or laid into table tops, drawer fronts, or legs as decoration. English furniture of the Regency period often was embellished with brass stringing.

STRUCK MOLDING

The decorative edging or molding that is carved, cut, or planed, and thus struck while being worked, directly onto a board or panel, post or rail, as opposed to molding made separately and then applied to the piece.

SUNBURST

A twentieth-century term for a semicircular decoration carved to represent stylized sun rays; used on eighteenth-century chests and tall chests.

SWAG

(See FESTOON.)

SWELL(ED) FRONT

The colonial term for what we usually today call a Bow-Front, *q.v.* "[Eliphalet] Chapin has for sale bureaus, and bookcases with china doors, chest on chest swel'd, and chairs, with a variety of other cabinet furniture, tea and wine servers, etc." *Connecticut Courant* (Hartford), October 5, 1795.

SWING LEG

A leg of a drop-leaf table so hinged that it can be swung out to serve also as a support for the leaf.

TABLE

Any flat surface or slab supported on a frame of legs or trestles. Until well into the eighteenth century, table generally was used to mean only the top board, not the supports.

TALON-AND-BALL FOOT

(See CLAW-AND-BALL.)

TALON MOLDING

Another name for the Reverse Ogee.

TAMBOUR

A flexible panel made of thin strips of light wood glued to a ground of linen or canvas so as to form a kind of shutter or fall. The tambour was fixed to slide or run in grooves so that it could be closed over some other part, such as the interior of a desk or the inner compartments of a cupboard. In *The Cabinet-Maker's and Upholsterer's Drawing-Book* (London, 1791–94), Thomas Sheraton showed a sideboard with a tambour covering the center section. George Washington owned a tambour-front bureau or desk, a forerunner of the more familiar late-nineteenth-century roll-top desk.

TAPER(ED) LEG
The square leg that gradually diminishes in size as it is "tapered" down to the foot; used after 1750 for chairs, tables, stands, and some sideboards.

TESTER RAILS
The narrow, flat lathlike lengths of wood fitted between the tops of bed posts to form a frame from which the tester or canopy was suspended. Sometimes spelled teaster because presumably this was the way it was pronounced during the seventeenth and eighteenth centuries when this type of canopy was used. (See also TESTER BED, Chapter 12.)

TRAY
Any large flat plate, oval, round, or rectangular, with or without a raised rim or gallery, but usually with handles. In the sense that we use the word today, trays probably were first popularized during the craze for tea drinking in the seventeenth century.

TRELLIS WORK
The same as Lattice or Fretwork, *q.v.*

TRIFID FOOT
The three-toed foot introduced during the Queen Anne period; also called a drake foot.

Trifid foot.

TRUCKLE
An early name for a small wheel or castor. (See also TRUCKLE BED, Chapter 12.)

TRUMPET TURNING
A furniture leg turning first popular during the William and Mary period; so called because in profile it has the appearance of a trumpet turned upside down.

Trumpet turning.

VALANCE
(See APRON.)

VASE AND RING TURNING
Introduced during the William and Mary period, this has the shape of a vase above a ring or disc and tapers to a bulbous base.

Vase and ring turning.

VASE SPLAT
An alternative term for Fiddleback, *q.v.*

VENEER
A sheet of any thin wood glued to other wood to enrich the appearance of a piece of furniture or accessory made of wood; a popular decoration first in vogue late in the seventeenth century. Such early veneers, cut by hand, were heavier (seldom less than ⅛ inch in thickness) than later machine-sawn veneers.

VITRUVIAN SCROLL
The classic Roman decorative motif named for the architect, Marcus Vitruvius Pollio, and which resembles a series of undulating or rolling ocean waves. Revived in the eighteenth century to ornament moldings and friezes of Neo-Classic furniture.

VOLUTE

The spiral scroll of the Ionic capital.

WAINSCOT

From the German *wagenshot*. During the seventeenth and early eighteenth centuries, the reference in colonial manifests was to unmilled wide boards meant for any interior use, including furniture, as opposed to the narrower planks shipped as "clapboards" for exterior work. By the close of the Colonial period, the term often referred to all "the timber serving to line the walls of a room, and painted to serve in place of hangings." (M) The twentieth-century reference usually is to wall paneling below the chair rail or bottom window sash-line of a room.

WHORL FOOT

An English name for the type of curled-up or scroll-foot design adapted by Chippendale from Louis XV styles in the eighteenth century; used also on Victorian-era French revival pieces.

Whorl foot.

YOKE

In furniture making, this is the name for the top rail of a chair back that resembles the shoulder yoke used for carrying pails.

6
Woods and Their Preferred Uses

The tools in this restored woodworking shop are those used from 1765 to 1868 by three generations of an East Hampton, Long Island, family. The shop room originally was attached to the shingled, salt-box type house of the family of Nathaniel Dominy IV (1737–1812). Behind the high-wheel lathe in the foreground long workbenches are set along the walls. Tools and templates used for cutting cresting rails, cabriole legs, and chair slats, are suspended from ceiling and wall pegs. The table in the center aisle was made in the shop about 1796 by Nathaniel Dominy V for his own family's use. (Courtesy, The Henry Francis du Pont Winterthur Museum.)

ABELE TREE *Populus alba*
A common early name for the poplar, *q.v.*

ACACIA *Robinia pseudoacacia*
Actually the locust, a durable, extremely hard, white or pale yellow wood with a dark heart. In the seventeenth and eighteenth centuries, acacia was prized chiefly for inlay work, sometimes employed in chair and table frames and for small boxes.

ALBESPYNE
An early synonym for the whitethorn, *Alba spina;* probably the English hawthorn or May tree.

ALDER *Alnus*
"The wood is used by turners, and will endure long under ground or in water." Phillip Miller, *Gardener's Dictionary* (London, 1760).

ALDERNE
A common colonial spelling for the wood of the elder tree.

ALOE *Agillochum*
The aloewood is from "a tree in the East Indies, brought to us in small bits, of a very fragrant scent . . . the best is of a blackish purple colour, and so light as to swim on water." (J)

AMARANTH, Purpleheart *Peltogyne*
A hard, heavy South American wood with a close, even grain used for inlays and turned work. The popular name comes from the fact that after it has been cut the wood develops a purple cast.

APPLE *Malus*
The wood is hard and fine-grained and thus provided easily cut inlays and veneers. Some was used for furniture; however, the tree's great popularity as a source of fruit for food and cider usually kept it from being cut for milling during the eighteenth century. During the hysteria of the nineteenth-century temperance movement when apple orchards were destroyed (on the theory that without the fruit, there would be no hard cider and thus no alcoholism) apple wood was for a time in good supply for small furniture, picture frames, boxes, and caddies.

ASH *Fraxinus americana*
Ash is a pale brown wood of great elasticity and strength. In the seventeenth century and somewhat less so in the eighteenth, it was used for fine furniture and for veneering: "Some Ash is curiously camleted and veined, so differently from other timber that our skilled cabinet makers prize it equal with Ebony and give it the name of green Ebony, which the customer pays well for; and when our woodmen light upon it they may make what money they will. But to bring it to that curious lustre so as 'tis hardly to be distinguished from the most curiously diaper'd Olive, they [have to] varnish their Work." John Eve-

lyn, *Sylva* (London, 1679). Near the close of the eighteenth century it was used mainly for chairs. "The wood is in great use among general artificars, as wheel-wrights, cart-wrights, carpenters, turners, Ec., also for making ploughs, harrows, axle-trees, oars, bales, Ec. It is said to be as lasting for building as oak and often preferred before it." (M)

ASPEN TREE
"A species of the poplar with trembling leaves." (W)

BAMBOO, BAMBOE, BAMBOU
Bambusa
"A plant in the Indies, after the manner of European reeds. It is of the largest kind of cane. With these the Indians make all sorts of furniture in a very ingenious manner. The wood is so hard and strong that they serve very well [for] all sorts of utensils for kitchens and tables." (M)

BASSWOOD, American Lime *Tilia americana*
Is a fine-grained, soft white wood, some-times tending to pale brown, used in furni-ture making and carving. Strips of its inner bark, or bast, were used for baskets, sieves, and chair seats. "Bass wood Plank. 2000 feet suitable for Chair Seats, for sale by Erastus Flint." *American Mercury* (Hart-ford, Connecticut), January 31, 1811.

BEECH *Fagus sylvatica*
Of a pale brown color with reddish over-tones, beech is easily turned and was popu-lar with joiners, especially the makers of chairs, throughout the seventeenth, eight-eenth, and nineteenth centuries. Because it is so easily stained, beech was also a favor-ite for any furniture which was to be painted or gilded. "The Beech is a high tree . . . and with a thicke body . . . the timber is white, hard and very profitable. Petrus Crescentius writeth, that the ashes of the wood is good to make glasse with." John Gerard, *The Herball or Generall His-*

torie of Plantes (London, 1636). "[The American beeches are] quite the same as European ones. Their wood is very good for joiners' planes." Peter Kalm, *Travels in North America* (Warrington, England, 1770). "The woods about Louisville [Ken-tucky] are of supurb beech trees. These, because of their thickness, smother the little trees." Edouard de Montulé, *Voyage en Amérique . . .* (Paris, 1821).

BILSTEAD *Liquidambar styraciflua*
A colloquial name for the sweet-gum tree wood which somewhat resembled mahog-any and often was used as a substitute for that expensive, imported wood.

BIRCH *Betula alba*
"Of the common Birch tree, saith Pliny, *Mirabile candore & tenuitate terribilis mag-istratium virgis,* and in our time also School-masters and Parents do terrifie their chil-dren with rods made of Birch." John Ger-ard, *The Herball or Generall Historie of Plantes* (London, 1636). "Birch is of use for the husbandmen's ox-yokes, for hoops, small screws, paniers, brooms, wands, bavin-bands, withies for faggots, arrows, bolts, shafts, dishes, bowls, ladles." (M) Birch, easily stained, was used for painted, gilded, and japanned furniture.

BOILED WOOD
Any wood boiled in water and wood-ash lye to make it easier to turn on a lathe.

BOX *Buxus sempervirens*
"The [pale yellow] wood is very useful for turners, engravers, and mathematical in-strument makers; the wood being so hard, close and ponderous as to sink in water which renders it very valuable for divers utensils." (M) Box also often was used as an inlay.

BRASILWOOD, BRAZILWOOD
Caesalpinia sappan
"An American wood of a red color and very heavy . . . It is much used in turned work and takes a good polish. But its chief

use is in dying where it serves for a red colour." (M) "The returnes made hence from England are chiefly sugar, molasses, logwood and brazillawood, for which we are beholden to the Wést Indies." John Higginson of Salem to his brother in London, 1700: *Higginson Letters,* Massachusetts Historical Society Collections 3, VIII, 218.

BURL, BURR
An unnatural dome-shaped, knoblike growth on deciduous trees caused by disease or worms. These extrusions are found in all sizes, often as much as two to three feet in diameter. Sheered off into thin slices, burls of walnut and maple were favored for veneering fine furniture. Others were used for bowls, plates, small boxes, mortars, and other containers. "Only the trees with deciduous leaves have these knobs, chiefly the oak, and also the ash and red maple. [Many] who settled here made dishes, bowls, etc. of the ash knobs. These vessels are very pretty and look as if they were made of curled wood." Peter Kalm, *Travels in North America* (Warrington, England, 1770).

BUTTONWOOD, American or Virginia Plane *Platanus occidentalis*
Sometimes called the Virginia maple or the water beech. Buttonwood was the popular colonial term, said to have been adopted because the wood was useful for making buttons. It is hard, red-brown, and cross-grained, and according to Sheraton, it was used by country joiners for chairs. (See also PLANE TREE, SYCAMORE.)

CANARYWOOD *Liriodendron tulipifera*
This was the British name for the straight-grained American whitewood grown in Canada and New England. The color ranges from pale yellow to brown, usually with an overcast of light green. Canarywood or whitewood was used for furniture meant to be painted, or for drawer backs and cabinet interiors.

CANDLEBERRY TREE *Myrica pennsylvanica*
"The English name for a species of myrtle common in Virginia, and other parts of the British Colonies in America. It has its name from a sort of green wax extracted from the berries by boiling and of which they make candles." (M)

CANE *Arundinaria gigantea*
"The great Reed or Cane is esteemed to make [slivers] for weavers, sundry sorts of pipes, as also to light candles that stand before Images, and to make hedges and pales, and also to make certain divisions in ships to divide the sweet oranges from the soure, the Pomecitron and lemmons likewise in sundry and many other purposes." John Gerard, *The Herball or Generall Historie of Plantes* (London, 1636).

CARVERS-WOOD *Tilia americana*
A general term for any wood easily worked by those who carved furniture ornaments; specifically, the reference was to wood of the lime or linden tree, *q.v.*

CEDAR, Cedar of Lebanon *Cedrus libani*
"The great Cedar is very big and high [and its] timber is extremely hard; it rotteth not nor waxeth old [and is] very odoriferous and somewhat red." John Gerard, *The Herball or Generall Historie of Plantes* (London, 1636). First popularized in the Carolean period, this cedar chiefly was used for small boxes, sometimes for paneling, and bedsteads, often for caskets, seldom for large case furniture.

Virginia Cedar *Juniperus virginiana*
Sometimes called pencil cedar or red juniper, this also is reddish brown in color; it was used for drawers, chest linings, desk pigeonholes. Peter Kalm thought it "the hardest wood in the country" because it resisted rot and thus was useful for canoes and other vessels, for fence rails, and for roof shingles. Care had to be taken, Kalm said, when the wood was used for furniture or

paneling because its highly prized color eventually faded, and then "looked very shabby; it will keep its color, however, if a thin varnish is put on it while fresh or just after it has been planed." Because of its pleasant scent, "some get bureaus of it." *Travels in North America* (Warrington, England, 1770).

CHERRY *Prunus*
"The cherry tree groweth to a high and great tree . . . The substance is brown in the middle, and the outer part is somewhat white." John Gerard, *The Herball or Generall Historie of Plantes* (London, 1636). "The wood of the wild cherry, *Prunus virginiana,* looks exceedingly well; it has a yellow color and the older the furniture which is made from it the better it looks. But it is already scarce, for people cut it without replanting." Peter Kalm, *Travels in North America* (Warrington, England, 1770). "The wood of the cherry tree is of great use to cabinet makers, chair makers Ec. as it is very durable, not liable to split, and looks nearly as well as the ordinary sort of mahogany." (M)

CHESTNUT *Castanea dentata* (*americana*)
"The chestnut is a very great and high tree . . . the body is thicke . . . the timber or substance of the wood is sound and durable," John Gerard said in *The Herball or Generall Historie of Plantes* (London, 1636). John Evelyn a century later agreed, calling it next to the oak, the most "sought after by the Carpenter and Joyner," not only for building, but because it "also does well for Columns, Tables, Chests, Chairs, Stools and Bedsteads." *Sylva* (London, 1679). To avoid the expense of the imported wood, carefully selected chestnut often was steeped in alum and water and then in logwood dye to simulate mahogany. Dyed or in its natural state, chestnut was a favorite with colonial country joiners. "This timber is equal in value to the best oak, and for many purposes, far exceeds it, particularly for making vessels for liquors; it having a property, when once thoroughly seasoned, to maintain its bulk constantly, and is not subject to shrink or swell like other timber." Philip Miller, *The Gardener's Dictionary* (London, 1736).

CORK *Quercus suber*
The outer layer of this oak sometimes was used to cover tobacco or snuff humidors, tea chests, and ink stands because it insulated the contents and/or absorbed moisture. "Poor people in Spain lay planks of it by their Bed-sides to tread on, as great Persons use Turkie and Persian Carpets, to defend them from the floor. Sometimes they line or wainscot the walls of their houses built of stone with this bark which corrects the moisture of the air." John Evelyn, *Sylva* (London, 1679).

RAILS WANTED.
THE subscriber wishes to contract for THREE THOUSAND Chesnut or Cedar rails, to be delivered by the first of May next.
JAMES BABCOCK.
Hartford, March 9.   58

American Mercury (Hartford, Connecticut), March 9, 1818.

COROMANDEL *Diospyros ebenum*
A dark, almost black ebony with lighter stripes imported from the Coromandel coast of India; chiefly used for inlays and banding.

CRABWOOD *Carapa guianensis*
The reddish-brown West Indian or South American wood with an even, slightly undulating grain, used in cabinetwork; sometimes erroneously called Brazilian mahogany.

CROTCH-WOOD
That section of wood cut from the V or fork of a tree; hence, crotch-walnut, crotch-maple, crotch-mahogany were the names

126

given these decoratively grained woods used in veneers.

CYPRESS *Cupressus*
"The cypress is a tall straight tree; always green, and never either rots or is worm eaten . . . being anciently used in funerals, it is the emblem of mourning." (J)

DEAL
"A thin kind of plank, sawn out of the fir-tree," (M) and thus a synonym, at times, for any pine board, and often used also as an adjective to describe a piece of pine furniture, as a deal table. Deal is Scots pine, either red or yellow, and was used for furniture carcasses. Deal also signifies any sawed pine or fir that is more than seven inches wide but less than three inches thick.

DOGWOOD *Cornus florida*
This is "very hard, and is therefore used for weavers' spools, joiners' planes, wedges, etc." Peter Kalm, *Travels in North America* (Warrington, England, 1770).

EBONY *Diospyros ebenum*
The hard, fine-grained Oriental wood first imported to Europe by Dutch traders in the seventeenth century. The color varied from yellow, green, pink, violet, brown, to black. Expensive and much prized for better cabinetmakers' work and for use in decorative panels and ornamentation. (See also COROMANDEL.) "To be sold behind Numb. 4, in the Long Wharffe, Lignum-vitae, Boxwood, Ebony, Mahogany, Plank, Sweet Wood Bark, and Wild Cinnamon Bark." *Boston Gazette,* August 22, 1737.

ELM *Ulmus procera* (English), *U. americana*
A light brown wood with a fairly coarse grain which, because it tends to warp, seldom was used for fine furniture other than for chair seats. It once was popular for "trunks and boxes which are covered with leather, kitchen tables and shovel [shuffle] board table tops," according to Evelyn, *Sylva* (London, 1679).

HAREWOOD
Also called eyrewood, this was sycamore or maple stained with iron oxide to simulate a kind of soft, gray ebony.

HAZEL *Corylus americana*
"This [small tree] has gained celebrity from its twigs, being believed by the common people, capable of pointing to hidden treasures [and are called divining rods] when in the hands of certain persons. Hazels are planted for spars, handles for implements of husbandry, hurdles, crates, fishing-rods, hoops for casks. Charcoal made from hazel . . . when prepared in a particular manner, is used by painters and engravers to draw their outlines. The roots are used by cabinetmakers for veneering." *Encyclopedia Americana* (Philadelphia, 1831).

HICKORY *Carya*
The term is applied in the United States to several species of walnut which, however, form a natural section "differing from the true walnuts, especially in the smooth exterior of the nuts." *Encyclopedia Americana* (Philadelphia, 1831). (See also WALNUT.)

HOLLY, AMERICAN *Ilex opaca*
"The Holly, Holme or Halver tree, sometimes growes to a tree of a resonable bigness . . . the boughs are tough and flexible [and] the substance of the wood is hard and sound, blackish or yellowish within." John Gerard, *Herball or Generall Historie of Plantes* (London, 1636). "The holly makes an excellent fence and for that purpose is preferable to most other plants. The wood is made into hones for setting razors; it is the whitest of all hard woods, and therefore used by inlayers [who sometimes dyed it to simulate ebony]. It is also used by mill-wrights and turners." (M)

HORNBEAM *Carpinus betulus*

A plain, somewhat yellow wood sometimes used for inlays and, when dyed, as a substitute for ebony. "The timber of this tree is very tough and flexible and can be converted to many useful purposes. The principal uses it has hitherto been applied to is turnery ware, for which it is excellent, and also for mill cogs, beetle-heads, etc." (M)

HORSE CHESTNUT *Aesculus hippocastanum*

It has a soft texture, is of a pale, almost white color, and was used for inlays and for carving.

IRONWOOD *Carpinus caroliniana*

"He had at his house a number of utensils made of ironwood, which is black, lightly streaked with yellow; it reverberates like the metal whose name it bears . . . and is harder and heavier than box." Edouard de Montulé, *Voyage en Amérique . . .* (Paris, 1821).

JUDAS TREE *Cercis canadensis*

"The wood of this tree is very beautifully veined with black and green; it takes a fine polish." (M)

KINGWOOD *Dalbergia*

This was the name given a rich violet-brown Brazil wood with dark streaks, similar to rosewood; and which was used for veneers. The seventeenth-century name was princewood.

LARCH *Larix europaea, L. americana*

"Being cut in sunder [it] is red within and in the other part something white . . . The substance is very hard of color, especially that in the midst and very profitable for works of long contenuance." John Gerard, *The Herball or Generall Historie of Plantes* (London, 1636). As Gerard noted, the straight-grained wood is tough, but it tends to warp and so seldom was used for fine work, but chiefly for carcasses.

LAUREL *Kalmia latifolia*

"Was called the spoon tree because the Indians used to make their spoons and trowels of its wood. The wood is very hard and some on that account make the axes of their pulleys from it. Weavers' shuttles are made from it, for it may be made very smooth. The joiners and turners use chiefly the root for all kinds of work. The chimney sweepers make brooms in winter of the branches with leaves on them because they cannot get others in that season." Peter Kalm, *Travels in North America* (Warrington, England, 1770).

LEATHERWOOD *Quercus palustris*

Or moosewood, was so called "because its bark is as tough as leather. The French in Canada call it lead wood because the wood itself is as soft and as tough as lead. The bark is used for ropes, baskets, Ec. The tree itself is very tough. Some people use switches from this tree for whipping their children." Peter Kalm, *Travels in North America* (Warrington, England, 1770).

LIGNUM-VITAE *Guaiacum officinale*

Deep, dark brown or greenish-black wood of an extremely hard, dense, solid, compact texture, and remarkably heavy. The wood, gum, and bark were boiled and used medicinally; perhaps for this reason as well as its hardness and durability lignum-vitae was favored for mortars and pill boxes as well as a variety of bowls, cups, and other containers. Its handsome color and figuring also made this West Indian wood a favorite for veneering and inlays. "This morning my cozen, Thos. Pepys, the Turner sent me a cup of lignum vitae for token." Samuel Pepys, *Diary* (November 21, 1660).

LINDEN or LIME *Tilia vulgaris*

"The female lime or Linden tree waxeth great and thicke [and] yieldeth a most pleasant shadow . . . The barke next to the timber is white, moist and tough serving for ropes and halters . . . The timber is whitish, plaine and without knots, very soft and gentle in the cutting or handling. The timber of the male Lime tree is much harder, more knotty and more yellow, not much differing from Elme." John Gerard, *The Herball or Generall Historie of Plantes* (London, 1636).

MAHOGANY

Mahogany, first called the "Jamaica wood," was introduced into England and the colonies during the reign of George I. Its quick popularity was due not only to its rich color and handsome figuring, but especially to the great width of the boards. The size meant large table tops could be made of one piece of wood; the texture of the wood made it easy to carve, thus it lent itself easily to fretwork and other decoration. "In the matter of interior decorations the English style is imitated throughout America. The furniture, tables, bureaux, bedsteads, Ec., are commonly of mahogany, at least in the best houses." Johann David Schoepf, *Travels in The Confederation, 1783–1784* (Philadelphia, 1911).

Cuban Mahogany *Swietenia mahogoni*
Known in the eighteenth century also as Havana wood, and today sometimes referred to as Spanish, San Domingo, and Jamaican mahogany, the cuban wood is

American Mercury (Hartford, Connecticut), November 30, 1810.

pale red when new, gradually deepening in tone. Its grain is straight and tight with remarkably handsome curlings. Sheraton noted its strong figuring, and that it was "without black speckles." He thought it did "very well for chair wood." *Cabinet Dictionary* (London, 1803).

Honduras Mahogany *Swietenia macrophylla*
Softer than similar woods from the West Indies, this Central American variety has an even grain and is of a deep, red-brown color when first cut; the color pales or fades with age. Sheraton noted its black or gray spots, and said this was the mahogany then (1803) in principal use amongst cabinetmakers. *Cabinet Dictionary* (London, 1803).

MAPLE *Acer*

"The great maple is a beautifull and high tree . . . The substance of the wood is tender and easie to work on." John Gerard, *The Herbal or Generall Historie of Plantes* (London, 1636).

"The red maple [*Acer rubrum*] is plentiful . . . out of its wood they make plates, spinning wheels, spools, feet for chairs and beds, and other kinds of turnery." Peter Kalm, *Travels in North America* [1750] (Warrington, England, 1770).

"The timber of the common maple is far superior to beech for turners use, particularly dishes, cups, trenchers, Ec., and when it abounds with knots as it very often doth, it is highly esteemed by joiners for inlaying Ec.; And also for the lightness of the wood, is often employed by those that make musical instruments; and for the whiteness of it, was formerly in great request for tables, Ec." (M)

Curly Maple
"There is a variety [called] the curled maple. The wood being marbled within; it is used in all kinds of joiners' work and utensils made of this wood are preferred to those of any other kind, and are much

dearer than those made of the wild cherry or of black walnut." Peter Kalm, *Travels in North America* [1750] (Warrington, England, 1770).

Bird's-eye Maple

This is the wood of the sugar maple, *A. saccharum,* distinguished by its small circular and ovoid markings with tiny specks or eyes.

American Mercury (Hartford, Connecticut), February 11, 1817.

NUTWOOD

"The popular name of hickory." (W)

OAK   *Quercus*

The popular wood for most furniture and interior house work in the seventeenth century. "There are a great number of trees that go under the name of oak in divers parts of the world, but there is nowhere so many different kinds as in America, though the wood is not near so valuable as the English oak. In times of scarcity a great many poor people have made bread of the acorns; and the poets tell us they were food of the golden ages. However, they are heavy, windy, and hard to digest; therefore mankind in those early ages must doubtless have had a better digestion than us. There is no timber in the world so good for ship building as the English oak which makes our formidable fleets as much superior in the strength of their parts as our seamen are in skill and courage to those of other nations." (M)

Our ships were British oak,
And hearts of oak our men.

Samuel James Arnold, *Death of Nelson*

American Red Oak   *Quercus rubra*

This is pale brown with a reddish cast, sometimes tending to pink; the grain is coarser than the English variety.

American White Oak   *Quercus alba*

This is pale brown with a yellow cast and a coarse grain. As with the English, it deepens in color with age.

English Oak   *Quercus robur*

This is the hardest and most durable of oak woods. The color varies from pale yellow to rich brown, gradually deepening so that some furniture of the seventeenth century and early eighteenth century now appears almost black. Many tables, stands, joint stools, and chests from the Jacobean, Cromwellian, and American Pilgrim century survive today because they were turned from this hardy wood.

Bog Oak

Oak deliberately submerged in a bog as a means of seasoning, to make it rot-resistant, and to give it a very dark, almost black color. Or, the trunks of any old trees recovered from peat bogs and prized for the black color thus achieved. Also called black oak.

OLIVE   *Olea europaea*

A fine yellow to greenish-brown wood with wavy figuring; the Spanish and Italian olives were used for veneers, frames, boxes, and a variety of turned work in the late seventeenth and early eighteenth centuries. Veneers of olive wood sometimes were called oyster wood.

OSIER   *Salix viminalis*

"The osier grows in woods and hedges, especially on boggy land, and flowers in April and May, a valuable shrub . . . its pliant twigs are woven into putcheons, wheels for taking eels, and into bird-cages. The branches are much used for making hoops, and large baskets, and hampers . . . The French Osier is preferred for making the smallest and finest baskets, hats, fans, and other light articles." *The Domestic Encyclopedia* (Philadelphia, 1821).

OWLER TREE
A contemporary colloquialism for the Alder, *q.v.*

PARTRIDGEWOOD *Caesalpinia granadillo*
Streaked in red and brown tones resembling partridge feathers, this close-grained heavy wood was imported from Brazil for use in inlays during the seventeenth century and for veneers in the eighteenth century.

PEAR *Pyrus communis*
"The Peare Tree is many times great, the timber or wood itself is very tractable or easie to be wrought, exceeding fit to make moulds or prints to be graven on, of colour tending to yellownesse. The Wilde Peare tree growes likewise great . . . The timber of the trunke is very firme and sollid and likewise smooth, a wood very fit to make divers sorts of instruments of, as also the hafts of sundry tools to worke withal, and likewise to be cut into many kinds of moulds, but also many sorts of pretty toys." John Gerard, *The Herball or Generall Historie of Plantes* (London, 1636). The close-grained hard wood, varying from pink to an ivory white, was used for carved decorations, inlays, sometimes for small boxes (some of Gerard's pretty toys), and chair parts, and "Your frames for glass painting are usually made of stained Pear-Tree with narrow mouldings . . . made with Rabets . . . If you approve of black Frames, command the frame maker to work them half round with Pear-Tree." Stalker and Parker, *Treatise on Japanning and Varnishing* (London, 1688).

PLANEWOOD
(See BUTTONWOOD.)

PINE *Pinus strobus*
"New England white pine, or Mast-tree; is styled the prince of the American forest in size, age, and majesty of appearance. Great use is made of the timber for masts, yards and bowsprits of ships. It is sawed into boards . . . for inside work of houses. The grain is smooth and when free from knots does not injure the workman's tools. Shingles are also made of this tree.

"Pitch-Pine, *P. rigida toda,* Virginian swamp, Frankincense pine, the loblolly . . . is chiefly used for fuel and for making charcoal; its knots being full of turpentine, afford a light surpassing candles. Its soot is collected and used for lamp-black. It also yields tar, and is sawed into boards.

"*P. pinea,* or Yellow-Pine, is harder and heavier than the white; its planks and boards are in great demand for decks of ships and floors of houses.

"*P. abies americana,* Hemlock or Hemlock Spruce fir tree [has] a grain that is coarse and is not easily split, but is sawed into planks, joists and laths. It holds a nail well." *The Domestic Encyclopedia* (Philadelphia, 1821).

"8000 Feet square white pine Timber, from 6 to 14 inches square and all lengths, 450,000 merchantable Boards and Plank, 70,000 clear and merchantable Clapboards, 60,000 Shingles. For sale by Frederick Bange, State Street." *American Mercury* (Hartford, Connecticut), November 25, 1817.

Connecticut Gazette (New Haven), December 12, 1829.

PLANE TREE *Platanus occidentalis*
"Its wood, when veined, makes beautiful furniture. *P. occidentalis,* the Western Plane-Tree, is indigenous in Virginia and other parts of North America and [is also] highly esteemed, excellent for various articles of domestic furniture, especially for tables, because at a certain age it abounds with veins and when rubbed with oil, surpasses in beauty that obtained from the finest walnut tree." *The Domestic Encyclopedia* (Philadelphia, 1821). "The next day I traveled through immense forests of oak, plane trees, linden, and sugar maples which almost covered the valleys and mountains of this pretty country. [Frankfort, Kentucky]" Edouard de Montulé, *Voyage en Amérique* . . . (Paris, 1821).

PLUM *Prunus*
"The Bullace Plum, or Black Bullace Plum, *P. insittia,* wood is beautifully veined, and highly prized by turners." *The Domestic Encyclopedia* (Philadelphia, 1821).

POCKWOOD
"A hard wood, lignumvita." (W)

POPLAR *Populus alba*
This grayish white wood has an exceptionally fine grain and has been used for inlays since the seventeenth century. "The white poplar or abele tree is a white, tough wood advantageously employed for wainscotting, floors . . . and turnery-wares." *The Domestic Encyclopedia* (Philadelphia, 1821).

PRICKLY YELLOW-WOOD, Yellow Hercules *Zanthoxylum*
"A native of Jamaica, and other tropical countries . . . where it grows to the height of 16 feet and is about 12 inches in diameter . . . and somewhat resembles the common ash. The bark is covered with numerous prickles and the wood is of a bright yellow cast . . . chiefly employed for the heading of hogsheads, for bedsteads, and numerous other purposes." *The Domestic Encyclopedia* (Philadelphia, 1821).

QUICKEN TREE *Sorbus americana*
"The mountain ash or Roan-tree, moosewood, *Sorbus* wood answers very well for hoops, being pliant, tough and durable." *The Domestic Encyclopedia* (Philadelphia, 1821).

ROSEWOOD *Dalbergia nigra*
This dark brown Brazil wood is striped with an even richer brown, tending to black, and was given its popular name from its fragrance while being worked. Extremely popular during the nineteenth century, rosewood rivaled mahogany in use for furniture and veneers. Indian rosewood, *Dalbergia latifolia,* a Bombay blackwood, came from India, the East Indies, and Java. Sheraton suggested a "Lady's Secretary in black rosewood with tulip cross banding and brass mouldings." *Cabinet-Maker's and Upholsterer's Drawing-Book* (London, 1791–94).

SALLOW, Goat Willow *Salix caprea*
"The tender shoots and suckers of this tree are, on account of their flexible nature, useful for baskets and wicker-work." *The Domestic Encyclopedia* (Philadelphia, 1821).

SANDALWOOD *Santalum album*
The aromatic Indian wood used for boxes, chests, and trunks.

SASSAFRAS *Sassafras albidum*
"In many parts of America, where the tree grows in great numbers in the woods, it is not unusual to make bed-posts of the wood . . . its powerful scent drives away disagreeable insects." *The Domestic Encyclopedia* (Philadelphia, 1821).

SATINWOOD
The East Indian *Chloroxylon swietenia* and the West Indian *Fagara flava* are both a deep gold in color. Their handsome figurings made them favorite woods for elegant inlays, veneers, paneling, and fine furniture. "Some chests and commodes are made of satinwood with the ornaments of suitable colours." A. Hepplewhite & Co., *Cabinet-*

Maker's and Upholsterer's Guide (London, 1794).

SERVICE TREE *Sorbus domestica (Pyrus domestica)*
"Its wood is remarkably hard, and therefore valuable to turners for screws or cogwheels, and to mathematical instrument-makers, for rulers, gauging-sticks, Ec." *The Domestic Encyclopedia* (Philadelphia, 1821).

SLOETREE, Blackthorn *Prunus spinosa*
"The wood is hard and tough on which account it is usefully converted into walking-sticks, teeth for rakes, and turnery ware." *The Domestic Encyclopedia* (Philadelphia, 1821).

SWEET BAY *Magnolia glauca (M. virginiana)*
"Is used for joiners' planes." Peter Kalm, *Travels in North America* (Warrington, England, 1770).

SWEET GUM *Liquidambar styraciflua*
"The wood can be made very smooth because its veins are very fine. Carpenters agreed this tree has the same properties as tulip wood." Peter Kalm, *Travels in North America* (Warrington, England, 1770). Sometimes called satin-walnut; the wood is reddish brown with dark brown streaks. "The planks of this tree being beautifully veined, are often used in America for wainscotting rooms." (M) (See also BILSTEAD.)

SYCAMORE MAPLE *Acer Pseudo-platanus*
A hard, tough, white wood excellent for turning and often used as an inlay. Dyed black, it was called harewood. In this country sycamore sometimes also was called Buttonwood, *q.v.* Early-nineteenth-century American country tables, stands, and desks sometimes were made from sycamore wood. Sycamore was also "the English name for the greater maple, *Acer major*." (M)

TEAK *Tectona grandis*
The rich, dark brown, heavy and durable wood from "A timber tree of Birma in Asia, equal or superior to the oak of Europe or America." (W)

TIMBER
Large pieces of wood "fit to build with." (W)

NOTICE.
WHITE & CROCKER,
Want immediately,
10,000 feet of TIMBER suitable for brick buildings.
They also want Three APPENTICES, to the House Joiner's business, about 16 years of age.
They have for sale, one good new canvas top CHAISE, with plated harness.
Hartford, May 3.

American Mercury (Hartford, Connecticut), May 3, 1810.

TOUCHWOOD *Boletus igniarius*
"Also called punk. [It] grows as a fungus or sponge on the trunks of trees, particularly those of cherry and plum trees. It is very hard and tough, of a tawny-brown colour, and is used as a substitute for tinder. It is boiled in a strong lye, or urine, after which it is dried, and boiled a second time in a solution of salt-petre." *The Domestic Encyclopedia* (Philadelphia, 1821). (See also TINDERBOX, Chapter 12.)

TREE-OF-LIFE
A popular name for Lignum-vitae, *q.v.*, "an evergreen; the wood esteemed by turners." Philip Miller, *The Gardener's Dictionary* (London, 1757).

TULIP TREE, American Whitewood *Liriodendron tulipifera*
"It is used for canoes, boards, planks, bowls, dishes, spoons, doorposts and all sorts of joiners' work. Some reckon it better than oak because it does not warp." Peter Kalm, *Travels in North America* (Warrington, England, 1770). "A plant which grows naturally in North America with a smooth

purplish bark." (M) The wood varies from pale yellow to a light brown, sometimes with a green overtone. Despite Kalm's enthusiasm, white wood seldom was used in fine work but was reserved for drawer and chest backs, although some country furniture was made of it.

WALNUT *Juglans*

English Walnut *Juglans regia*

This is believed to have been introduced first in Britain during the Roman occupation. The golden brown wood with deeper brown and sometimes black striping is easy to carve and takes an excellent polish. Walnut was popular with English furniture makers during the second half of the seventeenth century, but even during the reign of Charles II it had begun to become scarce. Thus, although walnut was used extensively as late as 1725, many English chairmakers had turned to beech, and cabinetmakers who wanted to use walnut imported the wood from France, Italy, or the American colonies. By the mid-eighteenth century, the most fashionable wood was mahogany.

American, Black, or Virginia Walnut *Juglans nigra*

Often called Black Virginia in early records, this wood was used in England and America throughout the eighteenth century. It is a much deeper brown in color but with a straight grain and fewer of the streakings or dark veins of the English variety. English craftsmen often stained and polished American walnut to simulate the then more popular mahogany. Sheraton noted in his *Cabinet Dictionary* (London, 1803), "Black Virginia was much in use for cabinet work about 50 years since in England but is now quite laid aside since the introduction of mahogany." Nevertheless, in the colonies the earlier English liking for walnut continued, and in 1750 the Swedish naturalist Peter Kalm wrote that "the joiners use chiefly the black walnut, the wild cherry and the curled maple. [Of] the black walnut, there is yet a sufficient quantity, although careless people destroy it and even use it as fuel." Americans continued to use native walnut as colonists moved westward and discovered great stands in each of the new settlements. Even those who could afford to import furniture made in England often ordered it in walnut, but some were disappointed, as must have been the Yorktown, Virginia, merchant John Norton in July 1772 when his brother wrote to him from London that "White, the Cabinet maker, says the [English] Walnut-Tree wood is very dear and scarce (little of it being used here) and that mahogany wood is full as cheap . . . [So we] have consented to let him make your chairs of the last mentioned." Thus the great English Age-of-Walnut is given usually as 1660 to 1720.

The lack of sufficient English walnut was lamented early: "Were the timber in greater plenty amongst us we should have far better utensils of all sorts for our houses, as chairs, stools, bedsteads, Tables, Wainscot, Cabinets, Ec., instead of the more vulgar beech, subject to the worm, weak and unsightly." John Evelyn, *Sylva* (1679).

Following the Revolution and especially the War of 1812, "homestead" towns and settlements were being built by veterans who put their military bounty bonuses to use. Their land hunger caused great numbers of walnut trees to be felled. Some were seasoned and used on the spot to build homes; many others were shipped to furniture makers. The result was the vastly increased use of black walnut for all forms of American furniture from about 1820 throughout the nineteenth century.

WHITEWOOD

A general term for any light-colored wood useful for furniture, but usually applied to a smooth, close-grained wood such as birch, and often to inferior cherry wood; any light-colored wood easily stained.

Chairmaker's advertisement for white wood.

WILLOW *Salix alba*

"The common willow's wood is white, tough and hard to be broken . . . The water willow bringeth forth slender wands or twigs good to make baskets and such like workes of . . . Withy trees [grow] above man's height, of which do grow great rods, profitable for many things, and commonly for bands wherewith tubs and casks are bound." John Gerard, *The Herball or Generall Historie of Plantes* (London, 1636). "Willow is of use to make wooden heels for shoes, for cricket bats, as also to the turners in many kinds of light wares." (M)

YELLOW BIRCH *Betula lutea*

This superior birch wood, native to North America, varies in color from pale ivory-yellow to dark brown with reddish overtones; because of its silky finish, it often was used instead of cherry for fine furniture and for veneers. All yellow birch has a slight curl or wave to the grain; when these markings are especially striking, it is called curly birch, a handsome substitute for curly maple.

YEW *Taxus baccata* (English), *T. canadensis* (American)

The common yew tree is a native of Britain, Europe, and America. "Formerly the yew tree was cultivated in Britain chiefly for the manufacture of bows, but since these implements of war have been superseded by fire-arms, it is generally raised as an ornament to parks and plantations. The wood is hard and smooth, beautifully veined with red streaks; admits of a fine polish, and is almost incorruptible. Hence it is advantageously employed by turners and cabinet-makers for spoons, cups, as well as tables, chairs and various other articles . . . usefully converted into cogs for mill wheels, axle-trees, flood-gates for fish-ponds and may be effectually substituted for box." *The Domestic Encyclopedia* (Philadelphia, 1821).

7
Paints, Dyes, Finishes, Varnishes

Six-board chest painted to simulate inlay. (Courtesy, Connecticut Historical Society, Inc.)

Early-eighteenth-century clothes chest painstakingly painted to simulate expensive inlay work. (Courtesy, Connecticut Historical Society, Inc.)

1816 painted stencil pattern as substitute for expensive wallpaper. (Courtesy, Antiquarian and Landmarks Society, Inc.)

1725 portrait in oil on wood panel.

In the Colonial and Early Federal periods, a myriad of paints, dyes, and stains were used to color furniture woods and inlays; the textiles and leathers used for clothing and household linens, draperies, curtains, and upholstery; for fine book bindings; wall and ceiling hangings, papers, and plasters. Color also was used in the decoration of pottery, porcelain, glass, and metal wares; in the creation of decorative papers for book boards, trunk linings, and box covers; in printing and the illumination of manuscripts; in engavings and etchings; and, of course, in the still-life pictures, the marines, landscapes, and portraits we also collect today:

"Christopher Marshall at the Golden-Ball, opposite the end of Strawberry Alley in Chestnut St. [sells] Most sorts of oyls, and colours that are used either in Face, Landskips, House or Ship Painting, with Brushes, Tools and pencils that are useful in those workes likewise sundry Patterns for painting on glass and for Japan (Called Lady's Japan with useful Directions) Sundry sorts of varnishes and lackers, Shell and Dutch gold, English Glew, Spirits of Turpentine, Gums of sundry sorts. Also glass, putty, sashweights, and sheet lead." *Pennsylvania Gazette* (Philadelphia), September 1, 1743.

Throughout the Colonial and Early Federal periods many ready-ground paints and dye substances were imported for sale here. Some shops specialized in the colors and other supplies specifically needed by dyers and similar artisans, as well as those wanted by professional painters or limners and the country's many amateur artists. For this was a time when drawing and painting were considered part of the education of all young gentlemen and ladies. In those days before photography, each genteel traveler was expected to bring home for the edification of family and friends, his own sketches or water-color paintings of the far places he had toured, whether overland by stage coach or chaise or overseas under sail.

Unhappily, the professional academy-trained painter, who kept a studio and exhibition room, seldom was accorded social status higher than that given the unschooled itinerant limner, or indeed the common workman, as William Dunlap (1776–1839) made clear in the first basic history of American painting: "The judge said to me, you must not expect anything from this stupid place. There are not three men in it that ever thought. I'll tell you an anecdote. At a time of yellow fever in New York, two miniature painters, Trott and Tisdale, came to this city; they took a room and painted some heads. This was about the year '96. It was a novelty, and the

Early-nineteenth-century amateur water-color painting of roses, dahlias, morning glories, and violas in original veneered frame.

Miniature portrait on ivory of American Revolutionary War officer.

Advertisement lists inventory of dyes and paints. *American Mercury* (Hartford, Connecticut), December 6, 1817.

gentlemen of Albany visited the painters and were pleased with them; and on occasion of a ball they were getting up, they sent them tickets of invitation. But before the ball took place they had time to reflect and consult, and the result was that a note was written to the painters to say that the gentlemen of Albany must recall the invitation as, according to the rules, no mechanics could be admitted." *A History of the Rise and Progress of the Arts of Design in the United States* (New York, 1834).

In addition to the merchant who specialized, most hardware stores featured large selections of paints and dyes. The typical advertisement of such a shop included: "India Ink; French Chalk; White Lead; Red Lead; Spanish Brown; Spanish White; Venetian Red; Patent, Spruce, Stone, Kings, Naples and Chrome Yellow; Vermillion; Prussian Blue; Ivory Black; Lamp Black; Dutch Pink; Flake White; Verdigrise; distilled Verdigrise; Sap Green; Drop Lake; Verditure; Umber, Litharge; Logwood; Fustic; Nicaragua; Red Wood; Saunders; Madder; Amiatto; Rocoe; Allum, Copperas, Various kinds of Indigo; Oil Vitriol; Blue Vitriol; Nutgalls; Gold, Silver and Brass Leaf; Reaves' Colours, Also Hair and Black Lead Pencils; Painters' Brushes, Varnishing Brushes." Joseph Lynde. *American Mercury* (Hartford, Connecticut, November 18, 1817.

The frugal and industrious, or those unable to afford to purchase colors, could manufacture their own at home from plant and tree roots, stems, leaves, blossoms, and barks, and from native clays and stones, as old formulae make clear. Many antiques today need cleaning and restoring of their colors. To do so properly an understanding of the materials used by their original manufacturers and owners is necessary. The list that follows does not include all the variations used by earlier Americans, but it does cover those colors and dyes commonly preferred.

PAINTS

CHALK

"Black chalk among painters denotes a kind of ochreous earth, and fine black colour used in drawing upon blue paper." (M) "Red chalk, an indurated clayey ochre, common in the colour shops, and much used by painters and artificers." (M)

MILK PAINT

Milk curds, whiting, slaked lime mixed with water. "For ceilings, gates, doors and furniture: Bruise fresh curds in an earthen pan, or in a mortar; after which mix with an equal portion of slacked lime; the result will be a white fluid that may be applied with as much facility as varnish; it must be used on the same day [prepared] as it dries very speedily, and is apt to become too thick, if

it be kept twentyfour hours. Ochre and all pigments that are miscible with lime, may be incorporated in various proportions, according to the colour to be communicated; but some caution is necessary in making such additions, to use the smallest possible quantity of water. When two coats have been applied, it may be polished with a piece of woolen cloth; in consequence of which it will become as bright as any varnish. If the ceiling, Ec., be exposed to moisture, it should be coated with the whites of eggs, by which expedient it will become as durable as oil painting. The principal advantage [of this paint] consists of cheapness, and the facility with which two coats may be applied and polished.

Hence it deserves the attention of those whose lungs cannot support the disagreeable smell arising from oil paint, and who are not disposed to encourage the extravagant charges of painters." M. Lubicke, *Bibliothèque Physico-économique* (1792).

OCHRES

"A genus of argillaceous earths, slightly coherent, and composed of fine, smooth particles, rough to the touch, and readily diffusable in water. Ochres are of various colours —yellow, red, blue, brown, green, Ec.; they are principally employed as pigments. Red chalk and reddle are red ochres." *The Domestic Encyclopedia* (Philadelphia, 1821).

OXBLOOD PAINT

An early-nineteenth-century formula, said to have been proposed by a Spanish physician named Carbonel who directed that "the serum (or water) of the blood of oxen instead of the solution of glue be used to mix up the colouring matter . . . After the blood has settled, the water must be poured off and strained, the adhesion of its integrant parts diminished by powdered quicklime, taking care to preserve the mixture of a proper fluidity to be easily spread with the brush. The colours [paint] so prepared should be used as quickly as possible; and when any particular colour is wanted, the material for the purpose must be added at the time the lime is mixed: but as these additions diminish the strength of the compound, a few whites of eggs must be added (too many whites will subject the paint to scale off). This paint can only be applied to wood or plaster not previously painted: a beautiful polish may be given to it by friction with cloths, greased with clean whale oil." *The Domestic Encyclopedia* (Philadelphia, 1821).

POTATOE PAINT

"Any quantity of newly made potatoe-starch should be boiled into a paste; a sufficient portion of which ought to be mixed with whiting after the latter has been diluted with water . . . [it is] much clearer, retains its whiteness longer and is less liable to crack or scale than such as is mixed with animal glue." *The Domestic Encyclopedia* (Philadelphia, 1821).

FLAX, Linseed Oil

"The oil which is pressed out of the seed, is profitable for many purposes in Physicke and Surgerie, and is much used of painters, picture makers, and other artificers." John Gerard, *The Herball or Generall Historie of Plantes* (London, 1636).

CHARCOAL CRAYONS

To prepare crayons for drawing, "Saw the finest grained charcoal into slips of the size wanted, and put them into a pipkin of melted bees'-wax; put them near a slow fire for half an hour, take them out, and when they are perfectly cool, they are fit for use. The advantages of these pencils are, that they can be made at the most trifling expense, and that drawings made with them are as permanent as ink. The above process will harden both red and black chalks, and make them permanent also." G. W. Francis, *The Dictionary of Practical Receipts* (London, 1847).

BASIC INKS

Ink was the "black liquor generally made of an infusion of galls, copperas, and a little gum-arabick." To make common black writing ink: "Take one gallon of soft water, and pour it boiling hot on one pound of powdered galls, put into a proper vessel; stop the mouth of the vessel, and set it in the sun in summer, or in winter where it may be warmed by the fire, and let it stand two or three days. Add then half a pound of green vitriol powdered, and having stirred the mixture well together with a wooden spatula, let it stand again for two or three days, repeating the stirring, when add further to it five ounces of gum arabick dissolved in a quart of boiling water; and lastly, two ounces of alum; after which the ink should be strained through a coarse linen cloth for use." (M)

INDIA INK

The name given "a black pigment brought hither from China, which on being rubbed with water, dissolves and forms a substance resembling ink, but of a consistence extremely well adapted to the working with a pencil [brush], on which account it is not only much used as a black colour in miniature painting, but is the black now generally made use of for all smaller drawings in chiara obscuro, or where the effect is to be produced from light and shade only." (M)

PRINTING INK

This is made by "boiling or burning linseed oil till it is pretty thick, adding a little rosin to it while hot, and then mixing this varnish with lamp black." (W)

DYES AND COLORS

Dyeing then as now was "The art of giving a lasting colour to silks, cloths, and other substances, whereby their beauty is much improved, and value enhanced." (M)

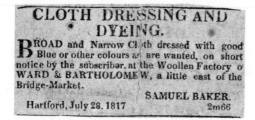

CLOTH DRESSING AND DYEING.

BROAD and Narrow Cloth dressed with good Blue or other colours as are wanted, on short notice by the subscriber, at the Woollen Factory of WARD & BARTHOLOMEW, a little east of the Bridge-Market.

SAMUEL BAKER.

Hartford, July 28, 1817.   2m66

American Mercury (Hartford, Connecticut), July 28, 1817.

BLACK

ACAJOU

"The cashew-nut tree . . . is a native of Brazil; the dyers make use of oil drawn from the kernel, in dying black." (M)

BLUE BLACK

"The coal of wood or other vegetable matter burnt in a close heat. The best kind is made of vine stalks and vine tendrils." (M)

COPPERAS

"A name given to the factitious green vitriol. It is the chief ingredient in the dying of wool, cloths, and hats, black; in making ink, in tanning and dressing leather, Ec. and from hence is prepared oil of vitriol, and a kind of Spanish brown for painters." (M)

CURRIER'S BLACK

"A tint or dye laid on tanned leather; one [kind is] first made of galls, sour ale, and old iron; the second of galls, copperas, and gumarabick." (M)

EARTH BLACK

"A soot of coals found in the ground, which the painters and limners use to paint in fresco after it has been well ground." (M)

IVORY BLACK

"The coal of ivory or bone formed by giving them a great heat." (M)

LAMP BLACK

"The soot of oil collected as it is formed by burning . . . in a number of large lamps in a confined place, the soot being collected against the top and sides of the room, may be swept together and collected." (M)

PERSIMMON TREE (PLUM-TREE BLACK)

"The unripe juice of the plum [*sic*] is preferable to oak bark, for tanning. Country tanners should attend to this useful fact. I have dyed silk with an ink made of this substance which was as black, and bore washing as well as that dyed with galls or logwood." *The Domestic Encyclopedia* (Philadelphia, 1821).

VERDIGRIS

This is the acetate of copper, "a kind of rust usually prepared from that metal by corroding it with vinegar . . . Verdigris is chiefly consumed for striking a black colour, when combined with a decoction of logwood." *The Domestic Encyclopedia* (Philadelphia, 1821).

BLUE

WOAD *Isatis tinctoria*

Flowers in the months of June and July, attaining a height of three to four feet. "The leaves are highly valued by dyers for the beautiful blue colour which they impart to wool. The leaves are cut with an edged tool, collected into baskets by women and children . . . ground and reduced to a kind of pulp, dried and formed into balls for sale. [However] the fresh leaves of woad with diluted bullock's blood, or with caustic soap boilers' ley [may be boiled]; in this simple manner, a dark green decoction of a blueish shade will be obtained; and, after clarifying the liquor, it will form a blue precipitate, which, dissolved in oil of vitriol, and properly diluted, imparts a beautiful colour to woollen cloth. Even the leaves, in a state of fermentation with pure water, on adding a small portion of caustic alkaline ley, afford a fine blue sediment, resembling the true indigo." *The Domestic Encyclopedia* (Philadelphia, 1821).

AZURE

"Among painters, the beautiful blue colour with a greenish cast, prepared from the *lapis lazuli,* generally called ultramarine. Azure (also) signifies that bright blue colour prepared from *lapis armenus,* a different stone, though frequently confounded together. This [latter] colour is, by our painters, called Lambert's Blue." (M)

BICEBEARS

"The best body of all bright blues used in common work, as house painting, Ec. but it is the palest in colour. It works indifferently well but inclines a little to sandy, and therefore requires good grinding. Next to ultramarine, which is too dear to be used in common work, it lies best near the eye of all other blues." (M)

Smalt: A pigment made from Azur d'Hollande or Holland cobalt which was fused with glass and then pulverized for use.

EGGSHELL BLUE

Also called robin's-egg blue. Made by burning and powdering eggshells, mixing the powder with vinegar to a thick paste, setting this mixture to ferment in dung, after which it was thinned with more vinegar and/or water.

ELDER TREE

"The elder has little berries, green at the first, afterwards blacke, whereout is pressed a purple juice, which being boiled with Allum and such like things doth serve very well for the Painters use." John Gerard, *The Herball or Generall Historie of Plantes* (London, 1636).

INDIGO

"I must tell you about the indigo plant, whose leaves after three boilings, yield a blue substance which collects in small particles." Edouard de Montulé, *Voyage en Amérique* . . . (Paris, 1821).

PLUNKET
"A sort of fine blue color." (W)

POMEGRANATE TREE *Punica granatum*
"From the deciduous leaves in autumn, when they present a brownish-red shade, may be obtained, by boiling them, a thick muddy liquor in which cotton, silk and woollen cloths acquire a good French-blue colour." *The Domestic Encyclopedia* (Philadelphia, 1821).

RED WORTLEBERRIES *Vaccinea rubra, V. vitis-idaea*
"Have small berries . . . of an excellent red colour and full of juice, of so orient and beautifull a purple to limne withall, that Indian *Lacea* is not to be compared thereunto, especially when this juyce is prepared and dressed with Allom according to art." John Gerard, *The Herball or Generall Historie of Plantes* (London, 1636).

SAXON BLUE
"A colour used for dyeing silk, also by washer-women as a liquid blue. Take indigo ground very fine and washed in clear water, 1 oz., strong oil of vitriol 8 oz. Let them digest together for 2 or 3 days in a flask or porcelain vessel. A few drops give a deep tinge." *The Domestic Encyclopedia* (Philadelphia, 1821).

SEA GREEN
The painter's name for a blue "resembling the colour of the distant sea; cerulean." (J)

ULTRAMARINE
This brilliant blue color "much estemed by painters . . . is manufactured from the mineral called *Lapis lazuli* . . . burnt or calcined, reduced to a fine powder, made into a paste with wax, linseed oil and resinous matters, and afterwards separated by washing. The powder that is left . . . is ultramarine. Few colours [are] so little susceptible of change." *The Domestic Encyclopedia* (Philadelphia, 1821).

ZAFFRE
This is the "oxyde or calx of cobalt, employed for imparting a blue colour to porcelain and pottery ware. [It is the] most permanent of the different colours employed in glass-works, as it resists the most intense heat. Hence, it is advantageously used for giving various shades of blue to enamels, and to the chrystal glasses made in imitation of lapis lazuli, turquoise, sapphire and other precious stones." *The Domestic Encyclopedia* (Philadelphia, 1821).

BROWN AND OTHER SAD COLORS

"Of this color there are various shades or degrees; Spanish-brown, sad-brown, London-brown, tawny-brown, clove-brown. Spanish brown is a dark, dull red of horse-flesh colour. It is an earth, and is of great use among painters, being generally used as the first and priming colour that they lay upon any kind of timber work in painting. That which is the deepest colour and freest of stones is the best." (M)

Sad: A contemporary adjective for anything heavy or "dark-coloured." (J) Pewter, for example, often was called sad-ware. "Scarce any tinging ingredient is of so general use as woad, or *glastum;* for though of itself it dye but a blue, yet it is used to prepare cloth for green, and many of the sadder colours, when the dyers make them last without fading." Robert Boyle, *Colours.*

ASPHALTUM
The name given a medium to dark brown color, produced from bitumen, used as a ground or undercoat in early painting; and because it dried slowly, was the cause of cracking in the top layers. It also was used extensively in the late eighteenth and nineteenth centuries as a glaze for paintings and as a protective coating for tinware.

BAY

"There are various degrees of this colour (from resembling the colour of dried bay leaves) from the slightest bay to the dark, that approaches the nearest to brown, but is always more gay and shining." (M)

BISTRE, BISTER

"The name of a warm, transparent, deep brown colour, extracted from wood soot." (M)

CAROLINA POPLAR   *Balsam fera*

"Provides a fine fawn, nut and similar grave color for wool, according to the quantity of wood employed and the length of time boiled." *The Domestic Encyclopedia* (Philadelphia, 1821).

DUN

"A color partaking of brown and black." (M)

HENNA   *Lawsonia alba*

The cyprus of the ancients, this is a shrub which has "acquired celebrity from being used [as a dye]; the leaves when dried, powdered, and made into a paste with hot water, leave a yellow color, requiring, however, to be renewed. It may be advantageously used for dyeing woollens, not only yellow, but brown of various shades, provided that alum and sulphate of iron be employed." *Encyclopedia Americana* (Philadelphia, 1831).

UMBER

The name of the painter's pigment that affords "a fine dark brown colour. It is an earth . . . formerly brought from Umbria in Italy. It is used in two states. The first, its natural one, with the simple precaution of washing. The second, that in which it is found after being burnt, [is called] burnt umber; the hues greatly differ." *The Domestic Encyclopedia* (Philadelphia, 1821).

WHITE WILLOW   *Salix alba*

"The bark communicates a cinnamon colour to yarn, and is advantageously used in tanning leather." *The Domestic Encyclopedia* (Philadelphia, 1821).

GREEN

ITALIAN or LOMBARDY POPLAR
Fustigata

"Affords a dye of as delicate a lustre, and equally durable, as the finest yellow wood. Its tinging matter is more readily extracted. Instead of striking a proper green with indigo, it changes to an olive shade." *The Domestic Encyclopedia* (Philadelphia, 1821).

PRIVET   *Ligustrum vulgare*

"Its juice [of the berries] when mixed with a solution of any acid salt, affords a black; with glauber's salt and spirit of sal ammoniac, a red; with urine, a purplish; and, with vitriol of iron, a green colour. On steeping these berries in a solution of salt of tartar, they yield a fine blue . . . which may be rendered still brighter by adding quicklime." *The Domestic Encyclopedia* (Philadelphia, 1821).

VERDITER

"A preparation of copper used as a pale green or blue." (W)

ORANGE, RED

ALBURN

"A compound colour formed by a mixture of red and white." (M)

ALOMA

A yellowish-red color.

ANCHUSA   *Alkanet*

"*Alkanet,* a species of bugloss; alkanet root is used in colouring oils, plaisters . . . which receive a fine deep red from one fortieth of their weight of the root." (M)

ANNOTTO

"In dying, an elegant red colour also called orlean and roncon." (M)

BASTARD SAFFRON *Carthamus*

An annual imported for use in England and America and "much cultivated for the use of dyeing and painting. It is sown in open fields in the spring and hoed out in the manner we do turnips. The flowers are used by the dyers." (M) "The only plant that gives a pink [dye] colour; wash out completely all the yellow colour first." *The Domestic Encyclopedia* (Philadelphia, 1821).

BRAZILWOOD TINCTURE

Take "ground Brazil wood 3 lbs., solution of Carbonate of soda 8 oz., sugar spirit (rum) 15 gallons." G. W. Francis, *The Dictionary of Practical Receipts* (London, 1847).

CARMINE

"A very beautiful red colour extracted from cochineal by means of water impregnated with alcaline salts, and precipitated with tin dissolved in an aqua regia." (M) "A bright red or crimson colour, bordering on purple, used by painters in miniature. It is the most valuable product of the cochineal mastick, and of an excessive price." (C)

CARMINE LIQUID

"Dissolve carmine in liquid ammonia or spirits of hartshorn. This makes a most beautiful ink, as also a fine colour for velvet painting and for staining maps, paper Ec." G. W. Francis, *The Dictionary of Practical Receipts* (London, 1847).

CARNATION COLOR

"Among painters is understood in general [to] represent flesh without drapery. The various colouring for carnations may be easily produced by making more or less red, blue, yellow, or bistre, whether for the first colouring or for the finishing. The colour for women should be bluish, for children, a little red, both fresh and gay; and for men it should incline to yellow, especially, if they are old." (M) "The Colours that shew best by candlelight are: white, Carnation, and a Kinde of Sea-water greene." Francis

Bacon: *Essay XXXVII, of Masques and Triumphs; The Essays or Counsels Civill and Morall* (London, 1625).

CINNABAR

This is made of "vermillion, quicksilver combined with sulphur and is called red sulphuret of mercury." (W)

CRIMSON

"One of the colours of the dyers, consisting of scarlet mixed with blue." (M)

FALLOW

"A pale red colour, like that of brick half-burnt." (M)

GRIDELIN

A color of "white and red mixed together." (W)

HEMLOCK *Picaea abies*

"The bark of the Hemlock spruce fir-tree, is used for tanning; it communicates a reddish appearance to the leather, and if used alone, burns the leather. The Indians dye their splints for baskets with it." *The Domestic Encyclopedia* (Philadelphia, 1821).

LADIES'-BEDSTRAW *Galium rubrum*

Provided a red dye.

MINIUM

"The red oxyd of lead." (W) (See also MINIATURE PORTRAITS, Chapter 12.)

ORCHAL, ARGOL, ARCHIL or CUDBEAR *Lichen roccella*

"Argol is of a light colour, though it is sometimes found of a dark grey. When mixed with lime, urine and alkaline salts, this moss is formed into a dark red paste, which has received the different names above mentioned and is much used in dyeing . . . a deep red or purple colour." *The Domestic Encyclopedia* (Philadelphia, 1821). This was the name given to archil or orchil, as a variation on his name, by Dr. Cuthbert Gordon in 1840 when he patented a dye made from lichens.

PLANE TREE *Platanus occidentalis*

The dry leaves and branches of the western plane tree "afford a decoration of a very bright red-brown, with advantage employed in dyeing." *The Domestic Encyclopedia* (Philadelphia, 1821).

POPPY *Papaver rhoeas*

The "corn-rose, cop-rose, or headwark, grows in cornfields . . . its flower-leaves yield, on expression, a bright-red juice, which imparts its colour to water and is greatly improved by the addition of vitriolic acid. Cloth, linen, and especially silk and cotton are dyed of a beautiful deep-red shade. The stuffs previously immersed in a solution of bismuth, acquire a yellow cast." *The Domestic Encyclopedia* (Philadelphia, 1821).

PUCCOON, Bloodwort, Indian Paint, Turmeric *Sanguinaria canadensis*

"It contains a large proportion of gum, some resin, and extractive matter. The juice of the root dyes a fine orange colour, and is much used by the Indians. The *murio sulphat* of tin, as a mordant, produces a handsome colour." *The Domestic Encyclopedia* (Philadelphia, 1821).

SANDAL, Sanders-the-Red *Pterocarpus santalinum*

"Red sanders is chiefly employed as a colouring drug in the compound tincture of lavender. Sandal wood communicates a deep red to rectified spirit." *The Domestic Encyclopedia* (Philadelphia, 1821).

SASSAFRAS *Sassafras albidum*

"The bark of the sassafras tree is used for dyeing worsted, which it does of a permanent and beautiful orange colour." *The Domestic Encyclopedia* (Philadelphia, 1821).

SLOE TREE, Blackthorn *Prunus spinosa*

"The dried berries of the black-thorn dye linen of a red hue, which on repeated washing, changes to a durable light blue. The bark boiled in ley, also yields a red tinge." *The Domestic Encyclopedia* (Philadelphia, 1821).

SUMACH *Rhus aromatica*

"The yellow Sumach, *cotinus,* has leaves and branches useful in tanning; the wood and bark yield an orange dye; the bark with the addition of Brazil wood imparts a chestnut colour." *The Domestic Encyclopedia* (Philadelphia, 1821).

VERMILION

Is the red pigment of a hue between scarlet and crimson. "There are two kinds; the one natural or native; the other artificial or factitious." *The Domestic Encyclopedia* (Philadelphia, 1821).

YELLOW

"The principal article affording a yellow dye is the Weld, or Dyer's green-weed, *Reseda luteola.* An excellent yellow dye may likewise be prepared from the flowers of the *Acacia,* the hickory and the barberry. These must be gathered before they be fully blown, and dried in an earthen vessel over a moderate fire, till they crisp, or curl up, in the same manner as tea leaves. The ripe seeds of the same tree are then added in the necessary proportions; and the whole, when boiled in river-water, with the addition of alum, will impart a yellow colour of any shade required." *The Domestic Encyclopedia* (Philadelphia, 1821).

ALCANNA

"An Egyptian plant used in dying; its leaves making a yellow infused in water, and a red in acid liquors." (J)

ARZICA

The illuminator's gold or yellow color produced from dyer's weed, *Resuda luteola.*

BERBERRY *Berberis*

The root was used for dyeing leather yellow.

148

FESTUCINE
The word for "a straw colour between green and yellow." (J)

FOLIOMORT
"A dark yellow; the colour of a leaf faded; vulgarly called philomot." (J)

FUSTIC
"A West India wood for dying yellow." (W)

GIALALINA
An Italian word adopted in English for "earth of a bright gold colour, found in the kingdom of Naples, very fine, and very much valued by painters." (J)

GOEL
The name is from the Old Saxon word for yellow.

> *In March at the furthest, dry season or*
> *   wet,*
> *Hop roots so well chosen let skillful go set*
> *The goeler and younger the better I love;*
> *Well gutted and pared the better they*
> *   prove.*

> Thomas Tusser, *Five Hundreth Points of Good House-wifery* (London, 1577).

MUSK ROSE *Rosa moschata*
"The white leaves stamped in a wooden dish with a piece of Allum and the juyce strained forth into some glazed vessell, dried in the shadow, and kept, is the most fine and pleasant yellow colour that may be devised to limne or wash pictures and Imagerie in books." John Gerard, *The Herball or Generall Historie of Plantes* (London, 1636).

ORPIMENT, KING'S YELLOW
Orpiment is a mineral, a combination of arsenic and sulphur and is poisonous. The color called King's Yellow is 43 parts sulphur to 57 of arsenic. Red orpiment, called Realgar, is 25 parts sulphur to 75 of arsenic.

PEAR TREE *Pyrus communis*
"The leaves impart a yellow dye, and are sometimes employed to communicate a green colour to blue cloth." *The Domestic Encyclopedia* (Philadelphia, 1821).

PLUM TREE *Prunus domesticus*
"The bark of the *P. domestica* or common Plum-tree imparts a yellow dye." *The Domestic Encyclopedia* (Philadelphia, 1821).

RAGWORT, Groundsel, St. James's-Wort
Senecio jacobaea
"If gathered before the flowers expand, and employed in a fresh state, the ragwort imparts to wool a fine green, though not permanent colour. But if woollen cloth be previously boiled in alum water, and then in a decoction of these flowers, a beautiful deep yellow shade will be produced. [Also] a decoction of the flowers and stalks while in blossom, the wool previously steeped in a solution of bismuth, [will acquire] a very permanent olive-brown colour, displaying a beautiful golden shade." *The Domestic Encyclopedia* (Philadelphia, 1821).

RUE *Ruta thalictrum*
"Meadow Rue. The root, branches, and leaves impart to wool a yellow colour; which, on adding sal-ammoniac assumes a pale shade; with oil of tartar, an orange colour." *The Domestic Encyclopedia* (Philadelphia, 1821).

SAW-WORT *Serratula tinctoria*
"This plant is employed by dyers to impart a yellow colour . . . chiefly confined to the coarser woollen cloths. In combination with indigo [it] strikes a permanent green colour. Its leaves readily yield a brownish-yellow decoction." *The Domestic Encyclopedia* (Philadelphia, 1821).

SAFFRON
"The [stamens] steeped in water serve to illumine or (as we say) limne pictures and imagerie." John Gerard, *The Herball or*

Generall Historie of Plantes (London, 1636).

> *Give us bacon, rinds of walnuts,*
> *Shells of cockles and of small nuts,*
> *Ribands, bells, and saffron'd linen,*
> *All the world is ours to win in.*

> Ben Jonson, *The Gyrnes Metamorphosel*

TURMERIC *Curcuma longa*
"A genus of exotic plants, natives of India, annually imported by the East India Company . . . [and] chiefly consumed in dyeing the finest yellow colours on silks, which are also the least prominent, and giving a brighter, though perishable shade to scarlet cloth." *The Domestic Encyclopedia* (Philadelphia, 1821).

TO DYE BONE

Bone, of which knife and fork handles; trinket, snuff, patch and other boxes; beads, seals, and other small articles were made, was dyed according to these or similar formulae:

"Red: Dissolve cochineal in spirits of hartshorn, into which immerse the bones after having put them in weak aquafortis a few minutes.

"Scarlet: First boil in madder dye or Brazil wood, and then in a solution of muriate of tin.

"Black: Soak for a day or two in ink or in a weak solution of lunar caustic.

"Purple: Boil for six hours with logwood and alum, not using an iron vessel.

"Yellow: First soak for 24 hours in a solution of sugar of lead, and afterwards in chromate of potass.

"Brown: Boil in a solution of turmeric, and afterwards boil in pearlash water.

"Blue: Soak or boil in a solution of sulphate of indigo, to which a little salt of tartar may be added.

"Green: Dissolve verdigris in vinegar and boil the bones therein." G. W. Francis, *The Dictionary of Practical Receipts* (London, 1847).

TO DYE HORN

"Black: Is performed by steeping brass in aquafortis till it is turned green; with this the horn is to be washed once or twice, and then put into a warm decoction of logwood and water.

"Horns receive a deep black stain from solution of nitrate of silver (lunar caustic). This is to be dissolved in water and diluted to such a degree as not sensibly to corrode the surface. It may be applied at two or three times, and an interval of some hours between each application. Exposing the article to the sun much hastens the blackening of the horn, which does not show at first any difference of color.

"Green: Boil the horn with alum water, then with verdigris, ammoniac, and white wine vinegar, keeping it hot therein, till sufficiently green.

"Red: First dye it green, then boil it in a strong lime water (strained), putting 3 oz. of Brazil wood in chips to every pint of lime water.

"Blue: First boil the horns in alum water and then soak them in a solution of blue stone, or boil them in a solution of the sulphate of indigo." G. W. Francis, *The Dictionary of Practical Receipts* (London, 1847).

TO DYE IVORY

"Black: Color is given it by a solution of brass and a decoction of logwood.

"Green: By a solution of verdigris.

"Red: By being boiled with Brazil-wood, in lime-water." *Encyclopedia Americana* (Philadelphia, 1831).

FINISHES

BRONZING

This is "the art of varnishing wood, plaster, ivory, Ec. so as to give them the colour of bronze." (M)

BRONZE POWDERS

"1) The *aurum musivum* or Mosaic gold, is used for inferior articles; this is a preparation of tin, quicksilver, and sulphur, possessing a bright gold-like appearance.

"2) A copper-coloured bronze may be obtained by dissolving copper in aquafortis [*q.v.*] until it is saturated, and then putting into the solution some small pieces of iron, when the copper will be precipitated in the metallic state, the fluid must then be poured off, and the powder carefully washed, dried, and levigated, when it may be put by for use.

"3) Bronze powder is sometimes made from Dutch gold, which is sold in books at a very low price. All these inferior bronzes require to be covered with a coat of clear varnish, or they will very soon lose their metallic appearance, nor will the varnish entirely prevent, although it will greatly retard, this change.

"4) Verdigris 8 oz., flowers of zinc or tutti powder 4 oz., borax and nitre of each 2 oz., corrosive sublimate 2 drams; made into a paste with oil and melted together. This is an inferior article, and is used in the commoner kinds of japanning tea-boards, Ec." G. W. Francis, *The Dictionary of Practical Receipts* (London, 1847).

AQUA FORTIS

"A corrosive liquor made by distilling purified nitre with calcined vitriol, or rectified oil of vitriol, in a strong heat. The spirit serves for dissolving silver and all other metals except gold. It is serviceable to refiners, in separating silver from gold and copper; to the workers in mosaick, for staining and colouring their woods; to dyers in their colours, particularly scarlet, and to other artists, for colouring bone and ivory. With Aqua fortis book-binders marble the covers of books, and diamond-cutters separate diamonds from metalline powders. It is also used in etching copper or brass plates." (M)

AQUA REGIA

The name of "an acid corrosive spirit, so-called because it serves to dissolve gold, the king of metals . . . Its basis is common sea-salt mixed with spirit of nitre or common Aqua fortis." (M)

ENAMELING

This is a "kind of coloured glass [which has for its] basis a pure crystal glass or frit ground up with a fine calx of lead and tin prepared for the purpose, with the addition usually of white salt of tartar . . . and by adding colours of this or that kind of powder . . . and melting them together. Enamels are used either in counterfeiting or imitating precious stones, in painting in enamel, or by enamellers, jewellers, or goldsmiths. The first two kinds are usually prepared by the workmen themselves. That used by jewellers, Ec., is brought to us chiefly from Venice or Holland, in little cakes." (M)

Amel: "The matter with which the variegated works are overlaid which we call enamelled." (J) "Glass melted with calcined tin compose . . . this white amel, the basis of all those fine concretes that goldsmiths and artificers employ in the curious art of enamelling." Robert Boyle, *Colours*.

For "**White** Enamel: Only manganese [should] be added to the basis.

"**Azure:** Zaffer mixed with calx of brass.

"**Green:** Calx of brass with scales of iron; or with crocus martis.

"**Black:** Zaffer with manganese or with crocus martis; or manganese with tartar.

"**Red:** Manganese or calx of copper and red tartar.

"**Purple:** Manganese with calx of brass.

"**Yellow:** Tartar and manganese.

"**Violet:** Manganese with thrice-calcined brass." (M)

TO ENAMEL EARTHENWARE

"Take of tin any quantity, inclose it in clay or loam and put it in a crucible, place the crucible in the fire, that the tin may calcine and then break it; there will be a quantity of calyx or oxyde of a very white colour." Or, "Mix together equal parts of white enamel, glass and soda, finely pulverized and sifted." G. W. Francis, *The Dictionary of Practical Receipts* (London, 1847).

GLAZES FOR POTTERY

(See in Chapter 10.)

FLITTERWORK

A rather crude form of luster painting. The iridescent effect was achieved by applying a thick coat of varnish which, when tacky, was sprinkled or dusted over with bronze powder. Used on glass, pottery, looking glass frames, and other small decorative accessories.

GILDING

To decorate any surface but especially wood or plaster with gold. "The art of spreading or covering a thing with gold,

either in leaf or liquid. We have this advantage over the ancients in the manner of using and applying the gold, that the secret of painting in oil, lately discovered, furnishes us with means of gilding works capable of enduring all the violences of time and weather which theirs could not." (M)

Gilding and Painting, BY **Sanford & Walsh**, Two doors South of the North Meeting House. PORTRAIT, Minature and Heraldry Painting, in all their various branches—*likewise*, Signs and Chaise Painting in the most elegant manner, equal to any done in America—*likewise*, Outside and room Painting, Fresco Painting upon walls, representing Landscapes, favorite Hunting Pieces, Shipping, &c. and various other pieces, too many to enumerate.

ALSO,

Engraving and Blazoning the Supplement of Ladies' and Gentlemens' Coats of Arms, &c. Engraving and Printing any other Device whatever.—*Likewise*, Painting Mezzotinto Prints on Glass, enlaying with hair, Lockets, Rings, Bracelets, &c. &c.

N. B. The Silversmith's business, is carried on at the same shop, by *Sanford & Jobonnet*—who make and have for sale, all kinds of Silver and Plated Shoe and Knee Buckles, Spoons, Creempots and Pepper Castors—also, plated Sturrups, Bridle-bits, Buckles, Tips and purrs—likewise, Gold Beads, and Earings, Stone, Gold, and Silver Sleeve-buttons ; Enamel'd Rings, Watch Seals, Chains and Trinkets ; and a variety of other matters not mentioned. Hartford, Nov. 2, 1789.

American Mercury (Hartford, Connecticut), November 2, 1789.

AMMOCHRYSOS

The name of a stone, "being a species of mica, with gold-coloured spangles. Reduced to powder, it is used to strew over writing," (M) that is, to illuminate manuscripts, initial letters, etc.

BORAX GILT

A less expensive method of gilding glass using gold leaf powdered with the mineral borax and gum arabic, then mixed with water. The painted object was fired at a low temperature to fuse the gilt to the glass.

GOLD LEAF

Or "beaten gold [is formed] with a hammer into exceeding thin leaves, so that an ounce may be beaten into 1600 leaves each three inches square. They use three sorts of hammers like mallets of polished iron, to chase or drive, to close, and to stretch and finish." (M)

American Mercury (Hartford, Connecticut), May 12, 1813.

PARCEL GILT

The term for anything partly gilt or decorated with gilt.

> *Thou didst swear to me on a parcel-gilt goblet . . .*
>
> *at the round table, sitting by a sea-coal fire.*
>
> Shakespeare: *King Henry IV*, Part II, II, i.

"If ye wish to decorate your work in some manner, take tin, pure and finely scraped, melt it and wash it like gold, and apply it with the same glue upon letters or other places which you wish to ornament with gold or silver; and when you have polished it with a tooth, take Saffron with which Silk is coloured, moistening it with clear of egg without water; and when it has stood a night, on the following day, cover with a pencil the places which you wish to gild, the rest holding the place of silver." Theophilus, eleventh century.

GRAINING

The technique or practice of finishing wood by painting it to resemble the color, texture, and figuring of a more expensive or fashionable wood. (See also STAINING, and see GRAINED FURNITURE, Chapter 12.)

JAPANNING

A method of decorating wood with lacquers (and later with spirit varnish) after the Oriental fashion, first introduced into Europe and England about the middle of the seventeenth century and from there to America. At that time the finest examples of such work came from Japan, hence the adjective japanning. Following their discovery that *Rhus vernifera* or lac-tree sap would harden into a translucent film, the Chinese had first used lacquers with low-relief and surface painting, as well as with incised designs, at least 1000 B.C. In 1688 the book *Treatise on Japanning and Varnishing* was published by Stalker and Parker. This English cabinetmakers' guide gave instructions for "guilding, burnishing, lackering, painting mezzo-tinto prints, counterfeiting tortoiseshell and marble" effects, etc. True japanning was time-consuming work, accomplished by applying as many as thirty-two layers of lacquer to the wood surface; each layer was burnished or polished after drying. The lacquered wood then was decorated with Oriental-style drawings painted with gold or vermilion powder mixed with sizing or gum water. Raised effects were created out of a paste of whiting and gum arabic which then was gilded or painted. Seventeenth- and early-eighteenth-century examples generally had a black background, although other colors sometimes were used.

The English and colonial "imitation" method followed in the 1770s called for wood "close-grained and smooth, [kept] in some warm place; then take the thickest seed-lack varnish six ounces, and lamp black enough to colour it. With this mixture wash over your piece three times, letting it dry thoroughly each time, and again wash it over three times more as before; then take of the thickest seed-lack varnish six ounces, Venice turpentine one ounce, and wash your work over with this six times; letting it stand twelve hours between the first three varnishes and as many hours between the three last. Last of all, take of the finest seed-lack varnish six ounces and of lamp black a sufficient quantity, which mix together and with it varnish your work twelve times, standing twelve hours between the first six and the last six washings. When it has stood to dry six or seven days polish it well with tripoli and rag till it be smooth; and then clean it up with oil and lamp black and you will have a good black japan, scarce at all inferiour to the true.

"As for the colour used in japanning, a common red is made of the thickest seed-lack varnish and pure vermilion; a dark red with fine sanguis draconies; a pale red with vermilion and white lead; blue with the finest smalt and in like manner may be done with gold colours or any others you please." (M)

Japanning was revived here in the early nineteenth century, resulting in the mass production of many types of furniture and accessories. At this time one to four coats of an inexpensive oil varnish were used for the base.

BANTAMWORK
A form of japanning with an incised design, also called coromandel and so named for the Dutch trading community in the East Indies from which early Oriental wares were exported in the seventeenth century.

PONTYPOOL
(See in Chapter 12.)

STAINING

"Mahogany, ebony, and the finer woods, being very expensive, artisans have contrived various preparations for tinging timber so as to be with difficulty distinguished from them." *The Domestic Encyclopedia*

Eighteenth-century clothes chest with grained decoration. (Courtesy, Antiquarian and Landmarks Society, Inc.)

(Philadelphia, 1821). The principal coloring stains used in the eighteenth and nineteenth centuries included:

Blue: To stain wood blue, (1) Take "two drachms of the best indigo reduced to a fine powder; put it in a glass with two ounces of oil of vitriol, and agitate them with a new clay pipe. After standing ten or twelve hours . . . in a temperate place, pour it into a large glass vessel, or china bowl, and add such a portion of pure water [needed] to give it the tint required."

(2) Dissolve "verdigris in distilled vinegar; then [make] a separate solution of 2 oz. of pure pearl ashes in a pint of water. The former liquid should be first repeatedly applied to the surface of the wood, till it be of a sufficiently deep green colour; when the latter preparation must be drawn over it with a soft painter's brush, as often as may be necessary to change it to a proper blue cast." Ibid.

Ebony: (1) This wood "may be imitated, by boiling clean, smooth box in oil, till it becomes permanently black."

(2) "By washing pear-tree wood that has been previously planed, with *aqua fortis,*

154

and drying it in a shady place in the open air; after which writing ink must be repeatedly passed over it, and the wood dried till it acquire a deep black colour. It may then be polished with wax and a woollen cloth, which will give it a fine lustre." Ibid.

Green: To color wood green, "Dissolve purified verdigris in distilled vinegar, or in *aqua fortis,* diluted with 15 or 20 times its weight of water, and apply the solution to wood previously warmed." Ibid.

Mahogany: (1) To communicate a "perfect mahogany colour finish to inferior woods, especially . . . elm, maple and sycamore . . . Dissolve two drachms of dragon's blood, one drachm of wild alkanet, *Anchusa tinctoria,* and half a drachm of wine. Previously to [applying], the wood ought to be moistened with *aqua fortis.*" Ibid.

(2) To stain wood through with "a beautiful red or mahogany colour, place a square piece of plane-tree wood, a line in thickness, into pounded dragon's blood, from the Canaries, mixed with oil of turpentine, over the fire, in a glass vessel; the wood will slowly assure the colour, even before the spirit has volatilized. After more than an hour, take the vessel from the fire, and let it stand the whole night, when it will appear of a mahogany colour, not merely on the surface, but also in the interior parts . . . The wood of the plane-tree is best for this purpose because it can be easily sawn and polished; because it has a white colour; is neither too hard nor too soft; neither contracts nor warps; has beautiful white spots with veins that cross each other; and because artists who make inlaid works, have long attempted to colour it by staining. The spirit of turpentine makes the wood more compact, and renders it more susceptible of a fine polish." Ibid.

Purple: To stain wood purple, "Take one ounce of logwood, and two drachms of Brazil wood; boil them together in a quart of water, slowly, over a moderate fire: when

one-half of the fluid is evaporated, it must be strained, and several times laid on the wood with a brush till it have received a dark-red shade. Thus prepared, and allowed to become perfectly dry, it may be changed to a fine purple by drawing over it repeatedly a weak solution of the purest pearl-ash, namely, one drachm in a pint of water. Some dexterity must be exerted on this occasion, as, by too sudden and frequent applications of either of the two liquids, the colour is very apt to assume a dark blue instead of a purple shade." Ibid.

Red: To stain wood with a red color finish, "take two ounces of Brazil wood, and 2 drachms of purified potash; mix them with a quart of water, and let the composition stand in a warm place for several days, stirring it occasionally. When sufficiently extracted, the coloured liquor must be decanted, moderately warmed, and in that state applied to the wood as many times as may be deemed necessary for giving it a more or less bright cast. Next, a solution of alum, in the proportion of two ounces to a quart of water, is to be laid on the wood, while it is still wet from the former stain, with a soft brush [or cloth]. After polishing the articles thus stained, their colour may be rendered still more beautiful and permanent, by giving them one or more coats with a varnish prepared of shellac." Ibid. (See also [2] under MAHOGANY.)

Walnut: "A fine walnut tree tint may be obtained by rubbing common wood with a mixture, prepared of the bark of trees, or the shells of walnuts, previously dried, pulverized, and reduced to a proper consistency with nut-oil." Ibid.

Yellow: (1) "This delicate tint may be easily imparted to wood which is naturally white. [To do so] take one ounce of pulverized turmeric, and a pint of rectified spirit of wine; shake them in a glass bottle; allow the infusion to stand for several days, closely covered; then decant the liquor, and lay it on the wood repeatedly, as may be found necessary." Ibid.

(2) A cheaper method: "[apply] weak *aqua fortis* to wood previously warmed, and immediately after the stain is given, hold it to the fire, at some distance, till it acquires the desired cast . . . The *aqua fortis* must be sufficiently diluted with water, as otherwise the wood is apt to acquire a brown or blackish hue." Ibid.

VARNISHES

Varnish is the clear liquid that becomes hard without losing transparency. It was used "by painters, carvers, gilders, and other artisans for imparting lustre to their works, while it defends them from the effects of dust, moisture, and air." *The Domestic Encyclopedia,* (Philadelphia, 1821).

Copal Spirit Varnish. "This recipe is kept a great secret [but] I have made it by dissolving copal in a warm place, in any of the following essential oils: bergamotte, lavender, orange, lemon, rosemary, of which the last is the cheapest; dilute it with twice the quantity of highly rectified spirit of wine. If the oil of rosemary is much adulterated with oil of turpentine, it will not succeed."

Copal "is a resin produced from certain trees in New Spain. The best is the clearest." Ibid. "Copal Varnish & Japan. Of a quality not surpassed by any heretofore offered for sale in this city, and as to price, as low as can be bought elsewhere, made and sold by the subscriber; who, having devoted a considerable share of his time for a number of years to the making and using of the same, is, he trusts enabled to accommodate purchasers with such as can be depended upon to be good. Orders from abroad attended to, at the Carriage Maker's Shop, next north of the South Meeting House. George Francis." *American Mercury* (Hartford, Connecticut), June 10, 1814.

ABEZZO

The name for a varnish made of silver fir resin diluted with oil.

CRYSTAL VARNISH

"This is a very easily prepared varnish and is used for a variety of purposes; for the varnishing of toys—for transferring engravings to wood, hence called transfer varnish —for varnishing maps, prints, and other paper works—for the making of transparent tracing paper, Ec. Mix together equal parts of pure Canada balsam and spirits of turpentine, leave the phial which contains the mixture, and which should be corked, in a warm place for a few days, shaking it occasionally, then strain for use." G. W. Francis, *The Dictionary of Practical Receipts* (London, 1847).

ELECTRICAL VARNISH

"This beautiful red varnish with which parts of philosophical instruments are ornamented is made by dissolving red sealing wax in spirits of wine; apply three or four coats." G. W. Francis, *The Dictionary of Practical Receipts* (London, 1847).

GLAIRE

The common term for albuminous varnish. "It is usually made as wanted, and is the best possible varnish for—indeed the only one—that can be used upon the covers of leather bound books; also, kid shoes that will not, of course, take blacking, may be readily polished by a little of this varnish laid on with a small sponge. [To make it] beat up the white of an egg with twice its weight of cold water, till it is well incorporated with it." G. W. Francis, *The Dictionary of Practical Receipts* (London, 1847).

SANDARACH

"A gummy resinous substance from the juniper tree, of a pale yellowish colour. Considerable quantities of this gum are consumed by varnish-makers who dissolve it in the oils of turpentine, or linseed, or in spirit of wine and thus prepare a kind of varnish, known under the name of vernix, which is used by cabinet-makers and painters." *The Domestic Encyclopedia* (Philadelphia, 1821).

TURPENTINE VARNISH

"Take of yellow resin four ounces, spirit of turpentine, six ounces; powder the resin, and digest with the turpentine in a gentle heat, till all is dissolved." *The Domestic Encyclopedia* (Philadelphia, 1821).

VARNISH FOR OIL PAINTINGS

"According to the number of your pictures take the whites of the same number of eggs, and to each picture take the bigness of a hazel-nut of sugar-candy, dissolve, and mix it with a tea-spoonful of brandy; beat the whites of your eggs to a froth; then let it settle; take the clear, put it to your brandy and sugar, and varnish over your pictures with it; this is much better than any other varnish, as it is easily washed off when your pictures want cleaning again." *The Domestic Encyclopedia* (Philadelphia, 1821).

VARNISH FOR PLASTER FIGURES

"Fuse ½ oz. of tin, with the same quantity of bismuth, in a crucible, when melted, add ½ oz. of mercury. When perfectly combined, take the mixture from the fire, and cool it. This substance, mixed with the white of an egg, forms a very beautiful varnish." G. W. Francis, *The Dictionary of Practical Receipts* (London, 1847).

VARNISH FOR WOOD CARVING

"To be used in the carved parts of cabinet work with a brush, as in standards, pillars, claws, Ec. Dissolve 2 oz. of seed-lac and 2 oz. of white rosin in 1 pint of spirits of wine. This varnish or polish must be laid on warm, and if the work can be warmed also it will be so much the better; at any rate moisture and dampness must be avoided." G. W. Francis, *The Dictionary of Practical Receipts* (London, 1847).

8
Cleaning, Polishing, and Repairing

CLEANING

TO CLEAN ALABASTER VASES, SMALL STATUES, ETC.

"Nothing is better than common soap and water if the objects be merely dirty; but if stained by time, smoke, Ec. they should, after being washed, be covered over with a white-wash made with lime, then suffered to stand with this upon them for some hours . . . being then washed off with clean water, and afterwards a little friction given with a piece of flannel, the figure will be equal to new. N.B. Alabaster is decomposed by too much water." G. W. Francis, *The Dictionary of Practical Receipts* (London, 1847).

TO CLEAN BEDS

"The house bug or *Cimex Sectuarius* is extremely troublesome about beds. In order to destroy the vermin let the bedsteads be washed with oil of turpentine or painted over with verdegrease ground in linseed and oil of turpentine. Or, boil wormwood, rue, common oil and water together till the water is consumed, then, after straining, make it into an ointment with a good quantity of grease or sulphur; with this rub the chinks and other places where the bugs are sup-posed to be. Or mix hemp, oil and ox-gall together with which rub the bedstead all over and the bugs will not come near it. Or, pound quantities of black soap and common soap together, then mixing as much of quicksilver with it. Let the buggy places be rubbed with this mixture." (M)

TO CLEAN COPPER-PLATE PRINTS or BOOKS

"Wet the print thoroughly. Expose it to the sun, by placing it on a grass plot, and to prevent the wind from having any effect upon it, fix four skewers into the ground near the corners, and tie a string to each of the skewers crossed from corner to corner so as to confine it completely. When it becomes dry, wet it again. And so on, if necessary. The foulness from flies may be gently brushed off with a wet sponge, when the print is thoroughly soaked. Spirit of salt, much diluted, will get whitewash off prints. Do not leave your prints on the grass plot at night." *The Domestic Encyclopedia* (Philadelphia, 1821). (See also BOOK PRESS, Chapter 12.)

TO CLEAN BOTTLES

"It often happens that glass vessels, used as pots for flowers and other purposes, receive an unsightly deposit or crust, hard to be removed by scouring or rubbing. The best method is to wash it with a little dilute muriatic acid." G. W. Francis, *The Dictionary of Practical Receipts* (London, 1847).

TO CLEAN FLINT-GLASS BOTTLES, DECANTERS, ETC.

"Roll up, in small pieces, some blotting paper, then wet and soap the same; put them into the vessel, with a little lukewarm water; shake them well for a few minutes; then rinse the glass with clean water, and it will be as bright and clear as when new from the shops." Thomas Tegg, *Book of Utility* (London, 1828).

TO CLEAN CLOTHES

SOAPWORT *Saponaria officinalis*

"A decoction of this plant is used to cleanse and scour woolen cloths; the poorer people

Soapwort, as shown by John Gerard, *The Herball* (London, 1636).

use it instead of soap for washing." *The Domestic Encyclopedia* (Philadelphia, 1821).

SOAPSTONE

So called because it is "as smooth as soap on the outside. They make use of it for rubbing spots out of their clothes. The ground color is pale green with some dark spots and a few of a greenish hue . . . The particles of talc in this stone are about 30 times as many as those of spar and garnet. Some of the stone is scraped off and used as a powder, strewed on a greasy spot. This absorbs the grease, and after rubbing off the powder the spot disappears." Peter Kalm, *Travels in North America* (Warrington, England, 1770).

STARCHWORT, Cuckow-pint, Wake-Robin, *Arum maculatum*

"The most pure and white starch is made of the roots of Cuckow-pint; but [it is] most hurtfull to the hands; the Laundresse that hath the handling of it, for it chappeth, blistereth, and maketh the hands rough and rugged and withal smarting." John Gerard, *The Herball or Generall Historie of Plantes* (London, 1636).

TO CLEAN LEATHER

"Mix together 1 lb. of Bath brick, 2 lbs of pipe clay, 4 oz. of pumice stone powder, and 6 oz. of ox-gall; color it with yellow ochre if desired. It is to be used over the leather by rubbing it with a little water, and when it has remained on to get dry, rub off the loose powder with a hard clothes brush. This was once very useful also in cleaning and coloring a then common article of dress, leather breeches." G. W. Francis, *The Dictionary of Practical Receipts* (London, 1847).

TO BLEACH IVORY

"Ivory is very apt to take a yellow-brown tint by exposure to air. It may be whitened or bleached, by rubbing it first with pounded pumice-stone and water, then placing it moist under a glass shade luted to the sole at the bottom, and exposing it to sunshine. The sunbeams without the shade would be apt to occasion fissures in the ivory. The moist rubbing and exposure may be repeated several times." G. W. Francis, *The Dictionary of Practical Receipts* (London, 1847).

TO DISINFECT LETTERS

"The best method of disinfecting letters and other articles coming from places that are supposed to be visited by the plague, is to expose them to the fumes of burning sulphur, mixed with saltpetre." G. W. Francis, *The Dictionary of Practical Receipts* (London, 1847).

TO CLEAN GOLD AND RESTORE ITS LUSTER

"Dissolve a little sal-ammoniac in urine, boil your soiled gold therein, and it will become clean and brilliant." Thomas Tegg, *Book of Utility* (London, 1828). (See also GILDING, Chapter 7.)

TO CLEAN MARBLE

"Take a bullock's gall, a gill of soap lees, half a gill of turpentine, and make it into a paste with pipe clay; then apply it to the marble, and let it dry a day or two, then rub it off; and if not clean, apply it a second or third time until it is clean." Thomas Tegg, *Book of Utility* (London, 1828).

TO CLEAN PAINTINGS

"Pictures form a valuable though not a necessary part of domestic furniture and . . . are liable to become obscured by dirt and smoke. As the ingredients used by the painter often vary, the safest process will be that in which the mildest means are employed: Let the picture first be taken out of the frame, then covered with a clean napkin, moistened with pure water, and suffered to remain in that state for a fortnight or longer according to circumstances. The cloth should be occasionally wetted till it has loosened all the particles on the surface. A small quantity of linseed oil is now to be passed over the picture which will thus, in most instances, resume its former lustre. Also recommended have been soap-water, spirits of turpentine, wine, Ec. but [they] require great precaution because they are apt to corrode the oil of the painting. Alkiline solutions or spiritous liquors should be used only for spots that have resisted simple water, oil of olives, or fresh butter." *The Domestic Encyclopedia* (Philadelphia, 1821).

TO RESTORE PAINTINGS ON VELVET

"To raise the surface or pile when pressed down, warm a smoothing iron moderately and cover it with a wet cloth and hold it under the velvet; the vapour arising from the heated cloth will raise the pile of the velvet, with the assistance of a rush whisk." Thomas Tegg, *Book of Utility* (London, 1828).

TO CLEAN PEWTER

"Great Horse-Taile or Shave-Grasse *Asprella* riseth up like a reed, and set at every joint with many stiffe Rush-like leaves, or bustles, which maketh the whole plant to resemble the taile of a horse, whereof it tooke his name. Small and naked Shave-Grasse, wherewith Fletchers and Combe-makers doe rub and polish their worke, riseth out of the ground like the first shoots of asparagus, jointed and kneed but without bristly leaves, yet exceeding rough and cutting. His ruggedness is not unknown to women, who scoure their pewter and wodden things of the kitchen therewith, and therefore some of our huswives do call it Pewter-Coat." John Gerard, *The Herball or Generall Historie of Plantes* (London, 1636).

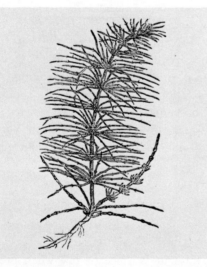

Shave grass, as shown by John Gerard, *The Herball* (London, 1636).

Pewter dinner plate, blackened by grime and showing a pitted surface, before and after scouring and polishing.

TO CLEAN FINE BLOCK-TIN DISH COVERS, PATENT PEWTER, Etc.

"Where the polish is gone off, let the article be first rubbed over the outside with a little sweet oil, on a piece of soft linen cloth; then clean it off with dry pure whiting, quite free from sand, on linen cloths, which will make them look as well as when new. The insides should be rubbed with rags moistened in wet whiting, but without a drop of oil. Always wiping these articles dry, when brought from table, and keeping them free from steam or other damp, greatly facilitates the trouble of cleaning them." Thomas Tegg, *Book of Utility* (London, 1828).

TO REMOVE RUST

"It consists in combining a proportion of quick lime with mutton fat, into balls, which must be rubbed on the utensils till it has entirely obliterated the rust; after their coating has remained for a few days on the metal, it is removed with coarse flannel or other rags; then another composition, made of equal parts of charcoal, red calx of vitriol and drying oil, is applied by continued friction, till the surface be restored to its pristine brightness." *The Domestic Encyclopedia* (Philadelphia, 1821).

TO PREVENT CUTLERY FROM TAKING RUST

"Case-knives, snuffers, watch-chains and other small articles made of steel, may be preserved from rust by being carefully wiped after use, and then wrapped in coarse brown paper, the virtue of which is such that all hardware goods from Sheffield, Birmingham, Ec. are always wrapped in the same." Thomas Tegg, *Book of Utility* (London, 1828).

TO CLEAN STEEL

"Methods of cleaning and polishing Rusty Steel [fire-irons, hearth utensils, fenders, footmen, etc.]. After well oiling the rusty parts of the steel, let it remain two or three days in that state; then wipe it dry with clean rags, and

1) polish with emery or pumice-stone or hard wood; or frequently,

2) a little unslaked lime, finely powdered, will be sufficient;

3) when a high degree of polish is requisite, [use] a paste composed of finely levigated bloodstone and spirit of wine;

4) Bright [fender] bars are admirably cleaned, in a few minutes, by using a small portion of fine corned emery, and afterwards finishing off with flour of emery or rotton stone; all of which may be had at any ironmonger's." Thomas Tegg, *Book of Utility* (London, 1828).

POLISHING

Polishing is "The act of smoothing and imparting brightness to hard substances such as metals, marble, glass, Ec. by rubbing them with certain matters adapted to that purpose." *The Domestic Encyclopedia* (Philadelphia, 1821). "When our chairs and tables were hand-polished the house wife took a certain pride in their sheen, produced by a vast amount of manual labour on the part of footmen or housemaids. The present system of French polishing, or varnishing furniture is destructive of all artistic effect in its appearance, because the surface of wood thus lacquered can never change its colour, or acquire that rich hue which is one of the chief charms of old cabinet-work." Charles L. Eastlake, *Hints on Household Taste, in Furniture, Upholstery and Other Details* (London, 1868).

CAST-IRON POLISH

"(1) Mix powder of black lead with a little common gin, or the dregs of red Port wine, and lay it on with a piece of linen rag; then, with a clean, dry but not too hard brush, dipped in dried black lead powder, rub it till of a beautiful brightness. This will produce a much finer and richer black varnish on the cast iron than either (2) boiling black lead with small beer and soap, or (3) mixing it with white of eggs which are the methods commonly practised." *The Domestic Encyclopedia* (Philadelphia, 1821).

CHARCOAL

"A kind of fuel, but [also used] for polishing brass or copper plates, Ec." (M)

FRENCH POLISH

"To 1 pint of spirits of wine, add ¼ oz. of gum copal, ¼ oz. of gum arabic, and 1 oz. of shell-lac. Let the gums be well bruised, and sifted through a piece of muslin. Put the spirits and the gums together in a vessel that can be closely corked; place them near a warm stove, and frequently shake them; in two or three days they will be dissolved. Strain the mixture through a piece of muslin, and keep it tight corked for use. Damp the rag sufficiently, then proceed to rub your work in a circular direction, observing not to do more than about a square foot at a time. Rub it lightly till the whole surface is covered; repeat this 3 or 4 times, according to the texture of the wood; each coat to be rubbed until the rag appears dry. Be careful not to put too much on the rag at a time, and you will have a very beautiful and lasting polish; be also very particular in letting your rags be very clean and soft, as the polish depends in a great measure on the care you take in keeping it clean and free of dust during the operation.

"Finishing Polish. This preparation is useful for finishing as it adds to the lustre and durability, as well as removed every defect which may happen in the other polish; and gives the surface a most brilliant appearance. Half a pint of the very best rectified spirits of wine, 2 drams of shell lac, and 2 drams of gum benzoin. Put these ingredients in a bottle, and keep it in a warm place till the gum is all dissolved, shaking it frequently; when cold, add 2 tea-spoonsful of the best clear white poppy oil; shake them well together, and it is fit for use. This preparation is used in the same manner as the foregoing polishes, but, in order to remove all dull places, you may increase the pressure in rubbing." G. W. Francis, *The Dictionary of Practical Receipts* (London, 1847).

FURNITURE OIL

"1) In 1½ pints of linseed oil, boil 4 oz. of rosin; or 2) Dissolve by a little warmth some yellow bees'wax in oil of turpentine, till of the consistence when cold of a thick jelly; a little red ochre may be mixed with it." G. W. Francis, *The Dictionary of Practical Receipts* (London, 1847).

FURNITURE-POLISHING WAX

"Take bees wax and a small quantity of turpentine in a clean earthen pan, and set it over a fire till the wax unites with the turpentine, which it will do by constant stirring about; add to this a little red lead finely ground upon a stone, together with a small portion of fine Oxford ochre, to bring the whole to the colour of a brisk mahogany. Lastly, when you take it off the fire, add a little copal varnish to it, and mix it well together, then turn the whole into a bason of

water, and while it is yet warm, work it into a ball, with which [a fairly stiff] brush is to be rubbed. And observe, with a ball of wax and brush kept for this purpose entirely, furniture in general may be kept in good order." Thomas Sheraton, *Cabinet Dictionary* (London, 1803).

METAL POLISH

"The stalks of *Asphodelus lateus* or Common Yellow Asphodel . . . when dipped in Colcothar, or Crocus Martis (which may be had of the druggist), reduced to a paste with sweet-oil, and properly applied to iron and brass utensils, will not only render them exceeding bright, but also prove a better preservative from rust than sand-paper, or other rougher materials." *The Domestic Encyclopedia* (Philadelphia, 1821).

Ash Brick: A ball or brick-shaped abrasive made from clay and coarse ashes used to polish metal.

PUMICE-STONE POLISH

"This hard, siliceous fossil is usefully employed in different mechanical trades, for rubbing and smoothing or polishing wood, pasteboard, metals and stone because it removes all inequalities from their surfaces." *The Domestic Encyclopedia* (Philadelphia, 1821).

ROTTEN-STONE GEM POLISH

"A variety of Tripoli . . . is used by lapidaries and other mechanics for grinding, polishing and sometimes for cutting stones." *The Domestic Encyclopedia* (Philadelphia, 1821).

SILVER POLISH

"Whiting, properly purified from sand, applied wet and rubbed till dry, is one of the easiest, safest, and certainly the cheapest of all plate powders; jewellers and silversmiths, for small articles, seldom use anything else . . . afterward rub bright with leather." Thomas Tegg, *Book of Utility* (London, 1828).

SILVER POLISH

"Take one ounce of red calx of vitriol, *Crocus martis,* and one ounce of fine whiting; pulverise and sift them through muslin; then diffuse the powder through a quart of water, and let it settle for two minutes; pour it off and use only the last and finest sediment." *The Domestic Encyclopedia* (Philadelphia, 1821).

TRIPOLI

A fine-grained abrasive; "an earthy substance used by lapidaries to polish stones and by the braziers to clean metalline vessels. *Alana gleba, tripolis* and *terra tripolitana* is a yellow white kind. The reddish tripoli is English. It is of great use in polishing brass." (M)

REPAIRING

TO REPAIR BOOKS

BOOKBINDERS' PASTE

"Mix wheaten flour first in cold water, then boil it till it be of a glutinous consistence; this makes common paste. When you wish it to be of a stronger nature, mix a fourth, fifth or sixth of the weight of the flour, of powdered alum; and where it is wanted [to be of a] still more tenacious quality, add a little powdered resin." *Domestic Encyclopedia* (Philadelphia, 1821). "The root of

Harebell, as shown by John Gerard, *The Herball* (London, 1636).

the blew Hare-bells or English Jacinth is bulbous, full of a slimie, glewish juice, which will serve to set leathers upon arrows in stead of glew, or to paste books with. Hereof is made the best starch next unto that of wake-robin roots." John Gerard, *The Herball or Generall Historie of Plantes* (London, 1636).

LEATHER BLACKING

"Take five parts tallow, seven ditto beeswax, twelve ditto size, one ditto brown soap, four ditto lamp-black; incorporate the whole over a fire, adding the ingredients one by one, (and stirring), then make it into cakes. The size is either glue dissolved in water to a jelly, or else strong jelly made of gum tragacinth in water; or a jelly made by boiling glue pieces, bought of tanners, to a proper consistency. Blacking feeds the leather and when brushed bright gives it the colour and appearance of new leather. To make it more shining, add more size." *The Domestic Encyclopedia* (Philadelphia, 1821).

CEMENT

"Any matter with which two bodies are made to cohere, as mortar or glue." (J)

"One of the finest and at the same time

167

strongest caements for joining broken glasses, porcelain, Ec. is the juice of garlick procured by stamping the herb in a stone mortar. This caement if the operation be done with care, leaves very little mark of the fracture.

Garlic, as shown by John Gerard, *The Herball* (London, 1636).

Eighteenth-century "black glass" rum bottle with a patch of glass cemented back in place. (Courtesy, Antiquarian and Landmarks Society, Inc.)

"Another caement is made by beating the white of an egg and mixing it with quicklime. With either of these caements the glasses, pieces of china, Ec., are to be joined and dried in the shade.

"A caement for cracked glasses may be prepared in the following manner. Take equal quantities of wheat flour, fine powdered Venice glass, and pulverized chalk; one half of the same quantity of fine brick dust and a little scraped lint; mix them all together with the whites of eggs. Spread this mixture upon a piece of linen cloth, and apply it to the cracks of the glasses. Remember to dry the glasses thoroughly before you apply the caement.

"Caement (among jewelers, engravers, Ec.) is a composition of fine brick dust, well-sifted, resin and beeswax." (M)

BOTANY BAY CEMENT
The common name for a nineteenth-century cement used to repair china and earthenware, made of "yellow gum and brick dust, of each equal parts." G. W. Francis, *The Dictionary of Practical Receipts* (London, 1847).

CEMENT FOR PEG LAMPS
To make "as good a cement as possible for fixing the necks of globes or cylinders or anything else that requires to be strongly fixed, for it is not easily melted again: Melt 1 lb. of resin in a pot or pan over a slow fire; add as much plaster of Paris, in fine powder, as will make it hard enough; then add a spoonful of linseed oil, stirring it all the while, and try if it be hard and tough enough for the purpose; if . . . not, add more plaster of Paris; and if not tough enough, a little more linseed oil." G. W. Francis, *The Dictionary of Practical Receipts* (London, 1847).

GLUE
"A very excellent glue or cement may be obtained by boiling small shreds of vellum [*q.v.*] so as to convert them into a jelly. Care should be taken that no fragments of parchment be used, because the skins of goats and sheep are unfit for such purpose [because of the odor]." *The Domestic Encyclopedia* (Philadelphia, 1821).

TO MEND CHINA

"Chinese methods of mending China: Take a piece of flintglass, beat it to a fine powder, and grind it well with the white of an egg, and it joins China without rivetting, so that no art can break it in the same place. You are to observe that the composition is to be ground extremely fine on a painter's stove." Thomas Tegg, *Book of Utility* (London, 1828).

"Jacob Da Costa . . . Gives notice to all Gentlemen and Ladies in this city or country, who have, or may have in their houses any broken China or Glass that they may have it mended in the neatest manner ever seen in this City, either by riveting or a cement so strong and durable that it may be used either in heat or cold without separating or loosening the joints. He also mends all sorts of marble or china furniture, such as is used for ornamenting chimney pieces, chests of drawers, Ec. He mends the necks of decanters that have been broken, and some of the pieces lost, cuts them even and makes them fit for use, likewise hoops glass and china rings that have been cracked, and makes them as strong and useful as ever. He also mends Lady's fans." *The New-York Journal or General Advertiser,* October 12, 1769.

by boiling liquids poured therein, or by being set too close to a flame; or, by careless handling. Discipline seldom was any more perfect in the colonial scullery than in the modern kitchen.

A covered sugar bowl with the so-called age crack or hairline in easily damaged soft paste.

Delft chocolate pot with riveted repair in the side. (Courtesy, Antiquarian and Landmarks Society, Inc.)

AGE CRACKS

The collector's euphemism for the hairline surface cracks sometimes found in antique porcelain or earthenware. They have been caused by application of too much heat, as

TO REPAIR WOODEN VESSELS

"To close and secure the chinks, flaws or other accidental defects in the most expeditious manner, it will always be more ad-

Twisted wrought-iron candle and rush light holder with block of wood serving as replacement for original broken-off base.

The largest portion of the plate of an iron oven shovel or peel has been replaced and riveted to reshaped remainder of the original plate and handle. (Courtesy, Antiquarian and Landmarks Society, Inc.)

visable to empty the vessels [first] and after drying them, to use a cement of pitch, bullock's blood, linseed oil, turpentine, and the finest brick dust, melted together in an iron pan . . . Before, however, this powerful lute be laid on, all the crevices or chinks ought to be properly caulked or filled up with tow or oakum. (2) A tough paste composed of whiting, a solution of gum arabick or tragacinth, and a proper quantity of oak bark reduced to a fine powder may be advantageously applied to tubs or casks to prevent farther leaking." *The Domestic Encyclopedia* (Philadelphia, 1821).

9
Metals – Antique Formulae and Uses

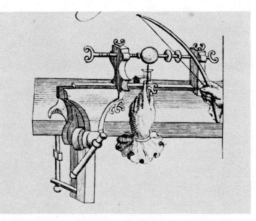

Metalworker's lathe for turning small work, illustrated in *The Dictionary of Arts and Sciences* (London, 1778).

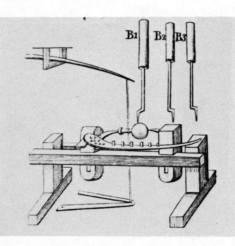

Brazier's lathe illustrated in *The Dictionary of Arts and Sciences* (London, 1778).

Metals, wrought and unwrought, mentioned in the House of Parliament rates, 1660, for imports and exports included "Lattin; Iron; gold; brass; Steel; Copper; Wyre; silver; gold foile; gold paper; leade; leaves of gold; white or ungilt silverplate; silver parcell gilt; silver gilt; Shruff or old Brass; gad steel; tinfozle; Copper, Gold and silver tinsell; Iron wyre; Lattin wire; steel wyre; Bell metall; old iron." Metals are those "hard, shining, mineral [bodies], fusible by fire, concrescible by cold, ductile, and capable of being amalgamated, or intimately united to quicksilver. There are properly but six metals—gold, silver, copper, tin, iron, and lead: to which some have added mercury, though it agrees in nothing but weight." (M)

"The American Bullion and Refining office, No. 1, Carter's Alley, Second Street, is just opened for the purchase of old gold, silver, copper, brass, pewter, and lead . . . as soon as a sufficient quantity can be collected, the refining will commence; also the button, buckle and plate manufactory, when artists bred to any of these branches will receive liberal encouragement and may be supplied with fine gold, silver, and plated metals. Wanted, the following tools and utensils: forging and raising hammers, triblets and beak irons; polishing wheels, collars and mandrils; ingots and skillets; a piercing press, a small anvil and spoon, moulds and screws; large and small weights, scales and vizes; draw bench and plates; a large iron pestle and mortar. Persons having such articles, new and old, will receive a fair price, by applying as above." *Pennsylvania Packet* (Philadelphia), October 21, 1789.

". . . wanted also, a good Caster, who is used to the fire and the moulding of large and small work—also, a number of Hands, large or small workers, finished workmen from Europe, who have been used to the button, buckle, plate or plating branches, will meet with good encouragement; and those who are not perfect in the above branches, and are willing to engage for a stated time will get reasonable wages; chamber masters, and all who are capable, may have work by the piece; Jewellers, Clock and Watch Makers, Options, Whitesmiths, and every man who is a good filer, willing and capable of working to instructions, sober and attentive, may be employed, by applying as above." *Pennsylvania Packet* (Philadelphia), October 28, 1789.

AES

Bronze, from the Latin word for alloys of copper.

ALBATA

A silver-colored alloy of copper, nickel, and zinc; or German silver.

ALCHEMINE

A variation of the term alchemy.

ALCHEMY, ALEAMINE

"The names given a kind of mixed metal used for spoons and kitchen utensils." (J) "White alchymy is made of pan-brass one pound, and arsenicum three ounces; or is made of copper and auripigmentum." Francis Bacon, *Physical Remains*. Alchemy was a form of fine sixteenth- and seventeenth-century pewter produced from copper and tin. The word also signified chemistry; black art, or magical effects. "January 30, 1713–14. I presented my son and daughter with six silver spoons; cost about 21s a piece . . . and 6 Alchimy spoons, cost 3s 6d." Samuel Sewall, *Diary*.

ALLOY

The term for any "combination of metals intended to produce a compound metallic substance, different in its character and superior or cheaper for some particular purpose than the metals separately. Alloys are always produced by melting the compound parts together, observing to melt first the more infusible metal, and then to add to it at as low a heat as possible the others." G. W. Francis, *The Dictionary of Practical Receipts* (London, 1847).

ANTIMONY

The metallic element first isolated and described by a German monk, Basil Valentine (Johann Tholde), in 1640. This is "a semi-metal . . . useful in refining; it gives [other metals] a finer polish. It makes a part in bell metal and renders the sound more clear. It is mingled with tin to make it more hard, white, and sound; and with lead . . . to render smooth and hard." (C)

ARGENTINE

The popular name for a type of German Silver, *q.v.* "The argentine contains 1 part silver for 1 part nickel of the formula for German silver." G. W. Francis, *The Dictionary of Practical Receipts* (London, 1847). Used for nineteenth-century tableware.

ARSIL

The alloy of arsenic and copper.

BATH METAL

"A composition of copper and zink melted together," (M) thus forming a type of brass. "Sometimes also called Prince's Metal; a kind of factitious metal of a beautiful yellow, and disposed to receive a fine polish and lustre. It is prepared as follows: take six ounces of copper, melting it in a wind-furnace; add to it one ounce of zink." (M)

BELL METAL

The name for "a composition of tin and copper, or pewter and copper, the proportion of one to the other is almost twenty pounds of pewter or twenty three pounds of tin to one hundred weight of copper," (M) from which bells were cast; as were candlesticks, other lighting devices, and hollow wares.

BIDDERY WARE

The term for items made of what also was known as Indian metal. "This is a white, and somewhat hard metal or alloy, made in India, and of which we have articles frequently (imported), particularly large hookohs, boxes, tea caddies, bottles, Ec. It is composed of 16 oz. of copper, 4 oz. of lead, and 2 of tin. These are first melted together and to every 3 oz. of the alloy are added 16 oz. of zinc. It is often made of a black colour, and inlaid with silver; the color is given by dipping the articles in a solution of sal-ammoniac, saltpetre, blut vitriol, and common salt. This acts upon the alloy, but not upon the silver."

G. W. Francis, *The Dictionary of Practical Receipts* (London, 1847).

BILLON
A kind of alloy of copper and silver.

BLACK METAL
A name given inexpensive pewter made with an overabundance of lead.

BLOCK TIN
"So the tradesmen call that which is pure or unmixed, and yet unwrought." Robert Boyle, *Colours.* Hence, block tinware was used to describe any utensil made of pure tin.

BRASS
The name of the "factitious metal composed of about five pounds of copper laid in seven pounds of *lapis calaminaris,* mixed with fine charcoal, in a melting pot . . . in a strong heat [for] eleven hours." (M)

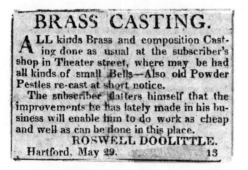

BRASS CASTING.

ALL kinds Brass and composition Casting done as usual at the subscriber's shop in Theater street, where may be had all kinds of small Bells—Also old Powder Pestles re-cast at short notice.

The subscriber flatters himself that the improvements he has lately made in his business will enable him to do work as cheap and well as can be done in this place.

ROSWELL DOOLITTLE.
Hartford, May 29.   13

American Mercury (Hartford, Connecticut), May 29, 1814.

Early-eighteenth-century or Queen Anne brass drawer pull.

BRITANNIA METAL
"The following mixture makes the article at once, fit for spoons, tea pots, Ec.: Melt together 8 oz. of brass, 2 lbs. of antimony, and 10 lbs. of tin, *or:*

"1) Melt together equal parts of brass, tin, bismuth and antimony. The brass is first to be melted, then throw in the tin, and afterwards the bismuth and antimony.

"2) Melt together 2 parts each of brass, tin, bismuth and antimony. When melted by the last receipt, add 1 part each of copper and arsenic previously melted together in a different crucible.

"3) Melt together 1 part of copper, 1 part of tin, and 2 lbs. of antimony." G. W. Francis, *The Dictionary of Practical Receipts* (London, 1847). This popular alloy of copper, antimony, and tin was first manufactured at Sheffield, England, after 1770 and was a substitute for silver or pewter tableware and flatware during the nineteenth century.

BRONZE
The name given the "compound metal, consisting of one part tin, ten of copper, and a little zinc." (M) However, "it appears from a number of experiments that the bronze of which the ancients formed their weapons and other articles, consists of 88 parts of copper to 12 of tin; and it is remarkable that the same admixture of the metals has been employed in nations so remote from each other.

"**To make bronze for Statuary:** a) Copper 88 parts, tin 9 parts, zinc 2 parts, lead 1 part. b) Copper 88½ parts, tin 5 parts, zinc 10½ parts; lead 2 parts. c) Copper 90 parts, tin 9 parts, lead 1 part. d) Copper 91 parts, tin 9 parts.

"**For Medals:** a) Copper 89 parts, tin 8 parts, zinc 3 parts. b) Copper 95 parts, tin 5 parts.

"**For Cutting Instruments:** Copper 100 parts, tin 14 parts.

"**For Mortars:** Copper 93 parts, lead 5

parts, tin 2 parts. They should be hardened after casting and turning smooth by heating to redress the thin upper edge, and while hot, plunging it into cold water, otherwise they will be apt to crack.

"**For Ornaments:** a) Copper 82 parts, tin 3 parts, zinc 18 parts, and lead 2 parts. b) Copper 83 parts, zinc 17 parts, tin 1 part, lead ½ part." G. W. Francis, *The Dictionary of Practical Receipts* (London, 1847).

BRONZE ARGENT
The name for a Chinese white bronze also called German Silver, *q.v.*

CASE HARDENING
The term among metalworkers meaning "to harden on the outside." (J) "The manner of case hardening is thus: Take cow horn or hoof, dry it thoroughly in an oven, then beat it to powder; put about the same quantity of bay salt to it, and mingle them together with stale chamber-lye, or else white wine vinegar. Lay some of this mixture upon loam and cover your iron all over with it; then wrap the loam about all, and lay it upon the hearth of the forge to dry and harden. Put it into the fire, and blow up the coals to it, till the whole lump have just a blood-red heat." Joseph Moxon, *Mechanick Exercises or The Doctrine of Handy-Works* (London, 1683–84).

CHASING, ENCHASING, INCHASING
"The art of enriching and beautifying gold, silver, and other metal work by some design, or figures represented thereon, in low relievo." (M)

COIN SILVER
A marking used after 1850 to designate an item manufactured from 900 parts pure silver to 100 parts of an alloy, and thus not as pure as sterling.

COPPER
"The lightest of all metals except iron and tin; it is, next after iron, the hardest metal. It is malleable much more easily than iron. It is beaten into leaves, which, not so thin as those of gold, serve for many purposes in their stead." (M) "As copper vessels are the best to make all kinds of made dishes in, you must be careful that they are well-tinned and kept clean." Richard Briggs, *The New Art of Cookery* (Philadelphia, 1792).

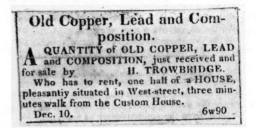

Connecticut Gazette (New Haven), December 12, 1829.

Eighteenth-century copper flagons.

TO TIN COPPER AND BRASS
"Boil 6 lbs. of cream of tartar, 4 gallons of water, and 8 lbs. of grain tin or tin shavings. After the materials have boiled a sufficient time, the substance to be tinned is put therein and the boiling continued, when the tin is precipitated in its metallic form." G. W. Francis, *The Dictionary of Practical Receipts* (London, 1847).

DAMASKEENING
"The art of adorning iron, steel, Ec. by making incisions therein and filling them up

with gold or silver wire . . . chiefly used in enriching sword blades, guards and gripes, locks or pistols, Ec." (M)

DUTCH GOLD
A synonym for brass.

ELECTRUM
The popular name for a type of German Silver, *q.v.* "Where more than 3 parts nickel are used to 8 of copper (in the formula for German Silver) the alloy is called Electrum." G. W. Francis, *The Dictionary of Practical Receipts* (London, 1847).

GERMAN SILVER
Also called Albata or Argentine, *q.v.;* this was "An alloy of different degrees of fineness used for imitating silver articles, such as spoons, forks, candlesticks, Ec. The real and original receipt is as follows—1 part nickel, 1 zinc, and 2 copper, melted together. When intended for rolling, 25 nickel, 20 zinc, 60 copper, to which, if for casting, 3 parts of lead may be added. The commonest [formula] is two nickel, 3½ zinc, and 8 copper." G. W. Francis, *The Dictionary of Practical Receipts* (London, 1847).

GOLD
The most precious of metals, the term perhaps derived from the Saxon *golo,* or the Welsh *golud,* meaning riches or "called gold in our English tongue, either from *geel,* which is, in Dutch, to shine; or of another Dutch word, which is *gelten,* and signifies in Latin *valere,* in English to be of price or value; hence cometh their ordinary word *gelt* for money." Henry Peacham, *The Compleat Gentleman* (London, 1661). It "is the yellow metal, being the heaviest, purest, most ductile and shining of any, and consequently the most valued . . . it is wholly incapable of rust, and is not sonorous, when struck upon." (M)

IRON *Mars*
The "greyish metal, soon tarnishing in the air to a dusky blackish hue, and in no time contracting a yellowish or redish rust. It is the most sonorous of metals except copper; the hardest and most elastick of all, hence its excellence for mechanick instruments. It is made into tools, by which others are filed, drilled and cut, and is the only one that strikes sparks with flint. It spreads under the hammer, [may be] drawn into wire. It is lighter, considerably than

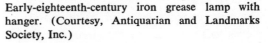

American Mercury (Hartford, Connecticut), August 6, 1813.

Early-eighteenth-century iron grease lamp with hanger. (Courtesy, Antiquarian and Landmarks Society, Inc.)

Eighteenth-century iron firewood tongs.

copper, and a little heavier than tin. It is the only metallick body which attracts, or is attracted by, the magnet, one of its own ores." (M)

Eighteenth-century iron skillet. (Courtesy, Antiquarian and Landmarks Society, Inc.)

Two eighteenth-century iron door plates. (Courtesy, Antiquarian and Landmarks Society, Inc.)

LACQUERING

The term in metalwork for "The laying on metals [of] colored or transparent varnishes, to produce the appearance of a different color in the metal, or to preserve it from rust. Thus lacquered brass appears gilt, and tin is made yellow. Seed-lac is the chief composition for lacquers, but turpentine makes a cheaper lacquer." *Encyclopedia Americana* (Philadelphia, 1831). See also JAPANNING; PONTYPOOL.)

LATTEN, LATOUN

This was the common name for plate tin in the late eighteenth and early nineteenth centuries or "iron plate covered with tin." (W) However, earlier it referred to a kind of mixed metal resembling brass in its colour and hardness, and was therefore much prized. Shakespeare gave his godchild, Ben Jonson's son, a dozen latten spoons, remarking that the poet should translate them. *He hadde a croys of latoun, ful of stones.* Chaucer, "Prologue," *Canterbury Tales.*

LEAD *Plumbum*

A coarse, impure metal "called Saturn by the chymists, is the heaviest of metals next after gold; it is, considerably lighter than quicksilver; it is the softest of all the metals, easily flattened under the hammer, and ductile in a very great degree though much less so than gold. Its colour is a pale bluish grey, it is very little subject to rust, and is the least sonorous of all the metals, except gold. It requires the least degree of fire of all metals, except tin, to put it in fusion . . . Lead is much used in building, especially for coverings, gutters, pipes and glazing, for which uses it is either cast into sheets in a mould, or milled." (M)

MALACHITE

The term for "a green copper ore or copper with aerial acid, capable of a high polish." (W)

MANGANESE

The name of "a whitish gray metal very hard and difficult to fuse; also the oxyd of the metal." (W)

MANHEIM GOLD

A type of brass.

MOLYBDEN, MOLYBDENITE

The name of "a metal of a whitish yellow color." (W)

OCCAMY

A contemporary corruption of the word alchemy, a compound metal meant to imitate silver.

Nineteenth-century American pewter.

PEWTER

A compound of metal employed in the manufacture of "plates, dishes, spoons, and similar domestic utensils. The basis of this metal ought to be tin, one cwt. of which being melted with 15 lbs. of lead, and 6 lbs. of brass, the whole forms what is called pewter. But there is another composition known by this name, which consists of different portions of tin, regulus of antimony, bismuth and copper; these, after being incorporated into one mass, over the fire, are manufactured into vessels like those of common pewter." *The Domestic Encyclopedia* (Philadelphia, 1821).

C. 1800 pewter spoons and molds in which similar spoons were made.

PINCHBECK

The name of the "factitious metal, the colour of which resembles gold, and which has received this appellation from its inventor. It is produced by melting one part of zinc with five or six parts of copper; Pinchbeck is manufactured principally into cases and chains for watches." *The Domestic Encyclopedia* (Philadelphia, 1821). "Christopher Pinchbeck, Senr. Clock, Watch maker and toyman at Pinchbeck's Head in Fleet Street, only maker of the true and genuine metal." Trade card used by the inventor in London. "To be had Ready made, for the very moderate price of One Dollar, at Joseph Cooke's, Goldsmith, Jeweler and Hair-Worker, in Second-Street . . . A Compleat Counting-House or Watch Seal, Made of the best Pinchbeck, not inferior in colour to gold, with the Initials of any Person's name, in a cypher engraved . . ." *Federal Gazette* (Philadelphia), January 21, 1789.

PLATE

(See in Chapter 12.)

PLATING

The term for "The art of covering baser metals with a thin plate of silver. The silver plate is generally made to adhere to the baser metals by means of solder [either] soft or hard, or tin or silver. The former of these [solders] consists of tin alone; the latter usually of three-fourths of silver with one of brass. The plate is first fitted to the article to be plated, by means of the hammer, and afterward fastened, by melting the solder." *The Domestic Encyclopedia* (Philadelphia, 1821).

PRINCE'S-METAL

A type of brass. (See also BATH METAL.)

SHEET IRON

"Iron in a thin plate." (W)

SHEET LEAD

"Lead in a thin plate." (W)

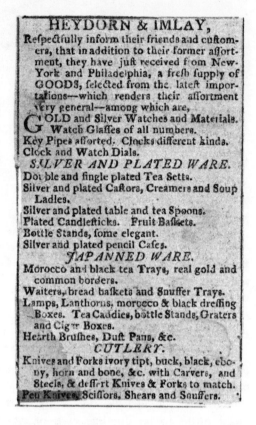

American Mercury (Hartford, Connecticut), April 19, 1810.

Sheet-iron, eighteenth-century lantern.

180

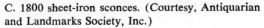

C. 1800 sheet-iron sconces. (Courtesy, Antiquarian and Landmarks Society, Inc.)

SILVER

The term from the Saxon *seolfer* for the "white and hard metal next in weight to gold . . . of soft splendour . . . having a pale lustre." (J)

STEEL

"Steel is a kind of iron, refined and purified by the fire with other ingredients, which renders it white, and its grain closer and finer than common iron. Steel, of all other metals, is that susceptible of the greatest degree of hardness, when well tempered, whence its great use in the making of tools and instruments of all kinds." (C)

TINFOIL

"Tin beat into thin plates." (W)

TRITANIA

A common synonym for Britannia Metal, *q.v.*

ZINC, ZINK

"A metal of a bluish white color, used with copper to form brass, pinchbeck, Ec." (W)

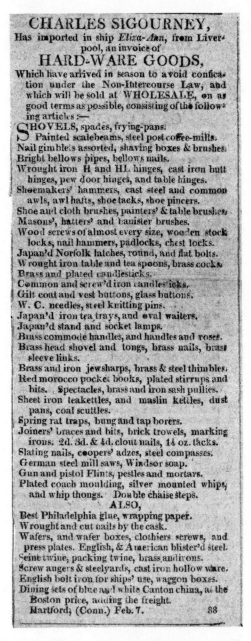

CHARLES SIGOURNEY,
Has imported in ship *Eliza-Ann*, from Liverpool, an invoice of
HARD-WARE GOODS,
Which have arrived in season to avoid confication under the Non-Intercourse Law, and which will be sold at WHOLESALE, on as good terms as possible, consisting of the following articles :—
SHOVELS, spades, frying-pans.
Painted scalebeams, steel post coffee-mills.
Nail gimblets assorted, shaving boxes & brushes.
Bright bellows pipes, bellows nails.
Wrought iron H and HL hinges, cast iron butt hinges, pew door hinges, and table hinges.
Shoemakers' hammers, cast steel and common awls, awl hafts, shoe tacks, shoe pincers.
Shoe awl cloth brushes, painters' & table brushes.
Masons', hatters' and banister brushes.
Wood screws of almost every size, wooden stock locks, nail hammers, padlocks, chest locks.
Japan'd Norfolk latches, round, and flat bolts.
Wrought iron table and tea spoons, brass cocks.
Brass and plated candlesticks.
Common and screw'd iron candlesticks.
Gilt coat and vest buttons, glass buttons.
W. C. needles, steel knitting pins.
Japan'd iron tea trays, and oval waiters.
Japan'd stand and socket lamps.
Brass commode handles, and handles and roses.
Brass head shovel and tongs, brass nails, brass sleeve links.
Brass and iron jewsharps, brass & steel thimbles.
Red morocco pocket books, plated stirrups and bits. Spectacles, brass and iron sash pullies.
Sheet iron teakettles, and maslin kettles, dust pans, coal scuttles.
Spring rat traps, bung and tap borers.
Joiners' braces and bits, brick trowels, marking irons. 2d. 3d. & 4d. clout nails, 14 oz. tacks.
Slating nails, coopers' adzes, steel compasses.
German steel mill saws, Windsor soap.
Gun and pistol Flints, pestles and mortars.
Plated coach moulding, silver mounted whips, and whip thongs. Double chaise steps.
ALSO,
Best Philadelphia glue, wrapping paper.
Wrought and cut nails by the cask.
Wafers, and wafer boxes, clothiers screws, and press plates. English, & American blister'd steel.
Seine twine, packing twine, brass andirons.
Screw augers & steelyards, cast iron hollow ware.
English bolt iron for ships' use, waggon boxes.
Dining sets of blue and white Canton china, at the Boston price, adding the freight.
Hartford, (Conn.) Feb. 7.   88

American Mercury, (Hartford, Connecticut), February 7, 1811.

10
Pottery, Porcelain, and Minerals

An eighteenth-century china and pottery shop re-created at Winterthur shows the typical multipane shop window with exterior shutters, closed at night to protect the expensive glass. (Courtesy, Henry Francis du Pont Winterthur Museum.)

POTTERY AND PORCELAIN

The term porcelain was derived, Samuel Johnson said in 1755, from the French *pour cent annees,* "because it was believed by Europeans that the materials of porcelain were matured under ground one hundred years [to make the] china ware, fine dishes of a middle nature between earthenware and glass, and therefore semi-pellucid."

"Porcelain is a fine sort of earthenware, chiefly manufactured in China and thence called China-ware . . . There are two kinds of earths used in the composition. The first, called Kaolin, is beset with glittering corpuscles; the second, called petunse, is a plain white, but exceedingly fine and soft to the touch. These are mixed with an oil or varnish drawn from the hard stone whereof the petunses are formed [and] oil of lime made from quick-lime . . .

"The French have been for several years attempting to imitate porcelain. The first essays made at Rouen are said to have succeeded tolerably well . . . in fact, for the beauty and turn of the vessels, exactitude of design, and the lustre of the colours, the French are not much behind the Chinese. But their grand defect is in the white of the ground, which is usually dingy and dull [not] the pure sprightly white of the Chinese. The Saxons have exceeded the French at Meissen where porcelains are painted and enamelled to such perfection, that they are more beautiful, as well as dearer, than those of China itself." (M)

Pottery, the common ware, signified the "manufacture of earthenware, or the art of making earthen vessels" (J) from indigenous clays.

AGATE BISQUE

The hard unglazed stoneware developed by Josiah Wedgwood, especially for the manufacture of flasks, mortars and pestles, and the vessels used by chemists and apothecaries.

AGATEWARE

A general term for any pottery with agate-like veining or mottling in the paste itself or in the glaze. In 1724, the English firm of Rendrich and Jones was granted a patent for staining and mottling stoneware, earthenware, and woodenware in imitation of agate; in 1729 a similar patent was granted for redware.

ARITA

The name for the Japanese porcelain produced since the early seventeenth century at Arita in Hizen province. Of these wares, the two decorations best known today are Imari and Kakieman, *qq.v.* The square, octagonal, and hexagonal paneled vases imported from Arita were copied extensively by continental factories.

BAMBOOWARE
The medium-to-light-brown stoneware, so named by Josiah Wedgwood when it was first manufactured in 1770.

BATAVIANWARE
A type of porcelain so named because it was transshipped from the trading center of the Dutch East India Company at Java; a lustrous medium to deep brown body decorated with *famille rose* panels.

BISCUIT
Pottery fired without a glaze.

BONE CHINA
First developed in England in the mid-eighteenth century, this was the hard and translucent artificial porcelain in which bone ash was substituted for kaolin, the natural clay.

BURNT BOWL
The adjective distinguished any porcelain, pottery, or earthenware piece fired [burned] in a kiln, from any similar vessel made of wood or metal.

CANEWARE
The fine-grained, pale tan or buff-colored unglazed stoneware made in the last quarter of the eighteenth century by numerous potters, particularly Wedgwood and Turner; sometimes with enameled decoration.

CELADON
Properly the translucent green glaze used over the gray stoneware of Lung Ch'uan in the Sung period; generally, the term for any sea-green color applied to porcelain, and thus by extension to the porcelain itself.

CHINA, CHINAWARE
Chinaware was so called from "the country where it is made; a species of (porcelain)

vessels made in China, dimly transparent, partaking of the qualities of earth and glass. They are made by mingling two kinds of earth, of which one easily vitrifies; the other resists a very strong heat; when the vitrifiable earth is melted into glass, they are completely burnt." (J)

CREAMWARE
The light-bodied, lead-glazed earthenware made from the palest of clays to which calcined flint was added. First produced in Staffordshire and later in Yorkshire in the mid-eighteenth century, it rapidly became the most popular of tablewares and was imported here by the shipload.

CROCKERY
(See in Chapter 12.)

DELFTWARE, DELF, DELPH
Earthenware coated with an opaque tin glaze; so named for Delft, the seventeenth-century Netherlands manufacturing center where it first was produced. That made in England is usually called English Delft; that imported from Holland, Dutch Delft.

EARTHENWARE
Potter's work; clay, turned and shaped into bowls, jugs or other vessels; fired in a kiln and glazed. "New York has some fine clay such as white, yellow, red and black, suitable for pots, dishes, plates, tobacco pipes and like wares." Adrien Van der Donck, *New Netherlands* (1653).

FAÏENCE, FAYENCE
"Potter's ware called delf." (W) The name now given any tin-glazed earthenware; the word originally was derived from the town Faenza, Italy, where faïence was manufactured. (See also DELFT.)

FLOWING BLUE
Sometimes also called Flow Blue or Flown Blue by collectors, this was a type of Staffordshire stoneware, made from 1825, in which the cobalt blue design was allowed to "flow" during firing, thus producing a

Early-eighteenth-century delftware covered posset pots and small milk pitcher. (Courtesy, Antiquarian and Landmarks Society, Inc.)

Nineteenth-century pottery pitcher, crocks and jugs with underglaze decorations in blue, brown, and red. (Courtesy, Antiquarian and Landmarks Society, Inc.)

American Mercury, (Hartford, Connecticut), December 22, 1818.

somewhat indistinct design with an overall paler blue "wash" appearance.

GLAZES

A glaze is the term in pottery-making for "a composition applied to vessels of earth, Ec., to render them more beautiful, and prevent fluids from penetrating them.

"**Black:** Is made of lead-ashes, 18 measures; iron filings, 3; copper ashes, 3; and zaffer, 2 measures. This, when melted will make a brown-black . . . if you want it black, add more zaffer to it.

"**Blue:** Take lead ashes, one pound; clear sand, two pounds; salt, two pounds; white calcined tartar, one pound; Venice, or other glass, 16 pounds; and zaffer, half a pound.

"**Brown:** Common glass and manganese, or brown stone, of each one part; and lead of glass, twelve parts.

"**Flesh Color:** Twelve parts of lead ashes, and one of white glass.

"**Gold Color:** Litharge three parts; of sand or calcined flint, one part.

"**Green:** Eight parts litharge, 8 parts of Venice glass; 4 parts of brass dust; or 10 parts of litharge, 12 of flint, and one of copper ashes.

"**Liver Color:** Twelve parts of litharge, 8 of salt, 6 of flint, and one of manganese.

"Purple-Brown: Lead ashes, 15 parts; clear sand, 18 parts; manganese, one part; white glass, 15 measures; and one measure of zaffer.

"Red: Of antimony, two pounds; litharge, three; and rust of iron, calcined, one.

"Sea-Green: Of five pounds of lead ashes, one pound of tin ashes; three pounds of flint, three quarters of a pound of salt, half a pound of tartar, and half a pound of copper dust.

"White: Take two pounds of lead, and one of tin; calcine them to ashes; of this take two parts, calcined flint one part, mix them well together.

"Yellow: Of red lead, 3 pounds; antimony and tin, of each 2 pounds.

"Citron-Yellow: Of 6 parts of red lead, 7 parts of fine red brick dust, and 2 parts of antimony." (M)

HARD-PASTE WARE

The general term for any of the fine, true porcelain made at the Bristol, New Hall, and Plymouth manufactories from the eighteenth century. The description distinguishes this ware from soft-paste or earthenware.

IRONSTONE

The first ware called ironstone was a cast-iron shell covered with a heavy tin glaze, then decorated as was porcelain. Although almost indestructible, it was expensive and never became popular. In 1813 in England, C. J. Mason patented a method of using scoria from iron furnaces as part of the clay body used for earthenware. The result was a thin, but strong ware. The thick, heavy ware usually called ironstone today was more properly termed graniteware when first produced in the nineteenth century.

REDWARE

The only type of pottery made in any great quantity in this country before the Revolution, this was made from local clays that turned reddish-brown when fired.

SLIP, SLIPWARE

"At the potteries in Staffordshire, the earths or clays of looser and more friable texture being mixed with water, they make into a consistence thinner than syrup, so that being put into a bucket, it will run out through a quill; this they call slip, and it is the substance wherewith they paint their wares, which from its several colours is called the orange-slip, the white slip, the red slip." Bishop White Kennet, *Antiques* (London, 1695).

Albany Slip: The chocolate-colored slip made from Hudson River Valley clay, sometimes used as a glaze but more often for finishing the interiors of salt-glazed stoneware.

Engobe: The slip coating on earthenware or porcelain.

STONEWARE

The common, hard, dense glazed pottery made from clay mixed with flint or sand, or made from very siliceous clay.

Nineteenth-century stoneware jugs, pitcher, and soda bottle. (Courtesy, Antiquarian and Landmarks Society, Inc.)

MINERALS

ALABASTER

"A kind of soft marble, easier to cut and less durable; some is white, some of the colour of horn, and transparent, some yellow like honey. The ancients used it to make boxes for perfumes" (J) and also urns, vases, candleholders, fruit bowls, and ornamental fruits for parlor decorations, etc. It was used also for small statuary and busts.

> Why should a man, whose blood is warm
> within,
> Sit like his grandsire cut in alabaster?
>
> Shakespeare, The Merchant of Venice,
> I, i.

Favored in the sixteenth century, alabaster statuary was purchased also by colonists in the eighteenth. "To be sold at Public Vendue, by William Nichols at the Royal Exchange Tavern, in King Street, Boston, precisely at 4 o'clock Afternoon, a Variety of Merchandize . . . some Household Goods such as . . . Paints, Draps, Alabaster Effigies . . . and many other things." Boston News-Letter, May 18, 1738.

"There are three species: (1) The snow-white shining alabaster . . . is large enough to make dishes of, or the like, cuts very freely, and is capable of a fine polish. (2) The yellowish alabaster is of a soft, loose texture, pretty heavy and nearly of the colour of honey. (3) Variegated, yellow and reddish alabaster is remarkably bright, and almost transparent, and admits of a fine polish. The ground is a clear pale yellow resembling amber and variegated with undulating veins. The alabaster, after being calcined and mixed with water may be cast in any mould like plaster of Paris." (M)

AMMOCHRYSOS

This is "A stone common in Germany being a species of mica, with gold-coloured spangles. Reduced to powder, it is used to strew over writing," (M) to illustrate manuscripts, decorate titles, etc.

AMPELITE

The proper name for "Cannel coal, a hard, opaque, inflammable substance of a black colour. It does not effervesce with acids; it is capable of a fine polish, and for that reason is turned into a number of toys, as snuff-boxes, and the like." (M)

BASALTES

"Coticula lapis heracluis and lapis lydius, a kind of marble, of a very fine texture, of a deep glossy black, resembling that of polished steel, and mixed with no other colour, nor any extraneous matter." (M)

CANNEL COAL

The common term for "a bituminous mineral, Ampelites [q.v.] often worked up into toys and utensils of various kinds and sold under the name of jet, with which it has often been confounded." (M)

CHINA STONE

Feldspar or petuntse, combined with China clay to manufacture porcelain.

KAOLIN

One of the substances "whereof china-ware is made; being no other than a kind of talc reduced to powder, and made into a paste with water. The peculiar property of kaolin is, that it is very difficult, if at all, [to render it] vitrifiable, so that being mixed with petuntse, a substance easily vitrifiable, the mixture produces a semi-vitrification in the fire, which is what we call china or porcelain." (M)

MICA

"June 8, 1642. One Darby Field, an Irishman, went to the top of the white hill . . . He found there much muscovy glass, they could rive out pieces of 40 feet long and 7 or 8 broad." John Winthrop, *Journal, History of New England* (Boston, 1825). The discovery in the White Mountains actually was of mica, since Muscovy glass is isinglass. However, both terms commonly were used throughout the Colonial period to describe mica; hills in a number of old towns still are called Isinglass Hill, denoting ancient quarrying sites.

OPHITE

The name for "a sort of variegated marble, of a dusky green ground, sprinkled with spots of a lighter green, otherwise called serpentine." (M)

PIPE CLAY

(See CLAY PIPE, Chapter 12.)

PORCELLANITE

The name given "a species of jaspar, a siliceous stone." (W)

PORPHYRY

"A stone of various kinds containing grains or dots of feldspar." (W) "The base is sometimes claystone, sometimes hornstone, feldspar, jade, pitchstone, pearlstone, and obsidian . . . its color is often red or green and, when polished, is valuable for ornamental work, being superior to marble on account of its great hardness. [It is found in] Egypt, northern Europe, in Mexico and South America; it also exists in the vicinity of Boston in Massachusetts." *Encyclopedia Americana* (Philadelphia, 1831).

SCAGIOLA

The term for a kind of imitation or artificial marble made of cement, isinglass, and coloring, to which chips of true marble might be added. This often was used for slab tops of some small eighteenth-century chests and tables.

SOAPSTONE

"Is very durable in fire [so] the country people make their hearths of it especially the part where the heat is the greatest. [Also] they use it for laying steps before the houses instead of bricks. Because it does not decay people commonly get the door posts in which hinges are fastened made of this stone." Peter Kalm, *Travels in North America* (Warrington, England, 1770).

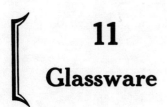

11
Glassware

In 1755 Samuel Johnson thought the word glass derived from the old British, *glâs,* for green, noting that "in Erse, glass is called *klânn,* primarily signifying clean or clear . . . from its transparency." Henry Peacham earlier noted that glass had its origin "in the Latin, *glacies,* which is ice, whose colour it resembles." *The Compleat Gentleman* (London, 1661). Glass was manufactured by "fusing salts and flint or sand together, with a vehement fire" (J) to make the metal, or molten mass which then was blown. "For the fine glass we use the purest of the finest sand, and the ashes of chali or glasswort [*salicornia,* salt-wort]; and for the coarser or green sort, the ashes of brake or other plants." Sir Thomas Browne, *Vulgar Errors* (London, 1646). In 1778, Middleton wrote that "of these materials we have many kinds of glass made, distinguished according to their beauty, as the crystal flint glass, the crystal white glass, the green glass, and the bottle glass. Again, these sorts are distinguished by their several uses, as plate or coach glasses; looking glasses; optick glasses, &c. The second sort includes crown glass, toys, phials, drinking glasses, &c. The third sort is well known by its colour, and the second by its form."

ART GLASS
The collector's general term for colored, decorative, or ornamental glassware, produced after about 1860. Those pieces that were blown or blown-in-the-mold generally are considered antiques because of the individual work or hand craftsmanship necessary. Mass-produced colored glassware, especially the types manufactured after 1900, such as carnival glass, are collected by some, but cannot be considered antiques.

Late-eighteenth-century blown wine glasses.

BLOWN GLASS
Until methods of manufacturing Pressed Glass, *q.v.,* were perfected early in the nineteenth century, all glass was free-blown, or blown into a mold. "The workman dips his blowing pipe into the melting pot . . . when he perceives there is enough metal on the pipe, he claps his mouth immediately to the

other end of it, and blows gently through the iron tube, till the metal lengthens . . . bringing the metal to the shape of a globe . . . this globe may be flattened by returning it to the fire and then brought into any form by stamp irons which are always ready." (M)

BLOWN-IN-THE-MOLD GLASS

Glass blown into a pattern mold, i.e., hollow block of metal, wood, or marble, thus impressing shape and decoration. Hinged molds were made in two, three, or more pieces.

BOTTLE GLASS

To make the green glass "such as is used for carboys and bottles, mix 11 lbs. of dry Glauber's Salts, 12 lbs. of soaper salts, ½ bushel of waste soap ashes, 56 lbs. of sand, 22 lbs. of glass skimmings, 1 cwt. of green broken glass, 25 lbs. of basalt; [or] yellow or white sand 100 parts, kelp 30 or 40, lixiviated wood ashes from 160 to 170 parts, fresh wood ashes 30 to 40 parts, potter's clay 80 to 100 parts, cullet or broken glass 100." G. W. Francis, *The Dictionary of Practical Receipts* (London, 1847).

Early-eighteenth-century rum bottle.

BULLION GLASS

The proper name for that section of blown glass popularly called a Bull's-eye, *q.v.;* the sear or pontil mark in the center of a disc of Crown Glass, *q.v.*

BULL'S-EYE GLASS

The center or least expensive portion of a crown of blown glass; the section including the pontil and thus, although translucent, the part that because of its thickness and irregularity distorted vision, and so was used only for over-door or fanlights, church windows, skylights or wherever a clear view was not necessary. "To be sold by Obadiah Wells . . . Window-Glass of all Sizes with large Bull-Eyes for Sky-Lights, or small ones for Dores . . ." *The New-York Evening-Post,* March 31, 1746.

CAPEWELL GLASS

Specifically, flint glassware made by John Capewell at Philadelphia after 1825.

CROWN GLASS

The name given "The finest sort of window glass." (W) A mass of molten glass was gathered at the end of the punty rod and spun or whirled rapidly until it formed a broad thin disc. The point where the punty rod was removed, that is, the center of the disc, was the thickest, and was called the pontil. The disc then was cut into smaller pieces or panes, used for windows, clocks, as a surface for painting pictures or for glazing generally. "Just imported and to be sold by Christopher Marshall next door to the Bird in Hand in Chestnut Street Best sort of Bristol Crown Glass from the largest to the smallest sizes for glazing Houses, Ships, Clocks, Beaufets, Pictures, Ec. Also an assortment of colours for Painting." *Pennsylvania Gazette* (Philadelphia), March 26, 1741. (See also BULL'S-EYE GLASS.)

CRYSTAL

The general term for the finest lead or flint glass, so called because it is the closest in quality to natural rock crystal.

CULLET

The common name for old or broken glass gathered for reuse because "glass is always clearer and tougher when not made wholly of new materials, but with old glass ground and melted up with them, hence the constant admixture of cullet or broken glass." G. W. Francis, *The Dictionary of Practical Receipts* (London, 1847).

FERRET

"The iron with which the workmen try the melted metal to see if it be fit to work. It is also used for those irons which make the rings at the mouth of bottles." (M)

FERRETO

"The substance which serves to colour glass; made by a simple calcination of copper. Take thin sheets of copper and lay them on a layer of powdered brimstone in the bottom of a crucible; over these lay more brimstone and over that another layer of the plates and so on until the pot is full. Cover the pot, lute it well, place it in a wind furnace, and make a strong fire about it for two hours. When it is taken out and cooled the copper with be so calcined that it may be crumbled to pieces between the fingers like a friable earth. It will be of a reddish and in some parts of a blackish colour. This must be powdered and made fine for use." (M)

FLINT GLASS

Originally this was made from crushed, calcined flint rather than common sand. Later, oxide of lead and sand, niter and black oxide of manganese were substituted to manufacture crystal-quality glassware. For "Flint, mix 71¾ of calcined flints with 12¾ of potash purified, 2¼ of soda, 10 of lime, ½ of white clay, $\frac{1}{12}$ each of oxide of iron and of manganese, and 100 of cullet or old glass. If too blue, leave out the manganese. The receipt is that used in the manufacture of the elegant glass articles lately brought here in such abundance." G. W. Francis, *The Dictionary of Practical Receipts* (London, 1847).

LEAD GLASS

Another name for flint glass or Crystal, *q.v.*

PATTERN GLASS

A general term for glass blown into a mold to give it a pattern, then removed and blown into its finished form.

PITTSBURGH GLASS

A general term to describe any glass made in that area of Pennsylvania near Pittsburgh. The earliest reference is to the glass house founded in 1808 by Thomas Bakewell and Benjamin Pears and called Bakewell, Pears and Company. This company manufactured lead glass and was its first successful general producer in this country, making glass tableware, bottles, decanters, vases, etc., as well as crystal chandeliers and other decorative wares. The furnaces were stopped in 1882. "At Pittsburg we saw a steam engine which drives all the machinery necessary to turn iron into bars, wire, nails, Ec. In general, metal work in America is very good. From there we went to visit a glass-blower's and a shop where cut glass is made. I can say that for finish and delicacy they are almost the equal of those I have seen in Europe." Edouard de Montulé, *Voyage en Amérique* . . . (Paris, 1821).

PRESSED GLASS

Molten glass pressed by means of a plunger into a mold; not blown. The process is said to have been perfected first in this country by Deming Jarves in the 1830s, thus making possible mass-production of glassware.

SANDWICH GLASS

Now a generic term for lacy pressed glass. Specifically, glasswares made at the Boston & Sandwich Glass Company, Sandwich,

Sandwich glass cup plate. (Courtesy, Antiquarian and Landmarks Society, Inc.)

Massachusetts. Blown glass was made there from 1825; pressed glass from the 1830s.

STAINED GLASS
(See in Chapter 12.)

WINDOW GLASS
One of the most inexpensive parts of a modern house, windowpanes in the Colonial period were a luxury not easily afforded by all. Many householders throughout the eighteenth and early nineteenth centuries, particularly in frontier settlements, continued the earlier practice of using only wooden shutters, or skins or sheets of horn stretched and scraped to translucence, or oiled paper as windowpanes. So relatively expensive was window glass that houses sometimes were sold, with a provision in the deed that the "lights" would remain the property of, and could be removed by, the seller. Through the mid-nineteenth century, most window glass was imported from England. When the double-sash window superseded the casement in the mid-eighteenth century, panes were cut to fairly standard sizes. "Cyprian Nichols has just received an assortment of goods which he offers for sale . . . at fair prices . . . Among his assortment are . . . 8 by 10, 9 by 7, and 8 by 6 [inch] English Crown and American Window Glas . . ." *American Mercury* (Hartford, Connecticut), November 17, 1817. Among the first of their products advertised by our early glass houses were windowpanes: "Any quantity of American Window-glass of different sizes to be sold at a lower Rate than can be imported from Europe. Enquire of Caspar Wistar near the Ship-Yards, where any Person may be supplied with York Distilled Rum." *The New York Journal or The General Advertiser,* September 28, 1769.

12

Furnishings Made Here or Imported for Use (including Apparel, Armorial Bearings, Jewelry, and Textiles and Leathers)

(There are separate listings of items of Apparel, Armorial Bearings, Jewelry, and Textiles at the end of this section.)

A

ABACK TABLE

A country colloquialism for a simple console, that is, a shelf or table board supported against a wall by brackets, not on legs or any free-standing frame. Aback, obviously, was contracted from the word Abacus, *q.v.*, which in 1806 Webster defined as "an old kind of desk or table." The term also has been given to those tables made with only one flap or drop leaf and intended to be set permanently "back" or against a wall.

ABACUS

Originally this was "A kind of cupboard, or buffet [which] had no frame or foot, but was fastened some way to the wall . . . Livy describing the luxury into which the Romans degenerated says they had their *Abaci*, beds, Ec. placed over with gold. [Eventually it meant] a little table strewed over with dust on which [mathematicians] drew their schemes and figures. Hence, a table of numbers." (M) That is, a tablet or board on which numerals were painted or carved. By the early eighteenth century the common English synonym was counter or counting board—and so today when we speak of a store sales counter we still mean the place, or board, on which goods are traded after they have been enumerated and their worth counted. Many such eighteenth-century *abaci* or counting boards were set in frames to serve as sales counters or table tops; as a result, some are identified, in error, today as types of gaming tables.

ABATJOUR

A common name for the Candle Shade or Hurricane Glass, *qq.v.*

A B C BOOK

"The little book by which the elements of reading are taught." (J) "A catechism, hornbook, or primer, used for teaching children but sometimes [containing] only the alphabet in general." (H)

A B C PLATE

Collector's name for a child's nursery plate around the rim of which was stamped, painted, or printed the letters of the alphabet, and/or maxims, many adapted from *Poor Richard's Almanack*. Made late in the eighteenth century and throughout the nineteenth century of pottery, porcelain, glass, pewter, or tin.

ABECEDARY

A kind of dial, "inscribed with the letters of the alphabet" and used to teach primary school children to read. Also, a kind of bracelet. "Two needles are touched with the loadstone, and placed in the center of two abecedary circles, or rings of letters, described round about them; one friend keeping one, and another the other, and agreeing upon an hour wherein they will communicate." (J) Friendship baubles or lover's tokens, these latter were ivory, metal, or polished wood dials set in gold, silver, pewter cases or lockets. (However, abecedarian was a common name for one we would call a kindergarten or primary school teacher today.)

Abecedary. (Courtesy, Antiquarian and Landmarks Society, Inc.)

ABRACADABRA

"A superstitious charm against agues." (J) "This word, written in a peculiar manner, was formerly worn about the neck [in a locket] as a cure for the ague." (II) As a result, the term also meant the locket or container. (See also AMULET.)

ABSEY BOOK

Another form of the common term for a primer or catechism, as Shakespeare used it in *King John,* I, i:

And then comes answer like an Absey book.

(See also A B C BOOK.)

ACADEMY FIGURE

"A drawing of a naked man or woman taken from life which is usually done on paper with red or black chalk, and sometimes with pastels or crayons." (M) A description of such class, studio, club, or academy study was given by an early-nineteenth-century American itinerant artist and silhouette cutter who, in Europe to perfect his craft, was almost undone by his introduction to Academy work: "[In London] I was introduced into a club of artists where they met once a week for the purpose of learning the human figure; the first subject we had was a young lady, stripped to the beef and placed on a pedestal, and we twenty Artists sitting round her drawing her beautiful figure, perfectly naked . . ." James Guild, *Travel Diary,* Vermont Historical Society Proceedings, New Series, V. Academy figures or life studies, particularly those by now-recognized artists, are sought by collectors today. (See also CHALK DRAWING, PASTEL DRAWING.)

ACCIDENCE

A corruption of accidents, from the Latin *acedentia;* this was the name given "the little book containing the first rudiments of grammar, and explaining the properties of the eight parts of speech." (J) (W)

I do confess I do want eloquence,
And never yet did learn my accidence.

John Taylor, the Water-Poet, *Collected Works* (1630).

Taylor, in fact, did fail his Latin accidence and was forced to leave school as a result.

ACCOUNT BOOK

Fascinating and useful sources of information concerning goods imported, exported, made and sold by earlier Americans. Account books often were made to the customer's order; the pages hand-ruled; the bindings chosen to match other books on the office shelf. "Books neatly Bound, Gilded and Lettered, Account Books Rul'd and Bound, in Vellum, Parchment, Calf, or Basil, by Henry De Forrest, enquire for him at the house of John Peter Zenger, or at his House opposite to the Sign of the Black-Horse." *The New-York Weekly Journal,* May 19, 1735.

ACHAUFFERN
An early form of the word for the utensil usually known as a Chafing Dish, *q.v.*

ACHIEVEMENT, ATCHIEVEMENT
(See ARMORIAL BEARINGS, at end of this section.)

ACROTERIA
(See in Chapter 5.)

ADDICE
One of the many old tools collected today. The name of this carpenter's, joiner's, and cooper's implement was derived from the Saxon word for ax, and is one "for which we corruptly write adz(e)." (J) "The addice has its blade made thin and somewhat arching. As the axe has its edge parallel to its handle, so the addice has its edge athwart the handle, and is ground to a basil on its inside to its outer edge." Joseph Moxon, *Mechanick Exercises or The Doctrine of Handy-Works* (London, 1683–84). Furniture makers used the addice to form any concave surface—the seat of a Windsor chair, for example. (See also ADZ, AX.)

ADZ, ADZE
Among the many tools collected today, and correctly called the Addice, *q.v.,* these were the popular spellings and pronunciation of the word designating "a cutting tool with an arching edge," according to Webster. "Just imported in the last vessels from England and to be sold cheap by Joseph Hallet . . . Ship carpenter's axes, adzes and mauls . . . house carpenter's broad axes, adzes and chisels . . ." *The New York Mercury,* June 8, 1761.

AEOLIAN HARP, AEOLIUS HARP
Introduction of this musical instrument generally is ascribed to the German scholar, Athanasius Kircher (1601–80); however, a form of it was described as early as the tenth century by Duncan, Archbishop of Canterbury. The harp or lyre, named for Aeolius, the classical Greek god of the winds, was a shallow, rectangular box set with strings tuned in unison, on which the wind produced the tones. "Robert Horne . . . from London . . . makes and repairs Violins, bass viols, tenor viols, Aeolius harps . . . in the neatest and compleatist manner . . ." *The New York Mercury,* September 14, 1767.

AEROMETER
A simple type of Hydrometer, *q.v.,* or measurer of the density of fluids. "A glass phial about two inches in diameter, and seven or eight long, is corked tight; into the cork is fixed a straight wire one twelfth of an inch in diameter and thirty inches long. The phial is loaded with shot so as to sink to the heaviest liquid, leaving the wire just below the surface." *Encyclopedia Americana* (Philadelphia, 1831).

AGATE MARBLE
The child's toy turned from agate stone; later examples were made of glass colored and streaked to resemble genuine agate; hence the familiar term, aggie, for a play marble.

Marble: "A little round ball of stone." (W)

AGATEWARE
(See in Chapter 10.)

AIGUIERE
A term adopted from the French word for "water-pot for a table." (H) (See also CARAFE.)

AIR GUN
"The common air gun is made of brass and has two barrels. The ball is put down into

its place with a rammer, as in another gun. There is a syringe fixed in the stock of the gun by which the air is injected into the cavity between the two barrels." (M) Leonardo da Vinci is given credit for designing the prototype of the Western air gun in 1495.

AIRING HORSE

The common term for a simple frame, set on a double base or standard; i.e., a horse on which linens were draped to dry or air.

Airing horse. (Courtesy, Antiquarian and Landmarks Society, Inc.)

Horse: "A machine on which anything is supported by laying it across." (H)

AIR JACK
(See SMOKEJACK.)

AISYLHE BOTTLE, AISYLL BOTTLE
Aisyll was a synonym for vinegar; hence, this was a Cruet, *q.v.*

ALBUM
The term, from the Latin *albus,* for white, was used to denote a portfolio or bound book of blank pages; the album was the nineteenth-century version of the early ta-

ble book. By the mid-nineteenth century, industrious Victorians printed ready-made albums or table books, prefilled with verses, drawings, pithy paragraphs, and mottoes. Still later, the parlor album was the repository of tintypes and photographs. (See also COMMONPLACE BOOK, TABLE BOOK.)

ALCOVE BED
"A couch with a Canopy . . . occasionally converted into a Bed [is the] sort of Couch very fit for Alcoves, or such deep Recesses as are often seen in large Apartments . . . The length of the Bed cannot be less than six Feet in the Clear, but may be more if required, the Breadth is three feet, or nine in proportion to the Length. The Height must be determined by the place it is to stand in." Thomas Chippendale, *The Gentleman and Cabinet-Maker's Director* (London, 1762).

ALEMBIC(K)
"A vessel or furnace used in distillation." (B) "A chymical vessel usually made of glass or copper, for condensing the vapours that arise in distillation . . . the head or upper part of the apparatus." (M) (See also STILL.)

ALE-SHOE
A warming vessel, usually made of brass or copper, in the shape of a high shoe or half-boot. Filled with ale or wine, the toe end of the shoe was set in or near embers on the hearth to warm the liquor.

Ale-shoe. (Courtesy, Antiquarian and Landmarks Society, Inc.)

ALE-YARD

The jolly tavern accessory once said to have been introduced by a glass blower who was also a practical joker. This is a drinking vessel, exactly a yard in length, its top opening in a flaring trumpet shape, its bottom a round ball that holds a pint of liquor. Adventurous antiquaries report it almost impossible to drain the contents of the glass without most of the ale dribbling over one's chin and collar.

ALIOTHUS, ALIOTHUSIAN WARE

Made from shellfish and sometimes referred to as "pearl of aliothus," the name is derived from *aliot* or seed pearl. Aliothus was used in japanning to imitate pearl; the term thus designated the small boxes, toilet articles, tables, or other items so ornamented.

ALMACANTAR'S STAFF

The name of a kind of quadrant, "an instrument commonly made of pear tree or box, with an arch of fifteen degrees, used to take observations of the sun about the time of its rising and setting, in order to find the amplitude, and consequently the variation of the compass." (C)

Almacantar: "A series of parallel circles drawn through the several degrees of the meridian," (J) and "generally called parallels of altitude." (M)

ALMANAC(K)

"A calendar of months, days, high waters, rising and setting of the sun and moon, the moons changes, fasts, Ec." (W) Paper pamphlets with self-covers, almanacs seldom were more than 6 by 9 inches in size, varied from 12 to 48 pages, and were illustrated with small wood cuts at the heads of pages. "November 9, 1685. New Almanack came out this Day intituled New-England's Almanack by Mr. Danforth." Samuel Sewall, *Diary*. Many early almanacs also included college vacation and commencement dates; post routes; stage-coach routes and the names of the inns at which they stopped; schedules of court sessions: "September 7,

1686. I goe with my wife, Cousin Ruth, Savages and Mrs. Baker and their children to Hay Island . . . I little thought of its being the day signed by the Almanack for the Court of Assistants, till coming home . . ." Samuel Sewall, *Diary*. Later, eighteenth-century and early-nineteenth-century almanacs included paragraphs of advice on a multitude of popular subjects, chiefly husbandry and gardening, and proverbs such as those familar from Benjamin Franklin's *Poor Richard's Almanack*.

1786 Boston Almanac.

ALMARIE, ALMARY

One of several ancient terms, revived by collectors today, to designate a large "cupboard, pantry, safe . . . The North Country word aumbry seems formed from this, glossed by the French *ameire*." (H)

Their avarice hath almaries,
and yren bounden cofres.

William Langland (?), *The Vision Concerning Piers Ploughman.*

(See ALMONRY, AMBRY, DOLE CUPBOARD.)

ALMONRY

"The place where the alms are distributed"; (J) by extension, a synonym for the cupboard or box in which provisions to be given the poor were kept. (See AMBRY; DOLE CUPBOARD.)

ALMORATTA

The Spanish or Portuguese wine jug with a rounded base and four spouts, often in a wicker container, suspended by cords from a wall or beam peg.

ALMS BASKET

The name of the covered "basket [in the kitchen] in which provisions are put to be given away." (J)

ALMS DISH, ALMYS DYSSHE

The dish or container kept "in the old hall in which was put the bread set aside for the poor." (H) (See ALMS BASKET, DOLE CUPBOARD.)

AMADOW

The tinder made of fungus boiled in lye and then dried with saltpeter; also called quickfire or touchwood. (See also TINDERBOX.)

AMBRY

This Middle English word was, according to Johnson in 1755, a corruption of Almonry, *q.v.,* and designated "the place where plate and utensils for housekeeping are stored; also, a cupboard for keeping cold victuals." (J) Johnson also indicated the term was obsolete amongst up-to-date mid-eighteenth-century English gentry, although he said the word was "still used in the northern counties and in Scotland." Webster in 1806 gave Ambry only as a synonym for Almonry. However, in 1823 John Walker defined Ambry as "a place where alms are distributed" and also as "the place where plate and utensils are kept." *Pronouncing Dictionary of the English Language* (Hartford, Connecticut, 1823). Earlier references support Johnson in his contention that Ambry correctly is a cupboard or press for the storage of food and table furnishings:

> Some slovens from sleeping, no sooner be up,
> but hand is in aumbrie, and nose in the cup.

> Thomas Tusser, *Five Hundreth Points of Good Husbandry* (London, 1577).

The word has been revived by modern collectors to describe a variety of large two-door cupboards with heavy cornice moldings, especially those with doors pierced to allow ventilation.

AMBULANTE

The term, from the French word for strolling, first appeared in the mid-eighteenth century to describe small tables and chairs that could be moved about as required. Thus, pembroke and tea tables, worktables and wine stands were ambulantes; today they would be called occasional or side tables.

AMERICAN EAGLE

In coin collecting, this term refers to one of the early gold pieces minted for use in the United States:

"American Standard of Money, Approved by act of Congress, April 10, 1806—

	pwt	gr
GOLD:		
Eagle, valued at Ten Dollars, must weigh	11	06
Half Eagle, at Five Dollars	5	15
Quarter Eagle, at Two Dollars and Fifty Cents	2	19½
SILVER:		
Dollar must weigh	17	07
Half Dollar	8	16
Quarter Dollar	4	04
French Crown, at One Dollar and Ten Cents	18	17"

Reprinted in *The Farmer's Almanack* (Boston, 1814).

AMERICAN EAGLE

The national symbol adopted by the United States, and often referred to as the Federal Eagle by collectors. Some, such as Franklin and Jefferson, thought the wild turkey a more apt choice; the majority, however, agreed that "the Bald Eagle is the most distinguished of the North American species, not only from his beauty, but also [now] as the adopted emblem of our country . . . In poetry and the fine arts, the eagle plays a very important part. As king of birds, the eagle was the bird of Jove, the carrier of the lightning, and thereby expressive of the sole or supreme dominion. In this sense he is used as the emblem and symbol of nations . . . The eagle of the United States stands with outspread wings, guarding the shield below him, in which are the stripes and stars representing the states of the Union, and the motto *E pluribus unum.*" *Encyclopedia Americana* (Philadelphia, (1831). "Improved Eagles. John Cook & Co., inform their friends and the public they have now finished a die for striking silver Eagles for American Cockades, and ready for sale." *The New-York Gazette,* June 30, 1798.

AMERICAN STOVE

The English name for the Philadelphia or "new Pennsylvania stove" invented by Benjamin Franklin. (See also FRANKLIN STOVE.)

AMPHORA

The Greek word, sometimes used in seventeenth-century England and the colonies, for a tall kind of ewer or container for oil and wine; the vessel itself being ovoid and wide-based.

AMPULLA

Originally this was a round, big-bellied vessel, such as a bath, but it "also signifies a cup made of glass, and sometimes of leather, for drinking out of at table." (M) (See also JACK.)

AMULET

"A charm against witchcraft, or diseases, etc. made of stone, metal . . . and in short, everything that imagination could suggest. Notwithstanding the progress of learning and refinement, there is not any country even at this day, who do not believe in some charm or other." (M) The use of amulets and charms to ward off evil and insure good luck was not limited to those of little education or low position. Some amulets were worn on silver or gold chains as necklaces and lockets, others were carried in handsome pocket boxes. Among the most popular amulets three centuries ago, just as today, were the four-leaf clover, shamrock, and the rabbit's foot. The Secretary to the Admiralty in the reigns of Charles II and James II noted in his diary: "So ends the old year, I bless God with great joy . . . I never have been in so good plight as to my health in so very cold weather as this, nor indeed any these ten years as I am this day . . . But I am at a great loss to know whether it be my hare's foot, or taking every morning of a pill of turpentine . . ." Samuel Pepys, *Diary,* December 31, 1664. (Pepys was subject to racking chest colds.)

ANCIENT

A synonym for ensign, "the flag or streamer of a ship [or of] a regiment." (J)

ANDIRON(S)

This word "is supposed to be corrupted from hand-iron, an iron that may be moved by the hand, or may supply the place of a hand [as a rest or something in which another thing is held]. Irons at the end of a fire-grate in which the spit turns; or irons in which wood is laid to burn." (J) Other spellings of the seventeenth, eighteenth, and nineteenth centuries included aundirons, aundiron, aundyren, awnderne. Those used at the kitchen hearth were almost invariably made of iron with attached spit hooks, rings, or rests. Those used in parlors and chambers were made of iron; iron with brass or pewter finials; polished steel; brass, copper, silver or silver-plated metal: "Brass andirons from $4.50 to $18., shovel and tongs to match, brass head andirons, brass candlesticks . . . brushes, bellows, tea-kettles . . . offered for sale by Ward & Bartholomew." *American Mercury* (Hartford, Connecticut), May 31, 1810. In many areas, andirons continued in use for the kitchen and parlor hearths, as a matter of preference, until later in the nineteenth century than now is commonly supposed—in some areas well into the twentieth century they were used out of necessity. The utility fireplace always was that heat source most easily contrived in hurriedly built frontier homes. Thus, it was in use in as late as 1912 when the 48th state, Arizona, was admitted to the Union.

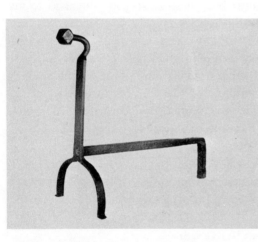

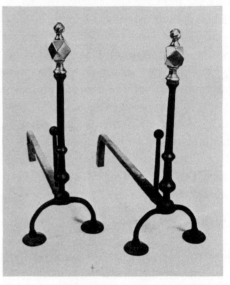

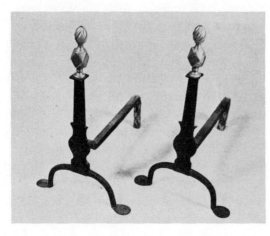

Andirons. (Courtesy, Antiquarian and Landmarks Society, Inc.)

ANEMOMETER

"An instrument contrived to measure the strength or velocity of the wind." (J)

ANEMOSCOPE

The term was derived from the Greek ἄνεμος for wind and the Latin *scopium,* to examine, and thus signified the instrument that enabled the user to observe the force and direction of the shifting wind: "The late ingenious Mr. Pickering published [1744] in *The Philosophical Transactions,* Numb. 473, an instrument which he called an anemoscope calculated to show [on an indoor dial] the velocity of the wind and the point of the compass on which it blows. Otto Guerick gave this name to a machine he invented consisting of a little wooden man, which by rising and falling in a glass tube, showed the change of the weather. But it is only an application of the common barometer." (M) A type of eighteenth-century weather vane: "A machine invented to foretel the change of the wind. It has been observed that hygroscopes, made of cat's gut proved very good anemoscopes, seldom failing, by turning the index about, to foretel the shifting of the wind." (C)

Anemoscope, as shown in *The New Dictionary of Arts and Sciences* (London, 1778).

ANGELOT

The name given to "a musical instrument somewhat resembling a lute." (J) Also the name of a gold coin.

ANGLE

An early synonym for the fishing rod. "An instrument to take fish, consisting of a rod, a line, and a hook." (J)

ANGLE ROD

And another. "The stick to which the line and hook are hung." (J) "The reed differs much in greatness, the smallest being fit for thatching of house; the second bigness is used for angle-rods, and in China for beating of offenders." Francis Bacon, *Essayes or Counsels, Civill and Morall* (London, 1625).

ANGLING CANE

And a third. "The great Reed or Cane makes the Angling-Cane for fishers." John Gerard, *The Herball or Generall Historie of Plantes* (London, 1636).

ANNAL(E)S

Usually used in the plural, annals were small books, published in parts each month or quarter and then stitched together in paper covers, or bound as a volume at the end of the year. Sometimes these were anthologies on individual subjects, or chronologies of events, as we have yearbooks today. "A species of history wherein events are related in chronological order, as a journal of what passes everyday. Annales require brevity only; history demands ornament." (M) (See also ALMANAC.)

ANODYNE NECKLACE

One of the many amulets worn in the hope or belief that it would mitigate or forestall pain. The principal ingredient was opium or other narcotics in some form. Necklaces were made from "little round pellets cut from different dried roots, sometimes from the roots of henbane, but mostly from orrice root. These pellets are strung into necklaces and hung round the necks of children cutting their teeth, under the impression that they lighten the pain of the gums . . ." G. W. Francis, *The Dictionary of Practical Receipts* (London, 1847). Anodyne necklaces, sold by apothecaries and jewelers alike, often were made with silver, gold, or ivory clasps; sometimes with amber beads strung alternately with those carved from roots. (See also ABRACADABRA, AMULET, CORAL-AND-BELLS.)

ANTHEMION-BACK CHAIR
A collector's term for a type of chair made in the late eighteenth and early nineteenth centuries. (See ANTHEMION, Chapter 5.)

ANVIL
"An instrument on which the smith hammers or forges his work, and is generally placed on a large wooden block; at one end there is sometimes a round pike, or beak-iron, for the rounding of hollow work, or bending iron into different curves." (M)

APOLLONICON
(See ORCHESTRION.)

APOSTLE SPOONS
Gift or souvenir spoons; from the custom below described, we gained the phrase "born with a silver spoon." "It was anciently the custom for sponsors at christenings to offer gilt spoons as presents to the child, which were called apostle-spoons, because very frequently the figures of the twelve apostles were chased or carved on the tops of the handles. Opulent sponsors gave the whole twelve; those in middling circumstances gave four; while the poorer sort contented themselves with the gift of one, [choosing] the figure of some saint in honour of whom the child received its name." (H) (See also note under LATTEN in Metals, Chapter 9; APOSTLE WARES.)

APOSTLE WARES
The collector's term for the spoons, mugs, jugs, carved plaques, or any other piece memorializing the twelve apostles, made from the mid-seventeenth through the mid-eighteenth centuries, and unfortunately, reproduced in quantity today.

APPARATUS
(See DRESSING APPARATUS, TOILET TABLE.)

APPAREL
(See separate list at back of this section.)

APPLE CORER
In the mid-eighteenth century, the term for a kitchen utensil with a wood haft and a small semicircle of sharpened iron or steel with which apples were cored and with which small ball shapes could be cut out of fruits or vegetables. A second form of apple corer was comprised of a small table-top stand and a handle which when turned caused two or more slender blades to re-

Early-eighteenth-century apple corer.

Late-eighteenth-century apple corer.

volve and so cut out the core. "I send you . . . a little Instrument to core Apples; another to make little Turnips out of great ones . . ." (Benjamin Franklin, from London, February 19, 1758, to his wife at Philadelphia.) *The Writings of Benjamin Franklin,* ed., A. H. Smyth. (New York, 1907). "Take two carrots, pare them, cut them about half an inch long, and with an apple corer cut them out . . ." Richard Briggs, *The New Art of Cookery* (Philadelphia, 1792).

AQUATINT

The name for a method, and thus the finished print, developed in the mid-eighteenth century, of tone etching designed to resemble water-color painting; the aquatint was and is produced by etching a copper plate with *aqua fortis,* or acid, through a resist or spirit ground (dissolved powdered resin) flooded over the plate. The plate then is bitten as in any Etching, *q.v.,* to the depth or amount of tone desired, highlights or white areas being stopped out; that is, protected against the bite of the acid by a coat of varnish.

ARAEOMETER, AIROMETER

The name of the "water-poise," or scale, "an instrument for measuring the density or gravity of fluids. [It was] generally made of a thin glass ball with a taper neck hermetically sealed at the top, having put as much mercury poured into the ball, as will keep it swimming in an erect position. The neck is divided into equal parts and properly numbered so that the lightness of the fluid is known by the depth the araeometer sinks in it." (M)

ARCHED VIOL

The name for a seventeenth-century variation of the harpsichord. "The new instrument was brought called the Arched Violl, where, being tuned with lute strings, and played on with keys like an organ, a piece of parchment is always kept moving; and the strings, which by the keys, are pressed down upon it, are grated in imitation of a bow, by the parchment; and so it is intended to resemble several vialls played on with one bow, but so basely and so harshly that it will never do." Samuel Pepys, *Diary,* October 5, 1664.

ARCHITECTURAL FRAME

A contemporary synonym for what also was called a Tabernacle Frame, *q.v.* In *The Universal System of Household Furniture* (London, 1762), Ince and Mayhew showed four designs for "Architectoral Frames."

ARGAND LAMP

The name given a type of late-eighteenth-century lamp burner first made with an iron chimney. The glass chimney was introduced in 1789; in 1808 the Argand burner was used by Samuel Glegg to burn gas. "The best lamps now in use are those invented by [Aimé] Argand at Geneva in 1784. The principle . . . is the admission of a larger quantity of air to the flame than can be done in the common way. This is accomplished by making the wick of a circular form, by which means a current of air rushes through the cylinder, on which it is placed, with great force and . . . excites the flame to such a degree that the smoke is entirely consumed. Thus both the light and heat are prodigiously increased . . . and what in common lamps is dissipated in smoke, is here converted into a brilliant flame. This lamp is now very much in use . . . It consists of two parts, viz., a reservoir for the oil, and the lamp itself . . . On the outside is placed a glass chimney which is capable of transmitting a current of air on the same principle as a common smoke flue. The flame does not waver." *Encyclopedia Americana* (Philadelphia, 1831).

ARGYLE, ARGYLL

The name given an English gravy warmer in form similar to the coffee pot, developed in the mid-eighteenth century and presumed to have been named in honor of the fourth Duke of Argylle. Made in silver, faïence, and pottery, the argyle kept gravy hot in a center interior tube—the pot itself serving as a hot-water jacket—by setting the argyle above a spirit lamp.

ARK

A large chest that could be locked; the term was derived from the Latin *arca,* for chest. "The large chests in farmhouses used for keeping meal or flour were so called. They are usually of oak, and are sometimes elaborately carved. From the name arkwright it would seem that the construction of them formerly constituted a separate trade." (H)

ARM CHAIR, ARMED CHAIR

In 1775, Johnson defined an Armed Chair as "an Elbow Chair [*q.v.*] or a chair with rests for the arms." The term arm chair was used more often in the nineteenth century for what earlier had been called simply a chair. In the seventeenth and early eighteenth century the term chair always carried

Seventeenth-century arm chair with modified crest on top rail. (Courtesy, Antiquarian and Landmarks Society, Inc.)

Wainscot arm chair of American red oak owned by Governor John Winthrop, the younger, c. 1640. (Courtesy, Connecticut Historical Society, Inc.)

Comb-back Windsor arm chair of late eighteenth century, attributed to John Wadsworth. (Courtesy, Connecticut Historical Society, Inc.)

the connotation of arms. What we now call a side, occasional, or single chair, in the early Colonial period was called a Back Stool, *q.v.*

ARMILLARY DIAL

A type of sundial made of rings forming an orb or kind of skeletonal open ball; the shadow of the gnomen thus falls on a curved surface and more accurately designates the time. (See also SUNDIAL.)

ARMOIRE

The French word for a Press or Wardrobe, each of which see.

ARMONICA

A musical instrument in which glass provided the tone medium; first invented in Nuremberg in the mid-seventeenth century and introduced in England in the mid-eighteenth century by the composer, Christopher von Gluck. An improved type was devised by Benjamin Franklin about 1761 during his stay in England. This consisted of a series of blown-glass bowls, graduated in size, tuned by grinding the edges, and mounted on a spindle above a trough filled with water. The edges of the bowls passed through the water, revolved on their axes by a wheel. The bowls or glasses were played by rubbing their moistened edges with the fingers. A variation of this instrument was fitted also with a keyboard and continued in favor throughout the nineteenth century: Mozart and Beethoven composed music for it. A third type was made of a row of small glass or metal bars, in graduated lengths, sounded by striking with a mallet, somewhat similar to the ancient Greek xylophone. "Let Sally divert you with her Music. Put her on Practising on the Armonica. Mr. Breuner with his Violin may assist and improve her there as well as on the Harpsichord." (Benjamin Franklin, from London to his wife in Philadelphia, February 14, 1765.) *Writings of Benjamin Franklin,* ed. A. H. Smyth (New York, 1907). "I did not forget the Armonica for Cousin Josiah: There is only one

Man that makes them well, his price no less than 34 guineas, asks 40 . . . He promised to make it now a 12 month since. He has not yet done a glass of it . . ." (Franklin to cousin Jonathan Williams, April 28, 1766.) Ibid.

ARMOR

The all-inclusive term for "all such habiliments as serve to defend the body from wounds, especially [those of] darts, a sword, or lance, Ec. A complete suit of armour [consists of] a helmet, a shield, a cuirasse, a coat of mail, a gantlet." (M) The parts of the helm or helmet were the skull, the top and back, the hinged visor over the eyes and cheeks; the hinged beaver over the mouth and chin. The gorget covered the neck; the pauldron or epauliere covered the shoulder and arm pieces; the rerebrace protected the upper arm; the coudiere, the elbow; the rambrace, the forearm; the gauntlet, the hand. Other upper portions or cuirasses were the breastplate and backplate; tassets or taces were metal strips forming a skirt over the abdomen. Guisses were the covers for the thigh; the genouillere protected the kneecap; the jamb the lower leg; the solleret, the foot. With the development of effective firearms and thus generally of long-range fighting, armor became superfluous; the exception, from the early eighteenth century, well into the nineteenth century was the cuirasse which was worn by cavalrymen, who, not unreasonably, were known as cuirassiers.

AROMATIQUE

The name given a nineteenth-century room freshener, a graduated series of small perforated paper boxes filled with cotton balls that had been impregnated with powdered spices, dried flowers, etc. The boxes were strung together and suspended from a beam or doorframe. When the string was tugged, the action shook out some of the powder and so perfumed the room.

ARQUEBUS

In weaponry, the term from the German *Hackenbusch,* for hooked gun, used after 1600 to describe a heavy carbine.

ARROW-BACK CHAIR

(See ARROW-BACK, Chapter 5.)

ARTIFACT

Any useful object made by man from existing materials.

ASHET

An old northern English and Scottish term for a Platter or Trencher, *qq.v.,* of wood; probably a variation of the Norman-French *assiette* or plate. The word was still in use, especially in southern colonies, late in the eighteenth century.

ASH PAIL

A contemporary term for a somewhat scoop-shaped container with a handle, usually made of wood or iron. "A Parcel of choice Iron Ash Pails, proper for taking up hot ashes from Hearths, to let them cool in; and are very useful as a Preservative against Fire; to be sold by Gerardus Beckman, opposite to the Fly Market." *The New-York Gazette and The Weekly Post-Boy,* January 27, 1752. (See also ASH TRUG, COAL SCUTTLE.)

ASH TRUG

An old term for "a coal scuttle," (H) usually made of wood. (See also ASH PAIL, TRUG.)

ASTRAL LAMP

The name of a type of early-nineteenth-century Argand Lamp, *q.v.,* popular because it was made with a shallow, ringed oil font that did not cast a shadow. "Pulpit Lamps, just received, and designed expressly for this purpose. Also, Study, or Reading Lamps, together with a good assortment of Astral and Mantel ditto. All of which are warranted to burn well, and give satisfaction, for sale by John J. Low & Co., Washington St." *Trumpet and Universalist Magazine* (Boston), August 18, 1835.

ASTROLABE, ASTELLABRE, ASTERLAGOUR, ASTRELABRE

"An instrument chiefly used for taking the altitude of the pole, the sun, or stars, at sea" (J) ". . . which consists of a brass ring, the limbs of which are divided into degrees and minutes . . . with two sights and a moveable index. When the instrument is used, the index is turned toward the sun, so that the rays may pass freely through both sights . . ." (M)

ASTROMETER

Another term for the Heliometer, *q.v.*

ASTRONOMICAL CLOCK

A contemporary term for the type of long-case clock generally called a calendar clock today: "May be had (at his Shop in Roxbury Street) Simon Willard's new constructed Astronomical Time Keeper, ascertaining the 60 or 20th part of a minute, by a second hand from the centre of the large circle, made upon a most simple plan, in which the friction and influence of the oil is almost annihilated, and has proved to keep time with the greatest accuracy . . . those that oscillate half seconds are portable, and are easily moved to any part of the room . . . to the pedestal of which is affixed (without obstructing the movement) a perpetual calendar, newly engraved, which shows at one view, the day of the month, the true and comparative time of the sun's rising and setting forever; as well as the age, increase, decrease, rising and setting of the moon, time of high water, Ec. The whole globe with its rotation every twenty-four hours, shewing the longitude, latitude, the hour and minute upon the most noted placed on the globe." *Thomas's Massachusetts Spy or Worcester Gazette,* March 11, 1784. Needless to say, not all calendar or astronomical clock works had every one of the extra features Willard offered.

ASTRONOMICAL QUADRANT

The term to describe an instrument "contrived to take the altitude, Ec. of the heavenly bodies in a very accurate manner . . . generally made of brass or wooden bars faced with plates of iron, having its limb divided either diagonally or otherwise into degrees, minutes and seconds, if possible, with two telescopes, one fixed on the side, and the other moveable upon the center . . ." (M)

ASTROSCOPE

The name of "An instrument with which to observe the stars." (J)   The contemporary term for a kind of telescope, described at the time as "an instrument composed of two cones, having the constellations delineated on their surfaces, whereby the stars may be easily known." (M)

ATLAS

Then as now, the term for "a collection of maps; a large square folio so-called probably from a picture of Atlas supporting the heavens, prefixed to some collections," (J) or, "A book of universal geography, containing maps of all the known parts of the world." (W)   As Johnson indicated, the term was used for any collection of maps, including: "A Modern Atlas, consisting of twenty-seven Plans of actions, fought in the present War, Charts of Rivers, Ec. Ec. amongst which are the following: Boston Harbour, its Works and Environs, the plan of the Town of Boston with the entrenchments. Plan of the action at Bunker Hill, Rhode Island with the Rebel works and batteries raised against it . . . Plan of Newport Town. Hudson's River from Sandy Hook to Fort Chamblee in Canada with the Soundings. The defeat of the Rebels under Mr. Arnold, 11th October 1776. The Action and Defeat of Mr. Washington at the White Plains, and all other operations in New York and the Jerseys from Oct. 12 to Nov. 28. The Battle of Brooklyn and Defeat of the Rebel Army on Long Island August 28, 1776. The forcing the Rebel lines near Fort Knyphausen 10 November 1776. A Plan of the City of New York, and

its Environs." *Royal Gazette* (New York), July 8, 1780.

AUGER, AUGURE

One of the tools for the carpenter to "bore holes with." (J)   "The auger hath a handle and bit; its office is to make great round holes. When you use it, the stuff you work on is commonly laid low under you that you may the easier use your strength; for in twisting the bit about by the force of both your hands, on each end of the handle one it cuts great chips out of the stuff." Joseph Moxon, *Mechanick Exercises, or The Doctrine of Handy-Works* (London, 1683–84). "Auglers for carpenters" were listed in the House of Parliament Rates, 1660, for Imports and Exports—*Statutes of the Realm* (London, 1819).

AUMBRY

(See AMBRY.)

AUTOMATON

Another contemporary name for the Physiognotrace, *q.v.*

AVOIDER

"The vessel in which things are carried away." (J)   (See also VOIDER.)

AWL, AUL

"Among shoemakers, an instrument wherewith holes are bored through the leather to facilitate the stitching or sewing the same. The blade of the awl is usually a little flat end bended and the point ground to an acute angle." (M)

AX, AXE

The colonial settler's indispensable tool, "an instrument consisting of a metal head with a sharp edge, fixed in a helve or handle, to cut with." (J)   "To be sold by Thomas Aston, Shipwright near the upper end of Water St. Several sorts of Nails, and other iron ware, viz. axes, adzs, Chissels, Gimblets, Hammers, Cross cut Saws, Whip Saws, Handsaws, files and sundry sort of other goods." *American Weekly Mercury* (Philadelphia), June 5, 1735. "Among carpenters, an instrument wherewith to hew wood. This implement differs from the joiners' hatchet as being deeper and heavier." (M)

B

BABBY, BABBY-BOOK, BABS
These were contemporary colloquialisms for "children's picture books." (H) (See also TOY BOOK.)

BABY
The common term from the seventeenth century well into the nineteenth century, not only for an infant, but for a "girl's doll, a little image," according to Webster in 1806. "Babies or Puppets for children," and "Babyes heads of earth [earthenware]" were listed in the House of Parliament Rates, 1660, for Imports and Exports—*Statutes of the Realm* (London, 1819). (See also DOLL.)

BABY-CLOUT
A contemporary term for a child's rag doll, "a puppet made of rags." (H) (See also BABY; DOLL.)

BABY HOUSE
A contemporary term for a child's doll house. "April 18th [1772]. Papa has promised he will bring up my baby-house with him. I [have made] a droll figure of a young lady in . . . a head-dress . . . taken from a print that came over in one of the last ships from London." *Diary of Anna Green Winslow* (Boston, 1894). (See also BABY.)

BACHELOR CHEST
The collector's term for a small eighteenth-century chest or set of Dressing Drawers, *q.v.*, with a board under the top which could be pulled out to form a table to hold toilet articles or to serve as a writing surface.

BACK BAR
"The bar in the chimney by which any vessel is suspended over the fire." (H) A contemporary synonym for a type of hearth utensil more commonly called a crane today; so named because it was centered in the back wall of the chimney rather than hung at one side. (See also CRANE, SWAY.)

BACKGAMMON
"From the Welsh word for a little battle," this is a "play or game at tables with box and dice." (J) The game requires a double board, the moves are determined by the throwing of dice; it thus provided an opportunity for the cabinetmaker to show his skill in executing handsomely inlaid tables, as it did the carver and turner who made the counters or pieces, the die and boxes.

BACKGAMMON TABLE
"William Hutton, Mathematical Instrument Maker . . . makes and sells . . . Backgammon Tables, Dice and Dice Boxes; Billiard Balls and Tacks . . . with a variety of other Articles too tedious to mention . . ." *The New-York Gazette and The Weekly Mercury,* May 4, 1772. (See PLAYING TABLE.)

BACKGAMMON WORKTABLE
A combination small work and gaming table designed for the parlor: "This ornamental piece of furniture will admit of every variety in execution; and, where expense is not an object, the whole frame may be gold [-lacquered], and the ornaments in bronze. The inside must be covered entirely with leather, to prevent noise, when used for play. The ends contain concealed drawers, which hold the chess and backgammon men. The casters are concealed in the plinths, supporting the whole." George Smith, *A Collection of Designs for Household Furniture* (London, 1808). (See also WORKTABLE.)

BACK PAINTING

A contemporary term for Reverse Glass Painting, *q.v.*

BACKSTAFF

One of the many small early navigation or colonial "scientific" instruments. This was "said to have been invented about 1590 by John Davis, a sea captain," (J) who first described it in his book, *Seaman's Secrets*. Used for taking the sun's altitude at sea, the backstaff was so called because the back of the observer was turned toward the sun when he made his observations.

BACKSTONE

A kitchen hearth utensil, this was "the stone [on which] to bake bread; the larger or double ones, as they are usually called, are about 28 to 30 inches by 16 to 20, and the smaller ones vary in size, 16 or 18 inches square." (H)

BACK STOOL

Literally, a stool with a backrest. This was the term in general use from the mid-seventeenth through the eighteenth century for what now is called a side chair. London cabinetmakers, Ince and Mayhew, showed eight designs for handsome back stools in *The Universal System of Household Furniture,* published in 1762, noting that one "has been executed in burnish'd Gold, and [the upholstered back and seat] covered with blue Damask." (See also ARM CHAIR.)

BACKSWORD

In weaponry, "A sword with one sharp edge," (J) so called because it was wielded with the same motion a tennis player uses in making a backswing or stroke.

BACON CUPBOARD

The contemporary colloquialism for a type of settle or long bench combined with a tall, shallow, one-door cupboard which served as the back to the bench. However, the qualifying term bacon refers specifically to the storage space below the box seat, an out-of-sight bin or drawer also often used in small farm or village houses as a handy repository for sides of smoked ham or flitches of bacon. "To save the bacon, is a phrase for preserving oneself from being hurt; borrowed from the care of housewives in the country—where they have seldom any other provision in the house than dried bacon—to secure it from marching soldiers." (J)

BACON DISH

Broiled bacon, which sometimes achieved the status of a delicacy, was served at better tables in a silver or plated rectangular or oval dish, the cover of which had a polished or painted wood handle.

BADGE

(See under ARMORIAL BEARINGS at end of this section.)

BAGATELLE

A popular game that Dr. Johnson reported was called also Troll-My-Dame, Troll-Madam, or Pigeon Holes. It was played on a board, at one end of which were arches, similar to pigeon holes, into which small ivory or wood balls were bowled.

BAGPIPE

"The well known musical instrument of the wind kind, greatly used in Scotland, Ireland and the northern parts of England," (M) brought to southern colonies by emigrants from those sections: "We danced to-night to the music of the bagpipe which made us beat the ground with prodigious force. Joining heartily in their amusement, we performed with much activity a dance which I suppose the emigration from Sky has occasioned; they call it America. Each of the couples . . . successively whirls round in a circle, till all are in motion, and the dance seems intended to show how emigration catches, till a whole neighbourhood is set afloat . . . Last year when a ship sailed from Portree for America the people on shore were almost distracted seeing their relations go off. They lay down on the ground, tumbled, and tore the grass with their teeth. This year not a tear was shed. The people all seemed to think that they [too] would soon follow." James Boswell, *Journal of a Tour* [1773] *to the Hebrides* (London, 1785). The bagpipe is "a musical instrument, which blows up like a football, by means of a little tube fixed to it, and stopped by a valve and three pipes or flutes . . . played on by compressing the bag under the arm, when full, and opening or stopping the holes, which are eight, with the fingers. The bagpipe takes in the compass of three octaves." (C)

BAG TABLE
Another name for the sewing or Worktable, *q.v.*

BAKE OVEN
A contemporary synonym for the Dutch Oven, *q.v.*, "John Carrell . . . has An Assortment of Ironmongery, Cutlery and Sadlery, to which he will receive considerable additions by the Vessels, now daily expected, from Bristol and Liverpool, and also . . . pots and kettles from ½ to 20 gallons, bake-ovens oval and round, of various sizes; bake-plates; cart-boxes, clock and sash-weights, Ec. Ec." *Pennsylvania Packet* (Philadelphia), September 8, 1791.

Bake Oven. (Courtesy, Antiquarian and Landmarks Society, Inc.)

BAKING PLATE
The kitchen utensil, sometimes called a bake iron, similar to a griddle in that it was flat with an extremely shallow rim; usually round in shape, with a short handle. "To roast or bake a Pike. Fill it with a stuffing, put it on an iron baking-plate . . . put some bits of butter here and there over it, bake it two hours in an oven." Richard Briggs, *The New Art of Cookery* (Philadelphia, 1792).

BAKING TIN
The flat, rectangular sheet of heavy tin or tin-plated iron, similar to that used today but with a short handle. "Make them as high and as big as a French roll . . . Put them on a baking tin, and bake them three quarters of an hour . . ." Richard Briggs, *The New Art of Cookery* (Philadelphia, 1792). (See also BAKING PLATE.)

BALANCE
A common synonym for the "balance scale." (J) "The modern balance now generally used, consists of a lever or beam suspended exactly in the middle, having scales or basons hung to each extremity." (M) "Ballances, Gold Ballances [for weighing gold], ounce Ballances [for apothecaries]" were listed in House of Parliament Rates, 1660, for Imports and Exports —*Statutes of the Realm* (London, 1819).

Balance Basons are the "two scales or dishes fastened to the extremities of the

Balance. (Courtesy, Antiquarian and Landmarks Society, Inc.)

strings, the one to hold the weight, the other the thing to be weighed." (M)

BALEEN
The whale bone or ivory used for Scrimshaw or Buttons, *qq.v.*

BALK, BAULK
From the Old English *balca,* or ridge, hence a bar or beam, for which this was the contemporary term. The bar which "locked" the door leading outside was called a doorbalk; the high bar or lug pole within the chimney was a galley-balk.

BALL
The "military art, comprehends all sorts of bullets for fire-arms, from the cannon to the pistol. Cannon-balls are of iron; musquet balls, pistol-balls, etc. are of lead." (M)

BALLAD, BALLET
Both were contemporary terms describing "a kind of song adapted to the capacity of the lower class of people, who, being mightily taken with this species of poetry, are thereby not a little influenced in the conduct of their lives." (M) Despite the lexicographer's disdain, the stanzas of many of these popular songs were printed on single or broadsheets to be sold by street hawkers, chapmen, and stationers. They are sought by collectors of antique printed ephemera whose special interest is in the woodcut or copper plate illustrations, the type ornaments or "printer's flowers" used to decorate the pages.

BALLIARDS
"A play at which a ball is driven by the end of a stick; now corruptly called billiards," (J) which, nevertheless, see.

BALLOON-BACK CHAIR
A popular design for dining and drawing-room chairs, developed between 1830 and 1860, whereby the classic chair back with horizontal top rail or yoke set over the uprights was replaced by a back formed by

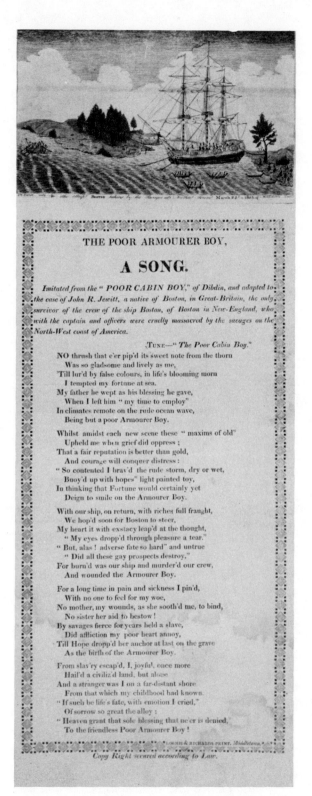

Ballad of *The Poor Armourer Boy,* the tale of a Boston sailing ship and its crew. (Courtesy, Connecticut Historical Society, Inc.)

ballooning or curving the uprights themselves to create a continuous rounded line or top.

Balloon-back chair illustrated in *The Cabinet-Maker's Assistant,* Blackie and Son (London, 1853).

BALLOT BOX

The ballot was "a little ball or ticket used in giving votes, being put privately into a box or urn." (J) Both boxes and ballots are collected today, particularly those that were made for the convenience of members of private clubs. Ballots and tickets were made of ivory and ivory stained black, or of dark marble, or of light- and dark-colored woods. The small boxes, or covered urns, often were richly inlaid or carved.

Ballot Glass: "Be pleased to send me . . . a set of balloting glasses such as are used in the house of commons." (Order, May 9, 1768, from George Wythe, Williamsburg, Virginia, to London.) Frances Mason, *John Norton and Sons, Merchants of London and Virginia* (Richmond, 1935).

Ballot box also was a cant term for the covered kitchen salt box, particularly one made of stoneware; so called because of the slit opening in the side of the box.

BALUSTER-BACK CHAIR
(See BALUSTER-BACK, Chapter 5.)

BAMBOO FURNITURE
The great Indian reed *Bambusa arundinacea* provided slender rods from which chairs, settees, and tables were made and which were exported to England and the colonies in the second half of the eighteenth century. So popular was such Eastern furniture that bamboo "turnings" were copied in beech and other light woods, and the furniture then painted in imitation of the natural bamboo color. By the early nineteenth century the turnings had become much less imitative of the natural bamboo and were increasingly stylized. The furniture was painted in other colors, including red, gold, black, green. The style of turnings was revived late in the nineteenth century at the time a great deal of wicker furniture was being made. "For Sale by Samuel Claphamson, Cabinet Maker in Market Street . . . French chairs, sophas, Bamboo chairs, settees . . . on the most reasonable terms." *Pennsylvania Packet* (Philadelphia), July 20, 1787. "William Challen, Fancy Chairmaker from London . . . manufactures all sorts of dyed, japanned, wangee and bamboo chairs, settees, etc. . . . in the neatest manner, and after the newest and most approved London patterns." *New-York Gazette and General Advertiser,* February 22, 1797.

BAMBOO WALKING STICKS
These elegant accessories for gentlemen who had leisure to stroll in gardens, courtyards or parks, were hand-carved and sold throughout the seventeenth and eighteenth centuries. Many were made with intricately carved heads; capped with silver or gilt knobs; given brass or silver ferrules. Early examples were made of cane. By the mid-nineteenth century many sticks were turned of other woods in imitation of the true bam-

boo. "The great sort of Reeds or Canes is used especially . . . of aged and wealthy Citizens and great personages to make them walking staves of, carving them at the top with sundry Scutchions and pretty toys of imagerie for the beautifying of them, and so they of the better sort doe garnish them both with silver and gold." John Gerard, *The Herball or Generall Historie of Plantes* (London, 1636).

BANDBOX

The small oval or round box first made in the seventeenth century to hold bands, falling bands, low ruffs, or gentlemen's other neckwear. Later, similar boxes were used for collars, caps, and hats. The earliest bandboxes were made of thin chip or splint wood and later, also, of cardboard covered with

Gilt-decorated, paper-covered bandbox.

Splint bandbox. (Courtesy, Antiquarian and Landmarks Society, Inc.)

paper. The latter often were decorated with freehand or stenciled pictures or cyphers, decoupage, gilt borders, and figures.

"Bandboxes. Wholesale and Retail, made in the neatest manner, cheap as the cheapest. Wm. S. Marsh." *American Mercury* (Hartford, Connecticut), November 11, 1812.

BANDORA, BANDORE

"An ancient musical instrument, whose strings resemble those of the lute." (M) A musical instrument somewhat similar to a guitar or banjo. Bass viols were also commonly called bandores. Bandores are said to have been invented in England by John Rose during the reign of Elizabeth I, but very probably the instrument he introduced was a variation, in both form and name, of the Italian *pandura*.

BANJO CLOCK

The twentieth-century name for an early-nineteenth-century American wall clock. From a circular dial at the top, the case curves in as to a narrow waist, then out to form a rectangular box base. It was first made in 1802 by Simon Willard (1770?–1839) of the famous clockmaking family, who called it his "Patent Timepiece."

Banjo: A corruption of *bandore,* this was an instrument made and used by southern slaves. It was brought to general attention during the heyday of minstrel shows in the late nineteenth and early twentieth centuries. The popularity of the shows, and the similarity of shape between banjo and clock, perhaps prompted the renaming of Willard's timepiece.

BANKS

(See DROP BOX, POOR BOX, THRIFT BOX.)

BANNER SCREEN

A wide, banner-shaped screen made to slide up or down a vertical pole attached to a base; a form of Fire Screen, *q.v.*

BANNIKIN

A contemporary colloquialism for "a small drinking cup" (H) of wood or plated tin; with straight sides, flat base, and a handle. The type kept at the well or in the kitchen beside a pail, water jug, or pottery cistern.

BANISTER-BACK CHAIR

(See BANISTER-BACK, Chapter 5.)

BANQUETTE

A nineteenth-century term for a variety of long low benches or stools; the name was applied variously to upholstered window seats, Hearth Stools, and Daybeds, qq.v.

BANTAM WARE, BANTAM WORK

(See under Chapter 7.)

BAR

Another contemporary name for the long, sturdy door latch or balk, this was "a piece of wood, iron or other matter [strips of heavy waxed leather sewn or riveted together; a single length or belt of leather; or a strong twisted rope] set into iron or wood catches or hold-fasts attached to the door posts and thus crossing a passage to hinder entrance." (J) Many of the carefully planed wooden bars, made of chestnut, oak, walnut, or maple, also were decorated with chip-carving, the owner's initials or the name given his homestead.

BAR-BACK SOFA

The contemporary name for the graceful, open-frame or shield-back settee with a cushion seat. "This kind of sofa is of modern invention, and the lightness of its appearance has procured it a favourable reception in the first circle of fashion. The pattern of the back must match the chairs [in the room]; these also will regulate the [wood] of the frame-work and the sort of covering." A. Hepplewhite, *The Cabinet-Maker's and Upholsterer's Guide* (London, 1788).

BAR BOLT

A type of door latch, similar to those still used today, this was the "piece of iron or wood fastened to a door, and entering into the post or wall to hold the door close." (J)

BARK

(1) A colloquialism for the "cylindrical receptacle for candles; a candle-box," (H) of wood or tin.

(2) A common term for "the tanner's tub." (J) (See also BARKER, Chapter 3.)

BARN LANTERN

Those lanterns made to light one's way to and from outbuildings, or to keep in the barn. They were especially fashioned to guard against mishap caused by sputtering flames or drops of hot grease. "The subscriber has on hand . . . American and English Jappan'd Lamps; Isinglass; Street, barn and hand Lanterns; Nurse Lamps . . . Richard Williams." *American Mercury* (Hartford, Connecticut), February 7, 1811. (See also PAUL REVERE LANTERN.)

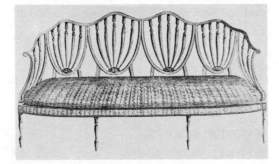

Bar-back sofa design from Hepplewhite's *Guide* (London, 1788).

Half-round barn lantern with handle and hanger.

BAROMETER

"A machine for measuring the weight of the atmosphere, and the variations in it, in order chiefly to determine the changes of the weather. The barometer was invented by [Evangelista] Torricelli at Florence in 1643. It is a glass tube filled with mercury, horizontally sealed at one end . . . as the weight of the atmosphere diminishes, the mercury in the tube will descend, and as it increases, the mercury will ascend." (J) One of the "scientific and philosophical machines" that delighted and bemused ladies and gentlemen of the Colonial period, the barometer was a triumph of the glassmaker's and the cabinet-maker's combined abilities. The majority were imported from England during the early period; it was not until well after 1800 that many were made here, although a number of jewelers advertised that they would have barometers made to order for customers who wished them. (See also WEATHERGLASS.)

Barometer by John M. Peddingham of Colchester, Connecticut. (Courtesy, Connecticut Historical Society, Inc.)

BAROSCOPE

"An instrument to show the weight of the atmosphere . . . the baroscope [differs from the barometer because it] only shows that the air is heavier at one time than another without specifying the difference." (J) (See also BAROMETER, WEATHERGLASS.)

BARREL

"A round wooden vessel to be stopped close." (J) "A vessel extending more in length than in breadth, made of wood, in form of a little tub and serves for holding several sorts of merchandise." (M) (See also in Chapter 4.)

BARREL CHAIR

The collector's term for a type of rustic chair resembling a barrel half cut away; also referred to as a grandfather's chair.

BARREL LANTERN

A contemporary synonym for the cylindrical lantern, as opposed to the flat front half-circle or the rectangular box lantern shapes. "John Arthur, near opposite Mr. William Walton's . . . has received in the last vessels from London . . . barrel and square glass lanthorns . . ." *The New-York Gazette and The Weekly Mercury,* November 22, 1773.

Barrel lantern with horn sides or "lights." (Courtesy, Antiquarian and Landmarks Society, Inc.)

BARREL ORGAN
(See HAND ORGAN.)

BARRIKET, BARRILET
Colloquialisms, combining the words barrel and kit, to describe "a small firkin." (H)

BARTHOLOMEW BABY, BARTHOLOMEW TOY

These once were common terms for the painted wooden or ceramic dolls and other small souvenirs such as patch boxes, collected today. Such toys were sold at the Bartholomew Fair, an annual outdoor market held from 1133 to 1855 in West Smithfield, London. "To Bartholomew fayre and there [saw] the dancing on the ropes, and several other best shows, but pretty it is. Then up and down to buy toys for my wife to give her maids." Samuel Pepys, *Diary*, September 2, 1664. "A Bartelmy Fair or Bartholomew Fair doll is often called a Bartholomew Baby." (H)

BASELRED, BASLARD

In weaponry, an early term for a kind of long dagger, "worn suspended from the girdle." (H)

BASE VIOL

This is "usually written bass-viol, an instrument which is used in concerts for the base sound." (J)

BASHRON, BASHRONE

Apparently a corruption in conversation of bason, used as a synonym for "a kettle." (H)

BASIN, BASON

"A small vessel to hold water for washing and other uses," (J) usually round and fairly shallow, and often spelled "bason" in early accounts. "I recd ½ dozn Basons of Mr. Davies on acct of old Pewter." Joshua

C. 1710 brass basin.

C. 1750 pewter basin.

Hempsted, *Diary*, May 14, 1714. *Collections*, New London, Connecticut Historical Society, Vol. I, 1900. Basins were made of hard woods, bone, horn, gourds, pewter, iron, tin, brass, copper, silver, pottery, porcelain, and sometimes glass. (See EWER and BASIN, BASIN STAND.)

BASIN STAND

During the second half of the eighteenth century this was a carefully made chamber stand with a circular hole in the top board to hold the wash basin. Often made with a lower shelf to hold the ewer, and a drawer below this for toilet articles; the basin stand usually was three-sided, being made to fit into a corner. It was by no means a common colonial household article: "The best chamber [was furnished with] the case of drawers handsomely carved, the chairs matched those below [in the parlor] and there was a novelty, the first wash-stand I ever saw, a pretty triangular one of mahogany, a light graceful pattern to fit into a corner of a room." (Description of a Newburyport home, c. 1790.) Sarah Anna Emery, *Reminiscences of a Nonagenarian* (Newburyport, Massachusetts, 1879).

By the end of the first quarter of the nineteenth century, the English term basin stand had given way to the American wash-hand stand, washstand, or washing stand; and most such stands then were made in square or rectangular shapes: "Aaron Chapin & Son [Laertes]. At their shop seventy rods north of the Court House

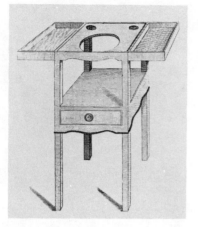

Hepplewhite bason stand. (*Guide,* London, 1794.)

have on hand a general assortment of mahogany and cherry House Furniture, both plain and elegant, Among which are sideboards, secretarys, desks, book-cases, bureaus, tables, bedsteads, wash-stands, candle-stands . . . Ec., Ec., which they offer for sale on liberal terms." *American Mercury* (Hartford, Connecticut), August 11, 1808.

BASKET

"A vessel made of twigs, rushes, or some other slender bodies interwoven." (J) ". . . to hold fruit, earth, Ec. It denotes a certain quantity of some commodities, as a basket of medlars is two bushels." (M)

Hepplewhite corner bason stand. (*Guide,* London, 1794.)

New England, late-eighteenth-century bason stand. (Courtesy, Antiquarian and Landmarks Society, Inc.)

Baskets. (Courtesy, Antiquarian and Landmarks Society, Inc.)

223

Baskets. (Courtesy, Antiquarian and Landmarks Society, Inc.)

BASKET CHAIR

The early description of a chair made of woven rushes or reeds, generally similar to the type we now call a wicker chair. From at least the sixteenth century when John Donne described one in *Elegie I,*

> *Nor when he swoln, and pamper'd with great fare*
> *Sits down, and snorts, cag'd in his basket chaire,*

through the nineteenth century, the plaiting or basket weaving of easily acquired rush,

slender sapling boughs or twigs provided the handy countryman with a chair, stool, or bench. During the same periods, similar woven chairs were manufactured for use in better homes; as garden and grotto seats; in summer sitting rooms, and later as Victorian porch furniture.

BASKET SPIT

A kitchen hearth cooking utensil; a spit rod in the center of which was a basket formed of iron strips in which small fowl or chunks of meat were roasted.

BASKET STAND

Usually nicely made, this small tripod parlor stand was designed specifically to hold a woman's "work" or sewing materials, the circular basket top having a gallery rim of 3 to 6 inches in height. Such a basket stand was a "prettier and more convenient arti-

Basket stands illustrated by A. J. Downing in *The Architecture of Country Houses* (New York, 1850).

cle" than the worktable, being "more suitable to the parlor," A. J. Downing said in discussing furniture proper to the country house, because it could be "easily lifted and carried about from one part of the room to another—wherever it may be most agreeable to sit." *The Architecture of Country Houses* (New York, 1850). (See also CANTERBURY, DUMB-WAITER.)

BASS, BAST

A stuffed or rushed chair seat, "a cushion made of straw [such as is] used in churches to kneel on," (B) or a straw mat. Bass, or bast, was the soft inner bark of white wood cut into strips for baskets and chair-seat splints.

BASSET TABLE

Basset or Bassette was a "game of cards invented at Venice," (J) introduced into France in the late seventeenth century and thence to England and the colonies in the eighteenth century. The Basset table was a small board designed for use in playing the game. (See also GAME TABLE.)

BASSON, BASSOON

"A musical instrument of the wind kind, blown with a reed, and furnished with eleven holes, which are stopped like other large flutes; its diameter at bottom is nine inches, and it serves for the bass in concerts of hautboys, etc." (J) Marching songs of the period were accompanied not alone by fife and drum—for "Musicians are wanted for a regiment; two good Horns, a Clarinet, a Bassoon, and a person capable of directing a band, to all of whom good encouragement will be given." *Royal Gazette* (New York), August 15, 1778.

BASS VIOL

"A musical instrument of the stringed kind, resembling a violin, but much larger," (M) and the first instrument permitted as accompaniment to the singing of psalms in colonial New England church meetings. "Aaron Chapin [has] now ready for sale cheap and good, various articles of mahogany and cherry tree furniture, sundry Bass Viols, complete for use; Pitch Pipes; Fifes; Watches do. Seals, Keys, Chains, Ec." *Connecticut Courant* (Hartford), December 17, 1798.

BASTER

A wood or iron cooking spoon or ladle. "To baste is to drip butter or anything else upon meat as it turns on the spit." (J)

BATH

During the Colonial period, this was "a sufficient quantity of water collected in some convenient receptacle, for people to wash in, either for health or pleasure." (M) A vessel or tub of wood, metal or marble, usually movable.

Tin Bath: The high, round- or oval-shaped tub of heavy sheet tin, sometimes given a painted exterior decoration; promoted during the early nineteenth century when concerned citizens took advantage of any opportunity to remind others that "every person should have, if he can afford it, a cold and a warm bath in his house. These can be had at any tinman's at a moderate expense." *The Domestic Encyclopedia* (Philadelphia, 1821); Because, frankly, "in our times it would be of great service if the use of baths were more general and frequent, and this beneficial practice not confined to particular places [seaside or spa] or seasons, as a mere matter of fashion." Thomas Tegg, *Book of Utility* (London, 1828).

BATH STOVE

The description of an ornamental as well as useful hearth grate, so called because the style was popularized at the famous hotels at Bath, England. "I intend to give Hirst the Dimensions of a bath stove for one of my Chimneys, which I beg the favor of you to send over by the first Opportunity. I think the Secy told me his did not cost above 50/ or £3 at most." (Order June 21, 1773 from Robert C. Nicholas, Williamsburg, to London.) Frances Mason, *John Norton & Sons, Merchants of London and Virginia* (Richmond, 1935).

"N.B. The Dimensions for a Bath Stove which in a former letter I told you should be sent was in a Hurry forgot. The Chimney Place for which it was intend is of the following Dimensions. In front it is exactly 3 feet seven Inches wide, it is contracted toward the back where it is only three feet wide. The Height from the bottom of the Hearth to the under part of the Arch in front is two feet eleven Inches—The Depth of the Chimney from the Face of the Jam to the Back is one foot 8½ Inches—this is the exact measure. So that some allowance must be made for the Stove to go in. I should be glad to have it sent over by the very first Opportunity. October 15, 1773." Ibid. (See also GRATE.)

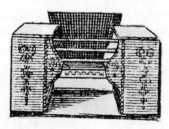

Bath stove, c. 1790 print.

BATLET

This was the name of a laundry utensil, the "square piece of wood with a handle used in beating linen when taken out of the buck." (J)

BATTER JUG

The collector's term for a large milk jug or pitcher in which batter sometimes was mixed and from which it was poured on to the griddle.

Batter jug.

BATTERSEA ENAMELED WARE

Small pocket, table, and cabinet objects made with a copper base coated with tin enamel and decorated with paint or transfer printing. Snuff boxes, patch boxes, decanter labels, watch cases, inkstands, and candlesticks were among the many products of the factory, opened in 1752–53 by Stephen Theodore Janssen at York House, Battersea, London. The company name was Janssen, Delamain and Brooks. Unhappily, Janssen was forced to declare bankruptcy in 1756; most of the small wares called Battersea today were not the products of his factory but of others. The ground colors used were white or yellow. Those items specifically noted as having been manufactured at the Battersea works, according to the bankruptcy auction sale notice, included "snuff boxes of all sizes and a great variety of patterns, of square and oval pictures of the Royal Family, History, and other pleasing objects, very proper ornaments for the cabinets of the curious; Bottle-tickets with chains for all sorts of Liquor, and of different subjects; watch-cases; Toothpick cases; Coat and Sleeve Buttons; Crosses and other Curiousities, mostly mounted in metal, double gilt." (See also BILSTONWARE, PAINTED ENAMELWARE.)

BATTLE-AX
"A kind of [short-handled] halbert used by the infantry; first introduced into England by the Danes." (M)

BATTLEDORE
An early cant term for "hornbook," (H) and also used to designate a beetle or wooden bat used in washing and beating clothes (see BATLET) because both resembled in shape the true battledore, "an instrument with a handle and a flat board, used in play to strike a ball or shuttlecock." (J)

BAUBLE
"A Gewgaw [q.v.], a trifling piece of finery, a thing of more show than use." (J)

BAXTER
An old term for baker, and by extension to anything flat or baked; thus, also a term for "an implement used for baking cakes upon." (H)   (See also BACKSTONE.)

BAYONET
"A broad dagger fixed at the end of a gun." (W)   First made to fit inside the muzzle, this was the short sword or dagger used to convert a gun into a pike during hand-to-hand combat. By 1700, the second or fixed type of bayonet was developed, being made to fit by means of a ring or tube over the muzzle, and with the blade offset so that the gun could be fired without removing the bayonet. "Charles Sigourney, Main Street Has imported in the brig Rhine from Am-

sterdam, arrived at Boston, A quantity of French muskets with bayonets *which were actually in use at the battle of Waterloo." American Mercury* (Hartford, Connecticut), August 19, 1815.

Bayonet attached to musket. (Courtesy, Antiquarian and Landmarks Society, Inc.)

BEADS
From the Saxon word for prayer, these were "small globes or balls of glass or pearl, or other substance, strung upon a thread . . . little balls worn about the neck for ornament." (J)   "Beades of Amber, Bone, Box [wood], Corall, Christal, Glass & Wood, Jasper Square" were listed in the House of Parliament Rates, 1660, for Imports and Exports—*Statutes of the Realm* (London, 1819).

BEAK
An old colloquial term for a kind of kitchen fireplace crane, "an iron over the fire [from] which boilers are hung." (H)

BEAKER
From the Middle English word *biker* or the Latin *bicarium,* for a large drinking glass with a wide mouth; originally perhaps, such a vessel with a cover. Johnson, however, said the name was derived from beak because it was "a cup with a spout in the form of a bird's beak." The English forms were followed here; the earliest were straight-sided with flaring rims, followed by the bell-shape on a low base favored during the Queen Anne period; the more egg-shaped or ovoid design was used between 1760–1810.

BEAM
In architecture, a horizontal timber support, but also, a colonial colloquialism for

candle, and so at times for a candle Sconce or a Chandelier, *qq.v.*

BEAU BRUMMEL

The collector's name for a gentleman's dressing stand, chest, or table fitted with a shaving mirror and drawers. It was made in the second half of the eighteenth century a number of years before George Bryan Brummel was born (1788). The top of the stand was comprised of two hinged leaves designed to drop at either side when the table was in use—that is, opened—and which folded over to "close" the table. This was a more elegant form of the small chest sometimes called a Bachelor's Chest, *q.v.*, today.

Beau: "A man of dress; a man whose great care is to deck his person." (J)

BEAUFET, BUFFET

Beaufet was the early spelling of the word now commonly written buffet, for a "kind of cupboard for plate or china;" (W) "a set of shelves where plate is set out to show in a room of entertainment." (J) The term was used interchangeably for a side or serving table, and for a type of corner cupboard. "Another corner was occupied by a beaufet, which was a corner closet with a glass door, in which all the china of the family and the plate was intended to be displayed for ornament as well as use." John F. Watson, *Annals and Occurrences of New York City and State in the Olden Time* (Philadelphia, 1846). (See also COURT CUPBOARD; SIDEBOARD.)

BECKY

A colloquialism among those of Scots-Irish descent for a "small wooden dish." (H)

BEDCHAIR

(See CHAIR BED, HUNTING CHAIR, SLEEPING CHAIR.)

BED CUPBOARD

The nineteenth-century term for the eighteenth-century Pot Cupboard, *q.v.*

BED-POLE

The New England colloquialism for the tester or canopy rail. (See also TESTER BED.)

BEDSTEAD

A place for a bed; that is, a rectangular frame on four legs or posts with side and end rails pierced with holes through which cords were threaded to support the bed, as the mattress was called. Above, either suspended from the ceiling, braced against the wall, or supported on the four high posts, was the tester or canopy. Curtains, sometimes referred to as bed curtains, listed among the "furniture" of the bed, were suspended from the tester. At night the curtains were drawn around the bed to keep out drafts.

Pencil-post bedstead with tester, curtains, and valance. (Courtesy, Antiquarian and Landmarks Society, Inc.)

"R. G. Allen has on hand 200 Bedsteads, consisting of mahogany carved, high and French panelled, cherry ditto, birch, high, and French, canopy, turn-up, cot, trundle ditto." *Literary Cadet and Rhode Island Statesman* (Providence), February 20, 1828.

Design for a bedstead from Hepplewhite's *Guide* (London, 1794).

BED-STEDDLE
An old corruption in conversation of the term "bedstead." (H)

BED STEPS
A kind of low step stool or set of steps to help the user enter the high bedstead of the eighteenth century with ease and dignity. Some served an additional purpose: "The tread of the top step is hinged and lifts up; the middle step pulls forward; and when drawn out, its lid lifts up and shows a space for a bidet or other convenience." John C. Loudon, *Encyclopedia of Cottage, Farm and Villa Architecture* (London, 1833).

BED TABLE
In the last quarter of the eighteenth century, this was a shaped lap table or tray with short, folding legs.

BED WARMER
(See VIRGIN, WARMING PAN.)

BED WINDER
The T-shaped wooden tool used to pull and tighten the cords stretched between the end and side rails of a bedstead to hold the bedding.

Bed winder.

BEEHIVE
A home for bees provided by the canny farmer or gardener who wanted to insure a supply of wax and honey; antique examples are sought by restorationists to complete garden settings; by interior decorators for use in conservatories and solaria. Roughly made, dome-shaped straw hives are being reproduced today in Europe, much larger than their prototypes: "Those made of straw are the best, on many accounts . . . As the ingenious Mr. Wildman's hives are reckoned to be of a preferable construction, we shall give an account in his own words: 'My hives,' says he, 'are seven inches in height, and ten in width. The sides are up-right, so that the top and bottom are of the same diameter. A hive holds nearly a peck.

Each hive should stand single on a piece of deal, somewhat larger than the bottom of the hive . . . that part at the mouth of the hive projecting some inches for the bees to rest on. The stand should be supported on a single post two and a half feet high to which it should be screwed very securely.' " (M) Hives were made of straw, rush, thatch, wood, and sometimes glass: "After dinner to Mr. [John] Evelyn's . . . we walked in his garden, and a lovely, noble ground he hath indeed. And among other rarities, a hive of bees. So as, being hived in glass, you may see the bees making their honey and combs mighty pleasantly." Samuel Pepys, *Diary,* May 5, 1665. In Scotland and northern English counties, beehives were called bee-skeps, a term used here by emigrants from those areas.

BEEHIVE CHAIR

A type of basket-woven seat, "a wattled straw-chair, common among cottagers." (H)   (See also BASKET CHAIR.)

BEER WAGON

Another term for the table Coaster, *q.v.,* or bottle slider.

BEE-SKEP

(See BEEHIVE, SCEP.)

BEETLE

"A large, heavy mallet; a rammer." (W) "A heavy mallet, or wooden hammer, with which wedges are driven." (J)

BELL

Then, as now, this was "a vessel or hollow body of cast metal formed to make a noise by the act of a clapper, hammer, or some other instrument striking against it . . ." Also, "a small, hollow globe of metal perforated and containing in it a solid ball, which when it is shaken, by bounding against the sides, gives a sound" (J) as, for example, a sleigh bell. Handsome table bells, with which the hostess signaled servants, were made of blown and cut glass, as well as metal and porcelain. Among bells col-

lected today also are the small sizes once hung by thongs about the necks of cattle and oxen, sheep, cats, and dogs; the sets or series of bells mounted on plates for use at shop entrances; school bells, both the large sizes hung in frames outside the building and the small brass, wood-handled desk bells used in the classroom; ship's bells; the medium-sized dinner bells kept at the kitchen door of the farmhouse. And, in addition, the bell was "a well-known machine ranked by musicians among the musical instruments of percussion. The metal of which a bell is made is a composition of tin and copper, or pewter and copper. The proportion of one to the other is almost twenty pounds of pewter or twenty-three pounds of tin to one hundred weight of copper." (M) "Hawkes bells; Horse bells; Doggs bells; Clapper Bells" were listed in the House of Parliament Rates, 1660, for Imports and Exports—*Statutes of the Realm* (London, 1819).

Brass hand bell or teacher's desk bell. (Courtesy, Antiquarian and Landmarks Society, Inc.)

Iron cow bell.

BELLARMINE JUG

The derisive name given by seventeenth-century Dutch protestants to stoneware jugs made in the shape of a bearded man's head; these were said to represent Cardinal Bellarmine, hence the name Bellarmine or Greybeard Jugs.

> . . . like a larger jug that some men call
> A Bellarmine, but we a conscience,
> Whereon the tender hand of Pagan work-
> man
> Over the proud ambitious head hath
> carved
> An idol large, with beard episcopal.
>   William Cartwright, *The Ordinary*
>   (London, 1651).

BELL GLASS

Another name for a type of Bell Jar, *q.v.* "Send . . . Three Bell Glasses for the Garden," order September 25, 1771 from Peter Lyons, Hanover, Virginia, to London. Frances Mason, *John Norton and Sons, Merchants of London and Virginia* (Richmond, 1935). (See also BEEHIVE, BELL JAR.)

BELL JAR

Any tall glass, open at the bottom but rounded and closed at the top, and thus, in form resembling a bell. Used on the sideboard, as a protective cover for food; elsewhere to keep dry flower arrangements and the like from dust or other damage. (See also BEEHIVE, BELL GLASS.)

BELLOWS

"The instrument used to blow the fire." (J) "Merchants and others may be supplied by the Dozen or single pair, of the best quality made of hard timber and best materials, and manufactured with Care. Old Bellows carefully repaired by Ebenezer Moore. N.B. to distinguish his from the inferiour qualities, his name will be stamped on each pair. Wanted—oak-tanned Sheep Skins." *American Mercury* (Hartford, Connecticut), October 14, 1812.

Bellows.

BELL PULL
(See HOUSE BELLS.)

BENCH

The general term for "a seat, distinguished from a stool by its greater length," (J) used at the hearth; as seats between or under windows, in halls or foyers, or as workstands.

C. 1720 painted bench. (Courtesy, Antiquarian and Landmarks Society, Inc.)

BENKIT

A type of bucket with a cover, "a wooden vessel with a cover that's loose, and fitted with notches in two prominent lags [ears] that have a string through them to carry it by." (H)

BERGERE

From the French word once used to describe a type of upholstered easy chair; bergere also is found in eighteenth-century inventories as burjair, bergier, booujar, etc. Sheraton said a bergere had "a caned back

231

and arms. Sometimes the seats are caned, having loose cushions." *The Cabinet Dictionary* (London, 1803). (See also CABRIOLE CHAIR; CABRIOLE, Chapter 5.)

BESOM
Originally, the Middle English word for a bundle of twigs used for birching or flogging; later it signified a bunch of broom twigs tied to a handle, and thus became a generic term for "A broom [of cane, rush, birch] to sweep with." (J)   (See also BIRCH.)

BETTY
The contemporary cant term for an "instrument to break doors open with," (W) a kind of iron or wooden rammer used by fire companies.

BETTY LAMP
The collector's common name for a type of Cruse, *q.v.,* the simple fat, grease, or lard lamp; the source of the name is much de-

Iron betty lamp with cover for bowl, hanger, and pick.

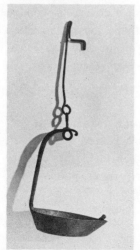

Iron betty lamp with hanger.

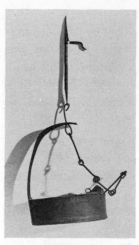

Tin betty lamp with cover, hanger, and pick.

bated. Perhaps from *petite,* meaning little; perhaps from *betying,* meaning leavings or crude fat. If it was a colonial colloquialism or cant term, it does not seem to have been included in dictionaries or encyclopediae of the period.

BEVEL
"An instrument used by masons, carpenters, joiners, Ec. for measuring angles. It is a kind of square, one leg of which moves on a centre, and may therefore be set to any angle." (M)

BIBLE
Although numerous early copies, based on Dutch and German translations were brought here by early colonists, these gradually were superseded in the seventeenth century by the Authorized Version, or King James Version, first published in 1611. Bible is "the name given by Christians to the collection of sacred writings, or the holy scriptures of the Old and New Testaments; known also by various other appellations, as the Sacred Books, Holy Writ, Inspired Writings, Scriptures, Ec. The Jews stiled the Bible (that is, the Old Testament) *Mikra,* which signifies Lesson or Lecture." (M) "Mrs. Nicholas desires the favour of you to chuse her a handsome Bible & Prayer Book for her own use, with her name Ann Nicholas on the outer cover." (Order, January 4, 1771, from Robert Nicholas, Williamsburg,

Virginia, to London.) Frances Mason, *John Norton and Sons, Merchants of London and Virginia* (Richmond, 1935). (See also DOUAY BIBLE.)

BIBLE BOX

The collector's misnomer for Desk Box, *q.v.* A romantic name, apparently adopted in the Late Victorian or Centennial period, for a type of small seventeenth- and eighteenth-century carved wooden box.

BIBLIOTHECA

The word, originally signifying a library or repository for books, was "often used as the title of a treatise, containing an account of all the writers on some particular subject," (M) as an anthology.

BICKER

A contemporary colloquialism for a "small wooden dish made of staves and hoops like a tub; also a tumbler," and when so used, another form of Beaker, *q.v.* (H)

BICKERN

One of the basic tools, the name "apparently corrupted from beak iron," (J) the pointed end of the smith's anvil.

BIDET

The small, painted and/or gilt-decorated chamber bath stool or low cupboard with a pierced seat or box top that held a metal or pottery pan. "Bathing in cold water and the daily use of the bidet contribute greatly to health as well as to cleanliness. No bedroom ought to want this useful article of furniture." *The Domestic Encyclopedia* (Philadelphia, 1821).

BIDET SHAVING TABLE

This was the description of a particular "Dressing or Shaving Table, with the usual conveniencies, and also a Bidet, which draws out and is supported by half-legs; this . . . has been much approved for its use and conveniencies." A. Hepplewhite, *The Cabinet-Maker and Upholsterer's Guide* (London, 1794). Shown was a rectangular shaving stand; a false drawer front at the base below the ewer shelf concealed the pull-out Bidet, *q.v.*

Bidet shaving table illustrated in Hepplewhite's *Guide* (London, 1794).

Bidet illustrated in Hepplewhite's *Guide* (London, 1794).

BIGGIN

A cap or nightcap.

> *As he whose brow with homely biggen bound,*
> *Snores out the watch of night.*
>
> Shakespeare, *King Henry IV,* Part II, IV, v.

Biggin also was "A kind of cap or coif used for a child." (W) Hence, it was a slang term for any small cup or wooden bowl.

BIJOUTERIE
This all-inclusive term for trinkets also was applied to a type of silk- or velvet-lined medal or display case set on a stand and having a framed glass lid.

BILBO
"A rapier; a fine or choice sword." (W) The term was "corrupted from Bilboa [Spain], where the best weapons are made." (J)

BILL
The name given "a kind of hatchet with a hooked point, used in country work, as a hedging bill, so-called from its resemblance to the beak of a bird of prey." This also was the name of "a kind of weapon carried by the foot [soldier], a battle-axe." (J)

BILLIARDS
"A game at which a ball is forced against another on a table." (J)

BILLIARD TABLE
"To be sold by Mathew Garrigue at the sign of the Prince Eugene in Second Street a good new Billiard Table with all its appurtenances for a reasonable price . . ." *American Weekly Mercury* (Philadelphia), February 11, 1723/24. "Charles Shipman, Ivory and Hardwood Turner . . . [makes] billiard balls . . . cups and balls, dice boxes, backgammons and chess men . . ." *The New York Journal or The General Advertiser,* August 6, 1767.

BILSTONWARE
The general term for painted or transfer-printed enameled wares produced after 1780 at Bilston, a town in south Staffordshire, England. Many of these are attributed in error to the Battersea factory. In the nineteenth century Bilston produced pottery. Ground colors used on Bilston enamelware were rose du Barry, royal blue, turquoise, yellow and pink. (See also BATTERSEA ENAMELED WARE.)

Bilston boxes.

BIN
The common term for any "repository for corn or wine; chest; or box." (W)

BINOCLE
The contemporary name for "a kind of telescope, fitted so with two tubes joining together in one, as that a distant object may be seen with both eyes together." (J) They are called binoculars today.

BIRCH (BROOM)
A long birch stick, one end of which was shaved so as to form long, slender shreds, used as a hearth or floor broom and for other cleaning needs: "To stew cockles. Put two hundred cockles into a pail of water, and wash them well with a birch broom . . ." Richard Briggs, *The New Art of Cookery* (Philadelphia, 1792). (See also BESOM.)

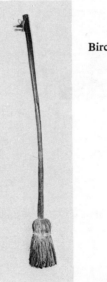
Birch broom.

234

BIRD CAGE

Then as now, "an inclosure with interstitial spaces, made of wire or wicker, in which birds are kept," (J) but sometimes much more ornamental and expensive than those we know today. "This night comes two cages, which I bought this evening for my canary birds." Samuel Pepys, *Diary,* January 25, 1660–61. The cages often were made of flat strips of tin or tin-plated iron, silver-plated tin, pewter or brass wire, sometimes with glazed pottery or porcelain floors; others were of wood or wicker. (See also advertisement quoted under NEEDLE-MAKER, Chapter 3.)

BIRD CAGE TABLE

(See BIRD CAGE, Chapter 5.)

BIRD CALL

They had other uses than in the decoy. "I saw an ordinary fellow carrying a cage full of little birds . . . for the opera . . . they are to enter towards the end of the first act, and to fly about the stage . . . to act the part of singing birds in a delightful grove . . . [However] though they flew in sight, the music proceded from a concert of flagelets and bird-calls which were planted behind the scenes." Addison and Steele, *The Spectator,* No. V (London, March 6, 1710–11).

Wooden bird call or turkey caller, also used as supper whistle. (Courtesy, Antiquarian and Landmarks Society, Inc.)

BIRDING PIECE

Another contemporary term for "A fowling-piece, a small gun to shoot birds with," (J) in the field, and sometimes in the home, to discourage the building of flue-choking birds' nests.

I'll creep up into the chimney. There they always use to discharge their birding-pieces.

Shakespeare, *The Merry Wives of Windsor,* IV, ii.

"To be sold Cheap by Edward Annely, Gun Smith, at the Fly Market . . . some Birding Pieces, with Bayonets in their Buts for Gentlemen's Use, and Guns with Bayonets fit either for Military Use or Fowling . . ." *The New-York Gazette and Weekly Post-boy,* August 1, 1748.

Birding or fowling piece used by Nathan Hale. (Courtesy, Antiquarian and Landmarks Society, Inc.)

BIRD SPIT

A wrought-iron or steel vertical rod fitted with projecting prongs, usually set above a footed pan to catch the drippings; used for roasting small birds such as quail. ". . . After they are picked and trussed, put them on a bird spit, toast on both sides, baste them often . . ." Richard Briggs, *The New Art of Cookery* (Philadelphia, 1792).

Bird spit.

BISHOP'S BOWL

A kind of punch bowl, usually of faïence, often designed in imitation of the shape of a bishop's mitre, and used for the mixing and serving of the drink called bishop.

"**Bishop:** This is a very old liquor; when made of old Rhine wine it was called Cardinal, and when of Tokay it had the name of Pope. It is at best a superior orange wine. The day before it is wanted, grill over a slow fire, till of a fine brown colour, 3 smooth skinned large bitter oranges; place them in the small punch bowl that will about hold them, and pour over them a half-pint of Bordeaux wine in which 1¼ lb. of loaf sugar is dissolved. Cover with a plate; when wanted to be served the next day, cut and squeeze the oranges into a small sieve, placed over a jug containing 1½ pints of the same wine, previously made very hot, add more sugar if it is wanted. Serve it in winter time hot in large glasses. In summer it need not be heated at all; on the contrary, it may be iced." G. W. Francis, *The Dictionary of Practical Receipts* (London, 1847).

BITTERS BOTTLE

Bitters was a general term for any liquor to which an extract of gentian, quassia, orange, or other citron was added to produce a stomachic. The old bottles, especially those that were labeled, are prized by some modern collectors. "500 Bottles genuine Stoughton's Bitters, made twelve months since, well worthy the attention of Tavernkeepers and others, who wish a superior article. The above, with an entire Fresh Stock of Drugs, Medicines and Wines, are for sale at the sign of the 'Good Samaritan', north side State-House square." *American Mercury* (Hartford, Connecticut), January 18, 1823. (See also BOTTLE, JUNK BOTTLE, MEDICINE BOTTLE, SNUFF BOTTLE.)

BITTLIN

A colloquialism for a small wooden "milk bowl." (H)

Bittlin.

BLACKING BOX

A type of shallow, covered, gallipot of pottery, porcelain, or tin, often mistaken for a kind of soap container; used to hold cakes of leather-blacking or dressing to keep them from drying out. Blacking was used to feed, improve the appearance, and to waterproof leather. (See also LEATHER BLACKING, Chapter 8.)

BLACKJACK

Another name for the waxed or varnished leather tankard or jug. (See also JACK, TANKARD.)

Early-eighteenth-century leather blackjack or tankard. (Courtesy, Antiquarian and Landmarks Society, Inc.)

BLACKPOT
Another name for the blackjack or leather tankard. (See also JACK, TANKARD.)

BLACK TEAPOT
The common early-nineteenth-century term for Jackfield or Jasper teapots, or teapots made of other basaltes. The inventory of the estate of Joseph Arnold, May 14, 1823, Haddam, Connecticut, thus included the listings, "1 red earthen wash bowl, .12; 1 black teapot, .10; 1 tin coffeepot, .12."

BLANKET
"A coverlet for a bed; also, a stuff [of which coverlets are made] commonly made of white wool, and wrought in a loom like cloth, with this difference that they are crossed like serges." (M) (See also COUNTERPANE.)

BLANKET BOX, BLANKET CHEST
Collector's terms for the Clothes Chest or Six-board Chest, q.v.

C. 1700 blanket box.

C. 1800 blanket box. (Courtesy, Antiquarian and Landmarks Society, Inc.)

BLANKET CRANE
(See DRYING CRANE.)

BLEEDING BOWL
Apparently a collector's term for any receptacle which may have been used by the barber, surgeon, or physician who bled patients as a method of purging. Some have believed the Porringer, q.v., was used for this purpose and others that a barber's Shaving Basin, q.v., was so used. Since some care was taken to extract exact amounts of blood, it would seem the name should be given only to those receptacles marked off to show the number of ounces contained. The term is not included in dictionaries of the period. It is possible the following reference is to this kind of utensil: "June 16, 1707. My house broken open in two places, and about twenty pounds worth of Plate [silver] stolen away . . ." "June 19. The measuring Bason is found . . ." Samuel Sewall, *Diary*.

BLIND FRAME
(See BACKBOARD, Chapter 5.)

BLOOD PORRINGER
A contemporary term. (See BLEEDING BOWL, PORRINGER.)

BLOWER, BLOWING PIPE, BLOWING TUBE
A hearth utensil. Forerunner of the more familiar bellows used to encourage embers to blow up and blaze, this was a hollow brass or iron tube, rather like a long peashooter. Those rare examples found are sometimes misidentified as extraordinarily tall single candle molds—and for good reason. The tube stood upright at the hearth on three small buttons—feet or braces—was given a slight rim or flange around the top or pipe end, and had an ear or lug handle. The user blew into the top, thus forcing a draft of air out the lower end of the pipe and under the kindling or embers of the fire. (See also BELLOWS.)

BLUDGEON

In weaponry, this was "a short stick, with one end loaded, used as an offensive weapon." (J)

BLUE GLASSES

(See GLASS INSERTS.)

BLUNDERBUSS

"A short wide gun," (W) with a flared muzzle, popular because the large mouth made it easy to load. Used in the army chiefly by the cavalry, and in the navy for firing at close range; the blunderbuss also was a favorite civilian weapon for the protection of households against intruders. Contrary to legend, it was not in use in this country until early in the eighteenth century. "A well known fire arm consisting of a wide, short barrel, capable of holding a number of small bullets at once." (M)

BLUNT

A colloquialism for the fencer's Foil, *q.v.* (See note under FENCING MASTER, Chapter 3.)

BOARD BED, BOARD BEDSTEAD

(See BOX BEDSTEAD.)

BOARD CHEST

The collector's term for any simple, little-ornamented chest made of wide boards nailed or mortised to stiles or end-to-end. A plain, bin-like chest.

BOARDING AX

(See POLEAX.)

BOB

"Something that hangs so as to play loosely; generally an ornament at the ear; an earring." (J) The term also was used to denote a clock pendulum.

BOBBIN

(See LOOM.)

BOBÈCHE

The disc of glass or metal set on the socket of the candlestick to catch drippings; or the Socket, *q.v.,* or socket pan, itself with a wide rim.

Candlesticks with bobèches.

BODDLE

One of the old tools, a small iron "instrument [with a flat blade] which woodmen use for peeling [the bark] from oaks and other trees," (H) especially used by those who supplied tanners. Another name for this tool was butting iron. To bod meant to husk.

BODKIN

Originally any short, pointed weapon such as a dagger, hence any small, pointed instrument used to pierce holes in cloth or leather to ease the passage of tapes or thongs; also a long pin used to fasten women's hair. ". . . Imported by the Ship Radius from London . . . Steel Bodkins, Steel tops for thimbles, Elastic knitting Pins, Superfine White Chapel Needles . . ." *American Mercury* (Hartford, Connecticut), November 23, 1809.

BOLEDISH, BOLEDYSSHE, BOLDYCHE, BOWLDISH

Old forms of the word for Bowl or Basin, *qq.v.,* combining bole and dish, to mean "a large round dish, chiefly used for lavatory purposes," (H) *i.e.,* a washbowl.

BOLSTER

The name, then as now, for "a long, stuffed pillow laid on the bed to raise and support the head; commonly a bag filled with down or feathers." (J)

BOLTER, BOULTYNG, BULTEL, BULTELLE

The name of "a sieve to separate meal from bran or husks." (J) "Bolting Cloths. H. & S. Chaffee have just received an assortment of Bolting Cloths, from No 1 to 12. They are real Dutch Cloths, of a superior quality, and will be Sold on the most reasonable terms. State St." *American Mercury* (Hartford, Connecticut), January 20, 1818.

BOLTING ARK

Bolting was a synonym for sifting; hence, this was a common country colloquialism for the box known also as an Ark or a Bolting Hutch, *qq. v.*

BOLTING HUTCH

The covered bin into which meal or flour was sifted and stored. Today we would say flour box or flour canister. Bolting hutch, as a container for a large amount of food, was one of Shakespeare's derogatory names for Falstaff in *King Henry IV*, Part I, II, iv. (See also ARK, BOLTING ARK.)

BOMBARD

A kind of large Blackjack, *q.v.,* or leather drinking vessel; also a wine keg, hence Shakespeare's description of Falstaff as that

Swollen parcel . . .
that huge bombard of sack.

King Henry IV, Part I, II, iv.

The ancient term is still echoed in today's cant phrase for someone who has imbibed too much, "he was bombed." (See also JACK.)

BOMBARDO

"A musical instrument of the wind kind much the same as the bassoon and used as a bass to the hautboy." (M)

BONBONNIERE

The term adopted from the French for a small, ornate sweetmeat box, made of gold, silver, porcelain, enameled ware; rarely of glass.

BONHEUR-DU-JOUR

The fanciful advertising name given a small Georgian writing table set on tall slender legs with a shallow cabinet and fitted drawers above.

BONNET BOX

A contemporary name for the covered storage or travel box specifically made to hold a woman's hat. These were fashioned of thin splint or pasteboard molded into round or oval shapes, lined, then covered with paper, which was decorated with watercolor or decoupage designs. Many other late-eighteenth-century and nineteenth-century boxes were covered with wallpaper samples. "Bernard Andrews . . . nearly opposite his Excellency General Gage's . . . makes and sells all kinds of Paper Work in the neatest manner, as Hat, Patch, and Bonnet Boxes, at the most reasonable Rates. If any Ladies should have an inclination to learn Embroidery or any of the above mentioned Work, he will attend them either at his lodgings or at their own Houses, as it shall best suit." *The New-York Gazette and The Weekly Mercury,* April 16, 1770. (See also BANDBOX.)

Bonnet box. (Courtesy, Antiquarian and Landmarks Society, Inc.)

BONNET CHEST

A tall, narrow chest fitted with deep drawers for the storage of wigs, hats, or bonnets.

Sometimes the term was applied to one of the deep drawers in the upper or lower parts of chests-on-chests, or to the deep drawers in the lower section of those tall chests now usually called highboys.

BONNET CUPBOARD
The tall, narrow cupboard with deep shelves, especially made for the dressing room or bed chamber, to be used as a wardrobe for wig stands, bonnets, or hats; sometimes made with only three sides so as to fit easily into a corner.

BOOK
The contemporary term for any written or printed matter, whether on a sheet of paper or other surface, as a horn book or a slate book, or as a series of sheets of paper stitched together. "The composition of a man of wit and learning, designed to communicate somewhat he has invented, experienced, or collected, to the publick, and thence to posterity; being withal of a competent length to make a volume. In this sense a book is distinguished from a pamphlet by its greater length, and from a tome by its containing the whole writing." (M)

> The "Olive Branch."
> FOR SALE, at this Office, a few copies of the "OLIVE BRANCH,"—the contents of which, every man in America ought to make himself acquainted with.— Price $1.

> AUCTION THIS DAY,
> AT TWO O'CLOCK.
> 20 BBLS. Canal APPLES, which must be sold to close a consignment. After which a lot of Miscellaneous BOOKS.
> J. ATWATER & SON, Auctioneers.
> Dec. 12. 90

Book advertisements. (Upper), *American Mercury* (Hartford, Connecticut), June 12, 1817; (Lower), *Connecticut Gazette* (New Haven), December 12, 1829.

BOOK BINDINGS
Books usually were purchased unbound and were sent to a bindery to be covered in the owner's choice of leather or cloth boards; the titles stamped on book tickets or Tags, *q.v.,* in gold leaf or a contrasting ink color: "Book Binding executed in the neatest manner. Old Books re-bound and repaired on the shortest notice. Those who hold the Classicks or Encyclopedia unbound, will be accommodated with the best of binding, and lowest prices. Merchant Account Books rul'd and bound to any pattern." *American Mercury* (Hartford, Connecticut), November 11, 1812. Handsomely tooled antique bindings are prized by collectors today, entirely apart from the literary worth of the book itself.

"To my bookseller's and there did give thorough direction for the new binding of a great number of my old books, to make my whole study of the same binding." Samuel Pepys, *Diary,* January 18, 1664–65. "The best binding at present [1778] is in calf . . . or sheepskin. [Anciently, books were bound in parchment.] The calf is stretched over the pasteboard with paste made of wheaten flour; afterwards the book is washed over with a little paste and water, then the cover is glazed fine with the white of an egg beaten, as painters do their pictures when they are finished, and at last, polished with a polishing iron, passed hot over the glazed cover." (M)

BOOK BOARDS
The common term in book binding for the piece of sturdy splint or pasteboard covered with paper and made into covers for books; cloth boards were "boards" covered with fabric, such as buckram. "Sole Agency for . . . The American Dictionary of the English Language . . . by Noah Webster, L.L.D.—a highly valuable work . . . will be printed on fine linen paper, in two volumes, quarto, and furnished to subscribers at twenty dollars, in boards, with cloth backs. No pains or expense will be spared to make it a superior specimen of America typography. It is expected the work will

appear in the course of the ensuing December. A prospectus . . . may be examined at the Book-store of Hutchens & Cory, First door west of the Bridge." *Literary Cadet and Rhode Island Statesman* (Providence), February 23, 1828.

Book boards.

Bookcase illustrated in Thomas Chippendale's *Gentleman and Cabinet-Maker's Director* (London, 1762).

BOOKCASE

A cupboard or set of shelves with glazed doors, sometimes referred to as a bureau bookcase or library case, developed from the Bookpress, *q.v.,* of the seventeenth century. In great early houses, these often were incorporated into the room by the architect, although the majority in the eighteenth century were free-standing. (See also BREAKFRONT, Chapter 5.)

BOOK CLASP

Clasps and catches often were attached to the covers of fine books not only as ornamentation but to hold the edges tight and thus help to prevent warping and curling. Fashioned from silver, gold, plated copper, heavy tin, or pewter, clasps usually were purchased from a goldsmith or jeweler and frequently engraved or embossed. "To the binder's, and directed the doing of my Chaucer, though they were not full neat enough for me, but pretty well it is; and thence to the clasp-maker's to have it clasped and bossed." Samuel Pepys, *Diary,* July 8, 1664.

BOOKPLATES

Bookplates, both the copper plates or woodcuts from which they were printed, and the engravings or impressions made from them, are collected today as examples of the engravers' and printers' arts. "Any Persons may have their Coats of Arms, or Names to paste on the Inside of the Covers of Books . . . Neatly executed by Adems, Schoolmaster and Engraver, on Golden Hill." *The New-York Gazette or The Weekly Post-Boy,* June 23, 1763. Bookplates were made also for library associations, schools, and for government offices: "You will oblige by sending a copper plate with the arms of Virginia neatly engraved and some impressions of them to be pasted in the books." (Order to London from Williamsburg, August, 1768.) Frances Mason,

John Norton and Sons, Merchants of London and Virginia (Richmond, 1935).

Bookplate engraved by Amos Doolittle for Linonia Society Library, Yale University. (Courtesy, Connecticut Historical Society, Inc.)

BOOKPRESS

In the seventeenth century the term was applied to a freestanding cupboard for books. "The truth is, I have bought a great many books lately to a great value; but I think to buy no more till Christmas next, and those that I have will so fill my two presses, that I must be forced to give away some, or make room for them." Samuel Pepys, *Diary,* January 10, 1667–68.

(2) During the eighteenth and nineteenth centuries, the term more commonly was applied to a pair of flat boards, one of which was adjustable, set between standards and held in place by a turnscrew or set of clamps. These were used to hold books being repaired, until, for example, glue had set, or until a warp had been straightened out.

Bookpress.

BOOKREST

The Georgian library table accessory designed to provide ease in reading large volumes or bound manuscripts. The book was rested or supported on a square frame made with horizontal bars on pivots in the uprights. The top bar was attached to a strut which could be adjusted to the angle required. (See also PORTFOLIO TABLE.)

BOOKSTAND

A freestanding set of bookshelves; a contemporary term for tiers of four or more shelves set between four corner posts and thus open on all sides. These also were called Moving Bookstands, Chiffoniers, or sometimes Canterburies. *qq. v.*

BOOK TAG

The small label of bookbinder's leather stamped with the name or cypher of the owner; usually ordered by the dozens, these were glued to the covers or spines of books in public and private libraries. "If the [bookbinding] is to be lettered, then a piece of red Morocco is pasted on the back, between the first and second bands to receive the title in gold letters, and sometimes a second between the next bands

Eighteenth-century book tag.

underneath, to receive the number of the volume." (M)

BOOTJACK

The contemporary term for "a tool for removing boots." (J) This was a dressing-room accessory of wood, iron, or brass, with the jack part in the shape of a V, or two arms, to hold the heel of the boot and thus allow the wearer to pull his foot free of the boot.

BOOT TREE

"Two pieces of wood, shaped like a leg, to be driven into boots, for stretching and widening them." (J) The shape of the boot tree sometimes was used as a shop sign by bootmakers.

BORACCHIO

"A lethern bottle" (W) or jack:

So I wish him joy wher'er he dwell,
That first found out the leather bottel.

Anonymous seventeenth-century ballad

(See also BLACKJACK, TANKARD.)

BOSTON CHAIR

The contemporary description of a high-backed chair made early in the eighteenth century in and around Boston, but almost equally popular throughout the rest of the country. The seats and backs either were covered in leather or were caned. The frames generally were of maple, painted red, black, or a deep green. The inventory of the estate of a Philadelphia house carpenter, Edward Warner, in 1749 listed "In the Front Parlor 1 large square walnut table £4; 1 oval square walnut Do. £1. 5s; 1 walnut tea table £1; Six Boston Chairs £ 3; 2 green chairs £ 1." Will Book K, p. 219. (See illustration, Chapter 1.)

BOSTON ROCKER

The popular designation for a plank seat stick or Windsor chair on rockers, developed in the 1830s, probably first in Connecticut. The earliest examples have shaped roll-front seats, nicely curved rockers, and decorations made with sharply cut stencils or free-hand painting. After 1840, thousands of these chairs were produced in factories throughout New England and the designation, Boston rocker, became a generic term. The variant is Salem rocker for a smaller —perhaps suburban?—size. The chairs were shipped to almost all U. S. ports and were exported to Europe, Asia, Africa, Australia, a variety of Scandinavian and Near East ports. (See illustration under CROOK-ED-FOOT CHAIR.)

BOTANICAL PRESS

The device used for pressing dry flowers or plants prior to preserving them in an Herbarium, *q.v.*, or *Hortus Siccus*. "Plants may be dried by pressing in a box of sand, or with a hot smoothing iron [between sheets of paper] or . . . a botanical press may be employed. The press is made of two smooth boards of hard wood, 18 inches long, 12 broad, and 2 thick. Screws must be fixed in each corner with nuts . . ." *Encyclopedia Americana* (Philadelphia, 1831).

BOTTLE

The name given any "vessel proper to contain liquors, made of leather, glass, stone or wood," (M) "with a narrow mouth" (J), usually stoppered. Bottle also was a synonym for Decanter, Flask, and Canteen, *qq.v.* "Bottles of Earth or Stone; of Glass covered with Wicker; of Glass with vices covered with leather; of Glass uncovered; Of Wood; [and] Sucking bottles" were listed in House of Parliament Rates, 1660, for Imports and Exports—*Statutes of the Realm* (London, 1819). "They have now in blast and good order the old glass Manufactory at Kensington in the Northern Liberties of Philadelphia, where they make among other glassware, green bottles of all sizes, claret bottles, olive bottles, caper bottles, anchovies bottles, and snuff bottles of all patterns . . . Christopher Trippel & Co." *Pennsylvania Packet* (Philadelphia), April 13, 1798.

C. 1700 rum bottle. (Courtesy, Antiquarian and Landmarks Society, Inc.)

C. 1740 rum bottle.

BOTTLE BOARD

This was the term for a serving tray specifically made to hold decanters and to prevent spilling and breaking. The tray had applied handles or cut-out handholds at each end; a one- to two-inch high gallery rim; and usually also interlocking dividers, of the same height as the rim, forming interstices in which the bottles were set. "Francis Trumble . . . makes and sells the following goods in mahogany, walnut, cherry-tree and maple, Ecc. viz. . . . corner cupboards, tea chests, tea boards, bottle boards, Ec. Ec. Likewise all forms of cabinet furniture, at reasonable rates. N.B. A great assortment of the above goods being ready made, after the newest fashions, any person may be supplied immediately, or on very short notice." *Pennsylvania Gazette* (Philadelphia), August 8, 1754.

BOTTLE CRANE

Crane was "the popular name for the siphon." (M) "To be sold by Joseph Leddel, Jun. . . . all sorts of Pewterware by wholesale or retail . . . worms for Stills of all Sizes. Likewise, makes Hogshead, Barrell or Bottle Cranes, either with or without Cocks . . ." *The New York Gazette or The Weekly Post-Boy,* March 23, 1752.

BOTTLE SCREW

A contemporary synonym for "a screw to pull out the cork." (J) (See also CORKSCREW.)

BOTTLE STAND

The silver, silver-plated, pewter, or Britannia protective frame or tray made to hold one or two bottles or decanters. Often set on tiny ball feet, the stands usually had stationary rod handles for ease in carrying from sideboard to table. "Joseph Lounes, Goldsmith . . . near the Drawbridge, has imported in the *William Penn,* from London, a very elegant Assortment of Plated Ware [including] Tea Urns, Coffee urns, Chocolate Pots, Dish rings, Dish covers, Caster Frames, Bottle Stands . . ." *Pennsylvania Packet* (Philadelphia), April 9, 1792.

BOTTLE TICKET

Another name for the Decanter Label, *q.v.* (See also note under BATTERSEA ENAMELED WARE.)

BOUGE
A leather bag or large wallet; i.e., a two-part pouch. The saddlebag was a form of wallet.

BOUGHPOT
(1) The seventeenth- and eighteenth-century term for what also was called a flowerpot; this was a decorated porcelain, pottery, or glass container or vase with a perforated lid to hold boughs or stems upright. The boughpot was set on the window enclosure, or on a sideboard or table: "The wind coming into the room for want [of a latch to the door] flung down a great bow-pott that stood upon the side-table, and that fell upon some Venice glasses, and did him a crown's worth of hurt." Samuel Pepys, *Diary,* September 13, 1665. (2) Boughpot also was the contemporary term for the arrangement of flowers or boughs, such as a spray of apple blossoms, either fresh or made of gilded and colored paper and foil. (See also BOUQUET.)

BOUGIE
"A thin, wax candle." (W) The term is from the Arabian word, *Bijiyah,* the Algerian town which was a large trading center for wax. Hence, the name for the night monster of the nursery, the boogy or bogeyman who owned the light and so took it away at will.

BOUQUET
The late-eighteenth-century term, from the French for little wood, used for a bunch of flowers or its container: "We have made her a boughpot. Say a bouquet . . . tis more genteel." William Makepeace Thackeray. (See also BOUGHPOT.)

BOUSING CAN
A contemporary term for "a drinking can or cup." (J)
 To Bouse: "to drink lavishly." (J)

As he rode he somewhat still did eat,
And in his hand did bear a bousing can,
Of which he sipt.

    Spenser, *Fairy Queen*

(See also CAN.)

BOW
(1) The "weapon of offence, made of steel, wood, horn or other elastic substances, which, after being bent by means of a string fastened to its two ends, in returning to its natural state, throws out an arrow with prodigious force." (M) The Britons' ancient weapon, for hunting game, as well as for making war, the bow continued in use in the colonies well into the eighteenth century. Also, (2) "A mathematical instrument, made of wood, used by seamen in taking the sun's altitude." (J)

BOW-BACK CHAIR
The popular name to describe the favorite Windsor chair design.

Bow-back Windsor chair. (Courtesy, Antiquarian and Landmarks Society, Inc.)

BOWET, BOWIT

From the Latin *bueta* and the French *boite* for box or case, and applied to a small lantern in a wooden case or frame.

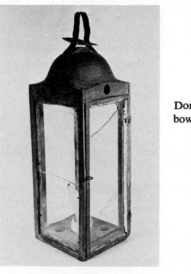

Dome-shaped bowet.

Rectangular bowet.

BOWIE

From the old English boll(e) or bowl, this word denoted a small vessel such as a milk bowl; sometimes a small, shallow tub.

Bowie.

BOWL

The common term for any wood, pottery, porcelain, metal, or glass vessel, rather wide than deep, to hold liquids; "distinguished from a cup which is rather deep than wide." (J) Johnson said that the term was derived from the Welsh *buelin* for anything made from horn, as drinking cups anciently were; however, it may more probably have been derived from the Old English *bolle* or *bolla,* so spelled because the Middle English pronunciation of ole was owl. The original meaning of bowl was a drinking vessel or cup, as Chaucer used it when he wrote "Bryngeth eek with you a bolle or a panne fful of water." (See also BASIN, CUP.)

Eighteenth-century pewter bowl. (Courtesy, Antiquarian and Landmarks Society, Inc.)

Late-eighteenth-century turned maple bowl.

Early-nineteenth-century soft paste bowl.

BOX

The term was derived from the Anglo-Saxon version of the Latin *Buxus* meaning box-wood, a kind of tree, and thus signified any case or container, usually with a lid or cover, that was made of wood. Later, box was used to designate containers made also of metal, glass, pottery, or porcelain. Small boxes, including "Fire or Tinder Boxes; Nest Boxes; Pepper Boxes; Spice Boxes; Round Boxes or French Boxes [decorated pottery] for Marmalade or Jelly; Sand

Eighteenth-century small brass desk box with false bottom.

C. 1700 box for a book. (Courtesy, Antiquarian and Landmarks Society, Inc.)

Early-nineteenth-century pasteboard box with decorated paper cover.

Early-eighteenth-century small leather-covered box.

An eighteenth-century painted storage box decorated with militia men.

A painted storage box. (Courtesy, Antiquarian and Landmarks Society, Inc.)

Boxes; Sope Boxes; Touch Boxes covered with leather, with velvet, of Iron or other Metall guilt; Tobacco Boxes" were listed in the House of Parliament Rates, 1660, for Imports and Exports—*Statutes of the Realm* (London, 1819). A box is "a case made of wood or other matter to hold anything. It is distinguished from chest, as the less from the greater." (J) (See combining forms, such as BANDBOX, DESKBOX, SNUFFBOX, etc.)

BOX BEDSTEAD

A rectangular open box set on four legs to hold a straw mattress or pallet. To save the construction of two sides, such bedsteads sometimes were built into a corner of a room. A medieval English farm and cottage style, box bedsteads continued in use here through the nineteenth century. They were the first bedsteads built in early homes in seventeenth-century Atlantic coastal colonies and for eighteenth- and nineteenth-century frontier cabins. Such low beds also were used in loft bedrooms. (See also JACK BED.)

BOX IRON

"A smoothing iron with an inner chamber to hold hot coals." (J) Similar in shape to the later flatiron, this was an iron box, with one pointed or half-lozenge-shaped end, and a fixed handle. Made with a lid at the top of the box or a sliding panel at the blunt end for insertion of coals or a piece of heated iron, these also were listed as [linen] smoothing irons, ironing boxes, or simply irons. "John Jackson . . . makes & mends Locks, Keys, and Ironing Boxes, at a reasonable rate." *Boston Gazette,* May 2, 1737.

BOX-ON-FRAME

The collector's term for the seventeenth-century box or simple small chest set on a separate stand or frame; the forerunner of the more elaborate set or case of several drawers called a chest on frame or highboy. (See also CHEST, DOUBLE CHEST OF DRAWERS, HIGHBOY, TALLBOY.)

BOX SETTLE

Another and more explicit term for the type of Settle, *q.v.,* the seat of which doubles as the hinged lid of a storage bin or box. (See also BACON CUPBOARD, SETTLE BED.)

BRACKET CANDLESTICK

Wall lighting fixtures lacking the large reflector back plate associated with the usual Sconce, *q.v.* These were (1) shaped tubular brass or silver arms with candle sockets made to fit into small hangers, or (2) candlesticks made to be used on a small wall shelf or bracket. "James Jacks . . . has imported in the Ship *Lexington,* from London, a large Assortment of Plated Goods . . . [including] a variety of Pillar Table and Bracket Candlesticks, of the newest patterns, from 5 to 14 dollars a pair . . ." *Federal Gazette* (Philadelphia), March 15, 1799. Ince and Mayhew illustrated "eight Designs of Brackets for Candles" in *The Universal System of Household Furniture* (London, 1762).

BRACKET SHELF

A narrow, ornamental shelf. "The bracket is intended to be fixed against the wall, in some blank space, where it serves the purpose of a table, as a place for books, vases of flowers, and rare articles of virtu." A. J. Downing, *The Architecture of Country Houses* (New York, 1850).

Bracket for bust designed by Thomas Chippendale, 1762.

Bracket for bust designed by Thomas Chippendale, 1762.

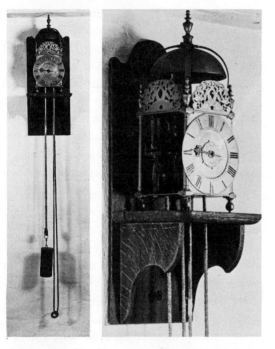

English brass seventeenth-century bracket or lantern clock and weights.

Same clock, side view. (Courtesy, Antiquarian and Landmarks Society, Inc.)

BRAISING PAN
(See BRASIER, CHAFING DISH.)

BRAKE
A word used variously for:

(1) a baker's kneading trough

(2) a large barrow

(3) a kind of crossbow (H)

(4) a tool for dressing hemp or flax

(5) a snaffle for horses

(6) an enclosure or pen or a kind of open cart, (H) and earlier

(7) in the sixteenth century, for a type of torture rack.

BRANCH
A common contemporary description of the wall candle Sconce, q.v., and sometimes also for the candelabrum or Branched Candlesticks, q.v. "To be sold Looking Glasses of many sizes some with Plain Walnut Frames, others very neatly Japann'd, Ec. Also Brass and Glass Branches, at very reasonable prices. Enquire at the Post Office. [Peter Turner]," *American Weekly Mercury* (Philadelphia), August 4, 1737.

BRANCHED CANDLESTICKS
A contemporary term for the candelabrum. "Just imported . . . from England by Joseph Hallet . . . dripping pans, pie pans and tea kettles, very neat branched brass candlesticks . . ." *The New York Mercury,* June 8, 1761.

BRANDER
A colloquialism of the period, this was a variation of brand iron or Brandreth, q.v., derived from the Middle English word brand, meaning to burn. It is sometimes found in estate inventories of kitchen utensils.

BRAND IRON
The Middle English combination of brand and iron, usually referring to a gridiron but sometimes to "andirons," (H) a trivet or a kettle stand, and so, generally, to any hearth utensil made of any combination of iron bars. When used in the plural form, this was a synonym for Ember Tongs, q.v.

BRANDRETH, BRANDELEDE, BRANLEDE, BRANLET
Four contemporary variations in spelling and pronunciation for a form of Brand

Brandreth.

Iron, *q.v.,* usually called a Brandreth; the term was derived from the Middle English *brand* plus *reio,* meaning grate or rest. A framework of iron used at the kitchen hearth, a high trivet or "an iron tripod fixed over the fire, on which a pot or kettle is placed." (H)

BRANDY WARMER
A small saucepan of brass, copper, or silver, in which spirits were warmed.

BRASIER, BRAZIER
"A pan to hold coals." (J) The term, from the French *brasier,* was used to describe a large, flat pan that held burning embers. Originally, it signified any brass vessel; later, an open pan on a footed base, used for braising or broiling. Thus, it was similar to a chafing dish, and so sometimes was called a Braising Pan, *q.v.* Brazier also was applied to any other hot coal carrier or portable stove.

BRASS RUBBINGS
Then as now, one of the traveler's favorite means of copying grave markers, memorial brasses, low-relief sculptures, or other carvings on flat surfaces, especially those found in cathedrals, churches, and public buildings. Thin paper was placed over the work, then rubbed with charcoal or chalk.

BRAZIER'S WARES, BRAZIERY
The all-inclusive term for copper or brass utensils made by the brazier or coppersmith. "Thom. Russell, Brazier, near the Draw-Bridge in Boston, Makes, Mends, and New-Tins all sorts of Braziery, viz. Kettles, Skillets, Frying Pans, Kettle-Pots, Sauce Pans, Tea Kettles, Warming Pans, Wash Basins, Skimmers, Ladles, Copper Pots, Copper Funnels, Brass Scales, Gun Ladles, Ec. . . ." *Boston News-Letter,* October 30, 1740.

BREAD BASKET
The container from which bread and rolls were served at the table; bread baskets were oval or round but seldom rectangular in shape. Some had cut-out handholds at both ends; others were set on small pedestals or bases and had bail handles. They were made of silver; plated copper or tin; Britannia ware; earthenware or porcelain, but rarely glass. Less expensive versions were available in wicker, lacquered papier-mâché, and many were made of japanned tin. "Henry C. Porter is now opening a general assortment . . . goods purchased with cash at the late Auction Sales in New York and are offered for sale for cash only at very low prices [including] Japanned teatrays and waiters, bread baskets, Real gold double border teatrays in sets, Plated, Britannia and iron sable tea spoons, plated sugar tongs . . ." *American Mercury* (Hartford, Connecticut), October 24, 1820.

BREADBOX
The kitchen cupboard or pantry storage container to keep bread fresh and moist. These usually rectangular boxes, with covers or attached lids, were made of hard wood; of plated tin or sheet iron; japanned tin; mocha ware; spatter- or sponge-decorated stoneware; slip-decorated redware, and other types of pottery. "Bread is in cities so heavy an article of expense that all waste should be guarded against; and having it cut in the room will lend much to prevent it. It should not be cut until a day old. Earthen pans and covers keep it best." *The Domestic Encyclopedia* (Philadelphia, 1821).

BREAD TRAY
Another name for the Bread Basket, *q.v.*

BREAD TROUGH
(See DOUGH BOX, KNEADING TROUGH.)

BREAKFAST TABLE
A fairly small table with two drop leaves or flaps. When fully open, the top might be rectangular, oval, square, or round. In colonial and early-nineteenth-century America, the breakfast table often doubled as the tea table. (See TEA BOARD.)

Chippendale illustrated two specific breakfast table designs: "One hath a stretching rail, and the feet are canted and sunk in. The other hath a shelf inclosed with a Fretwork. Sometimes they are inclosed with Brass Wirework: In the front is a Recess for the knees, Ec." *The Gentleman and Cabinet-Maker's Director* (London, 1762).

C. 1720 maple breakfast table. (Courtesy, Antiquarian and Landmarks Society, Inc.)

BREAKFRONT
(See LIBRARY BOOKCASE, and see also in Chapter 5.)

BREWSTER BED
An advertising name for a type of four-post bed, the posts made with roll-turnings; manufactured in the nineteenth century and having no connection with the type of bedstead used by Elder William Brewster in the seventeenth century at Plymouth.

BRIMMER
A Bumper, *q.v.,* "a bowl full to the brim." (W) A drinking vessel of wood, horn, metal, or pottery, and sometimes glass.

BRITANNIA WARE
The all-inclusive term for a type of bright pewter first developed in England in the mid-eighteenth century and produced in great quantities in this country after 1830. (See also BRITANNIA in Chapter 9.)

BROACH, BROCHE
A term applied variously to any item with a sharp point, and thus used as a synonym for (1) a skewer or larding pin; (2) a spindle stick or bobbin for winding yarn; (3) "a taper or torch" (H); (4) a horseman's "spur" (H); (5) "a fishing-hook" (H) (6) a buckle, clasp, or jeweled pin. "Brouches of Lattin or Copper" were listed in the House of Parliament Rates, 1660, for Imports and Exports—*Statutes of the Realm* (London, 1819); (7) another name for the "roasting spit," (J); and also a colloquialism for (8) "a musical instrument, the sounds of which are made by turning round a handle," (J) similar to the Hand Organ, *q.v.,* of the street organ-grinder.

BROACHER
A variation of the word for "a spit." (J)

BROADSIDE
The term generally used to describe any notice or advertisement printed on one side only of a large sheet of paper.

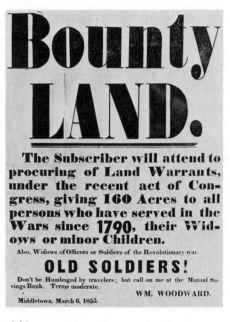

Broadside.

251

Broadside.

BROOM

The name sometimes given "a besom to sweep with," (W)   "so-called from the matter of which it is sometimes made," (J)   i.e., broom, attached by twisted wire or a thong to a rod handle or staff. (See also BESOM, BIRCH, BRUSH.)

BROWN BESS

The British and American Revolutionary War soldier's name for the flintlock musket, which often had a short brown walnut stock, and invariably a barrel "browned" with vinegar or other acid to reduce glare or visibility during battle. The length of the barrel was 46 inches. The musket was equipped with a bridle lock and was capable of firing six shots a minute.

BROWN BOWL

The common seventeenth- and eighteenth-century term for any wooden drinking vessel: "At night to sup, and then to cards, and last of all to have a flagon of ale and apples, drank out of a wood cup, as a Christmas draught, which made all merry." Samuel Pepys, *Diary,* January 4, 1667, perhaps because as John Dryden noted,

The rich, tir'd with continual feasts
For change become their next poor tenant's guests;
Drink heavy draughts of Ale from plain brown bowls,
And snatch the homely Rasher from the coals.

"They brought me a draught of their drink in a brown bowl, tipt with silver, which I drank off . . ." Samuel Pepys, *Diary,* February 27, 1659–60.

Brown bowl.

BRUSH

From the Middle English *brusche* or *brusshe* for the loppings of trees, and hence the utensil set with tufts or bunches; used for brushing or sweeping. (1) "An instrument to clean anything . . . generally made of bristles set in wood." (J)   Also, (2) "It is used [as a synonym] for the larger and stronger Pencils [*q.v.*] used by painters." (J) "Richard Fitzgerald, Brush-Maker from London, now living at the House of Mr. Taylor, Hatter, near the old Slip Market, Makes and sells all sorts of Brushes and Mops, such as Painter's, Hatter's, Scourer's, Barber's & Weaver's Brushes, Stair, House & Hearth Brushes, Hair Brooms and Flesh Brushes; with all sorts of double & single wired, besides several other sorts too tedious to mention . . . N.B. Said Fitzgerald gives ready Money for any Quantity of Hog's

Bristles." *The New-York Gazette,* July 29, 1751. "Bearde brushes, head brushes, rubbing and weaver's brushes" were listed in the House of Parliament Rates, 1660, for Imports and Exports—*Statutes of the Realm* (London, 1819).

BUCCANEER GUN

From the French *boucanier,* one who hunts wild oxen; literally, one who roasts meat on a *boucan* or barbecue frame; hence, the name for a heavy musket capable of discharging a greater-than-average load of shot, and thus a comfort when facing a large, wild animal. Buccaneer less politely, however, was the slang term of the period for a pirate or competing privateer, the name implying the renegade's need at times to hide out in the woods, if not his presumed wild and rude manner. Hence, a Buccaneer also signified a heavy murderous gun useful in fighting off privateers attempting to board and loot a ship: "To be sold by John Pim of Boston, Gunsmith, at the Sign of the Cross Guns, in Anne Street near the Draw Bridge, at very reasonable Rates, sundry sorts of choice Arms lately arrived from London, viz. Handy Muskets, Buccaneer-Guns, Fowling pieces, Hunting Guns, Carabines, several sorts of Pistols, Brass and Iron, fashionable Swords, Ec." *Boston News-Letter,* July 4, 1720.

BUCK

An old term, allied to bucket, but derived from the Middle English *bouken* or *bowken,* meaning to steep or boil in lye and thus to bleach or wash clean. Hence, it was a common term for the shallow, wooden, colonial washtub.

BUCK BASKET

The colonial term for what would be called a laundry hamper today. (See also BUCK.)

BUCKET

The term derived from the Old English word *buc* or pail and specifically referring to "the vessel in which water is drawn out of a

well, [and to that] in which water is carried, particularly to quench a fire." (J)

> . . . *like a deep well*
> *that owes two Buckets, filling one another.*

Shakespeare, *King Richard II,* IV, i.

Well buckets, unless sometimes those made of one hollowed-out section of a log, generally were bound with iron. The wood buckets used for carrying milk, cider, or water more often were hooped with splints of wood, such as hickory. (See also FIRE BUCKET.)

Oak bucket with iron hoops. (Courtesy, Antiquarian and Landmarks Society, Inc.)

BUCKET BENCH

The collector's name for the bench or stand near the kitchen entry kept as a repository for water buckets or milk pails.

BUCKLE

From the Latin *bucca, buccula,* for a helmet strap or fastener; hence in Middle English the term for any metal rim with a hinged tongue of one or more spikes for securing the "strap or belt passed through the rim and pierced by the spike." (J) Thus, a luxury counted as a piece of jewelry by many, as indicated by Franklin's letter from London, June 10, 1758, telling his wife that he had sent to Philadelphia "a pair of Buckles, made of French Paste Stones, which are next in lustre to Diamonds.

They cost three Guineas and are said to be cheap at that price." *Writings of Benjamin Franklin,* ed., A. H. Smyth (New York, 1907). On May 10, 1790, "Miles Beach and James Ward, South of the Bridge, Hartford . . . Have ready-made gold Buttons . . . a great variety of Plated and Silver shoe and Knee Buckles; Pinchbeck and Brass ditto." *Connecticut Courant* (Hartford). Those who could not afford silver, gold, ivory, pewter, or brass, used buckles fashioned of wood, bone, or iron.

Silver buckles owned by Nathan Hale, 1776. (Courtesy, Antiquarian and Landmarks Society, Inc.)

BUCKLER
Derived from the Latin *buccularius* or *buccula,* specifically to describe a small round shield worn or carried to ward off a blow.

BUDGE
Another spelling for Bouge, *q.v.,* sometimes also written budger.

BUDGE BARREL
In weaponry, the name of a "utensil for carrying powder. It consists of a barrel well hooped but having only one head, there being nailed on the other end a piece of leather, which draws together like a purse by means of strings." (M)

BUDGET
The diminutive of Budge or Bouge, *qq.v.,* for any small leather wallet, pouch, or bag, or any leather bottle, especially one carried while traveling; hence to budget originally was to store up or save in a wallet.

BUFFET
Now generally used to describe a combination of serving table and closed cupboard, the word in the mid-eighteenth century more often referred to what is called a corner cupboard today. "A kind of cupboard or set of shelves where plate is set out to show in a room of entertainment." (J) By 1778, it was "a small part of a room separated from the rest by slender pillars, glass-doors, etc. for china." (M) "A repository or sort of cupboard for plate, glasses, china-ware, etc. [but also] a large table in a dining room and called a sideboard for the plate, glasses, bottles, etc." (B) Sheraton illustrated a free-standing, elegant combination of cupboard surmounted by three open shelves which he said "may, with some propriety . . . prove ornamental to a break-fast room, answering as the repository of a tea equipage." *The Cabinet Dictionary* (London, 1803).

BUGLE, BUGLE HORN
"A hunting-horn." (J)

BULLET, BULLET MOLD
Originally meaning a small, round ball, bullet was derived from the French *boulette,* a diminutive of *boule* or ball; made of lead, iron, or stone and "usually shot out of guns." (J) Bullets for handguns usually were of lead, made in molds by the local pewterer, by the householder for his own use, or purchased from a hardware merchant or gunsmith.

BULLET CLOCK
The contemporary description of a type of table clock developed in the mid-seventeenth century and mentioned by Samuel Pepys in the diary he kept during the Restoration. According to the description here quoted, written 120 years later, such clocks would seem to have been the result of experiments based on the hopeful theory of perpetual motion: "Some clocks are still made with a small ball or bullet, on an inclined plane, which turns every minute.

Gainsborough, the painter, had a brother who . . . possessed a strong genius for mechanics. He invented a clock [that] told the hour by a little bell, and was kept in motion by a leaden bullet, which dropped from a spiral reservoir at the top of the clock, into a little ivory bucket. This was so contrived as to discharge it at the bottom, and by means of a counterweight was carried up to the top of the clock, where it received another bullet, which was discharged as the former." *Gentleman's Magazine* (London, 1785), p. 931.

BUMBARD
A contemporary variation, apparently based on pronunciation, of bombard or, as Johnson complained, "Wrong written for Bombard [q.v.]; a great gun, a black jack; a leathern pitcher." (J)

BUNG STARTER
(See CORK DRAWER.)

BUMPER
Traditionally, collectors have said this term for a drinking glass was derived from bump; that is, a heavy blow or knock. Such a glass was filled to the brim for a toast then bumped or thumped on the table for emphasis. However, Webster in 1806 said that bumper simply was "a glass filled with liquor to the brim" and indicated it was so called because bump meant "to swell." He also gave brimmer as a synonym for bumper. "She insisted on my staying one day longer that we might keep together my grandson's Birthday. At Dinner, among other nice things, we had a Floating Island, which they always particularly have on the Birthdays of any of their own Six Children. The chief Toast of the Day was Master Benjamin Bache, which the venerable old Lady began in a Bumper of Mountain [wine]." (Benjamin Franklin from London, August 14, 1771, to his wife, Deborah, at Philadelphia.) *Writings of Benjamin Franklin,* ed., A. H. Smyth (New York, 1907).

BUREAU
"A chest of drawers with a writing-board." (J) From the French colloquial word for desk or office; thus, bureau was used throughout the eighteenth century to describe a writing table, especially one fitted with drawers, document boxes, or pigeonholes. "To my compatriot in arms, and old and intimate friend, Dr. Graik, I give my bureau, or, as the cabinet-makers [now] call it, tambour-secretary, and the circular chair, an appendage of my study." (George Washington, last will and testament.) David Ramsay, *The Life of George Washington* (Hopkins & Seymour, 1807). By 1800, however, as Webster defined it, bureau was "a kind of small chest of drawers," a fashionable name then and still so used by many Americans today: "We found chests of drawers still called bureaus, sofas sittees, cups of tea dishes of tea; and a number of other things designated by names long out of fashion in genteel society in England." James Boardman, *America and the Americans by a Citizen of the World* (London, 1833).

BUREAU BEDSTEAD
A forerunner of the nineteenth-century Murphy bed, this was a bed enclosed in a case, made so that it could be folded up when not in use; the carcase had simulated drawer fronts to disguise the bed:

> *The white-wash'd wall, the nicely sanded floor,*
> *The varnish'd clock that click'd behind the door;*
> *The chest contriv'd a double debt to pay,*
> *A bed at night, a chest of drawers by day.*
>
> Oliver Goldsmith; *The Deserted Village.*

(See also PRESS BED.)

BUREAU PLAT
The eighteenth-century flat-top writing table with shallow drawers set beneath the top board.

BURETTE

From the French *buire,* or vase for liquor, originally this term was used to describe a small cruet for oil or vinegar.

BURNT BOWL

(See in Chapter 10.)

BUSH

The contemporary colloquialism for any tavern sign because anciently the ivy bush was depicted on such signs "to show that liquors are sold there." (J) (See also SHOWBOARD, TAVERN SIGN.)

BUTLER'S TABLE

A small fold-up table with collapsible legs; easily carried from place to place, this eighteenth-century standing tray or small sideboard was set on an X-shaped stand. Usually rectangular in shape, the tray top sometimes had drop leaves, sometimes a gallery or solid rim.

BUTLER'S TRAY

In the eighteenth and early nineteenth centuries this usually signified a series of trays, often with lift-up lid tops, set on a frame of four or six legs with casters; the whole somewhat resembling a fitted teacart.

BUTTER CUPBOARD

Any cupboard with pierced or ventilated

Maple and hard pine butterfly table with rarely found turned stretchers connecting the boldly splayed legs. The wide rake of the leg forms a wedge-shaped frame and thus more adequately supports the butterfly or reverse triangle of the bracket. (Courtesy, Connecticut Historical Society, Inc.)

doors, used for the storage of butter and cheese, and differing not at all from the pie cupboard or food safe.

BUTTERFLY TABLE

The type of drop-leaf table made with leaf supports of hinged pieces of wood similar in shape to the butterfly's wing.

BUTTER PADDLE

After butter was removed from the churn to a tray, it was worked with butter paddles until it was free from water or whey. These shapers, workers, or paddles were carved from hard woods or burl, in the shape of a thick, shallow plate or scoop. They were not used for scooping, however, but were pressed down on the mass of butter to press out water.

C. 1720 butter paddle.

BUTTER PRINT

"A piece of carved wood, used to mark butter." (J) This was the hand-carved stamp design or shallow-cut pattern with which a pat or pound of butter was impressed as a means of identifying the owner or shipper. The impression was called a print. Designs most often sought today include eagles, other birds, cows, representations of other animals, tulips, wheat sheaves, and flowers.

BUTTER SCALE

The term sometimes applied to a form of balance scale, many of which were made of porcelain plates suspended by brass chains from a central hook or rod. Country or homemade butter scales were simple

Buttons made between 1815 and 1830 by Anson Matthew, Southington, Connecticut.

wooden plates, similarly suspended by hemp, flax, or thong. Later types were made with brass or tin plates.

BUTTER TROWEL

The small broad-bladed serving knife for butter; usually of silver or silver-plated metal. "James Jacks, Jeweller and Watchmaker . . . has imported in the ship *Active* from London . . . a large and elegant assortment of goods [including] table, dessert and tea spoons; sugar tongs and butter trowels . . ." *Pennsylvania Packet* (Philadelphia), November 13, 1799.

BUTTING IRON

(See BODDLE.)

BUTTON

The Middle English term from the Latin *bottare,* meaning any knob, stud, or disc of bone, wood, ivory, or metal; sewn to clothing for the purpose of fastening one part to another. Buttons were a luxury of dress for many; were purchased separately; sometimes designed to special order by gold and silversmiths; or were chosen from ready-made assortments: Amos Bull, a drygoods merchant, offered "suited to the present season of festivity Federal and other elegant and common Buttons." December 28, 1789, in the *Connecticut Courant* (Hart-

ford), to enhance dress worn while making New Year's calls. "Buttons of Brasse, Steel, Copper, or Lattin; of Crystall; of Glass; of Thred; of silke; of fine damaske; of Bugle; for Handkirchers; of Hair," were listed in House of Parliament Rates, 1660, for Imports and Exports—*Statutes of the Realm* (London, 1819).

C

CABINET

The name given during the Colonial period and the early nineteenth century to any "set of drawers," (W) of any size. Cabinet meant "a curious piece of workmanship, being a kind of press with drawers" (M) developed first in France and Italy and, after 1650, in England and America. Its chief early uses were for the display of fine plate or porcelain on its upper open shelves and to provide a place of safekeeping for other valuables in the closed drawers set in the lower part of the case. Making the drawers and fitting them into the case called for more careful workmanship than was needed in average joinery. The term Cabinetmaker, *q.v.,* in Chapter 3, thus signified the most skillful of furniture craftsmen.

CABRIOLE CHAIR

The general eighteenth- and early-nineteenth-century name for an easy chair of the type commonly called a wing chair today. "It is an arm-chair stuffed all over. The legs are mahogany . . . a French easy chair." Thomas Sheraton, *The Cabinet Dictionary* (London, 1803). Chippendale showed ten designs for what he called "French chairs with elbows. The Backs and Seats are stuffed, and covered with Spanish Leather, or Damask, Etc. . . . Some of them are intended to be open below at the Back." *The Gentleman and Cabinet-Maker's Director* (London, 1762). These, however, were minus cheeks or wings. Lightly made chairs for the drawing room, cabrioles were "Chairs with stuffed backs" according to A. Hepplewhite, *The Cabinet-Maker and Upholsterer's Guide* (London, 1794). Those shown had upholstered backs and seats and open arms. "To be sold at Public Sale [from] the remaining stock in trade of William Long . . . a set of Mahogany Cabriole Chairs, fire screens, library table . . . William Shannon, Auctioneer." *Pennsylvania Packet* (Philadelphia), February 15, 1794. (See also CABRIOLE, Chapter 5.)

CACHEPOT

The French term for pot hider, and thus the name given any decorative metal, pottery, porcelain, or opaque glass container for the utilitarian flower pot. (See also BOUGHPOT.)

Cachepot.

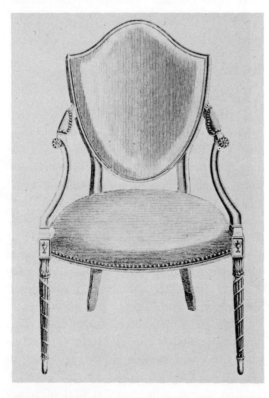

Cabriole chair illustrated in Hepplewhite's *Guide* (London, 1788).

Unglazed red-clay flower pots used alone in greenhouses or in cachepots.

CADET TABLE

The small breakfast table with one drop leaf or flap that could be used alone or as an adjunct to the main table. "William Long, Cabinet Maker and Carver from London . . . carries on the abovementioned business in all their various branches and executed in the most approved modern taste . . . elegantly put out of hand . . . new fashioned cadet breakfast tables, Ec. Ec. Orders from the country punctually attended to, and executed as if the persons were present . . ." *Pennsylvania Packet* (Philadelphia), July 11, 1788.

CADDY

Specifically, "a small box for tea." (W) The term was a corruption in conversation for *Kati,* a Malay weight of 1⅓ pounds, and thus the name given the wood, tin, pewter box in which the tea was exported from Eastern countries to Europe and the colonies. (See CANISTER, TEA CADDY.)

CADDY SPOON

The small spoon, scoop, or measure of silver or porcelain, with which tea is transferred from the caddy to the teapot. The spoon handle usually is just long and wide enough to be grasped between thumb and forefinger. (See also TEA CADDY.)

CADOGAN

A short-lived potters' fad of the late eighteenth century, this was a lidless or one-piece teapot filled from a bottom vent. Shaped somewhat like a peach, the cadogan was first made at Rockingham, Yorkshire, in the 1780s.

CAG

"A little barrel or cask," (W)   a keg, sometimes of leather, but usually of wood, in the shape of a miniature barrel.

CAKE CREEL

The Scottish-North Irish colloquialism, and hence a southern colonial term, for a wooden frame, a kitchen "rack to dry oat-cakes." (H)

CALABASH

For centuries gourds were planted for their eventual and specific usefulness as kitchen utensils. Thus in his *Herball,* John Gerard wrote, "Gourds are cherished especially [and] kept for the rinds wherein they put turpentine, oile, honey, and also serve them as pales [for] water and many other like uses." And in 1750, Peter Kalm reported that a kind of gourd "not fit for eating [these] are used for making all sorts of vessels. They are first dried well; the shells are scraped very clean within and then large spoons or ladles, funnels, bowls, dishes and the like may be made of them. They are washed to keep their white color." *Travels in North America* (Warrington, England, 1770). "The shells are used for cups, as also for making instruments of music, by making a hole in the shell, and putting in small stones, with which they make a sort of rattle." Philip Miller, *The Gardener's Dictionary* (London, 1736). "There are divers sorts of Gourds, bearing fruit in the forme of flagons and bottles, with a great large belly and a small necke. The Gourd groweth into any fashion that you would have it . . . according to the mold wherein it is put while it is yong." John Gerard, *The Herball or Generall Historie of Plantes* (London, 1636).

Calabash. (Courtesy, Antiquarian and Landmarks Society, Inc.)

CALDRON, CALDERON, CHALDRON, CHAULDRON

All names for a "very large kettle, pot or boiler," (W) usually the largest in the kitchen; made of iron, copper, or brass.

Seventeenth-century bronze cauldron.

Seventeenth-century brass cauldron. (Courtesy, Antiquarian and Landmarks Society, Inc.)

CALENDAR

One of the many small printed books or pamphlets collected today, this, then as now, was the political distribution of time, "accommodated to the uses of life, and taken from the motions of heavenly bodies. Of this kind are those annual books, wherein the days of the month, the festivals, the sign the sun is in, the sun's rising and setting, the changes of the moon, Ec., are exhibited which we also call almanacks." (M) A form of calendar was used in Egypt as early as 3500 B.C.; where also about 500 years later the civil year first was divided into 365 days or 12 months of 30 days each. In 239 B.C. they corrected their calculations, introducing a Leap Year. The Julian Calendar was introduced in 45 B.C. by Julius Caesar. Although the Gregorian Calendar reform was completed in 1582, when October 5 became October 15, the Gregorian Calendar was not adopted until 1752 in Britain and, hence, in the American colonies. (See also ALMANAC: WATCH CALENDAR.)

(2) One of the clothmaker's tools; "an engine to calendar, i.e., to give linen a gloss, or to smooth [it]; a hot-press." (W)

CALENDAR CLOCK

(See ASTRONOMICAL CLOCK.)

CALLIGRAPHY

"Fair, fine or beautiful writing." (W) The art of fine penmanship, and thus the collector's term for examples of highly stylized and ornate alphabets, or continuous-line pen drawings of birds, flowers, etc.

CALLIOPE

This term is a grand semantic triumph of hope over fact, for Kalliope (from *Kalos,* beauty, and *opos,* song) was the name of the Greek goddess who presided over eloquence and heroic poetry. Her name was given to a form of musical instrument that consists of a series of whistles activated by keys arranged on a keyboard similar to that of an organ.

CALUMET

The name, from the Latin *calamus* for reed, that French explorers gave to the Indian pipe, which was "The symbol of peace among the Indians of North America. It resembles our [English clay] tobacco pipes, but is much larger, and is adorned with fine feathers in the form of wings." (M)

CAMEL-BACK CHAIR

A term sometimes used to describe the Shield-back Chair, *q.v.*, the convex curve of the top rail somewhat resembling a camel's hump.

CAMEL-BACK SOFA

The collector's term for any sofa having a back with a double curve or hump-shaped top.

A camel-back or double-curve sofa shown in Thomas Chippendale's *Director* (London, 1762).

CAMEO

A type of carving on stone, bone, wood, coral, or shell on which the background is cut away; the opposite of Intaglio, *q.v.*

CAMERA LUCIDA

An aid to the artist, this was an optical device; a box in which mirrors were set to reflect an image onto a glass screen so that it might be traced on paper.

CAMERA OBSCURA

The term from the Latin for dark chamber, and the name for the darkened box into which light is admitted through a double convex lens to cast the image of some external object onto paper, glass, or metal.

CAMPAIGN CHEST

(See CAMPAIGN FURNITURE; CAPTAIN'S CHEST.)

CAMPAIGN FURNITURE

The all-inclusive term for any portable and/ or folding furniture first designed for use by army officers in the field, and which could be adapted for headquarters or home use. (See also FIELD BED.)

CAMP BED

(See FIELD BED, TENT BED.)

CAMPHENE LAMP

A type of fluid lamp made after 1835 and so called because it burned camphene, a mixture of 1.25 turpentine with 6.75 alcohol, which sometimes was scented with an oil, such as juniper, balsam, citron, or lemon. Camphene lamps were similar to whale-oil lamps. However, because of the fluid's highly flammable nature, the wick holders of camphene lamps were set at opposing angles of about 45° instead of the

Camera lucida, as shown in *The New Dictionary of Arts and Sciences* (London, 1778).

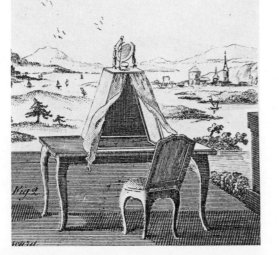

American pewter camphene lamps. (Courtesy, June and Bernard Cardé Collection.)

vertical or 90° angle common to the whale-oil lamp.

CAN(N)

"The can is the large vessel out of which the cup is filled; a cup made of metal." (J) To collectors today, can more often means a handleless cup made of silver, pewter, or tin, a type carried by soldiers:

> *Come fill up my cup, come fill up my can*
> *Come saddle your horse, and call up your*
> *men.*
>> Sir Walter Scott, *The Doom of Devorgoil,* II, 11.

Johnson's first definition, however, also was common during the Colonial period. "Send 4 white quart stone Cans, 4 pint ditto." Order from Mann Page, Stafford County, Virginia, February 15, 1770. Frances Mason, *John Norton and Sons, Merchants of London and Virginia* (Richmond, 1935).

CANAL LAMP, CANALBOAT LANTERN

A rectangular or box-shaped lantern with one open side and with a top ring-handle by which it was suspended from a ceiling or wall hook. These usually were made of tinned sheet iron and were large enough to hold three to five candles in a row.

CAN-BOARD, CANN-BOARD

An early synonym for Cupboard, *q.v.* (See also CAN.)

CANDELABRUM

The candleholder with two or more branches. The terms candelabrum or candelabra were first used in the nineteenth century. Branch or branches were the common earlier term.

CANDELSTAFFE, CANDELSTALK, CANDEL-TREOW

Early terms for the candlestick. (See also PRICKET.)

CANDLE BARK

A contemporary colloquialism for "a round cylindrical [wooden] box used for holding candles." (H)

CANDLEBEAM

Literally, a light suspended from a beam, this was the sixteenth- and seventeenth-century term, still in use in the colonies until the early eighteenth century, for the lighting device later called a Chandelier, *q.v.* According to one early description, "a candle-beame is such as hangeth in gentlemen's halls, with sockettes, to set candles upon." Huloet, *Abecedarium* (London, 1552).

CANDLE BOARD

The small pull-out shelf fitted below a table or desk top, just wide enough to hold a candlestick. Sometimes called a candle slide. The name also was applied to a type of work light: a board or a small table, upon which four X-shaped supports were set. A center socket held a lighted candle. The four supports held glass globes filled with water to reflect and thus magnify the candlelight.

CANDLEBOX

Any box, drawer, or small chest used for

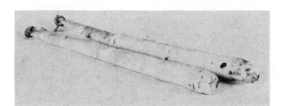

Dipped tallow candles made and stored away about 1800.

Candle storage box.

262

the storage of candles. The majority of eighteenth-century containers were wooden with lid tops, and shaped backs, and were made to be hung from wall pins or nails. Others were small, lidded table chests. "In ye fore [noon] I was at home, made a Candlebox contains 29½ lbs." Joshua Hempsted, *Diary,* January 7, 1715–16. New London (Connecticut) Historical Society, 1900. Many early-nineteenth-century candleboxes, elliptical or cylindrical in shape, were made of tin, usually japanned or otherwise decorated, and were made to be set on a shelf or to be hung by small attached wire bails from wall pins.

CANDLE BRANCH
(See CHANDELIER.)

CANDLE BRACKET
Another name for a type of Sconce, *q.v.,* sometimes used to designate a small shelf on which a candlestick was placed.

CANDLE CASE
Another name for the candlebox.

CANDLE CONE
The cone-shaped flame extinguisher, made usually with a ring handle and sometimes fitted with a long rodlike handle. (See also CANDLE EXTINGUISHER.)

Candle cones of painted tin.

CANDLE DRIER
Any bar or rack from which candles, just dipped or taken from the mold, could be hung to dry.

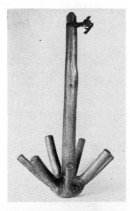

Candle drier made from natural tree or shrub branch. (Courtesy, Antiquarian and Landmarks Society, Inc.)

Candle drier suspended from original c. 1700 iron hooks.

CANDLE EXTINGUISHER

The small, cone-shaped utensil made from sheet iron, tin or pewter, steel or silver, for putting out the candle flame; it did not cut or trim the wick as did the snuffer. Extinguishers were made with small ring handles, set at the end of narrow rods for ease in reaching candles in sconce holders or chandeliers; and often were attached to individual candle holders, especially chamber sticks, by small chains. "There is also Snuffers, Snuffstand, and Extinguisher, of Steel, which I send for the Beauty of the Work. The Extinguisher is for Spermaceti Candles only, and is of a new contrivance, to preserve the Snuff upon the Candle." (Benjamin Franklin from London, February 19, 1758, to his wife at Philadelphia.) *Writings of Benjamin Franklin,* ed., A. H. Smyth (New York, 1907).

Candle extinguisher.

CANDLE MOLD

The name of the utensil used in households and shops to mold candles; usually a group or series of from eight to forty-eight hollow metal or pottery tubes set in a frame and in which candles were formed when hot wax or tallow was poured into the tubes and allowed to cool. Small molds in which one, two, or four candles only might be made were not uncommon. An apprentice to his father, a Boston tallow chandler, Franklin wrote that at ten, "I was accordingly em-ployed in cutting the wicks, and filling the moulds, taking care of the shop, carrying messages. Ec." Benjamin Franklin, *Life and Essays* (Boston, 1845). Before 1800, "they had no argand or other lamps in the parlours but dipt candles, in brass or copper candlesticks, was usually good enough for common use; and those who occasionally used mould candles, made them at home, in little tin frames, casting four to six candles in each." John F. Watson, *Annals of Philadelphia* (Philadelphia, 1830). "To Be Sold, by Robert Boyle, Pewterer . . . Limbecks and Cold Stills, Candle Molds of different sizes . . . Likewise the highest Prices in Cash for old Pewter, Copper, Brass and Lead." *The New-York Gazette or The Weekly Post-Boy,* December 22, 1755.

CANDLE PLATE

A confusing contemporary term because it had two uses; it was a synonym for the back piece or plate of what today is more commonly called a wall Sconce or Waller, *qq.v.,* and it was used also to describe the table plate or tray that held candlesticks and snuffers. "Candle Plates or Wallers of Brasse or Lattin" were listed in the House of Parliament Rates, 1660, for Imports and Exports —*Statutes of the Realm* (London, 1819). (See also CANDLESTICK.)

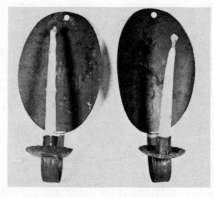

Candle plate sconces. (Courtesy, Antiquarian and Landmarks Society, Inc.)

CANDLE REFLECTOR
(See CANDLE SCREEN.)

CANDLE SCREEN

Two types of utensil were known as candle screens. One was a miniature or table-top version of the fire screen with a panel covered in tapestry or other needlework, a painting in oil or japan colors, or wood inlay, attached to a pole, and adjusted by being moved up or down the pole. These screened or protected the candle from stray breezes. A second form, also called a screen, actually served as a reflector as well. These often were adjustable round, square, or oval sheets or placques of brass or silver set on tiny tripod stands, miniature versions of the tilting-top table. "James Jacks, Goldsmith, Jeweller, and Watchmaker . . . has imported Among a rich assemblage of other articles . . . Pillar, bracket and chamber candlesticks . . . Bolton's patent shades, with spring candlesticks . . . silver patch boxes, candle screens." *Federal Gazette* (Philadelphia), April 15, 1797.

CANDLE SHADE

The 18- to 30-inch tall blown-glass cylinder, usually bulged near the center and open at both ends, set over a candleholder to protect the flame from draughts from open windows; sometimes also called an Abat-jour or Hurricane Glass, *qq.v.*

CANDLE SHEARS

A common name for candle snuffer, the small wick trimmer equipped with a box to catch the snuff.

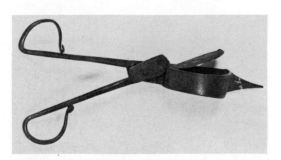

Late-eighteenth-century candle shears or snuffer.

Late-eighteenth-century candle shears or snuffer.

CANDLE SHIELD

Round, oval, or shield-shaped sheets of thin metal, horn, or wood attached to a ring or pincers which could be slipped over the candlestick or clipped to it to protect the flame from drafts and/or to reflect light.

CANDLE SLICE

(See under SLICE, CANDLE PLATE.)

CANDLE SLIDE

(See CANDLE BOARD.)

CANDLE SNUFFERS

"An instrument to crop candles with." (W) The hard candlewick, consumed by the fire of the candle itself, was not developed until the nineteenth century. Prior to that time, wicks were soft and thick and consequently a source of sooty snuff or snaft, a cause of sputtering flame, and in need of daily trimming. Until about 1750 snuffers usually were made with flat scissor-like blades, above the topside of which the snuff pan or box was set. During the reign of George III snuffers were designed with three small feet or rests. This improvement made it easier to pick up the snuffers from table or tray. Candles were themselves expensive; many of the snuffers were also. They were made of silver, gold, gilt-decorated silver, silver plate, polished steel, and japanned sheet iron or tin. They were ordered separately, often to match the design of the candlesticks; or with their own matching tray or stand holders.

CANDLE-SNUFFERS-AND-TRAY SET

After the Revolution, snuffers, with trays plated or japanned to match, were commonly for sale by local silversmiths, jewelers, hardware, and general dry-goods merchants. "Goodwin & Dodd have . . . Plated & Britannia Candlesticks; plated Snuffers and Trays, Britannia and iron Table & Tea Spoons, tea Trays, tea Caddies, Dressing Cases. Knives & Forks, Brass Andirons, Shovels and Tongs, Hearth . . . Brushes." *American Mercury* (Hartford, Connecticut), January 27, 1813. (See also CANDLE SNUFFERS.)

CANDLESTAND

Collectors today use this term to designate a small tripod base table of 26 to 30 inches in height. During the Colonial and Early Federal periods, however, the term signified a fairly high standard supporting a small top board just large enough to hold one candlestick holder, or, a series of arms or branches fitted with candle sockets. In describing his designs for candlestands, Thomas Chippendale noted, "They are from Three Feet, six Inches in Height. They have three Arms and Three Feet each." *The Gentleman and Cabinet-Maker's Director* (London, 1762). Hepplewhite said candlestands were "very useful in large suits of apartments, as the light may be placed in any part at pleasure—in drawing rooms, in halls and on large stair-cases . . . These designs may be executed in mahogany or wood japanned. The branches . . . should be of lacquered brass." *The Cabinet-Maker and Upholsterer's Guide* (London, 1794). (See CANDLE STOOL.)

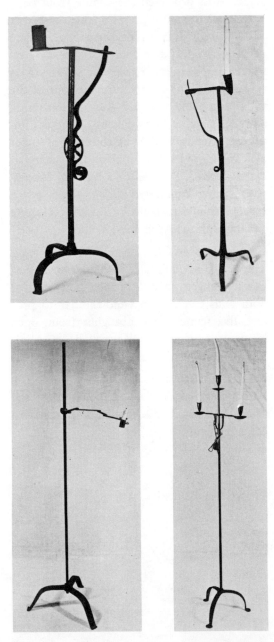

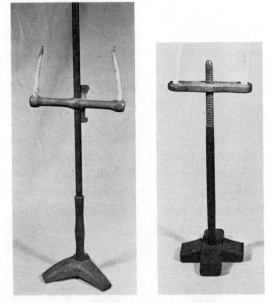

Six 1700–50 American wood and iron candlestands. (Courtesy, Antiquarian and Landmarks Society, Inc.)

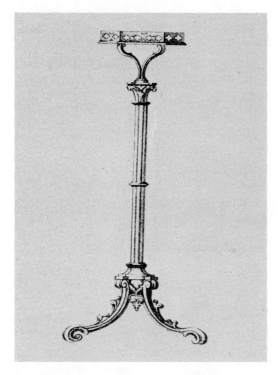

Candlestand illustrated in Chippendale's *Director* (London, 1762).

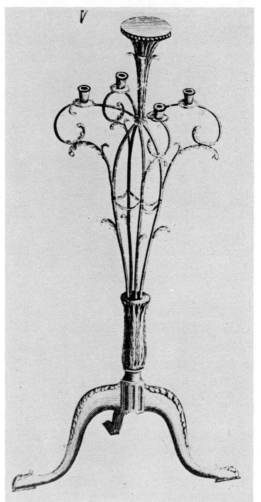

Candlestand illustrated in Hepplewhite's *Guide* (London, 1788).

CANDLESTICK

Any "instrument that holds candles," (W) either by impaling a candle on a spike, as does a Pricket Candlestick, *q.v.,* or by insertion of the candle into a nozzle or socket at the top of an upright stand. Candleholders or candlesticks were made of wood, metal, pottery, porcelain, glass, horn, stone. "I am about buying a compleat set of Table China, 2 cases of silver handled Knives and Forks, and 2 pair Silver Candlesticks; but these shall keep to use here till my Return, as I am obliged sometimes to entertain polite Company." (Benjamin Franklin, from London February 19, 1758, to his wife at Philadelphia.) *The Writings of Benjamin*

Dated pewter candlesticks.

Franklin, ed., A. H. Smyth (New York, 1907).

Eighteenth-century mid-drip candlestick. (Courtesy, Antiquarian and Landmarks Society, Inc.)

Seventeenth-century mid-drip candlesticks or holders.

C. 1700 tall mid-drip candlesticks. (Courtesy Antiquarian and Landmarks Society, Inc.)

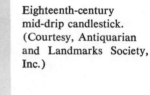

Eighteenth-century mid-drip candlestick. (Courtesy, Antiquarian and Landmarks Society, Inc.)

C. 1710 iron candleholders set in beams.

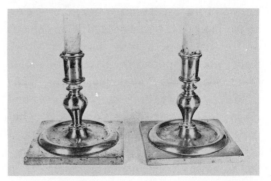

C. 1730 brass candlesticks. (Courtesy, Antiquarian and Landmarks Society, Inc.)

C. 1730 brass candlesticks. (Courtesy, Antiquarian and Landmarks Society, Inc.)

C. 1750 transition brass candlestick.

C. 1760 tin candlestick. (Courtesy, Antiquarian and Landmarks Society, Inc.)

C. 1780–1810 silver candlesticks.

CANDLE STOOL

The small table now generally called a Candlestand, *q.v.,* with a top board large enough to hold a candlestick and other small articles: ". . . Rested well last night, and am now writing on the candlestool by the fire,

Three-foot candle stool, c. 1740.

Candle stool with box for storage of candles, c. 1780. (Courtesy, Antiquarian and Landmarks Society, Inc.)

west side of the fireplace, in the corner . . ."
October 16, 1806 letter: Lyman Beecher, *Autobiography, Correspondence,* ed., Charles Beecher (New York, 1866). (See also CANDLESTAND.)

CANDLEWOOD
Light wood, any wood rich in resin, cut into small blocks or chunks or splints and burned to produce light. (See also CRESSET.)

CANE FURNITURE
First produced in England during the reign of Charles II, cane furniture was made until about 1750, prized because it was light and clean, and popular because it was comparatively inexpensive. Many caned chairs, day beds, and settees were brought here. Colonists who could not afford to import cane, substituted bannister-back chairs with rush or splint seats, copying as closely as possible the tall back with shaped crest and the bulbous, turned front stretcher of the imported chairs made with cane seats and

Cane chair.

C. 1700 chair with cane seat and back. (Courtesy, Antiquarian and Landmarks Society, Inc.)

backs. When first used, the cane strips were interwoven in a fairly open mesh; by the end of the period a tight, closely woven mesh was favored. Although often it was less expensive to import fine furniture than it was to manufacture it here, caned pieces were made in colonial urban centers, particularly Philadelphia, the second largest city, ranking after London, in the British Empire: "Cane Chairs of all Sorts made after the best & Newest Fashion; old chairs caned or holes mended, if not gone too far, at reasonable rates, by Nicholas Gale, next to the Sign of the Pewter Platter in Front Street, Philadelphia." *Pennsylvania Gazette* (Philadelphia), June 24, 1743.

CANISTER
"A box for holding tea; a small basket." (W) Canister was used to designate any box or case or container for tea, shot, biscuits, cookies, or bread. (See also CADDY, TOBACCO CANISTER.)

CANNIKIN
A little Can, *q.v.* (See also BOUSING CAN.)

CANNON-BALL BED

The cant term for a type of turned-post bedstead especially popular from about 1820 to 1850. Each of the posts had a large round finial, hence this descriptive common name.

CANNON STOVE

The popular name for an upright, free-standing stove, the pipe fitting into the chimney flue, made during the late eighteenth century in Pennsylvania and New York. "On Monday next . . . will be sold at Public Vendue [auction] . . . a quantity of unfinished walnut and mahogany furniture; . . . tools . . . work benches; a cannon stove with pipe, Ec. . . . with sundry other articles not enumerated. Wm. Shannon, Auctioneer." *Pennsylvania Packet* (Philadelphia), January 14, 1794.

CANOPY BED

(See BEDSTEAD, TESTER BED.)

CANOPY RAIL

(See BED POLE, TESTER BED.)

CANTEEN

The small, usually round wooden keg or cask, with stopper, used to carry water or other beverage for use while traveling, marching, or otherwise detained from a source of supply. "United States Deputy Commissary's Office, Norwich, Conn. December, 1813: The subscriber wishes to contract for several thousand CANTEENS to be delivered in Albany during the present Winter. Elisha Tracy, U.S. Deputy Commissary." The canteens used during the War of 1812 and the Civil War differed little from those carried during the Revolution. "A soldier's canteen contains three pints." *Treasury of Knowledge* (New York, 1833). The term also was used in the eighteenth century for what later was called a mess kit; that is, a traveler's case or box, usually with compartments, enclosing a dish, spoon, and cup. A second early use was as a synonym for a bottle case or chest. (See also CAN, CASE BOTTLE, RUNDLET.)

Canteen.

CANTERBURY

Originally, a kind of two-tiered tea wagon, or "supper-tray, made to stand by a table at supper, with a circular end, and three partitions cross-wise to hold knives, forks, plates." Thomas Sheraton, *The Cabinet Dictionary* (London, 1803). Shortly thereafter, as today, canterbury meant a low stand, often on casters, divided or partitioned to hold books of sheet music: "The Canterburies are intended for holding such music-books as are in Constant use . . . [and] may be manufactured in mahogany, rosewood, or bronzed and gilt, to suit the different rooms they may be placed in." George Smith, *A Collection of Designs for Household Furniture . . .* (London, 1808). By the mid-nineteenth century, the canterbury consisted "essentially of a drawer-case, on the top of which is placed a series of divisions, either in an inclined or vertical position, for holding music-books; while, the drawer, which extends the whole length, is a conventional deposit for loose sheets or manuscript." Blackie and Son, *The Cabinet-Maker's Assistant* (London, 1853). (See also BUTLER'S TABLE.)

CANTON CHINA

A general term that could be applied to any porcelain exported from that Chinese port;

but from the late 1780s it has been the popular specific designation for a type of blue-and-white dinner and tea services made at potteries near Canton and decorated with a Chinese scene including water, islands, bridges, boats, and trees painted in blue under the glaze, the forerunner of what later would be called the willow pattern. "Charles Sigourney . . . Eight dining sets of blue and white Canton china in boxes of 172 pieces each, and which, being bought at Auction, will be sold by the set, at the price it is usually sold for in Boston, with the addition of the freight only." *American Mercury* (Hartford, Connecticut), December 27, 1810.

CAPARISON
The horse cloth or "cover thrown over the saddle, Ec." (M)

CAP CASE
Another term for a "small travelling case, or bandbox." (H)

CAPE COD GLASS
Specifically, any pressed or cut glass produced at the Cape Cod Glass Company founded by Deming Jarves in 1858.

CAPSTAN TABLE
Another name for the Drum Table, *q.v.*

CAPTAIN'S CHAIR
The collector's term for the low-backed Windsor Chair, *q.v.*

CAPTAIN'S CHEST
The collector's term for an item of portable field or shipboard furniture, a plain chest of drawers made in two sections, each with brass side handles and with recessed drawer pulls. (See also CAMPAIGN FURNITURE.)

CAPTAIN'S DECANTER
The collector's term for the broad-based decanter, perhaps specifically designed for use aboard ship, and which at any rate could scarcely have been afforded by the average seaman or used with ease except in the cabin of an officer or distinguished passenger. These stoppered bottles were heavier than the house decanter and are distinguished by their flat base, much broader than ordinarily found, and presumably so made to prevent tipping over in high seas. Since no matter how wide its base, any ship bottle left out on a table top could have been tipped over when the main was bounding, it is more likely these decanters were designed for use in taverns or clubs ashore, the owners of which were just as apprehensive of broken glass.

CAP TREE
A type of hat rack or clothes tree made of pegs set in rows or tiers; also called a cap stock or "cap gallows." (H) "Capp hookes or ends" were listed in the House of Parliament Rates, 1660, for Imports and Exports —*Statutes of the Realm* (London, 1819).

CARABINE, CARBINE
In weaponry, the term for "a small sort of firearms, shorter than a fusil, and carrying a ball of twenty-four in the pound, hung by the light horse [soldier] at a belt over the left shoulder. It is a kind of medium between the pistol and the musket, having its barrel two foot and a half long." (J)

CARAFE
This term for a slender-necked water jug or pitcher with no stopper was derived from the French word *carafe,* the Spanish *garaffa,* the Italian *caraffa,* and the Arabic *gharafa,* meaning to draw water. Carafe sometimes was spelled craft, carrofft, or carf in the eighteenth and early nineteenth centuries. "Henry William Stiegel, Proprietor of the first American Flint-Glass Manufactory in Pennsylvania, is just arrived in this city, and opened a warehouse near the Exchange . . . he offers to the public a Quart, pint, and half pint decanters, pint crafts, half pint and jill tumblers; syllabub and jelly glasses; three feeted salts and creams; wine and water glasses; vinegar and mustard crewets; phials and other bottles, for Chymists and

Apothecaries, Ec." *New York Journal or The General Advertiser,* January 14, 1773.

CARBINIER, CARABINIER
"A short gun." (W) (See also CARABINE, CARBINE.)

CARCEL LAMP
A type of lamp first produced in France in 1800 and which also was called a mechanized lamp or patent lamp. This was a variation of the Argand Lamp, *q.v.,* and was made with a clockwork pump to fill the burner with oil from a lower reservoir.

CARD
This is the term "among artificers, for an instrument consisting of a block of wood, beset with sharp [iron] teeth, serving to arrange the hairs of wool, flax, hemp and the like; there are different kinds of them, as hand-cards, stock-cards." (M)

Carding is the operation of combing; i.e., "disentangling the wool, cotton, and other materials in order to render it proper for the work for which it is intended." (M)

"Card Manufactory, Nathan Allyn ten rods NW of the State-House, manufactures Machine Cards of all descriptions and of the very best quality. Hand Cards, Clothiers' Jacks, Steel Teeth do. and Cotton Filleting made of Steel Teeth. Card wire of various

numbers. He will supply on short notice, Double and Single Carding Machines complete, made by the Messrs. Kellogg's of New Hartford. Orders post-paid will be punctually attended to. One set of Card-Makers Machinery for sale cheap." *American Mercury* (Hartford, Connecticut), March 25, 1817. (See also PLAYING CARDS.)

CARDINAL'S HAT
A cant term for a deep pewter dish with a broad rim.

CARD TABLE
The term usually is applied to a small four-leg table, with a rectangular, oval, circular, or shaped two-piece top hinged in the center to make two folds or leaves. When open, one fold or one half of the top swings over and out, and is supported on a swing leg. "The inner part should be lined with green cloth; the fronts may be enriched with inlaid or painted ornaments; the top also admits of great elegance in the same style." A. Hepplewhite, *Cabinet-Maker and Upholsterer's Guide* (London, 1794). "Just arrived from Philadelphia . . . Two circular

Square card table of cherry with pine as secondary wood, has serpentine-shaped apron with conforming top, shaded satinwood inlay medallion, pierced brackets; rear swing leg has wooden hinge. (Courtesy, Connecticut Historical Society, Inc.)

Cards.

card tables; one Pembroke." *Charleston City Gazette* (South Carolina) January 30, 1790.

Card table from Thomas Sheraton's *The Cabinet-Maker's and Upholsterer's Drawing-Book* (London, 1791–94).

Round card table shown closed, Hepplewhite's *Guide* (London, 1788).

CARICATURA, CARICATURE

An "Italian word [that] in painting is principally applied to grotesque figures, which retain an extravagant and ugly, but real resemblance of the person they are designed to represent, and lash whomsoever the painter, carver, or graver has a mind to satirize, or divert himself with. But burlesque in painting, like burlesque in poetry, should be confined within bounds." (M)

CARPET

Now a generic term for any floor covering, this Middle English word originally meant a luxurious fabric used as a wall hanging, table, chest, or seat cover. By 1778 it connoted "A sort of covering of stuff, or other materials, wrought with the needle or in a loom, forming part of the furniture of a house, and commonly spread over table, or laid upon the floor. Persian and Turkey carpets are those most esteemed, though at Paris . . . they make them [as fine as] the true Persian. There are also carpets of Germany . . . We have likewise carpets made in England equal to any brought from the East." (M)

When Franklin in London ordered carpeting to ship to his wife in Philadelphia, he felt it necessary to send specific directions for its installation; when he said the purchase was "his fancy" he meant he had chosen the material himself, not leaving as he often did, the shopping to his housekeeper or a friend: "In the great Case is contain'd some Carpeting for a best Room Floor. There is enough for one large or two small ones, it is to be sow'd together, the Edges being first fell'd down, and Care taken to make the Figures meet exactly: there is Bordering for the same. This was my fancy." (February 19, 1758.) *The Writings of Benjamin Franklin,* ed., A. H. Smyth (New York, 1907).

By the end of the Colonial period, the term generally was used to mean floor coverings. "Carpets, Scottish and Turkish, are much used, and indeed are necessities where the houses are so lightly built; stairs and rooms are laid with them [by those who can afford the cost]." Johann David Schoepf, *Travels in the Confederation*

[1783–84] (Philadelphia, 1911). (Reference reflects the general European surprise at the number of American houses built of wood rather than of stone or brick.) Nevertheless, as late as 1806 carpet still was defined by Noah Webster as "a cover for a table or a floor." (See also FLOOR CLOTH.)

CARPET BALLS
Made in sets of seven for the Victorian era game of carpet bowls, these were white earthenware or brown stoneware balls, about 2 inches in diameter, some plain, the majority decorated with rings, lattice, star, or floral paterns. Each set included one plain ball and six decorated balls.

CARRIAGE LIGHTS
The general term used by collectors for any of the lamps specifically made for use in coach, carriage, gig, whiskey, chaise, buggy, or other horse-powered transportation. (See also GIG LAMPS.)

CART
The term for any "wheel-carriage, used commonly for luggage; a small carriage with two wheels, distinguished from a waggon, which has four wheels." (J)

CARTOON
The term is from the Italian *cartone* for a "painting or drawing upon large paper." (J) "The world beholds the cartoons of Raphael, and every one feels his share of pleasure and entertainment." Isaac Watts, *Logick* (London, 1725).

CARTOUCHE
"A case of wood about three inches thick at the bottom bound about with marlin holding about four hundred musket balls, sends six or eight balls of iron to be fired out of a hobit." (M)

CARTOUCHE BOX
Cartouche, from the French for scroll, signified a paper-wrapped charge of gun powder, or cartridge. The box carried such cartridges already made up, as opposed to the powder-horn or flask which held powder only. Worn suspended from the bandolier or belt, the boxes were of wood; metal-banded wood; varnished leather; pewter, tin, or brass. "Every listed soldier and other Householder shall be always provided with . . . good Fire Arms; a Cartouche Box, one Pound of good Powder. *Act for Regulating the Militia* (Boston, 1733). (See also CARTRIDGE POUCH.)

CARTRIDGE BOX
"A case of wood covered with leather holding a dozen musket cartridges." (M)

CARTRIDGE POUCH
"A cartridge [from the French *cartouche*] is a case of paper or parchment filled with gun powder, used in charging guns." (J) The pouch was of heavy leather and was carried suspended from bandolier or belt. "Every French soldier carries in his cartridge-pouch the baton of a marshal of France." [Napoleon I] E. Blaze, *La Vie Militaire sous l'Empire*. (See also CARTOUCHE BOX.)

CARVER AND STEEL
(See CARVING-KNIFE SET.)

CARVER CHAIR
The collector's term, in favor since the American Centennial period of the late nineteenth century, for a type of early-seventeenth-century English chair with turned back legs and posts and with front legs, also turned, and which rise as supports to the arms. The seat is rush; the back usually consists of three turned spindles. The name honors John Carver, first governor of Plymouth Colony, 1620–21, who is said to have owned a similar chair.

CARVING
The term for "wood, or stone or other matter cut into elegant forms," (J) as small statuary or other decorations.

CARVING-KNIFE SET
The large knife for use by the host at table or sideboard, sold *en suite* with its steel or

sharpening tool; the two were made with matching handles. "Henry C. Porter Has just received and is now opening a general assortment of Cutlery and Hardware Goods, which were purchased with cash at the late auction sales in New York, and will be sold at prices unusually low for cash only. Consisting in part of the following articles: Ivory, horntip, brick, bone and wood handle table and dessert Knives and Forks, Carvers and Steels, Butcher and Bread Knives . . ." *American Mercury* (Hartford, Connecticut), May 8, 1820.

CASE, CASE PIECE
The term derived from the French *caisse* for box, used to designate "something that covers or contains anything else; a covering; a box; a sheath." (J) Hence, a case of drawers was the term used in the Colonial period for what more commonly would be called a chest of drawers today; thus, also, a bookcase; a writing or letter case.

CASE BOTTLE
A single bottle, or set of matched bottles, blown to a specific size to fit into specially made cases or chests. Some sets included bottles in graduated sizes from half-pint to half-gallon, often etched or decorated and kept in handsomely inlaid chests. Others were made specifically, if not always successfully, to survive the rigors of travel: "The Carolina Gentlemen did . . . hire a clumsy . . . cart to transport their Effects as far as Roanoak. This wretched machine, at first setting out, met with a very rude choque, that broke a Case-Bottle of Cherry Brandy in so unlucky a manner that not one precious Drop was saved." William Byrd, *History of the Dividing Line* [1728–29] (Richmond, 1866.) (See also MEDICINE CHEST.)

CASE KNIFE
The term had several meanings throughout the early period. Johnson does not list it in his 1755 *Dictionary,* noting knife and case separately. "To case, to cover on the outside with materials different from the inside." (J) Thus, a case knife in the earlier eighteenth century was (1) "A large knife, kept in a sheath, and carried in the pocket." (H) (See note under KNIFE-AND-FORK SET; also CLASP KNIFE, JACK-KNIFE, PENKNIFE. At the beginning of the nineteenth century, however, the term also meant, at least in New England, (2) "A kitchen or table knife," (W) perhaps because these large utensils were kept in racks, drawers, or boxes when not in use. (See also CARVING-KNIFE SET.)

CASE OF DRAWERS
A contemporary synonym for a Cabinet, *q.v.,* and what today more commonly is called a Chest of Drawers, *q.v.* "A handsome new fashion'd Japan'd case of drawers, and chamber table to be sold by John Brown, Enquire of the Printer hereof." *Pennsylvania Gazette* (Philadelphia), June 23, 1737. (See also BUREAU.)

CASK
A synonym for barrel, "a wooden vessel to stop up liquor or provisions." (J) ". . . get a hogshead of wine vinegar and another of verjuice, both in good casks and iron-bound. We have lost much by bad casks." (John Winthrop at Charleston to his son, John, in England, September 9, 1630.) *Journal, History of New England* (Boston, 1825).

CASKET
The specific term, a diminutive of *caisse* or chest, to describe "a small box or chest for jewels, or things of particular value" (J) equipped with a lock. "Casketts of Iron and of Steele" were listed in the House of Parliament Rates, 1660, for Imports and Exports—*Statutes of the Realm* (London, 1819).

CASSETTE
A term sometimes used to describe a cash box, Casket, or Till, *qq.v.*

Seventeenth-century painted wood casket or jewel chest. (Courtesy, Antiquarian and Landmarks Society, Inc.)

CASSONE
The Italian term, often used by modern collectors, for the highly decorated and ornamented European Dowry Chest, *q.v.*

CASTANET
One of the musical instruments "much used by the Moors, Spaniards, and Bohemians, to accompany their dances." (M)

CASTER, CASTOR
A receptacle or container for dry condiments such as salt, pepper, sugar, made with a pierced top for casting the seasoning over the food; in silver, crystal with silver tops, silver-plated metal, soft or hard-paste porcelain. "New Goods, Goodwin & Dodd have just received an assortment, viz—Silver Tea Sets, Plated and Britannia do., Plated Castors . . ." *American Mercury* (Hartford, Connecticut), June 17, 1816.

Unmarked American pewter pepper caster.

Pepper casters in silver, delft, soft paste.

CASTING BOTTLE, CASTING GLASS
Two names for the bottle of metal, pottery, or glass, made with a perforated top and used for casting or "sprinkling perfumes." (H)   In the seventeenth century, the casting bottle sometimes also was called a Censer, *q.v.*

CAT
The modern collector's term for the small, narrow, tripod warming stand for plates; a plate warmer.

CATCAL(L), CATPIPE
The popular term for "a squeaking instrument, used in the playhouse to condemn plays." (J)   A small reed pipe, which when blown produced a sound imitative of the screech of an outraged alley cat.

CATHEDRAL CLOCK
The popular name for a type of Gothic shelf-clock case designed by Elias Ingraham about 1840; it had a rounded dome top rising to a sharp spirelike point, and pillars, somewhat resembling spires or turrets, at the four corners of the case.

CAUDLE CUP
A contemporary term for the small, covered drinking pot, usually made with two handles. The term caudle is derived from the French *chadeau,* a "mixture of wine and other ingredients given to women in childbed and sick persons." (W)   The cups were made in silver, pewter, wood, pottery,

and porcelain and used also for the service of any warm drink. (See also POSSET POT.)

CELESTIAL GLOBE
(See GLOBES.)

CELE, CELURE
The canopy suspended from the ceiling or wall above a bedstead; sometimes colloquially referred to as a bed-cellar. (See also FOUR POST BEDSTEAD, TESTER BEDSTEAD.)

CELLARET(T)E
Also called a *garde de vin,* this was "a case of cabinet work for liquors;" (W) a small rectangular, square, or polygonal box or chest with lid, set on legs or a frame "generally made of mahogany, and hooped with brass hoops lacquered; the inner part is divided with partitions, and lined with lead for bottles. [It] may be made of any shape. These are of general use where sideboards are without drawers." A. Hepplewhite, *The Cabinet-Maker and Upholsterer's Guide* (London, 1788). As Hepplewhite indicates, the name also was given to the deep drawer provided in some sideboards for the storage of wine bottles.

Cellarette, as shown in Hepplewhite's *Guide* (London, 1794).

CENSER
An incense pot; the thurible. This was "the pan or vessel in which incense is burned,"
but also a common term for "a pan in which anything is burned; a firepan." (J) Censer also was an early synonym for the Casting Bottle, *q.v.*

CENTERPIECE
An Epergne, *q.v.*

CERAMICS
The all-inclusive term from the Greek *keramos* for pottery or potter's earth, used to designate all types of pottery and porcelain.

CHAFFERN
"A vessel to make anything hot in, [using] a portable grate for coals," (J) a Chafing Dish, *q.v.*

CHAFING DISH
"A kind of dish to put hot coals in." (W) This term for a portable grate, that is, a vessel to hold burning fuel, was derived from the Middle English word chaufen and the old French *chaufer,* meaning to heat. It included a rectangular frame on four legs, had a wooden handle, and was set above a container of charcoal, or a spirit lamp. A covered pan or dish was set in the frame and thus was heated by the fuel. Usually nicely designed with the removable covered pan made of copper, brass, or silver, the chafing dish ensemble also was used to serve from: "Half roast a wild duck and cut up as for eating, put in gill of gravy, a gill of red wine . . . into a silver chaffing dish, and set it over the lamp till it boils up . . . Make it thoroughly hot, and send it to the table in the chafing dish." Richard Briggs, *The New Art of Cookery* (Philadelphia, 1792). "Chafing dishes of Brasse, Lattin or Iron" were listed in the House of Parliament Rates, 1660, for Imports and Exports —*Statutes of the Realm* (London, 1819).

CHAIR
The general term for any seat with a back support, with or without arms, and designed for the comfort of one person. "A moveable seat," (J) the first term for which was "back-stool," i.e., a stool or seat with a

back. In the late eighteenth century, Hepplewhite considered that "the general dimension and proportion of chairs [should be]: width in front 20 inches, depth of the seat 17 inches, height of the seat frame 17 inches, total height about 3 feet 1 inch," granting, however, that "other dimensions are frequently adapted according to the size of the room, or the pleasure of the purchaser." A. Hepplewhite, *The Cabinet-Maker and Upholsterer's Guide* (London, 1788).

CHAIR-BACK SETTEE

The collector's term to distinguish a settee with a back composed of two or more joined chair backs, from the settee with a single board or solid back. (See also DOUBLE CHAIR.)

CHAIR BED

The all-inclusive nineteenth-century term for any adjustable easy chair that could be converted for use as a bed, either by a back that could be let down or a kind of double-seat frame that could be pulled out. (See also BED CHAIR, HUNTING CHAIR, SLEEPING CHAIR.)

CHAIR TABLE

A chair with a separate back designed to swing over and rest flat on the chair arms, where, secured by pins, it can serve as a table board. This is called a hutch-chair table when the chair seat actually is a box with lid. "Supper was got before our eyes in the ample kitchen, by a fire which would have roasted an ox . . . and the dishes were soon smoking on the table, late the arm-chair, against the wall, from which one of the party was expelled. The arms of the chair formed the frame on which the table rested; and when the round top was turned up against the wall, it formed the back of the chair, and was no more in the way than the wall itself. This we noticed was the prevailing fashion in these log-houses, in order to economize in room." Henry David Thoreau, *The Maine Woods* (1864).

CHAISE LONGUE

"They have their name from the French which imports a Long Chair, Their use is to rest or loll upon after dinner." Thomas Sheraton, *The Cabinet-Maker and Upholsterer's Drawing-Book* (London, 1791–94). (See also DAY BED.)

CHALICE

The container for sacramental wine, this was, according to Webster, "a cup standing on a foot." Remarkably enough, many chalices are for sale and fine examples are included in numerous private collections. Those made for Roman Catholic, Anglican, and Eastern Orthodox congregations usually are of gold or silver only; New England Protestant congregations allowed the use of pewter also. "In old time we had treen chalices and golden priests, but now we have treen priests and golden chalices." Bishop John Janel, *Certain Sermons Preached Before the Queen's Majesty* (1609).

CHALK DRAWING

The contemporary term to describe any drawing done with chalk on paper usually in red or black line, but not necessarily confined to these colors. "Called at Faythorn's to buy some prints for my wife to draw by this winter, and here did see my Lady Castlemaine's picture, done by him in red chalke and other colours [from] which he hath cut it in copper to be printed. The picture in chalke is the finest thing I ever saw in my life, I think; and I did desire to buy it." Samuel Pepys, *Diary,* November 7, 1666. Today we would be more apt to describe such a drawing as a Pastel Drawing, *q.v.* (See also ACADEMY FIGURE.)

CHAMBER CANDLESTICK, CHAMBER STICK

The short candle socket set on a wide, shallow dish or saucer-like base, with a ringholder, and with a cone extinguisher attached by a fine chain; sometimes also

279

with matching snuffers hung from a hook on the candle socket. Made of brass, silver, pewter, silver-plated metal, tin, pottery. The broad saucer base was a safety measure, designed to catch drops of hot wax or tallow, and to keep the candleholder from being tipped or blown over. ". . . large plated candlesticks, card table ditto, bed chamber

Tin chamber sticks, c. 1780. (Courtesy, Antiquarian and Landmarks Society, Inc.)

Brass chamber sticks, c. 1800.

with snuffers and extinguishers ditto . . . William Dawson." *Pennsylvania Packet* (Philadelphia), April 26, 1793. "4 large fashionable brass Candlesticks; 1 large flat do. with a Slider." Order January 10, 1771, from James Carter, Williamsburg, Virginia, to London. Frances Mason, *John Norton and Sons, Merchants of London and Virginia* (Richmond, 1935).

Candlestick Slider: The plate or disc fitted within the shaft of the candlestick, and which could be pushed or slid up the shaft by means of a small external button or thumbpiece set in a vertical channel or groove.

CHAMBER CLOCK

A small table or shelf clock for the bed chamber. "James Jacks, Jeweller and Watchmaker [has] best London made chamber clocks, with mahogany, satin wood, and ebony cases, warranted . . ." *Pennsylvania Packet* (Philadelphia), November 13, 1799.

CHAMBER TABLE

A contemporary term for a dressing table; a small table with one drawer below the top board, and usually with an attached looking glass. (See advertisements quoted under CASE OF DRAWERS, TOILET.)

CHANDELIER

From the Middle English word, chaundler and the Latin *candelarius* for candle, this was the term used in the seventeenth and eighteenth centuries for any branched support for a number of lights; later it was used specifically for a light fixture suspended from a ceiling or beam. The older English common term had been candlebeam or candle-branch, terms that continued in use in this country well into the nineteenth century. Chandeliers seldom were used in the average home during the Colonial period because of the cost of candles; the simply formed iron, tin, or painted wood chandeliers originating here in the eighteenth century usually were made for use in taverns, inn common rooms, or church buildings. Well-to-do merchants, however, often imported handsome chandeliers of silver, pewter, brass, or crystal. Of those designs shown in *The Gentleman and Cabinet-Maker's Director* (London, 1762), Chip-

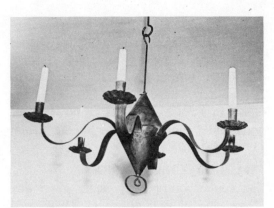

New England tin chandelier, c. 1810–20.

Gilt chandelier from Chippendale's *Director* (London, 1762).

C. 1810 brass chandelier. (*Hartford Times* photo by Einar Chindmark.)

pendale said, "They are generally made of Glass, and sometimes of Brass; but if neatly done in Wood, and gilt in burnished Gold, would look better, and come much cheaper." Chandelier, according to Johnson in 1755, was a synonym for candelabra, or, a "branch for candles."

CHAPBOOK

Or more literally, cheap-book; the contemporary term used to distinguish the pamphlets or other inexpensive, paper-covered booklets sold by chapman or peddlers, from the bound books sold by book sellers: "W. W. Marsh has just published and [has] now ready for sale *The History of America,* containing the Revolutionary War, and the principal Land and Naval Engagements since the present War. Price, $1.25. Will speedily publish an extensive assortment of CHAPBOOKS, which will be sold as low as can be purchased elsewhere of a superior quality. Peddlers take notice!" *American Mercury* (Hartford, Connecticut), January 15, 1814.

CHAPE

The term for the decorative "catch of anything by which it is held in its place, as the hook of a scabbard by which it sticks in the belt; the point by which a buckle is held to the back strap. Also, a brass or silver tip or case, that strengthens the end of the scabbard of a sword," (J) and sometimes for the entire buckle. "Just imported

281

in the *Sally,* from Bristol, an Assortment of Double and single shoe and knee chapes . . . George Dowig." *Maryland Journal* (Baltimore), April 16, 1790. "Lockers or Chapes for Daggers" were listed in the House of Parliament Rates, 1660, for Imports and Exports—*Statutes of the Realm* (London, 1819).

CHARGER, CHARYOWRE

The contemporary early name given any "large kind of dish or plate," (W) used for carrying meat; a platter to carry food to the table and from which it was served, as opposed to the trencher from which an individual served himself.

Charger of Lambeth delft commemorating coronation of King William III. (Courtesy, Antiquarian and Landmarks Society, Inc.)

CHART

The specific contemporary term for "a delineation or map of coasts, for the use of sailors. It is distinguished from a map by representing only the coasts." (J) Many were hand drawn; many more were printed from copper plates; decorated with handsome cartouches and illustrations of sailing ships, and were hand colored. They were made and/or sold singly and in sets or portfolios. (See also MAP.)

CHATELAINE

Derived from the French for mistress of the chateau and used to describe the early waist belt or chain, with a clasp in the form of

a ring or loop, to hold a work pocket or keys. Later, a chatelaine meant a metal plate or disc with several short chains from which a needle case, penknife, or keys could be suspended.

CHECKER TABLE
(See CHESS TABLE.)

CHEESE BRIGS
Another name for the Cheese Ladder, *q.v.*

CHEESE LADDER

A kitchen or dairy-room utensil, made of "two long pieces of wood, crossed toward the middle by two shorter ones, for the purpose of being placed over a large pan containing cream, to support the skimming bowl after it has been used so that it may drip into the liquid below." (H)

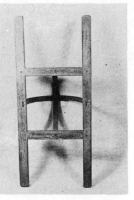

Cheese ladder.

CHEESE PLATE

A contemporary term for a small deep plate or shallow dish with a cover used to keep food warm at table; usually made of silver or Sheffield plate; less often of pottery or porcelain. "English Rabbit. Toast a slice of bread on both sides, put it into a cheeseplate, pour a glass of red wine over it . . ." Richard Briggs, *The New Art of Cookery* (Philadelphia, 1792).

CHEESE PRESS

In the kitchen or milk room, "the press in which the curds are pressed." (J)

Cheese press. (Courtesy, Antiquarian and Landmarks Society, Inc.)

CHEESE VAT
The kitchen or milk-room container, "a wooden case in which the curds are confined when they are pressed into cheese." (J)

CHEFFONIER
The same as Chiffonier, *q.v.*

CHESSBOARD
The common term for "the board or table on which the game of chess is played. Chess [is] a nice and abstruse game, in which two sets of men are moved in opposition to each other." (J) "Have just received from London, Chess Boards with men; portable Mahogany writing desks . . ." Hodyson & Nicholson. *Maryland Journal* (Baltimore), May 2, 1788. "Chess boards and Chess men" were listed in the House of Parliament Rates, 1660, for Imports and Exports—*Statutes of the Realm* (London, 1819).

CHESSMEN
Chess, the ancient game of wit and wits, "a difficult kind of game" required "a kind of board to play upon" with chessmen or "puppets." (W) Often beautifully executed, chessmen were made by the carver in ivory or fine woods, or by the silversmith, and sold in sets separately from the board, or as replacements for lost pieces. "Chessmen, cribbage boxes, tooth brushes, and gold and silver spangles . . ." [Joseph Anthony, Jr.] *Pennsylvania Packet* (Philadelphia), December 7, 1790.

CHESS TABLE
Any small stand or table with a top inlaid or painted with 64 alternating squares of black and white or black and red.

CHEST
The general contemporary term to describe

Chessboard table. (Courtesy, Antiquarian and Landmarks Society, Inc.)

Chest-over-drawer. (Courtesy, Antiquarian and Landmarks Society, Inc.)

Painted two-drawer chest; storage top part made to simulate drawers. (Courtesy, Connecticut Historical Society, Inc.)

C. 1680 oak two-sectional chest of drawers, geometric paneled front, ball feet. (Courtesy, Connecticut Historical Society, Inc.)

Typical of block-and-shell furniture identified with the Goddard and Townsend families of Newport. This chest of drawers from New London County, Connecticut, has stop-fluted pilasters, and a broad base molding and is set on boldly scrolled, edge-molded bracket feet. Made between 1755 and 1800 of mahogany with pine and whitewood. (Courtesy, Connecticut Historical Society, Inc.)

A cherry chest of drawers in the Yale University Art Gallery is inscribed "This Buro was made in the year of our Lord 1795 by Bates How" in pencil on the inside of the back. The date indicates the lengthy popularity span of the claw-and-ball foot in America, although, as shown here, by the end of the eighteenth century the size had diminished bringing the feet closer in feeling to the newer French bracket foot. Reverse curve or oxbow front; rope-carved skirt with carved lamb's tongue terminals. (Courtesy, Connecticut Historical Society, Inc.)

Chest of drawers with bow front, French feet. (Courtesy, Connecticut Historical Society, Inc.)

Chest of drawers illustrated in Hepplewhite's *Guide* (London, 1788).

any "box of wood or other materials, in which things are laid up." (J) A carefully made covered box, usually equipped with a lock; often decorated with carving or in-

lay; sometimes painted or gilded; sold singly or in sets. "Chests, of iron, large & small; of Cypresse wood, the nest of 3; of Spruce or Danske, the nest of 3; painted" were listed in the House of Parliament Rates, 1660, for Imports and Exports—*Statutes of the Realm* (London, 1819). The word also was a synonym for Casket, *q.v.*—as Shakespeare wrote of *A jewel in a ten-times-barr'd-up chest. King Richard II,* I, i.

CHESTERFIELD

A popular late-nineteenth-century term for a large, overstuffed couch or sofa, sometimes said to have been named for an Earl of Chesterfield, and which was "an indirect descendant of the Empire sofa, with the comfort kept, but all the grace left out . . . The obese, kindly-natured couch known to modern upholsterers as the Chesterfield is about as comely as a gigantic pin-cushion and as little convenient in a room of moderate dimensions as an elephant . . . decoratively, worse than useless . . ." Rosamund Marriott Watson, *The Art of the House* (London, 1897).

CHESTNUT ROASTER

A popular utensil for the kitchen or family sitting-room hearth of the eighteenth and early nineteenth centuries, these were round sheet-iron boxes 6 to 8 inches in diameter and approximately 3 inches in depth. The side and lid were perforated in simple decorative patterns. The main handle, also of iron, was from 2 to 3 feet long and had a wooden haft. The second handle, about half the length of the first, was attached to the lid and was fastened by a button or loop to the main handle when the roaster was in use over the fire. No contemporary record can be found to show that chestnut roasters ever were made of any metal other than sheet iron. An amazing number of reproductions, smaller than the prototype, and decorated with a variety of punched designs and chasing, unfortunately have flooded the market during the past fifty years. These gift-shop versions are still being made in brass and copper with turned wood handles. Chestnut roasting and popcorn toasting at the hearth were popular well into the nineteenth century. "Wanted. Two hundred bushels chestnuts for which a liberal price will be paid by James Goodwin. North end Main St." *American Mercury* (Hartford, Connecticut), November 6, 1802.

CHEST OF DRAWERS

The term for that useful item of furniture for storage originally called a Case of Drawers, or "a case with moveable boxes or drawers." (J) (See also BUREAU, CABINET, CASE OF DRAWERS.)

CHEVAL

This French word for horse was used to designate any support or frame having four feet or two standards. (See HORSE FIRE SCREEN, SWINGING CRADLE.)

CHEVERET, SHEVERET

The term for a small library table with a removable book shelf fitted to the top and set on a frame with tapered legs; often made with small drawers just below the shelf.

CHIFFONIER

A late-eighteenth-century bookstand or open cupboard, usually with one drawer set in the base; commonly equipped with casters and thus sometimes also called a moving library. "In almost every apartment of a house these articles will be found useful . . . their use is chiefly for such books as are in constant use, or not of sufficient consequence for the library; on the same account they become extremely serviceable in libraries, for the reception of books taken for present reading. The most simple are manufactured in plain mahogany or japanned in imitation of various woods; the more elegant in mahogany with decorations in imitation of bronze metal; rose-wood and gold come under similar recommendation, and gold with bronzed ornaments where expense is not an obstacle." George Smith, *A Collection of Designs for Household Furniture* (London, 1808). In the late nineteenth century, chiffonier came to mean a kind of bureau, a clothes chest or closed wardrobe; completely different in appearance and use from the piece of furniture originally so named.

CHILDREN'S PLAY CHINA
(See TOY CHINA.)

CHILD'S CHAIR

A small version of any chair design, including the popular Windsor, made in proper proportion and height to assure a child's comfort. "Alpheus Hews . . . carries on the business of Windsor Chair Making in Chapel Street in New Haven where may be had any Number of Windsor Settees, and Garden Chairs made in the neatest manner, and different fashions, also some very convenient for Children which he sells on the most reasonable terms for cash . . ." *New Haven Gazette* (Connecticut), February 22, 1787. (See also TABLE CHAIR, WINDSOR CHAIR.)

CHIMNEY BOARD
The board or panel designed to block the chimney opening when the fireplace was not in use. The majority of these boards were given the same background color used elsewhere in the room, against which stylized pictures of flowers, birds, or landscapes were painted.

CHIMNEY CORNER
This was the general term for the fireside and the specific colloquialism for a Settle, *q.v.;* that is, "The seat in each end of the firegrate; usually noted in proverbial language for being the place of idlers." (J) "With a tale forsooth he cometh unto you, with a tale which holdeth children from play, and old men from the chimney corner." Sir Philip Sidney, *The Defense of Poesy.*

CHIMNEY DOGS
A contemporary term for Firedogs or Andirons, *qq.v.* "1 pr. plain strong chimney Dogs for my Study no trap about them @ about 30/ [shillings]." Order January 10, 1771 from James Carter, Williamsburg, Virginia to London. Frances Mason, *John Norton and Sons, Merchants of London and Virginia* (Richmond, 1935).

CHIMNEY LOOKING GLASS
(See MURAL LOOKING GLASS.)

CHIMNEY ORNAMENTS
A common contemporary term for sets of garniture designed for the mantel shelf. "Joseph Anthony, Jr. Silversmith; has imported . . . a Large and General Assortment [including] chimney ornaments of the Derbyshire petrifaction, very elegant, . . ." *Pennsylvania Packet* (Philadelphia), December 7, 1790. (See GARNITURE SET.)

CHIMNEY PIECE
(1) Properly, the term for "the ornamental piece of wood or stone, that is set round the fireplace," (J) sometimes called the chimney surround. (2) Also a term sometimes used colloquially for any ornament, such as a porcelain vase or figure, set on the mantel shelf.

CHIMNEY PLATE
(See FIREBACK.)

CHINA, CHINAWARE
(See in Chapter 10.)

CHINA TABLE
Early-eighteenth-century term for a form of tea table, or as they were described by Chippendale, "Tables for holding a set of China, and [which] may be used as tea-tables. Those tables look very well, when rightly executed." *The Gentleman and Cabinet-Maker's Director* (London, 1762). Designed specifically for the service of tea, these tables had plain or fretted galleries around the edges of the top board, or scalloped or carved (piecrust) edges to prevent the china from sliding or being brushed off. The most popular types were oblong or circular; oval and hexagonal tops were made also.

China table. (Courtesy, Connecticut Historical Society, Inc.)

CHINESE CHIPPENDALE
The collector's term for any of the later eighteenth-century furniture inspired by

China stand from Chippendale's *Director* (London, 1762).

designs "in the Chinese taste" published by Thomas Chippendale in *The Gentleman and Cabinet-Maker's Director*. The reference today particularly is to any furniture with square legs and/or fretwork decoration. (See CHIPPENDALE PERIOD, Chapter 1.)

CHINESE EXPORT PORCELAIN

The correct term for any porcelain made and decorated in China specifically for export to the West; and often, in error today, called Lowestoft.

Chinese export porcelain.

Chinoiserie, c. 1720, American chest of drawers on bun feet; front and sides were japan-decorated in "the Chinese taste." (Courtesy, Connecticut Historical Society, Inc.)

CHINOISERIE

The name for the vogue and the pieces used; decorating with Chinese objects and/or English or Continental work in the Chinese manner, in fashion since the early seventeenth century and particularly reflected in textile embroideries, porcelain, and pottery decorations, as well as furniture design. Chippendale's *Director* is perhaps best known today for furniture "in the Chinese manner." So widespread was the fashion that one writer declared: "The simple and sublime have lost all influence; almost everywhere all is Chinese or Gothic; every chair in an apartment, the frames of glasses, and tables, must be Chinese; the walls covered with Chinese paper, fill'd with figures which resemble nothing in God's creation, and which a prudent nation would prohibit for the sake of pregnant women." B. Angeloni [pseud., John Shebbeare] *Letters on the English Nation* (London, 1756).

CHISEL

One of the carpenter's or carver's tools, "an instrument with which wood or stone is pared away." (J)

CHOCOLATE POT

Similar, but usually somewhat smaller in size, to the Coffee Pot, *q.v.,* the chocolate pot was made with an aperture in the lid for insertion of a stirring stick. Some lid finials were made to twist off to allow stirring.

CHOPPING KNIFE

In kitchenware, the broad-bladed "knife with which cooks mince their meat." (J)

CHRISTMAS CARD

The first such holiday greeting card is said to have been painted in 1844 by E. T. Dobson, R.A. Commercially printed Christmas cards were introduced in 1862 by Goodall and Son, London.

CHRONOMETER

This was a general contemporary name for any instrument used in the measuring of time; thus "serial clocks, watches, dials, Ec. are chronometers, though there are some other instruments peculiarly called by that name. [One] particularly, is a kind of clock, contrived to measure small portions of time with great exactness, even to the sixteenth part of a second, which is of great use in astronomical observations, the time of the full of bodies, the velocity of running waters, Ec. But these kind of chronometers must not be depended on for any long space of time, because all clocks which have short pendulums are liable to err more considerably than those with long pendulums." (M)

CHURCH WARDEN
(See CLAY PIPE.)

CHURN

The term from *kern,* the Dutch word for the dairy or kitchen "vessel in which butter is by long and violent agitation, coagulated and separated from the serous parts of the

Early-eighteenth-century wooden butter churn.

Early-nineteenth-century stoneware churn. (Courtesy, Antiquarian and Landmarks Society, Inc.)

Mid-eighteenth-century churners.

289

milk." (J) Early churns were tall, narrow cylinders made of wood staves banded or hooped as were barrels; stoneware churns were manufactured in quantities in the nineteenth century.

CIMETER

The correct spelling, according to Dr. Johnson, for a "sort of sword used by the Turks, short, heavy, and recurvated, or bent backward. This word is sometimes erroneously spelt scimetar."

CIPHER, CYPHER

The term for "a kind of enigmatic character, composed of several letters interwoven; which are generally the initial letters of the person's names for whom the ciphers are intended," (M) more commonly called a monogram today. Cyphers were cut in stone, such as quartz, carnelian, agate; in silver and gold; painted on fine-grained hard wood or ivory; done in hair work on ivory to be set in rings, lockets, or pins. "Claudius Fallize . . . draws pictures for rings and lockets, also, cyphers with human hairs on ivory, and of a very elegant taste . . ." *Federal Gazette* (Philadelphia), May 22, 1795. (See also SEAL.)

CIRCULAR-FRONT FURNITURE

This was a common c. 1800 description of bow or swelled-front designs in case furni-

Circular bow-front chest with ogee bracket feet, mahogany with cross braiding and inlay on drawers, bail brasses with oval-stamped plates. (Courtesy, Connecticut Historical Society, Inc.)

Circular-front commode design from Hepplewhite's *Guide* (London, 1788).

ture. ". . . Sundry kinds of good Cabinet Furniture . . . elegant Mahogany Circular Side-boards, Circular and plain Bureaus Ec. Connelly & Co. Auctioneers." *Independent Gazeteer* (Philadelphia), May 18, 1793.

CIRCUMFERENTOR
The name of an instrument used by surveyors for taking angles. "It consists of a brass index and circle, all of a piece. The Index commonly is about fourteen inches long, and an inch and a half broad; the diameter of the circle is about seven inches. On this circle is a chart . . . divided into three hundred and sixty degrees . . . A box for the needle . . . two sights . . ." (M)

Circumferentor, from *New Dictionary of Arts and Sciences* (London, 1778).

CISTERN
The term, from the Latin *cista* for box, for any "reservoir for holding rain water for the uses of a family," (W) given large containers kept in kitchen or cellar store rooms, and also to smaller, covered porcelain, pottery, or tinned metal jars or urns equipped with a spigot and used at table or sideboard for the service of iced water or punch. "To the Change, and I to see the price of a coppr cisterne for the table which is very pretty, and they demand 6£ or 7£ for one; but I will have one. Bought a nightgown for my wife; cost but 4s." Samuel Pepys, *Diary,* September 7, 1667. "Cesternes of Lattin" were listed in the House of Parliament Rates, 1660, for Imports and Exports—*Statutes of the Realm* (London, 1819). Four cisterns, all open basins, set on slender tripod stands, were shown by Chippendale who wrote "the Ornaments [all] should be Brass." He suggested one cistern in the form of an elegant open shell supported by a combination of amorini-mermen be made of marble. *The Gentleman and Cabinet-Maker's Director* (London, 1762).

Cistern from Chippendale's *Director* (London, 1762).

CITHARA, CITHER
Derived from the Greek *kithara,* a form of lyre with seven to eleven strings set above a wooden sound box.

CITHERN, CITTERN(E), SITTRON
An ancient form of guitar, with wire strings usually played with a plectrum, that is, a

quill, or a pick made of metal, horn, or ivory. "Citternes" were listed in the House of Parliament Rates, 1660, for Imports and Exports—*Statutes of the Realm* (London, 1819).

CITOLE
"A musical instrument with chords." (W) Chord, from *corda,* meant the string of a musical instrument.

CLAIR-OBSCURE, CLARO-OBSCURA
In painting, this is "the art of distributing the lights and shadows of a piece to advantage. It is also used to signify a piece consisting of two colours only," (M) and sometimes also was referred to as painting-in-shades. (See also SHADE.)

CLAP TABLE
An eighteenth-century colloquialism for the Console Table, *q.v.*

CLARICHORD
Defined in 1776 as "the name of a musical instrument resembling a spinet [with] forty-nine or fifty keys, and seventy strings," (M) with or without legs. "Claricords, the payre," were listed in House of Parliament Rates, 1660, for Imports and Exports—*Statutes of the Realm* (London, 1819). (See also CLAVICHORD, VIRGINAL.)

CLARION
This is the name of "a kind of small trumpet, whose tone is acuter than that of the common trumpet." (M)

CLASP KNIFE
"A knife which folds into the handle." (J) Many personal or travel knives meant for use at the table were clasp knives so that the owner could easily "pocket his knife" after dining. (See also JACKKNIFE.)

CLAVICHORD
The name from *clavis,* key, plus *chorda,* string, for the keyboard musical instrument developed after the harpsichord and before the piano forte, the keys operated small brass tangents that struck the horizontal strings.

CLAW TABLE
A contemporary term for a Georgian table with the type of foot called a claw to differentiate it from a claw-and-ball foot. Included in the inventory of the estate of Philadelphia house carpenter, James Davis, appraised March 20, 1748, "in the Lower Front Room" was "one walnut claw table, £1.10." *Will Book X,* p. 83.

CLAYMORE
The term from the Gaelic *claidheam-mor,* for great sword, used to describe the cumbersome two-hand weapon developed in Scotland during the sixteenth century, and often later used to denote any broadsword. (See also GLAYMORE.)

CLAY PIPE
The plain white-pottery smoking pipe, usually made with a small bowl and a long stem; the long version is sometimes called a Church-Warden or Church-Warden's Pipe. "The manufacture of pipes is a branch of pottery. The clay used . . . must burn white, be carefully cleansed, and kneaded up to a tenacious paste. Small lumps . . .

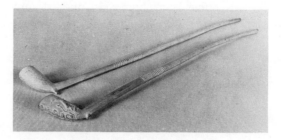

(Above), plain clay pipe; (below), long clay pipe, so-called church warden style, with lion and unicorn decoration.

Detail, showing lion decoration.

Detail, showing unicorn decoration.

are formed on the wheel into cylinders, bored by the laborer with a wire, and shaped in brass moulds. The head is then hollowed by a stopper pressed into it, and the whole is again smoothed and polished, and the pipes are then baked . . . They are polished with wax, gum tragacanth, or grease." *Encyclopedia Americana* (Philadelphia, 1831).

CLAY'S WARE
A term for papier-mâché because it was invented by Henry Clay. (See PAPIER-MÂCHÉ FURNITURE.)

CLEAVER
Then, as now, the broad, heavy kitchen knife that did double-duty. "Take three beef steaks cut half an inch thick, about ten inches long, flat them with a cleaver . . ." Richard Briggs, *The New Art of Cookery* (Philadelphia, 1792). "Cut some slices of veal very thin . . . beat them with a cleaver." Ibid.

CLEPSYDRA
The name for a kind of hourglass, "an instrument serving to measure time by the fall of a certain quantity of water," (M) and thus the proper name for an hourglass wherein water was used instead of sand. (See also HOURGLASS.)

CLICKET
"The knocker of a door; a clapper or clack." (W)

CLINCHER
"A Holdfast," *q.v.* (W)

CLOAK BAG
Another contemporary term for Portmanteau, *q.v.*, "a bag in which clothes are carried." (J)

CLOCK
From the French *cloche* and the German *glocke* for bell; the term originally designated the device that measured the passage of time by striking the hour on a bell. The word continued in use after a dial was added.

The iron tongue of midnight hath told twelve;
Lovers, to bed; 'tis almost fairy time.
Shakespeare, *A Midsummer-Night's Dream,* V, i.

"I open with a clock striking, to beget an awful attention in the audience: it also marks the time, which is four o'clock in the morning, and saves a description of the rising sun, and a great deal about gilding the eastern hemisphere." Richard Brinsley Sheridan, *The Critic,* II. (See also TIME-PIECE, WATCH.)

CLOCK GLASS
The contemporary term for the decorative mirror or painted pane of glass set above or below the clock face or dial of many shelf, mantel, or wall clock cases of the late eighteenth and early nineteenth centuries. "N. Ruggles' Looking-glass Store, on his usual liberal terms [has] some patterns just received from London, far more elegant than ever before offered for sale in this market. A constant supply of Clock Glasses, of superior quality, cheap." *American Mercury* (Hartford, Connecticut), January 9, 1816.

CLOCK JACK AND WEIGHT
The term to describe the kitchen hearth

Clock jack and weight. (Courtesy, Antiquarian and Landmarks Society, Inc.)

turnspit turned by a chain run by a clock-work device in combination with weights and pulleys. "At the Wolfe tavern and at the residences of some of the wealthier citizens, a jack turned by clock work had been placed in the wide fire place of the spacious kitchen." (Description of Newburyport homes c. 1790.) Sarah Anna Emery, *Reminiscences of a Nonagerian* (Newburyport, Massachusetts, 1879). (See also JACK.)

CLOCK PAPER

The collector's term for the printed or engraved label found in American clocks, placed there either by the clockmaker or the cabinetmaker. Because they identify the manufacturer and thus the date and place of origin, these papers add greatly to the value of the clocks. They should not be confused, however, with similar labels used by the retail merchants who sold the works and/or cases.

CLOSED FIREPLACE

A common, early-nineteenth-century colloquialism for a stove.

CLOSESTOOL

A portable necessary for use inside the house. Various interpretations have been offered for the origin of this term, in use since the Middle Ages, to denote a chamber pot set into the rim or just below the top of a stool, and which is covered by a hinged wooden lid. However, close was a common alternate for closed or covered. (See also COMMODE, CUPBOARD STOOL, NIGHT CHAIR, POT CUPBOARD.)

CLOSESTOOL CHAIR

The collector's term for any chair, such as a corner chair, the seat of which was cut out to accommodate a closestool pan or basin.

CLOSESTOOL PAN

The pan or basin made for use in a closestool; usually of pewter, sometimes of pottery, or porcelain, or tin; often today confused with a variety of other containers.

These pans were sold separately from the furniture. "2 Pewter Close stool pans large." Order October 2, 1773 from Thomas Everard, Clerk of York County, Virignia, to London. Frances Mason, *John Norton and Sons, Merchants of Virginia and London* (Richmond, 1935).

Eighteenth-century pewter closestool pan.

Colorfully painted and decorated clothes chest or box set on bun feet; early eighteenth century. (Courtesy, Connecticut Historical Society, Inc.)

Clothes chest from Thomas Chippendale's *Gentleman and Cabinet-Maker's Director* (London, 1762).

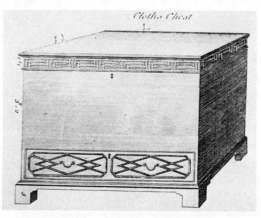

CLOTHES CHEST

The common contemporary term for the container or box with a top lid, usually set on feet or a separate frame, and equipped with a lock; often called a blanket chest by collectors today.

CLOTHES CRANE

(See AIRING HORSE, DRYING CRANE.)

CLOTHES PRESS

The clothes press differed from the chest in having one or two doors, and interior shelves.

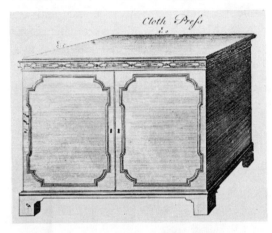

Clothes press from Thomas Chippendale's *Gentleman and Cabinet-Maker's Director* (London, 1762).

CLOTHING

(See APPAREL at end of this section.)

CLUSTER SHELF

(See SHELF CLUSTER, OVERMANTEL.)

COACHING GUN

The short-barreled weapon used by the stage-coach guard to ward off robbers or other non-paying passengers.

Coaching gun. (Courtesy, Antiquarian and Landmarks Society, Inc.)

COAL SCUTTLE

The name of a scoop-shaped container with a handle for holding coals for a fire, made of iron, brass, copper, polished steel, or wood. (See also ASH PAIL, ASH TRUG, SCUTTLE.)

COASTER

The eighteenth-century name for the small galleried tray also sometimes called a slider. Made with an underlayer of baize or felt to protect the table surface, or set on small castors or rollers, the coaster held bottles and decanters and was designed to be pushed back and forth across the table after dinner.

COATS OF ARMS

(See under ARMORIAL BEARINGS at end of this section.)

COB IRONS

"The irons which support the spit." (J) The prefix cob indicates a rounded or knobbed top. (See also ANDIRONS.)

COB MONEY

A term used to describe silver or gold coins struck in the seventeenth and eighteenth centuries in the form of slices from silver bars. "'At times to this day' [1793] says the historian of Wellfleet [Massachusetts] 'there are King William and Queen Mary's coppers, picked up, and pieces of silver called Cob money . . .' according to tradition, lost just off shore during the wreck of a ship piloted by a noted pirate named Bellamy." Henry David Thoreau, *Cape Cod*. (See also AMERICAN EAGLE, COIN.)

COCK

The common term for "the weathercock that shows the direction of the wind by turning." (J) This also was a word for "the style or gnomen of a dial." (C)

COCKED-HAT BOX

A collector's term for the eighteenth-century triangular box of wood, made to hold a man's tricorn or tri-cornered hat. (See also BAND BOX, CAP CASE, HAT CASE.)

COCK-FIGHTING CHAIR

The collector's misnomer for the early-eighteenth- through the mid-nineteenth-century Reading Chair, *q.v.* A study of early prints or paintings of cock fights show no such chair used by spectators, who, if phlegmatic enough to sit during a match, used stools or benches.

COFFEE CUP

The pottery or porcelain cup, with or without a handle, made specifically for coffee, was about one-fourth larger in overall size than the teacup. (See note under SLOP BOWL.)

COFFEE GRECQUE

Grecque, French for Greek, is a term used in architecture to indicate fretwork. The coffee grecque was a stand or ring usually set above a spirit lamp, and with a raised rim, pierced or fretted. Grecques were made of copper, silver, silver-plate, brass, and plated tin: "Tin-ware and Fan-Light Manufactory. The subscriber has on hand a complete assortment of Tin-ware, generally in use, besides a number of articles not carried into the country for sale, some of which consist of the following articles: Elegant Reflectors, Coffee Grecques, Wash Kettles from 14 gallons down to 4. Fan-Lights made as cheap as the cheapest (according to the quality of the work) and according to any pattern or dimensions. Richard Williams." *American Mercury* (Hartford, Connecticut), July 5, 1810.

COFFEE MILL

Introduced in the second quarter of the eighteenth century, the plate-iron coffee mill or grinder was similar to the spice grinder. Horizontal millstones, turned by a vertical iron shank, revolved on a corrugated iron sheet to grind the coffee, collected in a dish set underneath. After about 1750, the mills were made with drawers to catch the grounds. The cases usually were painted or japanned; some were gilded. Prior to introduction of the mill, whole coffee beans, first roasted over the fire in perforated iron cylinders, were boiled to make the popular drink. Later, many coffee-mill cases were made of wood.

COFFEEPOT

The container of silver, silver-plated metal, tin or porcelain, usually taller and narrower than the teapot, in which coffee was brewed. "James Jacks, Jeweller and Watchmaker, has imported from London Plated Coffee Pots from 3 to 4 pints . . . with and without spouts . . . Silver coffee and tea pots with stands, bread baskets and sugar dishes . . . Japanned urns and tea trays, with elegant paintings." *Pennsylvania Packet* (Philadelphia), November 13, 1799.

Early-nineteenth-century painted tin coffeepot. (Courtesy, Antiquarian and Landmarks Society, Inc.)

COFFEE TABLE

A term sometimes applied, in error, today to the eighteenth-century Teakettle Stand, *q.v.*

COFFEE URN

The larger, hot-water urn, similar in form and use to the somewhat smaller tea urn; although sensibly the same urn was used by many families in preparation of either beverage. "Joseph Anthony, Jr. . . . has imported . . . among other . . . Articles . . . Plated and bronzed tea and coffee urns, tea, coffee and chocolate pots . . ." *Pennsylvania Packet* (Philadelphia), December 7, 1790.

COFFER

Whatever else it may have been—and there are more definitions with their reasons, offered today to distinguish between coffer and chest as ever there have been for the authorship of Shakespeare's plays—a coffer was "a chest, generally for keeping money" and derived, according to Johnson, from an Old Saxon word *cofre*. To coffer was to "treasure up in chests," (J) and in 1806, coffer still meant a "chest, a treasure." (W) Chaucer in the Prologue to *Canterbury Tales* used the term in this sense:

> *For him was lever have at his beddes heed*
> *Twenty bokes, clad in blak or reed,*
> *Of Aristotle and his philosophye,*
> *Than robes riche, or fithele, or gay sautrye,*
> *But al be that he was a philosophre,*
> *Yet hadde he but litel gold in cofre.*

Shakespeare indicated a coffer was smaller than a chest, and that it was a jewel, money, or treasure box,

> *In ivory coffers I have stuff'd my crowns;*
> *In cypress chests my arras counterpoints.*
>
> The Taming of the Shrew, II, i.

If not made entirely of ivory, or veneered with sheets of ivory, such a small chest may well have had rich inlay. Reference to leather-covered coffers, based on the craft designation, in the fourteenth and fifteenth centuries, of a cofferer as a leather worker were ignored by Johnson in 1755 who said only that "a cofferer was a principal member of the King's household next under the Comptroller."

That coffers often were ornate and meant to be locked was indicated in the description "Coffers, covered with gilt Leather; covered with Velvett, with iron barrs; the nest of 3 plaine; the nest painted," listed in House of Parliament Rates, 1660, for Imports and Exports—*Statutes of the Realm* (London, 1819). Similar terms have had similar meanings in other languages: *Coffre-fort* is old French for a safe; the Dutch and German both use *koffer* to mean a chest, box, or trunk.

COFFIN CARRIER

Rather than coffin or joint stools, early Americans often used frames with supports and handles, which in time of need were draped and the coffin set thereon. After the memorial service, the carrier made transport to the family burying ground easier. Carrier shown was stored in the 1776 Hale Homestead, Coventry, Connecticut.

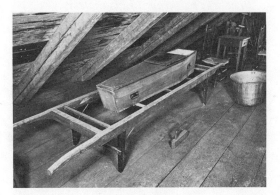

Pine and maple coffin carrier.

COFFIN CUPBOARD

The collector's term for a tall, narrow cupboard.

COFFIN STOOL

The collector's morbid misnomer for a joint stool. Coffins usually were set on any stand dictated by the necessity of the moment. The only justification ever given for the designation has been the often-quoted entry in Samuel Pepys' *Diary*. "July 6, 1661. My uncle's corps in a coffin standing upon joint-stools in the chimney [before the hearth] in the hall." This same inclination to so romanticize everyday household furniture has been responsible for calling some long dining tables Irish wake tables.

COIN

The term for money made of metal, such as gold, silver, or copper. Hence "coin differs from money, as the species does from the genus; money being any matter, whether metal, wood, leather, glass, horn, fruits, shells, Ec. (to which a certain value is attached). It is one of the royal prerogatives of any sovereign that he alone, in his own dominion, may order the quantities, value, and fashion of his coin." (M) It was in this sense that Shakespeare could have Richard II say,

An if my word be sterling yet in England . . .

it may show me what a face I have,
Since it is bankrupt of his majesty.

    IV, i.

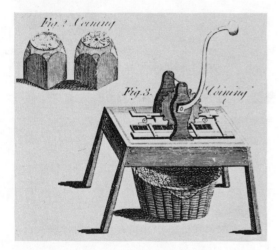

Stamp and press for making coins. (*New Dictionary of Arts and Sciences,* London, 1778).

Coin advertisement, *American Mercury* (Hartford, Connecticut), January 7, 1817.

Possession of, and sometimes even the knowledge of, the appearance of coins or hard money was not necessarily common in colonial America except among tradesmen and merchants. Of a visit to Boston in 1724, Franklin wrote that "My purse was furnished with nearly five pounds sterling in money . . . The workmen asked me with eagerness what sort of country [Philadelphia] was like . . . and what sort of money we had. I displayed before them a handful of silver . . . This was a curiousity to which they were not accustomed, paper being the current money at Boston." *Life and Essays* (Hartford, 1845).

English coins in use here prior to the Peace Treaty of 1783 included:

2 Farthings	=1 halfpenny
4 Farthings	=1 penny
12 pennies	=1 shilling
2½ shillings	=1 half Crown
2 half Crowns	=1 Crown
5 shillings	=1 pound
4 Crowns	=1 pound
1$\frac{1}{20}$ pound	=1 guinea
1¼ guineas	=1 Jacobus
5 Crowns	=1 Jacobus
4⅗ Crowns	=1 Carolus or laureat

It should be remembered that many Americans, particularly merchants, continued to use and specify English coins in business and advertising well into the nineteenth century; the most common in daily use were the penny, shilling, and pound. Following the Union, English coins were used in Scotland as throughout the rest of the island, thus doing away with minting of the peculiarly Scottish pound, shilling, pence, mark, noble, turnorer, half-pence, bodle, achison, babee, and plack. Irish coins always were the same as those of England, with the one exception of the shilling which in Ireland was valued at 26 half-pence.

Other coins current in England and the

colonies were the German, Dutch, and French. In 1776, French coins acceptable in many parts of the British Empire included the Denier, equal to ⅙ of a farthing sterling; Sol Paris, nearly equal to a half-penny; Livre, equal to 10½ pence; Eur, equal to 2 shillings, 7½ pence; Old Louis d'or, equal to 16 shillings, 9⅓ pence; New Louis d'or, equal to 1 pound, 6 pence. French coins were in common use in our far southern ports.

Acceptable Dutch coins included silver crowns or dollars, ducatoons, florins, and shillings; the copper duyt and penny; and the silver billion (a composition of precious and base metal, as a piece containing less than 12 carats gold, or less than 6 pennyweight of silver) stiver. Their equivalent values were ducat, 9 shillings, 3.2 pence; ducatoon, 5 shillings, 5.59 pence; patagon or rix dollar, 4 shillings, 4.28 pence; three-guilder piece, or sixty stivers, 5 shillings, 2.46 pence; guilder-florin, or twenty stivers, 1 shilling, 8.08 pence; the lion dollar, 3 shillings, 7.07 pence. The shilling equaled six stivers. Dutch and German coins were much in use in New York, Pennsylvania, New Jersey, Delaware, and to a lesser extent in other colonies. Thus, Franklin as a young man, having traveled from Boston to New York and thence to Philadelphia, wrote that in 1723, "On my arrival at Philadelphia . . . all my money consisted of a Dutch dollar, and about a shilling's worth of coppers, which I gave to the boatmen for my passage. As I had assisted them in rowing, they refused it at first; but I insisted on their taking it. A man is sometimes more generous when he has little than when he has much money, probably because . . . he is desirous of concealing his poverty." *Life and Essays* (Hartford, 1845).

German coins included a variety of gold ducats, issued by the different duchies; as well as the Rhine oboli and florin; and silver florin, vix dollar, and izelotte. Spanish coins were much more common here after the Revolution than before, filtering north and east from Florida and Mexico as frontier communities spread into new western and southern regions. Spanish gold coins included the half pistole, pistole, double pistole, and four-pistole piece. Silver money included the piaster of piece-of-eight real. Copper coins were the ochava or octava, quarta, double quarta, and maravedi. The piece of eight equaled 4 shillings, 6 pence. The pistole equaled 16 shillings, 9.3 pence. (See also AMERICAN EAGLE, PEAK, PIECES OF EIGHT.)

COIN BANK
(See DROP BOX, POOR BOX, PENNY BANK, THRIFT BOX.)

COIN SILVER
(See in Chapter 9.)

COLANDER, CULLENDER
In kitchenware, the term to describe a coarse sieve in the shape of a deep bowl. "A sieve made either of hair, twigs, or metal, through which a mixture to be separated is poured, and which retains the thicker parts; a strainer." (J) "Take two dozen large onions . . . boil them in plenty of water till they are very tender . . . then with a wooden spoon rub them through the cullender . . ." Richard Briggs, *The New Art of Cookery* (Philadelphia, 1792).

COLLAR BOX
(See BANDBOX.)

COLT PATERSON
(See REVOLVER.)

COLT REVOLVER
(See REVOLVER.)

COMB
"An instrument to separate and adjust the hair." (J) Combmaking was a separate craft, calling for skill in cutting and carving. "Curricombes; combes of wood, bone or horne; combes of bone; of box; lightwood combes; of horne for barbers; of ivory; Horse combes" were listed in the

House of Parliament Rates, 1660, for Imports and Exports—*Statutes of the Realm* (London, 1819).

COMMISSION, COMMISSION PAPER

The document given by someone in authority to designate right or privilege, as a militia officer's commission, that of a deputy, a justice, or other agent of government.

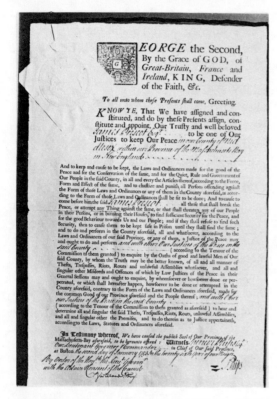

1752 Massachusetts Commission as a justice of the peace.

COMMODE

During the eighteenth century this French word was used to describe the elaborately carved or painted chest of drawers first made during the reign of George II. Chippendale called these chests commodes and commode tables. Of one, he said, "The Bass Relief in the Middle may be carved in Wood, or cast in Brass, or painted on Wood or Copper. That Part in the Middle may be a Door, with the Ornaments on it, and the End Parts in the same Manner . . . I would advise to model this Design before

Execution, as it will save Time, and prevent Mistakes." *The Gentleman and Cabinet-Maker's Director* (London, 1762). In the nineteenth century the prudish Victorians adopted commode as a euphemism for Pot Cupboard or Closestool, *qq.v.*

COMMODE CLOTHES PRESS

An eighteenth-century term for a clothes press or closed cupboard set above a chest of drawers with a shaped front. Chippendale, in *The Gentleman and Cabinet-Maker's Director* (London, 1762), showed two designs so titled.

COMMODE TABLE

Thomas Chippendale's name for commodes, i.e., chests or cupboards set on feet. (See COMMODE.)

COMMONPLACE BOOK

The term for a kind of personal scrapbook of facts and thoughts, "a book in which things to be remembered are ranged under general heads," (J) including "everything worthy of being noted in the course of a person's study, so disposed, that among a multiplicity of subjects, any one may be readily at hand." (M)

COMMUNION FURNITURE

The silver, silver plate, gold, or pewter furnishings used in the communion service. "Ward & Bartholomew have just received

Pewter communion flagon by Eben Smith, c. 1840. (Courtesy, Bernard Cardé Collection.)

300

Elegant Plated Communion Furniture Consisting of flaggons, cups, platters, and christening bason." *American Mercury* (Hartford, Connecticut), May 6, 1812. (See also CHALICE.)

COMPANION CHAIR

The mid-nineteenth-century term for the Confidante, *q.v.,* of the eighteenth century.

COMPASS DIAL

The term used to describe the "small horizontal dials fixed in brass or silver boxes for the pocket, to shew the hour of the day, by the sun's shadow, and the direction of the needle." (M) A kind of early pocket watch, used throughout the eighteenth century, described by Shakespeare:

And then he drew a dial from his poke,
And looking on it with lack-lustre eye,
Says, very wisely, 'It is ten o'clock.'

As you Like It, II, vii.

COMPASS CHAIR

The designations compass, compass seat, or compass bottom referred to chairs with rounded seat frames; these sometimes also were called horse-shoe seat chairs. The inventory of the estate of Nathan Levy of Philadelphia, appraised April 20, 1754, noted "in the Back Parlour, 1 walnut tree compass bottom arm chair, £1.10s; 4 ditto chairs 4." *Administrators Book F,* p. 527.

CONCERTINA TABLE

The twentieth-century collector's term for the kind of card table called a folding-top table or Folding Table, *q.v.,* in the eighteenth century; the term concertina refers to the jointed, fold-out undersection of the frame to which the swing leg was attached.

CONCHSHELL WORK

The general term for any item, from buttons, beads, and brooches to small horns, made of the large, spiral, univalve shells of the *strombis* or *cassis,* throughout the seventeenth and eighteenth centuries. "Daniel Carrell, Silver Smith and Jeweler, Conchshell Work, At the Sign of the Coffee Pot . . . executed in the best manner and most reasonable terms . . ." *Charleston City Gazette,* July 8, 1794. "Ladies silver set and Conchshell shoebuckles of the newest patterns . . . William Dawson." *Pennsylvania Packet* (Philadelphia), April 26, 1793. "Fancy Buttons of all kinds . . . of Tortoise Shell, Conk Shell, Clam Shell, or Mother of Pearl, ornamented with Gold, Silver, or Plate . . . (Made and sold by) Peter Geley." *Pennsylvania Packet* (Philadelphia), January 25, 1793. (See also under DRINKING VESSEL.)

CONFIDANTE

Originally this was a small sofa similar in

Confidante illustrated in Hepplewhite's *Guide* (London, 1788).

size to a loveseat. By the end of the eighteenth century, it had undergone both design and size changes, as Hepplewhite's *Guide* explains: "This piece of furniture is of French origin and is in pretty general request for large and spacious suits of apartments. An elegant drawing-room with modern furniture is scarce complete without a confidante. The extent of which may be about 9 feet, subject to the size of the room and the pleasure of the purchaser. This piece of furniture is sometimes constructed that the ends take away and leave a regular sofa: the ends [then] may be used as [separate] Barjier chairs." A. Hepplewhite, *The Cabinet-Maker and Upholsterer's Guide* (London, 1788). (See also BERGERE.)

CONNECTICUT CHEST

The collector's term for a type of chest made in the Connecticut Valley after 1650, distinguished by the use of panel and drawer fronts carved in a stylized tulip design and sometimes also ornamented with split balusters. (See also HADLEY CHEST).

CONSOLE TABLE

A collector's term for any large shelf or table, the back of which is affixed to a wall (in lieu of legs) and thus supported only by wall brackets plus a pair of shaped front legs. (See also ABACK TABLE, BRACKET SHELF, CLAP TABLE, PIER TABLE.)

CONSTITUTION MIRROR

A popular name for the long, rectangular looking glass, sometimes called a Federal mirror today, and often decorated with a reverse-glass painted panel above the mirror, and/or thirteen drops, symbolizing the original states, around the upper part of the frame.

CONVERSATION CHAIR

An occasional or parlor chair with a wide padded top rail, designed so that gentlemen might sit facing the back of the chair and thus keep their coat skirts from being wrinkled. "The parties who converse with each other sit with their legs across the seat, and rest their arms on the top rail, which, for this purpose, is made about three inches and a half wide, stuffed and covered." Thomas Sheraton, *The Cabinet Dictionary* (London, 1803).

CONVERSATION PIECE

The term for a group portrait or family painting, especially popular in the seventeenth and early eighteenth centuries. Seldom painted *in situ,* most had highly stylized background settings, the type of architectural or landscape detail left to the imagina-

Connecticut tulip-and-sunflower-decorated chest, dated 1672. (Courtesy, Antiquarian and Landmarks Society, Inc.)

tion of the artist. Colonial orders to English portraitists often requested the artist to dress his subjects according to the latest London fashion in wig and costume. The painter followed written descriptions as to the coloring, height, and weight of his subjects, and often was provided with miniatures to help him achieve facial likenesses. By the second half of the eighteenth century group portraits were no longer à la mode in London; nevertheless, many colonists continued to order them: "Send Sally's [miniature portrait] to me with your small picture, that I may here get all our little family drawn in one conversation piece. [November 22, 1757.] Yours is at the Painter's, who is to copy it, and do one of the same size; but as to Family Pieces, it is said they never look well, and are quite out of fashion; and I find the Limner very unwilling to undertake any thing of the kind. However, when Franky's comes, and that of Sally by young [Gustave] Hesselius, I shall see what can be done." (Benjamin Franklin from London to his wife at Philadelphia, June 10, 1758.) *Writings of Benjamin Franklin,* ed., A. H. Smyth (New York, 1907).

Throughout the eighteenth and nineteenth centuries, however, Americans continued to want conversation piece or family group portraits, for the fashion persisted into the age of the daguerreotype. Group portraits were often executed by the itinerant, unschooled limners of early-nineteenth-century America. For these paintings, the artist again sometimes provided convasses with set backgrounds, and costumed figures, minus only heads, having prepared the basic canvasses before he took to the road. The customer then was able to choose the setting and dress he preferred for his family; the artist had only to add the facial likenesses. (See also GROUP.)

COOP

The older name for "a barrel; a vessel for the preservation of liquids," (J) hence cooper, a maker of barrels and other wooden vessels.

COPIER

(See DELINEATOR.)

COPPER

The common Colonial- and Early-Federal-period term for a large kettle; "a vessel made of copper, commonly used for a boiler larger than a moveable pot," (J) "a large boiler." (W) "Miles Beach & Son, continue to manufacture all kinds of . . . Clothiers, Hatters and kitchen Coppers." *American Mercury* (Hartford, Connecticut), November 6, 1816.

Copper boiler advertisement in the *American Mercury* (Hartford, Connecticut), March 12, 1810.

COPPERPLATE

The engraver or printer's term for "a plate on which pictures are engraven for the neater impression, as distinguished from a wooden cut." (J) (See also ENGRAVING, WOODCUTS.)

COPYING PRESS

A common contemporary synonym for the Letter Copier, *q.v.* (See also the listing of such a press in the auction notice of Benjamin Franklin's estate under HARPSICHORD.)

CORAL

Imported to England and the colonies from the Mediterranean, *"Corallium* is the hard, brittle branched substance . . . usually about the thickness of a goose's quill . . . full of knots and sometimes variously bent . . . of a deep, bright red colour . . . found adhering to rocks in the sea . . . probably the work and nest of little animals." (M) "Artificial coral is made of cinnabar well beaten; a layer whereof is applied on a piece of wood well dried and polished, being first moistened with size; the whole is then again polished and for varnish rub it over with the white of an egg." (M) Real or man-copied, coral was used for amulets, necklaces, bracelets, and other knickknacks, especially children's rattles and teething rings. Hence, coral was a term for "a child's ornament," (W) or "the piece of coral which children have about their necks, imagined to assist them in breeding teeth." (J) (See also AMULET, CORAL-AND-BELLS.)

CORAL-AND-BELLS

The infant's necklace of beads of coral, real or reproduction, interspersed with small bells, and used as a teething ring from the Early Colonial period well into the nineteenth century: "The gravity of my behaviour at my very first appearance in the world . . . seemed to favour my mother's dream [that I would become a judge]; for she has often told me, I threw away my rattle before I was two months old, and would not make use of my coral until they had taken away the bells from it." Addison and Steele, *The Spectator,* No. I (London, March 1, 1710–11). By the end of the eighteenth century many of the "corals" were made of precious metals, semi-precious stones, ivory, or cinnabar: "Coral beads from 3–9 to 10 dollars a string. Silver and gold corals and bells, from 5 to 30 dollars . . . James Jacks." *Federal Gazette* (Philadelphia), March 28, 1798.

When coral was not available, or could not be afforded, other beads were substituted. For example, Mrs. J. C. Loudon wrote in 1840, "The wild Liquorice, *Abrus precatorius,* is a pretty climbing plant . . . the seeds, which are poisonous, are scarlet and black, and are sometimes made into necklaces for children, toward what end

Heaven only knows." *The Ladies' Companion to the Flower-Garden* (New York, 1843). (See also AMULET, CORAL.)

CORBAN

A term used during the eighteenth century for "an alm's basket"; (J) the earlier biblical sense was an offering to God.

CORK DRAWER

The bung starter or cork drawer was an iron ring to which was attached a lever or bar with a claw end. The ring was fitted over the bung or cork, the lever and claw then pushed down to raise the cork. "Joseph Lynde . . . has for sale a general assortment [including] bottle Corks, various qualities, Cork Screws, cork Drawers . . ." *American Mercury* (Hartford, Connecticut), November 11, 1812.

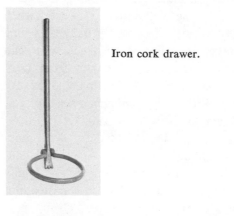

Iron cork drawer.

CORKSCREW

Then as now, the small metal device, a spike with a grooved or screw turning with which corks are pulled from bottle necks. Corkscrews were made with pewter, silver, gilt-washed metal, or carved hard wood hafts into which the iron or steel screws were inserted. Large-size cork or bottle screws were kept in the sideboard. Smaller sizes, often with their own cases, were made for the pocket or travel kit. Among "a general assortment of Silver, Plated-Ware, Jewellry and Cutlery . . . imported in the last ships from London" by Joseph Anthony, Jr., Silversmith, "were fancy lockets, Rings and bracelets . . . Silver pencil cases and cork-screws . . ." *Pennsylvania Packet* (Philadelphia), December 7, 1790.

CORKSCREW CANDLESTICK
(See HELIX CANDLESTICK.)

CORNER CHAIR
The chair with one leg in back and thus somewhat triangular in shape, specifically made to fit in a corner; often also called a roundabout chair.

Lightly framed Queen Anne corner chair with pad feet.

CORNER CUPBOARD
The first examples of these three-sided or triangular-shaped storage areas or enclosed shelves were built into the corner of the early-eighteenth-century room wherein guests were entertained, and thus are found in the parlors of many early houses. Whether attached permanently to the wall or made as separate movable units, corner cupboards generally were of two main sections; that is, made with separate doors for the upper and lower parts. The upper half usually had a glazed door; less often, the upper door was dispensed with and the shelves left open. The upper portion,

Pine corner cupboard, Connecticut, 1751.

Back of cupboard. (Courtesy, Connecticut Historical Society, Inc.)

whether open or glazed, was intended for the storage and display of tea equipage, the family's best plate or porcelain, and in this sense served as had the earlier Court Cupboard or Plate Cupboard, *qq.v.* (See also ENCOIGNURE, ETAGERE, HANGING CORNER CUPBOARD.)

CORNER TABLE
(See ENCOIGNURE.)

CORNET
The name of "an instrument much in the nature of a trumpet, which when it only sounded, the ensigns were to march alone, without the soldiers; whereas, when the trumpet only sounded, the soldiers were to move without the ensign." (M)

CORN MORTAR
(See QUERN, SAMP MORTAR.)

COROMANDEL
(See BANTAMWORK, Chapter 7, under JAPANNING.)

COROMANDEL SCREEN
The name generally given the tall, richly carved and colorfully detailed folding

Coramandel Screen. (Courtesy, William Boxter Collection.)

screens made during the late seventeenth and early eighteenth centuries, exported to Europe, England, and thus the colonies, from the Coromandel coast of India. Specifically, the term applies to the type of incised and painted carving on a lacquered base developed in India. The screens were made of three to a dozen leaves or panels, from five to ten feet in height. Unfortunately, and confusingly, Coromandel screens were reproduced, although in harsher colors and with less detail in the nineteenth century and early in the twentieth. (See also JAPANNING, Chapter 7.)

CORNUCOPIA
(See in Chapter 5.)

CORNUCOPIA SOFA
The name for a nineteenth-century fad, a couch or sofa with arms carved in the general shape of a cornucopia.

CORRIDOR STOOL
The description Sheraton applied in *The Cabinet Dictionary* (London, 1803) to a simple form of hall seat or bench, window seat, or any odd seat or bench that was not upholstered or supplied with cushions. A foyer seat wide enough to accommodate two persons.

COSTERIL, COSTREL
Derived "from coster or head," (J) and thus signifying a rounded object, this was another early term for a bottle or flask, often, but not necessarily made of leather. Specifically, it was a bottle with ears or tabs by which it might be carried or hung from a shoulder sling, bandolier, or belt. It was

a form of canteen or so-called pilgrim or traveler's flask, a small wooden bottle; "the ancient drinking cup made of wood." (H) (See also CANTEEN, COSTRET, ROUNDELET.)

COSTRET

A variation of the Costrel, *q.v.*, but the name today generally is understood to refer to a flask or bottle made of wood or earthenware rather than of leather. It was worn attached to a shoulder sling or belt held by a thong through the pierced ear, lug, or tab at the top of the bottle. (See also CANTEEN, RUNDLET.)

COTTAGE FIGURES

A general and modern term for inexpensive examples of what were called image toys and chimney ornaments in the late eighteenth and early nineteenth centuries. Most found today date after 1840, were almost always made in pairs, and were commonly sold house-to-house and at fairs. These were made of soft paste in most of the Staffordshire potteries, but were not always marked. Some American examples were made in stoneware. Potteries in both England and this country continued to manufacture cottage figures well into the twentieth century; care must be taken to differentiate between the antique and its later copy. (See also GARNITURE SET.)

COUCH

During the seventeenth and eighteenth cen-

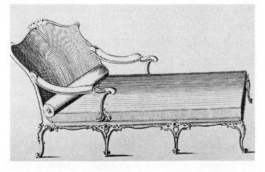

Design for a couch from Thomas Chippendale's *Gentleman and Cabinet-Maker's Director* (London, 1762).

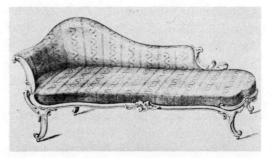

Couch from *The Cabinet-Maker's Assistant*, Blackie and Son (London, 1853).

turies this designated "a seat of repose, on which it is common to lie down dressed." (J) A day bed, or "a seat for ease." (W) "Before 1800 . . . they had couches of worsted damask, but only in the very affluent families, in lieu of what we now call sofas and lounges." John F. Watson, *Annals and Occurrences of New York City and State in the Olden Time* (Philadelphia, 1846).

COUCH BED

The seventeenth- and eighteenth-century synonym for Day Bed, *q.v.*

COUNTER DESK

A contemporary synonym for a flat-top desk; that is, a table fitted with a drawer for writing tools. "To be sold at Public Sale . . . stock in trade of William Long (including) Common counter desks . . ." *Pennsylvania Packet* (Philadelphia), February 15, 1794. (See also ABACUS, DRUM TABLE, LIBRARY TABLE.)

COUNTERPANE

"The utmost of the bed clothes; that under which all the rest are concealed." Thomas Sheraton, *The Cabinet Dictionary* (London, 1803). A decorative blanket or quilt often embroidered and thus also called a coverlet. "I forgot to mention another of my Fancyings, viz. a Pair of Silk Blankets, very fine. They are of a new kind, were just taken in a French Prize, and such were never seen in England before: They are called Blankets, but I think will be very neat to cover a Summer Bed, instead of a Quilt or Counterpane." (Benjamin Franklin from London, February 19, 1758.) *Writings of Benjamin Franklin,* ed., A. H. Smyth, (New York, 1907). "The counterpane procured for the bed of General Jackson at the American Hotel, was sold at auction for thirty dollars—it cost sixty. The President absolutely refused to sleep on the bed which was originally prepared for him. He said that he was not the King of England nor the Pope of Rome, but plain Andrew Jackson, and that plain furniture and a common counterpane was good enough for him. He had slept in the tented field with the covering of a blanket which cost but a dollar. He could not consent to encourage such extravagance. We need not add that the servants were called, the gaudy frippery removed, and a bed prepared in a style more congenial to the republican feeling of the Old Hero." *The Enquirer* (Hempstead, New York), June 27, 1833.

COUNTERPOINT
A contemporary term for the Counterpane, *q.v.*

COUNTERPOISE, POISE
These were common contemporary synonyms for the Stillyard, *q.v.*, or steelyard scale, because the counterpoise was the name of the "weight, which sliding along the beam of the steelyard, determines the weight of bodies weighed by that instrument." (M)

COUNTERS
The term for sets of smooth hardwood, metal, or ivory discs, a bit larger than ordinary poker chips; counters were an educational toy for colonial children as were the wooden play blocks also decorated with letters and numerals, used in the nineteenth century. "Charles Shipman, Ivory and Hardwood Turner lately from England [has] ivory counters engraved with alphabets and figures, very popular for children; backgammons and chess men." *The New York Journal or The General Advertiser,* August 6, 1767.

COUNTRY CHIPPENDALE
The collector's term for any furniture made in the late eighteenth century by joiners or turners in the smaller towns, using native woods rather than imported mahoganies, etc., and obviously influenced in part by styles fashionable following publication of Thomas Chippendale's *The Gentleman and Cabinet-Maker's Director* (London, 1754).

COUNTRY FURNITURE
The collector's term for the simple furniture made of native woods by village craftsmen. Some of the differences between such furniture, called cottage furniture by English collectors, and those produced in the skilled cabinetmaker's shop were discussed in an early-nineteenth-century text published to help young men choose a craft or trade: "All the arts of life have, no doubt, been the result of a gradual and progressive improvement in civilization. In nothing is this exhibited more than in an upholsterer's warehouse. What a difference is there between the necessary articles of furniture to be found in a cottage, and the elegantly furnished home of a merchant. In the former there is nothing but what is plain, useful and almost essential to the convenience of life. In the latter, immense sums are sacrificed to magnificence and show. The cottager is content with a deal table, an oaken chair, and a beechen bedstead, with other articles equally plain and inexpensive. The wealthy possess sumptious beds, inlaid tables, silk or damask chairs and curtains, sofas and carpets of great value; large looking-glasses, and brilliant lustres; together with a variety of carved work and gilding. The furniture of a small farm-house will cost but a few guineas; that of a single room in the wealthy parts will be valued at from five hundred to a thousand pounds." *The Book of Trades* (London, 1805).

COUPE
"A basket, cup, or vat" (H) and thus, also, a small bowl or basin.

COURT CUPBOARD
The massive cupboard of the seventeenth and early eighteenth century designed for use in the hall, parlor, or other best room, and on which a family's best plate or porcelain were set out. In 1647 Randle Holme said that "Side Tables, or Court Cubberts, for cups and Glasses to drink in, Spoons, Sugar Box, Viall and Cruces for Vineger, Oyle, and Mustard Pot" were among things necessary for and belonging to Dineing . . ." *The Academy of Armoury, or, a Storehouse of Armory and Blazon* (Roxburghe Club edition, 1905). Two hundred years later, Halliwell wrote that a court cupboard was "a moveable side board, generally covered with plate, in fact, used solely for that purpose, without drawers," as Shakespeare earlier used the term in *Romeo and Juliet:*

> *Away with the joint-stools; remove the court-cupboard; look to the plate.*
>
> (I, v.)

Thus, a court cupboard was the high sideboard with two shelves usually set above a frame with a pot board in the base, while the press cupboard, with which it sometimes is confused, had a cupboard with doors in the lower half, with a smaller cupboard space above, usually recessed to provide a shallow shelf.

COURTING CHAIR
The small settee or sofa, today commonly called a Loveseat, *q.v.* This apparently is a late-nineteenth-century term for the eighteenth-century Double Chair, which also see.

COURT DISH
"A kind of drinking cup," (H) often referred to as a standing-cup or state cup of the type we would be more likely to call a large goblet. (See also STATE DISH.)

COWL
The contemporary term for a kind of cask or "vessel in which water is carried on a pole between two [persons]." (J) (See also SOE.)

Cowl in use. (Early-nineteenth-century print.)

Late-sixteenth-century New England court cupboard of white oak. (Courtesy, Antiquarian and Landmarks Society, Inc.)

CRACKET
A contemporary cant term for "a low stool." (H) (See also CRICKET STOOL.)

CRADLE
This was the Old Saxon word for a "moveable bed in which children or sick persons are agitated with a smooth and equal motion, to make them sleep." (J) In form, these are cribs, or small, open boxes fitted with rockers. "One of the first settlers of Eastham was Deacon John Doane, who died in 1707, aged one hundred and ten.

Tradition says that he was rocked in a cradle several of his last years." Henry David Thoreau, *Cape Cod* (Boston, 1865).

Early-nineteenth-century cradle.

CRAN, CRANKS

The name for a type of Trivet, *q.v.*, a small, open rectangular frame with two feet at one end, and two prongs at the other. These engaged the bar of the firedog or andiron. The cran was specifically made to fit over the embers rather than in front of or to the side of the fire.

CRANE

The sway or rod of iron set in lugs at the back or side of the fireplace and from which cooking pots were suspended above the fire.

Late-eighteenth-century fireplace crane. (Courtesy, Antiquarian and Landmarks Society, Inc.)

CRATCH

"A kind of rack." (W) The term for any kind of wooden frame, cradle, or rack; thus, a pannier, a handbarrow, a clothes dryer—less often a wooden dish or tub—might each have been called a cratch.

CRATE

A wicker basket, especially one used to ship or store crockery; "a kind of hamper to pack earthenware in." (W) "In store, 300 crates and hogsheads Earthenware; 250 setts china from 6½ dolls. to 50 dolls. per sett; 40 blue printed and brown lined Dining Setts. The above ware is of the latest and most fashionable pattern. Frederick Bange." *American Mercury* (Hartford, Connecticut), November 19, 1816.

CRAYON

In painting, this "is a composition of colours reduced to the texture of chalk, and used dry, in the form and manner of Pencils [*q.v.*] for painting on paper." (M) "A kind of pencil, a roll of paste to draw with; [also] the drawing or design done with a crayon." (J) (See also ACADEMY FIGURE, CHALK DRAWING, PASTEL.)

CREAM BASON

A small, deep dish, sometimes footed, from which cream was ladled. "Joseph Anthony, Jr. . . . has imported . . . Oval and round sugar and cream basons. Castors, bottle stands and goblets, Wine and Water stands . . ." *Pennsylvania Packet* (Philadelphia), December 7, 1790.

CREAM JUG, CREAM POT

Early in the eighteenth century the majority of cream jugs were made in a helmet shape; by mid-century the fashion was for

Early-eighteenth-century English white delft cream pitcher.

Polychrome
soft paste
cream pitcher.

Cream jugs. (Courtesy, Antiquarian and Land-marks Society, Inc.)

CREEL
A wicker basket usually made with a lid or hinged top. (But see also CAKE CREEL.)

Creels. (Courtesy, Antiquarian and Landmarks Society, Inc.)

tall, cylindrical, and vase-shaped containers; by 1800 the jug was made as a low, round "pot."

CREAM PAIL
The name for a type of small cylindrical cream basin or bowl with straight sides and a rising bail handle, and thus resembling a miniature pail; made in porcelain, glass, faïence, silver, silver plate, or gilt-washed metal. "Standish Barry, Gold and Silversmith . . . From Liver-Pool . . . Plated Ware [including] Sugar-Basons; Cream-Pails, with Ladles; Boot and Shoe Buckles, Ladies Morocco Pocket-Books . . ." *Maryland Gazette* (Baltimore), November 15, 1792.

CREDENCE, CREDENZA
The Italian word for cupboard, credenza sometimes is used by collectors to denote a side table for food and beverages. Properly, this is the small table near the altar where bread and wine are set out prior to consecration.

CREEPER
The contemporary term for "an iron [or small andiron] to slide along the grate in kitchens," (J) more often used in the plural.

Creeper.

CREEPERS

The usual term for "the small low irons in a grate between the andirons," (H) that is, a pair of small andirons with short shafts set between the high andirons used at either end of any fireplace or grate. The itemization of household furnishings included in the marriage contract between Governor John Winthrop of Massachusetts and his fourth wife, the widow Martha Coytmore, December 10, 1647, thus listed "a pr. brass hollow andirons, fire shovell, tongs and creepers." John Winthrop, *Journal, The History of New England* (Boston, 1825).

CRESSET

Perhaps derived from *cresse,* an ancient word for rush, this was the name of an open lamp, suspended on pivots in a kind of fork or yoke, "set upon a pole and much used in parades." (H) The light was made of coiled, bound rope impregnated with pitch or rosin, stuck on a pin in the center of the lamp bowl; or a chunk of lightwood; i.e., a resin-filled pine block. Cresset also was used generally to designate any hollow vessel used to hold a light. (See also LINK.)

CRESSET ANDIRON, CRESSET DOG, CRESSET HOLDER

The andiron or firedog with a basket top or finial to the front post, specifically made to hold a cresset light; i.e., a knot or block of resinous wood, or resin-soaked rope. (See also CRESSET.)

CREST

(See under ARMORIAL BEARINGS at the end of this section.)

CREWET

The common colonial spelling for Cruet, *q.v.*

CRIBBLE

Another name for a "corn sieve," (J) a fan, or winnowing basket.

CRIB

Then, as now, a small, narrow, high bedstead for infants, made with protective side railings; sometimes also a synonym for Cradle, *q.v.* "R.G. Allen has on hand Cribs with and without rockers; mahogany, cherry, and cyprus Cradles, Ec." *Literary Cadet and Rhode Island Statesman* (Providence), February 20, 1828.

CRICKET, CRICKET STOOL

The name for a "low seat or stool," (J) derived from the German *kriechen,* to creep; the low wooden stool usually kept near the kitchen hearth.

CRICKET TABLE

The collector's name for any simply made, country-joiner's version of a high three-legged stool or plain tripod stand, apparently adapted in the sentimental late nineteenth century from the eighteenth-century name given a low hearth stool. The contemporary term was Trivet, *q.v.* (See also CRICKET.)

CRINZE

"A drinking cup." (H)

CRISPING IRON

The contemporary term for "A kind of curling iron" (W) used by men and women alike for dressing their own hair or for refurbishing wigs; also for smoothing lace and ruffles. (See GOFFERING IRON.)

Crisping or curling iron in holder. (Courtesy, Antiquarian and Landmarks Society, Inc.)

CROCK

The term for any (1) "cup; any vessel made of earth," (J) (2) the straight-sided, round jar used for storing food, as a pickle or sauerkraut crock, (3) the large pottery bowl used for "setting" milk, or (4) forming butter pats.

Early-nineteenth-century slip-decorated glazed redware crock.

Covered redware crock.

C. 1840 stoneware crock with blue underglaze decoration. (Courtesy, Antiquarian and Landmarks Society, Inc.)

Mid- to late-nineteenth-century stoneware crock. (Courtesy, Antiquarian and Landmarks Society, Inc.)

CROCKERY

From the Old English word crock or crocea, meaning clay or "earthenware," (J) hence, a general term for the latter or for any pottery vessels, jars, crocks, or tableware collectively. "New Crockery Store. Just opening, a complete assortment of Groceries, Crockery & Glass Ware, for sale on the most reasonable terms, by Lemuel Swift." *American Mercury* (Hartford, Connecticut), May 4, 1811. "New Goods, Solomon Porter Jr. Has just received a good supply of Groceries, Ec. which he offers for sale [including] 200 Doz. Plates, and some other Crockery." Ibid., October 23, 1812.

CROMWELLIAN CHAIR

The collector's term for a fairly plain, heavy, oak side chair made during the Commonwealth period in England (1649–60). Similar to a type of Spanish chair, these had leather backs and sling seats fastened with large nails or studs.

CROOK

Generally, "any crooked or bent instrument," (J) specifically, an iron spike fixed inside the chimney wall to hold a form of trammel chain, pothook, or the pot itself.

CROOK CHAIN

The iron chain suspended from a crook; i.e., a form of trammel made with a hook, from the lower end of which a pot could be suspended.

CROOKED-FOOT CHAIR, CROOK-FOOTED CHAIR

Contemporary terms for the chair made with bends or crooks—the contemporary term for rockers—attached to and joining each pair of legs front and back, a design assuredly developed in the first half of the eighteenth century, and perhaps much earlier. The rocking chair, a sensible extension of the cradle and thus a seat providing ease and comfort for children and their elders alike, probably was made first for use near the kitchen hearth. Not a type to be used in dining parlor, drawing room, or even in the chambers of great homes, crooked-foot (or rocking) chairs were not shown in major design books until the mid-nineteenth century. Perhaps because he designed, or at the least provided improvements in the design of numerous other contrivances, Benjamin Franklin often is given credit for suggesting

Eighteenth-century slat-back crooked-foot chair.

C. 1840 Boston rocker with stenciled decoration. (Courtesy, Connecticut Historical Society, Inc.)

Late-eighteenth-century comb-back Windsor crooked-foot chair. (Courtesy, Antiquarian and Landmarks Society, Inc.)

the rocking chair. If he was not the first to suggest the design, he nevertheless was an enthusiastic subscriber. In January 1742–43, Solomon Fussell billed "Benjamin Frankling 10 shillings" for "one Nurse crook't foot Chair," presumably a low rocking chair for the nursery; on March 2, 1748 for "3 Best Crook't Feet Chairs, £1.15.0" and April 23, 1748, 2 shillings 3 pence for "mending one crooked Foot Chair." Solomon Fussell Account Book, 1738–51, *Stephen Collins Papers,* Manuscript Division, Library of Congress.

CROSSBOW
"A missive weapon, formed by placing a bow athwart a stock." (J)

CROSS-STAFF
The exact name for the "instrument commonly called the fore-staff, used by seamen to take the meridian altitude of the sun or stars." (J)

CROW, CROWBAR

One of the tools, usually of iron, "a piece with a beak," (J) used as "a lever to lift up the ends of great heavy timber, and then they thrust the claws between the ground and the timber, and laying some stuff behind the crow, they draw the other end of the shank backwards, and so raise the timber." Joseph Moxon, *Mechanick Exercises, or The Doctrine of Handy-Works* (London, 1683–84). "A kind of iron lever, having a claw at one end and a sharp point at the other." (M)

CROWDY-KIT

A cant term for a fiddle or violin; from the old meaning of crowd, to move one thing across another and thus sometimes to make a grating noise. (See also FIDDLER'S KIT.)

Crowder: "A fiddler." (W)

CRUCIBLE

A small earthenware pot; this was a "chemist's melting-pot, made of earth, and so-called because they were formerly marked with a cross." (J) "Take a quantity of good silver, and put it in a crucible or melting cruse, and set them on the fire, well covered round about with coals." Henry Peacham, *Graphic or The Gentleman's Exercise* (London, 1606).

CRUET

From the Dutch *kruicke,* "a vial for vinegar or oil, with a stopple." (J) "A kind of large vial for vinegar or oil," (W) often spelled crewet. When made to be set by itself on the table, the cruet was a flat-bottomed small jug with a narrow neck, similar in shape to the carafe, but differing in that the cruet had a stopper and usually an applied handle. Cruets were free-blown, blown-in-the-mold, and often decorated with etching, cutting or enameling; many later examples were of pattern glass. Cruets made to be set in stands or frames did not have handles and were much narrower over-all. "Vinegar is placed in a special container on the table to be used on the kale." Peter Kalm, *Travels in North America* (Warrington, England, 1770). "To be sold by Gersham Flagg, in Hanover Street near the Orange Tree . . . five Jelly Glasses and Crewits of double Flint." *Boston Gazette,* August 6, 1745.

Needless to say, cruets were used to hold a variety of thin sauces, as well as oil and vinegar. "Take your white bait fresh caught . . . fry them quick two minutes, put them on a sieve to drain before the fire, and dish them in a hot dish, with plain butter in a boat, and soy sauce in a crewet." Richard Briggs, *The New Art of Cookery* (Philadelphia, 1792).

CRUET FRAME

The silver, silver plate, or plated tin holder or standard, often with a high, rising, bail-like handle, used on the sideboard or table to hold one or more cruets. "Charles Sigourney offers for sale the following articles . . . Plated Candlesticks, plated Cruet frames with glasses of a great variety of patterns." *American Mercury* (Hartford, Connecticut), November 4, 1812.

CRUSE

The word from the Dutch *kruicke,* for a "small cup," (J) or "a small vessel" of any kind. (W)

A little saint best fits a little shrine,
A little prop best fits a little vine,
As my small cruse best fits my little wine.

> Robert Herrick, *Hesperides, A Terniary of Littles.*

"Cruses of Stone, without covers & with" were listed in the House of Parliament Rates, 1660, for Imports and Exports—*Statutes of the Realm* (London, 1819). The word is used by collectors today to describe small grease or oil lamps, sometimes also called Betty Lamps, *q.v.*

CRUSET

A contemporary term for "a goldsmith's melting pot." (J) (W). (See also CRUCIBLE, CRUSE.)

CRUSKE

An "earthen vessel." (H)

CUP

From the Old Saxon term for any "small vessel to drink in," (J) and used in the same manner we say glass today. Cups were made of horn, wood, silver, pewter, tin, earthenware, porcelain, and glass. (See also DRINKING VESSEL; WATER CUP.)

CUP-AND-CAN

"Familiar companions. The can is the large vessel out of which the cup is filled, and to which it is a constant associate," Johnson wrote, indicating the use of can as a common synonym for a water carafe, a wine decanter, or a milk or cider pitcher. (J)

CUP-AND-SAUCER SETS

Pottery or porcelain sets for individual service of tea, coffee, or chocolate, purchased separately. "Phelps & Olmstead have just received a fresh supply of Goods [including] 50 sets china cups and saucers; 5 boxes china in Setts . . ." *American Mercury* (Hartford, Connecticut), November 18, 1812. (See also CUP, SAUCER.)

Soft paste cup and saucer.

CUPBOARD

A combination of cup and board, this was a "case with shelves, in which victuals or earthenware is placed." (J) Doors were a later addition. Included in the inventory of the estate of James Davis, Philadelphia carpenter, appraised March 20, 1748, was "one pine cupbour with some China, pewter porringers & 6 silver tea spoons, £2.26s" in the "lower front room." *Will Book I,* p. 83. Names used for various types of cupboards have included: ambry, armoire, bedside cupboard, clothes press, commode, commode press, corner cupboard, court cupboard, dole cupboard, hanging cupboard, hanging safe, kast, linen cupboard, linen press, larder, livery, pantry, plate cupboard, press, press cupboard, safe, schrank, wardrobe.

Early-nineteenth-century built-in cupboard. (Courtesy, Antiquarian and Landmarks Society, Inc.)

Early-eighteenth-century cupboard, closed, with butterfly or dovetail hinges. (Courtesy, Antiquarian and Landmarks Society, Inc.)

CUPBOARD STOOL

The collector's term for a rare type of early closestool. This was a joined stool with a lid top, usually hinged, closing off the small cupboard or bin that was formed by boards set below a deeper-than-average apron. Franklin described one such seventeenth-century stool: "Our humble family had early embraced the reformation. They remained faithfully attached during the reign of Queen Mary, when they were in danger of being molested on account of their zeal against popery. They had an English Bible, and to conceal it the more securely, they conceived the project of fastening it, open, with pack-threads across the leaves, on the inside of the lid of a close-stool. When my

Cupboard style used from early to late eighteenth century. (Courtesy, Colonial Williamsburg, Inc.)

great grandfather wished to read to his family, he reversed the lid of the close-stool upon his knees and passed the leaves from one side to the other, which were held down by the pack-thread. One of the children was stationed at the door to give notice if he saw the proctor, an officer of the spiritual court, make his appearance; in that case, the lid was restored to its place, with the Bible concealed under it as before." Benjamin Franklin, *Life and Essays* (Hartford, 1845).

CUPPING GLASS
Cupping was a form of bleeding "by scarification," (W) a popular treatment for a variety of physical ills used well into the nineteenth century. The glass was a kind of cup "used by scarifiers to draw out the blood by rarefying the air; a glass bell." (J) "Joseph Lynde at his old stand next door south of the Brick Meeting House has for sale, on the most reasonable terms, a general assortment of Drugs, Medicines, Groceries, Paints, Dye-Stuffs, Ec. Ec., among which are . . . a large assortment of Patent Medicines, salt of Lemons, flesh brushes, Lancets, Syranges, Cupping Glasses, Court Plaster, Tooth Powder, Tooth Brushes . . ." *American Mercury* (Hartford, Connecticut), November 11, 1812.

CURB
A fire curb or Fender, *q.v.*

CURRICLE
The term was first applied by Sheraton to a type of low-backed armchair that was "well adapted for dining parlours, being of a strong form, easy and conveniently low, affording easier access to a dining table than the common kind" of armchair. Thomas Sheraton, *The Cabinet Dictionary* (London, 1803). The back, rising no higher than the user's waist, curved round in a half circle to provide rests or arms.

CURTELASS, CURTLAX, CURTLEAXE
Early variations of the name of the Cutlass, *q.v.*

CUSKIN
An old name for "A kind of ivory cup." (W)

CUSTARD CUP, CUSTARD DISH
Synonymous terms for small, individual earthenware cups or bowls in which "to make little Hasty-puddings, to boil in Custard Dishes. Take a large pint of milk, put to it four spoonfuls of flour; mix it well together, and set it over the fire, and boil it into a smooth Hasty-pudding; sweeten it to your taste, grate nutmeg in it, and when 'tis almost cold, beat five eggs very well, and stir into it; then butter your custard-cups, put in your stuff, and tie them over with a cloth . . . let them boil [in the pot] something more than half an hour; pour in them melted butter." E. Smith, *The Compleat Housewife* (London, 1741).

Custard cup, redware with glazed interior, c. 1840.

CUSTREL
An early term for a "vessel for holding wine," (J) and apparently a variation of Costrel, *q.v.*

CUT-AND-THRUST WEAPONS
This broad term covers all blade and club weapons of bronze, steel, or iron used in battle or the hunt. These weapons are divided by collectors into sub-classifications:

1) Cutting weapons, made with a blade, a cross piece, hilt, and pommel, such as the sword or saber;

2) Stabbing weapons, such as the poniard, the dagger, and the dirk. Both of these were called also side arms or hand weapons,

because they were wielded with one or two hands;

3) Staff weapons refer to cutting and stabbing blades set at the end of wooden rods or staffs, and included the battle ax or bill, the pike or halberd, the spear, partisan, glaive, etc.

4) Striking or thrusting weapons, both side and staff arms, included any kind of battle club, bludgeon, or poleax.

CUTLASS
In weaponry, the term for a "broad, cutting sword . . . in much use among seamen." (J) Other contemporary spellings included cutlace, cutlash.

CUTLERY
The general term for any sharp-edged tools used for cutting. "Just received from New York and Philadelphia, latest importations of Cutlery; knives and Forks ivory tipt, buck, black, ebony, horn and bone, Ec. with Carvers, and steels, & dessert knives and forks to match. Pen knives, Scissors, Shears and Snuffers." Haydon & Imlay. *American Mercury* (Hartford, Connecticut), April 19, 1809.

CUT-PAPER PICTURE
The contemporary popular name for the intricate landscapes and still-life pictures cut out in white paper then mounted on colored paper or cloth. The colored stock thus reveals the substance of the picture's details. "Feb. 22nd, 1772. Uncle Ned was here just now & has fairly or unfairly carried off Aunt's cut-paper pictures tho' she told him she had given them to papa sometime ago." *Diary of Anna Green Winslow* (Boston, 1894). (See also PAPYROTAMIA.)

CUTWORK
One of the nineteenth-century "Ladies' Arts." (See also CUT-PAPER PICTURE.)

CYLINDER FALL DESK
The contemporary name for a type of Bureau, *q.v.,* eventually to be called a roll-top desk. The descriptive term is from the semi-circular or curved Tambour, *q.v.,* closure, which opened, or slid back, to provide access to the writing surface. Small desks or bureaus of this design were set above a stand containing one central map or print drawer, plus sometimes deeper drawers at either side. Others also had bookcases set above the desk portion. "Edward Johnson . . . has opened a Ware-Room in Meeting Street nearby opposite the Scotch Church where he has for sale . . . Modern and Elegant Cabinet work . . . Amongst which are Capital cylinder fall desks and book cases, side boards, ladies commodes, drawers of different patterns, card tables of various patterns and figures, breakfast do, do . . ." *South Carolina Gazette* (Charleston), April 23, 1796. (See also TAMBOUR TABLE.)

Cylinder desk and bookcase illustrated in Thomas Sheraton's *The Cabinet-Maker's and Upholsterer's Drawing-Book* (London, 1791–94).

CYPHER SEAL

The ready-made metal disc, with one incised initial letter or cypher, attached to a metal, wood, or ivory haft or shank; used to stamp or mark one's monogram in sealing wax on documents or to seal letters. "Dan Carrell, Silversmith and Jeweller . . . Has on hand for sale: A large quantity of Cypher Seals, at 1s–6d apiece, a variety of plated buckles, silver work, jewellry, and cutlery, which will be sold at the most reduced prices . . ." *City Gazette and Advertiser* (Charleston, South Carolina), April 20, 1790. (See also CIPHER, SEAL.)

D

DADING STRINGS

To dade was to lead children who were just learning to walk. The strings were a kind of harness made with leather thongs or tapes that could be held by a parent or nurse. (See also STAND STOOL.)

DAG, DAGGER

This was another term for the dagger, but it was used more often to describe "a handgun [or] a pistol, so called from serving the purpose of a dagger, i.e., being carried secretly, and doing mischief suddenly." (J) "Daggs with fire lockes or Snaplance" were listed in the House of Parliament Rates, 1660, for Imports and Exports—*Statutes of the Realm* (London, 1819).

DAGSWAIN

"A rough sort of coverlet or carpet used for beds, tables, or floors," (J) apparently derived from dags meaning locks or shreds of wool, and wain, for wood.

DAGUERREOTYPE

In 1839 the French inventor Louis Jacques Maude Daguerre perfected a method of producing silver photographic images on copper plates. Daguerreotype was the name given his invention, the popular forerunner of the modern photograph.

DANGLESPIT

In the kitchen fireplace, this was (1) a hanging spit or hook dangling on a chain from the lug pole; often made with a turn-buckle or swivel joint so that it might be turned easily, (2) a horizontal bar, pointed at one end and supplied with weights or balls with rings which could be slipped over each end of the spit rod to cause it to rotate as it hung from the lug pole, (3) two crossed iron bars with spit hooks, similarly suspended above the fire.

DARBY AND JOAN CHAIR

A cant term used throughout the nineteenth century for any double chair or small settee of any period, wide enough to seat two comfortably. The term came into use as a result of the popularity of the song, *The Joys of Love Ne'er Forgot* published in *The Gentleman's Magazine* (London, March 1735), and which described the devotion of two untidy elderly lovers:

Old Darby with Joan by his side . . .
They're ever uneasy asunder.

(See DOUBLE CHAIR, SETTEE.)

DARK LANTERN

The term for any hand lantern made with three solid metal sides and with a fourth

Dark lantern. (Courtesy, Antiquarian and Landmarks Society, Inc.)

metal section or quarter made to slide in channels so that when required, the open, or light, side might be covered. It was, thus, "one with only a single opening, which may also be closed up when the light is to be entirely hidden, or opened when there is occasion for its assistance to discover some object." *Encyclopedia Americana* (Philadelphia, 1831). Collectors today sometimes call this a policeman's lantern.

DART
In weaponry, the name from the French *dard* for "a missile weapon thrown by the hand; a small lance." (J)

DASHER
The staff or rod of a Churn, *q.v.*

DAVENPORT, DEVENPORT
The name given about 1800 for "drawing room cabinets used by ladies." J. C. Loudon, *An Encyclopedia of Cottage, Farm, and Villa Architecture and Furniture* (London, 1833). This was a small, high, writing desk-cabinet, in form appearing to be a chest of drawers with a slanted lectern-type top board. When needed for use, a writing board or slide was pulled forward and out from the dummy top drawer.

Davenport Bed: The term used in this country very late in the nineteenth century for a couch with an undersection that could be pulled out or extended for use as a bed; hence, our later use of the word to describe any parlor sofa.

DAVY'S SAFETY LAMP
A type of lantern or miner's lamp invented by Sir Humphry Davy, distinguished nineteenth-century English chemist, to offset damps or the deleterious carbonic acid gases formed in mines which extinguished candles and often caused death. The lamp "consists of a cylinder of [iron or copper] wire gauze, about four inches in diameter and a foot in length, having a double top, securely fastened by doubling over to a brass rim, which screws on to the lamp itself below. The whole of the wire gauze is protected and rendered convenient by carrying by a triangular wire frame and a ring at the top. The gauze is woven so as to leave 625 apertures in a square inch. The body of the lamp is of riveted copper, cast brass or cast iron, the screws fitting so as to leave no aperture into the body of the lamp . . . The effect of the safety lamp [depends] on the cooling agency of the wire gauze . . ." *Encyclopedia Americana* (Philadelphia, 1831).

DAY BED
The contemporary designation for a "bed used for idleness and luxury in the day time," (J) a long, narrow seat or couch

Day bed. (Courtesy, Connecticut Historical Society, Inc.)

with one adjustable end that could be raised to form a back support, or lowered to form a bed. Introduced during the Carolean period, day beds were in great favor throughout the eighteenth century, when they were known also as long chairs or chaises longues.

DAYBOOK
A diary, "a tradesman's journal; a book in which all the occurrences of the day are set down." (J)

DEATH'S-HEAD RING
A common form of Mourning Ring, *q.v.;*

> *They keep death's heads in rings,*
> *to cry "memento" in me.*

Beaumont and Fletcher, *The Chances.*

DECANTER
The term for a "glass vessel made for pouring off liquor clear from the lees" (J) and "for holding liquor." (W) The word was first used early in the eighteenth century, supplanting bottle, table bottle or wine bottle, as a common name for the slender-necked wine container from which glasses were filled. Bottles or decanters of the late seventeenth and early eighteenth centuries had round, fat bodies and high, narrow necks. Those with sloping sides or shoulders were first made about 1725. When used for storage, decanters were "stoppered" with

Blown three-mold decanter; nineteenth century, Massachusetts.

corks, corks with silver caps, or matching glass stopples. "To be sold by Delphane and Tatem, in Front Street between Market and Arch streets the second door below Coomb's alley. A large neat Assortment of Glass-Ware, amongst which are Quart, Pint and Half Pint Decanters, Pint and Half Pint Tumblers, Wine Glasses, of different sorts, a few Gross of Phials, etc. . . ." *Pennsylvania Gazette* (Philadelphia), July 21, 1777.

DECANTER FRAME
Frame was used to mean "a contrivance or projection," (J) "a shape or support." (W) The silver decanter frame was a small stand or tray with a slender shaft or rod rising from the center of the back to which one or two rings or hoops were attached to hold the bottles in place. Wood decanter frames were handsomely made cases with compartments or other fittings to hold bottles and drinking vessels. "James Jacks, Goldsmith, Jeweller, and Watchmaker . . . [has] Imported in the last ship from London, via Charleston [South Carolina] a large and general assortment of Goods . . . bought on the best terms, and warranted of the first quality [including] Tea Pots and Stands, Dish rings and Crosses, Decanter Frames with glasses . . ." *Federal Gazette* (Philadelphia), April 15, 1797.

DECANTER LABEL
The decorative label or tag hung on a chain about the neck of a bottle to designate its contents. Usually of silver, but also made of enameled tin, tin-glazed pottery, pewter, enamel on copper, and Sheffield plate, labels were engraved or otherwise marked rum, gin, sherry, sack, brandy, madeira, port, etc. Some labels were crescent-shaped, others were oval, rectangular, or round. "James Jacks, Jeweler and Watchmaker, has imported on the ship Lexington, from London and is now opening a Large

Assortment . . . of a Superior Quality . . . of Plated Goods [including] Patent Cork Screws, Castors . . . quart, pint and half pint Mugs and Goblets . . . Decanter Lables . . ." *Federal Gazette* (Philadelphia), March 25, 1799. "Silver and Plated Lables." Ibid., January 7, 1800.

DECEPTION TABLE

The contemporary term for a small, rectangular table with what appear to be drop leaves, and which was designed to look like a Pembroke Table, *q.v.* However, the "leaves" usually were hinged at the bottom so they might be pulled out and forward to disclose a hidden cupboard, and thus "answer the purpose of a pot cupboard, or any other secret use which we would hide from the eye of a stranger." Thomas Sheraton, *The Cabinet Dictionary* (London, 1803).

DECOY, DECOY DUCK

The decoy was a place or covert made for catching wild fowl; hence, a decoy duck "flies abroad, and lights into company of wild ones, which by her allurements she draws into the decoy." (M) The carved, turned, and painted wooden decoys now being collected were not commonly in use until the early twentieth century.

DEJUNE TABLE

The name is the English adaptation of the French *dejeuner,* for breakfast or luncheon, given to a much-ornamented breakfast or tea table of the late eighteenth and early nineteenth centuries. Some were stands; others had tilting tops. "These Tables, adapted for a breakfast set of superb china, are used for Ladies' Boudoirs or Morning Breakfast Rooms, and therefore portable of the richest decoration . . . agreeable to the style of china placed on them . . . They may be painted, gilded, made to imitate bamboo, or japanned black and gold, [or to] imitate ormolu." George Smith, *A Collection of Designs for Household Furniture* (London, 1808). (See also BREAKFAST TABLE, TEA TABLE.)

DELF CASE, DELF CUPBOARD

A colloquialism for any kitchen "shelves for crockery," (H) so-called from the popular delftware.

DELFT

(See in Chapter 10.)

DELINEATOR

A device for making silhouettes in exact proportion; the name given the instrument patented in 1806 by Charles Schwalkoelder. This was a contrivance of steel rods so arranged that one end was passed over the face of the sitter while the other "drew" an outline in chalk, or cut out a silhouette portrait. The instrument also was called a copier or a proportionometer. (See also PHYSIOGNOTRACE.)

DEMI-LANCE

In weaponry, "a light lance; a short spear; a half pike." (J) (See also LEADING STAFF.)

DEN-DARN, DEN-DDARN

The Welsh cupboard, sometimes called a Welsh dresser, with two shelves for the display of pewter or silver set above a cupboard base. (See also TRI-DARN.)

DERRINGER

Perhaps best remembered today as the type of pocket pistol used by John Wilkes Booth in the assassination of President Lincoln, this small percussion weapon was named for its first manufacturer, Henry Deringer, a Pennsylvania smith, who developed it in the late 1820s.

Derringer made in Whitneyville, Connecticut, factory. (Courtesy, Connecticut Historical Society, Inc.)

DESK

"An inclining table [board] for the use of writers or readers, made commonly with a box or repository under it," (J) as we more generally today would describe a Desk Box, *q.v.* The term also was used to mean "an inclined table; a pulpit," (W) or what more commonly now is called a lectern. "Desks or stayes for bookes" were listed in the House of Parliament Rates, 1660, for Imports and Exports—*Statutes of the Realm* (London, 1819). (See also BUREAU.)

DESK BOX

The portable, square or rectangular wooden box with a lift-up lid top, made from the sixteenth through the nineteenth centuries, and usually today miscalled a Bible box. In the seventeenth and eighteenth centuries many such boxes were decorated with carved or incised designs, among the most popular of which were a series of lunettes or a series of stars enclosed in circles. Some had tops with a so-called desk slope. This

angle, however, more often was meant to provide ease in reading, not writing: "Then Mr. Edward Holyoke made a Latin oration standing at a Desk on the Table next the Entry." Samuel Sewall, *Diary* (1707).

Similar but longer carved-wood boxes probably were meant to hold small attire

Desk box in use in c. 1720 chamber or hall. (Courtesy, Antiquarian and Landmarks Society, Inc.)

C. 1750 desk box on frame, made of cherry and pine by a country craftsman. (Courtesy, Antiquarian and Landmarks Society, Inc.)

Desk or document box with drawer for writing utensils; top compartment for records, books. (Courtesy, Antiquarian and Landmarks Society, Inc.)

Desk.

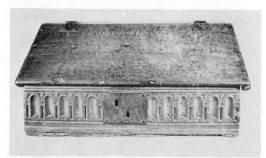

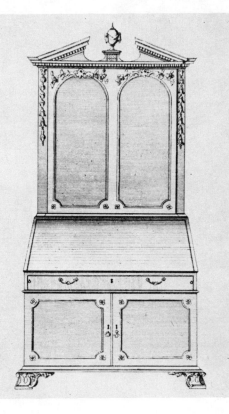

Desks and bookcases as illustrated in Hepplewhite's *Guide* (London, 1794).

Final, handsome late-eighteenth-century form of desk box, set on drawers, on a frame with scalloped plinth, claw-and-ball feet; center door, flanked by two turned pilasters, is removable and pulls out to reveal a covered well or "secret compartment." Cherry with white wood and pine. (Courtesy, Connecticut Historical Society, Inc.)

such as laces or gloves. Some small boxes were, of course, made to hold valuable books. These, however, usually were cut to the size of the individual volume and generally are much smaller than desk boxes.

DESK AND BOOKCASE

A contemporary description for what sometime in the late nineteenth century came to be known as a secretary. Of one such, Chippendale said, "the under Part hath Doors and sliding Shelves within for Cloaths; the

Cherry and pine desk and bookcase; mid-eighteenth-century American. Handsomely pierced pediment is made to lift off. Base has engaged fluted quarter columns, ogee bracket feet. Two adjustable shelves are enclosed in top section. (Courtesy, Connecticut Historical Society, Inc.)

Late-eighteenth-century fall-front Connecticut desk and bookcase with stop-fluted pilasters, serpentine front, scrolled bracket feet, shown open and closed. (Courtesy, Connecticut Historical Society, Inc.)

upper Doors are . . . Glass," and of another, "the upper Doors are Glass; within the Doors may be upright Partitions for Books . . . the Desk-Part [has] Drawers, Doors and Pigeon-Holes." *The Gentleman and Cabinet-Maker's Director* (London, 1762).

DESK SEAL
(See SEAL.)

DEY-CUP
Dey was the old name for dairy, and hence, dey-cup was a "milk cup or bowl." (H)

DIAL
The term for a metal or wood "plate marked with hours, where a hand or shadow shows the hour." (J) The simpler form of compass dial. "Dialls of wood and bone" were listed in the House of Parliament Rates, 1660, for Imports and Exports —*Statutes of the Realm* (London, 1819). (See also COMPASS DIAL, SUNDIAL.)

DIAPER
A common term throughout the eighteenth century for a fine "napkin, a towel," usually made of the linen called diaper, "the finest species of figured linen after damask." (J)

> Let one attend him with a silver bason
> Full of rose-water, and bestrew'd with
> flowers;
> Another bear the ewer, a third a diaper.
>
> Shakespeare, *The Taming of the Shrew,*
> Induction, i.

(See also EWER AND BASIN.)

DIARY
"An account of transactions, accidents and observations of every day; a journal." (J)

DIBBER, DIBBLE
The term from the Dutch *dipfel* or sharp point, for "a small spade, a pointed instrument with which gardeners make holes for planting." (J) The word continued in use here into the nineteenth century. "A gardener's planting tool, a spade." (W) "The tool employed in setting plants." (M)

DIBBLER
A cant term for a pewter plate; a term perhaps derived from dibble, a small spade used in the garden.

DICE
Small cubes of bone or ivory used in many games of chance. Dice are "marked with dots on each of their six faces, from one to six, according to the number of faces. Sharpers have several ways of falsifying dice: (1) By sticking a hog's bristle in them so as to make them run high or low, as they please; (2) by drilling and loading them with quicksilver, which cheat is found out by holding them gently by two diagonal corners, for the heavy sides will turn always down; (3) by filing and rounding them. But all these ways fall far short of the art of the dice-makers, some of whom are so dexterous [in loading dice] that sharping gamesters will give any money for their assistance. Dice are very old." *Encyclopedia Americana* (Philadelphia, 1831).

DICE BOX
The nicely carved or painted, polished hard wood, superior metal, or ivory cup or "box from which the dice are thrown." (J)

Dice and throwing box.

DICTIONARY
"A book containing the words of any language in alphabetical order, with explanations of their meaning; a lexicon; a vocabulary; a word-book." (J) The earliest dictionary is said to have been compiled in 1100 B.C. by the Chinese scholar Pa-out-tse; the first Latin dictionary about 60 B.C. by

Marcus Terentius Varro; the one that first stabilized the English language was published in 1775 in London, compiled by Samuel Johnson and immediately earning him the soubriquet "Dictionary Johnson." One of the first colonial orders placed for a copy of Johnson's dictionary was written by Benjamin Franklin, erstwhile Philadelphia printer, bookseller, and writer.

Nineteenth-century stenciled school dinner box.

DINNER BASKET
Dinner or lunch baskets, carried by workmen, by farmers to the field, or children going to school, generally were of splint, provided with lid covers and bail-like handles. The tin lunch pail was a nineteenth-century fashion. "When prayers were over every morning, the first move of the day was to get the boys out of the way: Our dinner was packed in a small splint basket, and we were started on our way to the district school, about a mile distant." (Description of New England Life, c. 1800.) Harriet Beecher Stowe, *Old Town Folks* (Boston, 1868).

DINNER WAGON
(See BUTLER'S TRAY, CANTERBURY, DUMB-WAITER.)

DIRK
The name generally given in America to the small dagger worn by naval officers during the eighteenth and early nineteenth centuries. The dirk was similar in form to the long knife of the same name used in the Scottish highlands: "Dr. Johnson asked about the use of the dirk with which he

imagined Highlanders cut their meat. He was told they had a knife and fork *besides* to eat with. How did the women do? he asked, and was answered, some of them also had a knife and fork, but in general the men, when they had cut their meat, handed their knives and forks to the women, and they themselves eat with their fingers. The old tutor of Macdonald always eat fish with his fingers, claiming that a knife and fork gave it a bad taste." James Boswell, *Journal of a Tour* [1773] *to the Hebrides* (London, 1785).

DISCHBANK
The Pennsylvania German term for a Sideboard, *q.v.*

DISH
"A broad wide vessel in which food is served up at table; [also] a deep, hollow vessel for liquid food." (J)

> *I'll give my jewels for a set of beads,*
> *My gorgeous palace for a hermitage,*
> *My gay apparel for an almsman's gown,*
> *My figur'd goblets for a dish of wood.*
>
> Shakespeare: *King Richard II,* III, iii.

DISH CRADLE
A scullery drainer; "a rack of wood used for drying dishes in." (H)

DISH CROSS
The late-eighteenth-century adjustable X-shaped stand set on tiny ball feet, used as a kind of coaster or in place of a trivet, at the table to protect the table finish from damage from hot bowls or platters. (See also DISH RING.)

DISH RING
The raised hollow ring or square, often set on tiny ball or bracket feet, on which hot dishes were set to protect the table finish; developed in the mid-eighteenth century and made of brass, iron, silver, or silver-plated metal; conversely, dish rings were sometimes fitted with candleholders or spirit lamps to keep food warm. "Joseph Anthony, Jr. Silversmith . . . has imported

... immediately from the manufactories ... slop basons, Dish rings and crosses, with and without lamps, quart, pint and half pint mugs ..." *Pennsylvania Packet* (Philadelphia), December 7, 1790.

DISPENSARY, DISPENSATORY
The term signifying "a repository or shop for selling medicines at prime cost for the benefit of the poor [hence] it is also the title of several books, containing the method of preparing the various sorts of medicines used in the practice of physick." (M) (See also PHARMACOPOEIA.)

DIVAN
The term, used in Turkey and other Eastern countries for a grand council or royal court, was adopted in the late nineteenth century to signify any low couch, having neither back nor arms, covered in richly embroidered silk or other cloth, because presumably such couches were similar to those with which Oriental halls were furnished.

DIVINING ROD
The term describing any long rod or wand "made with certain superstitious ceremonies; either single and curved, or with two branches, like a fork, of wood, brass, or other metal. The rod is held in a particular way, and if it bends toward one side, those who use the rod believe it to be an indication that there is treasure under the spot." *Encyclopedia Americana* (Philadelphia, 1831).

DOCUMENT BOX
Apparently a collector's term for a small lidded box, equipped with a lock and large enough to hold one's important papers, such as deeds or notes. Such boxes were made of thin wood, covered with leather or decorated paper, and usually lined with paper. Some so-called nineteenth-century decorated tin boxes are called document boxes today. When first made, these small boxes were used for trinkets, to hold thread, laces,

etc., as well as papers. (See also HANAPER, PAMPHLET BOX.)

Wood document box covered with marbled paper.

DOG GRATE
The name sometimes given the fireplace grate which did away with the need of separate firedogs or andirons. These grates, rectangular in overall form, were a kind of open, squared-off basket set between four uprights or legs. The bars, or "basket" ends, supported the larger logs. Some of these were made with vertical plates or firebacks set between the rear uprights.

DOG IRONS, DOGS
One of the popular names from the seventeenth through the mid-nineteenth centuries for small, short andirons. "I left him and hied home, buying several things at the ironmonger's; dogs, tongues, and shovells, for my wife's closet, and the rest of my house." Samuel Pepys, *Diary,* September 7, 1663. "Any Person that has occasion for . . . Chimney-Backs, Dog-Irons or any other Cast Iron Ware, may be provided with them by Richard Clarke, at his Furnace in the Gore, giving speedy Notice of the Sizes and Quantity they want to him there." *Boston Gazette,* July 13, 1741. (See ANDIRONS, CREEPERS, FIREDOGS.)

DOG-SPIT
(See SPIT-DOG.)

DOLE CUPBOARD
The collector's term for a type of almonry or Ambry, *q.v.,* with a pierced door or door

Dole cupboard. (Courtesy, Connecticut Historical Society, Inc.)

made of bars, placed in churches to hold bread or other food to be given to the poor.

DOLL

"A puppet or baby." (W)   Children's dolls were made with separate heads of carved and painted wood, ivory, bone, or wax, as well as pottery, and porcelain. Doll heads usually were purchased separately, the bodies and clothing made at home, or by a seamstress. Some early dolls were made of painted and stuffed leather. In New England it was not until well after 1850 that Christmas was celebrated or considered a proper time for giving presents, although such festivities were known in southern and other Anglican parishes. In the North, New Year's Day or the spring Militia Election Day were the times of festive dinners and balls; to make calls at friends' homes and to give gifts: "Charles Cottu, Fruit & Toy Store, has also an assortment of Dolls, and fancy Toys, that will be, he hopes very acceptable for election presents." *American Mercury* (Hartford, Connecticut), April 28, 1816. (See also BABY.)

DOLL DISHES
(See TOY CHINA.)

DOLLHOUSE
(See BABY HOUSE.)

DOMESDAY BOOK, DOOMSDAY BOOK

The reference is to the "very ancient record made in the time of William the Conqueror [1081–86], which now [1778] remains in the exchequer and consists of two volumes: the greater contains a survey of all the lands in most of the counties in England, and the lesser comprehends some counties that were not then surveyed." (M)   This was the first specific and intensive survey of lands, and inventory of private ownership of goods and chattels undertaken in Britain; once used as a basis for taxation, latterly as a prime reference source by genealogists and historians; it sometimes also is referred to as the tax book or the *magna rolla*.

DOMINO PAPER
(See WALLPAPER.)

DOOR BALK
(See BALK.)

DOOR KNOCKER

The often ornately wrought iron or brass ring or knob thumped against the door plate

New England iron door knocker and door nail, c. 1700. (Courtesy, Antiquarian and Landmarks Society, Inc.)

or nail to announce one's arrival. "It is a great pity that the old-fashioned brass knocker has become obsolete . . . There was something in its brightness indicative of a hospitable, well-ordered house. The present cast-iron knocker is a frightful invention; the only possible fact one can urge in its favour is that it saves work for the housemaid's arm . . . The work of the hammer and anvil is infinitely superior in every way to the production of the mould." Charles L. Eastlake, *Hints on Household Taste in Furniture, Upholstery and Other Details* (London, 1868). (See also DOORNAIL.)

DOORNAIL
The large, decorative, and useful iron or brass nail, flattened knob, or back plate set in the face of the door to be struck by the door knocker:

What! Is the old king dead?
As nail in door.

　　Shakespeare, *King Henry V*, Part II; V, iii.

DOOR PORTER
A porter was one who kept the door, or guarded the gate, hence this term for a pottery or metal doorstop, made in a variety of forms, particularly human and animal figures.

DOORSTOP
So long as H and strap hinges were used, doorstops were unnecessary. They first came into use during the last quarter of the eighteenth century when rising butt hinges were installed to cause a door to close automatically. Made of metal and earthenware and more rarely in glass, in a variety of patterns, many nineteenth-century examples also were painted or bronzed.

DOOR TREE, DORE TREE
Another name for the door balk, the bar especially planed or shaped, and some-times carved, set into iron or wooden holdfasts on either side of the doorframe, to secure the door against intruders.

DORMANT TABLE
(See TABLE DORMANT.)

DORSEL, DORSER, DOSSEL
All variations of the name for "a Pannier [*q.v.*], a basket or bag, one of which hangs on either side of a beast of burden, for the reception of things of small bulk." (J) Matched leather, wicker, or heavy cloth saddlebags.

DOSSER
Another name for the "Pannier [*q.v.*], or basket." (H).

DOUAY BIBLE
The Douay Bible, or Douay Version was so named from Douai, the town in France where it first was published. The transliteration of the New Testament appeared in 1582, that of the Old Testament in 1609–10, from the Latin Vulgate, approved specifically for the use of Roman Catholics. (See also BIBLE, HAGIOGRAPHIA.)

DOUBLE CHAIR
A contemporary term for the small settee introduced during the Carolean period, and simulating two or more chairs joined together with one seat; thus, September 14, 1754, Gedediah Snowden, joiner, billed John Reynell, Philadelphia merchant, " £3 for 2 Double Window chairs with 6 legs" and in October, for the same price made him a settee "with six feet & stretchers answerable." Historical Society of Pennsylvania: Coates-Reynell mss. 1751–54.

DOUBLE CHEST OF DRAWERS
A contemporary synonym for the chest-on-chest designs for which Hepplewhite's *Guide* gave two; the author remarking that "these may have the same depth [20

C. 1760 Connecticut double chest of drawers or cherry chest-on-chest with carved shell and roundels. Top drawer is actually single drawer with the front arranged to simulate the conventional two short and one long drawers. Sunburst and sunrise carving with dentil course on pediment. (Courtesy, Connecticut Historical Society, Inc.)

Double chest of drawers illustrated in Hepplewhite's *Guide* (London, 1794).

inches] as chests of drawers, and a height of 5 feet 6 inches." (See also TALLBOY.)

DOUBLER

A contemporary cant term for a large dish, plate, or bowl from which two people might dine at once. Thus, the platter Jack Sprat and his wife used would have been called a doubler.

DOUBLE ROCKING CHAIR

One of the many so-called Boston rocker designs, a double or settee-rocker, first made after 1820. "R. G. Allen . . . has on hand . . . Chairs. 2000 stained rose and elegant gilt, Fancy Fret; high back Rocking ditto; double back ditto; cane, rush and wood seats, made of seasoned stock, painted by experienced workmen, under my own inspection." *Literary Cadet and Rhode Island Statesman* (Providence), February 23, 1828. (See also MAMMY ROCKER.)

DOUBLE-TOP TABLE

A name sometimes given a c. 1800 form of Dumb-waiter, *q.v.* The table had two circular trays, one of which was supported on slender posts or turned spindles and thus raised above the other. The resultant "double top" then was set on a pedestal stand with three or four feet.

DOUGH BOX, DOUGH TROUGH

A trough or box with a separate lid set on a frame, and in which dough was mixed and kneaded. Also called a kneading trough

Dough box. (Courtesy, Antiquarian and Landmarks Society, Inc.)

Dough box. (Courtesy, Antiquarian and Landmarks Society, Inc.)

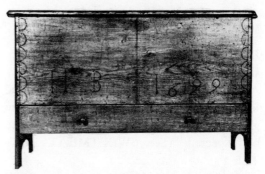

Dower chest over drawer with punch decoration. (Courtesy, William Putnam Collection.)

or box, a dough tray or trough. In addition, it was "one of the most economical of kitchen tables, a good deal in use in the cottages and small farmhouses [because the lid] when on the trough serves as a table." J. C. Loudon, *An Encyclopedia of Cottage, Farm and Villa Architecture and Furniture* (London, 1833).

DOUTER, DOUTERS, DOWTES, DOWSER

Common cant terms for the Candle Extinguisher, *q.v.,* "instruments for extinguishing the candles without cutting the wicks." (H)

DOWER CHEST

Correctly, Dowry Chest, *q.v.*

DOWRY CHEST

The general term for any blanket or linen chest made in any period, especially to hold a bride's trousseau. Usually decorated with carved or painted floral, leaf, or bird designs; marked with the wedding date and the bride's name or cypher. Often miscalled a dower chest, a strange error since dower usually refers to a widow's portion.

DOWLE STONES

A synonym for "land-marks." (M) Boundary markers, merestones, or property corner stakes.

DOWRYBBE, DOWRUB, DOWRYS

In the kitchen, the spatula-like wooden utensil used for "scraping and cleaning the kneading trough or dough-box." (H)

DRAGANALL, DRAGANEL

A container or covered dish for dragees, the

Early-eighteenth-century dover chest with painted and grained decoration.

333

old term for comfits derived from drage, a kind of spice.

DRAM CUP, DRAM DISH, DRAM GLASS, DRAM POT

A small, short-stemmed drinking glass. The lower half of the bowl usually was solid; the glass thus held less than might at first glance be expected. (See SWEETMEAT BOTTLE.)

1800–25 dram glasses.

DRAUGHTS, DRAUGHTBOARD, DRAUGHTSMEN

The name of a popular game; the checkered board on which it is played is similar to the chessboard; "with 24 pieces, which by angular movements are enabled to take each other, until one of the parties has lost all his men, or is placed in a situation to lose them all, when the game is at an end." *Encyclopedia Americana* (Philadelphia, 1831). Boards and men were the work of turners and carvers. The tops of some small stands were inlaid with small squares so they could serve as playing boards for the game. (See also CHESSBOARD.)

DRAWER(S)

"A sliding box or chest." (W) This also was a contemporary synonym for a chest of drawers or a double chest of drawers, so used for example in Hepplewhite's *The Cabinet-Maker and Upholsterer's Guide* (London, 1794). (See also TILL, and advertisement quoted under CYLINDER FALL DESK.)

DRAWING BOX

A contemporary term for "a drawer." (H) A box in a case. (See also DRAWER.)

DRAW TABLE

The early extension or extending table, made with leaves stored beneath a center board and which could be drawn or pulled out to rise on tapered bearers flush with the top board. (See also EXTENDING TABLE, IMPERIAL DINING TABLE, TELESCOPE DINING TABLE.)

One of the earliest surviving pieces of American oak furniture. The draw table shown is believed to have been made between 1650 and 1670. The bulbous baluster-turned legs are typical of the time. (Courtesy, Connecticut Historical Society, Inc.)

DRAWING-ROOM CHAIR

A general term for chairs, usually purchased in sets of four, six, eight or more to be used in the best room of the house; but not including lounge or easy chairs. "Chairs for Drawing Rooms admit of great

Drop seat for top chair shown next page.

334

Late-seventeenth-century banister-back "best" chair with drop-in seat. (Courtesy, Antiquarian and Landmarks Society, Inc.)

Queen Anne cherry chair of the type made here between 1730 and 1760 with yoke crest rail, solid vase or fiddleback splat, balloon seat, front pad feet. (Courtesy, Connecticut Historical Society, Inc.)

Drawing-room chair as shown in Thomas Chippendale's *The Gentleman and Cabinet-Maker's Director* (London, 1762).

Decorated chair with rush seat, c. 1830. (Courtesy, Antiquarian and Landmarks Society, Inc.)

taste and elegance as well as variety, and are constructed of rich and costly materials in accordance with the room . . . highly enriched; the seats covered with silks, painted satins, painted velvets, superfine cloth, or chintz." George Smith, *A Collection of Designs for Household Furniture* (London, 1808). (See also PARLOR CHAIR.)

DRAWING TABLE
The same as Draw Table, *q.v.*

DREDGER, DRUDGER
The common pronunciations of the French term *drageoir,* from the Latin *drageria,* for a little spice box, about the size and shape of a pocket watch, in which dragees or spiced comfits were carried. It was also the name of the larger box kept in parlor or dining parlor, which was used to sift powdered spices, such as cinnamon or nutmeg, onto food or punch. Needless to say, these differed greatly in size and in the quality of materials and workmanship from those wood, iron, or tin flour dredgers used in the kitchen: "I did carry home a silver drudger for my cupboard of plate, and did call for my silver chafing-dishes; and with my wife looked over our plate, and picked out 40 £ worth to change for more useful plate . . . and then we shall have a very handsome cupboard." Samuel Pepys, *Diary,* February 2, 1665–66.

DREDGING BOX
Another name for the drudger or kitchen Dredger, *q.v.;* "a box used for dredging meat." (W)

Dredge: "To sprinkle flower on roasting meat." (W) ". . . Turn the oysters about till you find them crisp; then put a pound of butter in a frying pan, and with a dredging-box dust in flower . . . then mix that and the oysters together." E. Smith, *The Compleat Housewife* (London, 1741).

DRESSER
During the Colonial period and well into the nineteenth century, this was the "bench in a kitchen on which meat is drest or prepared for the table," (J) or in Webster's terser phrase, "a kitchen table." "Take a turbot, large sole, or any flat fish that will boil well, lay the fish on the dresser and take away all the bones . . ." Richard Briggs, *The New Art of Cookery* (Philadelphia, 1792). It is the dresser or kitchen table that is romanticized by collectors today as a tavern table. The term also is given a type of kitchen cupboard that evolved early by adding tiers of two or three open shelves above the table or dressing board, and/or drawers, or a pot board below. (See WELSH DRESSER.)

DRESSING APPARATUS
The general term encompassing the furnishings of the chamber or dressing room other, of course, than the bedstead; including, according to Hepplewhite's *The Cabinet-Maker and Upholsterer's Guide* (London, 1794), "Dressing Glasses, Dressing

Tables, Dressing Drawers, Commodes, Rudd's Tables or Reflecting Dressing Tables, Shaving Tables, Bidets, Night Tables, Bason Stands, Wardrobes and Pot Cupboards," each of which see.

DRESSING BOARD
(See DRESSER, KITCHEN TABLE.)

DRESSING BOX
A small fitted box to hold toilet necessities, sometimes with a looking glass set in a frame above the box. Listed in the inventory of the estate of Israel Pemberton, Philadelphia, May 1754, were "in the Front Chamber, 1 mahogany chest of Drawers, 1 Dressing Table & Dressing Box, 4 . . ." *Will Book K,* p. 143.

DRESSING CASES
The leather, leather-covered wood, cloth-covered pasteboard, or splint box usually fitted with a looking glass and/or other small accessories helpful to the traveler; the type of case usually called a shaving kit or cosmetic case today. ". . . Gold, gilt, tortoise-shell, and leather boxes, Ladies dressing cases . . ." Joseph Anthony, Jr. [silversmith]. *Pennsylvania Packet* (Philadelphia), December 7, 1790. (See also BANDBOX, HATBOX, HAT CASE, TRAVEL CASE.)

DRESSING DRAWERS
A contemporary term for a small chest of drawers, "the top drawer of which contains the necessary dressing equipage; the other [drawers] are applicable to common uses," according to Hepplewhite. *The Cabinet-Maker and Upholsterer's Guide* (London, 1794) illustrated two such "drawers" with plain fronts, one with a bow front, a fourth with a serpentine front, "the drawers to which are elegantly ornamented with inlaid or painted work, which is applied with great beauty and elegance to this piece of furniture. Some made of satin-wood, with the ornaments of suitable colours, have pro-

duced a most pleasing and agreeable effect." (See also BEAU BRUMMEL.)

Dressing drawers illustrated in Hepplewhite's *Guide* (London, 1794).

DRESSING GLASS
A small, framed mirror set on swivel supports, usually above a small drawer or drawers, and designed to stand on a dressing table or low chest of drawers: "Mrs. Nicholas is in Want of a couple of small looking Glasses for Chambers; which You'll be pleased to send me; I would have them cheap and neat without Drawers." (Order from Robert Carter Nicholas, Treasurer of the Colony, Williamsburg, Virginia, November 12, 1771, to London.) Frances Mason,

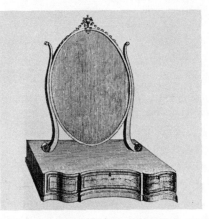

Dressing glass illustrated in Hepplewhite's *Guide* (London, 1794).

John Norton and Sons, Merchants of London and Virginia (Richmond, 1935). Sometimes also called a shaving mirror by collectors. (See DRESSING BOX, TOILET GLASS.)

DRESSING STOOL

The lightly made, handsome stool designed for use at the dressing table. "The frame work proper for a dressing or music stool may be of mahogany or japanned, as most agreeable, or to match [other furniture in the room] and should have the same sort of covering." A. Hepplewhite, *The Cabinet-Maker and Upholsterer's Guide* (London, 1794).

DRESSING TABLE

Often misnamed a lowboy. (See TOILET TABLE.)

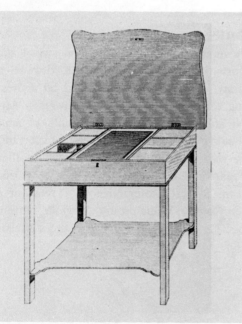

Ladies dressing table illustrated in Hepplewhite's *Guide* (London, 1794).

DRILL

One of the tools, "an instrument with which holes are bored. It is a point pressed hard against the thing bored and turned round with a bow and string." (J) "Drills are used for the making such holes as punches will not serve for; as a piece of work that hath already its shape and must have an hole made in it." Joseph Moxon, *Mechanick Exercises, or The Doctrine of Handy-Works,* (London, 1683–84).

DRINKING HORN

The drinking cup or goblet made of horn. "Remember to come well furnished with linnen, woolen, some more beddinge, brasse, pewter, leather bottels, drinkinge hornes Ec. . . ." (John Winthrop at Charleston to his wife in England, July 23, 1630.) *Journal, History of New England* (Boston, 1825).

DRINKING TABLE
(See SOCIAL TABLE.)

DRINKING VESSEL

A collective term describing any cup, bottle, bowl, dish, pot, or other container from which the user might imbibe any beverage. Many types and shapes of such containers, and the names by which they would have been known to English colonists in America, were thus listed by an early-seventeenth-century writer: "Of drinking cups, divers and sundry sorts we have; some of elme, some of box, some of maple, some of holly, etc. Mazers, broad-mouthed dishes, noggins, whiskins, piggins, creuzes, ale-bowles, wassel-bowles, court-dishes, tankards, kannes, from a pottle to a pint, from a pint to a gill. Other bottles we have of leather but they are mostly used amongst the shepherds and harvest people of the country; which when the Frenchmen first saw, they reported at their return unto their countrey that the Englishmen used to drink out of their bootes. We have besides cups made of horns of beastes, of cockernuts, or goords, of eggs of estriches, they made of the shells of divers fishes brought from the Indies and other places, and shining like mother of pearle. Come to plate, every tavern can afford you flat bowles, French bowles, prounet cups, beare bowles, beakers; and private householders in the citie, when they make a feast to entertain their friends, can furnish their cupboards with flagons, tankards, beere cups, wine bowles, some white, some parcell guilt, some guilt all over, some with covers, others without, of sundry shapes and qualities." John Heywood, *Philocothonista or Drunkard Opened, Dissected and Anatomized* (London, 1635).

DRIPPING HORSE
A contemporary cant term for a wooden, standing "frame to hang wet clothes on that they might dry." (H) (See also AIRING HORSE, DRYING CRANE.)

DRIPPING PAN
"The [iron] pan in which the fat of roast meat is caught," (J) set beneath the spit rack or stand. "Dripping and frying pans" were listed in the House of Parliament Rates, 1660, for Imports and Exports— *Statutes of the Realm* (London, 1819). (See advertisement quoted under BRANCHED CANDLESTICKS.)

DROP BOX
Another contemporary term for "a money box or coin-bank." (J) (See also BANKS, COIN BANK, MONEY JUG, POOR BOX, THRIFT BOX.)

DROP-FRONT DESK
(See ESCRITOIRE. See also DROP-FRONT, Chapter 5.)

DROP-LEAF TABLE
The American name for what in England still is called a flap table.

DROSOMETER
In appearance, a kind of small balance scale, this was an instrument to ascertain the quantity of dew which falls. "It consists of a balance, one end of which is furnished with a plate fitted to receive the dew. The other containing a weight protected from it." *Encyclopedia Americana* (Philadelphia, 1831).

DRUDGER
"The box out of which flour is thrown at roast meat [as it turns on the spit]." (J)

Also called a Dredger, *q.v.*, this was a type of small canister with a pierced top, made of hard wood, iron, tin, pewter, or brass.

DRUM
"An instrument of military musick, consisting of vellum strained over a broad hoop on each side, and beaten with sticks." (J) "Military Auction. Disposal of the property . . . of the late Uxbridge Grenadier Company, the following viz.—1 Good Bass Drum, 2 Camp Kettles, 1 Bugle Horn, 2 large Chests. *Independent Messenger* (Mendon, Massachusetts), September 9, 1831. "David Woolhaupter, Instrument Maker, in Fair Street, opposite St. Paul's Church, New York, Makes and sells all sorts of Drums and Fifes; Drums made of Mahogany, curled maple, and Beech wood, in the best and neatest manner, and now has a quantity ready made for sale." *The New-York Journal or The General Advertiser*, June 8, 1775.

Drum, c. 1800. (Courtesy, Antiquarian and Landmarks Society, Inc.)

DRUM TABLE
The name given a table with a circular or polygon-shaped top, and with a series of small drawers set in the apron below the surface board. This was the counting-out or so-called rent table, a separate drawer presumably being reserved for the account sheet of each individual client, customer, or tenant. (See also COUNTER DESK.)

DRUNKARD'S CHAIR

The Late-Victorian period collector's whimsical name for the type of wide easy chair first introduced in the early eighteenth century, and intended to provide a seat for two persons. The Confidante, *q.v.,* originally was such a small sofa or double chair.

DRYFAT, DRYVAT

A box, case, chest or trunk, or a large basket, used for shipping or storing dry goods, as opposed to fat or vat; specifically, a large barrel or cask containing liquids.

DRYING CRANE

A simple flat wood crane, shaped much as was the iron pot crane inside the fireplace, but hinged to the jamb above the hearth opening, so that it could be swung out when needed. This was used to hold linens to dry before the fire; also, for the drying of bunches of herbs. (See also AIRING HORSE; DRIPPING HORSE.)

DUCHESSE

One of the eighteenth-century forms of sectional furniture, the duchesse combined two easy chairs, with a stool set between them to create a kind of elegant day bed. The three pieces also, of course, could be used separately. The term for this piece of furniture "is derived from the French. Two Barjier chairs, of proper construction, with a stool in the middle form the duchesse, which is allotted to large and spacious antirooms; the covering may be various, as also

Duchesse illustrated in Hepplewhite's *Guide* (London, 1794).

the frame-work, and made from 6 to 8 feet long. The stuffing may be of the round manner or low-stuffed, with a loose squab or bordered cushion fitted to each part, with a duplicate linen cover to cover the whole or each part separately." A. Hepplewhite, *The Cabinet-Maker and Upholsterer's Guide* (London, 1794.) (See also BERGERE, CONFIDANTE.)

DUCHESSE BED

The elaborate and elegant bed formed by suspending a canopy above a Duchesse, *q.v.,* by fitting sockets to the chair backs to hold the slender posts necessary; a form of day bed.

DUCK'S NEST

A popular name for a type of eighteenth and nineteenth-century portable kitchen grate in the shape of a rounded or ovoid basket, and thus resembling a nest in outline; the grate was set between four uprights or standards, about a foot above the hearth stone.

DUDGEON

Now a term for Dagger, *q.v.,* this properly signified the root of the boxtree of which handles for daggers frequently were made; hence, such a dagger first was called a dudgeon-handled dagger or dudgeon-dagger; eventually simply a dudgeon.

DUELING PISTOLS

Always sold in sets or pairs of identical pieces, these had smooth-bored barrels and were kept in specially made cases; the cases also held the necessary cleaning and loading utensils. "I regret the passion for duelling here . . . no other nation offers more opportunities to deplore the mania which arms a man against his compatriot . . . Even more shocking is it to find everyone armed, as though in time of war. New Orleans, like all other great cities, has need of order and administration of justice." Edouard de Montulé, *Voyage en Amérique* . . . (Paris, 1821).

DUFFEL BAG

Duffel was strong, shaggy cloth manufactured chiefly in Yorkshire and often used for travel bags and trunks as well as cloaks.

DUG-OUT CHEST

(See TRUNK.)

DULCIMELL

Another name for the Dulcimer, *q.v.*

DULCIMER

This was "an old kind of musical instrument." (W) The term was derived from the Latin *dulce melos* and the Old French *doulcemer,* for sweet air, to describe the instrument developed in the fifteenth century and popular through the eighteenth century. The dulcimer had graduated wire strings stretched over a sounding board and which were struck with two small hand-held hammers.

DUMB SPINNET

(See MANICORDION.)

DUMB-WAITER

The handsome side serving table or tea stand designed as "a useful piece of furniture to serve in some respects the place of a waiter." Thomas Sheraton, *The Cabinet Dictionary* (London, 1803). An eighteenth-century ambulante, this was a movable stand on a three- or four-legged base with casters. The central stem supported a tier of three or more circular trays, graduated in size, the top tray being about one-third the diameter of the lowest. The bottom tray sometimes had shallow drawers, in which cutlery, etc., might be stored, set in an apron below the board. The inventory of the estate of Nathan Levy, Philadelphia, appraised April 20, 1754, listed "In the Front Parlour 6 old Rush Bottom chairs fineered with walnut, 18s; 1 walnut tree oval table £1.5s; 1 mahogany Dumb Waiter £2; 1 Windsor chair 7s. 6d; 4 pictures on glass fram'd & gilt £2." *Administrator Book F,* p. 527.

DUST COVERS

Any protective covering for furniture, draperies, paintings. "The whole range of rooms in his middle story is most grandly fitted up. But since it would be pity to soil such good furniture, his curtains, which we must suppose to be made of the richest damask, are carefully pinned up in paper-bags; and the chairs, of which the seats and backs are undoubtedly of the same stuff, are no less cautiosly skreened with ordinary checked linen. Thus does he answer, by the appearance of finery, all the purposes of pride and ostentation." *The London Magazine,* January, 1756.

DUTCH CROWN

(See GAME HANGER.)

DUTCH OVEN

A heavy footed pot or kettle for baking at the hearth. It was set above the embers, and coals were placed on the lid, thus providing overall heat, as in an enclosed oven. Usually made of iron, although other metals were used: "Send one copper Dutch Oven lined with tin 20 inches over the top." (Order from Attorney Peter Lyons, Hanover, Virginia, to London, September 25, 1771.) Frances Mason, *John Norton and Sons, Merchants of London and Virginia* (Richmond, 1935). The term is often used today in error to describe the recessed oven built into chimneys. (See also BAKE OVEN.)

DUTCH TEA TABLE

(See HAND BOARD.)

DWARF LIBRARY BOOKCASE

A contemporary term for a low set of bookshelves seldom over five feet in height. "Literature and the fine arts going hand in hand, this kind of Bookcase is well adapted to the connoisseur in sculpture and painting [because] from the lowness [of height] adopted, the walls remain free for paintings, at the same time figures or antique sculpture, placed this height before the spectator, will

afford the most pleasing appearance . . ."
George Smith, *A Collection of Designs for Household Furniture* (London, 1808).

E

EAR(E) DISH, EARED DISH
Seventeenth-century cant terms for the Porringer, *q.v.*

EAR RINGS
Then as now, jewels worn on or dependent from the earlobe. "Ear-rings of all Sizes, Fashions and Prices; Paste Shoe and Knee Buckles . . . Daniel Fueter, who was bred a Jeweller and Goldsmith will give full satisfaction to those Gentlemen and Ladies who will honour him with their custom . . ." *The New-York Gazette or The Weekly Post-Boy*, March 10, 1763. (See also PENDANT.)

EASEL PAINTING
The term for a painting small enough to be executed on an easel, as opposed to the painting of great size that covered a wall in the galleries or reception rooms of the large homes of the wealthy. The rise of a middle class of colonial merchants and shippers, and their desire for enrichments suited to their smaller homes, caused a demand for easel paintings.

EASEL PIECES
Another term for Easel Paintings, *q.v.* "A name given by painters to such pieces as are contained in frames, in contradistinction to those painted on ceilings, Ec." (M)

EASY CHAIR
The eighteenth-century term for what today is called a wing chair. The adjective easy carried the connotation of softness; that is, the use of upholstered surfaces on arms and backs, or the addition of stuffed seat cushions: "William Sheer, Cabinet and Chair-Maker . . . a little below the Market-House in Annapolis takes this method to inform the Public that he makes and sells . . .

Easy Arm, Parlour and Chamber Chairs; Corner Settees . . . Couches . . ." *Maryland Gazette* (Annapolis), September 10, 1769. ". . . As their name imports, [they] are especially adapted to those sedentary and reclining attitudes of person which are most favourable to repose or relaxation. They are usually large, low seated, and stuffed, with a sloping back." Blackie and Son, *The Cabinet-Maker's Assistant* (London, 1853). (See also ARM CHAIR, ELBOW CHAIR, FAUTEUIL, SADDLE CHEEK.)

Easy chair with walnut front legs, shell-carved knees; maple swell-turned stretcher and back legs, stained to resemble mahogany. (Courtesy, Connecticut Historical Society, Inc.)

ECRAN
The French term for the fire screen. (See also FOLDING SCREEN, HORSE SCREEN, POLE FIRE SCREEN.)

ÉCUELLE
The French word for a popular type of covered porringer with two flat pierced ears or handles; a continental style introduced in

England in the eighteenth century and thence transported to the colonies.

EDDYSTONE LIGHTHOUSE CLOCK
(See LIGHTHOUSE CLOCK.)

EEL SHEAR, EELER
The iron prong or spear with three or four points used for catching eels.

EGG CUP
The small container, in form a miniature stemmed goblet, made of silver, gilt-washed silver, pottery, porcelain, or glass, or the porcelain or glass insert or liner set in a silver or other fine metal frame, of similar shape, sold separately. "James Jacks . . . has imported, a Large Assortment [including] large and small Waiters, Egg Cups, and Stands, Decanter Lables . . ." *Federal Gazette* (Philadelphia), March 25, 1799.

EGG FRAME
A contemporary synonym for the small silver, gilt-washed silver, or silver-plated metal stemmed open bowl or holder into which a glass or porcelain liner (the actual egg cup) was set. "James Jacks . . . Has imported . . . from London . . . sterling plate, jewellry, plated goods, and a great variety of other articles, [including] Egg frames, salt-cellars, and bottle-stands . . ." *Federal Gazette* (Philadelphia), November 27, 1797.

EIGHT-DAY CLOCK
The contemporary term for the clock works designed to run for eight days before needing adjustment. "John Marshall, Cabinet Maker . . . has on hand . . . Useful and Elegant furniture [including] a very elegant eight day clock . . ." *City Gazette and Daily Advertiser* (Charleston, South Carolina), February 17, 1796. (See also CLOCK, FURNITURE.)

ELBOW CHAIR
The popular eighteenth-century description of "a large chair" (W) "with arms to support the elbows." (J) A type of easy chair with padded arms, but without wings or

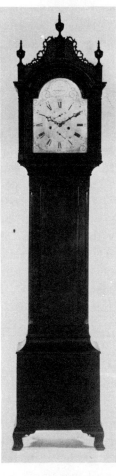

Tall-case clock (7 feet, 4 inches) of cherry and pine with gilded capitals and bases of columns. Bracket feet; eight-day wooden movement with engraved dial enscribed "E. Terry, Plymouth." Case believed made by Simeon Loomis and the dial or face by Daniel Burnap, whose ledger for May, 1793, notes, "One clock case finished for Eli Terry's Clock." (Courtesy, Connecticut Historical Society, Inc.)

Elbow or French chair design from Thomas Chippendale's *Director* (London, 1762).

cheeks. Chippendale offered "Two Designs of French chairs with Elbows . . . the Backs and Seats are stuffed, and covered with Spanish Leather, or Damask, Ec. and nailed with Brass Nails. The Seat is twenty-seven inches wide in Front, twenty-two inches from the Front to the Back, and twenty-three inches wide behind; the Height of the back is twenty-five inches, and the Height of the Seat fourteen inches and an Half, including Casters." Thomas Chippendale, *The Gentleman and Cabinet-Maker's Director* (London, 1762). "To be Sold at Public Sale on Thursday the 20th inst, at the corner of Chestnut and Seventh Streets, the following articles [including] a few sets of fashionable elbow painted chairs . . . William Shannon, Auctioneer." *Pennsylvania Packet* (Philadelphia), February 15, 1794.

EMANCIPATION EPHEMERA
(See SLAVE PAPERS.)

EMBER TONGS
The term sometimes applied to a pair of small fire tongs, used for transferring small coals from the hearth to a chafing dish, for example, or in place of Pipe Tongs, *q.v.*

Ember tongs.

Ember tongs with extension handles. (Courtesy, Antiquarian and Landmarks Society, Inc.)

EMBLEM
A decorative device or insignia, "a kind of painted enigma, or certain figures delineated or cut metaphorically, expressing some action, with reflections [mottoes] underneath, which in some measure explain the sense of the device, and at the same time instruct us in some moral truth or other matter of knowledge." (M)

EMBROIDERY
The term for a type of stitchery "work in gold, or silver, or silk thread, wrought by the needle upon cloth, stuffs, or muslin, into various figures." (M)

EMBROIDERY FRAME, LOOP
"In embroidering stuffs, the work is performed in a kind of loom because the more the piece is stretched, the easier it is worked." (M)

EMBROIDERED PICTURES
From the seventeenth through the nineteenth centuries fine needlework portraits, pastorales, landscapes, still-life arrangements of flowers and fruits were embroidered and framed for display in parlors and chambers. "At Mr. Debasty's I saw, in a gold frame, a picture of a fluter playing his flute, which, for a good while, I took for painting, but at last observed it was a piece of tapestry and it is the finest I ever saw in my life for figures, and good natural colours." Samuel Pepys, *Diary,* June 21, 1666. "George Stattler [sells] all kinds of . . . Girandoles, and looking glass frames of all patterns; Square, Oval, and Circular Frames for the Portrait Prints, Drawing and Ladies Embroidery Work from the Plainest to the most elegant, Gilt in oil or burnished Gold, equal to any imported." *City Gazette and Daily Advertiser* (Charleston, South Carolina), December 4, 1797. "Pictures and Embroidery framed in new and elegant patterns very reasonable. Hartford, Main Street, near the Bridge [N. Ruggles]."

Seventeenth-century embroidered portrait.

Embroidery and cut-work still-life picture in original frame.

Seventeenth-century embroidered landscape. (Courtesy, Antiquarian and Landmarks Society, Inc.)

American Mercury (Hartford, Connecticut), February 15, 1810.

ENAMELED KITCHENWARE
Although a process for enameling metal saucepans was invented in 1799, it was not until 1839 that a patent was issued. However, this type of kitchenware did not become popular until the late nineteenth century.

EN CAMAIEU
The French term adopted to describe painting executed in several tones or intensities of one color.

ENCOIGNEUR
The French word used to describe a shelf or set of shelves, made to fit into a corner. "The encoigneur, devoted to the same purpose (as the bracket-shelf) is intended to

be fixed in the corner of a room." A. J. Downing, *The Architecture of Country Houses* (New York, 1850).

END IRONS

Sometimes used as a synonym for andirons, but, properly, two vertical iron plates on standards or broad feet, used to contract the size of the fireplace, and thus reflect more heat out into the room.

ENGINE

The descriptive term for any "machine, instrument or agent, to aid human power in the application of force." (W) "Engines are extremely numerous; some used in war, as the battering-ram, ballista, waggons, chariots, Ec.; others in trade and manufacture, as cranes, mills, presses, Ec., others to measure time, as clocks, watches, Ec. And others for the illustration of some branch of science, as the orrery, and the like . . . in all, a certain power is applied to produce an effect of much greater moment." (M)

ENGRAVING

This is "the art of cutting metals and precious stones and representing thereon figures, letters, or whatever device or design the artist pleases. The original way of engraving on wood is called cutting on wood; that on metals with *aqua fortis* is named etching; that by the knife, burnisher, punch and scraper is called mezzotinto; that on tombs, Ec. stone cutting; and that performed with the graver, on metals and precious stones, keeps alone the primitive name of engraving." (M) The general term for any intaglio carving; that is, "to picture by incisions in any matter; to mark wood or stone; to impress deeply." (J) "Engraving by James Peller Malcolm, Done in a Neat and Expeditious Manner . . . For the satisfaction of those that please to honour him with their custom, he has engraved two Plates as Specimens of his Work, which may be seen at his house, . . . where he does Seals, Coats of Arms, Cyphers, Type Metal, Landscapes, Portraits, Ec. Ec." *Pennsylvania Packet* (Philadelphia), August 15, 1786.

Print from engraving for Essex, Massachusetts, trade card or label.

ENTAILE

An old Anglo-Norman word for shape and thus, "sculpture or a carving of any kind; a very common term in ancient art, and sometimes applied to ornamental work of any kind." (H)

ENTRY LIGHT

Before 1800 the term signified "a glass lanthern with square sides [that] furnished the entry light in the houses of the affluent." John F. Watson, *Annals of Philadelphia* (Philadelphia, 1830). (See also HALL LANTERN.)

EPERGNE

The center decoration for the table; a richly ornamented silver, porcelain, or crystal dish with rising branches to support several smaller dishes or baskets for sweetmeats, fruit, flowers. "James Jacks . . . has imported in the ship *Lexington*, from London . . . Bread and Cake Baskets; Epergnes with 7, 8, and 10 basons . . ." *Federal Gazette* (Philadelphia), March 25, 1799.

EPHEMERA

A term used in zoology for a "genus of flies so-called from their living only one day and a night," (M) and so, today the name collectors give to antique advertisements,

346

broadsides, political pamphlets, posters, etc. that originally were intended for short-term use.

ESCHUTCHEON, ESCUTCHEON
(See under ARMORIAL BEARINGS at end of this section.)

ESCRIN
A writing cabinet or small desk. (See also SCRINE.)

ESCRITOIRE, ESCRUTOIRE
"A kind of desk on a chest of drawers." (W) The eighteenth-century term for any piece of furniture, such as a chest of drawers or a table, fitted with a writing drawer that pulls out; the drawer has a hinged front that, when opened, lies flat to provide a writing surface. (See also BUREAU and note under HARLEQUIN TABLE.)

ESHIN
A colloquialism for a pail, no doubt because esh or esche was a common form of ash, a popular wood used for buckets.

ESPONTOON or SPONTOON
The term is derived from the French *sponton,* the Italian *puntone* or *punto,* for point, to signify a kind of half-pike or halberd carried by eighteenth-century infantry officers but continuing in use as late as 1835 in New England: "The commissioned officers [of the militia] shall each be armed with a sword or hanger, and espontoon." *Connecticut Statutes* (Hartford, 1835).

ESTUIFE
A word from the French for "pocket case." (H) (See also ETUI.)

ETAGERE
(See WHATNOT.)

ETCHING
The general term for "a way of making prints, by drawing with a proper needle upon a copper plate, covered over with a ground of wax, Ec., well blacked with the smoke of a Link [*q.v.*] in order to take off the figure of the drawing or print, which having its backside tinctured with white lead, will, by running over the strucken outlines with a stick, impress the exact figure on the black or red ground, which figure is afterwards with needles drawn deeper quite through the ground, and all the shadows and hatchings put in; and then a wax border being made all round the plate, there is poured on a sufficient quantity of well-tempered *aqua fortis* which insinuating into the strokes made by the needles, usually eats, in about half an hour, onto the figure of the print or drawing on the copper plate." John Harris, *Lexicon Technicum* (London, 1704). (See also ENGRAVING.)

Etching, "Fire and Water," published in 1799 and still in original painted and gilded frame.

ETUI
This French word for case or cover was adopted as a name for a small pocket box made of gold, silver, pewter, faïence, enameled metals, ivory, or wood, and in which comfits, patches, or pills were carried. "Myers & Halstead . . . make all kinds of work in gold and silver, and have to sell, a neat assortment of ready made plate, chased and plain . . . Silver, ivory and wood etwees, tooth pick cases and smelling bottles . . ." *The New-York Gazette or The Weekly Post-Boy,* November 10, 1764.

ETWEE
(See ETUI.)

EWAGE

A kind of magic stone or Amulet, *q.v.*

EWER

"A vessel in which water is brought for washing the hands," (J) "a jug to hold water to wash with." (W) (See EWER AND BASIN.)

EWER AND BASIN

A type of large pitcher and matching basin. When Gremio in *The Taming of the Shrew* boasted that

My house within the city
Is richly furnished with plate and gold,
Basons and ewers to lave her dainty hands,

he referred to the gentry's custom of keeping utensils for hand washing near the dining table, usually on a sideboard. It was an age when most food was eaten in the fingers; the nicer sort washed their hands between courses. By the end of the seventeenth century, even though forks were then more commonly used in homes of the well-to-do, the ewer and basin remained on the sideboard, as evidence of the owner's worth in silver, as well as his good table manners. By the middle of the eighteenth century, the greater use of individual napkins at table, as well as of knives and forks, did away with the need to wash greasy, food-stained hands between courses, if not at the conclusion of the meal. Thus, September 6, 1768, Robert Carter Nicholas of Williamsburg (Treasurer of the Colony) included in his annual order of household goods from England, "1½ dozen blue and white Slop Basons to wash in after Dinner at about 1/ each." Frances Mason, *John Norton and Sons, Merchants of London and Virginia* (Richmond, 1935).

The wall-hung lavabo common in better Continental and English bed chambers seldom was installed in colonial American homes. Instead, ewer and basin sets were provided. Early examples extant include many in handsome porcelain and faïence.

Development of comparatively inexpensive ironstone and the use of soft pasteware in the nineteenth century enabled the average family to purchase such sets for use in kitchen or chamber. During the nineteenth century in this country the ewer and basin commonly was called a wash pitcher and bowl set.

Seventeenth-century delft ewer; pewter top and base. (Courtesy, Antiquarian and Landmarks Society, Inc.)

EWERY

The term for the small cupboard in which ewers and basins were stored or the stand or table on which they were placed. (See BASIN STAND.)

EXTENDING TABLE, EXTENSION TABLE

A general term for any table extended or lengthened by the insertion of additional leaves. (See also DRAW TABLE, IMPERIAL DINING TABLE, TELESCOPE DINING TABLE.)

EYE MINIATURE

The term for a disconcerting type of miniature portrait in vogue late in the eighteenth century; fortunately not long-lasting. The miniature was a small painting of the eye of one's beloved, executed on ivory, glass, or parchment and set in a ring, broach, or locket; sometimes today mistaken for a kind of Masonic jewelry.

F

FABRIC(K)
The term for the "structure or construction of anything . . . [from the] Latin *fabrica* and derived from *faber,* a workman." (M)

FACE GLASS
A contemporary colloquialism for the Looking Glass, *q.v.*: "The Dining Parlour must be furnished with nothing trifling . . . [but] with the respectable and substantial-looking chairs; the large face glass; the family portraits . . ." Thomas Sheraton, *The Cabinet Dictionary* (London, 1803).

Late-eighteenth-century face or looking glass with gilt urn, leaf, flower, and wheat spray ornaments. (*Newtown Bee,* photo by R. S. Smith.)

FACE PAINTING
A contemporary term for "the art of drawing portraits" (W) and for the portrait itself. (See also IMAGE, LIKENESS, PORTRAIT.)

FACHELL, FACHON, FAUCHON
Variations of Falchion, *q.v.,* for a dagger or small sword.

FAD
A cant term for a popular fashion, in the sense of "a trifling whim; a colored ball." (H)

FADDLE
A colloquialism for "a pack or bundle," (H) or any small "trifle or toy." (W) (See also FARDEL.)

FAÏENCE
(See in Chapter 10.)

FAIRY PIPES
A colloquialism for "small tobacco pipes" (H) made of white clay with short stems; the opposite in length of the Church Warden, *q.v.* (See also CLAY PIPE.)

FALCHION
In weaponry, "a short crooked sword, a Cimeter," *q.v.* (J)

FALCON
In weaponry, a "small cannon of 2½ inch bore, carrying 2 pound weight of shot." (H)

FALLING TABLE
A seventeenth- and eighteenth-century name for a flap or Drop-leaf Table, *q.v.,* such as a Gate-leg Table, *q.v.*

FAN, FANN
Fan is derived from the Anglo-Saxon *fann* and the Latin *vannus,* for any 1) "instrument by which the chaff is blown away when corn [grain] is winnowed," (J) i.e., the sieve, basket or shovel in which grain is tossed in the air so that the chaff is blown off. Thus, a word for any utensil that caused or utilized air currents, and hence, 2) "An instrument used by the ladies to

move the air and cool themselves." (J) "French Paper Fanns for Women and Children" were listed in the House of Parliament Rates, 1660, for Imports and Exports—*Statutes of the Realm* (London, 1819). Often elegantly painted, embroidered, encrusted with semiprecious stones or pearls, fans were made of paper, fabric, or feathers mounted on a stick or handle; often were made to fold up when not in use, and so to radiate in an arc or sector of a circle when open.

Early-nineteenth-century American painted or fancy chair with rushed balloon seat.

Hitchcock fancy chair with stenciled decoration. (Courtesy, Antiquarian and Landmarks Society, Inc.)

Turkey feather fan. (Courtesy, Antiquarian and Landmarks Society, Inc.)

FANBACK CHAIR
(See under FANBACK, Chapter 5.)

FANCY CHAIR
The contemporary term for painted and gilded chairs made during the late eighteenth century and the first half of the nineteenth century, and especially applied to those which followed decorating suggestions made by the Adam brothers, and the designs issued by A. Hepplewhite & Co. and Thomas Sheraton, all of which see. Many simple country pieces, decorated by skilled amateurs, also survive. One method used

by a well-known New England minister's wife was described thus by her husband:

"She took some common wooden chairs and painted them, and cut out figures of gilt paper, and glued them on and varnished them. They were really quite pretty." (Furnishing the parsonage at East Hampton, Long Island, 1800), *Autobiography, Correspondence, . . . of Lyman Beecher, D.D.,* ed., Charles Beecher (New York, 1866). Perhaps the predilection of householders to make up their own fancy chairs inspired this advertisement by a Connecticut manufacturer: "Attention Economists! A penny sav'd by prudence, is as good as a penny earn'd by labour. Embrace the golden opportunity wherein you may procure for yourselves & children a very useful article of household furniture by calling at J. Choat's, about 15 rods south of the Brick Meeting house, who has in store and is constantly manufacturing a variety of FANCY and COMMON chairs, comprising most of the kinds now in use. In point of beauty and durability they will equal those of any other manufactory." *American Mercury* (Hartford, Connecticut), April 10, 1820. (See also PAINTED FURNITURE, Chapter 7.)

FANE
A colonial synonym for the Weather Vane, *q.v.,* made in various shapes, "seldom in that of the bird [cock] whence the modern term is derived." (H)

FANGLE
The ancient Anglo-Saxon term for a trifle or a Toy, *q.v.*

FARDEL
An old term for any bundle or "little pack," (J) or a "packfaddle." (W) (See also FADDLE.)

FARSET, FORCER, FOSSET
Old synonyms for a "Chest or Coffer," *qq.v.,* (H) perhaps because to farce or farse was to stuff or to fill.

FARTHINGALE CHAIR
The name collectors during the Victorian era gave to a type of back stool or single chair used in the late sixteenth through the early seventeenth centuries; the wide seat, lack of arms, and narrow back presumably were designed for the convenience of ladies wearing farthingales; i.e., gowns with extraordinarily wide hoops.

FAS
Another term for the "porridge pot." (H)

FASHION DOLL
The dressed doll or Baby, *q.v.,* used to advertise the latest in costume style. "To be seen at Mrs. Hannah Teatt's, Mantua Maker at the Head of Summer Street, Boston, a baby drest after the newest Fashion of Mantuas and Nightgowns & Everything belonging to a Dress . . . from London." *New England Weekly Journal* (Boston), July 2, 1733.

FASHION PATTERN BOOK
Catalogues, usually approximately 6×9 inches, of the latest fashions in dress for men, women, and children, printed from copper plate engravings and often handcolored. The catalogues, and single prints detached from them are collected today. "Latest London fashions. Hull, Townsend, Knevals & Co., Merchant-Tailors, Have just received from London, E. Minister's last report of Fashions, with printed instructions, which will enable them to make for their customers every article of clothing in the newest and most approved style. They have just received an assortment of Cloths . . . of the most fashionable colours . . ." *The Columbian Register* (New Haven, Connecticut), December 12, 1829. (See also note under BABY HOUSE.)

FASSET, FAUCET
A spigot or "tap to put into a barrel." (W)

FAT
The common colonial spelling for Vat, *q.v.*

FAUCHION

Another name for a small "crooked sword." (J) (See also FALCHION, of which this word is a variation.)

FAUTEUIL

The French term for a type of comfortable, upholstered, easy chair with open arms; the word was used without change in England and America. "This article, which is of French invention, and adapted only to an elegantly furnished Library, is made very deep (two feet six inches) in the seat; a stand for a lamp and another for books usually accompany this piece of furniture, of which one should be on each side the fireplace." George Smith, *A Collection of Designs for Household Furniture and Interior Decoration* (London, 1808). The term is a contraction of the ancient French word *fauldsteuil,* or folding stool; the modern version was used late in the seventeenth century for a padded chair with open arms, and in the eighteenth century for the upholstered chair with padded arms. (See also ELBOW CHAIR.)

FEATHER, FETHER

"A plume, an ornament or badge of honor." (W) (See also PLUME.)

FEDERAL EAGLE

(See AMERICAN EAGLE.)

FENDER

An "iron plate laid before the fire to hinder coals that fall from rolling forward to the floor." (J) The eighteenth-century safety device made necessary by the more shallow fireplaces then built and the consequent use of much narrower hearthstones, and of Grates, *q.v.,* the fender sometimes was called a Fend iron; that is, the iron which fended off sparks and embers. First examples were shaped strips of highly polished, flat, rolled iron welded on to wrought-iron bases. The use of saw-cut ornament dates from about 1740. Brass fenders of the second half of the century usually were orna-mented with chased and pierced designs. Others were of closely set vertical iron rods or wires.

"Charles Sigourney . . . Has imported . . . from London [and] Liverpool . . . a few polished bottom Copper Warming pans. Shovel and Tongs, plain & with Brass Heads. Green wire Fenders, with Brass Tops . . ." *American Mercury* (Hartford, Connecticut), November 23, 1809.

FENDER STOOL

A collector's term synonymous with the Hearth Stool, *q.v.*

FENDER TRIVET

The late eighteenth-century brass or iron trivet or holder specifically made to hang from the top rail of the fireplace fender and so serve as a stand for the teakettle or food warmer. These trivets were made with a circular or rectangular flat frame with two hooks or prongs which fitted over the bar, and an angled foot to serve as a kind of bracket-support or brace against the front or grill of the fender.

FEND IRON

(See FENDER.)

FERRE, FERRY CUP

A common synonym for the Caudle Cup, *q.v.* Ferre was an early term for caudle or thin gruel.

FERULA, FERULE

The term for "a wooden slapper used in schools," (W) derived from the Latin *ferula* for giant fennel; "an instrument of correction with which young scholars are beaten on the hand, so named because anciently the stalks of fennel were used for this purpose." (J)

FESCUE

The common term for "a small wire by which those who teach [others] to read point out the letters." (J) Sometimes also a slender wooden wand.

FIBLE, FIBBLE

The small "stirring stick or wooden spoon used in preparing oatmeal pottage." (H)

FIDDLE

The common term from the Saxon and Dutch *fidel,* for a "stringed instrument of musick, a Violin," *q.v.* (J)

FIDDLE-BACK CHAIR

(See in Chapter 5.)

FIDDLER'S KIT

(See KIT, VIOLIN.)

FIELD BED

A type of lightly framed bedstead originally made to fold up for easy transportation, or to save space, the name was derived from that of similar bedsteads carried by officers for use "in the field." Chippendale shows "Four Designs of Tent, or Field-Beds . . . The Furniture [hangings and canopy] of all these Bedsteads is made to take off, and the Laths [which support the canopy] are hung with Hinges, for Convenience of folding up." *The Gentleman and Cabinet-Maker's Director* (London, 1762). General Washington did not always expect to find accommodations in inns or private homes.

Field bed illustrated in Hepplewhite's *Guide* (London, 1794).

New England field bed with fluted posts.

Eighteenth-century New England field bedstead with urn finials and marlborough legs. (Courtesy, Connecticut Historical Society, Inc.)

Equipping for war duty, he charged £22 "To a Field Bedstead & Curtains, Mattress, Blankets, eca, eca, had of different Persons. October 2, 1775." Treasury Department: *Accounts, G. Washington with the United States Commencing June, 1775, and ending June 1783. Comprehending a Space of 8 years. A Monument to Washington's Patriotism.* Trustees of the Washington Manual

Labor School and Male Orphan Asylum, 1841. (See also TENT BED.)

FIELD BOOK
The surveyor's day book or work record, "wherein the angles, stations, distances, Ec., are set down," (M) and by extension used to describe any detailed travel journal or description of landscape and sites, such as Benson J. Lossing's *Field-Book of the Revolution* or *Pictorial Field-Book of the War of 1812.*

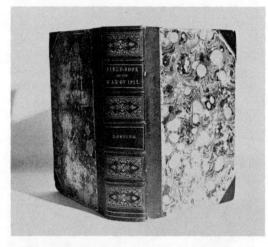

Field book, Benson J. Lossing's volume of drawings of War of 1812 battle sites.

FIELD COLORS
In war these signified the small flags about a foot and a half square, "which are carried along with the quartermaster general, for marking out the ground for the squadrons and battalions." (M)

FIELD STAFF
The weapon carried by the gunners, "about the length of a Halbert [*q.v.*], with a spear at the end; having on each side ears screwed on, like the cock of a match-lock, where the gunners screw in lighted matches, when they are upon command, and then the field staffs are said to be armed." (M)

FIFE
A sort of musical wind instrument, "being a small pipe." (M)

FIGUREHEAD
The carved and painted figure that adorned the bow of a sailing ship; representations of persons—real or mythical—animals, birds, were all favored. ". . . A stranger walking along the wharves, must be struck with the beautiful female figures of Peace, Plenty, Love, Harmony, Aeriel, Astronomy, Minerva, America, Ec., Ec., and also with the masculine statues of American warriors, Alexanders, Hannibals, Caesars, Ec., Ec., and amongst the rest of these heros the bold and striking likeness of the President on the General Washington, a ship which sailed yesterday for Dublin must give pleasure to every spectator. The artist who executed this we hear is Mr. [William] Rush; and as we may allow sea captains to be judges, they are generally of opinion that the carving of heads of vessels in Philadelphia is superior to any they have seen in any part of the world." *Pennsylvania Journal* (Philadelphia), November 23, 1791.

FILSTAR
A colloquialism for the "pestle and mortar." (H) (See also MORTAR and PESTLE.)

FINGER VASE
The term used to describe a ceramic vase made with five small flower holders or "fingers."

Pair of Staffordshire finger vases. (Courtesy, Antiquarian and Landmarks Society, Inc.)

FIREARMS

The general term for "all sorts of arms charged with powder and ball, as cannon, musquets, carbines, pistols, blunderbusses, Ec." (M)

FIREBACK

A cast-iron plate set vertically against the back wall of the fireplace to reflect heat and to preserve the stone; also called a fire plate or a chimney back.

Rare, early, iron fireback, dated 1679. (Courtesy, Antiquarian and Landmarks Society, Inc.)

FIRE BAG

(See under FIRE BUCKET.)

FIRE BALL

(See FIRE EXTINGUISHER.)

FIRE-BAR TRIVETS

The type of small iron or brass trivet, so-called, made to fit over the front fire bar of the andirons, grate, or curb. Such trivets or kettle supports thus had two feet only

at the back, where the handle was joined. (See also CRAN, FENDER, FOOTMAN, TRIVET.)

FIREBOARD

The painted, papered, carved, or otherwise decorated board made to fit the fireplace opening; used in warm weather for parlor and chamber fireplaces.

FIRE BRUSH

The hearth broom; "the brush which hangs by the fire to sweep the hearth." (J) (See also BESOM, BIRCH, BROOM, BRUSH, HEARTH BRUSH.)

FIRE BUCKET

Buckets, usually made of heavy oiled leather, twelve to eighteen inches high, narrow in shape, and with leather bails, were kept by each householder for use in the obvious emergency at his own home or to enable him to help a neighbor. Fire buckets also were made of wood or tin, but unless they retain a fire company insignia they are less easily recognized today. Often colonists were members of volunteer fire companies, and usually the buckets they used were decorated with a numeral identifying the company, or with the owner's name or monogram: "Each of us will keep constantly in good order in our Respective dwellings two leather or cedar buckets with a bar across and painted and shall be marked with ye first letter of ye owners Christian name and with his surname at length. [There] shall be one bag two yards in length and three quarters of a yard in breadth [owned by each member]. At a notice of fire we will immediately repair with our buckets and bag and use our best endeavours to Remove and Secure all his goods." Salem, Massachusetts Fire Club Regulations: *Salem Miscellaneous Mss. 1,* Essex Institute. Many buckets, however, were plain: "Ever since the Fire broke out in the House wherein *John Overing,* Esq; lately dwelt in New Boston, has been missing two Leather Buckets, belonging to Mr. John Phillips Merchant; whoever has got them are desir'd to send 'em home." *Boston Gazette,* September 25, 1738.

Such buckets were kept near whichever door was handiest to the well or cistern. They are collected today by fire buffs or to add authenticity to restorations. The fire-bags, usually of canvas, were containers for any household furnishings, papers, clothing, or food recovered from the burning building.

Late-eighteenth-century New England fire bucket. (Courtesy, Antiquarian and Landmarks Society, Inc.)

FIREDOGS
A contemporary popular name for short, small andirons. "William Coffin, at the Ostrich, near the Draw-Bridge, makes and sells . . . Fire-Doggs of all Sorts, Candlesticks, Shovels and Tongs . . ." *Boston News-Letter,* February 17, 1736. (See also ANDIRONS, CREEPERS, DOG IRONS.)

Brass and iron firedogs.

FIRE EXTINGUISHER
The round or ovoid bottle of thin glass filled with a variety of chemicals; thrown at the edge of a fire to smother the flames.

FIRE GUARD
A common term to describe a form of high Fender, *q.v.,* usually of slender, vertical iron or brass bars or wires.

FIRE IRON(S)
1) The all-inclusive term for the basic tools needed to tend the fire; sets of matching tongs, shovel, and poker. Many such sets, particularly those intended for the parlor or chamber, were made to match the fender and/or andirons. 2) Also, a synonym for Fusil, *q.v.,* "the piece of iron or steel used for striking a light with a flint." (H)

FIRELOCK
The name for an early type of gunlock in which sparks were produced, "by striking steel with flint" (J) to ignite the priming; also called a Wheel Lock, *q.v.,* the term was used to designate a certain type of Musket, *q.v.,* fitted with such a gunlock. "Newly imported, and sold by Samuel Miller, Gunsmith, at the Sign of the Cross Guns near the Draw Bridge, Boston: Neat Fire Arms of all sorts, Pistols . . . Firelocks, Ec." *Boston Gazette,* May 11, 1742. "The American army . . . firelocks are very long, some near seven feet; and they had fifes and drums." Report of John Clarke, First Lieutenant of (British) Marine, June 17, 1775, *Bunker Hill* (Boston, 1875). A much shorter barrel was acceptable after 1800: "The barrel of the musket or fire-lock for the infantry, shall be at least, three feet and six inches long, furnished with a priming-wire and brush." *Connecticut Statutes* (Hartford, 1835).

FIRE PAN
A kind of small iron, brass, or copper scoop, "a vessel of metal to carry fire." (J) Sometimes referred to as a coal carrier: "The house of John Page of Waterton burnt by

carrying a few coals from one house to another. A coal fell by the way and kindled the leaves." *Annals of New England.*

"1 copper Kettle abt. 36 Gallons; 1 Copper pan to remove fire Coals, 1 Shovel, pr. tongs and Poker." (Order October 2, 1773, from Thomas Everard, Clerk of York County, Virginia, to London.) Frances Mason, *John Norton and Sons, Merchants of London and Virginia* (Richmond, 1935). (See also FIRE SHOVEL.)

FIRE PIKE
A common early term for a poker, one of the Fire Irons, *q.v.*

FIRE PLATE
(See FIREBACK.)

FIRE POTTER
A contemporary colloquialism for "a poker." (H)

FIRE SCREEN, FIRE SCREEN HORSE
A framed panel of tapestry, embroidery, painted paper, painted or carved wood, or wicker, usually made to slide up and down on a pole set on a tripod base. Popular during the eighteenth and nineteenth centuries as a decorative means of diffusing heat from the parlor or chamber fireplace, and thus screening those who sat near the hearth. Fire screens also were made with fixed panels and with additional swinging side leaves. Others were set on a horse or cheval frame. Chippendale, showing nine designs for fire screens, included each of these types in *The Gentleman and Cabinet-Maker's Director* (London, 1754). Sheraton published designs for Horse Fire Screens with "The fyre screen [turning] on a swivel. It is carved, gilt and burnished and covered with blue silk or satin." His "Tripod Fire Screens [featured one that] may be furnished in white and gold, or japanned. The other two mahogany or japanned." *The Cabinet-Maker's and Upholsterer's Drawing-Book* (London, 1791–94). The third edition of A. Hepplewhite's

Fire cheval or horse screen shown in Thomas Chippendale's *Director* (London, 1762).

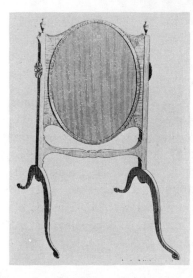

Cheval screen shown in Hepplewhite's *Guide* (London, 1794).

Cabinet-Maker and Upholsterer's Guide (London, 1794), illustrated screens "ornamented with maps, Chinese figures or needlework, weighted in the feet with lead." (See also FOLDING SCREEN, HORSE FIRE SCREEN, POLE FIRE SCREEN.)

FIRE SCREEN DESK
(See WRITING FIRE SCREEN.)

FIRE SHOVEL

The "instrument with which the hot coals are thrown up in kitchens." (J) One of the Fire Irons, *q.v.,* or hearth tools, used for carrying coals; for cleaning out ashes; usually made of iron for use in the kitchen, or brass or polished steel for the parlor and chamber hearths.

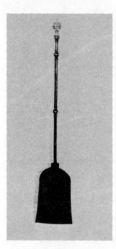

Fire shovel with brass finial, c. 1810.

FIRING GLASS

The name echoes the sound made when this heavy toasting glass was thumped in rapid succession on the table top, producing a "firing" or volley of raps. These glasses had thick, round, or cone-shaped bowls on extremely short stems, and are often found engraved with fraternal or other society insignia. (See also TOASTING GLASS.)

FIRKIN

The name of the small covered cask or keg holding, on an average, the fourth part of a barrel, or eight gallons, and used generally as a container for butter, or other liquid or semiliquid commodities. Once emptied, of course, the firkin could be put to other uses about the house and garden. "At the first frost I dig up the (flower) roots and put up or rather hide the roots in a butter ferkin, or such like vessell, filled with sand, until April." John Gerard, *The Herball or Generall Historie of Plantes* (London, 1636).

FISH KETTLE

The long, narrow, oval, covered kettle so shaped that the fish could be cooked whole. "Be careful that your fish-kettles are kept clean from sand, or anything sticking to the sides . . . and that they are well-tinned, and the frying pans the same." Richard Briggs, *The New Art of Cookery* (Philadelphia, 1792). "Charles Sigourney has imported from London . . . and Liverpool Hardware Goods . . . offered for sale, both at wholesale and retail . . . cast and sheet iron tea kettles. Sheet iron fish kettles, sauce and stewpans." *American Mercury* (Hartford, Connecticut), November 4, 1812. "1 small coper Fish Kettle; 2 spits 1 large & 1 small." (Order August 14, 1769 from Martha Jacquelin, York, Virginia, to London.) Frances Mason, *John Norton and Sons, Merchants of London and Virginia* (Richmond, 1935).

FISH SLICE

The perforated, flat, kitchen utensil of polished steel, tin, or tin-plated iron, similar in shape, although much smaller, to the bread slice or peel: "Put in the fish, then throw in a large handful of green parsley, and boil them five minutes, take them very carefully out with a fish slice . . ." Richard Briggs, *The New Art of Cookery* (Philadelphia, 1792).

FISH TROWEL

The serving utensil of silver or silver-plated metal, with a broad, flat, triangle-shaped blade. "In carving fish, care should be taken not to break the flakes, and this is best avoided by the use of the fish trowel, which not being sharp, divides it better than a steel knife." William Kitchiner, *The Cook's Oracle, and Housekeeper's Manual* (New York, 1830). "Joseph Lownes . . . near the Drawbridge has imported from London a very elegant Assortment of Plated Ware Consisting of . . . Dish rings, Dish crosses,

Fish knives and Trowels with silver edges . . ." *Pennsylvania Packet* (Philadelphia), April 9, 1792. (See also FISH SLICE.)

FIZGIG

The common term for "a kind of dart or Harpoon [*q.v.*], with which seamen strike fish," (J) a small lance attached to a rope so that it could be whirled in the air to gain momentum and force before being swung out toward the mark.

FLACKET, FLACK'ED

A colloquialism for flask; perhaps a form of Flasket, *q.v.*

FLAG BROOM

"A broom [commonly made of birch twigs] for sweeping flags or pavements." (J) That is, a hearth broom; flags referred to the stones of the fireplace.

FLAGEOLET(TE), FLAGELET, FLAGELL, FRAJOLET

All variations of flageolet, the name of a small sweet-sounding pipe or flute "used chiefly by shepherds and country people. It is made of box, or other hard wood, and sometimes of ivory, and has six holes beside that at the bottom, the mouthpiece, and that behind the neck." (M) The flageolet was appreciated also by the more urbane: "He took us into the cellar where we drank a most admirable drink, a health to the King. Here I played on my flageolette, there being an excellent echo." Samuel Pepys, *Diary,* February 27, 1659–60.

FLAGETTE

Another name for the Flagon, *q.v.*

FLAGON

The name given the large wood, silver or pewter "two quart measure of wine" (W) that was "a vessel of drink with a narrow mouth," (J) a handle, a pouring spout, and usually a lid. The flagon was kept on the sideboard, used to fill the table wine bottle, or individual drinking cups. "So at noon I find brought home in fine leather cases a pair of the noblest flaggons that ever I saw all the days of my life." Samuel Pepys, *Diary,* July 21, 1664. "Weighed my two silver flaggons at Steven's. They weigh 212 oz., 27 dwt. which is about 50£ @t 5s. per oz.; and then they judge the fashion [design and manufacture] to be worth 5s. per oz. nine; nay, some say 10s an ounce the fashion." Ibid., October 1, 1664. Originally of fine silver, gold, silver-plated ware, or pewter, the flagon was a sacramental vessel, and in form a tall, somewhat tapering tankard with either a flat or dome-shaped lid. In some areas, the flagon was used secularly as a beer tankard, thus continental versions in faïence, stoneware, and porcelain, such as the German stein, are in good supply. (See note under COMMUNION FURNITURE.)

Pewter flagon by T. D. and S. Boardman. (Courtesy, Bernard Cardé Collection.)

FLAKE

The fisherman's name for the wooden frame or "scaffold made of hurdles for drying codfish," (H) often also called a stage by early New Englanders.

Hurdle: "Sticks woven together, a cradle." (W)

"A great many of the houses here [Provincetown] were surrounded by fish flakes, close up to the sills on all sides, with only a narrow passage two or three feet wide, to the front door, so that instead of looking out into a flower or grass plot, you looked on to so many square rods of cod turned wrong side outward . . . There were flakes of every age and pattern, and some so rusty and overgrown with lichens that they looked as if they might have served the founders. [August] They were now, as elsewhere on the Cape . . . busily covering the wicker-worked flakes about their houses with salted fish." Henry David Thoreau, *Cape Cod* (Boston, 1865).

FLAMBEAU

A term collectors sometimes give ornate candleholders. Specifically, however, this was the term from the French for "a kind of large taper, made of hempen wicks, by pouring melted wax on their top, and letting it run down to the bottom. This done, they lay them to dry, after which they roll them on a table, and join four of them together by means of a red-hot iron; and then pour on more wax, till the flambeau is brought to the size required." (M) (See also in Chapter 5, and see CRESSET; LINK.)

FLAP TABLE

The English and hence colonial term for what today is called a drop-leaf table.

Oval top, maple flap or drop-leaf table popular in America, with restrained cabriole leg and cushioned pad or club foot. (Courtesy, Connecticut Historical Society, Inc.)

Flap: "Anything that hangs broad and loose, fastened only by one side." (J)

FLAT CANDLESTICK

A contemporary synonym for Chamber Candlestick, *q.v.*

FLASK

The term for "a kind of bottle or powder-horn," (W) the flask was a flat bottle of wood, horn, waxed leather, silver, pewter, tinned iron, or glass carried in the pocket, knapsack, or travel bag. Some flasks were meant to hold gunpowder, others a beverage. "Flaskes, of horne, covered with leather [or] with velvett" cases, were listed in the House of Parliament Rates, 1660, for Imports and Exports—*Statutes of the Realm* (London, 1819). (See also FLASKIN, POWDER HORN.)

Leather and brass flask. (Courtesy, Antiquarian and Landmarks Society, Inc.)

FLASKET

The term for "a sort of large basket, a kind of tray," (W) and also, of course, some-

Flasket or tray of hickory splint.

times a diminutive of flask. "A vessel in which viands are served." (J) "1 Tin Cullender and 3 Cloths Flaskets" were ordered from London August 14, 1769, by Martha Jacquelin, York, Virginia. Frances Mason, *John Norton and Sons, Merchants of London and Virginia* (Richmond, 1935).

FLASKIN
Another term for a small flask or pocket bottle, of wood, metal, stoneware, waxed leather, or glass.

FLATWARE
The all-inclusive term for flat tableware such as knives, forks, and spoons, as opposed to Hollow Ware, *q.v.*

FLEETING DISH
"A shallow dish" (H) or bowl for skimming, as cream from a pan of milk or fat from hot broth. (See FLIT.)

FLEMISH TILES
A contemporary synonym for delft or faïence tile. "Flemish or Dutch tiles, which are glazed and painted, formerly were much used in chimney jaumbs. Some thirty or forty years ago it was not uncommon to see a complete scripture history, and other curious devices, in a parlour fire place." *The Book of Trades* (London, 1805). (See also HISTORICAL TILES, TILES.)

FLESH FORK
"An iron prong to lift meat from the pot." (J) The common colonial term for the long-handled, two-pronged cooking fork.

FLESH HOOK
An iron kitchen utensil, "a hook to draw flesh from the caldron." (J) (See also FLESH FORK.)

FLESH POT
Flesh was the contemporary term for meat and so this was "a vessel in which flesh is cooked." (J) Any heavy kettle, pot, stewpan, or skillet might have been so designated.

FLINTLOCK
A type of gunlock in which a flint was screwed to the cock so that it struck against the hammer, producing sparks which ignited the priming; and thus the term used to designate a musket with this type of gunlock. (See also FIRELOCK, MATCHLOCK, WHEEL LOCK.)

FLIP GLASS
This may have been a contemporary term; however, no dictionary of the Colonial or early Federal periods lists it. The term is used by collectors to designate the thin blown-glass tumblers used to mix flip in, and from which to drink this concoction; "a liquor made by mixing beer [or hard cider or wine] with spirits and sugar." (J) Frothed in the mixing glass, flip was heated by insertion of a hot iron. According to Johnson, Flip was a cant word. "1 qt. tumbler .17, 4 pt. tumblers, .30" were listed in the estate inventory of Joseph Arnold, Haddam, Connecticut, May 14, 1823.

FLIP IRON
(See LOGGERHEAD.)

FLIT, FLITTER
Flit meant to take or steal away. In the kitchen, this was a colloquialism for the small round skimmer, with a ring handle, used to remove or skim the cream from milk. (See FLEETING DISH.)

FLITTER WORK
(See under Chapter 7.)

FLOCKBED
The term for "a bed [mattress or pallet] filled only with locks of wool." (W)

FLOOR CLOTH
A type of decorative floor covering or carpet, generally of duck or canvas, used throughout the eighteenth and nineteenth centuries. Some cloths were painted in geometric patterns from stencils, others in overall floral, leaf, animal, and bird designs in imitation of Far East carpets; some had painted borders only. Many designs were

painted to order. Some customers, however, left the choice of color and subject to friends or exporters in England: "Send 2 Kilmarnock [Scottish] carpets, 1 large and 1 small, 1 painted duck floor cloth." Order from Williamsburg, Virginia, August, 1769. Frances Mason, *John Norton and Sons, Merchants of London and Virginia* (Richmond, 1935).

For most families, of course, purchased floor carpeting of any kind was a luxury. Of the Parsonage in East Hampton, Long Island, in 1800, the Rev. Lyman Beecher wrote: "We had no carpets; there was not a carpet from end to end of the town, your mother introduced the first carpet. [I] went to a vendue, and bought a bale of cotton. She spun it and had it woven; then she laid it down, sized it, and painted it in oils, with a border all around it, and bunches of roses and other flowers over the centre. She sent to New York for her colors, and ground and mixed them herself. The carpet was nailed down on the garret floor and she used to go up there and paint. East Hampton folks thought it fine. Old Deacon Tallmadge came . . . stopped at the parlor door, and seemed afraid to come in. 'Walk in, deacon, walk in,' said I. 'Why, I can't,' said he, 'thout steppin' on't.' Then, after surveying it a while in admiration, 'Do ye think ye can have all that, *and heaven too?*' Perhaps he thought we were getting too splendid, and feared we should make an idol of our fine things." *Autobiography, Correspondence . . . of Lyman Beecher, D.D.,* ed., Charles Beecher (New York: Harper & Brothers, 1866). (See also CARPET.)

FLOUT, FLOWTE, FLOYTE
All old variations of Flute, *q.v.,* signifying the musical pipe or at times a child's whistle; thus, in the *Canterbury Tales* Chaucer wrote of playing the flute, as floyting.

FLOWER STAND
1) The small, circular-top eighteenth-century stand or pedestal with a high gallery or rim, specifically made to hold a single flowerpot. In the nineteenth century this type was made with much wider tops of varying shapes. 2) The term also described a wide bench or set of graduated-depth shelves, some of which ". . . wholly gilt or japanned, [are] very well adapted for the end of a long [room] or staircase, or to fill the space of a wide window, whether in a room or on the landing of an elegant staircase." George Smith, *A Collection of Designs for Household Furniture* (London, 1808). (See also JARDINIERE.)

FLOWERPOT STAND
Another contemporary term for the plant or Flower Stand, *q.v.* (See also note under MOVING LIBRARY.)

FLUID LAMP
Any lamp of metal, glass, or pottery, in which a liquid fuel was burned, as, for example, an Argand Lamp, Camphene Lamp, Carcel Lamp, Stand and Socket, or Peg Lamp, each of which see.

Fluid lamp.

FLUTE
"A musical pipe with stops for the fingers." (J) (See also GERMAN FLUTE, FLAGEOLET.) "30th November, [1771] We made four couples at country dansing. In

the evening young Mr. Waters hearing of my assembly, put his flute in his pocket and played several minuets and other tunes, to which we dansed mighty cleverly." *Diary of Anna Green Winslow* (Boston, 1894).

FLY
A colloquial term for "that part of a [weather] vane which points how the wind blows," (J) used also for the vane itself.

FOB
A contemporary description of "a small pocket," (J) hence watch fob originally was the pocket or purse hung from the sash in which a pocket watch was carried. (See also DIAL, POCKET, WATCH SEAL.)

FOIL
The light fencing practice sword made with a button at the point in order to protect one's opponent from any injury greater than a bruise. "Fencing is a genteel exercise, of which no gentleman ought to be ignorant. It is learned by practicing with foils." (M)

FOLDING FURNITURE
An all-inclusive term for any piece of space-saving furniture; i.e., with parts that could be folded up and thus kept out of the way when not in use. Thus, the bureau

Foldaway yarn winder, ready for use.

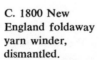
C. 1800 New England foldaway yarn winder, dismantled.

bedstead, chair bed, chair table, or hutch chair; any table with flap or drop leaves.

FOLDING MEASURE
This "four-foot gauging-rod [is] usually made of box-wood, and consists of four rules, each a foot long and about half an inch square, joined by three brass joints, by means of which the rod is rendered four feet long, when the four rules are quite opened, and but one foot in length when they are folded together." (M)

FOLDING SCREEN
A combination of two, three, or more hinged leaves or panels made to stand vertically and to serve as a decorative protection against drafts, to reflect heat back toward the fireplace or to divide space within a room. "Feb. 13th [1772]. Everybody says that this is a bitter cold day, but I know nothing about it but hearsay for I am in aunt's chamber with a nice fire, a [foot] stove, sitting in Aunt's easy chair, with a tall three-leav'd screen at my back, & I am very comfortable." *Diary of Anna Green Winslow* (Boston, 1894).

Such screens were as elaborate as the owner's taste and budget allowed: "These articles of general use admit of every species of decoration; viz. [gilding] of entire gold, bronze and gold, or japanned; of mahogany, rose, or satin wood; as the [room] they may be destined for shall require. The mounts, if expense be not regarded, may be carved solid in wood, and embellished with painted decorations; or painted on silk or velvet. Where the stands are wholly mahogany, the mounts may be covered with lustring in flutes, with tassels to suit." George Smith, *A Collection of Designs for Household Furniture* (London, 1808). (See also COROMANDEL SCREEN; FIRE SCREEN, HORSE FIRE SCREEN, POLE SCREEN.)

FOLDING TABLE
The term sometimes used to describe a table with one leaf or drop so hinged that it

can be folded back over the top board when not in use; or folded out over the back swing leg which served as support when needed; many card tables were also called folding tables.

FOLIO
The common term for "a book [printed] two leaves to a sheet" (W) of paper.

FOOD CHOPPER
A sharpened iron or steel blade, attached to a handle, and used for chopping or cutting vegetables or herbs.

Eighteenth-century food chopper and iron trough or bowl. (Courtesy, Paul Weld Collection.)

Early-nineteenth-century food chopper.

FOOLSCAP
"Paper of a small size." (W)

FOOTMAN
The contemporary term for "a stand" (W) with three or four feet; that is, the high trivet or frame of brass, iron, steel, or a combination of these metals, and sometimes made with a wooden handle; used near the hearth to hold the teakettle.

FOOTSCRAPER
The iron blade set between posts or standards, usually cemented into a paving stone near the door to a house, on which one could scrape the mud from one's boots.

Early-eighteenth-century wrought-iron footscraper. (Courtesy, Antiquarian and Landmarks Society, Inc.)

FOOTSTOOL
The common designation for the "stool on which he that sits places his feet," (J) a sometimes necessary adjunct to the high-seated chairs of the seventeenth and early eighteenth centuries. Some were made with hinged tops or removable lids and so also served as storage bins. Those of the nineteenth century were much lower, in keeping with the seat heights of the chairs, and usually much more elaborate in ornamentation.

C. 1790 footstool with painted, grained decoration.

FOOT STOVE

A small, perforated metal or wooden box, with a bail handle, and an interior, smaller sheet-iron box or container to hold hot coals, used particularly to make winter journeys more comfortable. "March 4, 1772. We had the greatest fall of snow yesterday we have had this winter. Yet Cousin Sally, Miss Polly, & I rode to & from meeting in Mr. Soley's chaise both forenoon & afternoon, & with a stove was very comfortable there." *Diary of Anna Green Winslow* (Boston, 1894). (See also note under PAUL REVERE LANTERN.)

Eighteenth-century American foot stoves with perforated wood outer cases; iron ember box or "stove." (Courtesy, Antiquarian and Landmarks Society, Inc.)

FOOT WARMER

The collector's term for what was called a Foot Stove, *q.v.,* or simply a stove.

FORK

In the view of sixteenth-, seventeenth-, and early-eighteenth-century gentlefolk and poorer classes as well this was the least necessary of eating utensils. The knife was used to cut food as well as to carry it to the mouth. When first introduced, forks were deemed mostly useful for holding food on the plate while it was cut. It was basically, "an instrument with two or three prongs" (W) "used on many occasions." (J) "There is a great want of that neatness and gentility which is practiced in Italy (where the fork was first introduced); for, on the English table there are no forks . . ." Count Lorenzo Magalotti, *Travels* [1669] *of Cosmo the Third, Grand Duke of Tuscany, through England during the Reign of King Charles II.* "In carving at your own table, distribute the best pieces first, and it will appear very comely and decent to use a fork; so touch no piece of meat without it." *The Accomplished Lady's Rich Closet of Rarities* (London, 1653). (See also EWER AND BASIN, KNIFE.)

FORELL

Another synonym for a "bag, sack or purse," (H) or a covering for something else; see the related word, FORREL.

FORM

A long wooden bench, used during the seventeenth and early eighteenth centuries for seating guests or family at dinner. "If a chair be defined as a seat for a single person, with a back belonging to it, then a stool is a seat without a back, and a form is a seat for several persons, without a back." Isaac Watts, *Logick* (London, 1725). (See also JOINT STOOL.)

FORREL

A colloquialism for "the cover of a book or the border of a handkerchief." (H)

FORTUNE BOOK

The contemporary term for "a book consulted to know fortune or future events." (J) A text usually based on the astrologer's generalized interpretation of horoscopes; i.e. "the configuration of the planets at the hour of birth," (J) of dreams or other signs, as similar books published today.

FOUR-POST BEDSTEAD

A contemporary term for a bedstead with four high posts, all of the same height, to support the tester or canopy frame. "To be sold . . . all the elegant and valuable household furniture of Richard Vassal, Esq. . . . consisting of . . . pictures, china, mahogany four-post bedsteads, bureaus, desks, tables . . . little if any the worse for wear . . ." *The New York Gazette and The Weekly Mercury,* June 29, 1772.

FOURQUETTE

In weaponry, the infantry gunner's weapon or musket rest.

FOWLING PIECE

A "light gun for [shooting] birds." (J)

The unwearied fowler roves,
When frosts have whiten'd all the naked groves.

Alexander Pope.

FRACTURED PIECE

The collector's common term for any piece that has been broken and obviously repaired; or for any piece, a missing part of which has been replaced with an unharmonious material, as for example, a pewter whale-oil lamp font set on a new wooden base. (See also SHELF PIECE.)

FRAIL, FRAYEL

A light kind of "basket made of rushes," (M) or matting and used especially for packing fruit, such as figs and raisins, and so identified with the latter that the word frail also signified a weight or "quantity of raisins of about 75 pounds." (M) "Provisions sent in the *Rebecca* . . . A frail of figs which I sent to yourself (in the barrel of raisins of the sun, the figs are in the end that hath your mark in black lead)." (John Winthrop at Boston to his "son, Mr. John Winthrop, Governour of the Plantation upon the mouth of the Conetecticott." June 4, 1636.) *Journal, History of New England* (Boston, 1825).

FRANKLIN CLOCK

The name Silas Hoadley of Plymouth, Connecticut, gave to a type of shelf clock with wooden works that he developed about 1825.

FRANKLIN STOVE

Today few eighteenth-century examples are to be seen outside museums. Those now available are usually free-standing "parlor" stoves, late-nineteenth-century interpretations of what originally was a simple cast-iron fitting to be used inside the fireplace opening. Franklin never patented his design.

"Since the Englishmen like to see the fire burn instead of confining it in a stove, Benjamin Franklin invented a new type which provides plenty of heat, saves fuel and brings fresh air into the room, but is so constructed that the flame may be seen. The bottom [is] elevated a little and an opening left to the air-box so the air which is heated can get out into the room. There are several types: some have dampers, called registers, and others have not; some have a front plate which can be moved up and down; when down the draft becomes stronger . . . Persons who could not afford to purchase the (cast-iron) stoves imitated them by making them either of brick or white Dutch tile, with only the top of iron. But these are not so warm." (Philadelphia, 1750.) Peter Kalm, *Travels in North America* (Warrington, England, 1770).

Franklin himself called his stove the "New Invented Pennsylvanian Fire-Place" when he described it in a pamphlet printed in 1744. One reason few early examples remain was the careless installation and use by first owners: "On the eleventh Instant early in the Morning, a Fire broke out at Mr. Pierpoints House, occasioned by the Heat of the Iron Hearth of one of the newly invented Fireplaces, whereby the floor was set on Fire; the People being in Bed, perceived a great Smoke, got up and happily discover'd and timely distinguished the Fire." *Boston Gazette,* December 22, 1747.

FRANKLIN WICK LAMP
Benjamin Franklin is said to have devised the first double-spout wick of the type usually seen on whale-oil and camphene lamps. Two wicks, lighted, create a greater air current and thus consume more oxygen and provide a clearer, brighter light than does a single wick.

FREED-MAN'S PAPERS
(See SLAVE PAPERS.)

FRENCH BEDSTEAD
A nineteenth-century term for a bedstead made usually with a high headboard and a low footboard, but no tester or canopy, and which "may be executed in mahogany, walnut, satinwood, or maple; they are finished plain on the side which stands next the wall, the exposed parts alone being decorated." Blackie and Son, *The Cabinet-Maker's Assistant* (London, 1853). (See note under HALF-TESTER BEDSTEAD.)

FRENCH CHAIR
(See description quoted under ELBOW CHAIR.)

French chair illustrated in Thomas Chippendale's *Gentleman and Cabinet-Maker's Director* (London, 1762).

FRENCH CORNER CHAIR
The name given in the mid-eighteenth century to an elegant, wide seat or chair resembling, to our eyes, a small sofa or loveseat, designed with a shaped, angled back and curving arms; the angle of the back allowing it to fit into a room corner. Two such designs were shown by Ince and Mayhew as "French Corner Chairs or Settees" in *The Universal System of Household Furniture* (London, 1762).

FRENCH HORN
A musical instrument. "The horn is bent into a circle, and goes two or three times round, growing gradually bigger and wider towards the end, which in some horns is nine or ten inches over." (M) The French horn was particularly favored as a military band instrument, if not always appreciated by the public at large. "A By-Law to prevent disturbance in the night season: no person or persons shall beat or play upon any drum, or play upon any trumpet, bugle, or bugle-horn, or any French horn at any time from sunset to sunrise within the following limits—Main Street, State Street, Front Street, Morgan Street, Church Street, Trumbull Street, Pearl Street, Ferry Street, Prospect Street, School Street, The-

French horn, as illustrated by Filippo Bonanni, *Cabinetto Armonica* (Rome, 1723).

atre Street, Commerce Street, Mill Street, Tower Hill . . . nor [anywhere] within the [other parts] of the city between the hours of nine o'clock in the evening and sunrise . . . Court of Common Council, Hartford, July 21, 1815." *American Mercury* (Hartford, Connecticut).

FRENCH SOFA

A contemporary description of the sofa that was light and delicate in appearance and that was made with an upholstered seat and back, the arms padded on top but open at the sides, and sometimes, as Chippendale described a "French chair," one that also was "open below at the back." The advertisement quoted here suggests that the description perhaps was applied also to pieces with woven rattan or cane seats and backs. "William Long, Cabinet Maker and Carver, late of London . . . makes French sophas in the modern taste, on as reasonable terms as them of the older fashion . . . and French Chairs on reasonable Terms. A good price will be given for a quantity of Rattan." *Pennsylvania Packet* (Philadelphia), April 30, 1787.

FRENCH STOOL

The term Ince and Mayhew gave what might otherwise best be described as a Window Stool, *q.v.,* in *The Universal System of Household Furniture* (London, 1762).

FRICKLE

A woven "basket for fruit" (H) large enough to hold a bushel.

FRIGGERS

An all-inclusive term for the improbable or nonsense "toys" blown by glassmakers, such as glass rolling pins, walking sticks, tobacco pipes, riding crops, etc.

FRIZZEN

A corruption of frizzle; frizzen was the slang term for the battery, hammer, or steel that was struck against the flint to produce sparks and thus fire a musket.

FROGON, FROGGON, FRUGGAN, FRUGGIN, FURGON

All variations of the name for a kind of oven fork or poker; a "curved iron scraper with which ashes in an oven are stirred." (H)

FROW, FROWER

The name for the house carpenter's "sharp edged tool to cleave laths." (W)

FRUIT BASKET

The decorative silver, silver-plated, pewter, or japanned, footed basket with bail or swing handle, in which fruit was displayed and served. "Goodwin & Dodd, Directly West of the State House, have this day received a large assortment of . . . Plated Tea Setts, Plated & Britannia tea Pots in pairs or single; plated Casters, fruit Baskets . . ." *American Mercury* (Hartford, Connecticut), November 11, 1812.

FRUIT KNIVES

Sold singly or in sets; small, slender, sharply honed steel blades, set in decorative, engraved hafts of ivory, bone, silver, gilt, or silver-plated metal. "For sale by James Jacks . . . Best warranted Razors, Sportsmen's and Penknives, Gold and Silver Fruit Knives . . ." *Gazette of the United States* (Philadelphia), August 2, 1798.

FRY

A common contemporary term for "a kind of sieve." (J)

FRYING PAN

In the kitchen, the "vessel in which meat is roasted on the fire" (J); "an iron pan to fry things in." (W) Early types in brass or iron were round, shallow containers usually suspended by a bail handle and pothook from the crane or lug pole. Later, the same type of shallow pan was attached to the now more familiar long wand type of handle. "After due Respects unto yor Self and Second [wife] request you Send me . . . a good Frying Pann . . . my wife presents her kind love unto your Self and to her

C. 1775 long-handled iron frying pan. (Courtesy, Antiquarian and Landmarks Society, Inc.)

deare Cozen your Second." (Order from Newport, Rhode Island, to Boston, December 7, 1666.) *The Letter Book of Peleg Sanford* (Providence, 1928). "Thomas Russell, Brazier, near the Draw-Bridge in Boston Makes, Mends, and New-Tins, all sorts of Braziery ware, viz. Kettles, Skillets, Frying-Pans, Kettle-Pots . . ." *Boston News-Letter,* October 30, 1740. (See also POSNET, SKILLET.)

FUDDLING CUP
"To fuddle," according to Dr. Johnson, was "to drink to excess." This pottery vessel was a trick mug formed of a number of cups joined together and opening one into another.

FUMING BOX
A common term for "a pastile-burner; an incense-burner," (H) usually of iron or brass.

FURNACE
The common eighteenth-century term for a stove, "an enclosed fireplace," (J) or "a large vessel," (W) to hold coals. "A vessel or utensil for maintaining a strong fire, either of coal or wood." (M) Also, a synonym for a free-standing oven or bake-kettle.

FURNITURE
The contemporary term for any "moveables; goods put in a house for use or ornament," (J) such as "utensils, decorations," (W) or the accessory pieces used with major pieces. Thus, "house furniture" re-ferred to major standing or set pieces such as bedsteads and cupboards; "bed furniture" referred to the linens, coverlets, curtains, and valance used on a bedstead; "harness furniture" included bits, snaffles, stirrups, bells, and decorative discs. "My furniture, part of which I made myself, consisted of a bed, a table, a desk, three chairs, a looking glass three inches in diameter, a pair of tongs and andirons, a kettle, a skillet, and a frying-pan, a dipper, a wash-bowl, two knives and forks, three plates, one cup, one spoon, a jug for oil, a jug for molasses, and a japanned lamp." Henry David Thoreau, *Walden* (Boston, 1864).

FURNITURE GUIDES
The collector's all-inclusive term to describe those books of designs published by architects and cabinetmakers, chiefly in the eighteenth and nineteenth centuries. These may be considered sales catalogues in that it was expected householders would order similar pieces made up from the patterns shown. Guides also were purchased by other cabinetmakers for use as shop style books. In the preface to *The Cabinet-Maker and Upholsterer's Guide,* Alice Hepplewhite said of what generally are presumed to have been designs suggested by her late husband, George: "We have exerted our utmost endeavours to produce a work which shall be useful to the mechanic, and serviceable to the gentleman . . . and convey a just idea of English taste in furniture for houses; [for] English taste and workmanship have, of late years, been much sought for by surrounding nations. The mutability of all things, but especially of fashions," necessitated frequent revisions to keep design books up to date; thus, "the labours of our predecessors . . . at this day can only tend to mislead those foreigners who seek a knowledge of [current] English taste. The same reason, in favour of this work, will apply also to many of our own Countrymen and Artizans, who [live at a] distance from

the metropolis . . . We flatter ourselves [these new patterns] will be found serviceable to young workmen in general, and occasionally to more experienced ones."

FUSEE
A contemporary term for the weapon, "firelock, from *fusil,* a small neat muskit, this is more properly written fusil." (J) Also used for "part of a watch," or for "a match." (W) (See also FUSIL.)

FUSIL
A firelock; "a small, neat Musket," *q.v.* (J) Hence, fusilier, a soldier armed with a fusil, "a musketeer." (J) Also, the fire steel kept in the Tinderbox, *q.v.*

G

GABSTICK
The cant term for a large wooden spoon, derived perhaps from the Anglo-Saxon word *geapan,* a Lincolnshire colloquialism brought here by settlers near Boston. (See also GOBSTICK.)

Gabstick.

GAD
A colloquialism for any "wedge of steel; club; graver," (W) derived from the Old Saxon word for a goad.

GAFF, GAFFLOCK
Another name for the whale-fishermen's "hook; harpoon," (W) but also for "an iron hoe," (H) or a crowbar.

GAGE
A common term for "a quart pot; a bowl or tub for cream," (H) and also for "a measure, more properly, gauge." (J)

GAIL, GAILKER, GALCAR, GUIL-VAT, GUIL-FAT, GYLE-FAT, GYLE-TUB
All terms for a wort tub, "the tub used for brewing." (H)

GAIL DISH
"A small dish, cup or funnel used for pouring liquor into a bottle or cask." (H)

GALLERIED TABLE
The collector's description of any table made with a rising rim or edge surrounding the entire top board. (See GALLERY, Chapter 5. See also TEAKETTLE STAND and URN STAND illustrations.)

GALLANTRIES
An eighteenth-century synonym for Toys, *q.v.,* especially those small decorative objects given in token of esteem, or collected as souvenirs.

GALLETYLE
"I suppose this word has the same import with Gallipot," *q.v.* (J)

GALLEYTILE
The term for "a kind of tile; an earthenware." (W) (See GALLIPOT.)

GALLIPOT
"A small pot painted or glazed," (W) and thus often the name of a grease or ointment pot, sometimes also called a gleypot or glumpot. This was a small earthen, faïence, or porcelain jar with a cover, used by apothecaries for salves or ointments and by housewives for conserves and jelly. "Black currant jelly. Put currants in an earthen pan and to every ten quarts put in a quart of spring water; tie a paper over them and set them in the oven for two hours, then squeeze out the juice through a fine cloth, and to every pint of juice put a pound of loaf sugar broke to pieces, stir it and boil it

gently for half an hour, skim it well all the time. While it is hot put it into gallipots; put brandy papers over it and tie another paper over that, and keep in a cool, dry place." Richard Briggs, *The New Art of Cookery* (Philadelphia, 1792).

GALLY-BALK, GALLEY-BALK
Perhaps originally gallows-balk; a term for the pole or rod within the chimney, or directly in front of the fireplace opening, from which trammels and pothooks were suspended.

GALLY DISH
A variation of the term, Gallipot, *q.v.* "Gally dishes" were listed in the House of Parliament Rates, 1660, for Imports and Exports—*Statutes of the Realm* (London, 1819).

GAME HANGER
A larder or kitchen utensil; this was a circle or band of iron to which spiked hooks were riveted and from which game was hung until ready for use. Such hangers were made to be suspended from the ceiling by means of an iron rod with a ring top. Another similar design was called a Dutch Crown.

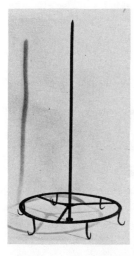

Eighteenth-century New England iron game hanger. (Courtesy, Paul Weld Collection.)

GAME TABLE, GAMING TABLE
Correctly, the term should be gaming table. Game meant the sport produced by the chase of fowl or animals while gaming signified a gambling contest.

GAMES TABLE
The contemporary term for a reversible board, inlaid with squares, for use in playing backgammon, chess, or checkers.

GANTRY, GANTREE, GAUNTRY
All variations of Gawntree, *q.v.*

GAPESTICK
A Scotch-Irish cant term for "a large wooden spoon." (H) (See also GOBSTICK.)

GARDE du VIN
The French term for a wine cupboard or safe used by Hepplewhite as a synonym for a Cellarette, *q.v.,* in *The Cabinet-Maker and Upholsterer's Guide* (London, 1794). (See also SARCOPHAGUS.)

GARDE MANGER
The French words for "a cupboard," (H) especially a food safe.

GARDEN FURNITURE
Any furniture of wood, wicker, or iron used in the garden summerhouse, grotto or arbor, ranging from the fairly elegant designs suggested by Chippendale to the rustic types popular with Victorian-era householders. In *The Gentleman and Cabinet-Maker's Director* (London, 1762), Chippendale described "Six Designs for chairs [suitable] for Halls, Passages, or Summer

Design for a garden seat from Thomas Chippendale's *Gentleman and Cabinet-Maker's Director* (London, 1762).

Houses made . . . of any Wood, and painted, and [that] have commonly wooden Seats; Two Designs of Chairs for Gardens, and a long Seat, proper [also] for Arbors or Summer-Houses, or Grottos. The Seat may be placed in Walks, or at the Ends of Avenues." Painted Windsor chairs often were advertised also as suitable garden furniture. (See advertisement illustrated under SETTEE.)

GARDE ROBE

"A wardrobe; a place or room where the clothes are kept." (H)

GARLAND

A common name for "small collections of popular ballads," (H) songbooks, pamphlets.

GARNISH

A colloquialism for "a service which generally consisted of sets of twelve dishes, saucers, Ec." (H) Thus, to garnish a table was to set out the dishes on it.

Garniture set includes vase and covered jar of polychrome delft. (Courtesy, Antiquarian and Landmarks Society Inc.)

GARNISHMENT, GARNITURE SET

"Ornaments," (W) "decoration, embellishments," (J) usually used on either side of the mantel shelf. (See also CHIMNEY ORNAMENTS, IMAGE TOYS; LUSTRES.)

GATE-LEG TABLE

The modern term for a table with a leg made to swing out, as a gate does, and so support the drop leaf. Made with two uprights and two horizontal pieces; i.e., with the stretcher attached to and swinging with the leg. The contemporary term was folding table.

Early-eighteenth-century gate-leg table with vase and reel turning. (Courtesy, Antiquarian and Landmarks Society, Inc.)

Early-eighteenth-century table with two gate legs, and long candle or utility drawer box. (Courtesy, Connecticut Historical Society, Inc.)

GAUBERT

A kind of trammel, "iron racks for chimneys." (H)

GAUDE

A term, perhaps derived from the Latin *gaudium* for joy, and thus "a bauble, an ornament, a token of joy," (J) a souvenir.

GAUGE

The proper term for any "measure, standard or rod." (W)

GAUGING ROD

(See FOLDING MEASURE.)

GAUGING RULE

One of the many carefully made instruments now collected, this was used by the official local inspector or surveyor of commercial weights and measures and was "commonly made of box, and sometimes ivory, exactly a foot long, one inch and 2-10ths broad, and ¾ of an inch thick; it consists of 4 parts, viz. a rule and 3 small scales or sliding-pieces filled nicely with grooves to slide in it." (M)

Gauging: "The art of measuring the contents of all kinds of vessels thereby to determine the quantity of liquids, Ec. they contain." (M)

GAUN PAIL, GAWN PAIL, GORN PAIL

A pail "with a handle [or long stave] at one side," (H) perhaps derived from gawn or gaun, an old term for a gallon measure. (See also LADE-GORN.)

GAVELOC

In weaponry, a kind of long iron bar such as "a pick-javelin, a war-like instrument." (W) (See also HALBERD, PIKE.)

GAWN

The word is a corruption of gallon, according to Dr. Johnson, and thus a provincialism for any "small tub or lading vessel."

GAWNTREE

Derived from Gawn, *q.v.,* and thus the term for a "wooden frame on which beer casks are set when tunned [filled]." (J)

GAY POLE

Another name for the lug pole, the "piece of wood that goes across the interior of a chimney on which the hangers for the kettles are hung." (H)

GAZETTE

Gazetta was a Venetian halfpenny, the price of a newspaper (the first of which was published at Venice) and thus gazette was the general term for any "kind of newspaper or public print." (W) "I am persuaded that the body of the British people are our friends; but they are changeable, and by your lying Gazettes may soon be made our enemies." (Benjamin Franklin at Philadelphia to a friend in England, October 3, 1775.) *The Writings of Benjamin Franklin,* ed., A. H. Smyth (New York, 1907).

GAZETTEER

"A book," (W) more exactly, a geographical dictionary. "Books & Stationary, Cook and Hale have lately received an extensive assortment . . . Liberal discounts made to individuals and public Library Companies . . . A pocket edition of Brookes' General Gazetteer, improved, containing a description of the Empires, Kingdoms, States, Cities, Towns, Rivers, Lakes, Seas, Capes, Mountains, Ec. in the known world."

C. 1810 *Gazetteer* in calf binding.

American Mercury (Hartford, Connecticut), September 4, 1816.

GAZOMETER
The term for "an instrument to measure gas." (W)

GEMEL, GIMMAL, JIMMAL
A corruption of the Latin *gemeleus* for twin, and thus a synonym for anything in pairs; two objects hinged or otherwise attached to each other.

GENTLEMAN'S REPOSITORY
A mid-eighteenth-century term for several pieces combined into one grand case piece at least seven feet wide: "The upper Part or Middle is a Book-Case; on each Side is Draws; the Top of the under Part or Middle, is a Desk Drawer; under that either Draws or Cloathes-Press; on each Side Cupboards." Ince and Mayhew, *The Universal System of Household Furniture* (London, 1762).

GEOGRAPHY
The name of the art or science was given to the books written about it; such texts were second only in number to works on religious and political history. In an age of shifting frontiers, of expanded horizons both literal and figurative, books of geography went into many editions, necessarily revised on an average of every two years. In great measure they also provided a knowledge of current world events and natural phenomena, although geography in a strict sense signifies "knowledge of the circles of the earthly globe, and the situation of the various parts of the earth, when it is taken in a little larger sense, it includes the knowledge of the seas also; and in the largest sense of all, it extends to the various customs, habits, and governments of nations." Isaac Watts, *Logic* (1725). "It is all important that every man should know the history and geography of his own country. But a vast many of us hardly know our right hand from our left in this respect. What more profitable employment can you have during the long winter evenings than reading Hutchinson's History of Massachusetts, Belknap's New Hampshire, William's Vermont, Life of Gen. Washington, American Revolution, Morses' and other Geographies, Ec.?" [December] *The Farmer's Almanack* (Boston, 1814).

"Woodbridge's Geography. Just published and for sale, the 11th edition of Woodbridge's Rudiments of Geography for Schools & Academics . . . exhibiting by means of Emblems, Figures, Ec. the various degrees of civilization, of the inhabitants of the Earth, the Population, Form of Government, Religion, Climate, Degree of Temperature and Productions of all countries—and the comparative size of Towns, Rivers, and Mountains, by the Rev. Wm. C. Woodbridge . . . Foreign correspondent of the Geographical Society of Paris . . . Care will be taken to introduce into each successive edition such corrections and additions as the state of the globe or new discoveries shall render advisable . . . For sale by A. H. Maltby, at the New Haven Bookstore." *Columbian Register* (New Haven, Connecticut), November 28, 1829.

1816 geography textbook.

GERMAN FLUTE

The ancient flute, a musical wind instrument, was a hollow pipe, blown through a mouthpiece at one end, with holes along the length of the pipe, or cylinder, stopped by the fingers. The German Flute, also called a transverse flute, is blown through an opening at one side near the upper end, stopped by the fingers or by keys opened by the fingers. There were numerous advertisements and notices of concerts where the German flute was mentioned, including this by a flautist who implies musical amateurs needed ready defense against critical neighbors: "To be sold by a Gentleman who lodges at Widow Darcey's nigh the Ship-Yards . . . and who is to go soon out of Town; exceeding good German Flutes, for Three Dollars each, likewise others with 2, 3, 4 or 5 middle pieces to change the Tones and Voice, do . . . German Flute Concerts, Sonatas, Duets and Solos [sheet music] and a great many other things in the musical way, imported by himself . . . and a foreign Pocket Gun." *The New York Mercury,* August 13, 1759.

GEWGAW, GUGAW

The modernized form of an Old Saxon word, this was the common term for a variety of trifles or small luxuries deemed "showy, without value." (J) According to Webster, at the beginning of the nineteenth century, a gewgaw was a "toy or bauble," popularized by a fad, thus echoing Dryden's earlier verses that

As children when they throw one toy away
Straight a more foolish gewgaw comes in
play.

The word also was a common eighteenth-century "synonym for flute" (H) or piccolo; in the seventeenth century, Blount said "a geegaw [was] a Jew's harp or trifle for children to play with."

GIB-CROKE

Another early term for pothook, sometimes spelled gib-crook; and perhaps so-called because gib or gibbous also meant crook-backed.

GIBSTAFF

The name of "a long staff to gage water." (J)

GIG

"Anything that is whirled round in play," (J) or "a top," (W) and thus, a whirligig, a kind of child's toy. "Playthings, as toys, gigs, battledores, should be procured them." John Locke, *An Essay Concerning Human Understanding* (London, 1726).

GIG LAMP(S)

Gig was a cant term for a type of small, light, fast, two-wheeled carriage. The lamps were smaller than many made for use on chaises and stage coaches. "Charles L. Sigourney Has Imported from Bristol . . . Hardware Goods [including] steel springs for gigs and coaches. Coach & Curricle steps—double steps for gigs. Plated gig lamps, whiskey joints, Plated Candlesticks . . ." *American Mercury* (Hartford, Connecticut), November 4, 1812.

GIMBAL, GIMMAL, GIMMEW RING

"A quaint device; something with a double or corresponding part," (J) and thus, "a kind of double ring" (W) exchanged by lovers as a token of betrothal. Gimmal or joint rings were two or three circlets held together with a clasp or rivet so as to appear as one. A design or motto (see POSY, POSY RING) was engraved over the combined hoops. The third hoop, if there was one, was given to the main witness to the marriage contract or ceremony. (See also JOINT RING.)

GIMBLET, GIMLET

One of the tools used by the leatherworker, shoemaker, upholsterer, etc. This was "a borer for nails" (W) "with a screw at its point." (J)

GIMCRACK

"A little pretty thing or device; a toy," (W) derived from gim, an old word for "neat, spruce, well-dressed." (J)

GIMLIN

In the kitchen, "The large, shallow tub in which meat was salted." (H)

GIN

The general term for any engine, trap, or snare, such as the cotton gin.

GINETTE

A cant term, literally small gin, for the Dram Glass, *q.v.*

GINGLE-BOY

(See JINGLE-BOX.)

GIRANDOLE

The French word generally used to describe an ornate wall sconce with one or more candle branches, made of wood, metal, crystal, or combinations of all three; often with a looking-glass back plate: "This kind of ornament admits of great variety in pattern and in elegance; they are usefully executed of the best carved work—gilt and burnished in parts. They may be carved, and coloured suitable to the room, [or with] cut glass, either white or coloured, ornaments." A. Hepplewhite, *The Cabinet-Maker and Upholsterer's Guide* (London, 1794).

Ince and Mayhew suggested that this type of "rich Candlestick or Girandole, which if executed in Wood gilt, in burnish'd Gold, or Brass, would be extremely grand, and might be equally the same executed in Silver, proper for a Stand or Marble Table." *The Universal System of Household Furniture* (London, 1762).

"Different only in the mode of fixing them from [chandeliers], the use is the same; in rooms of considerable length where a single Chandelier would not afford sufficient Light, Girandoles are fixed at the extremities of apartments in pannels against the wall; they are equally serviceable in [rooms]

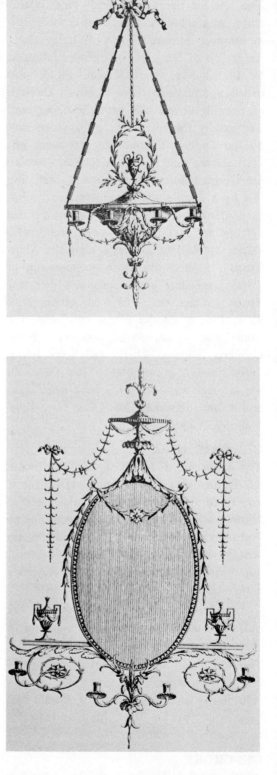

Girandoles illustrated in Hepplewhite's *Guide* (London, 1794).

376

Hepplewhite 1794 *Guide* design for a girandole with looking glass and an interpretation of the period in gilt, gesso, and pine with beveled mirror. (Courtesy, Mr. and Mrs. Guy Mankin Collection)

where Chandeliers are not used." George Smith, *A Collection of Designs for Household Furniture* (London, 1808).

GIRDLE

To all intents and purposes, and in appearance, this was the same as the griddle. Dr. Johnson did not list girdle in his 1755 *Dictionary,* but others have, defining it as a flat "round iron plate for baking," (H) possibly derived from gird, an old word for hoop. The girdle sometimes was supported on a cran, trivet, a brandeth, or other free-standing support. Some such baking plates had hoop or bale handles so they could be suspended by pothooks from

a crane. The term also was used anciently for a kind of purse, as we would use the word money belt today. (See also GRIDDLE.)

GISPEN

Another name for the Black Jack, *q.v.,* "a pot or cup made of leather." (H)

GLAIR(E)

In weaponry, "A kind of halbert." (W)

GLASS BELL

(See BELL, BELL GLASS.)

GLASS COLORED PRINTS

(See REVERSE GLASS PAINTING.)

GLASS INSERTS

The small colored-glass cups or basins to be set into silver or plated hollow ware or other serving pieces, were purchased separately, in addition to the main piece, or as later replacements. "Joseph Anthony, Jr. . . . has imported from London . . . Blue glasses for sugar and cream basons, Mustard Tankards and salts . . ." *Pennsylvania Packet* (Philadelphia), December 7, 1790.

GLASS LUSTRES

(See LUSTRES.)

GLASS SILHOUETTE

Silhouettes scraped and painted in eglomise; that is, painted on the reverse side of a piece of flat or of convex glass; many were backed with red or gold color and further decorated with geometric or floral designs outlined in the borders. (See also PROFILE, PORTRAIT, REVERSE GLASS PAINTING.)

GLAVE, GLAIVE

In weaponry, the name of a "broad sword, a large bill," (W)   or "a falchion" (J)

GLAYMORE

A variation of Claymore, *q.v.* "The gentlemen of the clan went away early in the morning to the harbor of Loch Braccadale to take leave of some of their friends who were going to America. We saw Rorie

More's bow, and his glaymore, which was wielded with both hands and is of a prodigious size. The broad-sword used [now] though called the glaymore is much smaller than that used before." James Boswell, *Journal of a Tour* [1773] *to the Hebrides* (London, 1785).

GLEYPOT
(See GALLIPOT.)

GLOBES
These "spheres in which the various regions of the earth are geographically depicted [the terrestrial globe], or in which the constellations are laid down according to their places in the sky [the celestial globe]," (J) usually were sold in pairs, set on handsomely made stands, and were considered a necessary furnishing in the well-appointed home library, as well as the schoolroom, and countinghouse. "Dined at home with my wife. It being washing-day, we had a good pie baked of a leg of mut-

Late-eighteenth-century celestial globe. (Courtesy, Antiquarian and Landmarks Society, Inc.)

ton; and then to Moxon's, and there bought a payre of globes cost me 3£, 10s., with which I am well pleased." Samuel Pepys, *Diary,* September 8, 1663. "A pair of globes nine inches Diameter with their appurtenances to be sold. Enquire of Andrew Bradford in Second St." *American Weekly Mercury* (Philadelphia), May 31, 1722.

GLOSSARY
The term to describe a "sort of dictionary explaining the obscure and antiquated terms." (M) "I am always sorry when any language is lost, because languages are the pedigrees of nations." Samuel Johnson, quoted by James Boswell, *Journal of a Tour to the Hebrides* (London, 1785).

GLOVE BOX
(See DESK BOX.)

GLUMPOT
(See GALLIPOT.)

GOAD
The term for "a sharp instrument used to drive oxen," (W) a stout wooden rod with a pointed iron end.

Late-eighteenth-century terrestrial globe.

GOBLET

The term for "a kind of bowl, a kind of large cup" (W) "that holds a large draught." (J) Technically, the goblet is a covered wine glass holding at least four ounces. In common usage, however, the term has been applied to any large wine glass, especially one made of fine silver or crystal. "Joseph Anthony, Jr. Silversmith, No. 76 on the South Side of Market Street . . . has imported in the last ships from London, a Large and General Assortment [including] Castors, bottle-stands and goblets, Wine and water stands . . ." *Pennsylvania Packet* (Philadelphia), December 7, 1790.

GOBSTICK

A spoon; the term was derived perhaps from gob, a colloquialism for the mouth, and also gobbet, a mouthful, or a morsel.
  Gob: "A small quantity; a low word." (J)
  Gobbet: "A mouthful." (J)

GO-CART

A contemporary synonym for the Stand Stool, *q.v.,* "a machine in which children are enclosed to teach them to walk, and which they push forward without danger of falling." (J)

GO-CHAIR

This was a contemporary term for the wheel chair or Machine Chair, *q.v.* "William Long, Cabinet Maker and Carver from London At the Rocking Horse in Fourth Street . . . has at present for sale . . . a most curious and completely furnished go-chair, calculated for the use of the sick or decreped, in which machine, a person having only a slight use of one hand, may conduct himself from room to room or where he pleases, on one floor, with care and expedition, without the assistance of a servant, and in which the invalid may take the air and exercise himself in his garden . . ." *Pennsylvania Packet* (Philadelphia), July 11, 1788.

GODDARD, GODDET, GOWBERT

A "wooden cup, goblet, or tankard." (H)

GOFFERING IRON

A slender, cylindrical rod or iron, with a wooden handle, used for crimping or fluting cloth. The iron was heated, then pressed against the cloth.

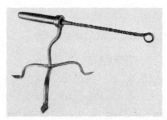

Early-eighteenth-century single goffering iron for pressing ruffles, in iron stand.

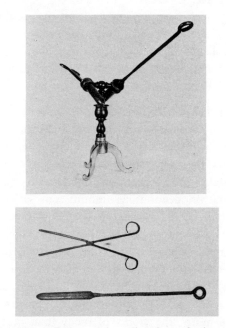

C. 1800 goffering and curling irons in iron and brass stands. (Courtesy, Antiquarian and Landmarks Society, Inc.)

GOGGLES

A particular type of spectacles with round lenses; often specified for those who squinted because of near-sightedness. "For myself, 1 pr. Goggles for a Man 60 yr. old set in Silver." (Order from Mann Page,

February 15, 1770, Stafford County, Virginia.) Frances Mason, *John Norton and Sons, Merchants of London and Virginia* (Richmond, 1935). (See also SPECTACLES, SUNGLASSES.)

GONFALON, GONFANON
Synonyms for an ensign or standard, but especially a battle flag.

GOOSE
A cant term for "a taylor's iron." (W)

GOTHIC CHIPPENDALE
The collector's all-inclusive term for any furniture based on designs by Chippendale and others of the eighteenth century who used Gothic-period motifs as ornaments.

GOTHIC CLOCK
Any clock case design made in the Gothic style. The reference today generally is to the sharp, pointed top, Connecticut shelf clock manufactured in the 1840s. (See also STEEPLE CLOCK.)

GOTHIC FURNITURE
The mid-eighteenth-century designation used by architects and cabinetmakers (of whom the most familiar to most is Chippendale) for any furniture made with ornaments or decorations reminiscent of the Gothic, "Old English" or Medieval period. The chief exponent of the style, Horace Walpole, whose home, "Strawberry Hill," reflected the Gothic in its architecture as well as its furnishings, noted that such designs of the eighteenth century, however, were more "the works of fancy than imitation." Furniture of this time was light in execution, its Gothic quality mainly achieved through the use of fretwork or carved arches or arcades. The designation also was used in the mid-nineteenth century during the so-called Neo-Gothic period, for furniture much heavier in appearance.

GOUGE
"A kind of chisel having a round edge" (W) "for the cutting of such wood as is to be rounded or hollowed." Joseph Moxon, *Mechanick Exercises, or The Doctrine of Handy-Works* (London, 1683–84).

GOURD
A cant term for "a bottle" (W) because "the large fruit so-called is often scooped hollow, for the purpose of containing and carrying wine and other liquors; from thence any leathern bottle grew to be called by the same name." (J) (See also CALABASH.)

GOUT STOOL, GOUTY STOOL
Any low stool on which an afflicted foot might be rested, and especially any stool with a top set on a notched frame so that the height of the cushion or board might be adjusted or inclined. "The mechanism of a Gouty Stool [by] the construction of which, being so easily raised or lowered at either end, is particularly useful to the afflicted." A. Hepplewhite, *The Cabinet-Maker and Upholsterer's Guide* (London, 1794). "Gout, arthritis, a very painful disease whose seat is in the joints and ligaments of the feet, and whose principal time of invasion are the spring and autumn." (M) Even though, throughout the generations, it was often assumed that "Gout seldom attacks those who live an abstemious and active life . . . [it is] brought on by full living and indolence," (G. W. Francis, *The Dictionary of Practical Receipts* [London, 1847]), high-ranking Puritans also were af-

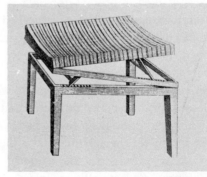

Gout stool illustrated in Hepplewhite's *Guide* (London, 1788).

flicted: "January 2, 1708–09. Cloudy cold day. Mr. Browfield is prayed for . . . is in much pain by reason of his disordered great Toe . . . Dr. Mather is kept in by the Gout." Samuel Sewall, *Diary*.

GOVERNOR WINTHROP DESK
None of the three Governors Winthrop ever used such a desk. This is a twentieth-century advertising term used to promote a reproduction similar to what in the eighteenth and early nineteenth centuries was called a Bureau, *q.v.*

GRACE CUP
A contemporary term for "the cup of health drank after grace," (W) the "large cup or goblet passed round the table after grace was said," (H) and that also was called a State Cup or a Loving Cup, *q.v.*

GRAINED FURNITURE
The all-inclusive term for any furniture, usually the product of the country craftsman or the homeowner himself, the surface finish of which has been painted to resemble the color, texture, figuration, i.e., grain, of a more expensive or fashionable wood. Chairs, chests, tables, picture and looking-glass frames all were so treated. "The extra cost of working hard wood renders its employment rare in economical cottages. As a substitute, however, we strongly recommend that the wood be either grained in imitation of the native wood of the district where the house is—such as maple, birch, ash, black-walnut or oak—, or in the cheapest cottages stained to have the same effect . . . The grained surface, being made smooth by varnishing, does not readily become soiled, and when it does, a moment's application of a damp cloth will make all clean and bright. While, if the same surface were painted only, it would require frequent and most vigorous scrubbing by the house-maid, to restore it to its original condition." A. J. Downing, *The Architecture of Country Houses* (New York, 1850).

GRAINING BOARD
This was the "board used by the curriers to give a grain to their leathers. It consists of notches quite across, into which the pliant leather being pressed, its surface readily takes the impression." (M)

GRANDFATHER CHAIR
A Late-Victorian period romanticism for any Easy Chair, *q.v.* The term probably came into common use at the same time Grandfather Clock became a popular synonym for the Tall- or Long-case Clock, *qq.v.*

GRANDFATHER CLOCK
Late-nineteenth-century American colloquialism for what was called a tall clock or long-case clock from the time of its introduction in this country during the second half of the seventeenth century. Cases were designed to follow the styles of the William and Mary period through the Sheraton era, usually made to order by cabinetmakers and sold directly to clock manufacturers who provided the works, or directly to

Shortened or "grandmother" version of the tall-case clock (Courtesy, Connecticut Historical Society, Inc.)

householders. The term came into use following publication in 1878 of the popular poem by Henry Clay Work, *Grandfather's Clock,* which included the stanza:

> *My grandfather's clock was too large for the shelf,*
> *So it stood ninety years on the floor.*

The first clocks, sans cases, were hung just below ceiling moldings to allow room for weights and later pendulums. The tall cases were designed to hold the clock, to hide the weights and/or pendulums, and to keep the mechanism free of dust.

GRANDMOTHER CLOCK

Where there is a grandfather, there assuredly is a grandmother, and thus this name has been given in the twentieth century to the smaller, shorter version of the tall-case clock, popularly called a Grandfather Clock, *q.v.*

GRAPESHOT

In weaponry, "a large kind of shot [made] in clusters." (W)

GRAPHOMETER

"The name of a mathematical instrument used by surveyors and generally called a semicircle"; (M)   that is, "an instrument to find an angle whose vortex is at the center of it." (W)

GRAPNEL

"A small anchor with four or five flukes." (W)

GRAPPLING

"An instrument with barbs to grapple." (W)

Wrought-iron grappling hook or grapnel.

GRATE

The term for a metal "fireplace," (W)   i.e., "a range of bars within which fires are made." (J)   An open basket formed of iron bars and set between the andirons; used to allow air to circulate beneath the coals and also to protect the hearth paving from being burned. Grates for parlor, dining parlor, and chamber hearths often were well designed, and handsomely ornamented with superior metals including brass, silver, and silver-plated metal. Designs for "Eight Stove-grates [are shown]. I would recommend the ornamental Parts to be of wrought Brass, and as they are made to take off, will be easily cleaned." Thomas Chippendale, *The Gentleman and Cabinet-Maker's Director* (London, 1762). (See also BATH STOVE.)

Grate, illustrated in Thomas Chippendale's *Director* (London, 1762).

GRATER

"A rough instrument to grate with.

   Grate: "To rub small," (W)   as with a Nutmeg Grater, *q.v.*

GRAVER

The name of the engraver's tool "by which all lines, scratches, and shades are engraved on copper, Ec. There are three sorts: round-pointed, square-pointed, and lozenge-pointed. The round are best for scratching, the square for cutting larger strokes; the lozenge for the most delicate strokes. A graver of the middle form, between the square and the lozenge, will make the stroke or hatches appear with more life and vigour." (M)

GREEN SPECTACLES
The popular contemporary term for Sunglasses, *q.v.* (See also GOGGLES, SPECTACLES.)

GREGORIAN CALENDAR
(See CALENDAR.)

GREYBEARD JUG
A popular synonym for the Bellarmine Jug, *q.v.*

GRIDDLE
Sometimes also spelled gredel, this was the "solid iron or earthen flat pan in which food is cooked over the fire"; (J) a shallow round pan suspended by its bail handle from a pothook or trammel above the embers. According to Webster, it was "a pan to bake cakes on," as we still refer to griddlecakes.

Eighteenth-century griddle with swivel hook.

GRIDIRON, GRYDERN, GRYDRYN
At the kitchen hearth, this was the flat iron "portable grate on which meat is laid to be broiled upon the fire," (J) and equally useful as a utensil around the campfire: "The men were so delighted with the buffalo, that the Gridiron and Frying-Pan had no more rest all night." William Byrd [1729], *History of the Dividing Line* (Richmond,

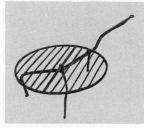

Eighteenth-century gridiron.

1866). "Send 1 Grid Iron & 2 pr. Tongs & Shovel & Pokers." (Order from Martha Jacquelin, August 14, 1769, York, Virginia, to London.) Frances Mason, *John Norton and Sons, Merchants of London and Virginia* (Richmond, 1935).

GRINDSTONE, GRIND WHEEL
Two colloquialisms for one of the house-yard tools, "a stone for grinding tools on," (W) the circular whetstone set so as to revolve on an iron axis above a frame or sawhorse. "Grindle stones" were listed in the House of Parliament Rates, 1660, for Imports and Exports—*Statutes of the Realm* (London, 1819). (See WHETSTONE.)

GROG TABLE
The collector's name for a portable tripod table, from which presumably a ship's master served grog (rum and water) to the crew. Similar to the Butler's Table, *q.v.*, such a table basically is a sturdy tray with a gallery rim and folding X-base stand.

Grog: "A general name for any spiritous liquor and water mixed together; but is more particularly applied to rum and water cold, without sugar." *Encyclopedia Americana* (Philadelphia, 1831).

GROUP
The word, from the Italian *groppo* or *guippo*, used to designate any painting or sculpture representing an assemblage of several objects such as "figures of men, beasts, fruits or the like, which have some relation to each other, arranged in such a manner as to present to the eye one connected whole . . . Thus in Historical Painting [*q.v.*] all the figures have reference to the principal one, to which the attention is chiefly directed." *Encyclopedia Americana* (Philadelphia, 1831). (See also CONVERSATION PIECE, HISTORY PAINTING.)

GUERIDON
A round Candlestand, *q.v.*

GUGLET

A cant term to describe a small pot with a drinking spout or tube. (See also PAP BOAT, POSSET POT.)

GUIL-FAT, GUIL-VAT

"A wort-tub"; (H) that is, the tub in which liquor ferments. (See GAIL.)

GUITAR

The name of "a musical instrument of the stringed kind, used greatly in Spain and at present in England." (M)

GUN

The general term for any firearm that "forcibly discharges a ball, shot, or other offensive matter, through a cylindrical barrel, by means of gunpowder. They may be divided into great and small: Great Guns are called also by the general name of cannons, culverins, demi-culvers; Small Guns include musquets, musquetoons, carabines, blunderbusses, fowling-pieces, Ec." (M) A cant term for a "large flagon of ale," (H) and hence the contemporary phrase, son-of-a-gun, for a cheerful, jovial drunk.

GUN LADLE

A small measure for powder wherewith the powder horn was filled. "Thomas Russell, Brazier, makes all sorts of Braziery Ware . . . Copper Funnels, Brass Scales, Gun Ladles . . ." *Boston News-Letter,* October 30, 1740. Made of copper, brass, pewter, tin, occasionally of horn.

H

HACKADAY, HAGGADAY

The term for a wooden door latch.

HACKBUSH

A colloquialism for "a heavy hand gun," (H) but see also ARQUEBUS.

HACK HOOK

A cant term for "a crooked bill with a long handle for cutting peas" (H) or beans. (See also SICKLE, SCYTHE.)

Hackaday or haggaday (wood door latch), c. 1720. (Courtesy, Antiquarian and Landmarks Society, Inc.)

HACKLE

Generally (1) "Any conical covering of hay or straw" but specifically, (2) a straw "cone of thatch placed over a Bee Hive," *q.v.* (H) (3) A shackle or hobble for oxen, horses, etc. (4) A colloquial variation for Hatchel, *q.v.* (See also HURDLE.)

HADLEY CHEST

The collector's term for the late-seventeenth-

The Hadley chest made in the Connecticut Valley during the last quarter of the seventeenth century. (Courtesy, Connecticut Historical Society, Inc.)

Book or Bible box allied in decoration to the Hadley chest. (Courtesy, Connecticut Historical Society, Inc.)

century New England dowry chest made in the Hadley, Massachusetts, area; distinguished by the lavish use of incised or shallow-carved leaves, vines, and/or tulips to decorate the entire front. (See also CONNECTICUT CHEST, DOWRY CHEST.)

HAGIOGRAPHIA
From the Greek *hagios,* sacred or holy, and *graphein,* to write, these are the holy writings; i.e., the name given to a "particular division of the Old Testament, as containing hymns to God, and moral precepts for the conduct of life. The books distinguished by this term were the Psalms, Proverbs, Ecclesiastes, and the Song of Solomon." (M) Or that portion not included in the Law and the Prophets. (See also BIBLE.)

HAIR PENCIL
A contemporary term for the artist's paintbrush, "a tool for drawing and painting." (W) "The following articles compose a part of the Assortment . . . India Inks, India Rubber, black lead pencils, Camels hair pencils, French Chalk, Red Chalk . . ." *American Mercury* (Hartford, Connecticut), November 1, 1815. (See also advertisement quoted under LIMNER, Chapter 3.)

HALBARD, HALBERD, HALBERT
In weaponry, a "soldier's long battle axe." (W) "A set of Halberts for a foot Company to be sold on reasonable Terms, by Nicholas Boone, Bookseller, to be seen at

his House near School-House Lane, Boston." *Boston News-Letter,* April 22, 1706.

Early-eighteenth-century halberd or pike. (Courtesy, Antiquarian and Landmarks Society, Inc.)

Halberds carried by eighteenth-century troops, as shown in a contemporary print.

HALE
In the sense of pulling or drawing, this was a colloquialism for a "Pot-hook or Kettle-tilter," *qq.v.* (H)

HALF-CHEST
A contemporary description of the dressing table now called a Lowboy, *q.v.*

HALF-CLOCK
(See MASSACHUSETTS CLOCK.)

HALF-COUCH

An eighteenth-century descriptive term for the Bergere, *q.v.* Ince and Mayhew, for example, published "two Designs of Birjairs, or Half Couches," in their book of designs, *The Universal System of Household Furniture* (London, 1762) one of which could be converted into a chair bed, having a "Back made to fall down at pleasure."

HALF-HOUR GLASS

The contemporary term for a type of sandglass "frequently called a watch-glass [which] is used at sea to measure the time each watch has to stay on deck. To 'flog' or 'sweat the glass,' is to turn it before the sand has quite run out, and thereby, gaining a few minutes each half hour, to make the watch too short." *Encyclopedia Americana* (Philadelphia, 1831). (See HOURGLASS, CLEPSYDRA.)

HALF-PIKE

"A small pike carried by officers." (W) (See also ESPONTOON, LEADING STAFF.)

HALF-TESTER BEDSTEAD

The bed frame with ceiling-high headposts from which a half-tester extended, supporting side curtains and valance. Such a design, according to one maker, was considered ". . . very suitable for moderately-sized apartments, their style is intermediate between French and tester bedsteads, being less expensive than the latter, and esteemed more elegant than the former." Blackie and Son, *The Cabinet-Maker's Assistant* (London, 1853).

HALL CHAIR

Plank seat side chairs designed more for service than decoration because they were made for the use "of servants and strangers waiting on business." Thomas Sheraton, *The Cabinet Dictionary* (London, 1803). For their designs, Ince and Mayhew offered "Hall Chairs in the Gothic Taste, the Ornaments of which, if thought too Expensive, may be painted, and have a very good Effect." *The Universal System of Household Furniture* (London, 1762).

Hall chair illustrated in Hepplewhite's *Guide* (London, 1794).

HALL CLOCK

Another name for the Long-case Clock, *q.v.*, or tall-case clock, because it usually was given a prominent setting in the main hall or parlor. (See also GRANDFATHER CLOCK.)

HALL LANTERN

The handsome lantern suspended from a ceiling hook to light the foyer, lobby, or antechamber; made of fine, clear glass set in a light decorative frame or case, often gilded and painted. Some of those made in the mid-eighteenth century were described thusly in one book of designs for the well-to-do home. "Two Hall Lanthorns [are shown]. The first is an Hexagon in the Gothic taste, and would have a very good effect [often a euphemism for impressive]; the other Square, with French Ornaments, two others [are] calculated for being made

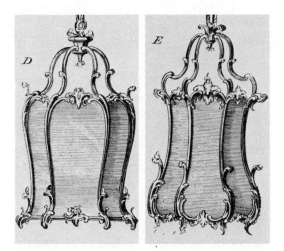

Hall or stair lanterns, as illustrated in Thomas Chippendale's *Director* (London, 1762).

Mid-eighteenth-century hall or hanging lantern with tin frame. (Courtesy, Antiquarian and Landmarks Society Inc.)

American eighteenth-century hall lantern with brass frame. (Courtesy, Antiquarian and Landmarks Society, Inc.)

in Brass or Wood; we have executed some which are much admired, and at a much less Expence than Brass." Ince and Mayhew, *The Universal System of Household Furniture* (London, 1762). (See advertisement quoted under GLAZIER, Chapter 3, and ENTRY LIGHT.)

HALL TABLE

Hall, the term for a large reception room in the seventeenth- and early-eighteenth-century house later was used to designate the front entrance area, lobby, or foyer.

Hall table from *The Cabinet-Maker's Assistant,* Blackie and Son (London, 1853).

The hall table was set against the wall, was fairly wide, but extremely shallow, usually had heavily carved and turned front legs. "As they stand to the wall, and the back legs are but little seen, two plain pilasters are usually employed for the back supports." Blackie and Son, *The Cabinet-Maker's Assistant* (London, 1853). (See also CONSOLE TABLE.)

HAMES

Part of the harness, "a kind of collar for draft horses" (W) supplied by the hardware merchant; made of fine-grained hard wood with brass or steel tips and rings, and usually painted to match the coach or wagon color; collected today and used to decorate restored tack rooms, so-called country store museums, and by some in home bars or playrooms. "James H. Wells, has received by the James Cooper, from Liverpool, a further supply of Hardware Goods. Locks, Hinges, Latches, low priced plated Sadlery, Spectacles, Needles, plated and iron Hames, superior Scotch Hones, Gun Flints, plated and gilt Buttons, Ec. Ec. Ec." *American Mercury* (Hartford, Connecticut), March 10, 1822.

HAMMER

The name of the tool used by the carpenter and cooper to drive nails, and by the smith to form and beat metal; made with a head, usually of iron or steel, fixed crosswise to a handle. "The most trifling actions that affect a man's credit ought to be regarded. The sound of a hammer at five o'clock in the morning, or nine at night, heard by a creditor, makes him easy six months longer." *Writings of Benjamin Franklin,* ed., A. H. Smyth (New York, 1907).

Hammer.

HAMPER

The word to designate "a large basket for carriage" especially one for bottled goods (J) with a cover that could be fastened or locked; made of splint, rush, or other sturdy material in a basket weave. "Pray add to my Invoice two Hampers of best bottled Porter, and a dozen packs of playing cards, and you will oblige . . . Peter Lyons." (Order November 20, 1770, from Hanover, Virginia, to London.) Frances Mason, *John Norton and Sons, Merchants of London and Virginia* (Richmond, 1935). (See also HANAPER.)

HANAPER

The Norman word was *hanapier* from *hanap,* a drinking vessel or bottle, and thus a kind of protective container for a bottle and, by extension, anything of worth. Hence, originally hanaper signified a hamper or box wherein documents were kept.

HAND

"A measure of four inches or of a clenched fist." (M)

HAND BELLS
(See BELL.)

HAND BOARD

A portable table board, and so a serving tray, or tea tray. "Lately arrived from London & are to be Sold by Giles Dulake Tidmarsh at his Warehouse No. 4 on the Long Wharfe, Five Dutch Tea Tables, as Hand Boards." *Boston Gazette,* November 19, 1722. (See also TEA BOARD.)

HAND CANDLESTICK

Another name for the candleholder designed to be carried from room to room as needed; hence, especially one for use in a bed chamber. (See also CHAMBER CANDLESTICK.)

HANDGUN

In colonial terminology, any gun that was carried by a man, including muskets, carbines, rifles, pistols, etc., as distinct from cannon.

HAND IRONS

A contemporary spelling and pronunciation of Andirons, *q.v.* "John Gientes, Bracier in Duke Street, intend selling off his Shop consisting of a large Sortment of Brass and copper Kettles . . . hard metal, and Pewter of all Sorts, Shovels and Tongs, Hand Irons, Grid-Irons . . ." *The New-York Gazette and The Weekly Post-Boy,* March 12, 1750.

HANDLE

The term for "that part of anything by which it is held." (J) A haft. In an age when tools are purchased complete with handles, and when, should a handle break, the tool itself is discarded, we sometimes forget that Americans from the seventeenth

"George James, Dr.

1 mo	11	1746/7	To 6 Best 5-Slat chairs	1.13.0
3 mo	4		To auger Handles & 2 Drawing Knive handles	0.1.10
4 mo	2		To putting handles to 15 Cards	0.2.6
8 mo	16		To 2 How handels & one Shovel handel	0.2.6"

Solomon Fussell Account Book, 1738–51, Stephen Collins Papers, Manuscript Division, Library of Congress.

through the nineteenth centuries generally purchased metal tool parts from the smith, then ordered handles or grips turned to order. Thus, it was common even for the country's finest cabinetmakers to supply their customers with tool handles turned from hickory, walnut, maple, or other hard woods. The entry on page 388 is from the work journal of one of Philadelphia's famed chairmakers.

HAND ORGAN

A minor musical instrument, the portable hand or barrel organ "consists of a movable, turning cylinder called a barrel, on which by means of wire pins and staples, are set the tunes it is intended to perform. These pins and staples, by the revolution of the barrel, act upon the keys within, and give admission to the wind from the bellows to the pipes . . . [it] is so contrived that the same action of the hand that turns the barrel gives motion to the bellows." *Encyclopedia Americana* (Philadelphia, 1831). "[At Orleans] we overtook two Italian boys, who had waded thus far down the Cape through the sand, with their organs on their back, and were going on to Provincetown . . . we concluded that they had chosen wisely to come here, where other music than that of the surf is rare." Henry David Thoreau, *Cape Cod* (Boston, 1865).

HAND TABLE
(See HAND BOARD; TEA BOARD.)

HAND VICE
The name for the tool used by smiths and carpenters, "a small kind of Vice [*q.v.*], serving to hold the lesser works in, that require often turning about." (M)

HAND WARMER
(See PULSE GLASS.)

HANDY
A cant term for "a Piggin," *q.v.* (H)

HANGER
The common colonial term for "a short broadsword, an iron," (W) in use well into the nineteenth century. "The officers [in each company of artillery] each to be armed with a sword or hanger, a fusee, bayonet and belt, with a cartridge box, to contain twelve cartridges." *Connecticut Statutes* (Hartford, 1835).

HANGING CUPBOARD
(1) The seventeenth- and eighteenth-century food safe often made with doors formed of turned spindles to provide the necessary ventilation. (2) The term may also have been used to describe a seventeenth-century cupboard tall enough to permit clothing kept therein to hang at full length. (See also LIVERY, LIVERY CUPBOARD.)

Hanging cupboard. (Courtesy, Antiquarian and Landmarks Society, Inc.)

HANGING CORNER CUPBOARD
The half cupboard, made with three sides to fit into a corner, hung well above the chair rail. (See also CORNER CUPBOARD.)

HANGING SAFE
The portable larder, suspended from a ceiling hook in the kitchen, storeroom, or attic; made with louvred, pierced tin, or side and front boards drilled through in decorative patterns for ventilation. "Very few modern-built town-houses have a proper place to preserve provisions in. The best substitute is a hanging-safe, which you may contrive to suspend in an airy situation . . . Larders,

pantries and safes must be sheltered from the sun, and otherwise removed from the heat; be dry, and if possible have a current of dry, cool air continually passing through them." William Kitchiner, *The Cook's Oracle, and Housekeeper's Manual* (New York, 1830). (See also LARDER, PANTRY.)

HANGING SHELVES

One to three or more shelves, usually graduated in depth, made to hang on the wall from brackets or hooks. Those with galleries or fretwork generally were intended for the display of china, that is porcelain or pottery ornaments. "These are often wanted as Book-shelves in closets or Ladies' rooms; they also are adapted to place China on [and] should be made of mahogany." A. Hepplewhite, *The Cabinet-Maker and Upholsterer's Guide* (London, 1794). Those from the cabinetmaker's shop were made from mahogany, walnut, maple, or cherry; some were decorated with gilt, japan work, or other paint. Many more, simply fashioned, were made by the householder himself because "though few cot-

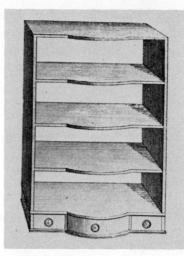

Hanging shelves, as illustrated in Hepplewhite's *Guide* (London, 1794).

Hanging shelf or bracket shelf. (Courtesy, Antiquarian and Landmarks Society, Inc.)

tages of moderate size have a room specially set apart for a library, no cottage in America need be without books. If no better means of placing them is within reach, the simple hanging book-shelves which may be made by any one, with a few pieces of board, will suffice." A. J. Downing, *The Architecture of Country Houses* (New York, 1850).

HANGLES

This was a colloquialism for the pothook or "the moveable iron crook, suspended over the fire for culinary purposes." (H)

HANKWINDER

The more explicit term for the spinner's accessory, usually called a Niddy-Noddy, *q.v.*

HAQUE, HAQUEBUT

An Arquebus, *q.v.*, or "a hand gun about 2 feet long." (H)

Hanging shelves, as illustrated in Thomas Chippendale's *Director* (London, 1762).

390

HARLEQUIN TABLE

The name, given the comedy or pantomime character who wore particolored tights, became a general term for anything particolored or divided, and so was used to describe a late-eighteenth-century design for a combined writing and dressing table, or in the words of one contemporary designer: "This elegant article, an appendage to the Ladies Boudoir, is so contrived, as to form a Writing, Work, Drawing, and Breakfast Table, as occasion may require. For the first purpose, a small Escrutoire [is] concealed in the body of the Table . . . The lefthand drawer is fitted up with the colours and other useful articles for Drawing. The two ends of the table, forming flaps, are supported by lopers thrown forward by Springs, making this article serve as the sofa or Breakfast Table. This piece of decorative furniture should be made of rose-wood, the ornaments of real *or molu,* or it may be made of mahogany and the ornaments of bronzed metal; the top should be covered with morocco leather . . ." George Smith, *A Collection of Designs for Household Furniture* (London, 1808).

HARMONIA CELESTIA

The musical instrument also known as a Harmonium, *q.v.* "This excellent and admired instrument, blended in sound between the grandeur of the Organ and the ravishing softness of the heart-thrilling Lute, never before introduced in this Country will be exhibited at Mrs. Armory's this evening . . ." *The Daily Advertiser* (New York), January 23, 1793.

HARMONICA

(See ARMONICA.)

HARMONIUM

A musical instrument invented in the late eighteenth century; in form a small pipeless organ with one or two keyboards.

HARNESS FURNITURE

The contemporary term for decorative metal accessories used on harnesses and usually called Horse Brasses by collectors today; made of plated iron, steel, brass, sometimes silver, or Sheffield plate. "Charles Sigourney, Main Street, Has imported . . . from London [and] Liverpool . . . Plated roller and sham roller buckles, and slides, harness buckles, Plated Stirrups, Spurs, Martingale Trimmings, Terrets, & other harness furniture . . ." *American Mercury* (Hartford, Connecticut), November 23, 1801.

HARP

"A lyre, an instrument strung with wire, and commonly struck with the finger." (J)

HARPING IRON, HARPAGO, HARPOON

All terms for a "large javelin of forged iron, five or six feet long, with a sharp triangular point, barbed like that of an arrow. It is fastened to a line, wherewith whales, sturgeons, Ec. are catched." (M) "They get commonly a barrel of oil, worth fifteen or twenty dollars, to a [black] fish. There were many lances and harpoons in the boats—much slenderer instruments than I had expected." Henry David Thoreau, *Cape Cod* (Boston, 1865).

HARPSICHON

A contemporary synonym for the Harpsichord, *q.v.* "After dinner, my wife and Mercer, and Tom and I, sat till eleven at night, singing and fiddling, and a great joy it is to see me master of so much pleasure in my house. The girle plays pretty well upon the harpsichon, but only ordinary tunes, but hath a good hand." Samuel Pepys, *Diary,* September 9, 1664.

HARPSICHORD

The name of the popular sixteenth- through the eighteenth-century "fine keyboard musical instrument" (J) resembling a piano; the strings were set in vibration by quill or leather points set in jacks connected with the keys by levers. Dr. Franklin, who particularly enjoyed music and music making (See ARMONICA) owned both pianoforte and harpsichord: "Furniture. This day at 10 o'clock at the House of the late Dr. Franklin, up Franklin Court, Market St. will be sold by Public Vendue a Variety of Valuable Furniture and Plate consisting of Mahogany Side-Board, Dining, Card and Pembroke tables, Mahogany chairs; Looking Glass; cloath's Presses; tea Urns, Plated candlesticks; Windsor Chairs; an elegant Sopha; chintz window curtains, Chests of Drawers; a Forte Piano; a Harpsicord; a copying Press, etc. China, Queen's Ware, Plated Knifes and Forks. 21 May, 1792." *Pennsylvania Magazine of History and Biography,* Vol. 23, 1899, p. 123.

Harpsichord, as illustrated in Bonanni's *Cabinetto Armonica* (Rome, 1723).

HARQUEBUSS

In weaponry, a "large hand gun," (W) and despite Webster, properly spelled Arquebus, *q.v.*

HASH DISH

The silver, copper, or Sheffield plate covered serving dish, usually round or oval and with a false bottom or pan to hold hot water, set on a frame above a candle-warmer or spirit lamp. "James Jacks, Jeweller and Watchmaker . . . Has Imported . . . Plated tea kettles, bread and cake baskets, steak and hash dishes with lamps . . ." *Pennsyl-*

vania Packet (Philadelphia), November 13, 1799.

HASP

The iron door catch that falls into a loop or staple.

HASSOCK

A reed or rush, or tuft of rushes; hence, "a basket made of hassocks was called a hassock," (H) and because of its rounded shape, the name was given to a thick, stuffed cushion used for kneeling on.

HASTER

Haste meant to roast and thus haster was a term describing (1) "a tin meat-screen, to reflect the heat while the operation of roasting is going on." (H) (2) Haster also was a late-eighteenth-century colloquialism for a type of plate-warmer. This was a narrow set of shelves or cupboard, about four feet high, made with one open side. Service plates were stacked within and the back or open side turned to the fire. The plates were removed through the door or doors at the front of the cupboard. (See also REFLECTOR OVEN.)

HATBOX, HAT CASE

The shaped leather or wood box or case used for the storage of hats, or as a travel

Eighteenth-century cocked hatbox or case. (Courtesy, Antiquarian and Landmarks Society, Inc.)

case; often decorated with gilt or other colors. "I pray if you Send any goods lett them be good goods & not Refuge and please to send me a good hatt Case with two very good Castors in it for my own Ware Let them be Fashionable: & one Gray the other Blake. They must not be very Beeg in the head . . . to Mr. William pate at the princes arms in Marke Lane in London. [January 10, 1667]." *The Letter Book of Peleg Sanford* (Providence, 1928). (See also CAP CASE, BANDBOX.)

HATCHEL
The instrument, a flat board with iron teeth or sharpened spikes, over which hemp or flax is drawn to comb or clean it.

Hatchel.

HATCHMENT
A type of memorial painting. (See under ARMORIAL BEARINGS at end of this section.)

HATTIL
A "Thumb-stall," *q.v.*, (H) or thimble.

HAUTBOY
"A wind instrument," (J) the high-pitched, double-reed wooden musical instrument that provided a treble to the bassoon and now usually is called an oboe.

HEARTH BRUSH
The nicely made broom or brush used to keep the hearth tidy, made and purchased singly, as indicated by the advertisement quoted; often made to match the fire tongs. The handles were of brass, iron, or steel with brass finials, of all iron or all steel; some were of turned wood. "Samuel M. Taber, Westminster Row, has just received from New York and Boston Tea Pots, Waiters, Candle-sticks, Knives and Forks, Pen

and Pocket Knives, Razors, Scissors, fancy Bellows, Hearth Brushes, Clothes do., Ec." *Literary Cadet and Rhode Island Statesman* (Providence), December 19, 1827.

HEARTH STOOL
The collector's term for any long stool used before the hearth, from the plain wood-plank type of the farmhouse kitchen to handsome stools with seats of cane, leather, or cloth-covered cushions. Hearth stools were of normal seat height and should not be confused with the low cricket stool used by children or as a step stool.

HEDDLES
(See WEAVER'S LOOM.)

HEDGINGBILL
The name of "a kind of axe used to [cut a] hedge with." (W) (See also BILL.)

HEIRLOOM
The term used to describe "such household furniture as is not inventoried after the owner's decease, but necessarily descends to the heir along with the house; such are tables, presses, cupboards, bedsteads, Ec." (M)

HELIOMETER, HOLOMETER
Contemporary terms for "a mathematical instrument for taking all sorts of measures, both on the earth and in the heavens; it is the same with the pantometer." (M) "An instrument to take the diameter of heavenly bodies." (W)

HELIOSCOPE
The contemporary name for "a sort of telescope peculiarly adapted [by blackening or smoking the glass] for observing the spots, eclipses, Ec. of the sun" (M) "without hurting the eyes." (W)

HELIX CANDLESTICK
Helix is the term for a spiraling corkscrew-like curve and thus was used to describe the candleholder with a column or shaft so formed. The open core and spiral provided

a groove for the manipulation of a "pusher" to eject candle ends.

Mid-eighteenth-century Helix candlestick.

HELMET
An ancient "defensive armour worn by horsemen, both in war and in tournament. It covered both the head and face, only leaving an aperture in the front secured by bars, which was called the visor." (M)

HELVE
A term used "among country people for the handles of a hatchet, pick-ax, mattock, or the like." (M)

HEPTACHORD
The term from the Greek for a system of seven sounds, and hence the name given a Lyre or Cithara, *qq.v.*, with seven chords.

HERBAL, HERBALL
A book "describing the figure, genus, species, properties, virtues, Ec. of herbs, trees, seeds, and plants. It also denotes a collection of specimens of the several kinds of plants dried in the leaves of a book." (M) "A treatise on herbs, a book of plants." (W) (See also HORTUS HYEMALIS, HORTUS SICCUS.)

HERBARIUM
A contemporary term for a collection of pressed flowers and leaves, arranged on pages and bound as a book. "Mr. Rossiter pursued all the natural science with an industry and enthusiasm only possible to a man who has . . . none of the thousand dissipations of time resulting from our sys-

tem of intercommunication . . . He had a ponderous herbarium, of some forty or fifty folios of his own collection and arrangement . . ." Harriet Beecher Stowe, *Old Town Folks* (Boston, 1868). "To preserve the natural colour in Petals of dried Flowers: Immerse the petals for some minutes in alcohol. The colours will fade at first; but in a short time they will resume their natural tint, and remain permanently fixed." Thomas Tegg, *Book of Utility* (London, 1828). (See also BOTANICAL PRESS, HERBAL, HORTUS HYEMALIS, HORTUS SICCUS.)

HERB BASKET
The hanging wall basket in which leaves and flower heads were set to dry.

Herb basket, c. 1800. (Courtesy, Antiquarian and Landmarks Society, Inc.)

HEXACHORD
The term from the Greek for a chord in ancient music, "equivalent to that which the moderns call a sixth [and] also the name for a lyre with six strings." *Encyclopedia Americana* (Philadelphia, 1831).

H, HL HINGES
The contemporary name for a type of hinge made of brass or iron in varying sizes during the seventeenth, eighteenth, and

early nineteenth centuries, for use on interior doors, cabinet or cupboard doors: "Imported in ship *Eliza-Ann,* from Liverpool, an invoice of Hardware Goods [including] Wrought iron H and HL hinges, Cast iron butt hinges, pew door hinges, and table hinges." *American Mercury* (Hartford, Connecticut), February 7, 1811.

Eighteenth-century iron H, HL hinges.

HIGHBOY

Originally a nineteenth-century New England slang term, and now used throughout the country to describe what, following its introduction during the William and Mary

The tallboy, chest-on-frame, or highboy in order of age and development in this country:
C. 1700 William and Mary period walnut chest-on-frame. (Courtesy, N. Liverant and Son, Colchester, Connecticut.)

New England Queen Anne period, c. 1720 pine-and-maple chest.

Elegant mid-Georgian or mid-eighteenth-century cherry chest-on-frame. (Courtesy, Connecticut Historical Society, Inc.)

period, was called a tall chest, high chest, or a chest-on-frame. Webster does not include highboy in his first 1806 dictionary, although it was included in later editions. The term seems to have developed about the time of General Lafayette's triumphal farewell tour (1824) and may be, in part, a corruption of *bois;* any number of French-sounding words and phrases were affected by Americans during that exuberant Francophile period; but see also Tallboy, for Highboy may simply be the American version of that English cant term.

HIGH CHAIR
(See CHILD'S CHAIR, TABLE CHAIR.)

HIGH DADDY
Not a correct term but another unfortunate choice of name for a fine piece of furniture, the tall chest that also labors under the designation Highboy, *q.v.,* used by latter-day Americans who believe an antique is enhanced by a cute, quaint nickname.

HINGES
These generally are the joints on which doors, gates, lids, or leaves of tables hang and turn in opening, shutting, or folding. "They are of different denominations, as butts used by joiners for hanging table-leaves, Ec.; casement for hanging casements [windows] upon dove-tails; esses for light doors and lockers; garnetcross for hanging large doors. Besides these, there are many others of different forms and uses, distinguished by different names, as coach, desk, bed, box, trunk, screw, shutter, Ec." (M) (See also H, HL HINGES, STRAP HINGE.)

HIRLAS
The ancient "Welch drinking-horn." (W)

HIRED-MAN'S BED
The collector's romantic term for an under-eaves or attic bed, better known to its original owners as a stump bed or box bedstead, each of which see. No doubt these low, single-width bedsteads were assigned for servants' use, however, one earlier chronicler notes an equally sensible explanation of their number: Before 1800, "bedsteads if fine were made of mahogany, but if for common purposes, or for the families of good tradesmen, they were of poplar and always (seem to have been) painted green. It was a matter of universal concern to have them low enough to answer the purpose of repose for sick or dying persons—a provision necessary for such possible events . . ." John F. Watson, *Annals of Philadelphia* (Philadelphia, 1830).

HISTORICAL TILES
The contemporary term for faïence tiles decorated with scenes of battles, explorers' ships, landscapes depicting distant lands, crusaders, historical sites. "To be sold by Nathaniel French in Second Street Fine tasted Jamaica Rum . . . also Historical Chimney Tiles at 3/6 per dozen." *American Weekly Mercury* (Philadelphia), September 25, 1735. (See TILES.)

HISTORY
The account of the past and thus the term for the printed book containing an account

Title page from *A Complete History of England* (London, 1706) by a variety of authors including John Milton, Thomas More, Francis Bacon.

of "such circumstances as are proper to be transmitted to posterity . . . History is of all others the most difficult province, [for] in other subjects there is a greater latitude for the writer's imagination, but, in history, he is confined to the occurrences he relates, and these, as they are not alike entertaining, require force and judgment. History will not admit those decorations other subjects are capable of . . ." (M) (See note under ANNALS, GEOGRAPHY.)

HISTORY PAINTING

A type of illustrative painting once considered the most worthwhile project to which the artist might aspire, and thus more important than landscapes, still-life work, or portraiture. Any theme from the Bible or classical writings, as well as a historical event, came under this heading. The purpose was to exemplify the heroic virtues and provide the viewer with a pattern for his own life. Factual detail or historical accuracy were subordinate to the dramatic theme. As one American artist wrote: "To such Gentlemen and Ladies as have thought but little upon this Subject, and might only regard painting as a superfluous Ornament, I would just observe that History-painting, besides being extremely ornamental, has many important uses. It presents to our view some of the most interesting Scenes recorded in ancient or modern History; gives us more lively and perfect Ideas of the things represented than we could receive from an historical account of them, and frequently recalls to our Memory a long Train of Events . . . They show us a proper expression of the Passions excited by every Event, and have an Effect, the very same in kind (but stronger) than a fine historical Description of the same Passage would have upon a judicious Reader. Men who have distinguished themselves for the good of their Country and Mankind may be set before our Eyes as Examples and to give us their silent Lessons, and, besides, every judicious Friend and Visitant shares with us in the Advantage and Improvement, and increases its Value to ourselves. John Durand." *The New-York Gazette or The Weekly Post-Boy,* April 11, 1768. Perhaps the two later works best known to Americans today, and which might be considered history paintings, are those depicting "The Landing of the Pilgrims" and "Washington Crossing the Delaware."

HOE

A tool "in country affairs, made like a cooper's adz, to cut up weeds in gardens, fields, Ec. This instrument is of great use and should be more employed in hacking and clearing the several corners, cracks, and patches of land, in spare times of the year." (M)

HOGARTH CHAIR

A modern term for a hooped-back chair made during the early eighteenth century, with a pierced splat and carved cabriole legs, and so called because it may be seen in prints of engravings by the famed English artist, Thomas Hogarth.

HOG SCRAPER

Probably a nineteenth-century cant term,

C. 1800 hog scraper candlestick with hanger and slide.

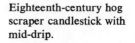

Eighteenth-century hog scraper candlestick with mid-drip.

C. 1800 hog scraper or flat-bottom candlestick with slide ring.

and certainly a collector's term today, for the common sheet tin or tinned iron candle-holder set on a simple disc base resembling an extremely shallow, inverted saucer. The sharp edges of the "saucer," when the base was unscrewed from the socket shaft, are said to have served as a handy tool with which to scrape or shave off bristles. (See advertisement quoted under STAND-AND-SOCKET LAMP.)

HOLDFAST

The name of a tool "used by joiners, carvers, Ec. which goes through their bench to hold fast such work as cannot be finished by its being held in the hand." (M) Also, the common colonial term for an "iron hook, catch or cramp" (W) to hold fire tools: "Send 2 Cinder shovells for my self at 1/ each, 2 pr. of fire Iron holdfasts for Do." (Order from Catherine Ratnell, Williamsburg, Virginia, January 31, 1772 to London.) Frances Mason, *John Norton and Sons, Merchants of London and Virginia* (Richmond, 1935). More often today called a Jamb Hook, *q.v.*

Holdfast. (Courtesy, Antiquarian and Landmarks Society, Inc.)

HOLLOW WARE

The all-inclusive term for metalware forms that were hollow, and thus essentially were containers, such as teapots, bowls, pitchers, jars, and jugs.

HOLSTER

"A lethern case for a horseman's pistols." (W) "The commissioned officers (of each troop of horse) to furnish themselves with good horses, of at least fourteen and one half hands high, and to be armed with a sword and pair of pistols. The holsters of which [are] to be covered with bear-skin caps." *Connecticut Statutes* (Hartford, 1835).

HOMESPUN

The general term for any textiles woven in the home as opposed to cloth purchased and ready for use. (See TEXTILES at end of this section.)

HONE

The term for "a fine kind of whetstone, used for setting razors, pen-knives, and the like," (M) usually set in their own small wooden frame or box. (See advertisement quoted under HAMES, see also GRIND-STONE.)

HONFLEURE

The name of a type of amateur transfer painting on china, wood, or metal, imitative of japanning, developed shortly after 1820 by a Boston art teacher named Honfleure, who sold instruction kits for the "six easy steps" needed. "S. M. Bassett, No. 131 Chapel-Street . . . has on hand . . . Transparent Paper for Honfleure's or other painting." *Columbian Register* (New Haven, Connecticut), May 23, 1829.

HOOKAH

The Eastern water pipe, brought here by seamen and merchant adventurers, and used for smoking tobacco. The pipe had a long pliable tube attached in a vase of water, through which the smoke passed before it was inhaled. A common cant term for the hookah or water pipe was hubble-bubble.

HOOKED RUG

A contemporary term for the carpets "made of wool, but wrought with the needle, and often embellished with silk." (M)

HOOP, HOOPED POT

A colloquialism for a quart pot or wooden-stave flagon, so-called because it was bound with hoops. "There was generally three hoops on a quart pot, and if three men were drinking, each would take his hoop, or third portion." (H) Hence, the allusion in Shakespeare to that happy day when

> There shall be in England seven halfpenny
>   loaves sold for a penny;
> the three-hooped pot shall have ten hoops;
> and I will make it felony to drink small
>   beer.

> *King Henry VI,* Part II, IV, ii.

(See also PEG TANKARD.)

Hoop or three-hooped drinking pot or tankard. (Courtesy, Antiquarian and Landmarks Society, Inc.)

HOOP-BACK CHAIR

A common contemporary description of the Windsor side chair, and also for a bended-back chair; that is, one the top rail of which forms a continuous curve.

HOPE CHEST

A colloquial term for a Dowry Chest, *q.v.*

HOPPER

The "box in which corn is put to be ground. Also, a basket for carrying seed." (J)

HORN

The common name for any "musical instrument of the wind kind chiefly used in hunting, to animate the hunters and the dogs, to call the latter together." (M) "A horn to cheer the hounds with." (W)

Horn, c. 1800 print.

HORNBOOK

Not a book as we think of such today, but a single sheet of paper on which was printed the alphabet, the ten digits, and sometimes also simple rules for spelling, or the Lord's Prayer. The paper was mounted on wood and covered with a thin, protective sheet of horn, and the "book" used to instruct children in primary school classes. By the end of the first quarter of the nineteenth century, the hornbook still was "a copy of the alphabet set in a [wooden] frame, and covered with a thin plate of horn to prevent the paper from being thumbed to pieces by the children who were made to study it [but] it is now almost, if not quite, antiquated, as an instrument of elementary education." *Encyclopedia Americana* (Philadelphia, 1831). (See also BATTLEDORE.)

HORN OF PLENTY

(See CORNUCOPIA, Chapter 5.)

HORNPIPE

The name of a country dance, so-called from the instrument played to accompany its performance. "The instrument called the hornpipe [originated in Wales and] . . . consists of a wooden pipe, with holes at stated distances, and a horn at each end, the one to collect the wind blown into it by the mouth, and the other to convey the sound as produced by the performer." *Encyclopedia Americana* (Philadelphia, 1831).

HOROLOGIUM

The general name for instruments to measure the hours, as a "watch, clock, dial," (M) each of which see.

HORSE

A contemporary description, adapted from the French *cheval* for horse; of a part or a piece of furniture that held or supported something else; hence, sawhorse, clothes-horse, towel horse. The word was applied to those pieces, the base of which simulated four feet. (See also HORSE FIRE SCREEN.)

HORSE BELL

Small bells, usually of iron, suspended from a leather thong or neck harness, or fitted in a metal arch or bar above the collar, ordinarily used to enable an owner to ascertain the whereabouts of his horse. "In the morning early the man who had gone astray the day before found his way to the Camp, by the Sound of the Bells that were upon the Horses' Necks." William Byrd, *History of the Dividing Line* [1729], (Richmond, 1866). (See also BELL.)

HORSE BRASSES

The collector's all-inclusive term for metal harness ornaments.

HORSE FIRE SCREEN

The term Hepplewhite used to describe the hinged fire screen set between two standards with two feet each. (See CHEVAL, FIRE SCREEN HORSE.)

HORSE FURNITURE

(See HARNESS FURNITURE. See also SADDLE; see under trade descriptions in Chapter 3, HORSE'S MILLINER, SADDLER'S IRONMONGER, TREE MAKER.)

HORSE SCREEN

(See FIRE SCREEN.)

HORSESHOE CHAIR

(See COMPASS CHAIR.)

HORSESHOE TABLE

(See KIDNEY TABLE, SOCIAL TABLE.)

HORTUS HYEMALIS

A contemporary synonym for the *Hortus Siccus* or *Herbarium, qq.v.*: "[on a visit] to Mr. Evelyn, he read to me very much of his discourse, he hath been many years and now is about, Gardenage; which will be a most noble and pleasant piece. He showed me his 'Hortus Hyemalis'; leaves laid up in a book of several plants kept dry, which preserve colour, however, and look very finely, better than an Herball. In fine, a most excellent person he is, and must be allowed a little for his conceitedness, he may well be so, being a man so much above others." Samuel Pepys, *Diary,* November 5, 1665.

HORTUS SICCUS

A dry garden or the name given to a collection of specimens of plants carefully dried and preserved. (See also HERBAL, HERBARIUM.)

HOSTER

A cant term, perhaps a variation of hoist, to raise high, for "a kind of jug without a handle," (H) a drinking cup.

HOST'S POT

(See SHOT FLAGON.)

HOT-WATER PAN

A sensible alternative to the Warming Pan, *q.v.,* and similar to it in basic design, the only difference being that a rather flat, round copper, brass, or pewter bottle replaced the perforated-top ember pan. The hot-water pan, by not using coals, obviated the problem of fumes. (See also VIRGIN.)

HOURGLASS

The common term for a timepiece, also called a sandglass. Two cone-shaped bottles of the same size and capacity, joined mouth to mouth with wax or cement and fixed in a frame of wood or metal, were used as a device for measuring a designated number of minutes or hours, the time needed for the sand to run from one bottle into the other having been predetermined. The most common measure was for one hour; however, glasses for three-hour and longer periods were made as were those to mark shorter times. "July 23, 1644. Then he called the master of the Bristol ship, and told him if he would yield himself, all his should have what belonged to them, and turning up the half hour glass, [required] to have his answer by that time of half an hour." John Winthrop, *Journal, History of New England* (Boston, 1825).

Today's three-minute kitchen egg timer is an example of a "short" hourglass still in use. The accurate hourglass was a tribute to the glass-blower's craft, not to be discarded if it could be kept in repair: "All sorts of Hour-Glasses to be made or mended on Reasonable terms by James Maxwell at his House in Water Street, near the Town House." *Boston News-Letter,* September 17, 1716. (See also WATCH GLASS.)

Early-eighteenth-century hourglass in wooden frame.

HOUSE BELLS AND PULLS

These were the means by which the master or mistress in an upper chamber or parlor signaled to servants belowstairs. Bell pulls, hung below the ceiling molding, were attached by wires to small house bells. The pulls, varying in width from three to five inches and averaging three or more feet in length were embroidered in overall designs of stylized flowers, leaves, and birds; in crewelwork or flame-stitch patterns, on silk, velvet, or fine linen, and sometimes were embellished with gold or silver threads or tassels. Lovely as the pulls were, the mechanism they were intended to activate did not always work well, as an advertisement by a famed Philadelphia cabinetmaker indicates. As did many craftsmen of the period, Elliott, remembered today mainly for fine looking glasses, also kept a retail store and provided repair services.

"Imported from London and to be sold by John Elliott, Cabinetmaker, in Chestnut-Street, the corner of Fourth Street, a Neat Assortment of Looking Glasses, viz. Piers, Sconces and Dressing Glasses, Joiners and Sadlers Furniture Ec. Fine Waisted patterns for Jackets, thread and cotton stockings. Looking Glasses new quick silver'd, or framed, in the neatest manner. He supplies people with new glasses to their own frames, and gives ready money for broken Looking-glasses and compleatly fixes up House bells and Cabbin bells in the neatest and most convenient manner as done at London, with cranks and wires, which are not liable to be put out of order, as those done with pullies. N.B. Said Elliott has on hand a few books, entitled, Second Thoughts Concerning War." *Pennsylvania Gazette* (Philadelphia), December 30, 1756.

HOUSE CLOCK

If not the only one, the main clock in a house by which other timepieces were set. "He had made it a rule for many years of his life—on the first Sunday night of every month throughout the whole year —to wind up a large house-clock, which we had standing on the backstairs head." Laurence Sterne, *Tristram Shandy,* Book I. (See also LONG-CASE CLOCK.)

HUBBLE-BUBBLE

A cant term for the water pipe or Hookah, *q.v.*

HUMBUZ, HURR

Cant terms for a kind of Rattle, *q.v.,* or child's toy made of a "thin piece of wood with a notched edge, which, being swung round swiftly on a string, yields a humming or buzzing sound." (H)   (See also GIG.)

HUM GLASS

A common early term for a kind of small cordial glass or taster, derived from the name of a popular and potent mixture of warmed ale and spirits.

> *They say that Canary sack must dance*
> *again*
> *To the apothecarys, and be sold*
> *For physic in hum glasses and thimbles.*
>
>   John Shirley, *Wedding*

C. 1825 hum glass or taster.

HUMMING TOP

A child's plaything, "a large hollow wooden top which makes a loud humming noise when it spins." (H)

HUMSTRUM

A colloquialism for the Jew's Harp, *q.v.*

HUNT BOARD, HUNTING BOARD, HUNT TABLE

Collector's terms, now used to enhance any high sideboard table, made with a center drawer and cupboard spaces at each side; and applied to such simply made pieces, usually of pine or walnut, found in southern areas. Needless to say, such a serving table would have been referred to in the eighteenth and early nineteenth centuries as a side table or sideboard; nor should it have to be pointed out to the sensible collector that the plain, poorly made, undecorated sideboards, usually called hunt boards today, are country pieces from farm kitchens, the original owners of which could scarcely have afforded the time or accoutrements of hunting, and assuredly could not have afforded to have built a separate, special sideboard to be used only on hunt days.

HUNT CUP, HUNTER'S CUP, HUNTING CUP

Collector's terms for the drinking cup or trophy, also called a Stirrup Cup, *q.v.*

HUNTING CHAIR

"A temporary resting-place for one that is fatigued, as hunters generally are." This was a type of easy chair "stuffed all over, except the legs, which are of mahogany, [with a front frame made to slide out] even with the seat of the chair" to support a loose cushion. Thomas Sheraton, *The Cabinet Dictionary* (London, 1803).

HUNTING HORN

(See HORN.)

HURDLE

"Sticks woven together, a cradle." (W)

HURLBAT

In weaponry, "an old kind of weapon, a whirlbat." (W)

HURRICANE GLASS

A New England colloquialism for the Candle Shade, *q.v.*

HUTCH

A term from the old French *huche* or *husche* for chest, applied to various containers, usually made of wood, given its exact meaning according to use, as a designation for bin, box, chest, or cupboard, as hutch table, for example.

HUTCH CHAIR TABLE, HUTCH TABLE

(See CHAIR TABLE.)

Two views of the hutch chair table of pine and maple. (Courtesy, Connecticut Historical Society, Inc.)

Hutch table. (Courtesy, Antiquarian and Landmarks Society, Inc.)

HYDRAULICON

Literally, a water-organ; a musical instrument "acted upon by water, the invention of which is said to be of higher antiquity than that of the wind organ." *Encyclopedia Americana* (Philadelphia, 1831).

HYDROMETER

One of the many "philosophical" or "scientific" devices developed in the eighteenth century, sometimes also called a proof glass. Its use is explained by two manufacturers: "Joseph Donegal from Philadelphia . . . makes and sells Hydrostatical Glass Bubbles, and Hydrometers for proving spirits . . . and glasses for making useful and entertaining experiments." *New York Daily Advertiser,* October 17, 1787. "Joseph Gatty, Artist from Italy . . . makes and sells . . . curious Glass Hydrometers for assaying spirits, which shew the actual strength with the Greatest precision, and are not liable to be corroded; also several new Philosophical instruments of his own invention." *The Diary, or Evening Register* (New York), November 3, 1794. (See also AEROMETER.)

HYDROSTATIC BALL, -BUBBLE
(See HYDROMETER.)

HYDROSCOPE

The contemporary term for "an instrument used for the measuring of time. The hydroscope was a kind of water-clock, consisting of a cylindrical tube, conical at bottom; the cylinder was graduated, or marked out with divisions, to which the top of the water becoming successively contiguous, as it trickled out at the vortex of the cone, pointed out the hour." (M) (See also CLEPSYDRA, HOURGLASS.)

HYGROMETER

The name for a "machine whereby to measure the degrees of dryness or moisture of the air." (M)

HYGROSCOPE

Another name for the HYGROMETER.

I

IDLE-BACK
A cant term, as was its counterpart lazy-back, for the Kettle Tilter, *q.v.*, because those who used it presumably were too indolent to lift the kettle from the pothook.

ILLUMINATED MANUSCRIPTS
The general term describing those manuscripts "adorned with paintings illustrating the text, or in which the initial letters were decorated with flourishes or gilding. This kind of bibliographical luxury was not unknown to the ancients, and the art of illumination was much practiced by the monks . . . We still see traces of this practice in the ornamenting of initial letters in printed books." *Encyclopedia Americana* (Philadelphia, 1831).

IMAGE, IMAGERIE
Popular synonyms for a Portrait or Likeness, *qq.v.*

IMAGE TOYS
A contemporary term for late eighteenth-century and early nineteenth-century Staffordshire figures, used as mantelpiece and shelf ornaments. (See also COTTAGE FIGURES, CHIMNEY ORNAMENTS, GARNITURE SET.)

IMPERIAL DINING TABLE
One of the late eighteenth-century terms for the dining table which could be extended by insertion of additional leaves or boards. (See also TELESCOPE DINING TABLE.)

INCENSE BURNER
Small brass- or iron-footed bowls fitted with pierced covers, used for "perfumes to burn," as incense was called in the seventeenth and eighteenth centuries.

INDIAN DRUM
The native percussion instrument often called a tom-tom. "The Instrument they danct to was an Indian-drum, that is, a large Gourd with a Skin bract tort over the Mouth of it." William Byrd, *History of the Dividing Line* [1728–29] (Richmond, 1866).

INDIAN QUILLWORK
The general term for certain native Indian wares, including baskets, small boxes, belts, and decorations on other articles of apparel, made from porcupine quills arrange in patterns. Porcupine "spines or quills are much used among the Indians to ornament different articles of dress; they dye them of various colors, in a very permanent manner." *Encyclopedia Americana* (Philadelphia, 1831).

INGLENOOK
The seventeenth-century fireside or chimney-corner seat; a settle or high-backed bench set within the side walls of the ancient, wide fireplace. As the chimney or fireplace became narrower and lower, the inglenook or chimney seat was moved out into the room. (See also SETTLE.)

INK BOTTLE
The container of metal, pottery, or glass in which prepared ink was sold or stored, and from which a sufficient amount was poured into the Inkpot or Inkwell, *qq.v.* These usually had a pouring spout and were stopped with a cork.

Pottery ink bottles.

Small brass incense burner.

Combination glass ink bottle and stand.

INKHORN

A small, cylindrical tapering or horn-shaped container, similar, except in size, to the larger gunpowder horn. Made of horn or varnished leather, both of which often were decorated with silver insets or rims; or of silver, pewter, or tin, to hold writing ink in powder form. "I told her in my Judgment she writ incomparably well [and gave her] a Quire of Paper to write upon . . . accompanied with a good leather Inkhorn, a stick of Sealing Wax and 200 Wafers in a little Box." Samuel Sewall, *Diary,* January 19, 1722. (See also INK in Chapter 7, INKWELL.)

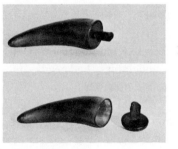
Inkhorn.

INK PAPERS

During the Colonial and Federal periods ink commonly was purchased and stored in powder form until needed for use, when the required amount was mixed with water in an Inkwell, *q.v.,* or any small container serving as such. "Ship by the earliest opportunity, 6 papers best Ink Powder [and] a box of largest wafers." Order from Robert C. Nicholas, Esq. 6 September, 1768, Williamsburg. Frances Mason, *John Norton and Sons, Merchants of London and Virginia* (Richmond, 1935). The spirals, skewers, or flat packets were colored papers; many were block-printed in a variety of designs and usually carried the name mark or label of the stationer-supplier; they often were re-used to line small trinket boxes or desk trunks. Modern fluid writing ink was invented by Henry Stevens in 1836 and sold in bottles. (See also INK BOTTLE, INKHORN, INKWELL.)

INKPOT

The small writing-table accessory more often called an Inkwell, *q.v.,* today; the pottery, porcelain, stone, glass, or metal vessel just large enough to hold the amount of prepared ink needed at a time. "A fresh supply of Drugs, Medicines, Groceries, Paints,

Eighteenth-century carved soapstone inkwells.

Late-eighteenth-century pewter inkwell with rests for quills. (Courtesy, Antiquarian and Landmarks Society, Inc.)

Pewter inkwell.

C. 1800 pewter inkwell with blown-glass well insert.

C. 1820 painted inkwell. (Courtesy, Antiquarian and Landmarks Society, inc.)

C. 1840 pottery inkwells.

Dye-Stuffs, Ec., Ec. Just received from New York, and selling on the most reasonable terms, by Joseph Lynde, [including] Ink-powder, Sealing Wax, Wafers, Quills, Pounce Boxes, Ink Pots . . ." *American Mercury* (Hartford, Connecticut), November 1, 1815. (See also INKSTAND, STANDISH.)

INKSTAND
The common term during the eighteenth century for the writing-table furnishing, earlier called a Standish, *q.v.* (See also INK BOTTLE, INKHORN, INKPOT.)

INKWELL
Another term for the Inkpot, *q.v.;* the well or dish for ink included in the desk Ink-stand or Standish, *qq.v.*

INSCRIPTION
The title or "writing carved, engraved, or affixed to anything, to give a more distinct knowledge of it, or to transmit some important truth to posterity." (M)   (See also EMBLEM.)

INTAGLIO
A general term for engraving on stone, used specifically to designate those "precious stones on which are engraved the heads of great men, inscriptions, and the like; such as we frequently see set on rings, seals, Ec." (M) (See also CAMEO, DEATH'S-HEAD RING, MOURNING RING.)

INVALID CHAIR
Another contemporary name for the Machine Chair, *q.v.* (See also GO-CHAIR.)

IRISH CHIPPENDALE
The collector's term for any elegant, heavily carved furniture made in Ireland from 1750 to 1800.

IRON BACK
A contemporary term for the cast-iron fire or chimney back, "To be sold by Nathaniel French . . . Figur'd Iron Backs." *American Weekly Mercury* (Philadelphia), September 25, 1735.

IRON FURNITURE
We are inclined to think of iron furniture in terms of the popular late-nineteenth-century lawn chairs and tables, bedsteads, and hall stands; iron, however, was used throughout the Colonial period, albeit not in as great quantities, for some furniture, particularly small stands and chests or lockers, and even bedsteads. "Oct. 3 [1733] I hear of iron bedsteads in London. Dr. Massey told me of them Sat. Sept. 29, 1733. He said they were used on account of the buggs, which have, since the great fire, been very troublesome in London." Thomas Hearne, *Reliquiae Hearnianae.*

IRONING BOX
(See BOX IRON.)

ITALIAN IRON
An early synonym for the Goffering Iron, *q.v.,* because this utensil for fluting or crimping cloth originated in Italy. (See also TALLY IRON.)

J

JACK

The name of "instruments which supply the place of a boy; foot boys, who had the common name of Jack given them, were kept to turn the spit, and when instruments were invented for these services they, too, were called jacks." (J) "My poor wife rose by five o'clock in the morning, before day, and went to market and bought fowles and many other things for dinner . . . The chine of beef was down also before six o'clock, and my own jacke, of which I was doubtful, do carry it very well." Samuel Pepys, *Diary*, January 13, 1662–63. Also a common cant term for the flagon made of hard polished leather. (See also AMPULLA, SMOKE-JACK.)

Black leather jack or flagon. (Courtesy, Antiquarian and Landmarks Society, Inc.)

JACK BED

A term used to describe the one-post type of stump bedstead, built into a corner. The location obviated the need for two side rails and three of the posts ordinarily used. The one post was called a jack because it served to lift and hold the two rails.

JACKKNIFE

A contraction of earlier colloquialisms, "Jack-a-Legs, and Jack-Lag-knife," (H) both of which referred to a large clasp knife enclosing not only a cutting blade but a hook and other miniature tools; hence, this was a Jack, *q.v.*, or tool, that could be carried on the leg, in a sheath or attached pocket. "On week-day evenings he used to have his jack-knife in active play in [the chimney] corner, and whistles and pop-guns and squirrel-traps for us youngsters grew under his hand." Harriet Beecher Stowe, *Old Town Folks* (Boston, 1869).

JACK ROLL

(See WELL-WINDER.)

JACOB'S STAFF

Another name for the cross-staff, a mathematical instrument for taking heights and distances.

JACQUARD

The name given the pattern-weaving loom invented by Joseph Marie Jacquard (1752–1854) in France in 1800. It was used in America and England after 1850, the year it first was exported. The jacquard weave or design was a substitute for Brocade, *q.v.*, under TEXTILES at the end of this section.

JAGGER

A contemporary term for the Jagging Iron, *q.v.*, or pastry wheel.

JAGGING IRON

In kitchenware, this was the pastry wheel, crimper, or decorator, so called because the disc was of iron, and its outer edge was made to cut jags or notches in the paste.

Jagging iron. (Courtesy, Antiquarian and Landmarks Society, Inc.)

JAMB, JAUM, JAUMB

The side posts of a door or fireplace.

JAMB HOOK

The horizontal S- or U-shaped hook set in the jamb beside the fireplace to hold the fire tongs, shovel, poker, brush; a synonym for Holdfast, *q.v.*

JAPANNED WARE, JAPAN WORK

(See in Chapter 7.)

JARDINIERE

The term from the French word for a flower stand, used during the eighteenth and the early nineteenth centuries for a handsome form of what generally today is called a plant stand; a kind of bench or set of open shelves in tiers. "These articles are appendages to drawing rooms, boudoirs, Ec., and may be executed with every variety of taste and elegance agreeable to the rooms they are intended for . . . in mahogany partly gilt; in rosewood." George Smith, *A Collection of Designs for Household Furniture* (London, 1808). Today, the term often is applied, rather loosely, to any outer pot or container for plants.

JAR

A term, from the Arabic *jarrah,* for an earthenware water vessel, usually cylindrical in form, and without spout or handle. The term is also used for any similarly shaped stoneware or glass container for water, wine, or oil.

Blown-glass storage jars with tin tops.

Ginger jar with blue decoration.

JAVELIN

In weaponry, "a sort of spear, five feet and a half long, the shaft of wood, with a steel point." (M)   A kind of "dirk, spear, half-pike." (W)   (See also HALBERD.)

JELLY GLASS

Jelly was a dessert, "a transparent fizzy broth, a sweetmeat." (W)   The glass was a dessert dish or cup, wide at the rim, narrowing toward the base and thus similar to the Syllabub Glass, *q.v.* "Removed from the store kept by Mr. Henry William Stiegel . . . for sale of the American manufacture . . . jelly and cillibut glasses, with and without handles . . ." *New-York Gazette and Weekly Mercury,* February 8, 1773.

JENNY-QUICK

A cant term for the "Italian-iron." (H) (See also GOFFERING IRON.)

JEWELRY

(See separate listing at end of this chapter.)

JEW'S HARP

Originally, this was more accurately called a jaw harp, for which gewgaw was a synonym. The later term apparently is a corruption in conversation for the small musical instrument made of brass or iron in the shape of a lyre, with a springy steel tongue fixed to the base or closed end of the lyre frame. The frame is held between the teeth, the metal tongue struck with the finger; gradations in tone are caused by altering the size of the

Wrought-iron-and-steel Jew's harp.

cavity of the player's mouth. "Charles Sigourney Has imported . . . from Liverpool an invoice of Hardware Goods [including] brass sleeve links, Brass and Iron jews harps, brass & steel thimbles, Red morocco pocket books, plated stirrups and bits . . ." *American Mercury* (Hartford, Connecticut), February 7, 1811. (See also GEWGAW, JEW'S TRUMP).

JEW'S TRUMP
The sixteenth- and seventeenth-century term for the Jew's Harp, *q.v.,* popular with emigrants from Scotland and the Northern Counties of England.

JIGGER
A cant term for an earthenware dish used in "toasting cheese." (H) (See also CHEESE PLATE.)

JIGGUMBOBS
Another term for toys, trinkets, "knickknacks." (H) (See also KNACKS.)

JIMCRACKS, JYMIAN
The same as Knickknacks, *q.v.* Jim was a cant word for something small, bright, or neat; hence, the burglar's jimmy or jimmyiron was a small, slender bar or rod with which doors or windows were forced.

JIMMAL
A form of joint, or gimmal ring. (See also GIMBAL.)

JINGLE-BOY, JINGLE-JACK
A popular term for the small leather Blackjack, *q.v.,* or leather drinking cup, decorated with bells. The jingling of the bells presumably added to merriment and at the same time notified the tavernkeeper that his customers were ready for another round. "They have little leather Jacks, tipped with silver, and hung with small silver bells . . . these are called Gyngle-Boyes, to ring peales of drunkenness." Decker, *English Villaines Seven Times Pressed to Death.*

JINGLEJANGLES
"Trinkets." (H)

JOINED STOOL, JOINT STOOL
A stool framed by joinery work, and first "so called in distinction to stools rudely formed from a single block." (H) Generally, a rectangular seat supported on four turned legs, connected by stretchers, and used at the dining table before chairs or back stools became common for this purpose.

Joined stool. (Courtesy, Antiquarian and Landmarks Society, Inc.)

JOINT RING
A synonymous term for the Gimbal, *q.v.,* or gimmal ring; a lover's token, an engagement or wedding ring, as inferred from Emilia's declaration that *I would not do such a thing for a joint-ring.* Shakespeare, *Othello,* IV, 3.

JONATHAN
A colloquialism for "the instrument used by smokers to light their pipes with. It is a piece of iron, of the size of a small poker, fitted at one end with a handle of wood, and having at the other a protuberance or transverse bar of iron, which is heated." (H) (See also EMBER TONGS, PIPE TONGS.)

JORDAN, JORDEN

A colonial cant term for a metal, glass, or pottery "chamber pot," (W) a name given first to a "vessel formerly used by physicians and alchemists. It was very much in the form of a modern soda-water bottle, only the neck was larger, not much smaller than the body of the vessel. Later the term came to be used for a chamber pot." (H)

Jordan or chamber pot with oriental flower decoration. (Courtesy, Antiquarian and Landmarks Society, Inc.)

Staffordshire chamber pot. (Courtesy, Antiquarian and Landmarks Society, Inc.)

JOUJOU

The word, adopted from the French, literally translated means play-play, was used to describe "a plaything, consisting of two thin circular plates of wood, about two inches in diameter, united in the center by a cylinder one sixth of an inch long. Fixed to the cylinder is a cord about a yard long or more, which is fastened with a noose to the finger. If the cord is wound round the cylinder and the joujou is let fall, you can by a pull before the whole cord is wound off, make the joujou wind itself up entirely. In this the whole play consists, and yet, from 1796 to 1794, the joujou was so fashionable in France, that the highest persons were seen playing with it on their walks, and in society. The fashion also extended [to other nations]." *Encyclopedia Americana* (Philadelphia, 1831). The toy described is more familiarly known today by its trade mark name, Yo-yo.

JOURNAL

The general term for a diary, "an account of daily transactions" (J) by those who kept to the land, as well as "among seamen, a diary of occurrances that happen from noon to noon in the course of the voyage, as winds, weather, setting and shifting of sails, and remarking on the various distances run . . . everything material that happens to the ship or her crew is observed particularly in the journal." (M) Thus, William Bradford's *History of Plimouth* was a journal, and John Winthrop's *Journal* was later called *The History of New England*. Both were accounts of day-to-day happenings. Most were bound in manuscript form by their writers for the safekeeping of annual records and correspondence. (See also DIARY, LETTER CASE, TRAVELS.)

JOWL

A contemporary cant term for a "large, thick-sided earthenware dish." (H)

JUBBE

"A vessel for ale or wine," (H) perhaps a variation of Juste, *q.v.*

JUG

"A large drinking vessel with a swelling belly." (J) "Among the China [is] a large fine Jugg for Beer, to stand in the Cooler. I fell in love with it at first sight, for I thought it look'd like a fat jolly Dame, clean and tidy, with a neat blue and white Calico Gown on, good natur'd and lovely, and put me in mind of—somebody." (Benjamin Franklin from London to his wife at Philadelphia, February 19, 1758.) *The Writings of Benjamin Franklin,* ed., A. H. Smyth (New York, 1907).

Brown-and-cream-colored pottery storage jug. (Courtesy, Antiquarian and Landmarks Society, Inc.)

Stoneware jug with incised blue decoration. (Courtesy, Antiquarian and Landmarks Society, Inc.)

JULIAN CALENDAR
(See CALENDAR.)

JUNK BOTTLE
The thick, sturdy green or "black" glass ale or beer bottle, used by retailers and home-brewers alike. (Junk tobacco, however, meant a lump or piece of tobacco cut off in the sense of chunk, hence junk.) "Ariel Hancock Has lately received and offers the following Goods at very low and reasonable prices . . . [including] Junk Bottles, Corks . . . Junk Tobacco, Pipes, Shaving Soap,

Bar do . . . A handsome assortment of Crockery, Glass and Stone Ware." *American Mercury* (Hartford, Connecticut), May 20, 1816.

JUNKET
A colloquialism for "a long basket for fish." (H)

JUSTE
An old term for a tall jug or flask, "a kind of vessel with a wide body and a long straight neck." (H)

K

KAFF
A corruption in conversation from gaff, for "a gardener's hoe." (H)

KAIL POT, KALE POT
Kale is a kind of cabbage; hence a kale pot was a "metal pottage pot for cooking meat and cabbage together, etc. It is a heavy globular iron vessel holding three or four gallons, and resting on three little spikes. Both the item and the term are now [1847] nearly out of use." (H)

KALEIDOSCOPE
A parlor amusement for adults, and in more simplified forms, a plaything for children. This is "an instrument for creating and exhibiting an infinite variety of beautiful forms, pleasing the eye by an ever-varying succession of splendid tints and symmetrical forms, and enabling the observer to render permanent such as may appear appropriate for any branch of the ornamental arts. This instrument consists of a tin tube, containing two reflecting surfaces inclined to each other at any angle which is an aliquot part of 360°. The reflecting surfaces may be two plates of glass, plain or quicksilvered, or two metallic surfaces . . . The instrument may be either covered up with paper, or leather . . . with an aperture for the eye . . . If the object be put in motion, the

combination of images will likewise be . . . and new forms will successively present themselves, sometimes vanishing, sometimes emerging . . . beautiful tints are developed in succession, and the whole figure delights the eye." *Encyclopedia Americana* (Philadelphia, 1831).

KAS, KASSE

The incorrect, but popular spellings of the Dutch *kast* for wardrobe. The reference in America is to the large cupboards or wardrobes with heavy moldings and cornices and ball feet, made by Dutch settlers in New York and Pennsylvania. (See also AMBRY, CUPBOARD, PRESS, SCHRANK.)

KAST

(See KAS.)

KEACHER

A ladle; the term is derived from the old verb keach, to lade out water.

KEALER

The term for a small "shallow tub used for cooling liquids." (H) Perhaps the same as Keeler, *q.v.*

KEELER

Any shallow, wooden tub; a cooler or basin.

> *Then nightly sings the staring owl . . . a merry note,*
> *While greasy Joan doth keel the pot.*
>
> Shakespeare, *Love's Labour's Lost,* V, ii.

Keeler. (Courtesy, Antiquarian and Landmarks Society, Inc.)

(Joan was the common nickname given the scullery girl, as Jack was the name for any kitchen boy.)

KEEP

A general term for any "large basket," (H) specifically a food safe to preserve meat in summer.

KEEVER, KIVER

Two old words to describe any large tub, but especially the one used in brewing; perhaps a corruption of keep. The term also meant a "bumper of liquor." (H)

KEG

The common term for a small barrel, "commonly used for fish." (J)

KELP, KILP

Two colloquial terms for an iron. "A crook for a pot or kettle, to hang it over a fire." (H) A Pothook or small Trammel, *qq.v.*

KEMBING, KEMELIN, KIMNEL

All forms of the same word for "a brewing vessel or tub" (H) or any kind of large tub for household purposes.

KEN

A cant term for "a churn." (H)

KENTUCKY RIFLE

The popular name given the early-eighteenth-century flintlock improved by German and Swiss immigrants working in Pennsylvania. These European-trained smiths developed a longer barrel with a smaller than usual caliber and thus produced a light, accurate rifle exceedingly popular with scouts and pioneer settlers along the Kentucky and Ohio frontiers. The handsomely engraved decorations, silver, brass, and gold stock inlays were first added well after the Revolution. "I got rid of my gun, not very suitable in these parts where they seldom use anything except very long, rifled carbines, charged with a very small ball. These carbines are astoundingly accurate. [Chillicothe, Ohio]." Edouard de Montulé, *Voyage en Amérique* . . . (Paris, 1821).

412

KERCHIEF PRESS

The small screw-type Linen Press, *q.v.*, used to smooth neckerchiefs and bands.

KETCH

An old term for a kind of water "tub or barrel." (H) (See also KEACHER.)

KETTLE

"A kitchen vessel to boil things in," (W) as a water kettle, soup kettle, or Fish Kettle, *q.v.*, of iron, copper, or brass. "I told her I had some Chocolett, if shee would prepare it; which with the help of some milk, and a little brass kettle, she soon effected to my satisfaction." Sarah Kemble Knight, *Journal* [1704] (New York, 1825). "Charles Sigourney, Main Street, Has imported this season by the ships from London . . . [and] Liverpool, an extensive assortment of Hardware Goods [including] Cast and Sheet Iron Tea kettles, Sheet Iron Fish-Kettles, Sauce and Stew-pans, Chafing-Dishes . . ." *American Mercury* (Hartford, Connecticut), November 23, 1809.

Brass kettle with iron rim and bail. (Courtesy, Antiquarian and Landmarks Society, Inc.)

KETTLEDRUM

The popular name for the "drums whose bodies are brass [or copper], called tymbals or kettledrums, used among the horse [cavalry]. They are laid across the shoulders of the horse before the drummer, who, with a variety of odd gestures, beats them with two little iron bars round at the ends. These are often used in operas, oratorios, tragedies and concerts," (M) and when so employed are set on a floor standard.

Kettle drums illustrated in Bonanni's *Cabinetto Armonica* (Rome, 1723).

KETTLE-TILTER

A frame to hold the kettle, while it remained suspended from the crane, with a lever and handle so arranged that the kettle could be tilted and hot water poured without lifting the pot off the crane.

KIBBLE

A colloquialism for the wooden bucket kept at the well for drawing water. Also, the "stick with a curve or knot at one end used for several purposes, but generally for playing the game of nurspell, which is somewhat similar to golf, or trap-ball." (H)

KIBBLE AX

One of the house-yard tools, the small ax or hatchet, "used for cutting kibbles, or firewood." (H)

KID

A cant term for a small tub, but also "a pannier or basket" because originally it meant a faggot or withe "used to bind up other faggots" or some other bundle. (H) (See also KIP, KIT.)

KIDNEY TABLE

An elegant late-eighteenth-century design so called because in shape it resembled a stylized kidney. The table given this name by Thomas Sheraton in *Cabinet-Maker's and Upholsterer's Drawing-Book* (London, 1791–94), today would be called a kidney-shaped kneehole desk. The side sections each had five drawers. A sliding shelf set under the top surface could be pulled forward and used flat for writing, or tilted at an angle, held upright on its own folding stand, for ease in reading. Sheraton recommended such tables be made of "mahogany with the drawers cross-banded with grain laid up and down."

A kidney table and detail drawing from Thomas Sheraton's *The Cabinet-Maker and Upholsterer's Drawing-Book* (London, 1791–94).

KILDERKIN

The wooden keg or cask made to contain sixteen to eighteen gallons.

KIP, KIPE, KYPE

Variations of an old term, possibly related to kit, for "a wicker basket, containing nearly a bushel." (H)

KIP TREE

An old synonym for the Jack Roll *q.v.,* at the well.

KIST, CHIST

Common early variations of Chest, *q.v.*

KIT

A common synonym for a "wooden box or case, or a wooden vessel," (H) especially a box for containing tools, hence a tool kit, sewing kit, etc. and by extension because of its boxlike or hollow nature, "fiddler's kit" for a violin: "A small fiddle; fishtub, bottle, pail." (W)

KITCHEN

A common eighteenth-century synonym for a "tea urn or large kettle," (H) or any container in which food was cooked. (See, for example, TIN KITCHEN.)

KITCHEN TABLE

The contemporary term, other than Dresser or Dressing Board, *qq.v.,* for the fairly small, rectangular table, often fitted with a utensil drawer in the apron, and which is given the idealized name, Tavern Table, *q.v.,* by some collectors today.

KITCHEN TONGS

Good-sized iron or wooden tongs for lifting heavy or otherwise unwieldy objects, including large pieces of meat. (See also KNAPPERS.)

KITTISOL

An eighteenth- and early-nineteenth-century name for a type of Umbrella, *q.v.,* "[Before the Revolution] they had no knowledge of umbrellas to keep off rain, but some few used kittisols—an article as small as present parasols now—they were entirely to keep off rain from ladies. They were of oiled muslin, and were of various colours from India by way of England. They must have been but rare as they never appear in any advertisements [of the period]." John F. Watson, *Annals of Philadelphia* (Philadelphia, 1830).

KNACKS, KNICKKACKS

The common term for a "nice trick [device], toy, or top," (W) usually applied to small wooden articles; later used for any small ornament, and with the connotation of uselessness; faddishness. "By knickknacks I meant to include that heterogeneous assemblage of modern rubbish which, under the head of 'Dresden China' and various other names finds its way into the drawing room or boudoir. (I do not intend) to discourage the collection of really good specimens. The smallest examples of rare old porcelain, of ivory carving, of ancient metal-work, of enamels, of glass, of anything which illustrates good design and skillful workmanship should be acquired wherever possible, and treasured with the greatest care." Charles L. Eastlake, *Hints on Household Taste in Furniture, Upholstery and Other Details* (London, 1868). (See also BAUBLE, GEWGAW, TOY.)

Knack: The term for any "pretty trifle," and specifically for "a kind of figure or doll made of corn at the end of the harvest." (H)

KNAPPERS, KNEPPERS, KNIPPERS

Cant terms for the "wooden tongs" (H) used in the kitchen for removing vegetables from the pot; larger ones were used in drawing fabrics out of the dye pot, and others for pulling up weeds in the garden.

KNAPSACK

A large carryall or pouch usually carried on one's back as it is now; of canvas or leather. "Every free, able-bodied white male citizen . . . under forty-five shall . . . be enrolled in the militia, and shall, within six months therefrom, provide himself with a good musket or fire-lock, a sufficient bayonet and belt, two spare flints, and a knapsack, a pouch, with a box therein to contain not less than twenty four cartridges." *Connecticut Statutes* (Hartford, 1835).

KNEADING TROUGH

One of the terms for a wooden "trough to work paste in," (W) a simply made, rectangular box with removable lid, set on a frame. The dough for bread or cake was mixed in the trough or box, then molded on the lid. "The process of making household bread is thus: to a peck of meal add a handful of salt, a pint of yeast, and three quarts of water, cold in summer, hot in winter. The whole, being kneaded in a trough by the fire in winter, away from it in summer, and a little yeast added, will rise in about an hour; then mold it into loaves, and put it into the oven to bake." (M) (See also DOUGH BOX.)

KNEEHOLE FURNITURE

Any writing table or desk, chest, or dressing table made with the center section below the top board recessed, thus providing a "convenient opening, or an aperture in any piece of furniture to admit a person to sit, or write, or dress at." Thomas Sheraton, *The Cabinet Dictionary* (London, 1803).

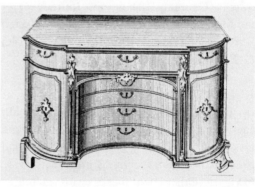

Kneehole or Buro dressing table illustrated in Thomas Chippendale's *Director* (London, 1762).

KNIFE

The general term for a small edged utensil or a "steel utensil to cut with." (W) Throughout the ages, the knife has been the most necessary of eating tools, surpassing, in all-round efficiency or multiplicity of use, both spoon and fork. As occasion demanded, the knife killed and dressed meat, cut it into pieces manageable in cooking, diced it into gobbets suitable for eating, and then conveyed "bites" to the mouth. (The fork was first introduced for individual use at table as a means of holding meat while it was cut.) Throughout the Colonial era, for the average person, and for those of sometimes well above average attainment, the knife continued to be the only essential tool with which to eat any solid food. "They generally boil the [sorrel] leaves in the water in which they cooked meat. Then they eat it alone or with meat. It is served on a platter and eaten with a knife." Peter Kalm [Philadelphia, 1749] *Travels in North America* (London, 1782).

Inn and tavernkeepers assumed wayfarers would carry their own knives with them, and so at times did the local gentry. "Traveled up to Solomon Hedge's, Esquire, one of his Majesty's Justices of the Peace in the county of Frederick . . . when we came to supper, there was neither a knife on the table nor a fork, to eat with; but as good luck would have it, we had knives of our own." (George Washington, Journey Over the Mountains, March 26, 1748.) *Collected Writings of George Washington*, ed., John G. Fitzpatrick.

KNIFE-AND-FORK SET

In the seventeenth and early eighteenth centuries, a combination set of knife and fork was an elegancy especially prized and needed by the traveling gentry. Sets were made of either two pieces with matching handles, or one utensil with a knife blade that folded out at one end and had a hinged fork at the other. Such sets were kept in cases for ease in carrying in one's pocket, purse, or muff. "July 25, 1718. I give her two cases with a knife and fork in each; one turtle shell tackling, the other long with ivory handles, squar'd. Cost 4s 6d." Samuel Sewall, *Diary*. (See also FORK, KNIFE.)

Wood- and bone-handled knives and forks. (Courtesy, Antiquarian and Landmarks Society, Inc.)

KNIFE-BLADE ANDIRONS

The collector's term for the andirons made with a thin, flat shank terminating in a brass finial.

KNIFE BOX

The more common eighteenth-century term for these handsome boxes of fine, highly polished mahogany, cherry, walnut, satinwood, or rosewood was knife case. These decorative cases were designed to stand on the sideboard, were made with top-hinged lids or covers, and enclosed fittings shaped to hold knives, forks, and spoons. Often in pairs, one to contain the knives, the second forks and/or spoons. Knife boxes were made in the Chippendale era, although he does not include designs for them in *The Gentleman and Cabinet-Maker's Director*. By the end of the century, however, they were commonly shown in design books; Sheraton included "a Side Board with Vase [urn-shaped] Knife Cases." *The Cabinet-Maker's and Upholsterer's Drawing-Book* (London, 1791–94). Many were inlaid with wood, ivory, and brass, or had silver cartouches for cyphers. Knife cases were ordered singly, and made in special sizes, as may have been the one requested by Justice William Reynolds, Yorktown, Virginia, from his London agents September 9, 1771: "Send 1 doz. Ivory handle table, & 1 doz. Dessert Knives & forks in a Mahogany Case with room for 1 doz. spoons, & a Carving knife and fork." Frances Mason, *John Norton and Sons, Merchants of London and Virginia* (Richmond, 1935).

KNIFE CASE

This was a contemporary synonym for the knife box and was so used in Hepplewhite's *Guide,* for that "piece of furniture the universal utility [of which] renders a particular description not necessary. They may be made of mahogany inlaid, or of Satin

Eighteenth-century knife boxes, mahogany crotch wood veneer, holly inlay. (Courtesy, Mr. and Mrs. Guy Mankin, Kent, Connecticut.)

Knife case closed, illustrated in Hepplewhite's *Guide* (London, 1794).

Knife case open, illustrated in Hepplewhite's *Guide* (London, 1794).

Knife case, illustrated in Hepplewhite's *Guide* (London, 1794).

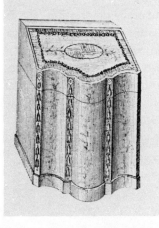

(wood), or other wood at pleasure." A. Hepplewhite, *The Cabinet-Maker and Upholsterer's Guide* (London, 1794). (See also KNIFE BOX.)

KNIFE TRAY

In appearance, more of a shallow, rectangular wooden box, made with a center divider which served also as a carrying handle; used to carry knives and forks to and fro between kitchen and dining room.

KNIFE URN

(See KNIFE BOX.)

KNITTING CUP

A contemporary cant term for the wedding bowl; a kind of loving cup used to pass wine around "immediately after the ceremony" (H) to members of the wedding party. A memento of the day, of turned hardwood, sometimes gilded; of pottery or porcelain, pewter, or silver, usually engraved with the name, initials, or arms of the two families, and with the date.

KNIVES

Knives were first manufactured in England in 1563. By the end of the Colonial period, social changes and skilled trade needs called for a multiplicity of knife designs and uses, some of which were listed by one Connecticut merchant: "Charles Sigourney, Main Street, has imported this season from London . . . and from Liverpool . . . A great variety of low priced table and dessert knives and forks and other cutlery; Pen knives, Barlow knives, Cutteaux; Cast Steel furriers' and skinners' knives, Straw knives, drawing knives; Butcher's, Cook's, Farmer's, Painter's, Book-Binder's and Shoemakers' knives, Cast Steel Bread knives, Mincing knives, Pruning and children's knives . . ." *American Mercury* (Hartford, Connecticut), November 23, 1809.

Bone: "Handles of knives, and several other useful articles are made of the bones of sheep, oxen, and other ruminating animals." *The Domestic Encyclopedia* (Philadelphia, 1821).

KNOP

The ancient form of knob, a word sometimes used for a small tub, or for anything round, such as a "knob, handle, or button," (H) as well as for the top part or finial of a spoon and for the collar, disc, or bulge used as a decoration on glass stems. "November 6, 1692. Joseph threw a knop of Brass and hit his sister Betty on the forehead and made it bleed and swell . . . for [this and] his playing at Prayer-time and eating when Return Thanks I whipt him pretty smartly." Samuel Sewall, *Diary*.

L

LABEL

The ancient term for a tassel, later given any name plate. (See under ARMORIAL BEARINGS, at back of this section.)

LABELED DECANTER

The collector's term for the glazed pottery, porcelain, flint-glass decanter or liquor bottle engraved with a self-label designating its thus predestined content, such as rum, gin, sherry, port. Often the name was added to a bottle in a wheel-engraved cartouche or embellishment of scrolls, flowers, vines, or leaves—grape being especially favored, although the hop vine was an obvious choice for ale bottles; the apple blossom and leaf for cider, etc. Most of those to be found date from the second half of the eighteenth century, or later. Colored-glass decanters with self-labels, such as those made at the Bristol factories, are early nineteenth-century examples, especially those with labels in gold or white. (See also BOTTLE TICKET, DECANTER LABEL.)

Labeled decanter.

LADE-GORN, LADE-PAIL

Old synonyms for the more familiar piggin, this was a wooden pail with one stave longer than the rest, forming a handle; used for drawing water from a spring or a large cistern. "A pail with which to ladle water." (H)

LACE BOX

A contemporary description of a fairly shallow, square, or rectangular box with a hinged lid; often handsomely carved or inlaid. These were used to hold laces or other small clothing accessories, and are often today confused with so-called Bible Boxes or Desk Boxes, *qq.v.*

LACQUER-WORK

(See JAPANNING, Chapter 7.)

LADDER-BACK CHAIR

The collector's term for a chair, the back of which is formed by a series of slats between the uprights. (See also in Chapter 5.)

LADIES' DRESSING TABLES

The late-eighteenth-century description for a table or chest fitted with a top section or drawer to hold a looking glass and toilet articles. Hepplewhite, for example, showed four designs, "of various constructions and conveniences; the partitions in which are adapted for combs, powders, essences, pincushions, and other necessary equipage. The glasses rise on hinges in the front, and are supported by a foot, affixed in the back . . . [They] may be made of mahogany, or of other, inferior wood." A. Hepplewhite, *The Cabinet-Maker and Upholsterer's Guide* (London, 1794). The designs illustrated were for tables with hinged tops that opened to show the partitioned sections; a four-drawer chest with a similar top part; a table with drawers at either side. (See also RUDD'S TABLE, TOILETTE.)

LADLE

A large Water Dipper, Spoon, or Scoop, *qq.v.*, "a vessel or receptacle" (W) of wood, pewter or other metal, or glazed pot-

Early-eighteenth-century ladle with hanger. (Courtesy, Antiquarian and Landmarks Society, Inc.)

C. 1700 wooden ladle, carved handle, (Courtesy, Antiquarian and Landmarks Society, Inc.)

Burl ladle or dipper. (Courtesy, Antiquarian and Landmarks Society, Inc.)

Gourd ladle or dipper. (Courtesy, Antiquarian and Landmarks Society, Inc.)

tery, sometimes made from a gourd. (See also CALABASH.)

LADY'S CABINET

A contemporary synonym for the Cheveret, *q.v.*

LADY'S WRITING FIRE SCREEN

(See WRITING FIRE SCREEN.)

LAMP

The all-inclusive term for any "vessel con-

Lamps illustrated in Hepplewhite's *Guide* (London, 1794).

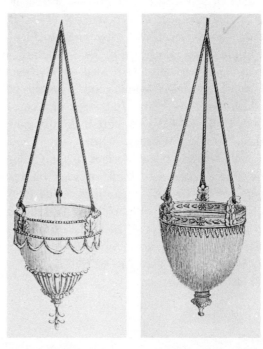

Blown-glass hall lamp with glass smoke shade, brass chain and fittings from 1795 Connecticut entrance hall. (Courtesy, Antiquarian and Landmarks Society, Inc.)

taining oil, with a lighted wick," (M) of wood, iron, pewter, tin, silver, glass, porcelain, or pottery.

LANCET CLOCK
The popular term for a nineteenth-century mantel-shelf clock case, so named because the top or spire of the case resembled the shape of the surgeon's instrument or appeared similar to the early English-Gothic pointed or lancet arch.

LANDSCAPE
In art, a "picture representing a [certain] extent of space, with the various objects in it . . . a prospect of a country." (J) "If thou should meet with—by any Accident cheap a Good Landscape or Two—the prospect Geometrically Extended—Well and beautifully shaded—and good painting in which thou may take Judgment of Somebody of Skill—I did not care if thou bought them—for my Garden Closett—as Thou Remembers my begun designs of the Chimney Piece there . . . think of such [in regard to] the figures, rivers, hills, fields Ec." (Isaac Norris of Philadelphia to Isaac Norris II, April 10, 1722.) Historical Society of Pennsylvania, *Norris Letter-Book, 1716–30*. (See also PROSPECTS, WINTERPIECE.)

LANDSKIP
A contemporary spelling for landscape; and thus the term to describe any drawing, painting, or engraving depicting inland scenery from a certain aspect. (See advertisement quoted under PAINTER, Chapter 3.)

LANGELL, LAWNGELLE
A cant term from long and ell for a long blanket; also a measure.

LANTERN, LANTHORN
The term from the French *Lanterne,* and the Latin *Lanterna,* for "a well-known invention for shewing light in the night." (M) This was, and is, a "transparent case

Multipurpose lanterns. Each could be carried, hung from a beam, or set on a table to provide light for colonists from 1700 to 1810.

for a candle," (J) anciently made with sides formed of thinly shaved, and thus translucent, sheets of horn. Later, glass or mica were used in place of the horn. The open framework, whether rectangular, round, square, oval, or multisided, was made of wood, lead, tin, sheet iron, brass, copper, or silver; the quality of workmanship and the superiority of the metal usually were determined by the use, or place in which the light was needed. (See also BARN LANTERN, DARK LANTERN, ENTRY LIGHT, HALL LANTERN, PAUL REVERE LANTERN, POCKET LANTERN.)

LANTERN CLOCK

The first English domestic clock developed in the early seventeenth century was given this name because its shape was similar to that of the dome-top lanterns of the time. Made to stand on a shelf or to hang on a wall, brass lantern clocks were imported here throughout the Colonial period. Care should be taken in ascribing too early a date to many examples found, however, for this type of clock was manufactured in England as late as the early nineteenth century and sold here. Basically it was a chamber clock equipped with a bell to strike the hours and was driven by weights; the works were enclosed in a rectangular frame surmounted by an arched or dome top capped by an ornamental finial. Clocks of this type gradually were superseded by the clock with a pendulum. Other collector's names, sometimes given the lantern clock, include bedpost, birdcage and bracket clock.

LANTERN-LEET, LEET

The horn or glass at "the sides of a lantern." (H) Leet was an Early English colloquialism for light, and so used in the colonies as it had been at home.

LARDER

The term to describe the piece of nineteenth-century kitchen furniture also known as a meat-safe; in form, a standing cupboard with ventilated front and sides made of louvres, pierced tin panels, or boards with small holes drilled through, often in decorative patterns. Wrought-iron hooks held the meat suspended from the top board. (See also BACON CUPBOARD, HANGING SAFE, PANTRY.)

LARDING STICK

In the kitchen, a kind of skewer of hard wood or iron used for larding fowls or roasts, and so "an instrument for piercing holes." (H)

LARK-SPIT

The specific eighteenth-century term for the smallest of the Bird-Spits, q.v., used at the kitchen hearth for any small dainty to be roasted: "Cut your veal steaks thin, season them with pepper and salt, and sweet herbs; wash them over with egg; put two steaks together, and lard them with bacon; wash them over with melted butter, and wrap them in white papers butter'd; roast them on a lark-spit . . ." E. Smith, *The Compleat Housewife* (London, 1741).

LATCH PAN

In kitchenware, another name for the Dripping Pan, q.v. Latch here is derived from the French verb *lecher,* to smear, with the connotation of dripping into, as when Oberon asked,

But hast thou yet latch'd the Athenian's eyes
With the love-juice, as I bid thee do? . . .
What has thou done?
Thou has mistaken quite,
And laid the love-juice on some true-love's sight.

> Shakespeare, *A Midsummer Night's Dream,* III, ii.

LATTICE, LEVESELE

A kind of hinged shutter or screen hung from the ceiling or lintel, made of crossed strips of wood or sometimes simply of equally spaced bars or spindles. The lattice anciently was the sign of a tavern. Chaucer mentions the "gay levesele" of the inn as a sign of the wine there sold. Throughout the Colonial period the lattice continued to be part of the architecture expected of a tavern, used as a kind of open shutter before the door or window, and especially in front of the serving bar itself to separate the tapster from his more exuberant customers.

LAVABO
(See EWER AND BASIN.)

LAVER
"A washing-vessel." (W) A common contemporary term for the wash basin. (See also BASIN, and EWER AND BASIN.)

LAZY-BACK
(See IDLE-BACK, KETTLE-TILTER.)

LEAD
The term, from the metal of which they were manufactured, given to "(1) a vat for dyeing, Ec.; (2) a kitchen boiler or other large pot." (H)

LEADING STAFF
The contemporary term for a parade marshal's baton. "Monday, October 6, 1701. Artillery trains this afternoon . . . inform'd the Company I was told the Hallberds, Ec. were borrowed . . . I understand the Leading-Staff was so, and ask'd their Acceptance of a Half-Pike which they very kindly did . . . the pike will stand me fourty shillings being headed and shod with silver." Samuel Sewall, *Diary*. (See also HALBERD, PIKE.)

LEADING STRINGS
A synonym for Dading Strings, *q.v.* "The duck does not take to water with a surer instinct than the [Cape Cod boy]. He leaps from his leading-strings into the shrouds, it is but a bound from his mother's lap to the masthead." Henry David Thoreau, *Cape Cod* (Boston, 1865.)

LEAD PENCIL
A sharpened length of lead, set in a holder, and used for drawing. "You must first get your black-lead sharpened finely, and put fast into quills, for your rude and first draught." Henry Peacham, *Drawing*. (See also HAIR PENCIL, PENCIL.)

Black Lead: "A mineral found in the lead-mines, much used for pencils." (J)

LEAR QUILLS
The term, from the Old English *lear,* meaning hollow or empty, for "the very small quills, such as are used to wind yarn on." (H)

LEATHER BOTTLE
(See BORACCHIO, BLACKJACK, JACK, and see also quotation under DRINKING HORN.)

LEAVEN KIT
The name for the "vessel or large bowl" (H) of wood, metal, or earthenware in which batter for small amounts of bread or cake was prepared. (See also DOUGH BOX, KIT, KNEADING TROUGH.)

LECTERN, LECTORNE, LETTERON
"A reading-desk, or stand." (H) A contemporary term for an inclined or sloping board, sometimes with a box or bin beneath to hold books or papers, set on a pedestal. (See also DESK, DESK BOX.)

LEECH, LETCH
A term for the tub or "vessel used in making lye." (H)

LEETS
A common term here for windows or lights, especially among those of Scots-Irish descent who had emigrated to the Southern colonies. (See also LANTERN-LEET.)

LETTER CASE
A leather desk folder, "a book to post letters, Ec. in." (W) (See under POCKETBOOK.)

LETTER COPIER
A form of pantograph with a writing board and a case for storage or carriage greatly appreciated by men such as Franklin and others who maintained extensive correspondence in an age when all letters and records

were handwritten. "Innes's improved Press for Copying Letters and other Writings . . . upon an improved plan . . . The utility of these Presses is too obvious to require any recommendations . . . Those intended for Gentlemen to copy their letters are of so portable a size as to be carried in one half the compass of the smallest travelling desk. With these improved presses the operation of copying may be performed in a few minutes." *Federal Gazette* (Philadelphia), April 14, 1798. (See also COPYING PRESS.)

LETTER OF MARQUE, LETTER OF MART

The term for one of the types of ship's papers or early marine memorabilia collected today; usually printed forms with blank spaces to be filled in, giving ship and shipmaster's name, extent of operations; that is, "a commission granted to the commander of a merchant ship, or privateer, to cruise against and make prizes of the enemy's ships and vessels, either at sea or in their harbors, under pretence of making reprisals for injuries received." *Encyclopedia Americana* (Philadelphia, 1831).

LEVESELE

(See LATTICE.)

LEWTE

An old synonym for "a kind of cup or vessel." (H)

LIBRARY BOOKCASE, LIBRARY CASE

Contemporary eighteenth- and early-nineteenth-century terms for the type of large bookcase and cupboard, often called a breakfront today. Of one, Chippendale said, "these [upper] Cases are fourteen or fifteen inches deep, and the lower Part must project four or five inches more than the upper Part, at least they look better so." *The Gentleman and Cabinet-Maker's Director* (London, 1762).

Library case illustrated in Hepplewhite's *Guide* (London, 1794).

LIBRARY FAUTEUIL

The name given a type of Elbow or Easy Chair by George Smith, each of which see. (See also FAUTEUIL.)

LIBRARY STEPS

The set of steps, whether designed as a

Library step table from Thomas Sheraton's *The Cabinet-Maker's and Upholsterer's Drawing-Book* (London, 1791–94).

form of stool or as a short ladder, used to help one fetch books from the higher library wall shelves or bookcase. Of a ladder-like design, Ince and Mayhew said, "this is intended for a large Room," however, "the other contrived for a little Room (is made) to fold up." *The Universal System of Household Furniture* (London, 1762).

LIBRARY STOOL

The name Thomas Sheraton gave to the large, rectangular box stool with a hinged lid. The lid when opened became a vertical back or brace for the set of two steps raised out of the box; thus, a form of library steps.

LIBRARY TABLE

The popular eighteenth-century pedestal ta-

Library table illustrated in Chippendale's *Director* (London, 1762).

Mid-eighteenth-century library table or bureau.

ble fitted with drawers, called a kneehole desk today. Some copies of French tables of this type were made by English craftsmen late in the seventeenth century, but the richly carved library table, made to stand in the center of the room, reached the height of its popularity in the 1750s. In his *Director,* Chippendale called such tables "commode-buroes." Instructions in Hepplewhite's catalogue recommended they be made of "mahogany covered on the top with leather or green cloth [in] dimension generally three to four feet long by three feet deep." *The Cabinet-Maker and Upholsterer's Guide* (London, 1794).

LIE-LEECK, LIE-LATCH, LIE-DROPPER, LIE-LIP

Variations of a term for the box or barrel, perforated at the bottom, "used for straining water for lie [lye]." (H)

LIGGER

A colloquialism for a bed.

LIGGYNG-STEDE, LIGGING-STEAD

A couch or bedstead, derived from the Anglo-Saxon term *ligge,* to lie down.

LIGHTHOUSE CLOCK

A type of c. 1800 shelf clock designed by Simon Willard and said to have been modeled after the Eddystone Rock in the English Channel. Cumbersome in design and weight, it proved unpopular and few were made.

LIGHT STAND

A common contemporary term for the stand specifically made to hold one or more candles. "We found Mrs. Bartlett fully established . . . The parlor was handsomely furnished, for that period, with a mahogany desk and book-case, two mahogany card tables, and a light-stand to match." (Description of a Newburyport home c. 1790.) Sarah Anna Emery, *Reminiscences of a Nonagenarian* (Newburyport, Massachusetts, 1879). (See also CANDLESTAND, and advertisement quoted under STAND.)

LIKENESS

The contemporary synonym for a portrait in any medium. "To the Publick. Likenesses Painted for a reasonable Price, by A. Delanoy, Jun., who has been Taught by the celebrated Mr. Benjamin West, in London. N.B. is to be spoke with opposite Mr. Dirck Schuyler's, at his Fathers." *New York Gazette,* January 7, 1771.

LIMBECK

A corruption of Alembic, *q.v.*

LINEN CUPBOARD

(See LINEN PRESS.)

LINEN MARKERS

(1) Small stencils cut out of plated tin or brass plates in the form of individual letters

Set of iron type linen markers.

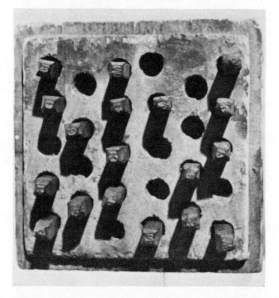

of the alphabet; (2) or a complete name cut in the plate; (3) or a set of individual letters cut on iron, usually kept in a divided box to avoid mislaying them. "[Please send a set of] Types consisting of the 26 Letters for marking Linning with the familys name, together with a paint & directions for staining the names. Another set of do. for a friend." (Order January 15, 1770 from John Robinson, York County, Virginia, to London.) Frances Mason, *John Norton and Sons, Merchants of London and Virginia* (Richmond, 1935).

LINEN PRESS

An upper and a lower board of fine-grained, polished hard wood set in a frame so as to form a vice or clamp when tightened by a turnscrew; similar to the small home library book press, and used to press and smooth napery. "April 13, 1641. A godly woman of Boston, dwelling sometimes in London, brought with her a parcel of very fine linen of great value . . . and had been at charge to have it all newly washed and curiously folded and pressed, and so left it in press in her parlour over night." John Winthrop, *Journal, The History of New England* (Boston, 1825). (2) Contemporary term for the large standing two-door cupboard, or the later chest of drawers with a cupboard top, used for the storage of linens. Thomas Chippendale showed this latter design in *The Gentleman and Cabinet-Maker's Director* (London, 1762). (See also BOOK PRESS illustration.)

LINK

"A torch of pitch," (W) carried in a cresset, and hence also a synonym for the Cresset Andiron, *q.v.* "Evens, the famous man upon the Harp, did the other day die for mere want, and was fain to be buried at the almes of the parish and carried to his grave in the dark of night without one link, but that Mr. Hingston met it by chance, and did give 12d. to buy two or three links." Samuel Pepys, *Diary,* December 19, 1666.

Link-Boy: "A hired boy who carries a torch." (W)

LINSET

The colloquial name given to the stool on which "women sat while spinning," (H) because lin was a common colloquialism for linen or flax.

LITHOCHROMICS

This term, often found in writings of the early nineteenth century, refers to a process of printing or reproduction perfected later in the century. At the time it was defined as "The art of painting in oil upon stone, and of taking impressions [thereof] on canvas. This process, which is designed to multiply the masterpieces of painting, was invented some years ago by Malapeau in Paris, [who] has an establishment for lithochromic productions . . . popular since 1823. This process is a substitute for the copying of portraits; it also serves as a cheap means of ornamenting walls. This art, however, is in its infancy. The lithochromic paintings yet produced are less valuable than the poorest copies. A similar but much superior invention has been made by Senefelder, which he calls *mosaic impression.*" *Encyclopedia Americana* (Philadelphia, 1831).

LITHOGRAPH

The term from the Greek *lithos,* stone, and *grapho,* to write, used to describe the surface-printing method developed by the Bavarian artist Alois Senefelder in 1798, and which is based on the incompatibility of grease and water, the disposition of greasy substances to adhere to each other, and the ability of oolitic limestone to absorb water. The stones were drawn on with lithographic ink or crayon. Best known of early American lithographers' work today are those of Nathaniel Currier, beginning in 1835 (the firm Currier and Ives was formed in 1859) and the Kellogg brothers of Hartford, Connecticut, from 1830.

LITTLE BOOKS

Another contemporary term for books specifically written for children. "The following Little Books for the Instruction & Amusement of all good Boys and Girls: The Brother Gift or The Naughty Girl Reformed. The Sister Gift or the Naughty Boy Reformed. Hobby-Horse or Christian Companion. Robin Good-Fellow, a Fairy Tale. Puzzling Cap, a Collection of Riddles. The Cries of London as Exhibited on the Streets. Royal Guide or Early Introduction to Reading English. Mr. Winloves Collection of Stories. Mr. Winloves Moral Lectures, History of Tom Jones, do. Joseph Andrews, abridg'd from the works of H. Fielding. History of Pamela, do. of Grandison, do. of Clarissa, abridg'd from the works of S. Richardson, Esq. Cox and Berry." *Boston Gazette and Country Journal,* January 20, 1772. (See also A B C BOOK, BABBY, TOY BOOK.)

LIVERY

An old term that generally signified possessions dispensed at the pleasure of a squire, landlord, or head of household, ". . . as they commonly use the word [it is] . . . derived of livering or delivering forth their nightly food; so in great houses, the livery is said to be served up for all night, that is, their evening allowance for drink . . . and livery is also called the upper weed which a serving man wears, so-called, I suppose, for that it was delivered and taken from him at pleasure." Edmund Spenser, *View of the Present State of Ireland* (London, 1597).

Livery was used in the colonies as a term for servants' clothing; for example, "10 yds of good cheap green livery cloth, Trimmings for ditto," were included in the order September 3, 1770 from Nathaniel Burwell, James City County, Virginia, to London. Frances Mason, *John Norton and Sons, Merchants of London and Virginia* (Richmond, 1935). A later order sent on behalf of the Royal Governor's household included, "2 Dozen Livery hats; 6 Postillion Caps; 30 Yds Blue Cloath for foot-Men; 30 do. Brown do. for do.; 6 Pieces of Brown Jeans for do.; 1 Piece of Green Shag for do. 1 do. Blue do. for do.; 30 Yds. Strip'd flannel for Grooms Waistcoats; Lining [and] Buttons Ec. for the Liverys." Order June 12, 1773, from James Minzies for the Earl of Dunmore, Williamsburg, Virginia, to London. Ibid. (See also COAT-OF-ARMS, at end of this section.)

In the sense of food for the night, the term livery was retained well into the twentieth century, or so long as the horse and carriage were a prime means of transportation, as a description of the stable where food, as well as grooming and stall space, was provided for horses.

LIVERY BOARD
This ancient term for a table or bench may, as some collectors believe, have signified a stand on which the livery cupboard was set, but it is just as likely a description of the old table at which liveries or rations were portioned out and, in the sense of livery as food, it would have been the supper board or table kept in the chamber. That livery, as a general term for food, was in common use in the early-seventeenth-century British Isles was reiterated by King James I's Attorney General for Ireland who wrote, "Fitz Thomas of Desmond began that extortion of coigne, and livery, and pay; that is, he and his army took horse meat, and man's meat, and money at pleasure." Sir John Davies, *Ireland* [1614] *Collected Works* (London, 1869).

LIVERY CUPBOARD
An ancient term, and a confusing one to modern collectors, for an early type of cupboard, probably similar to the court cupboard, in which liveries—anything meant to be distributed—were kept. Cupboard was the early word for a place to set out plate;

i.e., to display any silver, such as drinking vessels (cups), platters, or other fine food containers, and thus was generally a repository for any article of value. Hence, the adjective livery denoted: (1) A cupboard in which the badges of honor such as embroidered or painted helmet crests, ensigns, coats of arms, small weapons such as daggers or knives, or other distinguishing articles of apparel were stored; or (2) The chamber cupboard in which necessary serving utensils and a supply of food were kept for use, especially at night, either as a convenience for the owner of the house, or as a courtesy to his guests. (See also AMBRY, LIVERY, LIVERY BOARD.)

LIVERY TABLE
(See LIVERY BOARD.)

LOBBY CHEST
A late-eighteenth-century dwarf chest of drawers, "adapted for the use of a small study, lobby, or small lodging room," according to Thomas Sheraton, *The Cabinet Dictionary* (London, 1803).

LOCK
The instrument used for fastening doors, chests, etc., generally opened by a key. "The lock is esteemed the masterpiece in smithery; much art and delicacy being required in contriving and varying the wards, bolts and springs. From the different structure of locks, accommodated to their different uses, they acquire different names: thus those placed on outer doors are called stock locks; those on inner doors, spring-locks; those on trunks, trunk-locks, pad-locks, Ec. Of these the spring lock is the most curious. Its principal parts are the main-plate, the cover-plate, and the pin-hole." (M) "New Hardware Goods. Henry C. Porter has just received a general assortment of cutlery and hardware Goods . . . in part . . . knob-locks, mortise, chest, pad, cupboard, till, trunk and other locks . . ." *American Mer-*

cury (Hartford, Connecticut), October 23, 1820.

Seventeenth-century box lock and latch as used on a contemporary door. (Courtesy, Antiquarian and Landmarks Society, Inc.)

LOCKER

The term for "a drawer; cupboard; chest, or box," (W) supplied with a lock, but generally used to describe a small cupboard or trunk. It also was used for a small box built within a larger one, as a kind of Till, *q.v.* In addition, locker sometimes meant the drawer with a lock set just below the top of a table or at the base of a tall open cupboard. The term sometimes signified a belt loop or type of holster: "Lockers or Chapes for Daggers" were listed in the House of Parliament Rates, 1660, for Imports and Exports—*Statutes of the Realm* (London, 1819). (See also BUCKLE, CHAPE.)

C. 1775 country liquor chest or locker on frame with drawer; made of pine.

Set of matched bottles fitted compartments. (Courtesy, Antiquarian and Landmarks Society, Inc.)

LOGBOOK

"A book used to keep a ship's way in." (W) (See also JOURNAL.)

LOGLINE

"A line to measure a ship's way by." (W)

LOGGERHEAD

An iron haft with one lozenge or knob-shaped end, sometimes called a toddy iron or a flip iron. The knobbed end was heated over the fire, then plunged quickly into a bowl or other container of beer, ale, cider, or a mixed drink, such as flip, to warm it.

Loggerhead.

428

LOLLING CHAIR

A contemporary term for what we more commonly call a Martha Washington armchair today. Loll is an old form of lull, carrying a sense of relaxation or rest. The name was given to this type of chair because of its inclined back.

LONG-CASE CLOCK

Also called a tall-case clock. (See CLOCK, GRANDFATHER CLOCK, GRANDMOTHER CLOCK, HALL CLOCK.)

LONG GLASS

A synonymous term for the Ale-yard, *q.v.*

LONG SETTLE

A longer "Wooden seat, with back and arms." (H)   (See also SETTLE.)

LOO TABLE

The circular-top Georgian game table set on a center pedestal above a tripod base, especially designed for the round game of cards called Lanterloo or Loo. ". . . There is probably no article which requires so much care and experience in making as the Loo Table. The top, especially presenting to the eye a large level surface, under such circumstances, that the slightest irregularity, or imperfection, is brought distinctly into notice." Blackie and Son, *The Cabinet-Maker's Assistant* (London, 1853).

Loo table from *The Cabinet-Maker's Assistant,* Blackie and Son (London, 1853).

LOOKING-GLASS ARMS

Silver, brass, plated metal painted or gilded, carved wood arms, or branches made to be fitted into bracket holders at the front or sides of a looking-glass frame and so provide a wall light. Such arms usually were slender rods, in a horizontal or flat S curve, with a candle socket and drip plate at the end. "Just Imported and to be sold by Peter Turner at his Store under Mr. Thomas Leeches near Market St. wharf. Bohea and Green Tea, Tea Tables and Corner Cupboards, Branches and Lacker'd Arms for Looking Glasses, Brass Furniture for Chests of Drawers and Desks, Sadlery ware, Looking Glasses and Drinking Glasses . . ." *American Weekly Mercury* (Philadelphia), February 22, 1738–39. (See also BRANCH, CANDELABRUM, GIRANDOLE, SCONCE.)

LOOKING-GLASS CLOCK
(See MIRROR CLOCK.)

LOOKING GLASS

The contemporary term for a "glass that shows images of objects," (W) differing from mirrors which were "anciently made of metal, but, at present, are generally smooth plates of glass, tinned or quicksilver'd on the back part and are called Looking-glasses . . ." (M) Glass had replaced metal plates in the sixteenth century, at least in the homes of some:

My glass shall not persuade me I am old,
So long as youth and thou are of one date.

Shakespeare, *Sonnet 22.*

In the early Colonial period, "Looking Glasses, Halfe penny ware; Penny Ware; of Steele; small and large; of Christall, small and middle size," were listed in the House of Parliament Rates, 1660, for Imports and Exports—*Statutes of the Realm* (London, 1819). Even so, "[Before 1800] gilded [frame] looking glasses were unknown, and [were] much smaller than now. The looking-glasses in two plates, if large, had either glass frames, figured with flowers engraved thereon or was of scalloped mahogany, or of Dutch wood scalloped—painted

C. 1680–1750 looking
glasses. (Courtesy,
Antiquarian and Landmarks
Society, Inc.)

Looking glass with original label was made by
Kneeland and Adams who were in partnership between 1792–95, Hartford, Connecticut. Gilt span-
drel molding; mahogany veneer over pine and
white wood. Original label. (Courtesy, Connecticut
Historical Society, Inc.)

Late-eighteenth-century looking glass with phoenix gilt decoration.

Pine frame decorated with gilt over gesso. Stylized reverse painted panel above mercury-coated glass panel. Label on backboard from Nathan Ruggles' shop. (Courtesy, Connecticut Historical Society, Inc.)

white or black—with here and there some touches of gold." John F. Watson, *Annals of Philadelphia* (Philadelphia, 1830). "N. Ruggles has for sale Looking Glasses, of all descriptions, from 25 cents to 700 dollars a pair, which he is selling much lower than they are to be found in New-York or Boston. Likewise, for sale, Looking-Glass Plates [unframed] of all sizes." *American Mercury* (Hartford, Connecticut), February 15, 1810.

LOOM
"The frame in which the weavers work their cloth"; (J) that is, weave yarn into fabric by crossing the threads called the warp and the weft. (See also WEAVER'S LOOM.)

LOOP-BACK CHAIR
A synonymous term for the hoop- or loop-back Windsor chair.

LOOSE CASE
A contemporary term for what today is called a slipcover; that is, a separate fabric cushion-case easily removed either for cleaning or to exchange with another to vary a color scheme. "Thomas Elfe . . . having now a good upholsterer from London, does all kinds of upholsterer's work . . . chairs stuff covered, tight or loose cases for ditto." *South Carolina Gazette* (Charleston), January 7, 1751. (See also quotation under DUCHESSE.)

LOSSET
"A large flat wooden dish," (H) i.e., a Trencher, *q.v.*

LOVESEAT
The twentieth-century term for a type of small upholstered settee or double chair designed to seat two; a popular form from the early eighteenth century through the nineteenth.

LOVETOY
A common term for any "small present made by a lover." (W) (See also TOY, SCRIMSHAW.)

LOVING CUP
A term applied to various ornate drinking vessels with two handles. (See also GRACE CUP.)

LOWBOY

A mid-nineteenth-century American term for what should be called a Dressing Table or Toilet Table, each of which see.

LOW CASE OF DRAWERS

A contemporary colonial term for a small chest of two, three, or four drawers.

LOW DADDY

A silly term affected by modern collectors for that small dressing table afflicted also with the name Lowboy, *q.v.*

LOW-POST BED

(See HIRED-MAN'S BED, STUMP BED.)

LUCERN

An old name for a lamp, perhaps derived from *lucense,* the Anglo-Norman word for light.

LUSTRES

Originally this term was used to describe crystal chandeliers; late in the eighteenth century, it designated vases or candleholders with glass pendants or prisms, and sometimes was the term, loosely used, for a type of glass Sconce or Girandole, *qq.v.,* generally sold in pairs. "James Jacks . . . has imported Elegant glass Lustres and Chimney Ornaments; Imperial Paintings." *Gazette of the United States* (Philadelphia), August 2, 1798.

LUTE

"A stringed instrument of Musick," (J) the strings of which were struck with the fingers of the right hand and stopped on the frets with those of the left.

LYRE

"A harp; a musical instrument to which poetry is, by poetical writers, supposed to be sung" (J) and was by the ancient Greeks; hence, the word *lyric* for the stanzas of a song. "From the lyre, which all agree to be the first instrument of the stringed kind in Greece, arose an infinite number of others, differing in shape and the number of strings, as the psalterium, trigon, sambucus, pectis, magadis, barbiton, testudo, the two last being used by Horace with the lyre and cithara, epigonium, Simmicium, and pandura, which were all struck with the hand or a plectrum." (M)

LYRE-BACK CHAIR

A collector's term for any chair made with a back splat in the form of a lyre, a motif usually associated with designs used by Duncan Phyfe, New York City cabinetmaker of the Early Victorian period. Earlier, lyre-back chairs were designed by the Adam brothers, Hepplewhite, and Sheraton.

LYRE CLOCK

The term for the wall- or shelf-clock case design in the form of a lyre, attributed to Aaron Willard, Jr., of Boston, but a style also used in the early nineteenth century by numerous other manufacturers.

M

MACE

In ancient weaponry, "an iron club, short and strong . . . consisting of a handle two feet long, to which an iron ball was attached by a chain. It appears that the ball was frequently covered with iron spikes . . . At present the mace is used as an emblem of the authority of officers of state, before whom it is carried. [Such are] made of the precious metals, or of copper, gilt, and ornamented." *Encyclopedia Americana* (Philadelphia, 1831).

MACHINE CHAIR

In the Colonial period almost any article to which wheels, pulleys, or other "engines" or devices were added to provide easy movement, was called a machine. Chairs for invalids were as needed then as now; happily for the colonial owner his usually was an easy chair made according to the furniture style of the time, with only the addition of stretchers, connecting the chair feet, to which wheels or large casters were added. "Thomas Elfe . . . does . . . all kinds of Machine Chairs, stuffed and covered for sickly or weak people and all sorts of cabinet work . . . in the best manner." *South Caroline Gazette* (Charleston), January 7, 1751. (See also GO-CHAIR.)

MAGAS
In music, the name of "two instruments, one a stringed kind, and the other a kind of flute, which . . . yielded very high and very low sounds at the same time." (M)

MAGAZINE
"A Pamphlet," *q.v.* (W)

MAGIC LANTERN
The magic lantern or projector was invented in Italy in the late sixteenth century, improved in Germany in the early seventeenth century, and in 1665 was introduced in London, according to Samuel Pepys; "Comes by agreement Mr. Reeves, bringing me a lanthorn, with pictures in glass to make strange things appear on a wall, very pretty." *Diary,* August 19, 1666. It was "an instrument used to magnify paintings on glass, and throw their images upon a white screen in a darkened chamber. The lantern contains a reflector which is so situated as to have the light of a candle in its focus. On the forepart of the lantern there is a thick double convex lens, usually called a bull's-eye, of short focus. The lantern is closed on every side so that no light can come out but . . . through the lens. There is a tube fixed to the lantern . . . through this the glass slides with the painted small images, is moved in an inverted position. The forepart of the tube contains another sliding tube [with] a double convex lens. The thick lens throws a great deal of light from the candle onto the image [which] being thus well illuminated, sends forth rays from every point, which, by passing through the lens, are conveyed to a focus upon the

wall, and form large images." *The Domestic Encyclopedia* (Philadelphia, 1821).

MAID
A contemporary cant term for "the iron frame which holds the baking stone." (H)

MAIL
(1) Chain mail, or coat of mail, "a piece of defensive armour for the body, made of small iron rings, interwoven in the manner of a net." (M)   (2) Plate mail "consisted of small laminae or plates, usually of tempered iron, laid over each other like the scales of fish . . . so as to move freely." *Encyclopedia Americana* (Philadelphia, 1831).

MAIN HAMPER
A term for "a kind of basket used for carrying fruit" (H)   or vegetables, perhaps derived from the Old English word *mains* for the farm or fields near the house.

MAKRON
A kind of ash-peel, shovel, or "a rake for an oven." (H)

MAMMET
A synonym for "a puppet," (W)   another name for a Doll, *q.v.*

MAMMY BENCH
The collector's unfortunate popular name for a type of small Windsor settee-rocker developed in the mid-nineteenth century. Half or more of the seat is fenced off by a detachable crib siding. When in place, the fence or crib kept an infant from rolling off the chair, providing, of course, that mother or nurse occupied the other or open end of the seat.

MAMMY ROCKER
Another version of the term for the Windsor-type nursery rocker-settee, also called a Mammy Bench, *q.v.* (See also DOUBLE-CHAIR.)

MANGLE
"An instrument to smooth linen," (W)   this was a flat board with a rising handhold,

usually decoratively carved, especially when it was intended as a gift to a bride.

MANICORDION

The name of a contemporary "musical instrument in form of a spinnet, which consists of fifty chords and upwards, which are covered with pieces of scarlet cloth to deaden, as well as soften the sound; whence it is called the dumb spinnet." (M)

MANOMETER

The name of an early scientific "instrument to show the density and rarity of the air." (W)

MANTEL CLOCK

A modern term for the shelf or bracket clock.

MANTEL MIRROR

The modern term for the eighteenth- and early-nineteenth-century chimney glass, or chimney looking glass, or Mural Looking Glass, *q.v.*

MAP

The descriptive term for any black-and-white or colored, hand-drawn, engraved, or otherwise printed "delineation of lands, seas, countries." (W) Illustrated maps were collected by the colonists, often kept in sets or portfolios in the library, closet, or parlor, or framed for display in those rooms or stairwells. "Just printed, published and to be sold, This Map of Boston, Ec. is

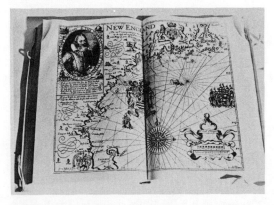

Captain John Smith's map of New England coast, first printed, London, 1624.

one of the most correct that has ever been published . . . taken by the most skilful Draughtsman in all America, and who was on the spot at the engagement of Lexington and Bunker's Hill. Every well-wisher to this country cannot but delight in seeing a plan of the ground on which our brave American Army conquered the British ministerial forces. Prices plain 5s., coloured 6s. and 6d. Pennsylvania Currency." *The New-York Gazette and The Weekly Mercury,* September 11, 1775. (See also PROSPECTS.)

MARBLE(S)

"Little balls supposed to be of marble, with which children play." (J) As Johnson intimated, these toys also were made of agate, wood, and of hard-baked clays. (See also AGATE MARBLE.)

MARBLE DECORATIONS

Use of marble slabs for the tops of serving tables, mixing tables, and sideboards, was popular in England and America from the seventeenth through the nineteenth centuries. In Pennsylvania, where much fine furniture was made, Peter Kahn noted in 1750 that "The land yields many kinds of marble, especially a white one with pale gray, bluish spots found a few miles from Philadelphia. People make tombstones and tables, enclose chimneys and doors and lay floors and flag in front of fireplaces of this marble." More than twenty years later southern homeowners, who wanted marble insets in furniture, still imported such pieces from England, Italy, or the northern colonies. Thomas Jefferson wrote that in Virginia in the 1770s, "There is very good marble and in great abundance on James River. Some [samples] are of a white as pure as one might expect to find [anywhere] but most are variegated, with red, blue and purple. None of it has ever been worked. It is said there is marble at Kentucky." *Notes on the State of Virginia* (London, 1787).

MARBLE TABLE, MARBLE-TOP TABLE

Twentieth-century terms for the slab-in-frame or slab table of the eighteenth century. (See also SLAB FRAME.)

MARMIT, MARMITE

The term from the French for "a pot with hooks [i.e., ears or lug handles] at the side." (H) A covered iron or earthenware pot, usually set on three feet.

MARQUISE

A term, adopted from the French for a Double-Chair or Settee, *qq.v.* with upholstered seat and arms.

MARROW SCOOP, MARROW SPOON

Both terms describe the popular late-eighteenth- and early-nineteenth-century long-handled, scoop-shaped silver spoon used to extract marrow from bones. "James Jacks, Jeweller . . . has for sale . . . Asparagus tongs, marrow spoons and soup ladles. Table, tea and dessert spoons . . ." *Federal Gazette* (Philadelphia), November 27, 1797.

MARTHA WASHINGTON CHAIR

A Late Victorian or centennial period name given the Lolling Chair, *q.v.,* because it was believed the first President's wife owned one of these at Mount Vernon.

MASELIN

A kind of drinking cup, so called because it originally "was made of maslin or brass." (H) (But see also MASER.)

MASER, MAESER, MAZARIN, MAZER BOWL

All terms for a handsome drinking bowl or large goblet without a footed base. Mazer is derived from the Old High German word for glossy, and was used to denote fine maple or other hard wood, and so, by extension, is the name of a richly carved and decorated bowl. These sometimes were "largely and finely edg'd about with silver, and double-gilt with gold," or sometimes "the outside whereof was black mazer [maple] and the inside of silver, double gilt, the edge finely wrought round about with silver, and double gilt." J. Davies, *Ancient Rites of Durham* (1672). When the bowls were ornamented with superior metals, the term mazarin or mazarine has been applied, although that term specifically denotes any deep dish or bowl made entirely of metal.

MASK

A cover for the face, specifically worn to keep the wearer from recognition, and sometimes from the ravages of winter cold or summer sun. "My grandmother wore a black velvet mask in winter with a silver mouth-piece to keep it on by retaining it in the mouth. I have been told that green ones have been used in summer for some ladies, for riding in the sun on horseback." John F. Watson, *Annals of Philadelphia* (Philadelphia, 1830). (See VIZARD.)

MASONIC WARES

The all-inclusive term for articles of apparel, personal jewelry, drinking and eating utensils, or other wares engraved or decorated with various insignia and identification de-

Masonic certificate "engraved by Brother Amos Doolittle, New Haven," issued in 1818. (Courtesy, Connecticut Historical Society, Inc.)

vices common to the semi-religious fraternal order of Free Masons: "Celebration. The Festival of St. John the Baptist will be celebrated by Moriah and Putnam's Lodges at Plainfield on the 28th day of June next. The procession will move from Eaton's Hall at 10 o'clock A.M. Brethren of adjacent Lodges are respectfully invited to attend. A Masonic Sermon and Oration are expected. Luther Paine, Nathan Williams, George Middleton, Charles L. Webb, Wm. Bowen, Isaac Davis, Committee. Coventry." *American Mercury* (Hartford, Connecticut), May 27, 1815.

"Taken out of the House of Mr. Todd, a small Silver Square, a Level, a Plumb-Rule, and Silver Pen, and other Utensils belonging to the Lodge of Free Masons in New-York. Whoever brings them to the Printer hereof shall be handsomely rewarded, and no Questions ask'd." *The New York Weekly Journal,* November 14, 1737. ". . . best gilt and other buckles, masons broaches and jewels, gold buttons and seals, silver ditto . . . [Simeon Coley]." *The New York Mercury,* October 5, 1767. "Removed from the store kept by Mr. William Henry Stiegel . . . to the store of James and Arthur Jarvis . . . who have for sale of the American manufacture . . . carrofts, enamel'd, mason and common wine glasses . . ." *New-York Gazette and Weekly Mercury,* February 8, 1773. (See also ORNAMENTAL PAINTING.)

MASSACHUSETTS CLOCK

The collector's term for the eight-day, brass-movement shelf clock manufactured by the Willard family and other Massachusetts makers; sometimes called a half-clock because of the size of the case.

MATCHBOX

A common name for any box used to hold splints, spills, or other fire-lighting aids. (See also TINDERBOX.)

Eighteenth-century match or tinder box; scratch-carved decoration. (Courtesy, Antiquarian and Landmarks Society, Inc.)

Painted tin mid-nineteeth-century wall matchbox.

Nineteenth-century decorated tin table matchbox with matches.

MATCHES

In 1680 Robert Boyle first made sulphur-tipped splints drawn through paper impregnated with phosphorus, but it was not until 1780 that phosphorus matches were introduced for general use in England. The first modern matches of potassium chloride, antimony sulphide, and sandpaper were sold in London in 1827, and by 1845 had superseded flint and steel as the common method of igniting fire. (Matches first were machine-made in 1842.) Safety matches first were made by the Swedish Lündstrom Brothers in 1852. Wax matches were introduced in 1860 in France. (See also TINDERBOX.)

MATCHLOCK

The type of gunlock in which a match (a wick impregnated with oil, wax, sulphur, or any easily inflammable material) was placed to ignite the powder; the term often was used as a synonym for a type of Musket, *q.v.* (See also FIRELOCK, FLINTLOCK, WHEEL LOCK.)

MATRASS

The term for a "long chymical glass vessel" (W) used in the apothecary's shop.

MATTRESS

The term for a pallet or "a kind of quilted bed to lie on." (W) (See also PALLET.)

MAULKIN

The common term for "a swab for the oven hearth"; (J) "a mop." (W)

MAUND

The name of a "handbasket with two lids or opening covers, chiefly used by market women to carry butter and eggs." (M) In shipping, maund was a term for a large hamper holding eight bales or two vats.

MAUNDREL

The early tool similar to a pickax, "sharpened at each end." (H)

MAWE

An old game of cards, played with a piquet pack of "thirty-six cards by any number from two to six." (H)

MAZARINE

A deep metal dish or plate, with an inner drainer, used both for cooking and serving. "Sprinkle on some fine bread-crumbs; butter a mazarine . . . place them on it very carefully and bake them three quarters of an hour . . ." Richard Briggs, *The New Art of Cookery* (Philadelphia, 1792).

MEASURE SETS

Sets of pewter, brass, tin, or iron open bowls for measuring liquids, similar in form to porringers or cups when they had handles, or small cans or beakers when they had not, were made for the use of careful housewives, owners of taverns, and retail shops. The amount the measure held usually was stamped just below the rim, under or on the

C. 1810 pewter powder measure.

Gill and half gill pewter measures.

Set of copper measures from gill to pint.

Seventeenth-century wood-grain measure. (Courtesy, Connecticut Historical Society, Inc.)

Early-nineteenth-century wood-grain measures. (Courtesy, Connecticut Historical Society, Inc.)

out the United States . . ." *Federal Gazette* (Philadelphia), March 20, 1790.

Silver medal ordered in 1687 by King James, commemorating recovery of Spanish gold by William Phipps; first medal struck honoring a colonial-born Briton. Shown one-third actual size.

handle. Those which carry a series of such stamps, sometimes dated, were used in taverns or shops, the additional stamps signifying they had been checked by local officials as giving a true measure. "The subscriber has on hand . . . Scales of all sizes; Scale beams; Measures from 4 gallons down to a Gill; Cast Iron and Lead weights. Richard Williams." *American Mercury* (Hartford, Connecticut), July 5, 1810.

MEASURING CUP

The blown-glass, funnel-shaped handleless cup, usually made with a pouring lip or spout and marked off in drachms and ounces, the type used by apothecaries, and also recommended for use in the kitchen. "At some glass warehouses, you may get measures divided into tea and table-spoons. No cook should be without one, who wishes to be regular in her business." William Kitchiner, *The Cook's Oracle, and Housekeeper's Manual* (New York, 1830).

MECHANIZED LAMP

(See CARCEL LAMP.)

MEDAL

The name for "a piece of metal in form of a coin, destined to preserve the memory of some great man and some memorable action." (M) "General Washington's Historical Medals, A Striking and approved Likeness taken from life, in silver, white and gold coloured metal—from one dollar to four—are now ready to be delivered to those patriotic Gentlemen who have subscribed and to every other citizen through-

MEDALLION

The term also for "a large medal." (W)

MEDDER

An old term, sometimes also spelled meader or mether and apparently a derivative of the ancient word mead, i.e., a drink made of honey, for a footed, wooden cup with handles. (See also LOVING CUP.)

MEDICINE BOTTLE

The amber, brown, green, sometimes clear bottles in which patent medicines were sold; especially prized by collectors if the name of the manufacturer was impressed in the glass, or if they retain some other original label. "Daniel Hopkins has replenished his stock . . . Important!!! 100 gallons Hopkins' Cordial Elixir for Gout, Rheumatism, Cholic, Indigestion, Debility Ec. (by measure and in quart, pint and half pint bottles) . . . which medicines are now generally prescribed by the most eminent physicians and preferred to all the Patent Grand Restorations . . . in circulation."

American Mercury (Hartford, Connecticut), June 1, 1813. (See also BITTERS BOTTLE, JUNK BOTTLE, SNUFF BOTTLE.)

MEDICINE CHEST
A fitted case or box, with lid, divided into compartments to hold a variety of blown and stoppered bottles. "To be sold . . . a large Medicinal Chest fitted with large and small square bottles, wanting but very Trifles to make it compleat for Sea, Inquire of the Printer hereof." *The New-York Mercury,* July 16, 1759. Undoubtedly there has been confusion between these and other chests and Case Bottles, *q.v.,* as well there might be, for minus labels, there is little other means of differentiating between them.

MELE
An Anglo-Saxon term for a cup or bowl.

MELL
A variation of mele for "a Warming-pan," *q.v.* (H)

MEMOIRS
In literature, "a species of history, written by persons who had some share in the transactions they relate." (M)

Memoirs.

MEMORANDUM BOOK
A private notebook for use at the writing table. "Send with all speed possible . . . 12 Asses Skin Memorandum Books in Gilt Leather Cases & Ribon to pull out . . ." Order December 29, 1771 from Catherine Rathell, Williamsburg, Virginia Merchant, to London. Frances Mason, *John Norton and Sons, Merchants of London and Virginia* (Richmond, 1935). (See also POCKET BOOK.)

MEMORIAL PICTURE
Another name for the Mourning Picture, *q.v.* "Something to preserve memory." (W)

MERIDIENNE
The French term for a type of graceful Day Bed, *q.v.,* popular between 1830 and 1850; specifically made with one arm higher than the other so that the back slopes in a rather undulating line from the higher to the lower arm.

METALLIC TRACTORS
Among medical curiosities collected today are many pseudo-scientific amulets and devices, such as copper, brass, and silver bracelets and lockets, touted as prevent-alls and cure-alls by early American quacks. Among the most popular were small devices said to be able to draw energy out of the atmosphere and, on application to the patient's body, to still pain and provide rejuvenating strength. The nation's first Vice-President described the claims made for metallic tractors: "There is a Dr. Somebody here from Connecticut who pretends, with an instrument made of some kind of metal . . . by a sort of mesmerian rubbing, or stroking, or conjuration, to cure rheumatisms, headaches, pleurisies, and I know not what . . . They have got him into the president's house among some of his servants, and Mrs. Washington told me a story on Tuesday so ineffably ridiculous that I dare not repeat it in writing. The venerable Lady laughed as immoderately as [did all the rest who heard it]." Letter from John Adams at Philadelphia, February 13, 1796, to his wife at Cambridge, *Letters of John Adams* (Boston, 1841).

METE-FORM(E)
A form; i.e., a long seat or bench used for "sitting on at dinner-time." (H)

METE-ROD

"A measuring rod," (H) the same as metewand.

METEWAND, METE YARD

"A rod to measure with," (W) today called a yardstick. (See FOLDING RULE.)

MEZZOTINT, MEZZOTINTO

The term to describe "a kind of engraving on copper," (W) sometimes called also the scraping art, invented by Ludwig von Siegen shortly before 1650. In the late seventeenth and eighteenth centuries, it was called *la manière anglaise,* being used much in England to reproduce the tonal effects of oil paintings. Perhaps the most familiar mezzotint engravings today are reproductions of Turner, Constable, and Landseer paintings. The copper (or in the nineteenth century, steel) plate was roughened by a tool called a rocker to create an even burr. This held the ink and produced a deep velvet-black. Those areas to be printed in lighter tones were scraped out by the engraver; highlights or white areas were burnished smooth. "By water to Deptford, and there made a visit to Mr. [John] Evelyn, who, among other things, showed me most excellent painting in little; in distemper, in Indian incke, water colours; gravery; and above all, the whole secret of mezzo-tinto, and the manner of it, which is very pretty, and good things done with it." Samuel Pepys, *Diary,* November 5, 1665. (See also REVERSE GLASS PAINTING.)

MICROMETER

The name of "an instrument to measure the magnitudes of objects viewed through telescopes and microscopes." (W)

MILK SELE

"A milk pail." (H)

MINIATURE FURNITURE

True, many small pieces of furniture and furnishings were made for use as children's toys. However, most of the small-size furniture now collected was made by cabinet-makers as display samples to be used in early shop windows. Throughout the eighteenth and early nineteenth centuries, windows were made up of small panes of glass, interlaced by glazing bars of lead or wood. Scale models were necessary in order that the "window shopper" might see the entire piece. After larger plate-glass windows became common, miniature or scale model display samples no longer were needed.

MINIATURE PAINTINGS

"The Queen [Elizabeth I] opened a little cabinet in her bedchamber, wherein were divers little pictures wrapped in thin Paper, and their Names written with her own hand upon the papers." James Melville, *Memoirs.*

These early sixteenth-century souvenirs of friendship, believed to have been originated by Hans Holbein, were described by the Elizabethan artist and goldsmith Nicholas Hilliard (1547?–1619), in his *Treatise,* as "small pictures to be viewed in the hand." Their popular early name was limnings or little paintings. Originally the word miniature, as applied to portraits, was derived from *minium,* the Latin for red lead or vermilion. Illuminating with *minium* was *miniare,* and the artist became known in England as a miniator. The earliest portraits in miniature were round; Hilliard introduced the oval shape. Many were enclosed in lockets, either open or closed; others were kept in specially made boxes of fine wood or precious metals. From the sixteenth through the eighteenth centuries, miniatures usually were painted against solid blue or gold grounds, although detailed backgrounds also were used. Early portraits were painted on parchment, which then was glued to a heavier paper or card stock; parchment or vellum continued in use throughout the eighteenth century. After 1700, thinly shaved sheets of ivory were used also and some miniatures were executed on tin.

"I Hear there is a miniature painter gone

Washington memorial picture; reverse glass painting in beaded, gilded pine frame (Courtesy, Antiquarian and Landmarks Society, Inc.)

Miniature. Officer's portrait on ivory, set in gold brooch. (*Hartford Times,* photo by Einar Chindmark.)

over to Philadelphia, a relation to John Reynolds. If Sally's picture is not done to your mind by the young man, and the other gentleman's a good hand and follows the business, suppose you get Sally's done by him, and send it to me." (Benjamin Frank-

Eighteenth-century miniature, oil on wood, snuff box top.

Eighteenth-century miniature on canvas, set in gold locket. (Courtesy, Connecticut Historical Society, Inc.)

lin from London to his wife at Philadelphia, November 22, 1757.) *The Writings of Benjamin Franklin,* ed., A. H. Smyth (New York, 1907).

"I fancy I see more likeness in her Picture than I did at first, and I look at it often with Pleasure, as at least it reminds me of her." Franklin, June 10, 1758, Ibid. Harriet Beecher Stowe said of her mother, a gifted amateur painter, "Her forte [about 1805] was drawing likenesses on ivory. She took many of her scholars and friends. There were about two dozen in all, which used to be kept as a treasure to be shown us children when we were good." *Autobiography, Correspondence . . . of Lyman Beecher, D.D.,* ed., Charles Beecher (New York, 1866).

MINUTE BOOK

A contemporary term for "a book to note short hints in"; (W) a memorandum or Pocketbook, *q.v.*

MIRROR

The proper term for any reflecting surface. "An opaque body whose surface is finely polished so that it will reflect light and thus represent the images of objects. Mirrors are made of metal or glass, polished on one side and silvered on the other." *Domestic Encyclopedia* (Philadelphia, 1821). The term, mirror, was revived as a synonym for looking glass during the Late-Victorian era. (See also LOOKING GLASS.)

MIRROR CLOCK
The collector's term for a shelf-clock case with a looking glass placed in the top portion, above the dial, designed in 1825 by Chauncey Jerome of Bristol, Connecticut, to compete with other pillar-and-scroll types of cases. Jerome listed these as "Looking-Glass Clocks."

Mirror clock. (Courtesy, Connecticut Historical Society, Inc.)

MONEY
Anything accepted as having a certain specified value. (See also AMERICAN EAGLE, COIN, PEAK, PIECES OF EIGHT.)

MONEY JUG
An early nineteenth-century cant term for a coin bank made of pottery.

MIXING TABLE
Collectors tend to call any small side table with a marble or slate top a mixing table. However, when the term first was used in the late eighteenth century, the reference was to a kind of sideboard table, with a shallow back cupboard or set of shelves or drawers recessed above the top board, with or without a marble slab on the board. This back area held the mixing glasses, decanters, corkscrews, and other utensils. When not in use, the shelves or drawers often were covered or enclosed by a tambour slide or roll top.

MONK'S CHAIR
A collector's handy term, enabling the user to give an aura of greater value to the space-saving kitchen chair table or Hutch Table, *q.v.*

MONOCHORD
The name of a musical instrument, "composed of one string, to try the variety and proportion of musical sounds. The ancient monochord consisted of a rule divided and subdivided into divers parts, whereon there was a string pretty well stretched upon two bridges, at each extremity. In the middle was a moveable bridge whereby, in applying it to the different divisions of the line, the sounds were found to be in the same proportion to one another as the divisions of the line cut by the bridge were." (M)

MONOGRAM
The common term for a "character or cypher, composed of one, two, or more letters, interwoven, being a kind of abbreviation of a name, used as a Badge, Cipher, Seal, Ec.," *qq.v.* (M) (See also ARMORIAL BEARINGS at end of section.)

MONOPODIUM
The term, from the Greek meaning single foot, used to describe small Regency and Empire tables supported by triangular-shaped pedestals, which often had claw-foot terminals. (See also CLAW TABLE.)

MONTEITH
The name given to a handsome scallop-rimmed bowl first designed in the late seventeenth century as a glass cooler. "This yeare

[1683] in the summer time came up a vessel or bason notched at the brim to let drinking glasses hang there by the foot so that the body or drinking place might hang in the water to cool them. Such a bason was called a 'Monteigh' from a fantastical Scot called 'Monsieur Monteigh,' who at that time or a little before, wore the bottome of his cloake or coate so notched." *Life and Times of Anthony Wood, antiquary of Oxford, 1632–95, described by himself,* Vol. III, ed. by Andrew Clark (Oxford, 1894). As a glass cooler, the silver or porcelain monteith was expensive and unsatisfactory. It was, however, of a good size for serving punch, and soon was so used. Some Monteith bowls were made with removable scalloped rims or collars and some also had handles. The flat-rim punch bowl, however, was preferred, and the Monteith type seldom was made after 1730, until the mid-nineteenth century when the design was revived.

MOON CLOCK

A contemporary term for the long-case clock with an eight- or thirty-day movement, specifically made with a face to which was attached an engraved or painted revolving plate showing the phases of the moon. "For Sale by Ephraim Clark . . . on hand plain, arched, and moon clocks, and one lady's elegant gold watch . . ." *Federal Gazette* (Philadelphia), September 22, 1790.

MOP

"Pieces of cloth or locks of wool fixed to a long handle [with wire or cord] with which maids clean floors." (J)

MOPPET, MOPSY

Another name for a child's doll or "a puppet." (W) (See also BABY, BABY CLOUT, DOLL.)

MORTAR, MORTAR AND PESTLE

This common colonial kitchen utensil was the one in which cooks of the period

Small burl mortar with pestle. (Courtesy, Antiquarian and Landmarks Society, Inc.)

Tall-case clock with plate showing moon phases. (Courtesy, Connecticut Historical Society, Inc.)

Burl mortar and pestle. (Courtesy, Antiquarian and Landmarks Society, Inc.)

Painted wood mortar and pestle. (Courtesy, Antiquarian and Landmarks Society, Inc.)

Brass mortar and pestle.

"flayed, brayed, bruised, beat, pounded, and broke" foods, that today would be ground, blended or pureed in electric mixers and blenders: "A strong vessel [of wood, iron, brass, pewter, marble, or stone] in which materials are broken by being pounded with a pestle." (J) "Take veal or chicken, with as much marrow as meat; with a little thyme, lemon-peel, marjoram, two anchovies boned; a little pepper, salt, mace, and cloves; bruise the yolks of hard eggs [and] mushrooms, mix all these together, and chop them, and beat them in a mortar very fine . . ." E. Smith, *The Compleat Housewife* (London, 1741). Mortars were carved or turned in all sizes from miniature ones holding a scant ounce and used for grinding a few peppercorns, to those of two-quart capacity. Many cooks and apothecaries kept several sizes.

Marble Mortar: The wooden mortar was preferred for dry foods. Smoothly polished marble mortars and pestles were used in the preparation of moist foods because they were less likely to absorb and retain scent or taste. "Chop the meat small, with half a pound of beef suet, and as much crumbs of bread. Beat them well in a marble mortar . . ." Richard Briggs, *The New Art of Cookery* (Philadelphia, 1792). (See also SAMP MORTAR.)

MOSAIC IMPRESSION
An early nineteenth-century term for Lithograph, *q.v.,* because such printing was made from a stone. (See also note under LITHOCHROMICS.)

MOTTO CUP
The collector's term for any small cup or mug made of pottery, porcelain, pewter, silver, or glass and painted or etched with a name or phrase.

Early-nineteenth-century soft paste motto cup.

MOTTO RING
A term used variously to describe a type of Mourning Ring, *q.v.,* or rings engraved with the mottoes or devices of clubs, civic groups, such as library associations or volunteer fire companies, clan rallying cries, military organizations, cyphers. "Charles Webb, Jeweller, from London, makes all sorts of Jewellry work and Motto Rings after the newest fashion and is as cheap as in London." *American Weekly Mercury* (Philadelphia), August 17, 1738.

MOLDING PLANE
One of the tools made for and used by the furniture maker and house joiner. "Every carpenter or joiner should provide himself with planes to form mouldings of different

styles since it is as easy to finish woodwork correctly as incorrectly." A. J. Downing, *The Architecture of Country Houses* (New York, 1850).

MOURNING LOCKET

A popular form of memorial jewelry, these were gold, silver, or pinchbeck cases, sometimes engraved with date and cipher or with the cipher worked in plaited hair. "A Variety of Gold, Silver, Jewellery and Plated Articles for sale . . Mourning Rings, lockets, Ec., Ec., made and worked with the real hair given, in any device that fancy can suggest, in the modern taste with dispatch. James Askew." *Evening Gazette* (Charleston, South Carolina), October 5, 1785. "Samuel Brooks . . . executes every article . . . in the most elegant manner, of the best materials, Bracelets, Lockets, Rings, Ec., Ec., made in the newest fashions, and hair laid in love mourning, and fancy pieces." *Federal Gazette* (Philadelphia), June 10, 1793.

MOURNING PICTURE

The general term for a water color, pen and ink drawing, or embroidered picture memorializing a friend or relative recently deceased; the name, dates, and sometimes a suitable motto were inscribed in a shield, cartouche, or on the face of a symbolic monument. "Miss Titcomb . . . taught history, and geography, and also gave special attention to female accomplishments. These, so far as I could observe, consisted largely in embroidering mourning pieces, with a family monument in the center, a green ground worked in chenille and floss silk, with an exuberant willow-tree, and a number of weeping mourners, whose faces were often concealed by flowing pocket handkerchiefs." Harriet Beecher Stowe, *Old Town Folks* (Boston, 1869). (See also EMBROIDERY PICTURE.)

MOURNING RING

Rings made up, usually of silver and often with a design enameled in black, and given as a memento of the deceased to those invited to attend the funeral service. "July 15, 1698. John Ive, fishing in Great Spie-pond, is arrested with mortal sickness; dies next day . . . I was not at his Funeral . . . Mr. Mather came in just as I was ready to step out, and so I staid at home, and by that means lost a Ring." Samuel Sewall, *Diary*. Mourning rings also were made for sale to the general public to be worn as a gesture of respect to the memory of eminent personages: "J. B. DuMoutet . . . has for sale . . . a quantity of those Rings so much in Demand, with striking likenesses of the late General Washington in uniform dress . . ." *Federal Gazette* (Philadelphia), January 27, 1800. (See also DEATH'S-HEAD RING, MOURNING LOCKET, MOURNING PICTURE, MOURNING SWORD.)

MOURNING SWORD

The name for a type of dress or ceremonial sword, usually with a silver-mounted hilt decorated in black enamel and/or worn in an all-black or a similarly incised and enameled scabbard; sometimes with a black silk tassel affixed. "May 2, 1709. Artillery Day, and [because] Mr. Higginson dead, I put on my Mourning Rapier and put a black ribband into my little cane." Samuel Sewall, *Diary*.

MOUSE TRAP

Always a necessary furnishing of any home, and one recorded early in English literature, for "she wolde wepe, if that she sawe a mouse Caught in a trappe . . ." Geoffrey Chaucer, *Canterbury Tales,* Prologue. Early traps usually were small cages with solid top and bottom boards, and sides of closely set wire rods or wooden spindles, or later, perforated boards; a small door was held partially open by a stick-brace, which when dislodged caused the door to swing down, and inward, and close. The design theoretically was proof against opening, but not actually, hence the need for the better version lamented (presumably) by Ralph Waldo Emerson: "If a man . . . make a better mouse-trap than his neighbor tho' he build his house in the woods, the world will make a beaten path to his door." Quoted by Mrs. Sarah S. B. Yule in *Borrowings* (1889), although Elbert Hubbard claimed he said it first.

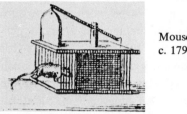

Mouse trap, c. 1790 print.

MOVEABLE

A common contemporary term for any portable piece of furniture, such as a small table.

 —*Why, what's a moveable?*
 —*A join'd stool.*

  Shakespeare, *The Taming of the Shrew,* II, i.

(See also AMBULANTE, WORK-TABLE.)

MOVING BOOKSTAND

(See BOOKSTAND, CANTERBURY, CHIFFONIER, MOVING LIBRARY.)

MOVING LIBRARY

A contemporary description of the bookstand, open on all four sides and equipped with casters for easy removal from one room to another or from one place within a room to a different spot. "The tea-room or breakfast-room, may abound with beaufets, painted chairs, flower-pot stands, hanging book shelves or moving libraries, and the walls may be adorned with landscapes, and pieces of drawings, etc. and all the little things which are engaging to the juvenile mind." Thomas Sheraton, *The Cabinet Dictionary* (London, 1803). (See also BOOKSTAND; CANTERBURY, CHIFFONIER.)

MUFFINEER

The term used since about 1830 for what earlier would have been called a sugar castor, which is exactly what it still was, whether or not it was used to sprinkle sugar or powdered cinnamon over muffins. Also, the small covered dish or cake plate used to keep muffins or biscuits warm.

MUFFLE

A contemporary term for the "small earthen oven or vessel," (W) better known today as a baking pot, such as is used for beans.

MUG

The general contemporary term for a "cup used to drink out of," (W) made of wood, metal, pottery, or glass.

Late-seventeenth-century polychrome-decorated, tin-glazed, or faïence mug. (Courtesy, Antiquarian and Landmarks Society, Inc.)

English delft mug; design indicates union of England and Scotland. (Courtesy, Antiquarian and Landmarks Society, Inc.)

Stoneware mugs with incised decoration. (Courtesy, Antiquarian and Landmarks Society, Inc.)

Mocha mug with applied handle.

Pewter mug. (Courtesy, Connecticut Historical Society, Inc.)

Polychrome soft paste mug.

1780–1820 blown-glass mug with enamel-painted decoration.

MULE CHEST

The collector's term for a type of clothes chest or chest-over-drawers popular in the seventeenth and eighteenth centuries. This was a low chest with two or more drawers in the plinth.

MUNDLE

A colloquialism for "a slice or stick used in making pudding." (H)   A stirring spoon or cooking ladle.

MURAL CLOCK

An obvious synonym for the wall or shelf clock.

MURAL LOOKING GLASS

The general term for any large looking glass meant to be affixed to a wall as a decoration and thus distinguished from the hand mirror or the sconce glass. "[There are] glasses of the newest fashion, proper to be placed over Chimney Pieces, Sofas Ec. They must be fixed very low. The pannels of the sides are frequently made of various coloured glass." A. Hepplewhite, *The Cabinet-Maker and Upholsterer's Guide* (London, 1788).

MURDERER

The common colonial term for the small cannon used not only in the field but to defend private dwellings—especially those remote from neighbors, as were the homes of southern planters—the auction wharfs, or traders' storage places. "May, 1643. Mr. Vines landed his goods at Machias, and there set up a small wigwam [the common term for a roughly built cabin], and left five men and two murderers to defend it." John Winthrop, *Journal, History of New England* (Boston, 1825). It was the firing of this type of small cannon (called for in the action of the play) during a performance of *King Henry VIII* that set fire to the thatched roof and so destroyed the Globe Theatre.

MUSICAL GLASSES

A popular name for the Armonica, *q.v,* ". . . with other fashionable topics, such as pictures, taste, Shakespeare, and the musical glasses." Oliver Goldsmith, *The Vicar of Wakefield* (1766).

MUSIC BOX

A name sometimes given the Canterbury, *q.v.*

MUSIC CANTERBURY

(See CANTERBURY.)

MUSIC DESK

(See DESK, LECTERN.)

MUSIC RACK

(See CANTERBURY.)

MUSIC STAND

(See DESK, LECTERN.)

MUSIC STOOL

The contemporary term for what is known more commonly today as a piano stool. "The whole of the seat raises from the stand by turning round the top, which raises a screw that works in a nut contained in the pillar. The screw is sometimes made of wood, but iron is preferable, as working better and lasting longer." John Hall, *The Cabinet-Maker's Assistant* (Baltimore, 1840).

MUSKET

From the French *mousquet* meaning a small hawk, the name for the long gun carried by the infantry. "Many of the fire arms are named from animals." (J) "Every listed Soldier and other Householder shall be always provided with a well fixt Firelock Musket, the Barrel not less than three Foot and a half long, or other good Fire Arms to the satisfaction of the Commission Officers of the Company . . . Twenty Bullets fit for his Gun, and twelve Flynts . . . fit for his gun, on penalty of six Shillings." *Act for Regulating the Militia* (Boston, 1733).

Whether kept by every householder to repulse French, Indians, or privateers, or to help implement community disapproval, the musket was ever a handy Colonial weapon:

"John Oldham suffered his unruly passion to run beyond the bounds of all reason and modesty . . . Reproofs were but oil to the fire [so] they committed him until he was tamer, and then appointed a guard of musketeers, which he was to pass through, and every one was ordered to give him a blow on his hinder-parts with the butt end of his musket; he was conveyed to . . . where a boat was ready to carry him away, with this farewell, Go and mend your manners. He was a man of parts, but high spirited." Nathaniel Morton, *The New England's Memorial* (1669). (See also FIRELOCK, FLINTLOCK, MATCHLOCK, WHEEL LOCK.)

MUSKETOON

A Blunderbuss, *q.v.,* "a short gun of a large bore." (J)

MUSKET REST

Another contemporary term for the artillery man's musket stand or fourquette, a long iron or wooden rod with a U- or V-shaped top or "rest." "A Man may think, if he will, that a Musket may be shot off, as well upon the Arme, as upon a Rest." Francis Bacon, *Essay XXVII, of Friendship; The Essays or Counsels, Civill and Morall* (London, 1625).

MUSTARD CRUET

A contemporary term for the mustard container for the table or sideboard. (See advertisement quoted under CARAFE.)

MUSTARD POT

The small pottery, porcelain, or glass-cov-

C. 1830 soft paste mustard pot.

ered container from which prepared mustard was served at the table.

MUSTARD SPOON
The small slender ladle, often somewhat flat or spade-shaped, and seldom more than two inches long, used to take prepared mustard from the pot. These spoons usually were of silver, sometimes given a gold wash, and often were sold separately for use with the porcelain, glazed earthenware, glass, or porcelain-lined silver mustard pots. "Heydorn & Imlay [have] on hand a great variety of silver Table, Tea, Desart, Mustard & Cream Spoons . . ." *American Mercury* (Hartford, Connecticut), September 27, 1810.

MUSTARD TANKARD
The name given to a type of mustard pot, made in silver or silver plate, so called because it had a hinged top, similar to that of the tankard, as much as because its shape was similar to that of the drinking vessel. "Joseph Anthony, Jr. has imported . . . from London . . . Sauce boats and mustard Tankards . . . Blue glasses for sugar and cream basons, mustard tankards and salts . . ." *Pennsylvania Packet* (Philadelphia), December 7, 1790.

MUSTERBOOK
The local militia register, or "a book in which soldiers are registered." (W) One of the manuscript records collected today.

N

NAILS
Nails of iron and brass, as well as pegs of wood and wire staples, were used to strengthen and combine woods; to fasten leather and upholstery fabrics to wood frames; and, in addition, to serve as bright decorative accents. They were burnished, such as those of copper or brass, or were tin-plated, for this purpose. Among types of nails sent here during the first Colonial period were "chaire nailes, copper nailes, rose nailes, Sadlers nailes, Head nailes, Harness nailes, spring nailes, Tente hooks," as listed in the House of Parliament rates, 1660, for Imports and Exports—*Statutes of the Realm* (London, 1819). Even in time of war, Americans continued to import English nails, although by the early nineteenth century many were being made by smiths here. "Charles Sigourney has imported from Liverpool . . . English fine rose head nails, wrought iron tacks, and nails of all sizes. Fine slating nails [roofing] nails, tin'd tacks for bellows makers, Brass nails, tinman's rivets . . . has 60 casks of 8d, 10d, 12d, 20d, cut and wrought nails and 4d cut shingle nails, cut Brads and tacks of various sizes." *American Mercury* (Hartford, Connecticut), November 4, 1812.

NAKER
An old term for "the kettle-drum," *q.v.* (H)

NAN
A cant term for a "small, earthen jar." (H)

NAPERY
A general term for table linens, especially napkins or towels.

NAPIER'S BONES
A device for counting, so named for its inventor, Lord Napier. This was an instrument consisting of small rods "used in the seventeenth century to expedite arithmetical calculations," (H) "whereby the multiplication and division of large numbers are much facilitated." (M) (See also TALLY, NICKSTICK.)

NAPKIN
(See DIAPER.)

NAPKIN PRESS
A synonymous term for the Linen Press, *q.v.*, in which napery was pressed and smoothed.

NECESSARY STOOL
(See CLOSESTOOL.)

NECROMANCER

A cooking vessel with a "magic" lid, and in which food was steamed and from which it was served. "Take the large silver or pewter dish, made like a deep soup dish, with an edge about an inch deep in the inside, on which the lid fixes (with a handle at top) so fast, that you may lift it up by that handle without letting it fall; this dish is called a necromancer . . ." Richard Briggs, *The New Art of Cookery* (Philadelphia, 1792).

NEGUS

The name of a kind of punch made from "wine, water, sugar, nutmeg and lemon," (W) and thus also for the cup from which it was drunk.

NELSON CHAIR

To commemorate Lord Nelson's triumph at Trafalgar, Thomas Sheraton designed two chairs to which he gave this name: (1) A type of elbow chair with a back shaped to represent an anchor, the error in taste compounded by using two carved dolphins for the front legs. (2) A side chair with the same type of anchor as a back splat.

NEST

A contemporary synonym for a chest or "a box of drawers," (W) or "any quantity or collection of articles together. Mr. Dyce tells us that a nest of goblets is a large goblet containing many smaller ones of gradually diminishing sizes, which fit into each other and fill it up. [Also] the phrase, 'a nest of shelves' is in common use." (H)

NEST OF DRAWERS

A contemporary term for a Chest or Case of Drawers, *qq.v.* (See also in Chapter 5.)

NEST OF TABLES

The contemporary term for a set of three or four small tables of diminishing height, so made that one could fit beneath another and thus all could be stacked in the space ordinarily taken by one. Thomas Sheraton called these worktables; when in sets of three, a trio; in sets of four, quartetto tables. *The Cabinet Dictionary* (London, 1803).

NEWSPAPERS

News, according to Dr. Johnson, is "a fresh account of anything; something not heard before" and thus a synonym for "papers which give an account of the transactions of the present times." Single copies, particularly those including the first intelligence of historic events; and runs, i.e., a complete series in chronological order, of a quarter, year, or longer, of our early newspapers are prized by collectors today. Early papers, published at weekly intervals, usually were single sheets printed on both sides, and folded once to provide two pages or four sides. "In 1720 or 1721, my brother began to print a new public paper. It was the second that made its appearance in America, and was entitled the *New-England Courant*. The only one that existed before was the *Boston News-Letter*. Some of his friends, I remember, would have dissuaded him from this undertaking, as a thing that was not likely to succeed; a single news-

1813 Connecticut newspapers.

450

paper being, in their opinion, sufficient for all America. At present, however, in 1771, there are no less than twenty-five." Benjamin Franklin, *Life and Essays* (Hartford, 1845).

In 1806, as part of the appendix to his *Compendious Dictionary,* Webster listed as the first newspapers, "public prints to circulate news," printed in various colonies, the *News-Letter* (Boston), 1704; the *American Weekly Mercury* (Philadelphia), 1719; the *New-York Gazette,* 1725; the *Rhode Island Gazette,* 1732; the *Connecticut Gazette* (New Haven), 1755. The *Connecticut Courant,* later renamed the *Hartford Courant,* first published in 1763, is now the oldest newspaper in continuous publication in the United States. (See also GAZETTE.)

NICKSTICK
"A tally notched for reckoning," (H) a colloquialism for the ancient Tally, *q.v.,* and thus, generally, also any tangible record of remarkable events. Thus, to "cut your stick" was to make a tally, or accounting, of assets at year's end. Hence, also, to arrive "in the nick of time" was to be present just as the notch was being cut. The sense of this old custom is retained today by those families who annually mark children's heights on a chamber or nursery doorpost.

NIDDY-NODDY
The hank winder, a central bar with crosspieces or ends set at right angles; in use, it was turned in a half circle to wind yarn from spindles and so form a hank or skein.

NIGHT CHAIR
This was a common contemporary synonym for the Closestool, *q.v.* "Jacob Sass . . . has for sale at his Ware-room . . . Mahogany Chairs of the newest fashion; sofas, Easy Chairs, Night Chairs . . ." *Charleston City Gazette and Advertiser* (South Carolina), February 27, 1797.

NIGHT COMMODE
A late-Victorian term for the Night Table or Closestool, *qq.v.*

NIGHT CLOCK
A seventeenth-century table clock with a double set of hour numerals, the second set pierced so that when a lighted lamp or candle was set behind the dial, the numerals were reflected onto a curved piece of metal set above the dial.

NIGHT GLASS
A common term for a kind of telescope with which to view objects after dark; the Scotoscope, *q.v.* "It was candle-light, and my eyes could not distinguish the wharves jutting out toward us . . . The Captain stands aft with his hand on the tiller, and the other holding his night-glass . . ." Henry David Thoreau, *Cape Cod* (Boston, 1865).

NIGHT STOOL
Still another contemporary description of the Closestool or Night Table, *qq.v.*

Seventeenth-century child's night chair. (Courtesy, Antiquarian and Landmarks Society, Inc.)

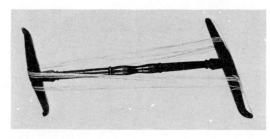

Niddy-noddy.

NIGHT TABLE

The c. 1800 description of a combination of small table and closestool, *q.v.,* for the bed chamber. "The seat part draws out in front like a common drawer, and contains a pan hid from the eyes by a deep front rail, which is sometimes made to appear like two drawers." Thomas Sheraton, *The Cabinet Dictionary* (London, 1803). (See also CLOSESTOOL.)

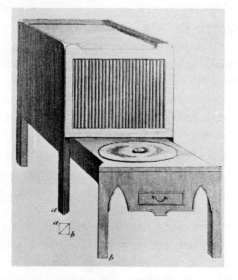

Night table illustrated in Hepplewhite's *Guide* (London, 1794).

NIP

The term for a measure of half a pint of ale, and thus, also, for the drinking mug from which the ale was quaffed.

NIPERKIN

The larger Nip, *q.v.,* a popular name for a drinking cup. "Lost or taken away from the House of Mr. Samuel Kirk at Brandywine Ferry in New Castle County, the 14 September a silver pint or Niperkin, mark made by Philip Syng of Philadelphia." *American Weekly Mercury* (Philadelphia), November 14, 1723.

NOGGIN

A small mug, usually of wood; "a small wooden cup or mug, a small measure," (W) as a noggin of ale. "A mug or a pot of earth with a large belly and a smaller mouth; in some areas a wooden Kit, *q.v.,* or Piggin, *q.v.,* was called a noggin." (H)

NONESUCH FURNITURE, NONSUCH FURNITURE

Nonesuch, or the palace without equal, symbolized for Elizabethan Englishmen the wonders and riches of their age. Built for King Henry VIII, and based on designs by the Italian Toto del Nunziata, the palace survived the additions and redecorating ideas of a series of owners until 1670 when Lady Castlemaine gutted the buildings. "I much admired how it had lasted so well and entire since the time of Henry VIII . . . There are some Mezzo-Relieves as big as the life. The storie is of ye Heathen Gods, emblems, compartments, Ec. . . . These walls [are] incomparably beautified," John Evelyn wrote in his *Diary* January 3, 1666. The term nonesuch now is given to that ornately inlaid furniture of the late sixteenth and early seventeenth centuries which was decorated with stylized designs of buildings reminiscent of the Palace of Nonesuch, and to the later reproductions of similar pieces.

NOON-MARK

The contemporary colloquialism for a small, portable sundial set on the window sill, moved as necessary as the seasons changed. Because basically it was accurate only in showing the noon-time, it was called a noon-mark. (See also SUNDIAL.)

Pewter noon-mark or window-sill sundial.

NORFOLK LATCH

The c. 1800 flat iron door plate with an applied, projecting half-round handle. "Charles Sigourney has imported in Ship *Eliza-Ann* from Liverpool, an invoice of Hard-ware Goods, which have arrived in season to avoid confiscation under the Non-Intervention Law, and which will be sold on as good terms as possible [including] wood screws of almost every size, wooden stock locks, Japan'd Norfolk latches, round and flat bolts." *American Mercury* (Hartford, Connecticut), February 7, 1811.

NOUCHE

(See OUCH.)

NURSE CHAIR

The nurse chair or nursing chair, as it sometimes was called, was made with a low seat, seldom more than sixteen inches high. Some chairs may have been rocking chairs with similarly low seats. Such a chair was billed to "Benjamin Frankling, 11 mo., 12, 1742/3 [as] one Nurse Crookt Foot Chair, 10 [shillings]" by Philadelphia chairmaker Solomon Fussell. Solomon Fussell Account Book, 1738–51, *Stephen Collins Papers,* Mss. Division, Library of Congress.

NUTCRACKER

Then as now, sturdy tongs or pliers for breaking the shells of nuts. (See note under TEA TONGS.)

NUTMEG GRATER

Small graters or rasps enclosed in engraved or etched silver or silver-plated two-piece cases, made in a variety of shapes, but usually round or ovoid, and just large enough to hold a nutmeg in one half and the grater in the other. Made for use at the tea table or to carry in the pocket or purse. "James Jacks has imported from London . . . and is now opening a large assortment of goods [including] Cream pots and nutmeg graters, Salt sellers, salt spoons . . ." *Federal Gazette* (Philadelphia), November 27, 1797.

O

OAST

"A kiln for malt or hops." (H)

OBOE

(See HAUTBOY.)

OBSCURA CAMERA

(See CAMERA OBSCURA.)

OCCASIONAL TABLE

The term Thomas Sheraton used to describe small games tables, such as those used for chess. *The Cabinet Dictionary* (London, 1803). The term, as we use it today, for any small, easily portable table did not come into use until this century. (See AMBULANTE, MOVEABLE.)

OCTANT

The term from the Latin means a half quadrant and thus an arc forming one-eighth of a circle. It was the name given in 1730–31 to an instrument used by astronomers (mostly amateurs) and navigators and made in the form of a graduated eighth of a circle for taking angular measurements. "The late invented and most curious Instrument call'd an Octant, for taking the Latitude or other Altitudes at Sea, with all other Mathematical Instruments for Sea or Land, compleatly made by Anthony Lamb in New York . . . and sundry other small works in wood, ivory, or brass, and Books of Navigation . . . Proper Direction given with every Instrument. Ready Money for curious hard wood, Ivory, Tortoise-Shell and old Brass." *The New-York Gazette or The Weekly Post-Boy,* January 23, 1749.

OGEE CLOCK

The name given by collectors to a simply made rectangular shelf clock, chiefly manufactured in Connecticut after 1830, characterized by the ogee molding used to frame the front of the case. (See also CYMA, Chapter 5.)

OGLING GLASSES
Opera glasses. (See also POLEMOSCOPE.)

OLIVER'S-SKULL
A contemporary cant phrase to describe a chamber pot; the Oliver so derided, was, of course, Cromwell. Other such slang terms included Jordan and Tom, *qq.v.*

OMBRE TABLE
One of the many small drawing-room card tables popular from the mid-seventeenth through the first half of the nineteenth century, at which Ombre, "a game of cards played by three" (J) persons might be dealt. Ombre was a Spanish improvement of primero: "There are several sorts of this game called L'Ombre but that which is chief is called Renegado, at which three only can play, to whom are dealt nine cards apiece; so that discarding the eights, nines, and tens, there will remain thirteen cards in the stock; there is no trump but what the player pleases; the first hand has always the liberty to play or pass, after him the second, Ec." *The Compleat Gamester* (London, 1721). Ombre tables were triangular. As a result, the name has been applied rather loosely at times to any three-sided table or corner table. (See also CARD TABLE, TRAYDRILL TABLE.)

OMBROMETER
The name of "an instrument to measure the quantity of rain that falls"; (W) a Rain Gauge, *q.v.* "I had observed for several years past a great inequality in the Quantity of Rain which fell; and judged that in the Gust of 1769 and some other heavy Showers there fell as much as fell in the same time in any part of Europe; and I had fancied that our Dews were greater than in most Parts of the world. I had also supposed that not only our Crops, but our Health must be greatly affected by this Inequality of Moisture, and that both must depend on a certain due Proportion of Heat and Moisture to be satisfied in this Point, I con-

trived a simple instrument by which I could easily Measure to the 1/300th Part of an inch of Rain. Mr. David Jameson by Mr. Hunt's means procured such an Instr. from London. Mr. Hunt causing it to be made after his Direction. Mr. Jameson imported 2 and gave me one. We have now for 13 Months kept an exact Journal of the Weather, and most accurately measured the Rain and Dews . . . We several times found near four divisions of Dew in our Glasses, equal to 1/100th of an Inch on the Earth. I have troubled you with this long Acct of our Observations partly because I thought it might be acceptable to you and your curious Friends, as being I believe the first that ever were made of this kind in America, and I may say, with such an Instr in the World; and partly, because I must beg the Favour of you to procure me another, as I have unfortunately broke mine. I have given Mr. Davis a Description of the Instrument which he will deliver to you." Letter from John Page, Jr. (President of the Society for the Advancement of Useful Knowledge, Later Governor of Virginia), Rosewell, Virginia, July 21, 1773 to London. Frances Mason, *John Norton and Sons, Merchants of London and Virginia* (Richmond, 1935). (See also PLUVIOMETER.)

OMNIUM
Another name for an étagère or Whatnot, *q.v.*, because it held "all," or a little bit of everything.

OPERA GLASSES
(See POLEMOSCOPE.)

ORCEL
An Anglo-Norman word for any small vase.

ORCHESTRION
The term for an instrument called an "automatic" orchestra; a type of organ, introduced by the French Abbé Vagler in 1789; a similar instrument called the Apollonicon was made in London in 1810.

ORNAMENTAL PAINTING

An all-inclusive term for ornamental illustrations apart from specific portraits, landscapes, etc., and especially for the decorative emblems or insignia of trades, associations, military organizations, or mercantile establishments. ". . . Pratt, Ruttle & Co. . . . Ornamental paintings, such as Emblematical, Masonic, Historical, and Allegorical Devices and Designs for Pictures, Regimental Colours and Standards; Ships' Flags, Drums, and every other decoration of that kind on linen, silk, bunting, muslin, or other substances . . ." *Aurora* (Philadelphia), February 15, 1796.

ORPHARION

A musical instrument, similar to the Lute, *q.v.*

ORRERY

The term to describe the late-eighteenth-century "instrument to show the revolutions

Orrery. (Courtesy, Antiquarian and Landmarks Society, Inc.)

of the planets." (W) "A curious machine for representing the motions of the heavenly bodies so called because one, copied from the original invention of a Mr. [George] Graham, was first made for the Earl of Orrerry, and otherwise known by the name of planetarium. It consists of representations of the planets and of the zodiac and other lines imagined by astronomers. By means of an orrery, persons who have not the leisure to study astronomy may, in the space of a few days, obtain a competent knowledge of several of the celestial phenomena and especially release their minds from the common prejudices respecting the motion of the earth; its principal use being to render the theory of the earth and moon intelligible, and to make evident the causes of those appearances that depend on the annual or diurnal rotation of the earth, and the monthly revolutions of the moon." *The Domestic Encyclopedia* (Philadelphia, 1821). David Rittenhouse of Philadelphia, famed colonial inventor and scientist, constructed if not the first, one of the first orreries used in this country. "We have supposed Mr. Rittenhouse second to no astronomer living: that in genius he must be the first because he is self-taught. As an artist, he has exhibited as great a proof of mechanical genius as the world has ever produced." Thomas Jefferson, *Notes on the State of Virginia* (London, 1782).

OTTOMAN

Basically a backless sofa, the ottoman was one of the symbols of the mid-nineteenth-century search for upholstered comfort in the grand manner. "The ottoman is a piece of furniture we borrow from oriental countries and which has become quite popular among us of late . . . in hot climates it affords a more agreeable lounge than any other seat—while, if made of a good breadth, it will also serve as a bed, should occasion require. Ottomans are made in various forms, from the simple continuous seat ex-

Ottoman seat from *The Cabinet-Maker's Assistant,* Blackie and Son (London, 1853).

George Washington's ottoman stool. (Courtesy, Connecticut Historical Society, Inc.)

tending around the wall, to the octagonal stuffed seat." A. J. Downing, *The Architecture of Country Houses* (New York, 1850).

OUCH, OUCHE, NOUCHE

The form of the Old French or Teutonic *nusche* or *nosche* for collar or necklace, used well into the eighteenth century to mean a necklace set with a precious stone or stones, a clasp, a brooch, and often as a synonym for an Amulet, *q.v.* In this latter sense, Johnson in 1755 noted wryly that the only cure for the bite of a tarantula was an ouch.

OVERMANTEL

The term for the late-Victorian chimney glass to which was added sets of shelves, above, below, and often also to each side of the looking glass itself, the better to display collections of small ornaments.

OVERMANTEL MIRROR

The collector's term for what was known, and more correctly, as a Chimney Looking Glass, *q.v.*

OVERMANTEL PAINTING

The collector's description of any painting, usually a landscape, executed directly on the mantel panel itself.

OYSTER RAKE

"We saw many boats in which the men were busy catching oysters. They made use of a kind of rake with long iron teeth bent inwards. They use these singly, or two tied together so that the teeth are turned towards each other." Peter Kalm, *Travels in North America* (Warrington, England, 1772).

P

PACK STAFF

A synonym for "the pedlar's staff, on which he carried his pack. We now say pike-staff." (H)

PACKTHRE(A)D

"A strong thread for packing with"; (W) cord or string.

PAD

A common term for "a low soft saddle; a cushion or bolster; properly, a Saddle or Bolster [*qq.v.*] stuffed with straw." (J) (See also BASS, HASSOCK.)

PAIL

A "wooden vessel for water, milk, Ec." (W) (See BUCKET.)

PAINTED ENAMEL WARE

A general term for many small objects designed for table and desk use; small furnishings such as looking-glass knobs, curtain holders, wall pegs; for trinkets, toys, or souvenirs, produced at various Staffordshire factories, notably Battersea and Bilston, in the eighteenth century, and numerous others in the early nineteenth century. Best known are the nineteenth-century small boxes for patch or snuff, often decorated with a painted motto, such as "A Trifle from Liverpool," "From a Friend," "Remember Me," etc. Some had mirrors inset in the underlid. To make this ware, an opaque base coat of enamel was laid on copper front and back, then fired. After firing, the design was applied in transparent enamels and refired. Transfer printed patterns were used in addition to hand coloring and lettering. The first transfer painting on enameled ware was accomplished by John Brooks, a Dublin engraver, at the Battersea factory. (See BATTERSEA ENAMELED WARE, BILSTON WARE.)

PAINTED FURNITURE
(See in Chapter 7. See also quotation under FANCY CHAIR.)

PAINTED PAPER
This was a contemporary synonym for Wallpaper, *q.v.* "Charles Hargrave in Front Street next door to the Bank Meeting House . . . Pistols, Cutlasses, pictures, painted paper for Lining of Rooms, Blue and White China plates . . ." *Pennsylvania Gazette* (Philadelphia), July 10, 1746.

PAINTED PARSON
An irreverent nineteenth-century cant term for a painted sign post, especially one cut in the shape of a pointing finger; so called, of course, because it pointed the way for others' benefit. One of the misnamed "folk art" items collected today.

PAINTING
The general term for the result of applying skill, genius, and imagination, to "the art of laying on colors; a picture." (W) The art of "filling up the outlines of objects represented on a flat surface, and giving them, by colour and shadows, or by shadow alone, the appearance of reality. The subject must be well imagined, and if possible, improved in the painter's hands . . . It must be strong, perfectly and readily understood . . . well-connected and contrasted

so as to make the whole as grateful to the eyes as a good piece of music to the ear . . . Nature must be the obvious foundation . . . but raised and improved from what is commonly seen to what is rarely met with and even yet higher from a judicious and beautiful idea in the painter's mind." *The Domestic Encyclopedia* (Philadelphia, 1821). (See also MINIATURE PAINTING, PAINTED ENAMEL WARE, PAINTING IN DISTEMPER, PAINTING IN LITTLE, PAINTING BY SUBSCRIPTION, FACE PAINTING, IMAGE, LANDSCAPE, LIKENESS, SEAPIECE, SILHOUETTE, WINTERPIECE, WAX FIGURES.)

PAINTING BY SUBSCRIPTION
This was the term used to describe a contemporary method of selling and circulating prints of engravings on copper plate or steel, copied from original portraits and historical scene paintings. The subscriber might thus build up a library or parlor-table portfolio of prints, or purchase prints to frame and hang. Details of the system were described by two of early America's best-known artists as they announced plans to publish the first of several subscription paintings or prints, now familiar to most. "Proposals by John Trumbull for Painting by Subscription; Two Prints from Original pictures painted by himself; One representing the Death of General Warren at the Battle of Bunker's Hill. The other, the Death of General Montgomery in the Attack of Quebec . . . The prints will be engraved by two of the most eminent Artists in Europe. The Size will be 30 inches by 20. The price to Subscribers, Three Guineas for each Print, one half to be paid at the Time of subscribing, the Remainder on the Delivery of the Prints, which will be as soon as the work . . . can possibly be completed . . . These Prints are the first of a series in which it is proposed to represent the most important Events of the

American Revolution." *General Advertiser* (Philadelphia), December 15, 1790.

"Gilbert Stuart, having been appointed by the Legislatures of Massachusetts and Rhode Island to prepare full length portraits of the late General Washington . . . [will] publish Engravings . . . from the Mount Vernon Portrait, executed upon a large scale, by an eminent artist . . . He therefore respectfully solicits the assistance of the Public on the following Conditions: 1. That a full length engraving of General Washington shall be delivered to each subscriber at the price of Twenty Dollars. 2. That towards defraying the expenses of the work, each Subscriber shall pay in advance the sum of Ten Dollars, and the remainder of the price on delivery of the print . . ." *Aurora* (Philadelphia), June 12, 1800.

PAINTING IN DISTEMPER
A painting medium, the name derived from *tempera,* and which in the words of a famous taste-maker of the nineteenth century, "is nothing more than a water-color wash, the color being mixed with clear, thin sizing, instead of oil." A. J. Downing, *The Architecture of Country Houses* (New York, 1850). "Ship and House painting, glazing, and graining mahogany, gilding in oyl, and distemper . . . in the neatest and best manner, by the subscriber to be found at Capt. Doran's on the dock. William Downal . . . [If his work] does not please the employer, no reward will be required." *The New-York Gazette and The Weekly Mercury,* June 1, 1772. As implied by this advertisement, distemper was used commonly in painted and stenciled wall designs, as well as in the finer arts.

PAINTING IN LITTLE
A contemporary synonym for painting in miniature, or for the Miniature Painting, *q.v.,* itself.

PAINTING IN SHADES
(See CLAIR-OBSCURE, SHADE.)

PAINTING ON VELVET
(See THEOREM, STENCIL PAINTING.)

PAIR-OF-GRAINS
A two-headed wrought-iron fish spear. "August 15, 1648. There came a snake into the seat where many of the elders sate behind the preacher . . . Divers shifted from it, but Mr. Thomson, one of the elders of Braintree trode upon it, and so killed it with his foot and staff with a small pair of grains." John Winthrop, *Journal, History of New England* (Boston, 1825).

PAIR OF TABLES
(See BACKGAMMON, PLAYING TABLE.)

PALLET
A small bed, as a folded blanket or quilt, or at best a long, stuffed cushion, or mattress filled with straw, pine boughs, corn shucks, moss, bits of cloth:

> *Why rather liest thou . . . upon uneasy pallets*
> *Than under the canopies of costly state . . . ?*
>> Shakespeare, *King Henry IV,* Part II, III, i.

"[Each night] Lay down before the fire upon a Little Hay Straw Fodder or bairskin . . . and happy is he that gets the Birth nearest the fire." George Washington: "Journey Over the Mountains," 1748. *Collected Writings of George Washington,* ed., John C. Fitzpatrick (1876).

PALLET(E)
The term, among painters, for a "little oval table or piece of wood, or ivory, very thin and smooth; on, and round which the painters place the several colours they have occasion for, to be ready for the pencil. The middle serves to mix the colours on, and to make the tints required in the work. It has no handle, but instead thereof, a hole at one end to put the thumb through to hold it." (M)   (See also PENCIL.)

PAILLIASE, PALLIASE
(See PALLET.)

PAMPHLET

"A small book," (W) "properly a book sold unbound, and only stitched," (J) with a self-cover serving also as the title page. Often, after accumulating several, an owner had his collection of pamphlets bound together in one volume. One of America's earliest booksellers, Judge Samuel Sewall, owned a shop in Boston where he was also a manager of the colony's printing press (although he delegated the actual work to the New London, Connecticut, printer Samuel Green). Sewall acted as the Mathers' publisher, as well as serving others. His own pamphlet, *The Selling of Joseph,* probably was the first forthright colonial publication deploring Negro enslavement. "Having been long dissatisfied with the Trade . . . I had a strong Inclination to write and began to be uneasy that I had so long neglected doing anything . . . There is a Motion by a Boston committee to get a Law that all Importers of Negros shall pay 40s p head, to discourage the bringing of them . . . Mr. C. Mather resolves to publish a sheet to exhort Masters to labour their Conversion . . . which makes me hope that I was call'd of God to Write . . ." Samuel

Sewall, *Diary,* June 4, 1700. *The Selling of Joseph, A Memorial* [Published at] "Boston of the Massachusetts" Printed by Bartholomew Green, and John Allen, June 24th, 1700. *Proceedings of the Massachusetts Historical Society,* October, 1863.

PAMPHLET BOX

The wood, metal, or waxed leather desk box in which papers and unbound pamphlets were stored to keep them safe from dust and mussing. "Out of the box where my lord's pamphlets lay, I chose as many as I had a mind to have for my own use, and left the rest." Samuel Pepys, *Diary,* March 1, 1659–60.

PANCHEON

"A large broad pan," (H) glazed within to hold milk. (See PANSHON.)

PANCROCK

A term to describe "an earthen pan," (H) because crock or crockery was a synonym for earthenware or pottery.

PANEL-BACK CHAIR, PANNELED CHAIR

Collectors' terms for what their ancestors called a Wainscot Chair, *q.v.*

PANNEL

"The treeless pad or pallet, without cantle," (H) upon which to ride, as a Saddle, *q.v.;* "a mean saddle." (W)

PANNIER

The name for a "wicker basket by which fruit or other things are carried on a horse." (J)

Eighteenth- and nineteenth-century pamphlets.

Panniers, shown in c. 1800 print.

PANSHON

A common corruption of pancheon; "an earthenware vessel, wider at the top than at the bottom, used for milk when it has to be skimmed; also for other purposes." (H)

PANTOGRAPH

(See PENTAGRAPH.)

PANTRON

Another colloquialism for "a small earthen pan." (H)

PANTRY

This term was applied also to a bread safe or bread box; a small, ventilated bin or cupboard for the storage of pastry from bake day to bake day. (See also HANGING SAFE, LARDER.)

PAP BOAT

The silver or ceramic ovoid or pear-shaped container with a tube-spout especially made for ease in feeding invalids and infants. Pap was a term for a thin gruel or "food made for infants, with bread boiled in water." (J) "James Jacks, Jeweller and Watchmaker . . . Has imported . . . elegant stock of goods [including] bottle stands and sugar dishes; fish spades, pap boats, and mustard pots . . ." *Federal Gazette* (Philadelphia), November 27, 1797.

PAPER CARPET

"Francis Guy, of Baltimore, Introduced [in 1812] a new kind of carpet, made of common paper hangings, which, it was thought, would prove as durable as canvas floor cloth, and be much more beautiful, and fifty per cent cheaper. It was patented in 1819, but a specification of the invention was filed as early as 1806, since which time he had been engaged in testing the value of the article. It was invented principally for summer use." J. L. Bishop, *History of American Manufactures from 1608 to 1860,* Vol. 2 (Philadelphia, 1861–68). (See FLOOR CLOTH.)

PAPER HANGINGS

This was a contemporary term for what commonly is called wallpaper today. When one manufacturer could not sell his papers on the basis of their attractiveness, he suggested their purchase as insulation, for they would at least cover the cracks between sheathing or paneling boards. "A great saving may be made in wood in the course of the ensuing winter by paying a few shillings for Paper Hangings; particularly in old rooms, besides the comfort derived from it in not being obliged to roast one side and freeze the other. Call at the Hartford Paper-Hanging Manufactory next door north of the Brick Meeting House." *American Mercury* (Hartford, Connecticut), October 24, 1820. (See PAPER LINING, WALLPAPER.)

PAPER HOLDER

A mid-nineteenth-century term for what today are better known as paperweights, "Ancient Egyptian Glass Globes filled with colored flowers like the paper holders now sold in the shops." News item reporting an exhibit of Near Eastern antiquities, *New York Illustrated News,* July 16, 1853.

PAPER KNIFE AND TRAY SET

The paper knife was a decorative but utilitarian reading-desk accessory, used to cut the pages of books, rather than to slit open envelopes, in those days when letters were folded and sealed with wax rather than enclosed in separate covers as they are today. Many knives were provided with small matching trays. "James Jacks, Goldsmith, Jeweller, Watchmaker, No. 1 South Third Street . . . has imported . . . from London Cutlery, Japanned Goods, Ec. . . . Table, dessert and carving knives and forks, with green and ivory handles, silver caps and ferrols . . . Sportsmen's, pen and fruit knives . . . Japanned paper knife trays and waiters . . ." *Federal Gazette* (Philadelphia), April 15, 1797.

PAPER LINING

Another contemporary term for Wallpaper, *q.v.* "Richard Wenman . . . in Little Queen Street near the Scot's Meeting-House . . . take this method to inform the Gentlemen and Ladies of this City that he . . . Puts up Paper Linings of Rooms, and Performs all Parts of the Upholsterer's Business in the neatest Manner." *The New-York Gazette or The Weekly Post-Boy,* January 6, 1763.

PAPIER-MÂCHÉ FURNITURE

Numerous ornate, incised, inlaid, painted, and lacquered pieces of furniture as well as smaller objects, all made of papier-mâché were shown in the mid-century Crystal Palace Exhibition at London, testifying that "The manufacture of a great variety of useful articles of large size [is now possible]. It is not many years since the limits of the trade were circumscribed to a tea-tray, but now we find articles of furniture,

Papier-mâché chair shown at the Crystal Palace Exhibition, London, 1851.

not only of a slight and ornamental character, such as ladies work-tables or boxes, but . . . chairs and sofas for the drawing-room or the entire casings of pianofortes." Illustrated were an inkstand, a nautilus-shaped couch, a boudoir table, an "Elizabethan" chair, a worktable, and a "Pompeian" flower stand. *The Art-Journal Illustrated Catalogue* (London, 1851). (See also PAPIER-MÂCHÉ, Chapter 5.)

PAPYROTAMIA

The Latin term for paper cutting and the proper name for Cutwork, or a Cut-paper Picture, *q.v.*

PARAPHERNALIA, PARAPHERNA

The descriptive term for those "goods which a wife brings her husband besides her dower, and which are still to remain at her disposal exclusive of her husband." (M)

PARASOL

"An umbrella to guard against the sun." (W) (See also KITTISOL, UMBRELLA.)

PARCHMENT

"The skins of sheep or goats prepared in such a manner as to be subservient to the binding of books; engrossing deeds, and other purposes. The skins are reduced to one half of their thickness by paring, and rendered by the pumice-stone." *The Domestic Encyclopedia* (Philadelphia, 1821). The name was derived from Perganum, the city where parchment is believed to have been invented in the second century B.C. To make parchment the skins are dried, but not tanned, then stretched, the hair or wool removed, and the skin scraped smooth. Parchment also was used for diplomas and citations; many military and naval commissions; drum and banjo heads; for painting in oils, especially miniature portraits.

PARGANWYNE

"A reel for winding yarn." (H)

PARLOR CHAIR

The term to describe the best chairs in the household, kept in that main room wherein guests were entertained; thus they were Hall Chairs in the sixteenth and seventeenth centuries; Parlor Chairs or Drawing-Room or Dining-Parlor Chairs in the late seventeenth and eighteenth centuries. All major design books from the mid-eighteenth century through the nineteenth illustrated parlor chairs specifying their use in such rooms. Chippendale, for example, in describing a plate showing three chairs, distinguished between them as "That in the Middle is proper for a Library; the two others [are] fit for Eating-Parlours." *The Gentleman and Cabinet-Maker's Director* (London, 1762).

PARLOR STOVE

The nineteenth-century term for the freestanding "sheet iron stoves [that] are a convenient method of quickly warming [those] rooms and apartments not in common use. Open fireplaces in large rooms are admirable contrivances to waste wood, to roast the front and freeze the rear of those who sit near the fire; to produce cricks in the neck, colds, coughs, and pleurisies, no invention can be more ingeniously or completely effect these purposes. Those who prefer the cheerful aspect of open fireplaces ought to be aware of the price they pay for them." *The Domestic Encyclopedia* (Philadelphia, 1821). (See also FRANKLIN STOVE, PORCELAIN STOVE.)

PARTISAN, PARTIZAN

In weaponry, the ancient thrusting weapon with a long, broad head, used in the eighteenth century as a symbol of rank by noncommissioned infantry and grenadier officers. The Espontoon, *q.v.,* or spontoon, was a type of partisan.

PARTNERS' DESK

The collector's term for the type of double pedestal desk that Thomas Chippendale called a Library Table, *q.v.* This is the flat-top writing table with a pedestal, fitted with drawers or cupboard space, at either end, and large enough so that two persons may sit at it facing one another.

PASTE ROLLER

A contemporary term for the kitchen utensil better known as a rolling pin, and made of blown glass, bone, and ivory, as well as hardwood; many rollers, carefully made and sometimes decorated with chip carving, were given as bride's presents. "Charles Shipman, Ivory and Hardwood Turner . . . purposes . . . on the most reasonable terms ivory tooth-pick-cases, eggs, nutmeg graters, ivory thimbles, paste rollers . . ." *The New York Journal or The General Advertiser,* August 6, 1767.

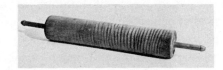

Maple paste roller.

PASTRY CRIMPER
(See JAGGING IRON.)

PASTETHE
A perfuming ball. (See also POMANDER.)

PASTEL, PASTEL DRAWING

In the sixteenth and early seventeenth centuries, pastel, from the Italian *pastella,* was used as a synonym for the plant woad, or the blue dye produced from it. Late in the seventeenth century the word was used to mean a crayon, literally a blue paste. The term to signify a drawing in various dry colors does not seem to have been used before the mid-nineteenth century. (See also ACADEMY FIGURE, CHALK DRAWING, PASTIL.)

PASTIL, PASTILLE

The term from the French *pastille* now more commonly written pastel, for an artist's crayon. "To draw with dry colours, make long pastils by grinding red lead with strong wort, and so roll them up like pencils, drying them in the sun." Henry Peacham, *The Compleat Gentleman* (London, 1661).

PATCH BOX

(1) The small, sometimes jeweled container for beauty spots or patches; made of silver, gold, ivory, japanned wood, papier-mâché, Battersea, or Bilston enameled ware, each of which see. (See also advertisement quoted under WASHBALL BOX.)

(2) The small space carved in the butt of a rifle, serving as a box to hold the greased patches in which ammunition balls were wrapped.

PATCHWORK, PATCHWORK QUILT

"Bits of different cloth sewed together," (W) to form one top piece of a quilt.

Quilt: "two pieces of cloth sewed together." (W)

PATENT LAMP

(See CARCEL LAMP.)

PATTERERO, PETTERERO

In weaponry, the term for a small piece of ordnance, "used on board ships for the discharging of nails, broken iron or partridge shot, on an enemy attempting to board ship. They are generally open at ·the breech, and their chamber made to take out to be loaded that way, instead of at the muzzle." *Encyclopedia Americana* (Philadelphia, 1831). (See also BUCCANEER GUN.)

PATTERN BOOK

(See FASHION PATTERN BOOK, FURNITURE GUIDES, and quotation under BABY HOUSE.)

PATTEPAN, PATTIPAN, PATTYPAN

Patty was the common seventeenth- and eighteenth-century term for a small pie or "pasty," and thus the pattypan was the small, metal plate or pan in which such meat or fruit-filled tarts were baked: "Take a tin or copper patty-pan and butter it . . ." Richard Briggs, *The New Art of Cookery* (Philadelphia, 1792).

PAUL REVERE LANTERN

An unfortunate but common misnomer for the cylindrical, pierced tin barn lantern used throughout the eighteenth and nineteenth centuries. Had the Sons of Liberty depended on the weak signal such lanterns provided, the Revolution would have ended April 17–18, 1775. They were made to provide only the minimum light needed by a farmer to make his way along the familiar path from kitchen to cowshed. The design provided the necessary illumination and was a safeguard against sparks causing fire in hay-filled, meal-dusty barns. Their original owners kept the lanterns, when not in use, on a kitchen shelf, or hung from a peg in the back entry. Most of these lanterns were made with little attempt at decoration. Some, however, were punched so that the tiny holes formed decorative overall stars or starburst patterns, or a series of intricate circles or diamonds. These are sought by collectors today. Few are found in good or complete condition. Many, now being recovered, need repair so extensive as to diminish any antique value. Unhappily, hundreds of these lanterns were gathered up in wholesale lots of ten to thirty during the early 1960s, purchased by decorating firms for restaurant chains to provide "atmosphere" for a variety of "ye olde" dining salons and cocktail bars. Candle sockets and doors were removed and bottom plates replaced in order to restyle the lanterns as electric lamps. (When it became difficult to find enough lanterns to supply the fad, small tin footstoves in turned-wood frames

Pierced tin lantern, in error called Paul Revere type.

463

similarly were stripped of their doors, fireboxes, and back or bottom plates.) Many that escaped the restaurant sweep were collected a few years later to enhance the decor of so-called country stores. (See also LANTERN.)

PEA BLUFF, PEA SHOOTER

The term for "a tube, one, two, or three feet long, usually of tin, through which boys blow a pea with considerable force and precision." (H) One of the many early toys collected today, such pea shooters usually were decorated in bright primary colors.

PEAK

The contemporary term for what generally today is called Wampum, q.v., by collectors of Indian artifacts; used as money by the settlers as well as by the native Americans. "This peak Consists of Small Cylinders cut out of a Conque-Shell, drill'd through and Strung like Beads. It serves both for Money and Jewels, the Blue being of much Greater Value than the White, for the same reason that Ethiopian Mistresses in France are dearer than French, because they are more scarce." William Byrd, *History of the Dividing Line* [1728–29] (Richmond, 1866).

PEALER

An old name for a wooden, long-handled ladle, spatula, or stirrer, used to reduce the action of boiling. "To peal is to stir with some agitation, as to peal the pot when it boils, to stir the liquor therein with a ladle." (J)

PÉCHÉ MORTEL

The French term for a kind of couch similar to the Duchesse, q.v., this was a combination of upholstered chair and stool, and thus a type of elegant mid-eighteenth-century Day Bed, q.v. Chippendale showed "two designs of Couches, of what the French call Peche Mortel . . . the Dimensions are six Feet long in the Clear, and two Feet, six inches, to three Feet broad." His patterns called for an easy-chair back, with a bolster, to be used as the head of the couch. "This style," Chippendale wrote, "is Sometimes made to take asunder in the Middle; one Part makes a large Easy-chair, and the other a stool, and the Feet join in the Middle, which looks badly. Therefore, I would recommend their being made, as in these Designs, with a pretty thick Mattress." *The Gentleman and Cabinet-Maker's Director* (London, 1762). When the couch was separated, the two pieces were similar in appearance to today's armchair and matching footstool.

PED(DER)

A contemporary term for a "small packsaddle; hamper; basket," (W) or, "a species of hamper without a lid." (H) Thus, Ped-Market was a fair or market to which farmers carried their fruits and vegetables in baskets, and a peddler was one who carried his wares about the streets or countryside in a basket.

PEDESTAL(S)

The term for a tall, decorative four-sided stand, a kind of narrow, closed cupboard fitted with shelves; placed at either end of

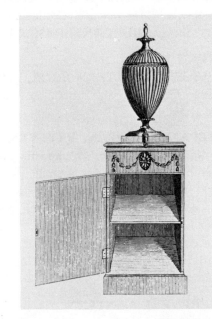

Pedestal and vase shown in Hepplewhite's *Guide* (London, 1794).

the side table. These "are much used in spacious dining-rooms where the kind of sideboards without drawers are chosen. One pedestal serves as a plate-warmer, being provided with [interior] racks and a stand for a heater; and is lined with strong tin; the other pedestal is used as a pot cupboard," *q.v.* "The height of the pedestal is the same as the sideboard and 16 to 18 inches square." A. Hepplewhite, *The Cabinet-maker and Upholsterer's Guide,* London, 1794. (See also TERMS for BUSTS.)

PEDESTAL DESK
(See LIBRARY TABLE.)

PEDESTAL TABLE
A term describing any table, whether rectangular, round, oval, square, or polygonal, set on a single column or pedestal above a low base.

PEDLERY
A general term for any "wares sold by pedlers." (W) (See also CHAPBOOK, TRADE GOODS.)

PEDOMETER
The name of "an instrument to measure distances by the steps in walking," (W) also called a way-wiser or Perambulator, *q.v.*

PEEL
From the Latin *pala* or shovel, this was the term for the broad, thin board with a long handle used to put bread in and out of the

Iron peel. (Courtesy, Antiquarian and Landmarks Society, Inc.)

oven; sometimes also called a slice or a thibble. A peel is a "wooden instrument of about a yard and a half long, and broad, on which pastry cooks put pies and tarts; the instrument to be put into the oven to draw breads and pies with." (H)

PEG LAMP
(1) A small bowl or reservoir, usually of glass, but sometimes of metal or ceramic, with a top fitting of brass, pewter, or steel to hold the wick or wicks, and with a bottom stub or peg by which the reservoir or lamp was inserted and held in a candlestick. Most known today date from 1800 or later and were made to use whale oil or camphene as fuel.

Early peg lamp or font made to be set in candlestick.

Wooden peel. (Courtesy, Antiquarian and Landmarks Society, Inc.)

Iron peel. (Courtesy, Antiquarian and Landmarks Society, Inc.)

465

(2) After about 1830, lamps, also called peg lamps, were made with the reservoir more or less permanently held in the stand by means of cement or plaster of Paris. (See also SOCKET and STAND-and-SOCKET LAMP.)

PEG TANKARD

Originally this was a two-quart ale measure or communal drinking vessel divided by pegs or pins into eight draughts, and meant to be passed from hand to hand, each drinker imbibing no more than one peg's worth or eight ounces. Ancient English law, promulgated under King Edgar, attempted to discourage intemperance; pegs were ordered fastened at intervals in tavern drinking horns; whoever drank beyond the peg or mark at one draught was liable to punishment. Hence the phrase still heard today "to take one down a peg," that is, to embarrass or punish someone publicly.

PELL

A term for "an earthen vessel." (H)

PEMBROKE TABLE

A type of small breakfast table, first developed in the mid-eighteenth century, with drop leaves supported by brackets. Usually

Connecticut, c. 1800 Pembroke table with shaped leaves, pierced leg brackets, and tapered legs with medallion and string inlays. (Courtesy, Connecticut Historical Society, Inc.)

made with a shallow drawer, the Pembroke, said to have been named in honor of Frances, Countess of Pembroke, also served as a worktable, *q.v.* "The most useful of this species (tables) of furniture (Pembrokes) may be various shapes. The long square and oval are the most fashionable [1790]. These articles admit of considerable elegance in the workmanship and ornaments, [with] tops inlaid, or painted and varnished." A. Hepplewhite, *The Cabinet-Maker and Upholsterer's Guide* (London, 1794).

PEN

The common term for the quill or quill-pen, from the Latin *penna* for feather or wing. The quill was shaped to an arrow-like point where it was split into two nibs. John Schaffer invented a fountain pen with a quill-shaped nib in 1819, following development of mid-eighteenth- and early-nineteenth-cen-

Pembroke table, shown open for use in Hepplewhite's *Guide* (London, 1794).

Pen or quill, c. 1790 print.

466

tury French and British pens or nibs made of steel, horn, and tortoise shell. These "permanent" points superseded quills about 1850. (See also PENHOLDER, PENKNIFE, QUILL BOX.)

PENCIL
The contemporary term for what today would be called an artist's brush; the "instrument used by painters for laying on their colours. Pencils are of various kinds, and made of various materials, the larger sorts are made of boar's bristles, the thick ends of which are bound to a stick, these when large, are called brushes. The finer sort of pencils are made of camels, badgers, and squirrels-hair, and of the down of swans; these are tied at the upper end with a piece of strong thread, and enclosed in the barrel of a quill. All good pencils, on being drawn between the lips, come to a fine point." (M) (See also HAIR PENCIL, LEAD PENCIL.)

PENCIL-POST BED
The collector's term for the high-post bedstead, the four posts of which are slender, taper toward the top, and usually are cham-

Maple bedstead with tester and so-called pencil posts. (Courtesy, Connecticut Historical Society, Inc.)

fered or turned in the familiar pencil shape, that is, are hexagonal or octagonal. (See also BEDSTEAD, FOUR-POST BEDSTEAD, TESTER BED.)

PENDANT
The term for "an ornament hanging at the ear, frequently consisting of diamonds, pearls, and other precious stones," (M) an earring.

PENDANTS
The term to describe "two paintings or prints of equal dimensions, which are attached in corresponding positions to the same wall . . . [they] are called pendants to each other." *Encyclopedia Americana* (Philadelphia, 1831).

PENHOLDER
The slender, cylindrical shaft into which the pen or quill was fitted for ease in writing. During the Colonial period these were of two types: the long holder, as it is envisioned today, or a small band or circlet one-half to one inch in length. The quill or pen point was inserted into the former. When the plume was retained, the circlet was slipped above the pointed quill and provided the brace or sturdiness needed for writing. At times both types were used at once, the circlet covered and thus kept the juncture tight and stable. These small circlets often are mistaken for a sort of necklace slide today. Both types were made of silver, gold, ivory, semiprecious stones, such as onyx, horn, tortoise shell, bone, or fine polished hardwoods. Despite common current belief the plume was not used alone if a holder could be afforded, for it was too pliable, and its retention made shaping of a good quill difficult. (See also QUILL BOX, PEN, PENKNIFE.)

PENKNIFE
A small knife, honed to a razor-like edge, used for shaping or mending quills for writing or drawing. An elegancy for a gentleman's desk, the colonial penknife was fitted

to a handle of silver, ivory, gold, polished wood, such as ebony, or semiprecious stones such as onyx, and was kept in a separate case: "I beg the favour of you to send me some best razors and pen knives." (Order from G. Wythe, Williamsburg, Virginia, 3 August, 1769.) Frances Mason, *John Norton and Sons, Merchants of London and Virginia* (Richmond, 1935). "My pen is as bad as a skewer and not worth mending." George F. Norton. Letter 26 April, 1773. Ibid. The folding pocket-knives of the nineteenth and twentieth centuries were called penknives because of their small size and their sharpness as much as for any use in shaping quills. (See also PEN, QUILL BOX.)

Penknife, c. 1790 print.

PENNER
A contemporary cant term for "a pencase," (J) a desk box for quills. (See also QUILL BOX.)

PENNON, PENON
The name given "a kind of standard with a long tail, anciently belonging to a gentleman. It is opposed to the banner, which was square." (M)

PENNSYLVANIA RIFLE
(See KENTUCKY RIFLE.)

PENNY MUG
The cant term for a small drinking cup or mug. "And ale in penny mugs not so big as a taylor's thimble." *Character of a Coffee-House* (London, 1673).

PENNY PRINT
The inexpensive sheet illustrated with simply made wood cuts, in black or white or primary colors, of animals, games, trades, the alphabet, or household articles. Some of these were used to teach children to read. (See PICTURE.)

C. 1790 penny prints illustrating some "Cries of London."

PENTACHORD
A musical instrument with five strings, whence the name. "The strings were of bullock's leather, and struck with a plectrum made of goats-horn." (M)

PENTAGRAPH
The parallelogram, "an instrument whereby designs of any kind may be copied on what proportion you please, without being skilled in drawing." (M)

PEPPERBOX
A cant term for the popular multibarreled pocket pistol of the early nineteenth century. (See also REVOLVER.)

PEPPERBOX
The peppercaster; "a box used for holding [ground] pepper." (W)

PEPPERQUERN
A contemporary term for "a pepper-mill." (H)   (See also QUERN.)

PERAMBULATOR
A pedometer or instrument for measuring distances in walking. (W)   "Once in three years, in March, April, October, or November, the select-men shall appoint two or more persons to perambulate the lines, and renew the bounds and monuments between the towns . . . The select-men of the most ancient town to give six days notice to the select-men of the adjoining town of time and place . . . for such perambulation." *Connecticut Statutes* (Hartford, 1835). "Its advantages are its handiness and expedition; its contrivancy is such, that it may be fitted to the wheel of a coach, in which state it performs its office, and measures the road without any trouble at all." (M)

PERIAPT
"A charm." (W)   (See also AMULET.)

PERIODICALS
These are publications that appear at regular intervals. "The periodical press, comprising newspapers, reviews, magazines, annual registers, Ec., devoted to religion, politics, the sciences, arts, amusements, husbandry, Ec., is one of the most interesting and most momentous consequences of the invention of the art of printing, [and] have now become one of the most important parts of the machinery of society, particularly in England, France and the U. States." *Encyclopedia Americana* (Philadelphia, 1831).

PERPETUAL CALENDAR
(See WATCH CALENDAR.)

PERSPECTIVE, PERSPECTIVE GLASS
The contemporary term for "a reflecting-glass" (H) or "a spying-glass" (W); a type of telescope. "If you want to use a Glass, your Father has a better, which he will lend you. But a Perspective Glass is not so good as the Eye for Prospects, be-cause it takes in too small a Field. It is only useful to discern better some particular objects." (Benjamin Franklin at Philadelphia to his grandson, W. T. Franklin at school, June 13, 1775.) *The Writings of Benjamin Franklin,* ed., A. H. Smyth (New York, 1907).

PERSPECTIVE
The term "also denotes a kind of painting frequently seen in gardens, at the end of galleries, Ec., especially designed to deceive the sight." (M)

PESTLE
"A tool to beat in a mortar." (W)   (See also MORTAR, MORTAR AND PESTLE.)

PETRONEL
The short hand gun or large pistol, popular in the seventeenth century, made with a curved stock that was rested against the chest when fired.

PEWTER CUPBOARD
A term for the set of slanted, open shelves set above a cupboard-base. (See PEWTER PRESS, PLATE CUPBOARD.)

PEWTER PRESS
A contemporary colonial synonym for the cupboard with shelves designed for the display of pewter or plate. The inventory of the estate of James Logan, Philadelphia, appraised in part July 31, 1752 by Benjamin Franklin and Richard Peters, included "In the Back Dining Room on the first story 1 maple Desk £2.15; 1 couch & couch Bed & Cushion £1.15; 2 walnut tables £1.17.-6; 10 Leather chairs with cushions 17s 6d; corner cupboard 10s; a tea table 5s; a pewter press." *Will Book I,* p. 510. (See also COURT CUPBOARD, PLATE CUPBOARD.)

PHANTASMAGORIA
One of many early machines or lanterns designed to provide moving pictures for parlor entertainment. This was similar to the Magic Lantern, *q.v.,* "only instead of paint-

ing the figures on transparent glass, all the glass is opaque, except the figure only, which being painted in transparent colours, the light shines through it, and no light can fall on the screen but what passes through the figure. The screen is very thin silk between the spectators and the lantern, and by moving the lantern backwards or forwards, the figures seem to recede or approach." *The Domestic Encyclopedia* (Philadelphia, 1821).

PHARMACOPOEIA
A contemporary term for a "Dispensatory [*q.v.*], a book containing rules for the composition of medicines," (J) useful equally to the physician or layman.

PHIAL
A common term for a small, stoppered bottle of pottery or glass. (See VIAL and advertisement quoted under SWEETMEAT BOTTLE.)

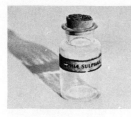

Blown-glass phial or medicine bottle.

PHILADELPHIA STOVE
The popular colonial term for what is now called a Franklin Stove, *q.v.* (See also VENETIAN STOVE.)

PHILOSOPHER'S STONE
(See ALCHEMY, Chapter 9.)

PHILTER
"A love charm." (W) (See also AMULET.)

PHOEBE LAMP
Apparently a collector's term for the "double" grease lamp; the term does not appear in any dictionary of the eighteenth or early nineteenth centuries when these lamps still were in use. Perhaps the word is derived

from the Greek *phoebe,* for bright, the name sometimes given Artemis, the moon goddess, or *phoebus,* literally bright and shining. (See also BETTY LAMP; CRUSE.)

Phoebe or double-cruse lamp.

PHOTOMETER
One of the late-eighteenth- and early-nineteenth-century scientific devices, this was "an instrument to indicate the different quantities of light, as in a cloudy or bright day, or between bodies illuminated in different degrees . . . the essential part is a glass tube, like a reversed syphon, whose two branches should be equal in height, and terminated by balls of equal diameter . . . one is of black enamel, and the other of common glass, into which is put sulphuric acid . . . The motion of the liquor, tinged red with carmine, is measured . . . and the intensity of the incident light is then estimated by the number of degrees which the liquor has runaway." *Encyclopedia Americana* (Philadelphia, 1831).

PHYSIOGNOTRACE
A device used early in the nineteenth century for drawing silhouette portraits: "The outline of the human face may be taken in a minute. The person whose portrait is to be taken, is seated upon a chair, with his cheek

resting on a projecting piece of board, that the head may be kept steady in one position. A brass ruler is then passed over the head and face, and a metallic pin, which makes parallel movements with the ruler, marks the exact profile upon a small sheet of paper. One of these machines is placed in Peale's Museum in Philadelphia, and has been used with success." *The Domestic Encyclopedia* (Philadelphia, 1821). "J. J. Boudier . . . has just now established a Phisiognotrace, an Instrument of a late inventor in Europe, by means of which likenesses from any point of view, are taken necessarily in a most striking manner, in a single setting of about one hour. The price of his likenesses, ornament with an elegant vignette . . . will be but two dollars for the present, in order to get some publicity to the invention." *Federal Gazette* (Philadelphia), September 26, 1796. (See also DELINEATOR, PROFILE.)

PIANOFORTE

The term from the Italian *pian e forte,* meaning soft and strong, was chosen by the inventor Bartolomeo Christofori of Padua, in the eighteenth century to designate the gradations in tone the pianoforte is capable of producing. Basically a dulcimer with keys and dampers, the piano resembled in shape the older harpsichord and clavichord. Small hammers are operated by levers from the keyboard which strike metal strings; the vibrations are stopped by the dampers. When first developed, the sound-box and that for the keyboard formed the case for the pianoforte; it was not necessarily sold with a matching supporting frame and legs as we are accustomed to seeing today.

Less than fifty years after its introduction, "The Forte-Piano is become so exceedingly fashionable that few polite families are without it. This much esteemed instrument forms an agreeable accompaniment for the female voice, takes up but little room, may be moved with ease, and consequently kept

C. 1830 pianoforte. (Courtesy, Antiquarian and Landmarks Society, Inc.)

in tune with little attention so that it is on that account superior to the harpsichord [Dodds and Claus]." *The Diary, or London's Register,* September 19, 1792.

So popular an instrument was the piano that numerous new companies were formed for its manufacture between 1800 and 1840 to compete with European houses and with each other. "We the Subscribers have formed a copartnership under the firm of Gould, Wilder & Co., as makers of Piano Fortes. Being experienced in the business, we intend to make as good instruments as any made in this city; and respectfully invite ladies and gentlemen to call at our establishment, Boylston Street, near Washington Street. S. L. Gould, B. G. Wilder, L. Wilkins, D. B. Newhall. Tuneing and repairing. Also instruments taken in exchange." *Trumpet and Universalist Magazine* (Boston), May 1, 1835.

By 1850 "the piano-forte is the universal accompaniment of the drawing-room or parlor in America. Even in simple cottages, where such a thing would excite astonishment in Europe, the piano will be found. It by no means follows that a knowledge of music is equally universal—but the desire for it certainly is; and, if, as we suspect, music demands more age and higher culture than our young nation has yet attained, we will have faith that, by and by, we may be as musical a people as the Germans." A. J. Downing, *The Architecture of Country Houses* (New York, 1850).

PIANO STOOL
(See MUSIC STOOL.)

PIB-CORN
Another name for the Hornpipe, *q.v.*

PICKAX
One of the tools, "a kind of ax that has a sharp point." (W)

PICKLE GLASS
Small dishes made of engraved or cut glass in the eighteenth century as well as of pattern glass in the nineteenth. "8 cut Glasses for Pickles; 1 Dozen Sweet Meat Glasses; 2 small Cruits . . ." (Order, February 15, 1770, from Mann Page, Fredericksburg, Virginia, to London.) Frances Mason, *John Norton and Sons, Merchants of London and Virginia* (Richmond, 1935).

PICKTOOTH, PICKTOOTH CASE
A common contemporary term for (1) "an instrument by which the teeth are cleaned," (J) and its case: (2) "If a gentleman leaves a picktooth case on the table after dinner, look upon it as part of your vails." Jonathan Swift, "Advice to Butlers," *Essays.* (See also TOOTHPICK CASE.)

PICTURE
Then as now a common term for "a resemblance of persons and things in colours; the work of painters." (J) "As soon as he begins to spell, as many pictures of animals should be got him as can be found with the printed names on them." John Locke, *Advice to Parents.* (See also PAINTING.)

PIECE
A common early term for a firearm, or in combination form, as a fowling piece or birding piece.

PIECES OF EIGHT
Hard money of silver or gold always was scarce in the colonies, and indeed also during the Early Federal period. A common practice was to cut the Spanish milled dollar into pieces or bits equal to twenty-five cents or twelve-and-one-half cents. These pie- or triangular-shaped pieces still are found in trinket and jewel boxes and treasured by collectors: "The money here [Lexington, Kentucky] is paper, issued by banks, or of silver, which is not common and which is Spanish. Small change, therefore, is rare, and for this reason they cut dollars into quarters and eighths. This facilitates fraud, for those so inclined find it easy to make five parts instead of four, or nine rather than eight." Edouard de Montulé, *Voyage en Amérique* . . . (Paris, 1821). It was as a result of this practice that the phrases two bits for a quarter of a dollar, and four bits for a half dollar, became part of our everyday language.

PIECRUST TABLE
(See PIECRUST, Chapter 5.)

PIER GLASS
The tall, narrow looking glass intended to be set between two windows, and for which richly carved and gilded frames often were made to order. Of his designs for such "Pier-glass-Frames," Chippendale said, "a skilful Carver may, in the Execution of this, give full Scope to his Capacity." *The Gentleman and Cabinet-Maker's Director* (London, 1762).

Pier table shown in Hepplewhite's *Guide* (London, 1794).

Pier Tables.

472

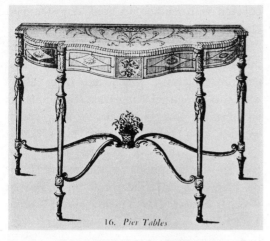

16. *Pier Tables*

Pier table from Thomas Sheraton's *The Cabinet-Maker and Upholsterer's Drawing-Book* (London, 1791–94).

PIER TABLE
The usually more or less D-shaped table, with the "vertical stroke" set against the wall, specifically made to place between two windows, and usually beneath a Pier Glass, *q.v.*

PIGGEN, PIGGIN
A common term for "a wooden dipper," (W) brought to the colonies by settlers of Scots-Irish descent, because it had been a word particularly "used in the northern provinces for a small vessel." (J)

PIG-IRON
In the kitchen, this was "a flat piece of iron which the cook interposes between the fire and meat roasting when she wants to retard or put back that operation. It is hung on the bars by a hook." (H)   A thin, flat circle, or rectangle of iron or tin with a top ring of hooks by which it was suspended from pot-hooks attached to the Trammel or Lug Pole, *qq.v.*, and thus hung between the spit and the fire.

PIKE
(1) In weaponry, "a long lance used by the foot soldiers, to keep off the horse [soldiers]; to which bayonets have succeeded." (J)   "Pikeheads; pikes, with and without heads" were listed in House of Parliament Rates, 1660, for Imports and Exports—*Statutes of the Realm* (London, 1819). (2) "A fork used in husbandry; a Pitch-fork," *q.v.* (J) (See also HALBARD, HALF-PIKE, LEADING STAFF.)

PILE
Originally a name for the head of an arrow, and thus later for "a kind of poker with a long flat handle used by bakers," (H) to stir the embers in the oven. Because of some similarity of shape and perhaps because of pronunciation, it often today is confused with the wooden Peel, *q.v.*

PILLAR-AND-CLAW TABLE
(See CLAW TABLE.)

PILLAR-AND-SCROLL CLOCK
A contemporary term for the shelf-clock case designed with narrow side pillars, a double scroll or broken-arch top, and slender bracket feet; first developed by Eli Terry, and used also by Silas Hoadley, Seth Thomas, and others during the first quarter of the nineteenth century.

PILLION
A type of small saddle or "a cushion for women to ride on behind a person." (W)

PILLOW
The term from the Saxon *pyle* for a "bag of down or feathers laid under the head to sleep on." (J)

PILLOWBEER, PILLOWCASE
Any "cover for a pillow." (J)   "When you put a clean pillowcase on your lady's pillow, fasten it well with pins." Jonathan Swift, "Advice to Butlers," *Essays*.

PIN
The name for "a well known little instrument, usually made of brass wire, blanched, and which is chiefly employed by females in adjusting their dress." *The Domestic Encyclopedia* (Philadelphia, 1821).

Pin Money was "an allowance for a wife's pocket," (W)   with which presumably she might purchase these necessary instruments. (See also PINCUSHION.)

PINCASE

A contemporary term for "a Pincushion," *q.v.* (J)

PINCUSHION

Then as now, the term for a small stuffed cushion or pad for the safekeeping of the seamstress' sewing needles and straight pins. This also was a customary gift of congratulation to a new mother; the design formed by pins. "Decr. 30th [1771]. My aunt stuck a white sattin pincushion for Mrs. Waters. On one side is a planthorn with flowers, on the reverse, just under the border are, on one side stuck these words, Joseph Waters, then follows on the end, Decr. 1771, on the next side & end are the words, Welcome little Stranger." *Diary of Anna Green Winslow* (Boston, 1894).

PINCUSHION CHAIR

A descriptive term sometimes applied to the Compass Chair, *q.v.*

PIPE BOX

The name collectors generally give to the tall, shallow wooden wall box deep enough to hold several long-stemmed clay pipes; often with a small drawer for tobacco.

Pipe box with drawer for flint and steel.

PIPE CASE

A fitted desk or table case, or box with lid, of metal or wood, sometimes painted or covered with leather, to hold long-stemmed clay pipes and packets of prepared tobacco. "In those days [pre-1800] the [Calvinistic] ministry had not yet felt the need of that generous decision which led them afterwards to forego all dangerous stimulants, as an example to their flock. A long green, wooden case, full of tobacco pipes and a quantity of papers of tobacco, used to be part of the hospitable stock prepared for the reception of the brethren." Harriet Beecher Stowe, *Old Town Folks* (Boston, 1868).

PIPE-STOPPER, PIPE-STOPPLE

Those stoppers or tampers prized by many collectors of small objects made from the mid-seventeenth century through the mid-nineteenth were used to press tobacco down in the pipe bowl. Many were handsomely decorated and ornamented, or carved in animal and human figural shapes, in silver, brass, steel, hardwood, ivory, stoneware, and porcelain, or combinations of these, as metal and wood.

PIPE TONGS

The specially made iron or steel small tongs used by the smoker to lift a small coal from the fireplace with which to light a pipe; often with a rasp and tamper added to the handle. (See also PLIERS.)

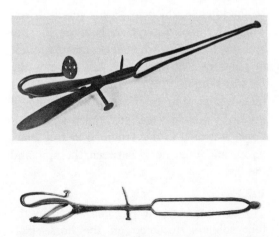

Smoker's pipe tongs with tampers and router, New England, eighteenth century. (Courtesy, Antiquarian and Landmarks Society, Inc.)

474

PIPKIN

"A small earthenware boiler or pot." (J)
". . . Then put it into a pipkin and cover it
with wine and water, and put into a hand-
full of good herbs . . . Let it boil for two
hours." Sir Kenelm Digby, *The Queen's
Closet Opened* (London, 1667).

Sometimes, a jam pot:

A little meat best fits a little belly,
As sweetly, Lady, give me leave to tell ye,
This little pipkin fits this little jelly.

Robert Herrick [*Hesperides*], *A Ter-
nary of Littles.*

PIPPIN

A kind of apple, but also another spelling
"for pipkin." (H)

PIRN

An old term for a spool or "a piece of wood
turned to wind thread on." (H)

PISTOL

The smallest of firearms, designed to be
fired with one hand, the pistol first was used
by cavalrymen and carried in saddle holsters. Small versions were designed later to
be carried in the pocket. "Military Goods
such as Swords, Guns, Pistols, Epaulettes,
Sergeants' knots, silk and worsted Sashes,
sword knots, horseman's Caps and Holsters,
Valices, Cartouch-Boxes, priming Wires and
Brushes, sword Belts, Flints; gold, silver,
and plated Laces, Cords, and Fringes;
Feathers of various colours and lengths,
Base-Drums for bands of music, common
martial do. Files, French horns, Ec. . . .
on as good terms as can be bought in these

parts, by Ward & Bartholomew." *American
Mercury* (Hartford, Connecticut), May 31,
1810. "Horsemen's swords and Pistols.
Charles Sigourney Has recently imported
. . . from Amsterdam and now offers for
Sale—100 pair of ordinary horsemen's
Pistols, 20 pr. of fine do. for officers. A few
pair of low priced pocket pistols . . ."
American Mercury (Hartford, Connecti-
cut), April 21, 1817.

PITCHER

The general term for any "earthen vessel; a
water pot," (J) or a "large earthen pot,"

Blue decorated delft pitcher. (Courtesy, Antiquarian and Landmarks Society, Inc.)

Glazed redware pitchers. (Courtesy, Antiquarian
and Landmarks Society, Inc.)

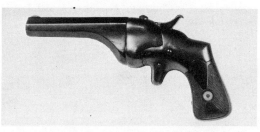

Pistol, Connecticut Arms and Manufacturing Company, c. 1863. (Courtesy, Connecticut Historical
Society, Inc.)

Glazed earthenware milk
pitcher. (Courtesy,
Antiquarian and
Landmarks Society, Inc.)

Small polychrome creamware cream pitcher. (Courtesy, Antiquarian and Landmarks Society, Inc.)

(W) with a pouring lip; also, of course, made in wood, porcelain, plated metal, silver, or glass. (See also EWER, JUG, POT.)

PITCHER AND BOWL
(See EWER AND BASIN, WASH BASIN.)

PITCHFORK
One of the farm tools, "a long fork to pitch hay." (W) "She wears her clothes as if they were thrown on her with a pitchfork." Jonathan Swift, "Polite Conversation," *Dialogues.*

PLANCHER
An old name for "a plate," (H) derived from planch or planchen, an ancient term for board or boards, and thus the same as Trencher, *q.v.*

PLANETARIUM
(See ORRERY.)

PLANT HORN
A contemporary colloquialism for the Horn of Plenty, or Cornucopia, *q.v.,* in Chapter 5. (See also note under PINCUSHION.)

PLANT PRESS
(See BOTANICAL PRESS.)

PLANT STAND
The collector's term for a Flower Stand, *q.v.*

PLASTIC, PLASTICE
The "plastick art, a branch of sculpture, being the art of forming figures of men, birds, beasts, fishes, Ec., in plaster, clay, stucco, or the like." (M)

PLASTRAN, PLASTRON
A term for "a piece of stuffed leather" (W) used to designate a cushion, sometimes a saddle. (See also PILLION, SADDLE.)

PLATE
In addition to its meaning as a flat surface, tray, or platter, of wood, ceramics, or

Seventeenth-century delft wedding plate. (Courtesy, Antiquarian and Landmarks Society, Inc.)

Late-seventeenth-century delft plate. (Courtesy, Antiquarian and Landmarks Society, Inc.)

Early-eighteenth-century delft plate. (Courtesy, Antiquarian and Landmarks Society, Inc.)

Chinoiserie design on dinner plate, early eighteenth century. (Courtesy, Antiquarian and Landmarks Society, Inc.)

Eighteenth-century pewter plate. (Courtesy, Antiquarian and Landmarks Society, Inc.)

Creamware perforated-edge plate. (Courtesy, Antiquarian and Landmarks Society, Inc.)

Staffordshire dinner plate. (Courtesy, Connecticut Historical Society, Inc.)

Glazed redware plate.   Mid-nineteenth-century pewter plate. (Courtesy, Antiquarian and Landmarks Society, Inc.)

metal, plate was a common contemporary and specific synonym for silver pieces, especially tableware: "We had twelve at table, and very good and pleasant company . . . but, Lord! to see with what way they looked upon all my fine plate was pleasant; for I made the best show I could, to let them understand me and my condition, to take down the pride of Mrs. Clerke, who thinks herself very great." Samuel Pepys, *Diary,* April 8, 1667. (See also COURT CUPBOARD, PLATE CUPBOARD.)

PLATE BASKET, PLATE CARRIER

A deep bucket with a lid and a bail handle; often made of mahogany or other fine wood and used to carry dinner plates to and from the kitchen or pantry. "Send . . . One Plate Basket lined with tin, One Plate Basket not lined." (Order, September 25, 1771, from Peter Lyons, Hanover, Virginia, to London.) Frances Mason, *John Norton and Sons, Merchants of London and Virginia* (Richmond, 1935). (See also VOIDER.)

PLATE CUPBOARD

A seventeenth- and early-eighteenth-century description of the set of shelves, usually ornately and handsomely carved, made for the display of pewter, silver, porcelains: "I was as merry as I could, giving them a good dinner . . . They eyed mightily my great cupboard of plate—I this day putting my two flaggons upon my table; and indeed it is a fine sight, and better than ever I did hope to see of my own." Samuel Pepys, *Diary,* September 9, 1664.

Again, on May 15, 1666, Pepys noted "my new plate sets off my cupboard nobly." Ibid. (See also COURT CUPBOARD.)

PLATE WARMER
(See HASTER.)

PLATTER
"Any large dish," (J) plate, or tray, or common food container of wood, pewter, silver, earthenware, or porcelain. (See also CHARGER, DOUBLER, PLANCHER, TRENCHER.)

PLAYING CARDS
The term "among gamesters, implies a small piece of fine pasteboard, in the form of a parallelogram; cards are of various sizes, but those commonly used are about three inches and a half long, and two and a half broad." (M) Playing cards were listed in the House of Parliament rates, 1660, for Imports and Exports—*Statutes of the Realm* (London, 1819). (See note under HAMPER.)

PLAYING TABLE
A common colonial synonym for the gaming table, today usually called a Card Table, *q.v.* "Playing Tables of Wainscott" and "Playing Tables of walnut-tree, the payre" were listed in the House of Parliament Rates, 1660, for Imports and Exports—*Statutes of the Realm* (London, 1819). This description probably referred to the early game called Tables, a form of Backgammon, *q.v.*, played on a double board. Such hinged boards were called pairs of tables.

PLIERS
The term also used for "a kind of tongs used by smokers for taking up a lighted wood coal." (H) (See also EMBER TONGS, PIPE TONGS.)

PLUME
The common term for "the feathers of birds which are frequently worn by military men, and females, as ornaments to the head-dress; a custom derived from barbarous nations." *The Domestic Encyclopedia* (Philadelphia, 1821). Nevertheless, plumes were favored as gown decorations, for women's hats, and for military caps. "Normand Smith keeps all kinds of military and plain Saddlery Work; Caps and Holsters; elegant gilt morocco Belts; Gilt and plain Cockades; Feathers; White and red military Web, in abundance, silver mounted Whips and Spurs; travelling trunks, Ec." *American Mercury* (Hartford, Connecticut), May 9, 1811.

PLUVIOMETER
A common name for the rain gauge; a device for measuring the quantity of rain that falls. (1) "One of the best is a hollow cylinder, having within it a cork-ball attached to a wooden stem [marked in graduated degrees] which passes through a small opening at the top, on which is placed a funnel [to catch the rain]. (2) A very simple rain-gauge . . . consists of a copper funnel, the area of whose opening is exactly ten square inches. This is fixed in a bottle and the quantity of rain caught is ascertained by multiplying the weight in ounces by 173, which gives the depth in inches and parts of an inch." *Encyclopedia Americana* (Philadelphia, 1831).

POCKET
The contemporary term for a kind of "small bag" (W) or purse, usually worn attached to the sash or girdle. "June 21, 1707. Billy Cowell's Shop is entered by the Chimney, and a quantity of Plate stolen . . . They find James Hews hid in the hay in

Pocket in crewel embroidery. (Courtesy, Antiquarian and Landmarks Society, Inc.)

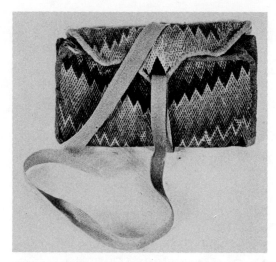

Pocket in flame stitch. (Courtesy, Antiquarian and Landmarks Society, Inc.)

Cabal's barn; while seizing him under the Hay, he stripped off his Pocket . . . [with] Cowell's silver in it." Samuel Sewall, *Diary*. (See also WALLET, WORK POCKET.)

POCKETBOOK

The common term for "a writing book for the pocket," (W) a kind of memorandum book or one "carried in the pocket for hasty notes." (J) "T. Anderson, Book-Binder, Letter-Case and Pocket-Book-Maker, makes and sells all sorts of letter cases, desk cases, travelling cases and boxes with or without shaving equipage; Ladies travelling writing desks, fishing cases, solo cases. New pocket books, made to old instruments." *The New York Mercury,* December 24, 1764.

"Feb. 12th 1772. The following lines Aunt Deming found in grandmama Sargent's pocket-book & gives me leave to copy 'em here—

Dim eyes, deaf ears, cold stomach shew
My dissolution is in view
The shuttle's thrown, my race is run
My sun is set
My work is done . . .

Diary of Anna Green Winslow (Boston, 1894). The verses quoted are from the epi-taph attributed to Governor Thomas Dudley.

"FIVE DOLLARS REWARD. Lost between the little Bridge in Hartford and New Gate Prison in Granby, a Red Morocco Pocket Book containing between 42 and 47 Dollars, together with some small change. Whoever will return said Pocket Book to the subscriber shall receive the above reward. William Gleason." *American Mercury* (Hartford, Connecticut), February 22, 1814.

POCKET CLOCK
A contemporary synonym for "a watch." (H)

POCKET DIAL
(See COMPASS DIAL.)

POCKET GLASS
The term for "a looking glass for the pocket." (W)

POCKET HYDROMETER
"Southworth's Patent Hydrometers . . . contain one weight only, and that is attached to the Instrument. It is portable for the pocket, the case of which with ease may be plunged into a cask of Liquor, and its strength ascertained in one minute. The instrument is made of Silver, about eight inches in length . . . The great use of ardent spirits in this country, whether criminally so or not, does not make it criminal of the purchaser to know whether he is purchasing grog, or good proof spirits. The Hydrometer is plunged into the liquor, which keeps erect, the stave of which is marked with degrees. The stronger the liquor the deeper it will sink . . . it weighs the liquor with as much accuracy as we can weigh the most precious metals, [and] never errs; the proof glass may . . . under the most favorable circumstances, [but] the use of the proof glass is guess work . . . Accompanying the instrument is a card from Gilpin's Tables of Specific Gravity . . . The above Hydrometers are for sale

at his store in Ferry-Street . . . [by] Joseph Belden." *American Mercury* (Hartford, Connecticut), November 11, 1812.

POCKET LANTERN

A small fold-up tin lantern, 3 to 4 inches in width and height, made with all sides and top and bottom plates hinged; the "light" sides usually of mica. "Hodgson, Nicholson & Co. Have Just Received, An assortment of Patent Lamps and Lanterns . . . The Pocket-lanterns, with Reflectors, are portable, and convenient for either Ladies or Gentlemen." *Maryland Journal* (Baltimore), December 11, 1792. (See also LANTERN.)

POCKET STANDISH

An early term for the Inkhorn, *q.v.*, carried by the traveler. (See quotation under STANDISH.)

PODGER

A contemporary colloquialism for a "platter or dish," the word formed from "podge," (H) a contraction of porridge; hence, another name for a shallow Porringer, *q.v.*

POISE

(See COUNTERPOISE, STILLYARD.)

POKE

A "small bag or Pocket," *q.v.* (W)

POKER

The "iron bar with which men stir the fire." (J) One of the fire irons commonly kept near the hearth.

POLEAX

In weaponry, the term for "a sort of hatchet nearly resembling a battle-axe, having a handle about fifteen inches long, and . . . a sharp point being downward from the back of its head. It is principally used on board ships to cut away the rigging of an adversary . . . They have also been used by driving the points into [the] side [of a hull] one above another, forming a kind of scaling-ladder, whence they are sometimes called boarding-axes." *Encyclopedia Americana* (Philadelphia, 1831).

POLE FIRE SCREEN

A type of decorative sliding screen fixed on a pole standard and used in parlors and chambers to deflect the too-intense heat of the hearth fire. "The Screens may be ornamented variously, with maps, Chinese figures, needle-work, Ec. The screen is suspended on the pole by means of a spring in the eye through which the pole goes; the feet are loaded with lead to keep them steady; they may be made of mahogany, but more frequently [are] of wood japanned." A. Hepplewhite, *The Cabinet-Maker and Upholsterer's Guide* (London, 1794). (See also FIRE SCREEN.)

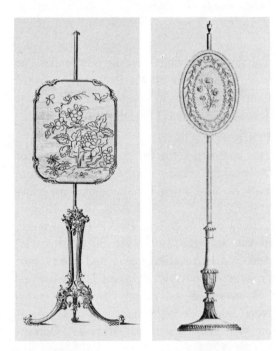

Pole fire screen illustrated in Chippendale's *Director* (London, 1762).

Pole fire screen from Hepplewhite's *Guide* (London, 1794).

POLEMOSCOPE

The term for an "oblique kind of prospective glass, contrived for seeing objects that do not lie directly before the eye. It was invented by Henelius in 1637 . . . This kind are now known among us, under the name of ogling-glasses, or opera glasses,

480

through which one sees a person, in appearing to look at another." (M)

POKING STICK

Another and earlier term for the Goffering Iron, *q.v.* Originally, "this tool was made of wood or bone," (H) to put the plaits of a ruff in proper form. Later it was made of steel in order that it might be used hot.

POLICEMAN'S LANTERN
(See DARK LANTERN.)

POLYGRAPH

The name given the instrument or press "invented by Mr. J. Hawkins, and improved by Mr. [Charles Wilson] Peale, of Philadelphia, is the most simple and complete writing apparatus yet invented. Two or three copies (or rather originals) are taken at the same time. The apparatus folds up in a large portable writing desk, and is sold for 50 dollars." *The Domestic Encyclopedia* (Philadelphia, 1821).

POLYOPTRUM

A name for "a glass through which objects appear multiplied." (W) (See also KALEIDOSCOPE.)

POLYSCOPE

A term for "a glass which makes a single object appear as many," (W) and so the same as Polyoptrum, *q.v.*

POMANDER, POMANDER BALL, POMANDER BASKET

The term for "a kind of perfume, generally made in the form of a ball and worn about the person," (H) pomander also designated the locket or container in which the pomander was kept. The lockets or pendants were usually ball-shaped, hinged to open into two equal halves, and made of perforated pewter, silver, or gold. Some were a kind of open-work formed of thin gold, silver, pewter, or plated tin wire. In addition to the lockets intended for wear as pieces of jewelry, larger containers were made to be suspended from a beam or ceiling hook as a kind of room air-freshener. These usually were plated tin, pewter, or iron.

"**To Make Pomanders:** Take two penny-worth of labdanum, two penny-worth of storax liquid, one penny-worth of calamus aromaticus, as much balm, half a quarter of a pound of fine wax [beeswax] of cloves and mace two penny-worth, of liquid aloes three penny-worth, of nutmegs eight penny-worth, and of musk four grains: beat all these exceedingly together till they come to a perfect substance, then mould it in any fashion you please, and dry it." Gervase Markham, *The English House-Wife* (London, 1675).

POMPADOUR

A fanciful name sometimes used to designate a lady's easy chair.

PONIARD

The name of a "little pointed dagger, very sharp-edged. It was anciently borne in the hand, at the girdle, or hid in the pocket, but is now set aside, except among assassins and at the theatres." (M)

PONTYPOOL, PONTYPOOL JAPANNING

A popular method of japanning or decorating tin, so named because such handicraft work was carried on extensively during the eighteenth century at Pontypool, Monmouthshire, England, based on the process developed by Thomas Allgood, a resident of Pontypool, during the reign of Charles II. Ground colors chiefly used were black, blue, white, green, yellow, bright red, or scarlet. These were heavily varnished to protect the paint. Decorations used were mainly swags or festoons, garlands, flowers, simple landscapes. "James Jacks, has imported in the last ships from London, via Charleston . . . An elegant assortment of real Pontypool and bronzed tea and coffee urns." *Federal Gazette* (Philadelphia), April 15, 1797.

POOR BOX

The common term for any small slot-top receptacle specifically used, as a storage coffer for coins or odd amounts of money, to encourage personal thrift, and to provide an extra means of giving to those less fortunate, sometimes, by self-imposed fines: "To the pewterer's, to buy a poore's box, to put my forfeits in, upon breach of my vows [breaking Lenten resolutions]." Samuel Pepys, *Diary,* March 5, 1662. One's private poor box could also be a visual reminder of the necessity to save for the inevitable rainy day, and a goad to sometimes restricted ambition: "He that gets all he can, and saves all he gets (necessary expenses excepted) will certainly become rich. Unless, of course, that Being who governs the world, in whom all should look for a blessing on their honest endeavours, doth not, in his wise providence otherwise determine." Benjamin Franklin, "Advice to a Young Tradesman," *Collected Works* (Hartford, 1845). (See also THRIFT BOX.)

POPGUN

Then as now, a cant term for "a child's wooden gun," (W) usually hand-carved or whittled by the youngster himself or an indulgent parent.

PORCELAIN STOVE

The decorated and more decorative free-standing Parlor Stove, *q.v.,* used in Europe in the eighteenth century but more commonly designating "The French white porcelain stoves, very beautiful and economical . . . One dollar in charcoal will go as far whether [in the home] of the poor or the rich as 4 dollars in wood." *The Domestic Encyclopedia* (Philadelphia, 1821).

PORRIDGE POT

A contemporary synonym for the large "pot in which meat [food] is boiled for a family," (J) as alluded to in the nursery rhyme inventory:

Brave news is come to town,
Brave news is carried;
Brave news is come to town,
Jemmy Dawson's married.
First he got a porridge-pot,
Then he got a ladle;
Then he got a wife and child,
And then he bought a cradle."

James Halliwell, *Popular Rhymes and Nursery Tales* (London, 1849).

PORRINGER

"From porridge; a vessel in which broth is eaten." (J) Sometimes listed as pottager or pottinger, this originally was a large, shallow dish made to hold any pottage; the earliest examples often had two flat, horizontal handles and were meant to be used by two persons. The smaller porringer for

Late-seventeenth-century New England covered wood porringer. (Courtesy, Antiquarian and Landmarks Society, Inc.)

Dolphin-handle porringer by Samuel Danforth, Hartford, 1795–1816. (Courtesy, John Carl Thomas, Syracuse, New York.)

individual use had but one handle, usually pierced to reduce discomfort caused by heat and to provide a built-in hanger. Porringers were made of wood, horn, silver, pewter, iron, and tin. Sixteenth-century records sometimes referred to these small dishes as "eare dyshes" but the word porringer was in common use in the seventeenth century. In 1659 the English Worshipful Company of Pewterers set regulations for the weight in which various sizes of porringers were to be made, including in that list "ordinary blood porringers" of about 3 inches in diameter; thus perhaps accounting for the Bleeding Bowl label given some. Other small porringers were made for specific use as winetasters. The great majority, however, were intended for use as food dishes: "To ward off the gripe of poverty, you must pretend to be a stranger to her . . . If you be caught dining upon a half penny porringer of pease-soup and potatoes, praise the wholesomeness of your frugal repast." Oliver Goldsmith: *Essay 5: The Merchant's Clerk*.

PORRINGER-TOP TABLE
A collector's term for a round tea or breakfast table, the top or table board decorated with carving reminiscent of the rounded porringer shape.

Porringer-top table with scrolled apron, turned legs, and H stretchers. (Courtesy, Connecticut Historical Society, Inc.)

PORTABLE DESK
The small box or case, fitted with a hinged writing board below the lid and with space below that for paper, ink, inkwell, pens; sometimes referred to as a travel desk. "John Marshall, Cabinet Maker . . . has on hand a great variety of Useful and Elegant Furniture, Consisting of Desks and Bookcases of different patterns . . . Ladies and Gentlemen's Portable Writing Desks; N.B. Produce taken in payment at the market price." *Charleston* (South Carolina) *City Gazette and Daily Advertiser,* February 17, 1796.

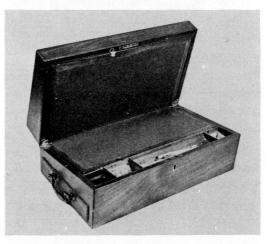

Portable desk. (Courtesy, Antiquarian and Landmarks Society, Inc.)

PORTABLE STOVE
(See FOOT STOVE.)

PORTASS, PORTESSE, PORTHOSE, PORTUIS
Variations of the term for "a breviary; a prayer-book." (J)

PORT-FEUILLE
A writing case for the traveler, a briefcase. "It is prudent [when traveling] to keep all writings together in a large, well-defended port-feuille; a preference is to be given to those of Russia leather, because water cannot penetrate to, and distroy the contents." Count Berchtold, *An Essay to Direct and*

Extend the Enquiries of Patriotic Travellers . . . (Philadelphia, 1821).

PORTFOLIO TABLE

A table for the library or parlor, made with a rising ledge or rest [or lectern's slanted top] to support a portfolio of prints. "The table is intended for displaying a portfolio or book of large prints; the top of it lifts up like a reading-desk, and its great recommendation is that it avoids the necessity of stooping. By removing the ledges in the front and sides, it is converted into a table for the purpose of writing, drawing." *The Art Journal Illustrated Catalogue* (London, 1851). (See also BOOK REST, TABLE BOOK).

PORTMANTEAU

The name given a "cloak-bag of cloth, leather, Ec., in which the cloak, linen, and other habiliaments of travellers are disposed and laid on the horse's crupper." (M) (See also TRUNK.)

PORTRAIT

The term used by painters for a Likeness, *q.v.,* or "the representation of a person, and especially of a face done from the life." (See also MINIATURE PAINTINGS, PROFILE.)

Portrait of George Codwine by John Trumbull. (Courtesy, Mattatuck Historical Society, Inc., Waterbury, Connecticut.)

C. 1780 American oil portrait on canvas of Major John Hale. (Courtesy, Antiquarian and Landmarks Society, Inc.)

Charles H. Charlot's water-color self-portrait for front of his journal, nineteenth century. (Courtesy, Connecticut Historical Society, Inc.)

484

POST BED, POSTED BED

A descriptive term for the bedstead with posts or pillars to support a tester; the four-post bedstead.

POSNET

"A little bason, porringer or skillet" (J) usually set on three stubby legs and having a long handle.

Early-eighteenth-century iron posnet. (Courtesy, Antiquarian and Landmarks Society, Inc.)

Early-eighteenth-century brass posnet. (Courtesy, Antiquarian and Landmarks Society, Inc.)

POSSET POT

An earthenware or porcelain vessel or cup used to serve hot, spiced drinks that could be sucked through the strainer spout. Posset meant to curdle or change, hence the basic beverage was milk or cream curdled with ale or wine, although there were other more extravagant versions. The recipe for sack-posset attributed to Sir Walter Raleigh called for boiling "a quart of cream with *quantum suffict* of sugar, mace and nutmeg; take half a pint of sack and the same quantity of ale, and boil them well together, adding sugar; these being boiled separately are now to be added. Heat a pewter dish very hot and cover your basin with it, and let it stand by the fire for two or three hours." Many earthenware pots were decorated with slip; faïence, or porcelain pots were colored in the glaze with floral motifs or the owner's cypher. (See also CAUDLE CUP.)

Late-seventeenth-century blue-and-white delft posnet pot. (Courtesy, Antiquarian and Landmarks Society, Inc.)

Late-seventeenth-century delft posnet pot. (Courtesy, Antiquarian and Landmarks Society, Inc.)

POSY, POSY RING

Posy meant a nosegay, but also a "motto on a ring," (W) and so was a synonym used throughout the seventeenth and eighteenth centuries, for the Motto Ring, *q.v.* Some romantic Victorians said posy referred to the "garland" or the circlet of words engraved around or within the ring. Johnson said "the word was a contraction of poesy and its primary definition is a motto in a ring." Hence,

What posies for our wedding rings,
What gloves we'll give and ribbonings.

Robert Herrick, *Hesperides;*

and Gratiano's explanation that he quarrel'd with Nerissa because the

Hoop of gold, [was] a paltry ring that she
did give me whose posy was
For all the world like cutler's poetry
Upon a knife, 'Love me and leave me not.'

Shakespeare, *Merchant of Venice,* V, i.

POT

A "vessel in which meat is boiled on the fire; also a vessel to hold liquid," (J) and thus often a synonym for cup or bowl or tankard:

I would give all my fame for a pot of ale, and safety.

Shakespeare, *King Henry V*, III, ii.

And in combining forms, as stew pot, jam pot, mustard pot, honey pot. "We'll sit contentedly and eat our pot of honey." George Meredith, *Modern Love,* XXIX. "Covered and uncovered Potts of Earth or Stone" were listed in the House of Parliament Rates, 1660, for Imports and Exports—*Statutes of the Realm* (London, 1819), as were "Gally pots; goldsmiths melting pots; Iron pots."

Early-eighteenth-century footed iron pot. (Courtesy, Antiquarian and Landmarks Society, Inc.)

POTATO RAKE

The eighteenth- and early-nineteenth-century iron utensil for drawing baked potatoes from the ashes of the hearth fire, the rake

(Courtesy, Mr. and Mrs. Paul Weld, Hartsdale, New York.)

resembled a modified sickle hook in form, having a handle of 6 to 10 inches in length and a slightly curved, flat hook or rake.

POTATO RING

Another popular name for the Dish Ring, *q.v.,* when it was used to hold a bowl of hot baked or boiled potatoes.

POT BOARD

The name given the storage shelf set below the work area or table of the open dresser and sometimes to a low, plain bench set below the Dresser, *q.v.,* for the same purpose.

POT BRACKET

A term sometimes used to describe the small fireplace crane which was just long enough to accommodate the teakettle or other single pot.

POT BRAKE

A trammel to hold pots; a claw or lifter, as a Kettle-Tilter, *q.v.*

POT CRATE

A colloquialism for a hamper for crockery. (See also CRATE.)

POT CROOK

A common term for a pothook of a crooked or S-shape, but also used as a synonym for a pot brake or lifter.

POT CUPBOARD

The contemporary term for the small, table-high cupboard specifically designed to hold the chamber pot. The piece of boudoir furniture that would be more commonly known in the Late-Victorian period as a commode or night commode. "These ornamental articles are calculated for Chambers, to be placed on each side of the bed; the upper shelf serving for china, either for ornament or use, and forming at the same time a table useful in case of indisposition. Casters may be concealed in the plinths . . ." George Smith, *A Collection of Designs for Household Furniture* (London, 1808). Hepplewhite showed three specific designs for

Pot cupboard illustrated in Hepplewhite's *Guide* (London, 1794).

POT LIFTERS

Iron hooks in S or C curves, usually equipped with wooden handles, to enable the cook to lift pots and kettles off the crane without burning her hands.

Early-eighteenth-century pot-lifter. (Courtesy, Antiquarian and Landmarks Society, Inc.)

Late-eighteenth-century pot lifter. (Courtesy, Antiquarian and Landmarks Society, Inc.)

pot cupboards that he described as "an article of much use in bed-chambers, counting-houses, offices, Ec. [with] the door in front [to] swing on hinges at the side." A. Hepplewhite, *The Cabinet-Maker and Upholsterer's Guide* (London, 1794). (See also CLOSESTOOL, PEDESTAL.)

POT HANGER

Sometimes used as a synonym for the fireplace crane as "a hook or branch on which the pot is hung over the fire." (J)   (See also POT BRACKET, TRAMMEL.)

POTHOOK

At the kitchen hearth, the wrought-iron "hook to hang a pot on," (W)   "to fasten kettles with." (J)

Pot lifter for pots without bails. (Courtesy, Antiquarian and Landmarks Society, Inc.)

Wrought-iron eighteenth-century pothooks. (Courtesy, Antiquarian and Landmarks Society, Inc.)

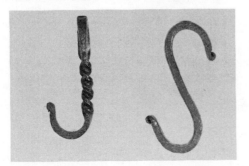

POTTAGER

Another term for "a vessel for spoonmeat." (W)   The term derived from pottage, the food cooked in a pot. (See also PORRINGER.)

POTTINGER

(See PORRINGER.)

POTTLE

The term for a two-quart measure, "sometimes used for a Tankard, or Pot [qq.v.] out of which glasses are filled." (J)

POUCH

"A small bag, purse, pocket," (J) "with a drawstring closure." (W)

POUCH TABLE

A synonymous term for the Sewing Table or Worktable, qq.v., with a cloth bag suspended below the top board.

POUNCE BOX

A small wood, porcelain, or metal container with a pierced top, similar to a Sander, q.v. "Powdered pounce or pumice stone, or charcoal, [is] used by embroiderers and other artists to transfer their patterns from paper on stuff or any other body. This is done by pricking the outline, in consequence of which, the pounce, passed over the whole, is left wherever the pin has pierced. Oyster shells scraped and sifted are used as pounce." *The Domestic Encyclopedia* (Philadelphia, 1821).

Because both were powdered, pounce also was a synonym for snuff, and for a mixture of dried and powdered lavender and rose petals; a Snuffbox, q.v., often was called a pounce box.

> *He was perfumed like a milliner,*
> *And 'twixt his finger and his thumb he*
> *held*
> *A pouncet-box, which ever and anon*
> *He gave his nose and took 't away again.*
>
> *Shakespeare, King Henry IV, Part I, I,*
> iii.

"A Fresh Supply of Paints, Dye-Stuffs, Ec., Ec., Just received from New York, and selling for the most reasonable terms, by Joseph Lynde . . . Liquid Blacking, Ink-Powder, Sealing-wax, Wafers, Quills, Pounce-Boxes, Ink Pots . . ." *American Mercury* (Hartford, Connecticut), November 1, 1815.

POWDER BOX

One of the toilet accessories, "a box to keep hair powder in," (W) usually purchased from the silversmith or jeweler; made of silver, gold, plated metal, polished or painted wood, ivory, and often with a small looking glass set inside the cover.

POWDER HORN

The hunter and soldier's accessory, "a horn case, in which powder is kept for guns." (J)

Powder horn with carved hickory stopple.

POWDERING STAND

A synonym for the Wig Stand, q.v.

POWDERING TUB

A large container in which meats were powdered, that is, "covered with salt to preserve them; also a tub or vessel for salted meat," (W) or fish.

"August 6, 1642. There arrived another ship with salt, which was put off for pipe Staves, etc., so by an unexpected providence we were supplied of salt to go on with our fishing, and of ships to take off our pipe staves, which lay upon men's hands." John Winthrop, *Journal, History of New England* (Boston, 1825). The powdering tub, a larger version of the kneading

Early powdering tub formed from hollowed out tree trunk. (Courtesy, Antiquarian and Landmarks Society, Inc.)

trough, was kept in the larder, cellar, or garret or wherever meat and fish were prepared for storage in the larger houses, or in the kitchen of the small house. After powdering, the meat was transferred to other tubs or barrels and packed between layers of more salt.

PRESS
A general term for any (1) "machine of wood or iron, serving to squeeze any body very close. Presses [usually] consist of six pieces; two flat smooth planks, between which the things to be pressed are laid; two screws or worms fastened to the lower plank, and passing through two holes in the upper; and two nuts in form of an S, that serve to drive the upper plank, which is moveable, against the lower, which is fixed." (M) (See also BOOK PRESS, BOTANICAL PRESS, NAPKIN PRESS.)

Press cupboard, New England, 1670–1700. (Courtesy, Connecticut Historical Society, Inc.)

(2) In furniture, this was the early, general term for any tall cupboard or wardrobe with doors.

PRESS BED, BEDSTEAD
The term to describe "a bed that shuts close up in a case," (W) often used in inns and small homes where space saving was essential. "The Judge and I lay in one press-bed, there being two more in the same room; my boy sleeping on a bench by me." Samuel Pepys, *Diary,* May 14, 1660. Sometimes, but not always, they were equipped with casters: "At the Inn I was to sleep in a little press-bed . . . I had it wheeled out into the dining-room, and there I lay very well." James Boswell, *A Journal of a Tour to the Hebrides* (London, 1785). (See also BUREAU BEDSTEAD.)

PRESS, PRESS CUPBOARD
(See COURT CUPBOARD.)

PRICKET, PRICKET CANDLESTICK
The ancient Anglo-Saxon terms for candleholder were candel-stick, candelstalf, candelstaffe, or candel-treow, all suggesting that the first were made of wood, as very probably they were; wood was the handiest and most easily worked medium. The earliest form of candlestick we know was that called a pricket, a tall sharp spike set in a standard or on a base, and on which the candle was stuck. The earliest documented English candleholders of fine metals were made in the twelfth century. The socket type of candleholder familiar to us today was developed about the beginning of the sixteenth century.

PRICKLE
A cant term for "a wicker basket." (H)

PRIG
A contemporary colloquialism for (1) "a small pitcher" or (2) "a small brass skillet." (H)

PRIMER
The term for "a first book for children." (W) See also A B C BOOK, ABSEY

489

BOOK, BABBY, LITTLE BOOKS, TOY BOOK.

1777 reprint of the 1690 *New England Primer*.

PRIMERO
The name of "an old game at cards," (W) played on a triangle-shaped table. (See also OMBRE TABLE, TRAYDRILL TABLE.)

PRINTER'S FLOWERS
(See TYPE ORNAMENTS.)

PROFILE
"A half-face. To profile: to draw or represent in profile." (W) Specifically, after 1800 in the United States, this meant the cut or solid black-painted silhouette, as opposed to the detailed portrait executed in oil or watercolors: "Here I went to cutting profile likenesses . . . I put up at a tavern and told a young lady if she would wash my shirt I would draw her likeness. Now I [had a chance] to execute my skill in painting . . . the poor Girl sat nipped up so prim and look so smiling [but the result] could not be called painting, for it looked more like a strangled cat than it did like her. However I told her it looked like her and she believed it, but I cut her profile [also] and she had a profile if not a likeness." *The Travel Diary of James Guild* (itinerant Massachusetts silhouette artist,

1797–1841), Vermont Historical Society Proceedings, New Series V, 1937. Although profile portraits also were painted in colors with highlights and shadows, today the collector, as did Guild, refers to the solid black silhouette type when he speaks of a profile. These solid profiles or likenesses generally were of two types, those cut either by machine or hand, and those that were painted. The most common was that usually referred to as the hollow-cut Silhouette, *q.v.* The second most popular was cut with scissors from black or other dark-colored paper or fabric and then pasted to a thicker piece of paper or cardboard. Others were painted in solid black India ink. Often each of these solid profile types was highlighted with bronze, gold, or silver. "Cutting a profile likeness" was a popular pastime of young ladies and other amateurs as well as the livelihood of the itinerant professional. As Guild's diary note makes obvious, however, the silhouette-cutter seldom was considered a true artist but more of a handicraftsman. No matter how accurate the likeness achieved, the fee he charged usually was from fifty cents to three dollars, including a frame, while the fee the itinerant limner or painter in oils could charge usually was from five to thirty dollars. The popularity of cut or painted profile diminished rapidly after 1840 with the introduction of various forms of photography. Collectors today accord much more respect to the work of the early silhouette artists than was given them by their contemporaries.

PROPORTIONOMETER
(See DELINEATOR, PHYSIOGNOTRACE.)

PROSPECTS, PROSPECTIVES
The contemporary terms for engravings from copper plates and woodcuts, and in the nineteenth century also for lithograph prints of views of townships. Many prospects illustrated a grander and more imaginatively detailed panorama than actually existed.

Nevertheless, they remain excellent sources of visual information concerning building methods of houses, public buildings, shops, and mills; of wharves and shipping; of costumes and customs of early America. The earliest of this country were published in London to show those "at home" how colonial townships looked. There they spurred investment in export and import adventures and were helpful in promoting colonization. They were the travel posters of the period. Equally popular here, prospects of their own as well as of distant towns, were collected by colonists and kept in parlor table books or portfolios; or framed as wall decorations for their "closets" or libraries, family parlors, and stairwells. As the frontier was extended, prospects of new towns promoted settlement in the lands beyond the Cumberland Gap, the Alleghenies, and the White Mountains, and once again served to keep those who had gone West in touch with families and friends who remained at home in the older Atlantic Coast communities. "Birch's Views of Philadelphia . . . intended to represent the City . . . in the most picturesque and advantageous light, will consist of about thirty Plates, (including) a general view of the City from the great tree at Kensington, with the Port and River; exhibiting the principal buildings; the prospective of the streets . . . it will point out beauties to its inhabitants as well as hold forth to foreign countries the rapid progress made in so young a country . . . The plates are One dollar each, plain, and One dollar and a half colored . . ." *Federal Gazette* (Philadelphia), January 29, 1799.

". . . Four select Engravings in Aquatinta, Three upon the River Shenandoah in the State of Virginia; and One upon the Schuylkill in the State of Pennsylvania . . . Subscriptions [will be] received at Mr. Dobson's, Bookseller, at the Stone House, Second Street, and at Mr. Joseph Anthony's, Silver Smith, Market Street . . ." *Gazette of the United States* (Philadelphia), July 11, 1794.

PSALTERY, PSALTERION, PSALTERIUM

A musical instrument, the ancient form of which probably resembled the modern harp. "The psaltery now in use is a flat instrument in the form of a trapezium, or a triangle truncated at top. It is strung with thirteen wire cords, tuned in unisons, or octaves, and mounted on two bridges. It is [played] with a plectrum, whence it is usually ranked among the instruments of percussion." *Encyclopedia Americana* (Philadelphia), 1831.

Psaltery illustrated in Bonanni's *Cabinetto Armonica* (Rome, 1723).

PUDDING MOLD

A ceramic or metal bowl, usually round or oval, with an intaglio or countersunk design in the bottom interior. When the baked pud-

Nineteenth-century ironstone pudding mold turned to show interior design.

ding was removed, it retained such shape and decoration.

PULSE GLASS

The name given a form of handwarmer discovered by Benjamin Franklin during his visit to Germany. This was a small vial partly filled with water, the air removed, and the bottle sealed. The low pressure in the vacuum was such that the heat of the hand was enough to cause the water to boil. Copies were made at Henry William Stiegel's American Flint Glass Manufactory at Manheim, near Philadelphia.

PUNCH BARREL

(See PUNCHEON.)

PUNCH BOWL

Any wide and fairly deep vessel in which punch was prepared or from which it was

Nineteenth-century punch bowl. (Courtesy, Mary J. O'Neil, East Hampton, Connecticut.)

Polychrome delft punch bowl, dated in bottom. (Courtesy, Antiquarian and Landmarks Society, Inc.)

Early-eighteenth-century polychrome delft punch bowl.

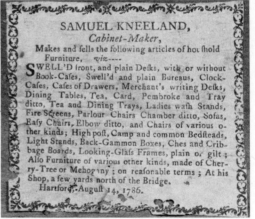

SAMUEL KNEELAND, Cabinet-Maker, Makes and sells the following articles of houshold Furniture, viz----
SWELL'D front, and plain Desks, with or without Book-Cases, Swell'd and plain Bureaus, Clock-Cases, Cases of Drawers, Merchant's writing Desks, Dining Tables, Tea, Card, Pembroke and Tray ditto, Tea and Dining Trays, Ladies wash Stands, Fire Screens, Parlour Chairs Chamber ditto, Sofas, Easy Chairs, Elbow ditto, and Chairs of various other kinds; High post, Camp and common Bedsteads, Light Stands, Back-Gammon Boxes, Chess and Cribbage Boards, Looking-Glass Frames, plain or gilt; Also Furniture of various other kinds, made of Cherry-Tree or Mahogany; on reasonable terms; At his Shop, a few yards north of the Bridge.
Hartford, August 14, 1786.

Punch bowl box with label. (Courtesy, Connecticut Historical Society, Inc.)

served, following the introduction of this mixed spice-fruit-and-wine beverage during the 1630s. Many large and elegant porcelain and soft paste bowls were made especially for the service of punch; silver bowls were used after the early 1680s. (See also MONTEITH.) Throughout the eighteenth and nineteenth centuries fine bowls

were made from glass and from highly polished hardwoods, such as maple.

PUNCH POT

These large porcelain, earthenware, silver, or silver-plated vessels, similar in shape to teapots but made without a strainer in the spout, were used to serve hot punch. Cold punch was taken up with ladles from the punch bowl. (See also MONTEITH, PUNCH BOWL, PUNCHEON.)

PUNCHEON

Properly, this was the term for a large cask, its capacity depending on what it was to contain, from seventy-two beer gallons to eighty-four wine gallons; it also was a slang term for a punch barrel or urn made of silver, silver plate, earthenware, or porcelain, from which the punch was drawn off by means of a cock. "James Jacks, Jeweller and Watchmaker . . . has imported . . . Plated quart and pint canns. Plated puncheons, goblets, and bottle stands . . ." *Federal Gazette* (Philadelphia), November 27, 1797.

PUNCH STRAINER

A small, shallow perforated bowl with one or two ears or short stubby handles; punch was poured through the strainer to keep fruit seeds and pulp or bits of spices such as cloves, from reaching the cup. "James Jacks, Jeweller and Watchmaker . . . has imported Sterling plate and plated goods [including] Table, tea and dessert spoons. Plain and engraved punch strainers, Cream pots . . ." *Federal Gazette* (Philadelphia), November 27, 1797.

Leeds creamware punch strainer. (Courtesy, Mr. and Mrs. Guy Mankin, Kent, Connecticut.)

PUPPET

A puppet or child's Doll, *q.v.*

PURDONIUM

The nineteenth-century Coal Scuttle, *q.v.*, with a tidy Victorian-era cover, so called for its manufacturer, whose name was Purdon.

PURSE

The common term for "a small bag used for money," (W) made of any textile or leather. (See also GIRDLE, POCKET, WALLET.)

PUZZLE RING

(See GEMEL.)

PYROGRAPHY

The name of pictures on hardwood, made from the seventeenth through the nineteenth centuries by burning the wood with heated iron or steel points. Tone gradations from a pale brown to deep black were produced by regulating the heat of the iron, the lightness or heaviness of touch, the amount of time the iron was kept in contact with the wood. Pyrography was used to decorate wall paneling, chest lids, and furniture backs, as well as to make plaques to hang as pictures.

PYROMETER

One of the scientific devices, "an instrument to measure expansion by heat." (W)

Q

QUADRANT, QUADRANT SET

A mathematical instrument "of great use in astronomy and navigation, for ascertaining the altitudes of the sun and stars, and for taking angles in surveying." *The Domestic Encyclopedia* (Philadelphia, 1821). "The Quadrant, called improperly Hadley's, was invented by T. Godfrey of Philadelphia in 1730." Noah Webster, *Chronology* (1806). One of the many instruments collected today, quadrants were kept in boxes or cases which usually were painted and decorated with the owner's name or initials. "Charles Sigourney . . . Has imported from London [and] Liverpool . . . a complete assortment [including] Brass pocket Compasses, Brass Candlesticks, Clock Balls and Capitals, Quadrant Setts . . ." *American Mercury* (Hartford, Connecticut), November 23, 1809.

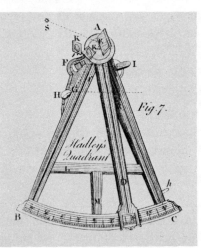

Hadley's Quadrant as illustrated in *The New Dictionary of Arts and Sciences* (London, 1778).

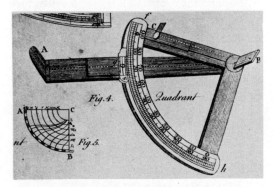

Quadrant, illustrated in *The New Dictionary of Arts and Sciences* (London, 1778).

QUAICH

A word derived from the Gaelic *cuach,* and also spelled *quaigh.* Orginally a wooden-staved cup hooped together and with two ears; later a small, shallow wood, metal, or ceramic cup with two ears, similar to a small porringer.

QUAIL PIPE

A hunter's birdcall, usually carved of wood; "a pipe used to allure quails by." (W) "Hen birds have a peculiar sort of voice, when they would call the male, which is so eminent in quails, that men, by counterfeiting this voice with a quail-pipe easily drew the cocks into their snares." John Ray, *Ornithologia* (London, 1676). (See also BIRDCALL.)

QUAKER CHAIR

Another name for the Balloon-back Chair, *q.v.,* a term apparently first used about the time of the Centennial celebration in 1876.

QUARIER

A wax candle, consisting of "a square lump of wax with a wick in the center. It was also called a quarion." (H)

QUARTETTO TABLE(S)

Thomas Sheraton apparently was the first to use this designation for a nest, or set, of four small tables for the parlor, generally used for individual service of tea or dessert. Sheraton said it was "a kind of small work table made to draw out of each other, and may be used separately." *The Cabinet Dictionary* (London, 1803). "As with Tea Poys [*q.v.*], Quartetto Tables are used in Drawing Rooms, Ec. to prevent the company rising from their seats when taking refreshments." George Smith, *A Collection of Designs for Household Furniture* (London, 1808). (See also NEST OF TABLES.)

QUARTO TABLE

(See NEST OF TABLES, QUARTETTO TABLE.)

QUEEN'S WARE

(See CREAMWARE, Chapter 10.)

QUERN

"A handmill, a churn." (W) A small mill for grinding corn at home. "We stopped at a little hut, where we saw an old woman grinding with the quern, the ancient Highland instrument, which it is said was used by the Romans." James Boswell, *Journal of a Tour* [1773] *to the Hebrides* (London, 1785).

QUIFFING POT, QUIFTING POT
Old terms for "small drinking pots holding half a gill," (H) apparently a corruption in conversation for quaffing.

QUILL BOX
A container for writing quills or pens. Although sometimes stored in wall boxes similar to those used for pipes, quills more often were kept in flat boxes or tills with slide or lift-up top lids. Quill boxes in merchants' and shippers' countinghouses were simple and utilitarian in comparison with the often elegantly inlaid polished wood or engraved silver boxes used in private homes. Quills were the large feathers plucked from the end of the wings of geese, crows, etc., and principally used for writing or drawing. "To prepare goose quills for writing, immerse in water almost boiling; leave it there till it becomes sufficiently soft to compress it, turning it on its axis with the back of the blade of the knife. This friction, as well as the immersions in water, being continued till the barrel of the quill be transparent, and the membrane as well as the greasy kind of covering, be entirely removed, it is immersed a last time, to render it perfectly cylindrical, which is performed with the index finger and the thumb; it is then dried in a gentle temperature. The yellow colour is given to quills by dipping them for an instant in *aqua fortis." The Domestic Encyclopedia* (Philadelphia, 1821). (See also PEN, PENKNIFE, STANDISH.)

QUILT
The Counterpane, *q.v.* or bed coverlet, formed of two outer pieces of cloth, between which any soft material such as cotton, moss, feathers, or other filling has been sewn. Quilts originally were used as Pallets or Mattresses. *qq.v.,* later as bed covers. (See also PATCHWORK QUILT.)

QUINQUETS
The name given certain lighting devices imported from France because there "the Argand lamps are called *lampes a Quinquet,* or more briefly, *Quinquets,* from an artist of the name Quinquet in Paris, with whom Argand was connected." *Encyclopedia Americana* (Philadelphia, 1831). (See also ARGAND LAMP.)

QUISSIN
The ancient form of cushion from the Old French *coissin.*

QUIVER
The term to describe "a case for arrows," (W) worn by means of a sling over the shoulder, or carried by the hunter who preferred the bow and arrow to the musket or fowling piece. Bows and arrows were common weapons in the seventeenth century and still in use on the American frontier well into the beginning of the nineteenth century.

R

RABIT
A cant term for a "wooden drinking can." (H)

RACK
A common term for "the cob-iron of a grate." (H)

RAPIER
The long, straight-blade sword used in fencing. (See also FENCING FOIL.)

RAIN GAUGE
One of the small so-called scientific instruments of the eighteenth and nineteenth centuries, often called a Pluviometer, *q.v.*

RAM'S-HEAD, RAM'S-HORN ORNAMENTS
This ancient classical decoration was revived during the late-eighteenth-century Neo-Classic era and was the basis of carved

and gilded decorations on fine furniture, such as chimney surrounds, wall cases, the knees of chairs, vases, and pedestals. Its popularity was reflected even in such mundane country blacksmith's work as finials for Slices and Peels, *qq.v.*

RANGE

"A kitchen grate," (J) the shallow openwork iron basket that held the coals or embers. "The implements of the kitchen are spits, ranges, cobirons and pots." Francis Bacon, *Physical Remains.*

RANGE TABLES

A contemporary description of sets of small dining tables that could be ranged or assembled to form a single large table, according to the requirements of the occasion.

RANTER

A cant term for a "large beer-jug." (H)

RATTLE

Then, as now, the term for any small wooden noisemaker with which youngsters amuse themselves. "Rattles and Rattles with Bells for Children" were cited in the House of Parliament Rates, 1660, for Imports and Exports—*Statutes of the Realm* (London, 1819). Also a substitute for a Hand Bell, used by patrols or night watchmen making the rounds of the streets. This was a small wooden plate or disc, made to swivel on a rod handle; when swung about, a clapper or small ball attached by a thong was struck or rattled against the plate. (See also BELLS, CORAL-AND-BELLS.)

RAZOR

An improvement over the pumice stone for removing a beard. The steel blade set in a wood, silver, or ivory haft came into use during the seventeenth century. "This morning I began a practice, which I find by the ease I do it with that I shall continue; that is, to trimme myself with a razer, which pleases me mightily." Samuel Pepys, *Diary* (January 6, 1663–64).

READING CHAIR

A combination of chair and desk, so made that the reader sat facing the back of the chair, his elbows supported on wide arm rests, his book supported on the inclined desk or stay that was attached to the chair back. Somewhat similar to the Conversation Chair, *q.v.*

READING SEAT

A type of early-nineteenth-century Day Bed, *q.v.;* an upholstered couch with one high, almost vertical end or rest; not "elegant in form; we can assert from experience . . . is exceedingly comfortable to sit on; not only the back, but the head being supported by the peculiar form of the upper part of the end, or support for the back." J. C. Loudon, *An Encyclopedia of Cottage, Farm and Villa Architecture* (London, 1846).

REBEC, REBECK

The ancient, early viol, "a fiddle of three strings." (W)

RECLINING CHAIR

Baltimore architect John Hall designed two such "easy chairs [that] may be covered with morocco, or velvet, with tufts, and [are] quite easy to sit on . . . the position of the back of this chair can be varied at pleasure, and the projecting part [an extension foot rest] in front can be elongated and adjusted to any angle with the seat. When it is required to be used as an easy chair, the back can be fixed upright, and the front projection slid in, so as to have the appearance of a common easy chair." John Hall, *The Cabinet-Maker's Assistant* (Baltimore, 1840). (See also GOUT STOOL.)

RED LEATHER CHAIR

A contemporary term for what sometimes also was called a Boston chair; a side chair of walnut, or mahogany, sometimes of cherry, with the back splat and seat covered in bright red leather. "Very good

Red Leather Chairs, the newest fashion. Fine Flanders Bed-Tick . . . and choice New-England Hopps, and very good Beavour Hats, and Silk Stockings to be sold by Peter Baynton, Living at the Lower End of Front Street." *Pennsylvania Gazette* (Philadelphia), January 20, 1729–30.

REEKING CROOK

A colloquialism for "the Pot Hook," *q.v.* (H) Reek or reech meant smoke, vapor, or soot, and so often was used to describe anything within the chimney.

REEL

(See WEAVER'S LOOM.)

REFECTORY TABLE

The collector's term, used to give added dignity and retail value to any long, heavy oak or pine table with four to eight turned legs connected by thick, square stretchers. At the time these were made in this country, following the English prototype, or when used earlier in England, they were known simply as long tables.

REFLECTING TABLE

A contemporary synonym for Rudd's Table, *q.v.*

REFLECTOR OVEN

A later term for what first was a kind of roasting jack, or portable covered spit or rotisserie enclosed in a tin container made with a sliding front panel that opened to the fire. The top and back reflected heat onto the roasting meat and at the same time kept grease from spattering the hearth and cook. One "improved model" was thus described by its manufacturer, Simon Willard:

"A new invented Roasting Jack, a compleat apparatus of Kitchen Dripping-Pan, Spit, Skewers and Baster Ec. which is so constructed with tin plates as to reflect back upon the meat all the heat the tin receives, which occasions the saving of almost one half of that important article fire-wood; it is also recommended for its being portable, which can be placed to any small fire-place, in any room, and which is made upon so simple a plan that it it is not subject to get out of repair and the friction upon every part being so trifling, that it will continue for longer duration than any mechanical performances of that kind is known to do. N.B. The above Jacks may be had of Col. Paul Revere, directly opposite Liberty-Pole, Boston." *Massachusetts Spy or Worcester Gazette,* March 11, 1784.

REGALS

A musical instrument made with pipes and bellows and thus similar to an organ, but small and portable.

> *Praise him upon the claricoales,*
> *The lute and simfonie;*
> *With dulsemers and regalls,*
> *Sweete sittrons melody.*
>
> John Leighton, *Teares or Lamentations* (1613).

RENT TABLE

(See DRUM TABLE.)

REREDO

Another name for the Fire-back, *q.v.*

REST

A support for the ancient musket. It consisted of "a pole of tough wood, with an iron spike at the end to fix it in the ground, and a semi-circular piece of iron at the top to rest the musket on. The soldier carried it by strings fastened over the shoulder." (H) (See also MUSKET REST, FOURQUETTE.)

RESTORATION CHAIR

The collector's name for any tall chair with a cane back and seat made during the Carolean period or those years following restoration to the throne of Charles II.

REVERSE GLASS PAINTING

In the Colonial period, this type of decoration usually was called back painting. The term today is used to describe either of two methods of painting on glass.

(1) Painting directly on the reverse side of the glass with oil paints ground in shellac, varnish, or linseed oil. The landscape, portrait, or still life usually was "backed" with a layer of white paint to reflect light through the pigments and to enhance the colors. This backing also protected the painting proper from chipping. Painting directly on the back side of the glass was an ancient method of decoration revived in the eighteenth century and one that increased in popularity throughout the nineteenth century. Many examples, created by professional artists and by untrained, so-called primitive painters, alike, survive today in the form of framed pictures, decorative inserts in clock cases, looking glasses, box lids.

So-called Federal looking glass with pine frame finished in gilt and gesso, labeled Spencer and Gilman (1807–27) on back; reverse glass painting in panel above mercury-coated glass. (Courtesy, Connecticut Historical Society, Inc.)

(2) Painting a design transferred from a mezzotint. This kind of transfer-glass or back-painting became popular in England sometime after 1650 when "This most ingenious way of painting justly claims applause and admiration, if skill and dexterity are [used. It] is lookt upon to be the womens more peculiar province and the ladies are almost the only pretenders." Stalker and Parker, *Treatise on Japanning and Varnishing* (London, 1688).

The number of exactly similar copies of portraits of public figures, popular scenes, and still-life arrangements found today, and the excellence of their execution, make it clear—despite Messrs. Stalker and Parker—that mezzotint transfer painting also was produced in commercial art studios. A great variety of mezzotint subjects was available in both English and American shops throughout the eighteenth century. "Prints and maps and fine Metzotints for painting on glass, in frames or without . . . William Prince," *Boston News-Letter,* June 1728.

Transfer paintings were made thusly: "Take your mezzotint print and lay it on clean water for forty eight hours, provided the print be on very strong, close and hard gummed [sized] paper, but if the paper be open, soft and spongy, two hours will sometimes be sufficient. [Then] take it out and lay it upon two sheets of paper and cover it with two more, and let it lie there a little to suck out the moisture. In the meantime take the glass the picture is to be put upon and set it near the fire to warm; take Stransburg turpentine, warm it over the fire till it is grown fluid; then with a hog's hair brush spread the turpentine very smoothly and evenly on the glass. Take the print from between the papers and lay it on the glass, beginning first at one end, rubbing it down gently as you go on, till it lie close, and there be no wind bladders between. Then, with your fingers, rub or roll off the paper from the back side of the print, till it looks black, i.e., till you can see nothing but the print, like a thin film left upon the glass, and set it by to dry. When it is dry, varnish it over with some white transparent varnish that

Reverse glass painting.

the print may be seen through it and then it is fit for painting." (M)

Old glass paintings were made on very thin crown glass with a somewhat uneven or wavy surface. Those of the late nineteenth century and the copies still being made today are on thicker, even-surfaced glass.

REVOLVER

The term generally used to describe any firearm made with a rotating cylinder to fire a series of charges from one barrel. The first Flintlock, *q.v.,* revolver with an automatic primer was patented in England in 1818 by Elisha H. Collier. In 1835 Samuel Colt patented the percussion revolver in England and in France, and in 1836, in the United States. Although now his name is synonymous with the firearm he developed, Colt had so much difficulty selling early models that his first factory at Paterson, New Jersey, was closed for lack of orders. The revolvers made at that plant are today called Colt Patersons by collectors, and are much sought after. Following suggestions made by Captain Samuel

Walker of the Texas Rangers, Colt improved the design and in 1847 was given a government contract for one thousand long-barreled pistols. These today are known to collectors as Walker Colts.

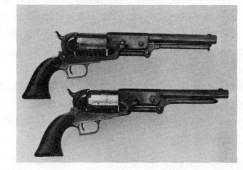

The 1847 Colt. (Courtesy, Connecticut Historical Society, Inc.)

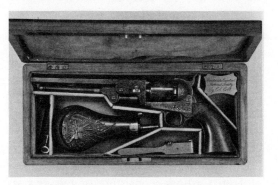

Colt in presentation case. (Courtesy, Connecticut Historical Society, Inc.)

RIBBON-BACK CHAIR
(See RIBBAND BACK, Chapter 5.)

RIBBON SHUTTLE
"The ribbon weaver's shuttle is different from that of most other weavers, though it serves for the same purpose. It is made of box, and is six or seven inches long, shod with iron at both ends, which terminate in points that are crooked, one towards the right, the other towards the left." *The Book of Trades* (London, 1805). (See also WEAVER'S LOOM.)

RICE
A yarn winder; "a turning wheel for yarn." (H)

RIDDLE
"A wide Sieve." (W)

RIFLE
The name given to a firearm with a rifled barrel; that is, a barrel made with spirals or grooves inside so that the projectile is rotated and thus flies more accurately toward the target. "Each militia man may furnish himself with a good rifle, knapsack, shot-pouch and powder horn, twenty balls suited to the bore of his rifle, and a quarter of a pound of powder." *Connecticut Statutes* (Hartford, 1835).

RINGE, RONGE, RUNGE
Familiar variations of an old term for a wooden "tub for carrying water," (H) a long tub; a kind of Flasket, *q.v.*

RITTENHOUSE STOVE
Named for its developer, the famed Phila-delphia scientist-inventor, David Ritten-house, this was the term to describe a type of iron stove similar to the stove first in-vented by Benjamin Franklin. "John Carrell at No. 32 Market Street the Corner of Laetitia-Court . . . has a constant supply of Iron Castings, consisting of ten and six plate stoves, Rittenhouse Open Stoves, some of a large size." *Pennsylvania Packet* (Phila-delphia), September 8, 1791. (See also FRANKLIN STOVE.)

RO(A)STER
A contemporary colloquialism for "a roast-iron, the iron grate used in roasting; a Gridiron," *q.v.* (H)

ROCK
The forerunner of the spinning wheel, "a distaff held in the hand from which the wool was spun by twirling a ball below." (J) "Children such as are set to keep cattle shall be set to some other employ-ment, withal such as spinning upon the rock, knitting, weaving tape [1642]." John Winthrop, *Journal, History of New England* (Boston, 1825).

ROCKER
"A long wooden sieve used in dressing beans." (H) The term is derived from the action used.

ROCKING CHAIR
The nineteenth-century term for any chair, the feet of which are connected with two curved stretchers or bends so that the chair can be rocked backward and forward. The earlier term was Crooked Foot Chair, *q.v.* (See also BOSTON ROCKER.)

ROLLING PIN
(See PASTE ROLLER.)

ROLLING TABLE
A colloquialism for the early-nineteenth-century breakfast or small dining table equipped with casters for easy removal from parlor to chamber. "Thus the Vermonters have made some advances from the rustic towards the elegant . . . the urbane and polished . . . Where they might once have been seen dining over a barrelhead, a board placed across it; or on a rough four-legged stool; you may find them at a polished cherry or mahogany rolling table." Hosea Beckley, *The History of Vermont; with De-scriptions, Physical and Topographical* (Brattleboro, 1846). (See also PEM-BROKE TABLE.)

ROLL-TOP DESK
(See CYLINDER FALL DESK.)

ROMKIN, RUMKIN
The old Anglo-Saxon term for "a drinking cup." (H) (See also RUMMER.)

ROSE NAIL
Contrary to popular belief, the terms rose nail or rose-head nail are not modern col-lector's descriptions, but those used in the Colonial period for the hand-wrought iron nail, the head of which was finished with five blows about the perimeter and thus simulated a simple rose blossom. Such nails were used for decoration as well as strength in the studding of doors, chests, and boxes,

and some picture frames. Many rose-head nails are being reproduced today; however, the color and high gloss finish usually betrays the new. (See also NAILS.)

C. 1700 New England door plate with rose head nails. (Courtesy, Antiquarian and Landmarks Society, Inc.)

ROSE-WATER DISH
A contemporary term to describe the basin which, with the ewer, was presented to guests between courses and at the conclusion of dinner. The name refers to the practice of pouring rose-water from the ewer over the guests' hands, held above the dish or basin. (See also EWER AND BASIN.)

ROUNDABOUT CHAIR
A name sometimes given the Corner Chair, *q.v.*

ROUNDEL
Anything round, as a circle, and therefore a colloquialism for "a Trencher," *q.v.* (H) or a round tray.

ROUNDELET
A contemporary colloquialism for "a rundlet, especially for wine." (H) (See also CANTEEN.)

Runlet: The old name for a soldier's canteen; also spelled rundlet. "A small barrel" (J) that held three pints. "To Col. Moylan QMG. Sir; Please to Supply Capt. Nathan Hale with fifty five Canteens or Runlets that being the Number wanted for his Company. New York." *Nathan Hale: Army Accounts,* Connecticut Historical Society Collections. (See also CANTEEN.)

ROUT CHAIR
Rout, which meant "a clamorous multitude" (J) or "an assembly for gaming," (W) was a popular late-eighteenth-century term for a large evening party. When the guest list became too extensive, the host or hostess rented "small painted chairs with rush bottoms, lent out by cabinet makers for hire, as a supply of seats at general entertainments or feasts." Thomas Sheraton, *The Cabinet Dictionary* (London, 1803).

ROUTIER
The French word for a sea chart, a map, or road guide. (See also WAGGONER.)

RUDD'S TABLE
The popular name for a complicated dressing table made with three drawers, each partitioned to hold toilet articles; this also was called a reflecting dressing table, denoting the inclusion of two looking glasses, so situated that the owner might view figure and dress from any desired angle. It was "the most complete dressing table made, possessing every convenience which can be wanted, or mechanism and ingenuity apply. It derives its name from a once popular character, [not otherwise identified] for whom it is reported it was first invented. The middle drawer of this table slides [out] by itself. The two end drawers are framed to slide, fastened at the catch; and when disengaged, each drawer swings [out] horizontally on a centre pin, and may be placed at any station. The glasses turn upward, and are supported by a spring at the bottom; when pushed in, they fall down and slide under with the two end drawers. [There is also] a slide covered with green cloth for writing on." A. Hepple-

white, *The Cabinet-Maker and Upholsterer's Guide* (London, 1788). By the early nineteenth century, the piece's popularity seems to have been on the wane, for Sheraton described it as "a kind of dressing table for ladies, not much in present use." *The Cabinet Dictionary* (London, 1803).

RUET, RUWET
"A small trumpet or cornet." (H)

RUG
The contemporary term for a table cover, or a "rough woolen coverlet for beds." (W) (See CARPET, FLOOR CLOTH.)

RULE-JOINT TABLE
A rule joint is a hinge so contrived that when open no separation shows between the two joined parts. It was used on table flaps, cabinet doors, and folding screens. Its use was a selling point for flap or dropleaf tables in the eighteenth century: "All sorts of Tea-Tables, Side Boards and Waiters, Rule Joint Skeleton Tables, Frames for Marble Tables, all made after the newest and best fashions, and with the greatest Neatness and Accuracy by Josiah Claypoole . . . at his shop next door to Mr. Lorimer's near the Market Square. He has Coffin Furniture of all sorts, either Flowr'd, Silver'd or Plain. N.B. He will warrant

C. 1770 tea or breakfast Pembroke table with rule-joint hinges.

his work for 7 years, the ill usage of careless Servants only excepted." The *South Carolina Gazette* (Charleston), March 22, 1740.

RULES, RULERS
One or two-foot measuring sticks marked off in inches and their fractions for desk, school, shop, or countinghouse use; made of hard wood, metal, ivory, whalebone. "James H. Wells Has received by the *Pacific* from Liverpool . . . Improved 2 ft brass rules, common do. ivory rules . . ." *American Mercury* (Hartford, Connecticut), February 7, 1811. (See also METEROD, FOLDING MEASURE, SLIDE RULE.)

RUMFORD OVEN, RUMFORD ROASTER
"A contrivance for roasting meat, which promises to be a great convenience." *The Domestic Encyclopedia* (Philadelphia, 1821). A replacement for the older beehive oven set in the fireplace wall. "No process of cooking is more troublesome or attended with a greater waste of fuel, than roasting meat before an open fire . . . Meat roasted by this new process, is more delicate, more juicy, and higher flavored, than when roasted on a spit before an open fire . . . The body of the roaster is a hollow cylinder of sheet iron, which, for a roaster of moderate size, may be made about 18 inches in diameter, and 24 inches long; closed at one end, and set in a horizontal position in brickwork in such a manner that the flame of a small fire made in a closed fireplace directly under it, may play all around it. The open end should be closed with a double door of sheet iron (set even with the front of the brick work) or a door of sheet iron covered on the outside with a pannel of wood. In the cylinder there is a horizontal shelf, a flat plate of sheet iron, supported on ledges about three inches below the centre . . . and serves as a support for a dripping pan over which the meat to

be roasted is placed . . . on a gridiron . . ." Count Rumford, *Essays,* Vol. III.

RUMMER

A contemporary term for a "drinking cup; a large glass." (W)

RUNLET, RUNDLET

(See ROUNDELET, CANTEEN.)

RUNNING SIDEBOARD

An early-nineteenth-century synonym for the Supper Canterbury, now more often called a tea wagon or dinner wagon. (See CANTERBURY, DUMB WAITER.)

RURAL CHAIR

An eighteenth-century term for Rustic Furniture, *q.v.* "Rural chairs for summer houses [are] made with the Limbs of Yew or Apple Trees, as Nature produces them, but . . . very dry and well seasoned . . . the Bark peeled clean off . . . they are generally painted in various Colours," were shown by Robert Manwaring in *The Cabinet and Chair-Maker's Real Friend and Companion* (London, 1768).

RUSH JACK

A contemporary term for the Rushlight Holder, *q.v.*

RUSHLIGHT HOLDER, RUSHLIGHT STAND

An iron or iron-and-wood table stand in which rushes, impregnated with grease, were used in lieu of candles. "The rushes are carried about by hand; but to sit by, to work by, or to go to bed by, they are fixed in stands made for that purpose. These have an iron part something like a pair of pliers to hold the rush, which is shifted forward as it burns. These rushes give a better light than a common dip-candle and they cost next to nothing." William Cobbett, *The Rushlight* (London, 1799). Iron work lights, meant to be suspended from a ceiling hook or beam, also were made to hold rushes, and sometimes were fitted with both pliers for the rush and a socket for a candle.

RUSTIC FURNITURE

The all-inclusive term for a type of furniture, especially chairs and tables; the rails, arms, legs, and other supporting parts of which were carved in imitation of tree branches. These first were made in the mid-eighteenth-century Gothic Revival period and again in the mid-nineteenth century. Many were made in cast iron for use as garden furnishings. (See also RURAL CHAIR.)

Early-eighteenth-century rushlight holders with candlestick sockets. (Courtesy, Antiquarian and Landmarks Society, Inc.)

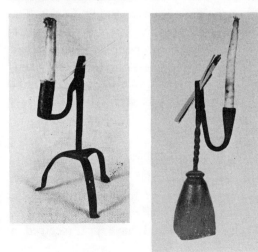

S

SABER, SABRE

The cavalryman's single-edge cutting weapon with a curved blade: "The sabre for the cavalry shall be at least three feet long, exclusive of the hilt; the arms, accoutrements and uniform of the horse-artillery shall be like those of the cavalry." *Connecticut Statutes* (Hartford, 1835).

SACK BUT, SACKBUT

The name for an ancient "bass trumpet," (H) the ancestor of the modern slide trombone. The term is the English form of the French *Sacquebute,* from the Middle French words, *saquer,* to pull, and *bouter,* to thrust.

SACK

A leather "pouch; commonly a large bag." (J)

SADDLE

The custom-made "seat which is put upon the horse for the accommodation of the rider." (J) "Such coverings [are] very costly . . . decorated with many ornaments. Saddles as they are now made consist of a wooden frame called the saddle-tree, on which is laid a quantity of horse-hair, wool, Ec. and this is covered over with tanned leather, neatly nailed to the wooden tree. To keep the saddle steady on the horse, the crupper is used, which passes under the creature's tail; and girths, to prevent it from turning round. To support the legs of the rider a pair of stirrups is also added; one of which is very useful in assisting to mount the animal. There are many different kinds of saddles, as the hunting saddle, the riding saddle, ladies' saddles, Ec. Ec." *The Book of Trades* (London, 1805). (See also HORSE FURNITURE; and in Chapter 3, trade descriptions of the HORSE'S MIL-LINER, SADDLER, SADDLER'S IRON-MONGER, TREE MAKER.)

SADDLE CHEEK

This was a Hepplewhite term for an "Easy Chair," *q.v.* "the construction and use of which is very apparent; they may be covered with leather, horse-hair; or have a linen case to fit over the canvas stuffing as is most usual and convenient." A. Hepplewhite, *The Cabinet-Maker and Upholsterer's Guide* (London, 1788).

The term often is given incorrectly today as saddle check chair, due to a typographical error in Hepplewhite's editorial paragraph, part of which is quoted above, explaining the construction of the chair. The name as printed in the 1788 *Guide* contained several wrong-font characters, including a *c* in a size larger than the rest of the word, incorrectly set in place of an *e*. However, the name of the chair design was given

Saddle cheek chair, as illustrated in Hepplewhite's *Guide* (London, 1794).

correctly in the table of contents of the *Guide,* where it was listed as Saddle Cheek Chair. The incorrect term, Saddle Check, does not make sense. The correct term, Saddle Cheek, while somewhat fanciful, does, if it is remembered that in the eighteenth century the term cheeks was used for what we now call the wings of a chair. Hepplewhite's design for the cheeks or wings of this easy chair resembled the sides of a saddle of the period, hence Saddle Cheek. The confusion suffered by later readers and collectors, caused by poor typesetting and proofreading in the essay portion, was compounded by the fact that the title under the illustration itself was given simply as Easy Chair, *q.v.*

SAD IRON

The flat, smoothing iron of solid construction, as opposed to the Box Iron, *q.v.* This was an oval or lozenge-shaped, thick, heavy piece of iron with a rising handle. "Phelps & Olmstead have just received a

Eighteenth-century sad iron. (Courtesy, Antiquarian and Landmarks Society, Inc.)

Salamander. (Courtesy, Antiquarian and Landmarks Society, Inc.)

fresh supply of Goods which will be sold at a small advance [including] English & American Shovels and Spades, Frying-pans, Sad-Irons, and Iron Hollow Ware." *The American Mercury* (Hartford, Connecticut), November 18, 1812.

Toy Sad Irons: "Allen & Belcher have just received, direct from the manufactories per ship *New York,* via New York, an extensive assortment of Hardware [including] Sad Irons, Shovels and Tongs, Bed Keys, Iron Spoons, Toy Sad Irons, Iron Candle Sticks . . ." *Literary Cadet and Rhode Island Statesman* (Providence), February 23, 1828.

SAFE

"A kind of buttery." (W) A general term for any box or closed cupboard in which anything of value might be kept securely. The term was used here to indicate a small kitchen food cupboard. Today it is used by collectors in combining forms, as a butter-safe, pie-safe, etc.

SAILORS' TOYS

Another description of Scrimshaw, *q.v.,* work. Toys meant the small objects, gifts, or baubles whittled or carved by sailors.

SALAMANDER

"A salamander [a mythical lizard-like spirit] is a kind of heroine in chastity, that treads upon fire, and lives in the midst of flames without being hurt." Joseph Addison, *The Spectator,* October 13, 1711. This was a browning iron with a long handle used to brown or toast the surface of roasts or pastry. Because many had handles of the same length as the Peel, or a Pile, *qq.v.,* salamanders sometimes go unrecognized today.

The "iron" end, however, was much smaller than that of a peel or shovel, usually about the size of the cook's hand. "To make a Welch Rabbit: Toast the Bread on both sides, then toast the Cheese on one side, lay it on the Toast, and with a hot Iron brown the other side." Hannah Glasse, *Art of Cookery* (London, 1747). "Let the ham braize . . . then sprinkle bread crumbs over it, and brown it with a hot salamander." Richard Briggs, *The New Art of Cookery* (Philadelphia, 1792).

The name Salamander also was given to any hot loggerhead or poker used to light a pipe or to ignite gunpowder.

SALT BOX, SALT KIT

A small round wooden box with a fitted cover; later a round or rectangular box with a hinged lid, made of wood or pottery.

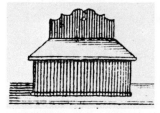

Wood salt box, c. 1790 print.

SALT CUP

A contemporary term for the footed, open, so-called master salt dish with one or two handles, usually equipped with a matching ladle or spoon. "Standish Barry, Gold and Silver Smith . . . A Handsome Assortment of Plated Ware . . . Salt Cups and Spoons; . . . Monumental Vinagarets, mustard frames . . . with an extensive Variety of Other Articles too tedious to enumerate . . ." *Maryland Gazette* (Baltimore), November 15, 1792.

Pewter salt cup. (Courtesy, John Carl Thomas, Syracuse, New York.)

C. 1700 turned wood standing salt cup.

Mid-eighteenth-century turned wood salt cups.

SALVER

The term from the Spanish *salva* to designate "any plate on which anything is presented." (J) A tray on which something is carried or offered, such as food or drink.

SAMBUKE

From the Latin, a term for a kind of harp.

SAMPLER, SAMPLAR, SAM CLOTH, SAM PLETH

All names for "a piece of girl's needlework; a pattern." (W) "A piece worked by young girls for improvement." (J) The proof or "sample" of skill in needlework, made by apprentices and other children; generally worked on a rectangle of linen to show proficiency in various stitches and/or

their use in designs. Samplers most sought are those which in addition to the name of the embroiderer, date, and place of execution, include representations of buildings and landscapes.

Early long sampler. (Courtesy, Antiquarian and Landmarks Society, Inc.)

SAMP MORTAR, CORN MORTAR

A common term to distinguish the great standing mortar from the much smaller mortars used at the kitchen worktable or pantry ledge. Samp was an Indian word for boiled ground corn. "When the [corn]

Grain is ripe and hard, there are several Ways of using it. One is to soak it all night in a Lessite [a lye of wood ashes], and then pound it in a large wooden Mortar with a wooden Pestle; . . . each Grain boil'd swells into a white soft Pulp, and eaten with Milk, or with Butter and Sugar, is delicious." "Observations on Mayz or Indian Corn," *Writings of Benjamin Franklin,* ed., A. H. Smyth (New York, 1907).

Hand-hewn samp mortar and pestle. (Courtesy, Antiquarian and Landmarks Society, Inc.)

SANDBOX, SANDER

The small silver, pewter, tin, or wood desk box or pot made with a perforated lid. The box was made specifically to contain the fine sand which was cast over a finished piece of writing to absorb and thus "dry" the ink. Sometimes more unusual materials were used to make the box: "The sand box (or Devil's Tree of San Domingo) tree [has] fruit as large as an orange, but rather flat, and divided into twelve sections . . . Picked

C. 1800 pewter sander.

C. 1825 lignum vitae sander.

before ripe, [the hard rind of] this fruit is used as a sand box." Edouard de Montulé, *Voyage en Amérique* (Paris, 1821). (See SAND CASTER, STANDISH.)

SAND CASTER

A common contemporary synonym for the ink sander or sandbox. Many, made in forms similar to sugar dredgers or muffineers, were of crystal combined with silver or gold, of silver or pewter, as well as of polished hard woods. (See also SANDBOX, STANDISH.)

SANDGLASS

(See HOURGLASS.)

SAP BUCKET

The open wooden bucket, generally holding up to three gallons, used to gather the sap of maple trees of which a form of sugar and/or syrup was made. "There is now more reason than ever for attending to making sugar from the maple tree—as we are deprived from obtaining it abroad. Those, therefore, who have the means will not neglect to manufacture this all important article." *The Farmer's Almanack* (Boston, 1814).

SARCOPHAGUS

The very late-eighteenth-century and early-nineteenth-century name for the cellaret or *garde du vin* designed to be part of, or to be set beneath, the sideboard; so called because it was "in some faint degree, an imitation of the figure of these ancient stone coffins, on which account only the term can with any colour of propriety, be applied to such wine cisterns." Thomas Sheraton, *The Cabinet Dictionary* (London, 1803). These generally were made with covers of mahogany or other fine wood and with a lead lining.

SATCHEL

A small sack of cloth or leather with a drawstring closure; "a little bag, commonly a bag used by schoolboys to carry their books." (J)

SAUCEBOAT

A contemporary term for a low, squat pitcher used for the service of gravy. "I thank you for the Sauceboats, and am pleased to find so good a Progress made in the China Manufactory." (Benjamin Franklin in London January 28, 1772, to his wife in Philadelphia.) *Writings of Benjamin Franklin,* ed., A. H. Smyth (New York, 1907).

C. 1835 soft paste sauce boats.

SAUCEPAN

"A small Skillet [*q.v.*], with a long handle in which sauce or small things are boiled." (J) In the colonial vocabulary, sauce meant any accompaniment to meat; the reference often was to vegetables. "Boil all your greens by themselves in plenty of spring water with salt in it; and never use iron pots or saucepans, as they are very improper vessels for [greens]; let them be copper or brass well-tinned, or silver." Richard Briggs, *The New Art of Cookery* (Philadelphia, 1792).

SAUCER

Until the close of the eighteenth century, this term had two definitions: (1) "A small pan or platter in which sauce is set on the table." (J) "Put the chops into a hot dish, with a spoonful of ketchup under them, and horse-radish and chopped shallots in saucers." Richard Briggs, *The New Art of Cookery* (Philadelphia, 1792). (2) "A piece or platter of china into which a tea-cup is set," was Johnson's second choice in 1755, and by 1806, the only one given by Webster as "a small plate used for a

teacup." By the turn of the nineteenth century, the words saucedish or Sauceboat, *q.v.,* more commonly were used to designate separate serving pieces for sauce.

SAUCE SPOON

The earliest meaning of sauce was any food other than bread or meat, including cooked vegetables as well as butter or liquid condiments. By the turn of the nineteenth century sauce was "something to improve the relish [taste] of food," (W) the sauce spoon or small ladle was a polite table utensil. "Send . . . 3 pair of Plated Soup Ladles; 4 pair of Silver Sauce Spoons with round Bowls & Crooket handles like the Ladles." (Order December 29, 1771, from Catherine Rathnell, Merchant, Williamsburg, Virginia, to London.) Frances Mason, *John Norton and Sons, Merchants of London and Virginia* (Richmond, 1935).

SAVE-ALL

The common term for "a small pan to save candle ends." (W) about the depth of a thimble and usually made with a slight rim, for use in candleholders made without push-ups or slides; of brass, tin, pewter, iron; rarely of silver. "Economy in Candles. Candles are frequently permitted to burn in the socket to a great waste, and to the injury of the Candlestick; this may be prevented by taking out early the short piece of candle, placing it betwixt three common pins stuck in an old cork, and putting the cork in the candlestick. Or rather, give a penny for that ingenious utensil, a save-all. It is at least as cheap, and prevents the risk of setting fire to the house." Thomas Tegg, *Book of Utility* (London, 1828).

SAWS

One of the basic tools for forming by cutting with a thin blade having a continuous series of sharp teeth. Some of those used by carpenters and cabinetmakers are listed here: "Charles Sigourney, has imported from London . . . and from Liverpool, an extensive assortment of Hardware Goods [including] Thick Mill Saws; Cross cut, Pit, and Ship Carpenter's turning saws; Cast Steel veneering saws, Hand, Pannel, Tennon, Sash, Dovetail, Compass, Keyhole, narrow Frame, Pruning & Wood saws . . ." *American Mercury* (Hartford, Connecticut), November 23, 1809.

SAXAMELODICON

A kind of small organ; an early-nineteenth-century musical instrument fad. "We have seen an instrument with a key-board like that of an organ, the tones of which were produced by the friction of wood; and the newspapers lately announced the invention of an instrument which produces agreeable sounds by the striking together of flints [called] the *saxamelodicon*." *Encyclopedia Americana* (Philadelphia, 1831).

SCABBARD

"The sheath of a sword," (J) and in an age when all gentlemen, as well as officers, might carry such arms, an important and often elegant costume accessory, made and sold by silversmiths and jewelers. "Scabbards made for Swords at the shortest Notice at different prices. Gun Screw Drivers and double Worms fit to draw a Ball, at 2s. All the Gentlemen of the American Army who are not supplied may have them at the above [silversmith's] shop . . . Charles Oliver Bruff." *The New-York Gazette and The Weekly Mercury,* July 8, 1776.

SCALE DISH, SCALING DISH

The shallow, saucer-like plate or dish used as "a milk skimmer." (H)

SCATE, SKATE

The term for "a kind of wooden shoe, with a steel plate underneath, on which they slide over the ice." (J) "An iron to slide with." (W) The iron or steel runner or blade was screwed to a wooden platform or sole and secured to the booted foot with leather straps. "Skates for amusement on the ice. A large quantity of various patterns, with excellent leathers, may be had . . . on ap-

plication to James Rivington." *Independent Journal or The General Advertiser* (New York), January 11, 1786.

SCEP, SKEP

The old Saxon word scep referred to a box or basket made of straw or rush; thus, a Beehive, *q.v.,* often was called a bee skep. The term has been revived by collectors today.

SCHRANK

A mid-colony name for a large clothes press or cupboard. "We passed many wagons of emigrants from Pennsylvania of German origin, each encumbered with a huge heavy mahogany press or *schrank* which had once, perhaps, come from Westphalia. These antique pieces of furniture might well contain the penates of these people, or be themselves their household god as they seem to be as religiously preserved." Lyell, *Travels in North America* (New York, 1845), describing a trip over the National Road to Cumberland in 1842.

SCISSORS

The small shears; the blades usually were of fine steel with steel, silver, silver-plated, or gilded metal shanks and handles. Those noted here were of steel with silver: "Joseph Anthony, Jr., silversmith . . . has imported . . . from London . . . Fine razor mettle Scissors, with silver cases and bows." *Pennsylvania Packet* (Philadelphia), December 7, 1790. (See also SHEARS.)

SCKREEN

"A riddle or coarse sieve," but also "anything by which the sun or weather is kept off." (J) (See also PARASOL, SCREENS, UMBRELLA.)

SCOLE

An ancient name for the cup or bowl from which revivifying drinks and toasts were quaffed by early Saxons and Celts; the name was derived from the term for skull, because such ale bowls originally were made from the skulls of fallen foes. Later victors were content to drink each other's healths from cups similarly deep in their rounded shape but formed of horn or wood. (See also BOWL, CUP, DRINKING VESSELS, SKILLET.)

SCONCE

"A pensile candlestick, generally with a looking glass." (J)   The decorative as well

C. 1775 polished tin sconce. (Courtesy, Antiquarian and Landmarks Society, Inc.)

C. 1710 polished tin sconces. (Courtesy, Antiquarian and Landmarks Society, Inc.

C. 1750 polished tin sconce. (Courtesy, Antiquarian and Landmarks Society, Inc.)

C. 1800 sheet-iron sconces. (Courtesy, Antiquarian and Landmarks Society, Inc.)

C. 1760 polished tin sconces. (Courtesy, Antiquarian and Landmarks Society, Inc.)

C. 1775 mirrored sconce. (Courtesy, Antiquarian and Landmarks Society, Inc.)

C. 1775 polished tin sconces. (Courtesy, Antiquarian and Landmarks Society, Inc.)

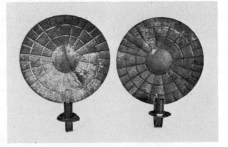

as useful wall light, made with a back plate from which a candleholder or branch extended. The plate usually was of metal or mirror glass used to reflect the light; polished tin, brass, silver, and pewter were used: "James Jacks . . . has imported . . . from London A Large Assortment of Plated Goods, of a Superior Quality [including] Sconce plates with two Branches . . ." *Federal Gazette* (Philadelphia), March 25, 1799. "At home, hanging up pictures, and seeing how my pewter sconces that I have bought will become my stayres and entry." Samuel Pepys, *Diary,* January 4, 1661–62. (See CANDLE PLATE; WALLER.)

SCOOP, SCOPE

The common contemporary term for any "kind of small basin with a handle for lading water," (H)   that is, "a kind of large ladle." (W)   Scoops also came in smaller sizes, defined as "an instrument used for scooping out anything," (H)   as, for example, one recipe suggested ". . . Pare half a dozen middle-sized turnips and with a scoop, cut them out round and as big as a nutmeg." Richard Briggs, *The New Art of Cookery* (Philadelphia, 1792). Scoops were made of steel, tinned iron, brass, pewter, sometimes silver, or gourds. (See also CALABASH.)

Scoop. (Courtesy, Antiquarian and Landmarks Society, Inc.)

SCOOTER
A cant term for a "syringe or Squirt," *q.v.* (H)

SCOPE
A kind of small basin [or ladle] "with a handle used for lading water." (H)

SCOPPERELL, SCOPPERIL, SCOPPERING
A child's plaything; a small button through which a piece of wood or quill is put so that it may be spun like a top. "A little sort of spinning top for boys to set up between the middle finger and the thumb." (H)

SCOTOSCOPE
The term *scoto,* from the Greek for darkness, plus scope (or *scopium,* to examine) to describe a small glass or instrument that enabled the user to see in the dark. This was one of the many small devices developed in the mid-seventeenth-century with which the curious and speculative sought to satisfy their desire for "greater philosophy" or scientific knowledge. Many of these glasses, set in handsomely wrought and engraved silver and/or gilt cases, survive today. "Comes Mr. Reeve with a microscope and a scotoscope. For the first I did give him 5£, 10s, a great price, but a most

curious bauble it is, and he says, the best he knows in England. The other he gives me, and is of value, and a curious curiosity it is to discover objects in a dark room with." Samuel Pepys, *Diary,* August 13, 1664. (See also NIGHT GLASS.)

SCOVEL
The term for "a sort of mop for cleaning an oven; a maulkin." (B)

SCREENS
Any wood, leather, textile, or paper panel used for protection from excessive heat or draughts, or to insure privacy. (See COROMANDEL SCREEN, FIRE SCREEN, FOLDING SCREEN.)

SCREEN WRITING TABLE
(See WRITING FIRE SCREEN.)

SCRIMSHAW
A specific nineteenth-century term for small souvenirs or toys made by sailors to while away time during long voyages. Among scrimshaw pieces most sought by collectors today are the small boxes, necklaces, bracelets, locket slides, pastry crimpers and cutters, button hooks, stays, or busks, etc. These were whittled from wood, whalebone, or ivory and decorated with light tattoo carving, into which color sometimes was rubbed. The origin of the term scrimshaw is usually listed as obscure; a tidy way of saying no one is certain from what other words it is derived. Some believe it may refer to a surname, but whose has never been determined; others, that it is related to another slang word, scrimshank, also of obscure origin. Scrimshanking, however, was the nineteenth-century term for what a later generation would call gold-

Scrimshaw pie crimper or jagging iron. (Courtesy, Antiquarian and Landmarks Society, Inc.)

bricking, both of which may be freely translated as making something out of nothing. So perhaps the collector now may hazard another guess; scrimshaw may have been a contraction of scrimp and shave, or scrimp and shaw: Scrimp today still means scant and meager, and carries a sense of economizing and saving, just as it did in the late eighteenth and early nineteenth centuries, but then it had also an additional meaning; an object of small dimension. "A scrimpy little thing," "just something I scrimped together," are phrases still heard in rural America. Shavings are bits and pieces left over or discarded from other work. Perhaps the seamen who saved odd bits of whalebone, teeth, and wood, in the vernacular of the time were said to scrimp the shavings or leavings; from there to scrimpshaving as the description of a whittled or carved toy is an easy jump.

If the leap from shave to shaw—because it was easier to say—seems too broad, then consider that shaw is the older English word (related in origin to shave, and familiar to the colonists) for scanty woods, or underbrush of little value, but a fine source of small branches and twigs suited to whittling. The man who picked up a stick there, when carving it of an evening, might have explained it was just something he scrimmed or scrimped from the shaw. And so scrimpshaw to scrimshaw.

Whatever its source, scrimshaw is a folk word evolved to describe a kind of folk art: small pieces of embroidery, needlework pictures on canvas, whittled and carved canes and candlesticks, all, also, were scrimshaw made by seamen as well as small toys and boxes of whalebone and ivory.

"I have never seen more ingenuity in the use of a knife [than that shown by a Nantucket man]. In the many leisure hours which their long cruises afford them, they cut and carve a variety of boxes and pretty toys, in wood, adapted to various uses, which they bring home as testimonies of remembrance to their wives or sweethearts." Hector St. John de Creveceour, *Letters from an American Farmer* (1783).

SCRINE
"A bookcase, a repository for writings." (W)

SCRIPTOR, SCRIPTOIRE
Another common synonym for the writing desk or *Escritoire, q.v.*

SCRIPTURE TILES
A contemporary term for ornamental glazed delft or pottery tiles, decorated with biblical scenes. (See also FLEMISH TILES, HISTORICAL TILES, TILES.)

SCROLL-TOP CLOCK
The "Terry Style" wooden works case, also called a Pillar-and-Scroll Clock, *q.v.*, developed by Eli Terry for use on the mantel shelf or wall bracket. These cases were, on an average, about 21 inches high, and had white-painted wooden dials about 11 inches square set above square or rectangular plates of reverse-painted or decorated glass.

SCRUBBOARD
The contemporary term for the ribbed wooden board later called a washboard.

C. 1810 scrubboard. (Courtesy, Antiquarian and Landmarks Society, Inc.)

Seventeenth-century scrubbing stick. (Courtesy, Antiquarian and Landmarks Society, Inc.)

SCUMMER

In the kitchen, the "vessel with which liquor is scummed, commonly called a Skimmer," q.v. (J)

SCRUTOIRE

A popular attempt to Anglicize the word, *Escritoire, q.v.,* for a writing desk or case for papers.

SCUPPIT

A "shovel, or spade, of uniform width the sides turned a little inward." (H)

SCUTTLE

An Old English term from the Latin, *scutella,* for dish or platter: (1) a slightly hollowed-out trencher or platter; later (2) "a wide, shallow basket" (J); a winnowing basket for sifting cereal grains from chaff; (3) the shovel used to cast the grain into the winnowing basket; (4) any large open basket that was wider at the top than bottom, especially one used for carrying grain, fruit or vegetables. (See also COAL SCUTTLE.)

SCYTHE, SITHE

"The instrument of mowing, a crooked blade joined at right angles to a long pole." (J) "Time is commonly drawn upon tombs, in gardens, and other places, as an old man, bald, winged, with a sithe and an hour-glass." Henry Peacham, *The Compleat Gentleman* (London, 1622). ". . . You will buy Some good Shipps that first Come in the Spring of the yeare Send me such goods as are Expressed heare following, in Nayles of Sisable Sorts not Exceeding double teens in bigness . . . and Siths to the value of Sixe pounds worth . . ." (Order from Newport, Rhode Island, to London, December 7, 1666.) *The Letter Book of Peleg Sanford* (Providence, 1928).

SEA CHEST, SEAMAN'S CHEST

The collector's term for the simple, painted, six-board wooden box or locker in which seamen kept personal belongings or changes of clothing aboard ship. Such boxes differ from similar small chests in that the sides usually are canted so that the base is wider than the top and the box thus less easily tipped over. Generally made with rope handles at both sides, and marked with the owner's initials or name, those most prized are decorated with paintings of ships or other marine scenes on the lid top or front board, or with incised or chip-carving.

SEAL

The term for a cypher, crest, or other insignia cut in metal, stone, or wood, and thus "a stamp engraved with a particular impression which is fixed upon the wax that closes letters, or affixed in a testimony," (J) as to a deed, indenture, will, or affidavit. "Brooks & Warrock, Jewellers, Respectfully inform the public that they have commenced Business at the Sign of the Dove and Locket, Market Street, three doors above Church Street, Norfolk . . . Society and Compting House Seals, made and beautifully cut with any Device; also, Gold, Silver, Steel, and other Metal Watch Seals, to any pattern, and cut with Cyphers, Crests, Coats of Arms, or any Device whatever." *American Gazette* (Norfolk, Virginia), October 9, 1795.

SEAL-SKIN TRUNK

The contemporary term for the colonial and nineteenth-century round-top trunk, made of wood, but covered with seal skin. "Trunks, Hair and Seal-Skin Trunks, assorted sizes . . . the best Philadelphia Leather, Calf, Kid, Morocco and Seal Skins, and good workmen . . . prepared to make to measure at short notice . . ." *Columbian Register* (New Haven, Connecticut) November 7, 1829.

Seapiece, 1814 engraving commemorating Perry's victory. (Courtesy, Connecticut Historical Society, Inc.)

SEAPIECE

The contemporary term for "a picture representing anything at sea," (J) more commonly called a marine painting today.

SEARCE

An old term for "a fine sieve." (W)

SEARCH

A common colonial spelling of Searce or sierce, for a kind of Sieve, *qq.v.*, perhaps resulting from contemporary pronunciation.

SEAT CURB

A synonymous term for the Fender Stool or Hearth Stool, *qq.v.*

SECRETARY

When those pieces of fine case furniture that we now call secretaries first were made, they were called a set of drawers, a bookcase with drawers, or perhaps drawers and bookcase. In 1806, Webster still defined secretary as "one who writes for another." When first in use to designate an inanimate secretary, the word referred to a single drawer with compartments for paper, books, inkstand, quills, and wafers, or to a pullout slide or writing surface with a back piece similarly fitted with a tier of small drawers. Thus, Sheraton offered a "Library Table with a Secretary Drawer." By 1840, John Hall, in *The Cabinet-Maker's Assistant* (Baltimore) advertised a "Secretaria Book Case;" that is, a case piece with a "writing drawer [that] pulls out to nearly its whole depth, and has a writing top that is hinged in front, and can be adjusted, by a rack underneath the top, to any angle required; at each end of the writing drawer, there are receptacles for pens, inks, Ec." In 1853, Blackie and Son (London) in their similarly named text, still described a "secretaire-bookcase." At times what we now call either a secretary or a highboy was known to its original owner simply as drawers or a set of drawers: "Every householder [in the eighteenth century] deemed it essential to his convenience and comfort to have an ample chest of drawers in his

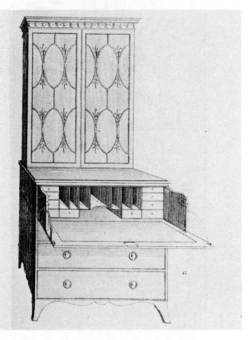

Secretary and bookcase illustrated in Hepplewhite's *Guide* (London, 1794).

Early-nineteenth-century New York secretary. (*Newtown Bee,* photo by R. Scudder Smith.)

parlour or sitting-room, in which the linen or cloths of the family were always of ready access. These Drawers were sometimes nearly as high as the ceiling. At other times, they had a writing desk about the centre with a falling lid to write upon when let down." John F. Watson, *Annals of Philadelphia* (Philadelphia, 1830). It seems reasonable to conclude that as a descriptive word, secretary, as we now use it, is a collector's description. (See also BUREAU; DESK; ESCRITOIRE.)

SEEDLIP, SEEDLOP
The woven basket or "vessel in which the sower carries his seed." (J)

SEETHER
A contemporary colloquialism for a "boiler, a pot to boil things in." (W)

SELOUR, SELLORE
Variations of celure. (See also CELE.)

SERVER
Server was a contemporary term for a serving tray, and also for the small sideboard, usually called a lowboy today. These varied in width from 36 to 48 inches, in height, from 36 to 60 inches, and often had a rim or gallery at the back and sides to prevent bottles, glasses, and cups from sliding off. "Aaron Chapin begs leave to acquaint the public . . . that he has lately removed from East Windsor to Hartford, where he now carries on the Cabinet and Chair making business in both Mahogany and Cherry Tree of which he has now a good stock . . . and he has now on hand a few good Tea and Kitchen Tables, a variety of Tea and Wine Servers to dispose of on reasonable terms for good pay in hand." *Connecticut Courant* (Hartford), December 9, 1783. (See also SIDEBOARD, HUNT BOARD, LOWBOY, TEA BOARD.)

SET
The general term for a group of matched articles, or "a number of things suited to each other; things considered as related to

each other; a number of things of which one cannot conveniently be separated from the rest." (J) Also a tea set. (See also NEST, QUARTETTO TABLE, TRIO TABLES.)

SETTEE
The term, apparently devolving from Settle, *q.v.*, for a wide seat with back and arms, made in the seventeenth, eighteenth, and nineteenth centuries. Settees usually were not as long as sofas. Early terms included the descriptive Double-Chair, *q.v.*, or double-seat and more than one mid-eighteenth-century maker thus classed settees with large chairs: "Francis Trumble . . . makes and sells the following goods in mahogany, walnut, cherry-tree, maple, Ec., viz. . . . Chairs of all sorts such as settees, easy chairs, arm chairs, parlour chairs, chamber chairs, close chairs, and couches, carv'd or plain . . ." *Pennsylvania Gazette* (Philadelphia), August 8, 1754. In comparison with the upholstered sofa, the settee was defined as a "large, long seat" (J) "with a back to it." (W) Although many settees were furnished with loose cushions, there does not seem to have been much connotation of softness or luxury. One social historian yearned for the eighteenth-century days before sofas were introduced, noting that "Since the year 1800, the introduction of foreign luxury, caused by the influx of wealth, has been yearly effecting successive changes in [furniture] . . . the former simple articles which contented . . . our forefathers could hardly be conceived. Plain

Windsor settee with modified bamboo turnings.

New Haven (Connecticut) *Gazette,* February 22, 1787.

people used settees [which had] a very high back of plain boards . . ." John F. Watson, *Annals and Occurrences of New York City and State in the Olden Time* (Philadelphia, 1846).

SETTEE ROCKER
(See DOUBLE ROCKING CHAIR, MAMMY ROCKER.)

SETTING STICK
A cant contemporary term for "a rod used in making plaits or sets of ruffs." (H) The Goffering Iron, *q.v.*

SETTLE
The term for "a long seat, a bench with a back." (W) Perhaps evolved from the basic low six-board chest, the settle was a long bench for two or more persons; it was made with a high back and arms, the actual

seat often doubling as the lid for a chest. Numerous settles, of course, were made with a plain, single-board bench seat without the box. In others, the box, rather than serve as a storage bin, enclosed a bed: "Plain people [before 1800] used settees and settles—the latter had a bed concealed in the seat, and by folding the top of it outwards to the front, it exposed the bed and widened the place for the bed to be spread upon it. This was a common sitting room appendage, and was a proof of more attention to comfort than display. It had a very high back of plain boards, and the whole was of white pine, generally unpainted . . . They were a very common article in very good houses . . . the proper property of the oldest members of the family . . . placed before the fireplace in the winter to keep the back guarded from wind and cold." John F. Watson, *Annals and Occurrences of New York City and State in the Olden Time* (Philadelphia, 1846). (See also BACON CUPBOARD, CHIMNEY CORNER, SETTEE.)

Late-seventeenth-century American curved back settle. (Courtesy, Antiquarian and Landmarks Society, Inc.)

SETTLE BED
The contemporary term for the kind of "folding bed" (H) formed by the box seat of one type of Settle, *q.v.*

SETTLE TABLE
The collector's term for the Chair-Table, *q.v.*, which was large enough to seat at least two persons when the hinged table top was raised to a vertical position, pegged tight, and so formed a high back.

SEXTANT
The navigator's and surveyor's instrument for measuring angular distances or observing altitudes in order to ascertain latitude and longitude. "The Subscriber [Andrew Elliot] . . . has for sale an excellent new Sextant, and an elegant pair of new Globes, containing all the late improvements with the tracts of Captain Cook and other celebrated Navigators." *Maryland Gazette* (Baltimore) April 15, 1788.

SHADE
This was a contemporary synonym for a Profile or Silhouette, *qq.v.*, particularly one with highlights brushed on in bronze paint. "Just received, from Charleston and for Sale (Price One Dollar) by Rice & Co., Baltimore, A Few Shades or Profiles, of the President of the United States, Done in a New Method, and his likeness correctly delineated by an American Artist." *Maryland Journal* (Baltimore), July 5, 1791.

SHALM, SHAWM
The name of an ancient reed "musical instrument or pipe, somewhat resembling the hautboy." (H) The term is the Anglicized version of the old French, *chalemie* or *chalemel,* derived from the Latin *calamus,* for reed.

SHARP
A colloquialism for the Fencer's Sword, *q.v.* (See also note under FENCING MASTER, Chapter 3.)

SHAUL
Any shallow receptacle, especially "(1) a small washing-tub, made hollow, and without staves; (2) a wooden shovel [or scoop] without a handle, used for the purpose of putting corn into a winnowing machine." (H) (See also SCUTTLE.)

SHAVING BASIN

The barber's bowl. The general term for the ceramic or metal shallow bowl with a portion of the rim cut away so that the bowl could be held under the chin.

Eighteenth-century brass shaving basin. (Courtesy, Antiquarian and Landmarks Society, Inc.)

Eighteenth-century delft shaving bowl or barber's basin.

SHAVING BOX

A small covered jar, pot, or box for slightly soft soap used to make lather; made of pottery, silver, pewter, tin. "Stolen . . . a small red leather Trunk, with several little articles in it . . . a pewter shaving box with soap." *New York-Gazette and Weekly Mercury,* March 3, 1777. (See also SOAP BOX.)

SHAVING MIRROR

The collector's term for a Dressing Glass, *q.v.*

SHAVING TABLE

(See BASIN STAND, DRESSING BOX, DRESSING DRAWERS, DRESSING CASE.)

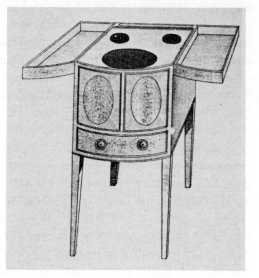

Shaving table illustrated in Hepplewhite's *Guide* (London, 1794).

SHAW-FOWL

The combination of shaw, an old word for thicket or wood, and fowl, to describe "an artificial bird, made for fowlers to shoot at." (H) A target for practice in marksmanship.

SHEARS

The iron or steel "instrument to cut, consisting of two blades moving on a pin, between which the thing cut is intercepted. Shears are a larger, and scissors a smaller instrument of the same kind." (J) "Shears for Shearmen, glovers, Seamestres, and Taylers" were included in the House of Parliament Rates, 1660, for Imports and Exports—*Statutes of the Realm* (London, 1819). (See also SCISSORS.)

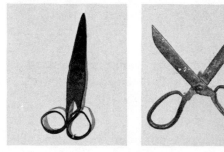

Eighteenth-century iron shears.

SHEATH
The general term for "the case of anything; (especially) the scabbard of a weapon" (J) such as a sword.

SHED
An old word for divide or separate, used colloquially for "(1) the handle of a pail, (2) the sheath of a knife, (3) a tub for cream." (H)

SHEET MUSIC
Hymns, popular ballads, chamber music, arias, and oratorios were printed on separate sheets that usually were decorated with handsomely drawn titles and other illustrations. Sheets could be purchased separately and later bound in a volume, or could be purchased as a ready-made collection in a paper or board binding. They are collected today as examples of the engravers' and lithographers' arts and for the variety of scenes, costumes, and objects illustrated. "Just published, neatly Printed on fine paper, and to be sold by A. Thorne, next Door to the Green-Dragon near the Moravian Meeting-House, in New York, *The Mock Bird,* or *New American Songster*; Being a Collection of all the newest and most approved Songs, Designed for the Entertainment of the Ladies and Gentlemen of New York and other Parts of North America." *The New-York Gazette or The Weekly Post-Boy,* March 19, 1761.

Not all music published was transcribed correctly; a special selling point often was the fact that the engraver himself was a musician or employed one to read proof: "Music Engraving in all its branches correctly performed by Wm. Priest, Musician of the New Theatre. For particulars inquire at No. 15, Apple Tree Alley between 4th and 5th Streets. *Pennsylvania Packet* (Philadelphia), January 3, 1795.

By the end of the first quarter of the nineteenth century, new, less expensive printing and lithographic reproduction methods, and a recession period, lowered the cost of popular sheet music: "SHEET MUSIC. At six cents the page. Just received at the Providence Music Saloon, a large quantity of good Music, for the Piano Forte, which having been bought low, will be sold for six cents per page—also, some at 4 cents. Those desirous of making up volumes will do well to call soon. Also, just received and on hand, as usual, a good assortment of Piano Fortes . . . of the best workmanship and tone." *Literary Cadet and Rhode Island Statesman* (Providence), September 6, 1828.

SHEFFIELD PLATE, SHEFFIELD PLATEWARE
Any item, especially table hollow ware, candlesticks, vases, urns, or picture frames, made of copper thinly coated with silver. (See in Chapter 9.)

SHELF
The general term for any "board fixed against a supporter so that anything may be placed upon it." (J) (See also BRACKET, in Chapter 5; BRACKET SHELF, CONSOLE, ENCOIGNEUR.)

SHELF CLUSTER
Or, as it also was known, the cluster shelf, was an alternative term for the Victorian Overmantel, *q.v.*

SHELF-PIECE
The collector's euphemism for an object that has been broken (or fractured) and, though mended, is not usable. Because of its beauty of color or form, the mended piece is kept "on the shelf," for the enjoyment the sight of it provides. Shelf-pieces always have had a second advantageous use: "In middling genteel families it is not uncommon to have things more for shew than use. And I cannot but applaud the ingenious thought of a friend of mine, who has contrived to furnish his house in the most elegant taste at a very small expence. He is pleased, it is true, to eat off your common stone ware, because it looks so

clean; but you see his beaufet crowded with a variety of curious enamelled China plates, which are ranged in such manner as to conceal the streaks of white paint that cement the broken pieces together." *The London Magazine,* January, 1756.

Shelf-piece. (Courtesy Antiquarian and Landmarks Society, Inc.)

SHELLS
A colonial cant term for money. (See also PEAK, WAMPUM.)

SHEVERET
(See CHEVERET.)

SHIELD
(1) The soldier's wooden, waxed leather, sheet iron, or steel "weapon of defence, worn upon the arm, to fend off lances, darts, and hand-arms." *The Domestic Encyclopedia* (Philadelphia, 1821). (See also under ARMORIAL BEARINGS.) (2) A carved, painted, and/or gilded wooden or-

nament decorated with a family's arms. In *The Gentleman and Cabinet-Maker's Director* (London, 1762), Chippendale illustrated designs for "eight shields, which, as they are often placed very high, should be very bold. They may serve as Ornaments to Pediments" or walls.

SHIELD-BACK CHAIR
The collector's term for a type of chair design based on those illustrated in Hepplewhite's *The Cabinet-Maker and Upholsterer's Guide* (London, 1794). The frame of the back was made in the shape of a shield, sometimes filled with a thinly stuffed or upholstered section, canework, or carved and curved bars.

SHIP FIGUREHEAD
(See FIGUREHEAD.)

SHOD-SHOVEL
A wooden shovel, shod or rimmed with iron along the outer edge of the scoop.

SHOEING HORN
The contemporary term for the shoehorn, "a horn to draw on shoes," (W) so called perhaps because its shape was somewhat reminiscent of a horn. Some were made of horn or molded bone, the majority were of tinned sheet iron or brass. "Shooing hornes" were listed in the House of Parliament Rates, 1660, for Imports and Exports—*Statutes of the Realm* (London, 1819).

Eighteenth-century brass shoeing horn. (Courtesy, Antiquarian and Landmarks Society, Inc.)

Design for a shield illustrated in Thomas Chippendale's *Director* (London, 1762).

SHOPBOARD
A "bench on which any work is done" (J); a worktable.

SHOT FLAGON, SHOT POT

Not a specific small container as such, but the name for the taverner or host's pot, given when "a guest has drunk above a shilling's worth of ale." (H) Shot was a term for the reckoning up, or bill, given at an inn.

SHOVEL

"An instrument consisting of a long handle and broad blade with raised edges." (J) The shovel was the gardener's and farmer's utensil that was "broader than a spade," (W) made, depending on its anticipated use, either with a squared-off edge, or a rounded edge. Many were entirely of wood; some had scoop edges rimmed in iron, others had plates or scoops made entirely of iron. In the Early Colonial period, shovels were made by the cooper or turner, assisted by the blacksmith if a metal edge was wanted. Later the wood handle and the iron scoops were made and sold separately or were assembled by hardware merchants. "Phelps & Olmstead have just received a fresh supply of Goods, [including] English and American Shovels and Spades, Frying Pans, sad-irons, and Iron hollow Ware . . ." *American Mercury* (Hartford, Connecticut), November 13, 1812. The shovel was of prime importance to the settler: "Yourself know what will be needful . . . Remember steel spades and shovels, two hand saws and small axes, the best of all, whatever they cost." (John Winthrop at Boston

Eighteenth-century wooden shovel.

to his son, John, in London, November 6, 1643.) *Journal, History of New England* (Boston, 1825).

SHOWBOARD, SHEWBOARD

This was the common contemporary term for a trade or business shop sign, usually shaped in the form of a symbol of one's trade, or with such a symbol painted thereon to show passers-by what was manufactured or for sale within. "To be sold at Public Sale . . . an elegant shewboard or sign, suitable for a Cabinet Maker, and a small assortment of fine tools . . . Wm. Shannon, Auctioneer." *Pennsylvania Packet* (Philadelphia), February 15, 1794. (See also SIGN.)

Showboard. (Courtesy, Connecticut Historical Society, Inc.)

SHUTTLE
(See WEAVER'S LOOM.)

SICKLE

The gardener's and harvester's hand tool, "the hook with which corn is cut; a reaping-hook." (J) A slender half-circle or crescent of wrought iron set in a wooden haft. The inner edge was serrated and ground to razor-sharpness.

SIDEBOARD

The late eighteenth century and nineteenth century description of the large fitted serving board in the dining parlor. "The sideboard being the chief article of furniture in the [dining parlor] having to contrast with plate, . . . should have a species of richness that looks well alone, and, at the same time, sets off the service of plate to the best advantage. Sufficient effect may be obtained by the use of beautiful woods, carefully wrought, of different shades, but not colours, that may with advantage be used together . . ." Blackie and Son, *The Cabinet-Maker's Assistant* (London, 1853).

This word was also a common contemporary synonym for a large serving tray, especially one designed to be kept on display in the dining parlor. "Tea-Sets and Side Boards of Plate, Made in the most fashionable manner of Silver equal to dollars, not inferior to any from Europe, at 13s., 6d. per oz. for Silver and making; or those that choose to find their own Silver shall have it well made for 4s, 6d per oz." *Federal Gazette* (Philadelphia), January 21, 1789. (See also TEABOARD, TRAY, WAITER.)

SIDEBOARD TABLE

The eighteenth-century term for a side table with a marble or slate top, and also for a side table with shallow drawers set in the frieze below the board, designed for "a dining equipage, on which the silver plate is placed." Thomas Sheraton, *The Cabinet Dictionary* (London, 1803). Ince and Mayhew illustrated six "Side Board Tables," approximately 6 feet wide by 3 feet deep and 34 inches high in *The Universal System of Household Furniture* (London, 1762). Chippendale illustrated twelve designs for what were listed as "Sideboard Tables" and "Side Board Tables," with tops varying from 5 feet by 2 feet, 6 inches and 30 inches high to 6 feet by 3 feet and 34 inches high, noting "these vary according to the Bigness

of the Rooms they stand in." Two of the designs had "the Feet and Rails cut through, which gives it an airy Look, but will be too slight for Marble-tops. Therefore the Tops will be better made of Wood." *The Gentleman and Cabinet-Maker's Director* (London, 1762).

Sideboard table illustrated in Thomas Chippendale's *Director* (London, 1762).

Sideboard or sideboard table illustrated in Hepplewhite's *Guide* (London, 1794).

Small c. 1800 sideboard table. (Courtesy, W. F. Schwind, Rumford Point, Maine.)

SIDE CHAIR

A common term for any chair without arms, a single chair, a straight chair. The

Slat-back side chair, early eighteenth century. (Courtesy, Antiquarian and Landmarks Society, Inc.)

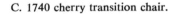

The maple, walnut, or cherry side chair popular from 1730 to 1750 carried over a type of medial stretcher found on William and Mary chairs, combined with the cabriole leg and cushioned pad foot of the American Queen Anne period. (Courtesy, Connecticut Historical Society, Inc.)

Banister-back side chair, early eighteenth century. (Courtesy, Antiquarian and Landmarks Society, Inc.)

C. 1740 cherry transition chair.

Connecticut side chair of cherry and pine, with a Gothic splat, is similar in design and proportion to eighteenth-century Philadelphia work, but is attributed to Eliphalet Chapin (1741–1807) and is an interpretation of Chippendale era English designs popular here from the 1760s through 1800. (Courtesy, Connecticut Historical Society, Inc.)

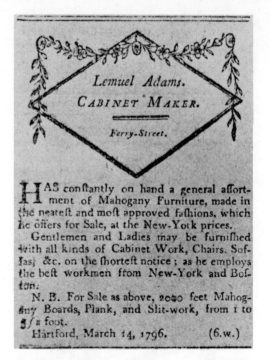

American Mercury (Hartford, Connecticut), March 14, 1796.

Federal period side chair by Lemuel Adams. (Courtesy, Connecticut Historical Society, Inc.)

American "Empire" period curly maple side chair. (Courtesy, Connecticut Historical Society, Inc.)

term devolved from the practice of ordering dining parlor chairs in sets with six or more "side" chairs for guests and one "armed" chair for the host at the head of the table.

SIDE TABLE

A common contemporary synonym for the Sideboard Table, *q.v.*, this was the "table on which conveniences are placed for those who dine at the other table." (J) "In the sitting room, besides food, was a broad side table covered with decanters and bottles, and sugar, and pitchers of water." (Description of an 1810 dinner meeting.) Lyman Beecher, *Autobiography and Correspondence,* ed., Charles Beecher (New York, 1866).

Eighteenth-century country side table with semi-circular pine top, cherry apron and legs.

SIEVE

A general term for any "bolter, searce [or] thing used to sift with," (W) made of "hair or lawn strained upon a hoop, by which flower is separated from bran, or fine powder from coarse." (J)

"2 Wheat Sives brass wire, 1 doz. Meal Sifters—6 Searches [Sierces]" were included in an order October 2, 1773 from Thomas Everard, Clerk of York County, to London. Frances Mason, *John Norton and Sons, Merchants of London and Virginia* (Richmond, 1935).

SIGN

Then, as now, the term for "a picture hung at a door to give notice what is sold within." (J) (See also BUSH, SHOWBOARD, TAVERN SIGN.) None of these, however, necessarily included an inscription or name, for one picture was worth any number of words in an age when literacy was not taken for granted.

SILHOUETTE

A contemporary term, evolved in the second half of the eighteenth century for an inexpensive shadow portrait or profile, so called for Etienne de Silhouette, discredited French Minister of Finance whose name became a cant term for anything cheap. Any solid-color profile painted, cut out with scissors, or cut with the aid of a mechanical device

Full figure silhouette. (Courtesy, Antiquarian and Landmarks Society, Inc.)

C. 1820 cut-paper silhouettes in original pine, gesso, and gilt frames. (Courtesy, Antiquarian and Landmarks Society, Inc.)

525

such as the Delineator, Physiognotrace, Proportionometer, *qq.v.* (See PROFILE.)

SIMITAR
In weaponry, the name for "a crooked or falcated sword with a convex edge." (J) (See also CIMETER.)

SINUMBRA(L) LAMP
Another name for the Astral Lamp, *q.v.*

SIPHON
(See BOTTLE CRANE.)

SIX-BOARD CHEST
The collector's term for the simple bin or blanket chest made of six wide boards: four sides, a bottom, and a top or lid-board.

Early-eighteenth-century six-board chest made of shadow-molded sheathing boards. (Courtesy, Antiquarian and Landmarks Society, Inc.)

SKAIL, SKALLE, SKAYLE, SKOLE
Variations of the Old Anglo-Saxon term Scole *q.v.*, for a drinking cup or goblet.

SKAIN, SKAYNE, SKEAN, SKEEN
An Old English term for "a short sword, a knife," (J) this was the crooked sword or scimitar used by the Irish, as the Glaymoor, *q.v.*, was used by the Scots.

SKEEL
A colloquialism for "a pail," (H) perhaps allied to Skail, *q.v.*

SKEWER
Then, as now, the cooking utensil, made of iron, steel, or wood. "A kind of pin to truss meat, Ec. with." (W) "A wooden or iron

pin, used to keep meat in form." (J) "Take a sirloin of beef . . . skewer it down tight, paper it, put it on a spit, and roast it four hours." Richard Briggs, *The New Art of Cookery* (Philadelphia, 1792).

Skewers also served as racks or frames to keep food from burning: "Take veal . . . wash it very clean, lay three or four wooden skewers at the bottom of a stew-pan, with two quarts of water, a bundle of sweet herbs . . ." Ibid.

C. 1720 skewer holder and skewers. (Courtesy, Antiquarian and Landmarks Society, Inc.)

SKEWER HOLDER
The decorative as well as useful small wall rack from which skewers were hung when not in use.

SKILE
In kitchenware, "an iron slice used for skimming the grease off broth." (H)

SKILLET
"A small pot of iron or copper or brass with a long handle." (H) Many today use the terms frying pan and skillet as synonyms; these utensils were different in form in early kitchens. The vessel of the skillet was similar to the modern saucepan; early colonial alternative terms for the skillet were Pipkin or Posnet, *qq.v.* The early skillet, made to be set over the fire, was a small pot or cauldron, on three legs, and had a wand or

rod-type of handle. It was made of iron, bronze, or brass, and sometimes tinned copper. By the end of the eighteenth century the skillet-vessel was broadened and the bottom made less round in shape, similar to today's saucepan.

"A copper tea kettle, to hold six quarts, of the best sort, a Bell metal skillet, to hold a gallon." (Order, September 23, 1770, from Peyton Randolph, Williamsburg, Virginia, to London.) Frances Mason, *John Norton and Sons, Merchants of London and Virginia* (Richmond, 1935).

The term for what Johnson defined in 1755 as a "small kettle or boiler," as did Webster in 1806, makes more sense to modern collectors when it is remembered that skillet was derived from the ancient Saxon word *Scole,* meaning a cup or bowl; scole originally was the word for the drinking cup made of the skulls of recently felled foes from which the victors drank each other's health.

Eighteenth-century iron skillets. (Courtesy, Antiquarian and Landmarks Society, Inc.)

SKIMMER

A long-handled, shallow, perforated pan or small round ladle used to skim grease from food while it simmered in the pot. The handle usually was of iron, the skimmer pan of brass, copper, or tinned iron.

SKIPPET

A colloquialism for "a small round wooden vessel with a long handle, used for lading water into troughs," (H) or tubs. (See also LADE-GORN.)

SKIVER.

A colloquialism for "a Skewer," *q.v.* (H) Skiverwood was the name colonists gave to the dogwood tree, the small twigs or branches of which were whittled or turned for skewers.

SKREEN

"A coarse sieve." (W)

SLAB FRAME

The common term for a frame or base to support a marble slab or top; a name used to distinguish this type from those called Tables for Slabs, *q.v.* However, either would be called a marble-top table today. Design books of the eighteenth century showed a variety of handsome designs for use beneath pier glasses, or as Ince and Mayhew said, "in Piers under Glasses." Many frames were ornate and "must be very elegant and grand, work'd by the Hand of an ingenious Carver." *The Universal System of Household Furniture* (London, 1762).

Bracket or frame for a slab, illustrated in Thomas Chippendale's *Director* (London, 1762).

SLAT-BACK CHAIR

The simple, country ladder-back chair. (See LADDER BACK, SLAT BACK in Chapter 5.)

SLATE BOOK

The contemporary term for the writing slate or Tablet, *q.v.*

SLATE TABLET

The slate, or slate tablet, was the memo pad of the merchant and householder, and the class exercise book of school children during the Late Colonial and Federal periods. Because it could bȩ reused, slate was much less expensive than paper. Although slate was found here, it was less costly to import sheets of it, already smoothed and polished, from Europe; have it cut to size at the shop, where also when required, simple wood frames often could be added: "Imported in the Ship Galen from London and Brig Ann from Rotterdam, 18 cases of English and Dutch Slates and Slate Pencils . . ." *American Mercury* (Hartford, Connecticut), October 18, 1815.

SLAVE PAPERS

This is the collector's general description of Americana concerned with slaves and slavery. Ship manifests, sale or auction notices, broadsides offering rewards for runaways, and "Freed-man's" papers—those letters or documents declaring a former slave's happy change in status—usually are included in this category, as are letters, newspapers, and broadsides concerning Emancipation Laws. Although much of this material has been lost, great numbers of such documents, covering a broad period in colonial and national American history, remain and are collected today. Although slavery was abolished in the British Empire in 1807, the practice continued in the United States until after the country suffered the five years of material and emotional devastation called variously the Civil War, the Great Rebellion, and the War Between the States. Until that time thousands of African Negroes were imported to work here, the majority in Southern colonies and states. Their numbers were increased drastically in the nineteenth century just prior to the outbreak of war, so much so that by 1840, twice as many were brought here as had been landed in 1790. In addition to the docu-

ments, broadsides, pamphlets, and books now collected, paintings of the period showing wharf and cabin scenes, and workers in fields are sought.

SLAW, SLEW, SLUE BED

Three cant terms for any type of bedstead that folded up, such as the Bureau Bedstead or the Turn-up Bedstead, *qq.v.* Slaw was a variation of the word slew or slue, meaning the turning, swinging, or twisting around of anything on its own axis without changing place; hence, an apt description of the hinged bedframe.

SLEDGE

The name of "a large heavy hammer." (J) "The uphand sledge is used by under workmen, when the work is not of the largest, yet requires help to batter and draw it out; thcy use it with both their hands before them, and seldom lift their hammer higher than their head." Joseph Moxon, *Mechanick Exercises, or The Doctrine of Handy-Works* (London, 1683–84).

SLEEPING CHAIR

A contemporary term for a bedchair; i.e., an easy chair with an adjustable back that could be let down to form a couch or bed. (See BEDCHAIR, HALF-COUCH, HUNTING CHAIR.)

SLEEPY HOLLOW CHAIR

The collector's term for a mid-nineteenth-century sling-back chair with an X-framed seat and open arms; the name undoubtedly inspired by Washington Irving's description of repose in the "sequestered glen" in his *Sketch Book* story, "The Legend of Sleepy Hollow."

SLEIGH BED

The name given the American version of the French Empire bed, because its silhouette resembled that of a sleigh.

SLICE

(1) The term for "a broadhead fixed in a handle; a Peel, *q.v.*, a spatula"; (J) generally used to describe "an instrument of the

kitchen to turn meat that is fried. The slice is still [1847] used for many purposes, particularly for taking up or turning fish in a kettle or stew pan. It was early described as a 'thin bit of wood to stir meat in pots.' " (H) (2) Slice also was a term for any flat piece, as a tray or salver: "This afternoon, Mr. Harris, the sayle-maker, sent me a noble present of two large silver candlesticks and snuffers, and a slice to keep them upon, which indeed is very handsome." Samuel Pepys, *Diary,* March 16, 1665.

SLIDE RULE, SLIDING RULE
A mathematical calculating instrument combining a ruler and medial slide, each being graduated with similar logarithmic scales and with corresponding antilogarithms; made of silver, polished steel, brass, or ivory, in both desk and pocket sizes. "Abroad to find out one to engrave my tables upon my new sliding rule with silver plates, it being so small that Browne that made it cannot get one to do it. So I got [Edward] Croker, the famous writing master, to do it." Samuel Pepys, *Diary,* August 10, 1664.

SLIP COVER
(See LOOSE CASE.)

SLOG IRON
The same as Box Iron, *q.v.,* the name having reference to the heated bar or slog of iron inserted in the box.

SLOP BASIN, SLOP BASON
The common term for the small waste bowl, considered part of the proper equipage for brewing and serving tea; this was the repository for used tea leaves. These small basins or bowls were made of well-glazed, decorated porcelain, faïence, earthenware, or silver and silver plate, often chased, and sometimes decorated with gilt or enamel. "Standish Barry . . . just received by the latest arrivals from Liver-Pool, A handsome Assortment of Plated Ware, consisting of Tea and Coffee Urns, plain and chased; Teapots, Slop Basons, Gilt and Plain . . ." *Maryland Gazette* (Baltimore), November 15, 1792.

Slop Bowl: "Send . . . 1 Dozn. Tea Cups, 1 Dozn. Saucers, 1 Dozn. Coffee Cups & 1 Dozn. Saucers, 1 Slop Bowl of Queen China." Order, February 15, 1770, from Mann Page, York, Virginia, to London. Frances Mason, *John Norton and Sons, Merchants of London and Virginia* (Richmond, 1935).

SMELLING BOTTLE
A pocket elegancy, usually of glass, sometimes equipped with a separate silver, gold, carved wood, or decorated leather outer case. These were small stoppered bottles or phials for perfume, lavender or rose water, or smelling salts, useful as a restorative in case of faintness or headache. "James and Arthur Jarvis, at their Glass and Earthen Store . . . Have . . . a variety of smelling bottles, cut and plain, with and without cases . . ." *The New-York Gazette and The Weekly Mercury,* December 6, 1771. These useful articles were carried by both sexes: ". . . Ladies and gentlemens smelling bottles, pen and fruit knives . . . William Dawson." *Pennsylvania Packet,* (Philadelphia), April 26, 1793. (See also POMANDER, VINAIGRETTE.)

"Lavender water. This perfume is most excellent for smelling bottles, and otherwise, to cure head-aches, recover from fainting, Ec. [to make it take] English oil of lavender 2 oz., essence of ambergris 1 oz., eau de luce 1 pint, spirits of wine, 2 pints." G. W. Francis, *The Dictionary of Practical Receipts* (London, 1847).

SMOKEJACK
A type of revolving spit "so called from its being moved by means of smoke, or rather by means of rarefied air, moving up the chimney, and striking against the tail of the horizontal wheel, which being inclined to the horizon, is thereby moved about the axis of the wheel, together with the pinion which carries the chain and turns the spit."

The Domestic Encyclopedia (Philadelphia, 1821). (See also JACK.)

SMOOTHING IRON
A contemporary synonym for the Box Iron, *q.v.*

SNAFT, SNAT
A colloquialism for "the snuff of a candle." (W) (See also SNUFF DISH, CANDLE SNUFFERS, TINDER BOX.)

SNAPSACK
A common term for a travel bag, especially "a soldier's bag; more usually written knapsack." (J)

SNAP TABLE
An eighteenth-century term sometimes used to designate the tip-and-turn, or so-called tilt-top, tea or breakfast table.

SNEAKER
A contemporary cant term for "a large vessel of drink," (W) applied variously to punch bowls and brandy snifters.

SNEEZE-HORN
Sneeze was a cant term for snuff; the sneeze-horn was a Snuffbox, *q.v.,* made of horn.

SNICKERSNEE
A cant term for a large clasp knife, derived from snick, meaning "to notch or cut." (H)

SNUFF
The common term for "the burnt or burning wick of a candle; a candle's end [or] tobacco powdered." (W) (See also SNUFF-BOX, SNUFF DISH, CANDLE SNUFFERS.)

SNUFF BOTTLE
Snuff, perhaps from the Dutch *snuf* or *snuiftabak,* is prepared powdered tobacco inhaled through the nose. It was sold in packets, by the jar or small bottle; many such containers were impressed with the manufacturer's name or trade-mark and are collected today. "Elisha Shepard & Sons, Have just received and offer for sale . . ."

Leiper's and Lorrillard's Scotch and Maccuboy Snuff in jars and bottles . . ." *American Mercury* (Hartford, Connecticut), July 12, 1815. (See also BITTERS BOTTLE, JUNK BOTTLE, MEDICINE BOTTLE.)

American Mercury (Hartford, Connecticut), February 1, 1818.

C. 1800 snuff bottle label. (Courtesy, Connecticut Historical Society, Inc.)

SNUFFBOX
The container for snuff or powdered tobacco made from the seventeenth through the nine-

teenth centuries. Boxes for the pocket usually had hinged lids and generally held a half ounce or less; larger boxes for the table usually were made with detachable covers and in a variety of sizes. Throughout the seventeenth and eighteenth centuries snuffboxes were fitted with rasps to grate the tobacco. Prepared snuff sold in the nineteenth century made the rasp unnecessary. Snuffboxes were made of gold, silver, pewter, brass, copper, polished steel, and japanned tin; of horn, bone, ivory, and tortoiseshell; papier-mâché; polished hard woods; porcelain, pottery, painted enamelwares; easily carved stone such as alabaster, soapstone, amber, etc.

Sir Plume, of amber snuff-box justly vain,
And the nice conduct of a clouded cane.

Alexander Pope, *The Rape of the Lock*
C. IV.

"I am much obliged to you for the snuffbox. The wood is beautiful. The manufacturer should be encouraged." (Letter July 4, 1771, to Cadwallader Evans of Philadel-

Late-eighteenth-century silver snuffbox. (Courtesy, Antiquarian and Landmarks Society, Inc.)

C. 1820 painted wood snuffbox *on the left;* horn snuffbox, *right.*

phia.) *Writings of Benjamin Franklin,* ed., A. H. Smyth (New York, 1907).

SNUFF DISH

A contemporary synonym for the large, often ornate, Snuffbox, *q.v.,* made for table use: "This night comes home my new silver snuffedish, which I do give myself for my closet [study]." Samuel Pepys, *Diary,* February 2, 1666–67.

SNUFF SPOON

The extremely small silver, gold, or gilt spoon with which the fastidious took snuff from the box; with it the powder was placed on the back of the left hand whence it was sniffed.

SNUFFERS STAND

A holder for the candle snuffers. Although stand might signify a tray, in this case the term generally is applied to an upright holder; that is, (1) a base from which a flat vertical rod rises with a hook at the top from which the snuffers can be suspended. (2) Another type of vertical stand is made with an upright rectangular receptacle, about the size and shape of a modern pocket matchbox, set on a short stem above a base in which the snuffers may be set and held when not in use. (See note under CANDLE EXTINGUISHER.)

SNUFF STAND

The small, covered, desk or table box, usually *en suite* with the candle snuffers, to hold snuff or snaft to be reused for tinder; made of silver, silver-plated metal, polished steel, painted tin. (See quotation under CANDLE EXTINGUISHER.)

SOAPBOX

These boxes for soft toilet soap were sometimes also referred to as Shaving Boxes, *q.v.,* and were often elegantly chased, covered containers of silver with glass inserts; or were turned from richly grained hardwoods such as mahogany, walnut, lignum vitae, ivory, porcelain, faïence, or soft paste. "Charles Shipman, Ivory and Hardwood Turner . . . having served a regular apprenticeship at a very considerable Turning Manufactory in Birmingham . . . purposes carrying on that business here in all the various undermentioned articles [including] soap boxes, washball boxes, patch boxes, pounce boxes . . ." *The New-York Journal or The General Advertiser,* August 6, 1767.

SOCIAL TABLE

A late-eighteenth-century small kidney-shaped dining-room table with a self-contained revolving cellaret or bottle board—a sort of Lazy Susan—fitted into the concave curve. "This table was placed in front of the [dining parlor] fire, with its convex side outwards, and the guests—the gentlemen after the ladies have retired to the drawing room—sit round that side, with their feet to the fire." J. C. Loudon, *An Encyclopedia of Cottage, Farm and Villa Architecture and Furniture* (London, 1833).

SOCKET

The term for "any hollow pipe; generally the hollow of a candlestick" (J) and sometimes, the candlestick itself.

Two goodly Beacons, set in watches stead
Therein gave light, and flam'd continually;
For they of living fire most subtilly
Were made, and set in silver sockets
　　bright.

Spenser, *Faery Queen*

SOCKET CHISEL

One of the tools, "a stronger sort of chisel." (J) "Carpenters, for their rough work, use a stronger sort of chisels, and distinguish them by the name of socketchisels, their shank made with a hollow socket a-top, to receive a strong wooden sprig made to fit into the socket." Joseph Moxon, *Mechanick Exercises, or The Doctrine of Handy-Works* (London, 1683–84).

SOE

An old name for a kind of cask or bucket; "a large wooden vessel with hoops, for holding water; a cowl," *q.v.* (J)

SOFA

The term, first used just prior to 1700, for an upholstered couch, "a splendid seat covered with carpets" (W) having an upholstered or cushioned back and two ends or arms. Of his four designs for sofas shown in *The Gentleman and Cabinet-Maker's Director* (London, 1762), Chippendale wrote, "when made large, they [should] have a Bolster and Pillow at each end, and Cushions at the Back, which may be laid down occasionally, and form a Mattress . . . The

Sofa with Marlborough legs illustrated in Thomas Chippendale's *Gentleman and Cabinet-Maker's Director* (London, 1762).

Late-eighteenth-century Connecticut sofa with front and rear corner legs in mahogany, others of cherry; secondary framing woods are tulip, poplar, cherry, and pine; 41 inches high, 9 feet, 4 inches long, seat height 16 inches. (Courtesy, Connecticut Historical Society, Inc.)

sizes differ greatly, but commonly [sofas] are from six to nine, or ten feet long; the Depth of the Seat, from front to Back, from two Feet, Three Inches, to three Feet; and the height of the Seat one Foot, two Inches, with Casters."

According to Hepplewhite, "The dimensions of Sofas vary according to the size of the room and pleasure of the purchaser. The following is the proportion in general use: length between 6 and 7 feet, depth about 30 inches, height of the seat frame 14 inches; total height in the back, 3 feet 1 inch." *The Cabinet-Maker and Upholsterer's Guide* (London, 1788).

SOFA BED

A popular late-eighteenth- and early-nineteenth-century piece of dual-purpose furniture "so contrived that the seat draws out, to form a comfortable bed in a moment, with very little trouble . . . in a house where the number of bed rooms is limited —or as seats for dressing-rooms, enabling the mistress of the house, when her hospitality is severely taxed, to turn a dressing-room into a bed room at a moment's notice." A. J. Downing, *The Architecture of Country Houses* (New York, 1850).

Sheraton suggested a sofa bed with an ornate canopy, bolsters, and upholstery in "rich silk [and] frames in white and gold with the ornaments carved." Thomas Sheraton, *The Cabinet-Maker's and Upholsterer's Drawing-Book* (London, 1794).

"For sale A new, large, and elegant sofa, covered with crimson, so constructed on a simple principle as to be converted at once, if occasion require, into a commodious double bedstead. Enquire of the printer." *The New-York Independent Journal, or The General Advertiser,* March 12, 1785. (See also BUREAU BEDSTEAD, PRESS BEDSTEAD.)

SOFA TABLE, SOFA WRITING TABLE

Similar to the Pembroke, this, too, was usually rectangular with short, rounded drop leaves, and with a drawer at either end. Of such low side or end tables, Sheraton said, "The Ladies chiefly occupy them to draw, write, or read upon." *The Cabinet Dictionary* (London, 1803). Sometimes a synonym for a breakfast table. (See quotation under HARLEQUIN TABLE.)

SOON

A cant term for an Amulet, *q.v.,* perhaps allied to the Anglo-Saxon *soune* for sound or noise.

Sooner: a spirit or ghost.

SOR

The wooden tub reserved by brewers and housewives "in which to wash their best glasses." (H)

SOY FRAME

A small stand with a ring frame to hold a soy or other sauce bottle. (See also CRUET.)

SPACE LAMP

Another contemporary term for the Argand or Astral Lamp, *qq.v.* "New and Elegant Glass Ware [from] the New England Glass Company [including] Plain and Ornamental Space Lamps." *American Mercury* (Hartford, Connecticut), February 17, 1823.

SPADDLE

A small tool, "a little spade" (W) used in the house garden rather than in the field.

SPANGLE

"Anything sparkling and shining," and thus a contemporary cant term for "a buckle; a locket; earrings." (J)

SPARVER

The canopy or wooden frame set at the top of a bed to hold the bed curtains and valance. (See also CELE, TESTER BED.)

SPATULA

A flat plate attached to a long handle, used for turning food; usually of iron or steel. "A spreading slice, used by apothecaries." (W)

Carved wood spatula.

SPECTACLES

Lenses could be purchased ready-ground to aid those who were near- or far-sighted. These were set in steel, silver, or gold frames, called cases by a silversmith or jeweler. Many side pieces were made to fold. "You take notice of the failing of your eyesight. Perhaps you have not spectacles that suit you, and it is not easy there to provide one's self. People, too, when they go to a shop for glasses, seldom give themselves time to choose with care; and, if their eyes are not rightly suited, they are injured. Therefore I send you a complete set, from number one to thirteen, that you may try them at your ease; and, having pitched on such as suit you best at present, reserve those of higher numbers for future use, as your eyes grow still older; and with the lower numbers, which are for younger people, you may oblige some other friends." (Benjamin Franklin from London, July 17, 1771, to horticulturist John Bartram in Philadelphia.) *Writings of Benjamin Franklin,* ed., A. H. Smyth (New York, 1907).

"Spectacles without cases [and] Glass stone plates for spectacles, rough," that is, unpolished glass for lenses, were listed in the House of Parliament Rates, 1660, for Imports and Exports—*Statutes of the Realm* (London, 1819). Listed separately were "Cases for spectacles guilt; ditto unguilt." Case, in this instance, meant the frame, with nose and ear pieces, not a box or container. (See also GOGGLES.)

Silver-framed or -cased spectacles and leather container. (Courtesy, Antiquarian and Landmarks Society, Inc.)

SPICE BOX, SPICE CUPBOARD

General terms for the small enclosed set of drawers kept, often under lock and key, in parlor, kitchen, or the chamber, for storing expensive spices. Thus, in the inventory of the estate of Samuel Powell, Philadelphia cooper, appraised March 5, 1749, were listed, "in the Parler Below, 1 8-day clock,

Late-seventeenth-century table-top spice cupboard. (Courtesy, Antiquarian and Landmarks Society, Inc.)

Interior of spice cupboard. (Courtesy, Antiquarian and Landmarks Society, Inc.)

£12; 1 Deask & Spice Box £1.15 . . ."
Will Book I, p. 231.

SPICE PLATE

A kind of saucer or small dish: "It was formerly the custom to take spice [any sweetmeats, gingerbread, cake, or dried fruit] with wine, and the plate on which the spice was laid was termed the spice-plate." (H)

SPIDDOCK-POT

Spiddock was a variation of spigot. The spigot or spiddock-pot was an "earthen jar perforated to admit a spiddock." (H)   (See also PAP BOAT; POSSET POT.)

Spiddock-pot with name used as slip decoration. (Courtesy, Antiquarian and Landmarks Society, Inc.)

SPIDER

The common term for a kind of fairly shallow frying pan with a handle and which was set on three high legs, so that it might be used safely and easily over the coals. The term sometimes also was used to designate a trivet or stand to support separate pots over the coals. "Ward & Bartholomew have . . . brass wash basons, sadd irons, chafing dishes, coffee roasters, fish kettles, skimmers

Eighteenth-century spider. (Courtesy, Antiquarian and Landmarks Society, Inc.)

and ladles, cast iron pots, dish kettles, bake pans, spiders, skillets, fire dogs and tea kettles." *American Mercury* (Hartford, Connecticut), May 6, 1812.

SPIGOT

The term used for any "peg to put into a fasset; a pin, a stopple" (W)   "to keep in the liquor" (J)   in a cask. (See also SPIDDOCK-POT.)

SPILE

Another name for (1) "a peg or pin to stop a hole in a cask," (W)   but also used by those who harvested maple sap for (2) the wooden funnel inserted in the tree and through which the sap dripped into buckets or troughs.

SPILLS, SPILL-BOX

A spill was a "small shiver of wood," (J) thus, the thin slips of wood or twisted paper used for lighting candles, and which were kept in a wall box or holder near the fireplace.

Late-eighteenth-century spill or pipe box with tinder drawer. (Courtesy, Antiquarian and Landmarks Society, Inc.)

C. 1800 spill or pipe box with tinder drawer. (Courtesy, Antiquarian and Landmarks Society, Inc.)

SPINET, SPINNET

"A small Harpsichord, *q.v.*, an instrument with keys." (J)   The popular eighteenth-century instrument, similar to the harpsichord, but smaller. "The Spinet takes its name from the quills which are resembled to *Spinae,* thorns." *The Domestic Encyclopedia* (Philadelphia, 1821). "William Pearson . . . strings, quills, and tunes harpsichords, spinnets, clarichords, and hand or barrel organs, all at a reasonable rate . . ." Rivington's *New-York Gazetteer,* April 14, 1774.

Spinet illustrated in Bonanni's *Cabinetto Armonica* (Rome, 1723).

be tax'd at will and pleasure by the Parliament of Great Britain without being at all represented there, they will no longer be free-born Englishmen, but vassals and slaves to Great Britain. My wife has got a new spinning wheel and is spinning away already and rather than fail I will give up my beloved article of tea and put on a leather jacket." John Reynell to Henry Groth, February 2, 1769. *Reynell Letterbooks,* Historical Society of Pennsylvania.

A spirit of inter-colony competition grew apace and prodigious feats of spinning were praised in newspapers throughout the country: "We hear from New Fairfield in Connecticut, that the wife of Samuel Hungerford (who is 43 years of Age, and has now living 12 of her own children, and 5 grandchildren) on the 21st Day of September last, spun by Day-light in about 12 Hours, on a common spinning wheel, 126 skeins of good fine Worsted Yarn, tho' under the Disadvantage of having a sucking Child to take care of . . . The laudable Ambition of both Sexes, and all Degree of People

SPINNING WHEEL

"The wheel by which since the disuse of the rock, the thread is drawn." (J)

Spinning: "Is the art of twisting flax, hemp, silk or cotton, wool or similar matters, so as to reduce them into yarn or thread." *The Domestic Encyclopedia* (Philadelphia, 1821).

Although during the first 150 years of settlement, few homes were without spinning wheels, spinning and weaving were tasks assigned to servants in the homes of the well-to-do and the cloth thus manufactured was used mainly for the wardrobes of kitchen and stable employees. With the institution of new taxes during the reign of George III, however, the work of spinning, and the wearing of homespun were to become the symbol and badge of British colonial rebellion: "If they are to

Saxon or Dutch wheel. (Courtesy, Antiquarian and Landmarks Society, Inc.)

Flax spinning wheel. (Courtesy, Antiquarian and Landmarks Society, Inc.)

Flax spun into thread. (Courtesy, Antiquarian and Landmarks Society, Inc.)

in the British Colonies still increases, to encourage Industry, Frugality and Manufactories among ourselves that we may not long depend upon those who would ungratefully take Advantage of our Necessities to deprive us of our natural Rights and Liberties." *The New-York Gazette and The Weekly Mercury,* October 29, 1770. (See also REEL, YARN WINDER.)

SPIT
Made of iron or steel, this was "a long prong on which meat is driven to be turned before the fire." (J)

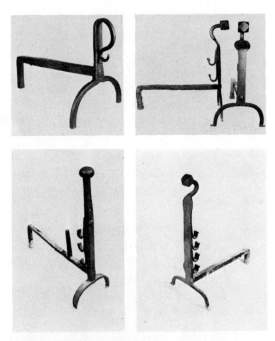

Eighteenth-century spit-dogs or -irons. (Courtesy, Antiquarian and Landmarks Society, Inc.)

SPIT-DOG, SPIT-IRON
A seventeenth- and eighteenth-century description applied to the "firedog" or andiron made with rings or hooks to support a spit. Andirons used in the kitchen hearth to support the spit rod were called Firedogs, *q.v.,* or spit-dogs because they replaced the small live dog anciently trained to be kept in the treadmill or enclosed wheel that once turned the large spit in manor house and inn kitchens.

SPONK, SPUNK, SPUNK BOX
Sponk was another name for "touchwood or tinder," (J) hence this was a match or tinderbox.

SPONTOON
(See ESPONTOON.)

SPOOL
The hand-shaped, carved, turned, or whittled "small piece of cane or reed, with a knot at each end; or a piece of wood turned in that form to wind yarn upon; a quill." (J)

SPOOL HOLDER, SPOOL RACK, SPOOL STAND
A small worktable accessory to hold spools of thread. The slender wire rods slipped out of the top board for easy insertion or removal of a spool.

Spool holder or stand turned about 1800, and painted red.

SPOON
The term is derived from the Old English *spon,* a synonym for chip or shiver of wood.

Later the wood was formed or carved to provide a hollowed out bowl at one end. Second only to the knife as an early, basic utensil in the preparation and service of food (when it usually has been styled a ladle), and later, for partaking of liquids, the spoon has been called "a kind of ladle to eat with," (W) or "a concave vessel with a handle, used in eating liquids." (J) Good spoons still were scarce even in fairly affluent families in the eighteenth century, as Mrs. Courtenay Norton of London indicated in a letter to her son at Williamsburg, August 30, 1775: "Your Aunt Turner intended to send you & my Daughter a couple of spoons that you might not fall out which should eat first." Frances Mason, *John Norton and Sons, Merchants of London and Virginia* (Richmond, 1935). Spoons were considered such a necessary article that, as late as the first part of the nineteenth century, they sometimes were exempt from taxation: "Silver plate, except spoons, shall be valued and set in [the tax assessor's] list, at six per cent of value." *Connecticut Statutes* (Hartford, 1835). (See also FORK, KNIFE.)

up and sold in tall, cylindrical stoneware bottles with wide mouths, as noted by John Adams in a letter December 27, 1786. (See quotation under VIRGIN.)

SPYGLASS
A small telescope, a useful device for the astronomer or traveler: "M. Fremont, an ingenious young Italian, who was lately here, gave me a little SpyGlass of his Making; it is indeed a very good one." (Benjamin Franklin from London, September 30, 1773, to Jan Ingenhousz at Vienna.) *Writings of Benjamin Franklin,* ed., A. H. Smyth (New York, 1907). The spyglass was considered by some an indispensable part of the military kit: "Those not possessed of a portable Spy-Glass may be accommodated with this sine qua non in Reconnoitering the Foe . . . Please to apply to James Rivington; the prices from Seven to Sixteen Dollars each. Those of the supreme quality are fixed in strong Cases, and slung over the shoulders, stand buff to all weather." *Royal Gazette* (New York), May 27, 1778.

Pocket spyglass.

C. 1720 horn spoons. (Courtesy, Antiquarian and Landmarks Society, Inc.)

Eighteenth-century pewter spoons. (Courtesy, Antiquarian and Landmarks Society, Inc.)

Seventeenth-century flame-stitch embroidered squab or seat cushion. (Courtesy, Antiquarian and Landmarks Society, Inc.)

SPRUCE BEER BOTTLE
Spruce beer, ginger beer, mineral springs water, and other such beverages were put

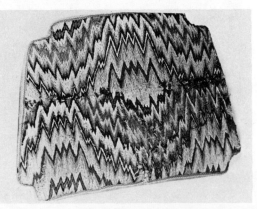

SQUAB

A contemporary term for a small, flat loose cushion used since the seventeenth century to add comfort to chairs or a larger, separate cushion for a couch.

SQUARE

One of the tools, "a rule or instrument by which workmen measure or form their angles," (J) made of polished hardwood with brass edgings; all brass or steel.

SQUIRT

A cant term for the pewter, copper, or tin tube for decorating pastry. "Bramble biscuits [are] so-called because of a round form, like a piece of bramble stick cut off. Sometimes the two ends are bent round and united . . . When made the dough may be pushed through a kind of squirt made for the purpose, called a syringe mould . . ." G. W. Francis, *The Dictionary of Practical Receipts* (London, 1847).

STADLE, STADDLE

The term from the Saxon word for foundation for "anything which serves for support to another." (J) (See also STAND, TRESTLE.)

STAFF

The term to describe a variety of utensils: (1) "a stick with which a man supports himself in walking; also, any prop or support; (2) a stick used as a weapon, a club, the handle of an edged or pointed weapon. A club properly includes the notion of weight, and the staff of length. (3) An ensign of office; a badge of authority." (J) (See also BAMBOO WALKING STICKS, HALBARD, LEADING STAFF.)

STAGE

(See FLAKE.)

STAINED GLASS

This was (1) the ancient art of transparent painting or coloring of glass, fixed by firing, and used for windows and plaques; it was also (2) the term used to describe Euro-pean tablewares made by covering the glass with a metallic oxide film, which also was fixed by firing. Ruby and green were the favorite colors for this kind of glassware, however, yellow, blue, lavender, and pink also were made. Most such glass now available was produced after 1840, although much was manufactured earlier. "Mr. John Smith, lately from England, begs leave to inform the admirers of the polite arts and the public in general that he will open his exhibition of paintings on vitrified stained glass, an art supposed to have been lost for several centuries . . ." *Aurora* (Philadelphia), January 3, 1798.

"Exhibition of Stained Glass. Wm. Redding respectfully announces that the numerous productions in the art of painting and staining on glass which has been his indefatigable employment for some few past years, will be exhibited from 5 o'clock in the afternoon to 10 in the evening, at the American Gallery of Fine Arts in Summer Street . . . This [is] the first display of what has been done on this side of the Atlantic in this beautiful and difficult art. Admittance, 25 cents." *Trumpet and Universalist Magazine* (Boston), July 24, 1835.

STAIRCASE LIGHT

The encased candleholder or ornate lantern in a rectangular, globular, hexagonal, or octagonal-shaped glass, with gilded or japanned framework, set in a bracket or base, or, as Ince and Mayhew explained, "Different Designs for Stair-Case Lights [are] mostly designed to fix on the Hand Rail," or the wall of the stairway. *The Universal System of Household Furniture* (London, 1762).

STAKE

One of the tools, "The stake is a small anvil, which stands upon a small iron foot on the workbench, to remove as occasion offers; or else it hath a strong iron spike at the bottom, let into some place of the workbench, not to be removed. Its office is to set small cold work strait upon, or to cut or punch upon with the cold chissell or cold punch." Joseph Moxon, *Mechanick Exercises, or The Doctrine of Handy-Works* (London, 1683–84).

STALDER

An old word to describe "a wooden frame to set casks on." (W)   (See STADLE.)

STAND

The all-inclusive term for a variety of (1) bases or free-standing frames to support chests, cupboards, or cabinets; (2) any

C. 1750 stretcher-base stand-table. (Courtesy, Antiquarian and Landmarks Society, Inc.)

C. 1700 cross-base stand-table. (Courtesy, Antiquarian and Landmarks Society, Inc.)

C. 1760 splayed-leg stand-table. (Courtesy, Antiquarian and Landmarks Society, Inc.)

C. 1720 stand-table. (Courtesy, Antiquarian and Landmarks Society, Inc.)

small table, such as a candlestand, urn stand, wine stand, and so the general term for any "frame or table on which vessels are placed." (J)   "R. G. Allen has on hand, at his new Ware Rooms . . . Light Stands; Wash hand Stands; Mahogany, Toilet and painted ditto . . ." *Literary Cadet and Rhode Island Statesman* (Providence), February 23, 1828. This term also was used to mean the large oval, round, or rectangular type of plate today commonly called a serving tray. "James Jacks . . . has imported . . . from London . . . silver

C. 1780 tripod stand-table.

One-drawer stand-table with pierced cross-stretcher base, chamfered legs; applied molding or raised-rim top. (Courtesy, Connecticut Historical Society, Inc.)

coffee and tea pots with stands . . . decanter stands . . ." *Pennsylvania Packet* (Philadelphia), November 13, 1799. (3) In weaponry, "a musket and its apparatus." (W)   (See also FOURQUETTE.)

STAND-and-SOCKET LAMP

The explicit contemporary synonym for the lighting device more familiarly known today as a Peg Lamp, *q.v.* "Charles Sigourney Has imported in the ship *Eliza-Ann* from Liverpool, an invoice of Hardware Goods [including] Common and Screw'd Iron Candlesticks . . . Japan'd stand. and Socket Lamps . . ." *American Mercury* (Hartford, Connecticut), February 7, 1811.

C. 1830 stand-and-socket or peg lamp with glass font, brass pedestal, and marble base.

STANDING CUP

The ornately engraved ceremonial cup with cover; sometimes inlaid with gem stones or other ornaments, and often referred to as a state cup or State Dish, *q.v.*

STANDISH

"A case to hold pens and ink." (W)   The term is a combination of stand and dish and was the name given from the seventeenth through the early nineteenth centuries for what eventually was more commonly known as an inkstand or a desk tray. The simplest

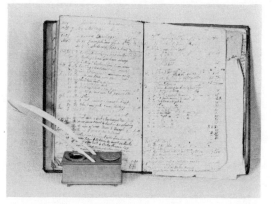

Mid-eighteenth-century pewter standish. (Courtesy, Antiquarian and Landmarks Society, Inc.)

541

Early-nineteenth-century silver standish with shell-and-scroll decoration. (*Hartford Times,* photo by Einar Chindmark.)

form was a tray or stand on which were fixed dishes or wells for ink and sand, and grooves or small holes to hold the pens. More complicated designs had, in addition, receptacles for wafers and sealing wax, and sometimes holders for papers or letters. "Standishes of wood; Brasse & covered with Leather; also Pocket Standishes" were listed in House of Parliament Rates, 1660, for Imports and Exports—*Statutes of the Realm* (London, 1819).

STANDS for CHINA JARS
This was the contemporary designation for a variety of small, delicate, ornate stands

Stand for a China jar from Thomas Chippendale's *Director* (London, 1762).

designed in the eighteenth century to help satisfy the craze for furniture and decorations "in the Chinese taste," as Chippendale described such work. They were made to display the handsome porcelain covered jars imported from Far Eastern centers or the same types of urns imitated by British potters. Chippendale provided "Three Stands for China Jars [that] may be either gilt or japanned" in *The Gentleman and Cabinet-Maker's Director* (London, 1762), and Ince and Mayhew illustrated "Six designs of Stands for Figures and China Jars, [of which] one has been executed to hold a Jar and two Beakers." *The Universal System of Household Furniture* (London, 1762). Obviously, these should not be confused with the squat, bulbous urn stands mass-produced in heavy dark wood in the late nineteenth century. (See also CHINOISERIE.)

STAND STOOL, STANDING STOOL
A common name for the four-sided box on castors or truckles in which infants were stood to keep them from harm and to help them learn to walk. Other descriptive terms included child's walker or Go-Cart, *q.v.* "Thus far his infancy . . . 'tis pitie to dangle him longer . . . The elf dares peep abroad, the pretty foot can wag without a truckling standing-stoole." John Fletcher, *Collected Works.*

STATE DISH
A piece of fine silver, a presentation piece, a bowl or plate meant more for display than use, except possibly on important occasions or at a formal dinner. "This day Captain Taylor brought me a piece of plate, a little, small state dish, expecting that I should get him some allowances for demurrage of his ship, William, which I shall." Samuel Pepys, *Diary,* November 7, 1663.

STEAK DISH
The same as a Hash Dish, *q.v.*

STEAM DISH

The name given an early-nineteenth-century improvement of the common cooking pot. Meat was held on rests above and apart from vegetables stewing in the base of the pot; the rising steam cooked the meat. "In Philadelphia it is a common practice to surround meat with potatoes in an earthen dish, which is sent to the oven. The potatoes are thus soddened, the meat hard and dry . . . the steam-dish obviates these inconveniences. It is made of tin or earthenware (for a family of six or eight); twelve inches by nine at the top, and nine by seven at the bottom, four and a half inches deep on the slant rim, and three inches in the clear, under four resting knobs (a little below the top) which space is to be occupied by the meat." *The Domestic Encyclopedia* (Philadelphia, 1821).

STEAN, STEANWARE

A common seventeenth-century variant of stone, still in use in nineteenth-century rural families, especially among those of North-England and Scottish descent. Specifically, Stean was used to designate "a large upright jar of baked clay." (H)

STEIN

The German word for stone and thus a mid-colony colloquialism for a tall Tankard, *q.v.*, made of pottery; i.e., stoneware or porcelain.

STEEPLE CLOCK

The collector's term for the pointed top Gothic-style Shelf Clock, *q.v.*

STEELYARD

The correct term for a kind of scale, "An iron rod to weigh goods with," (W) usually written Stillyard, *q.v.*

STENCIL PAINTING

The proper term for a type of painting from stencil patterns, often called theorems. Among the most popular subjects were arrangements of flowers and fruits; others included stylized landscapes and animal portraits, etc. Individual stencils were cut for sections of the picture. The paintings or theorems were painted on a variety of grounds other than linen or cotton "canvasses." "A Saturday School. Miss H. Brownell respectfully informs the ladies of Providence and its vicinity that . . . She intends opening a school the 16th inst. for the purpose of instructing young Ladies and Misses in the art of Painting on Velvet, Paper, Satin-Wood and White Marble, with India Ink and Fancy Colours . . . Young ladies who wish to attend so pleasing a study are invited to call at her room, No. 148 Westminster Street, where are specimens of her Painting to be seen." *Literary Cadet and Rhode Island Statesmen* (Providence), February 9, 1828. Care should be exercised in purchasing theorems today; many reproductions have been made on carefully stained and "aged" velvet with a view to cheating buyers eager to own theorem paintings.

STEPS

(See BED STEPS, LIBRARY STEPS.)

STEWPAN

The covered pan in which food was lightly boiled, seethed, or simmered over the embers. "The most useful size is 12 inches diameter by 6 inches deep; this we would have of silver, or iron, or copper, lined, not plated, with silver. Their covers also must be kept perfectly clean and well tinned . . . not only on the inside but about a couple of inches on the outside . . . The health and even the life of the family depend on this, and the cook may be sure her employers had rather pay the tinman's bill than the doctor's." William Kitchiner, *The Cook's Oracle, and Housekeeper's Manual* (New York, 1830).

STILL

"A vessel of distillation," (W) the parts of which included an alembic, a close vessel, a retort, a boiler, and in which the substance to be distilled is subjected to the action of heat, and the still so arranged that the vapor produced is condensed; thus, the essence of the substance is distilled. The word still also was used to mean alembic only. "The copper alembeck or Cole Still leaked in so many places and was so badly tinned that no use could be made of it . . . Pray sell it to some other person and send me one of the best Pewter stills proper for distilling Roses and simple Waters." (Order, September 1768, from Williamsburg, Virginia, to London.) Frances Mason, *John Norton and Sons, Merchants of London and Virginia* (Richmond, 1935). "Miles Beach . . . having resumed the Coppersmith business . . . will keep an assortment of well made STILLS, from 30 to 300 gallons . . . also Pewter and Copper WORMS . . ." *American Mercury* (Hartford, Connecticut) May 17, 1810.

STILETTO
"A small dagger, of which the blade is not edged, but round, with a sharp point." John Walker, *Pronouncing Dictionary* (New York, 1840).

STILLING
A wooden frame or "a stand for casks." (J)

STILLIARD, STILLYARD
The name given to the common scales; originally called steel-yard or yard of steel, indicating the length of the scale lever: "One of the most ancient machines for ascertaining the weight of bodies, by its counterpoise. [It] consists of a lever of unequal arms." *The Domestic Encyclopedia* (Philadelphia, 1821). The stillyard, however, seldom was as accurate as the balance-scale: "I put on iron peices on the poze [poise] of both pair of Stillyards and Made them Exact, only the Great Sid goes slow, and ye little Side Quick of the Great stillyards." Joshua Hempsted, *Diary*, January

7, 1748, New London (Connecticut) Historical Society Collections, Vol. I, 1900.

STIRRUP CUP
The stirrup is the iron loop suspended from the saddle "in which the horseman sets his foot when he mounts" (J) preparatory to riding. The stirrup cup, if not precisely "one for the road" was a cup from which to quaff a fortifying drink before setting out on, or on returning from, the hunt. It also was a favorite sporting trophy, made in the form of a fox or other animal head, but without a foot or handles; of silver, silver-plated metal, porcelain, or pottery.

STOCK LOCK
A lock fixed in wood and so differing from a movable lock such as a padlock. "There are locks for several purposes; as street-door locks, called stocklocks; chamber-door locks called spring-locks; and cupboard locks." Joseph Moxon, *Mechanick Exercises, or The Doctrine of Handy-Works,* (London, 1683–84).

STONE BIRD
A contemporary term for the whistle made of earthenware, or carved from soapstone, alabaster, or marble. "Stone birds or whistles" were listed in the House of Parliament Rates, 1660, for Imports and Exports —*Statutes of the Realm* (London, 1819). (See also BIRDCALL, QUAIL PIPE.)

STOOL
Correctly, this word was defined as any "seat for a single person without a back," Isaac Watts, *Logick* (London, 1725). In ordinary conversation, however, it sometimes was used to designate a small stand, viz., Candle Stool, *q.v.* (See also CRICKET,

C. 1730 New England country householder's all-purpose pine stool. (Courtesy, Antiquarian and Landmarks Society, Inc.)

Carved walnut stool with pad feet made by John Elliot of Philadelphia. (Courtesy, Henry Francis du Pont Winterthur Museum.)

Design for a scroll-foot footstool from Hepplewhite's *Guide* (London, 1794).

DRESSING STOOL, GOUT STOOL, JOINT STOOL, MUSIC STOOL.)

STOOLS

Different forms of stools, civilization's oldest type of seat furniture for one person, listed herein include BACK STOOL, BIDET, CLOSESTOOL, COFFIN STOOL, CORRIDOR STOOL, DRESSING STOOL, FENDER STOOL, FOOTSTOOL, FRENCH STOOL, GOUT STOOL, JOINED STOOL, LIBRARY STOOL, MUSIC STOOL, STOOL TABLE, TABOURET, WINDOW STOOL.)

STOOL TABLE

The collector's term for the late-seventeenth-century stool made with a drawer below the seat. (See also CUPBOARD STOOL.)

STOP(PE), STOOP, STOUK, STOUP

Used variously for any small pitcher, pail, or bucket, or for a drinking cup with a handle.

STOVE

Any free-standing iron, brick, or stone box or other container in which a fire is built; these differ from fireplaces by enclosing the fire so as "to exclude it from sight, the heat being given out through the material of which the stove is composed." *Encyclopedia Americana* (Philadelphia, 1831). (See also FOOT STOVE, FRANKLIN STOVE, PARLOR STOVE.)

STRAIGHT CHAIR

The middle-colony colloquialism to designate a simple Side Chair, *q.v.,* with no refinement of design such as a curve to the back or splay to the legs; later and now, a New York and mid-West colloquialism for any chair without arms. "Formerly [before 1800] their chairs of the genteelest kind were of mahogany or red walnut (once a great substitute for mahogany in all kinds of furniture, tables Ec.) or else they were of rush bottoms, and made of maple posts, and slats, with high backs, and perpendicular." John F. Watson, *Annals and Occurrences of New York City and State in the Olden Time* (Philadelphia, 1846).

STRAP HINGE

The name for the early wrought-iron hinge

Late-seventeenth-century strap hinge. (Courtesy, Antiquarian and Landmarks Society, Inc.)

Strap hinges.

Combination strap hinges.

used on exterior doors and some interior batten-type doors in kitchens and store-rooms. "The old hinges were not half-butts, as our ordinary ones are called, but stout straps of iron, which, more or less decorated, stretched across the surface of the door on either side, and being bolted through the thickness, gave it ample support." Charles L. Eastlake, *Hints on Household Taste* (London, 1850).

STRIKE BLOCK

One of the tools, "a plane shorter than the jointer, having its sole made exactly flat and straight, and is used for the shooting of a short joint." Joseph Moxon, *Mechanick Exercises, or The Doctrine of Handy-Works* (London, 1683–84).

STUDY TABLE

A term sometimes used to describe a type of library or writing table. The study table shown by Ince and Mayhew in *The Universal System of Household Furniture* (London, 1762), was made "with a writing Drawer [that pulled out] to give room for Books or Papers" plus a built-in Standish, *q.v.*, a double row of pigeon holes above the board. The base was similar to that of the modern so-called kneehole desk with three drawers at either side.

STUMP BED

Low, paneled box bedstead or rope bedstead made with short, stubby posts and no footboard; often referred to as an attic bed, and the type to which twentieth-century collectors have given the name hired-man's bed.

STUSNET

A colloquialism for "a Skillet," *q.v.* (H) (See also POSNET.)

SUBSCRIPTION PRINT

(See PAINTING BY SUBSCRIPTION.)

SUCKET FORK

Made for eating sweetmeats, this was a flat stem with a two-tined fork at one end, a spoon at the other.

SUCKING BOTTLE

A contemporary term for a baby's bottle. (See PAP BOAT and note under BOTTLE.)

SUGAR BASON

The contemporary term for the open container, now generally called a sugar bowl, in which sugar, after being cut from the loaf, hammered or powdered, was served. "Joseph Lownes, Goldsmith . . . has now made and ready for sale, Silver Coffee Pots, Tea, do. Sugar Basons, Slop Bowls, Tankards, Canns, Ladles, Milk Pots, Soup ladles, Table spoons, Tea do. Ec. Ec." *Pennsylvania Packet* (Philadelphia), April 9, 1792.

Blue-and-white soft paste sugar bowl with beehive finial.

Staffordshire sugar bowl made for the American market. (Courtesy, Connecticut Historical Society, Inc.)

SUGAR BOX

A contemporary term for a small covered box, chest, or canister to hold powdered sugar; often set on tiny ball or bracket feet, and when not set out for use at the tea table, displayed in the plate cupboard. In the mid-seventeenth century Pepys recorded his pride in being able to afford the luxury of expensive, imported sugar, as well as his interest in adding to his silver inventory what then was a fairly rare piece. "To several places to pay away money, to clear myself in all the world, and among others paid my book seller 6£ for books I had from him this day, and the silversmith 22£ 18s for spoons, forks, and sugar-box." Samuel Pepys, *Diary,* December 30, 1664. (See SUGAR BASON, SUGAR HAMMER.)

SUGAR CUTTERS

Often also called sugar nippers, this was

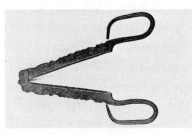

Eighteenth-century sugar cutter. (Courtesy, Antiquarian and Landmarks Society, Inc.)

Eighteenth-century sugar cutter. (Courtesy, Antiquarian and Landmarks Society, Inc.)

Late-eighteenth-century steel sugar cutters on brass-and-wood stand.

a common seventeenth- and eighteenth-century kitchen or dining-room pantry utensil, used to break up the loaf of sugar.

SUGAR HAMMER

The term for the small mallet of hardwood, ivory, or silver; or sometimes a combination of two of these, used to "powder" loaf sugar, preparatory for use. "Charles Shipman, Ivory and Hardwood Turner [makes] . . ., bell handles, pack thread boxes, drum sticks and walking stick heads . . . round rulers and sugar hammers . . ." *The New York Journal or the General Advertiser,* August 6, 1767.

SUGAR KIT

In the kitchen, the covered wooden box or earthenware jar in which sugar, already pounded and powdered, was kept for use. "I noticed that the [clam] shells were such as I had seen in the sugar-kit at home." Henry David Thoreau, *Cape Cod* (Boston, 1865). The shell, of course, formed a handy scoop at no expense. (See also SALT BOX.)

SUGAR TONGS

Similar to such tongs today, these, too, were needed to lift a lump of sugar from the bowl. "James Musgrave has on hand . . . sugar tongs and every article in the silver line." *Pennsylvania Packet,* (Philadelphia), November 6, 1800. (See also TEA TONGS.)

SUMMER BED
The term used by Sheraton to describe a pair of single-width four-post bedsteads, with testers connected by a cornice, in *The Cabinet-Maker and Upholsterer's Drawing-Book* (London, 1791–94.)

SUNDIAL
Man's oldest device with which to count the passing hours, this basically is a "plate to show time by the sun;" (W) "a marked plate on which the shadow points the hour." (J) "Sundials have lost much of their value in modern times by the general introduction of instruments which indicate the time at any period of the day or night; but clocks and watches require to be regulated, and the shadows projected by the sun are the most convenient standard for this purpose. Dials are of various kinds, but the horizontal and vertical are most com-

monly used." *Encyclopedia Americana* (Philadelphia, 1831).

SUNGLASSES
These were called green spectacles or goggles, "glasses to cure squinting or defend the eyes," and usually were available also with blue-glass lenses, set in the same type of silver, gold, or steel frames as clear lenses. "This morning did buy me a pair of green spectacles to see whether they will help my eyes or no." Samuel Pepys, *Diary,* December 24, 1666. (See also GOGGLES, SPECTACLES.)

SUPPER CANTERBURY
(See CANTERBURY, DUMB-WAITER, RUNNING SIDEBOARD.)

SWAY
A colloquialism brought here by settlers from the north of England and Scotland, for the fireplace crane specifically attached to the center of the back wall of the kitchen chimney; it thus could be swung from one side to the other of the fireplace.

SWEET BAG
A small silk bag filled with fragrant spices and used as a sachet. (See also ARO-MATIQUE, POMANDER.)

SWEETMEAT BOTTLE
"James and Arthur Jarvis have for sale of the American [Flint Glass] manufactory mustard and cream pots, flint and common; salts, salt linings, and crewets, wide-mouthed bottles for sweetmeats, rounds and phyals for doctors, wine and water glasses, ink and pocket bottles." *New York Gazette and Weekly Mercury,* February 8, 1773.

Sweetmeat: "Delicacies made of fruits preserved with sugar." (J)

SWEET-STAND
This was a contemporary synonym for the sweetmeat jar or covered vase, usually made with a footed base. "Standish Barry . . . just received by the latest arrivals from Liver-Pool sugar tongs; mustard

Engraved and dated eighteenth-century sundial. (Courtesy, Antiquarian and Landmarks Society, Inc.)

Tankards; snuffer Trays; Fish Knives; Punch Ladles; Sweet-Stands . . ." *Maryland Gazette* (Baltimore), November 15, 1792.

SWIFT
The common term for a revolving wooden frame used for winding yarn or thread, and sometimes also called a swing-devil. "I have sent Sally two little Reels. The Reels are to screw on the edge of a Table, when she would wind Silk or Thread. The Skein is to be put over them and winds better than if held in two Hands. There is also an Ivory Knob, to which she may with a Bit of Silk Cord hang a Pinhook to fasten her Plain Work to . . ." (Benjamin Franklin from London April 6, 1766, to his wife in Philadelphia.) *Writings of Benjamin Franklin,* ed., A. H. Smyth (New York, 1907).

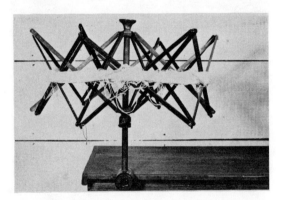

Swift or swing-devil in use. (Courtesy, Antiquarian and Landmarks Society, Inc.)

SWILL
(1) "A wicker basket of a round or globular form, with open top in which red herrings and other fish and foods are carried to market for sale." (H)   (2) "A keeler to wash in, standing on three feet;" (H) i.e., a laundry tub.

SWING OR SWINGING GLASSES
A contemporary synonym for the Cheval, *q.v.,* or horse dressing glass, "Hodgson & Nicholson . . . have just received . . . from London Neat square-carved and gilt Pier glasses, 20×12, to 30×16 inches; neat square and oval Glasses to hang and swing . . ." *Maryland Journal* (Baltimore), May 2, 1788.

SWINGING CRADLE
A contemporary term for the crib or cradle suspended in an open framework or horse, rather than set on rockers. "Aaron Chapin & Son, At their shop north of the Court-House have on hand . . . mahogany and cherry House-Furniture, both plain and elegant, Among which are swinging cradles, Ec." *American Mercury* (Hartford, Connecticut), August 11, 1808. (See also CRIB, CRADLE.)

Adjustable-height swinging cradle. (Courtesy, Connecticut Historical Society, Inc.)

SWORD
The term from the Old English *sweord* for the cut and thrust weapon with one or both

Federal-period sword; hilt decorated with eagles, shield, stars. (Courtesy, Antiquarian and Landmarks Society, Inc.)

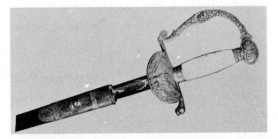

blade edges sharpened, and with a sharp point.

SWORD CANE

A thin, rapier-like sword or knife carried in a hollow case or sheath, having the outward appearance of a cane or walking stick. Made so that the sword could be drawn out of the cane by unscrewing the cane cap, or released from the lower end by a spring device set just under the cap. "James Jacks . . . has imported from London . . . silver mounted dress swords, Gilt and plated swords . . . Sticks and canes, with or without swords." *Federal Gazette* (Philadelphia), November 27, 1797. "I likewise want 3 Dozen Sword Canes from Mr. Masden in Fleet Street near Temple Bar, such as I had from him at 7/." (Order, November 16, 1771, from Catherine Rathnell, Merchant, Williamsburg, Virginia, to London.) Frances Mason, *John Norton and Sons, Merchants of London and Virginia* (Richmond, 1935).

SYLLABUB GLASS

Syllabub was considered a dessert as well as a beverage, but however it was served, it had to be frothing. Syllabub glasses, therefore, were made much wider at the top than most other wine bowls, then were narrowed at the center of the bowl to form a small cup just above the stem. They were made of silver, silver plate, and glass: " . . . Removed from the store kept by Mr. Henry William Shiegel . . . for sale of the American manufacture . . . Jelly and Cillabub glasses, with and without handles. Mustard and cream pots, flint and common . . ." *The New-York Gazette and The Weekly Mercury,* February 8, 1773.

There were a variety of recipes for the popular drink including this for a "Whipt Syllabub. Take a quart of good sweet cream, put it into a broad earthen pan, with a gill of sack, the juice of a lemon or Seville orange, and the rind of a lemon cut thin; make it pretty sweet with fine sugar, whip it with a whisk, and as the froth rises take it off, put it on a sieve to drain for half an hour; then half-fill your glasses with some red, and some white wine, and with a spoon put on your syllabub as high as you can; or you may half fill your glasses with different coloured jelly." Richard Briggs, *The New Art of Cookery* (Philadelphia, 1792).

SYRINGE MOLD

(See SQUIRT.)

SYRUP JUG

A small pitcher or pot with a lid cover and a pouring spout, made of silver, silver-plated metal, tin, pewter, pottery, and used in serving syrups or molasses.

Nineteenth-century pewter syrup pitchers. (Courtesy, Mr. and Mrs. Bernard Cardé, Centerbrook, Connecticut.)

T

TABERNACLE FRAME

The contemporary description of ornate, rococo frames designed to surround or face a wall recess. The name evolved from the architect's term, tabernacle-work, designating the kind of decorative tracery used on shrine niches in Gothic church buildings. Chippendale illustrated two tabernacle frames "proper for a Stair-case." *The Gentleman and Cabinet-maker's Director* (London, 1762). (See also ARCHITECTURAL FRAME.)

TABLE
(See in Chapter 5.)

TABLE BEDSTEAD
A space-saving fold-up bedstead that was concealed by day in a cupboard beneath a wide, hinged table board that doubled as a side table. At night the top or "table" folded back against the wall, the cupboard doors were opened and the bed was pulled forward and out. Some styles were made with a single "door" hinged to the top board. (See also BUREAU BEDSTEAD, PRESS BEDSTEAD.)

TABLE BOOK
The contemporary name, used from the seventeenth century until well into the nineteenth century, for a type of portfolio in which collections of prints, broadsides, or of one's own drawings or writings were kept. This was a kind of large commonplace book or scrapbook because, as John Dryden wrote, one might "put into your table-book whatsoever you judge worthy"; Webster in his 1806 *Dictionary* defined table book as a "book to grave or note down on." "Vellum for Table Bookes; Parchment; Bookes unbound; Paste boards for books; Table Bookes" were listed in the House of Parliament Rates, 1660, for Imports and Exports—*Statutes of the Realm* (London, 1819). (See also ALBUM, COMMON-PLACE BOOK.)

TABLE BOTTLE
A contemporary synonym for the Decanter, *q.v.*, less rarely used to describe the water Carafe, *q.v.*

TABLE CHAIR
This was a contemporary description of a type of child's high chair; i.e., one with the seat raised high enough for a youngster to sit at an ordinary breakfast table, not a chair with its own tray or table board. Philadelphia chairmaker Solomon Fussell thus billed the well-known local printer:

"Benjamin Frankling, Dr.:

10 mo. 30—To child's chair	0.2.6
11 mo. 24 1743/4—To one child's Table Chair	0.5.0
9 mo. 29 1744—To white child's Chair	0.2.6″

Solomon Fussell Account Book, 1738–51;

C. 1700 slat-back table chair. (Courtesy, Antiquarian and Landmarks Society, Inc.)

C. 1700 banister-back child's table chair. (Courtesy, Connecticut Historical Society, Inc.)

Stephen Collins Papers., Mss. Division, Library of Congress. The two "child's chairs" would have been small-size copies of those used by adults. The designation "white" probably was a short form of the common term "in-the-white," meaning an article that was not painted or stained. (See also CHAIR TABLE.)

TABLE DESK
(See DESK BOX.)

TABLE DORMANT, DORMAND
The early term, retained throughout the Colonial period, for the Sideboard, *q.v.,* or serving table set permanently in place, particularly one affixed to a wall. Thus, Chaucer indicated the Franklins' hospitality when he wrote,

> *His table dormant in his halle alway*
> *Stood redy covered al the longe day.*
>
> Prologue, *Canterbury Tales.*

TABLES
The sixteenth- and seventeenth-century term for backgammon, a description continuing in use late in some rural areas. (See also BACKGAMMON.)

TABLE SERVANTE
The French term for the French version of the Dumb-waiter, *q.v.,* made during the reign of Louis XVI.

TABLES for SLABS
The term indicated a base or pedestal with a wooden top board rather than an open frame into which a marble slab could be set. (See also SLAB FRAME.)

TABLET
A general term for any flat surface on which one could write; *i.e.,* Slate Tablet, *q.v.,* and sometimes for "a little table," as Sheraton defined the word in *The Cabinet Dictionary* (London, 1803), and as did Webster in 1806.

TABLET CHAIR
The term sometimes used to describe a type of Windsor chair also called a writing-arm chair. These chairs were made with one arm flat and broad enough to serve as a Tablet or Desk, *qq.v.*

TABOR, TABORET, TABORIN, TABOUR, TABRET
These were all contemporary names for a "kind of small drum beaten with only one stick" (W) "to accompany a pipe." (J)

TABOURET
The name given a small upholstered French stool early in the eighteenth century.

TACK
A colloquialism for a kind of "shelf made of crossed bars of wood suspended from the ceiling, on which to keep supplies." (H) Tack apparently was a shortened form of tackling, in the sense of provisions, and thus this was a place to keep necessary tools or other supplies. (See also HANGING SHELVES.)

TALISMAN
The term, derived from the Arabic word for figure; a "figure cast or cut in metal or stone, at some particular moment in time; as when a certain star is at its culminating point [It] is supposed to exercise extraordinary influences over the bearer, particularly in averting disease . . . the Amulet, *q.v.,* is much the same. In the middle ages, relics, consecrated candles, and rods, rosaries, images of saints, Ec. were employed, and still are, in some parts of Christendom . . . astrology and the knowledge of the virtues of talismans and amulets, formed an important part of medical science; and the quacks of modern times sometimes have recourse to similar means." *Encyclopedia Americana* (Philadelphia, 1831).

TALLBOY
A type of chest-on-chest or double chest. This was the popular circa 1800 name used in England and sometimes in America for the tall two-section chest of seven or more drawers, usually constructed with a top of three drawers plus two small or "half" draw-

C. 1720 painted tall chest-on-frame with scalloped apron, the early-eighteenth-century forerunner of the tallboy, or chest-on-chest. (Courtesy, Connecticut Historical Society, Inc.)

Tallboy, or chest-on-chest, has bonnet top, dentil course on cornice molding, fan carving on upper center drawer, and ogee-bracket feet. (Courtesy, Connecticut Historical Society, Inc.)

ers directly beneath the cornice, and with three or four full-length drawers in the lower section. Hepplewhite in *The Cabinet-Maker and Upholsterer's Guide* (London, 1794), stated that tallboys generally are five feet six inches high by twenty inches deep, and were thus smaller than many similar chests made earlier in the eighteenth century. (See also DOUBLE CHEST OF DRAWERS, HIGHBOY.)

TALL-BOY
A cant term for high cups or glasses or "bottles or two-quart pots." (H) (See also POTTLE.)

TALL-CASE CLOCK
A contemporary term for what novice collectors call a Grandfather Clock, *q.v.*

TALLY
During the seventeenth and early eighteenth centuries, accounts were kept and funds paid and received by the king's Exchequer, with the exchange or delivery of tallies. These were pieces of wood notched or scored; matching pieces or tallies being kept by the two parties. "By water to the Exchequer, and strike my tallys for 17,500£ which me thinks is so great testimoney of the goodness of God to me, that I, from a mean clerk there, should come to strike tallys myself for that sum and on the authority that I do now . . ." Samuel Pepys, *Diary,* May 12, 1665. From this custom, one of the head officers at the Exchequer was called the Tallier or Teller, and we retain the word today to describe a bank employee. Similar thin, narrow pieces of polished hardwood or ivory were used by merchant shippers and importers in the colonies. At times, these old tallies are mistaken for a kind of game or game scorer. (See also ABACUS, NICKSTICK.)

TALLY IRON
A cant term for the Goffering Iron, *q.v.* Tally was a corruption of the Italian iron,

so named because the utensil was first used in Italy early in the seventeenth century.

TAMBOUR, TAMBOUR FRAME

Tambour also means a kind of embroidery. The frame is "an instrument of spherical form, upon which is stretched, by means of a string and buckle, or other appropriate means, a piece of silk or [other fabric] which is wrought with a needle, and, by means of silver or gold, cotton or silk, into leaves, flowers, or other figures." *Encyclopedia Americana* (Philadelphia, 1831). (See also EMBROIDERY, EMBROIDERY FRAME.)

Tambour frame. (Courtesy, Connecticut Historical Society, Inc.)

TAMBOURIN(E)

"A small drum," (W) shallow, with one head and metal discs at the side that jangle; also a colloquialism for "a sieve." (W)

TAMBOUR TABLE

Tambour was the term for a roll-up shutter made of thin strips of wood glued to canvas or linen and which thus when closed or in use, presented a reeded (or reided) appearance. These were used to close in desk compartments, and anything to be hidden from view; they thus were used whenever

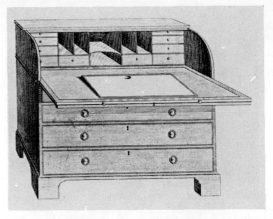

Tambour table illustrated in Hepplewhite's *Guide* (London, 1794).

"no great strength or security is requisite, as in night tables, and pot cupboards," according to Sheraton in *The Cabinet Dictionary* (London, 1803). Hepplewhite showed what we would call a roll-top desk as a tambour table, saying it had "four long drawers, with a slide to write on, the flap in which lifts up and may be adjusted to any height." *The Cabinet-Maker and Upholsterer's Guide* (London, 1794). (See also BUREAU.)

Tambour writing table with bookcase, illustrated in Hepplewhite's *Guide* (London, 1794).

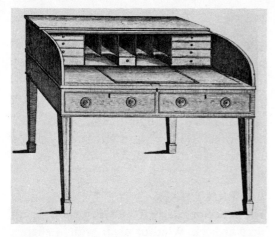

Tambour writing table, illustrated in Hepplewhite's *Guide* (London, 1794).

TAMBOUR WRITING TABLE

This, said Hepplewhite, is "a very convenient piece of furniture, answering all the uses of a desk, with a much lighter appearance . . . with two drawers and shown with the reids thrown back." *The Cabinet-Maker and Upholsterer's Guide* (London, 1794).

TANK

The contemporary term for any "large cistern or basin," (J)   each of which see.

TANKARD

"A large vessel with a cover, for strong drink." (J)   The early tankard was made of wooden staves hooped together. Later, drum-shaped mugs with one handle and a lid were called tankards. "To be sold by Robert Boyle, Pewterer, at the Sign of the Gilt Dish in Dock Street . . . at the most reasonable Rates . . . Dishes and Plates of all Sorts, Basons, Tankards, and Porringers

Early-eighteenth-century wooden tankard.

Pewter tankard marked Wallingford (Connecticut), 1725. (Courtesy, Connecticut Historical Society, Inc.)

of all Sizes . . ." *The New-York Gazette or The Weekly Post-Boy,* December 22, 1755. Originally, tankard was a term for a vessel containing three gallons, made in England from the fifteenth century, and used for carrying water.

TAPE

"A narrow linen, fillet, a kind of fine inkle." (W)

TAPE LOOM

A small wooden loom to use on lap or

Table tape loom. (Courtesy, Antiquarian and Landmarks Society, Inc.)

Standing x-base tape loom. (Courtesy, Antiquarian and Landmarks Society, Inc.)

table for weaving tapes that were used to face hems.

TAPER LADDER
The common name for "a kind of small rack having one end broader than the other," (H) and so, of course, tapered at the top; similar to the short kitchen stepstool or stepladder used today.

TAPER JACK
A writing desk accessory; a small stand on which was set a candlestick and a wheel or other spring device to hold and dispense wax for use in sealing documents and letters. The wax, or taper, came in a coil or spiral. "Send 24 Spring Brass candlesticks such as they use in Offices with half a pound of taper green candle wax on 12 of them and a pound of do. on each of the other 12, with 12 pound of white wax do. in paper for a Supply. You can't misunderstand me as what I mean is those usually used by Merchants to Seal Letters . . ." (Order, November 16, 1771, from Catherine Rathnell, merchant, Williamsburg, Virginia, to London.) Frances Mason, *John Norton and Sons, Merchants of London and Virginia* (Richmond, 1935).

TARGE, TARGET
In weaponry, "a kind of buckler or shield," (W) "worn on the left arm . . . for a defensive weapon." (J)

TAROC
The name of a card game, often considered "the most interesting, but also the most difficult" [and of the cards themselves, collected by many today]. "It is played with seventy-eight cards and derives its name from the twenty-two trumps or tarocs in it . . . faithful to its Oriental origin." *Encyclopedia Americana* (Philadelphia, 1831).

TARPAWLING
"A cloth covered with tar," (W) hence, a tarpaulin.

TASSE, TASSAKER
A cup or "goblet," (H) perhaps a variation of taste or of Tazza, *q.v.*

TASTER, TASTOUR
A "little cup; a dram cup." (W) "To taste wine." (H) More often today called a winetaster; the smallest of wine or brandy glasses.

TAVERN CHAIR
The collector's term for a type of low, semi-circular-back Windsor chair with a shaped wooden seat and plain spindles. The spindles, which connect the chair seat and curved back rail, are slightly raked, making this a chair easy to lean or loll back in.

TAVERN SIGN
The painted sign board, affixed to the facade, or to a post near the front entrance, of a place of public entertainment duly licensed to sell food, drink, or to provide lodging for wayfarers and travelers: "All inn-holders, taverners, and common victuallers, shall, at all times, be furnished with suitable provisions and lodging, for the refreshment and entertainment of strangers and travellers, pasturing and stable-room, hay and provender . . . for their horses and cattle, on pain of being deprived of their license. And every licensed victualler, inn-holder, or taverner, shall, at all times, have a board or sign affixed to his or her house,

1780 tavern sign by a professional sign painter. (Courtesy, Connecticut Historical Society, Inc.)

Early-nineteenth-century tavern sign by an un-schooled painter. (Courtesy, Connecticut Historical Society, Inc.)

New England tavern sign shows Regency-era gentlemen tipplers. (Courtesy, Connecticut Historical Society, Inc.)

or in some conspicuous place near the same, with his or her name at large thereon, and the particular employment for which he or she is licensed . . ." Act passed February 28, 1787, *Laws of the Commonwealth of Massachusetts* (Boston, 1801).

TAVERN TABLE

Two types of fairly plain rectangular or square tables were in common use in early taverns. One was the long "common" board at which six to a dozen guests might be seated. The second was a lightly made, smaller table, without a drawer, made to stack easily at night when it was time to sweep up or, if the tavern also was an inn, make room for travelers to spread their pallets. The term is often given today to heavier tables, with drawers and sometimes stretchers, and which originally would have been found in the kitchen. (See DRESSER, KITCHEN TABLE.)

Stretcher base painted pine and maple kitchen worktable, commonly called a tavern table today. (Courtesy, Antiquarian and Landmarks Society, Inc.)

Maple table with squared flaps above stretcher base. Such long, tavern or common tables used in inns are a transition style between the draw table and gateleg table. (Courtesy, Connecticut Historical Society, Inc.)

TAZZA

An Italian term for a tall drinking cup with an extremely wide and shallow bowl.

TEABOARD

A serving tray, and often today called a Butler's Tray, *q.v.* "In the box are six coarse diaper Breakfast cloths, they are to spread on the Tea Table, for nobody breakfasts here on the naked Table, but on the cloth set a large Tea Board with the cups." (Benjamin Franklin in a letter to his wife from London, 1765.) *Writings of Benjamin Franklin,* ed., A. H. Smyth (New York, 1907). These elegancies usually were of polished mahogany, cherry or walnut, sometimes of oak or other woods with handsome grains; either plain or set with inlays, sometimes lacquered or japanned. Usually rectangular or oval in shape, round, hexagonal, and octagonal shapes are to be found, also.

TEA CADDY

Originally the word signified a covered container to hold a pound or more of the luxury imported from China; those jars first so used generally were of porcelain. By the eighteenth century caddies were being made of a variety of handsomely grained woods, fine metals, tortoiseshell and horn, as well as ceramics. When made of silver, copper, pewter, or other metal, caddies usually were called canisters. Whatever its design, or material from which it was made, the caddy was an individual receptacle for one kind of tea.

TEA CANISTER

(See CADDY, TEA CADDY, TEA CHEST.)

TEA CHEST

Although this term often was used interchangeably with caddy or canister, by the eighteenth century it had come to mean specifically a container larger than the caddy.

Tea caddies illustrated in Hepplewhite's *Guide* (London, 1794).

Tea caddy from Thomas Chippendale's *Gentleman and Cabinet-Maker's Director* (London, 1762).

Painted tin New England kitchen tea caddy, c. 1840.

Tea chests illustrated in Thomas Chippendale's *Gentleman and Cabinet-Maker's Director* (London, 1762).

Three inlaid tea chests illustrated in Hepplewhite's *Guide* (London, 1794).

Chests usually had at least two inner lidded compartments, to hold black and green teas, and sometimes a third for sugar. These chests usually were fitted with locks to forestall pilfering. "Send pr very first ship . . . a neat Mahogany Tea Chest & Canisters . . ." (Order, September 9, 1771, from William Reynolds, York, Virginia, to London.) Frances Mason, *John Norton and Sons, Merchants of London and Virginia* (Richmond, 1935).

TEACUP
"A small cup used to drink tea out of," (W) of fine porcelain or soft paste, usually with a matching plate or saucer.

TEA JAR
A term sometimes used to designate the Tea Caddy, *q.v.,* made of pottery or porcelain.

TEAKETTLE
The covered kettle made with a pouring spout, in which water was boiled. At the kitchen hearth, these were usually of iron; those used in the parlor at tea time were often made of brass or copper. Thus Peyton Randolph, September 23, 1770 ordered "a Copper tea kettle, to hold six quarts, of the best sort" from London for his Williamsburg home. Frances Mason, *John Norton and Sons, Merchants of London and Virginia* (Richmond, 1935).

Late-eighteenth-century brass teakettle. (Courtesy, Antiquarian and Landmarks Society, Inc.)

TEAKETTLE STAND
Thomas Chippendale said designs of these low tripod stands, usually made with circular or shaped tops, were "so easy to understand, that they want no explanation." *The Gentleman and Cabinet-Maker's Director* (London, 1762). They were made just large enough to hold the teakettle and spirit lamp; were low so that the hostess might easily lift the kettle. The collector's whimsy is to call them coffee tables or candlestands. (See also TEA POY, URN STAND.)

Teakettle stand illustrated in Thomas Chippendale's *Director* (London, 1762).

TEAPOT

The elegant tea service necessity; the handsome covered porcelain, pottery, or silver pot with pouring spout and interior strainer;

Late-eighteenth-century tin teapot. (Courtesy, Antiquarian and Landmarks Society, Inc.)

C. 1800 popular pear-shaped soft paste teapot.

C. 1820 Staffordshire teapot with "historical view" of early Connecticut State House. (Courtesy, Connecticut Historical Society, Inc.)

Early-nineteenth-century pewter teapot. (Courtesy, Connecticut Historical Society, Inc.)

C. 1835 luster-decorated teapot. (Courtesy, Antiquarian and Landmarks Society, Inc.)

in which the proper amount of tea was placed, covered with boiling water from the teakettle, allowed to brew, then poured into the teacup or bowl, as the early handleless cups often were called. (See advertisement quoted under FRUIT BASKET.)

TEA POY

Properly, this was the name given the small tray table, a miniature tripod stand, intended for individual service of tea or dessert. "Tea Poys are used in Drawing Rooms, Ec., to prevent the company from rising from their seats when taking refreshment." George Smith, *A Collection of Designs for Household Furniture* (London, 1808). The term has often been used incorrectly to designate outsized tea caddies set on small footed stands.

TEASTER

A common contemporary spelling and pronunciation of Tester, *q.v.*

TEA SERVICE

The important pieces needed for the serving of tea, made according to the same design. "James Jacks . . . has imported from London A large and elegant assortment of goods, viz. . . . Plated tea and coffee urns, tea pots, caddies, sugar vases and milk pots to match . . ." *Pennsylvania Packet* (Philadelphia), November 13, 1799.

TEASPOON

"A small spoon used in drinking tea," (W) almost invariably of silver; often ordered singly, although sometimes sold in matched sets.

TEA TABLE

A general term for any table, round or rectangular, on which the tea service was set out and from which the hostess served her guests. Such tables often were made with gallery-rims to prevent the china from sliding off. "[Before the Revolution] they had mahogany tea boards and round tea tables, which, being turned on an axle underneath the center, stood upright, like an expanded fan or palm leaf, in the corner." John F.

Connecticut tea table, Queen Anne period, with tray top and double slides. (Courtesy, Connecticut Historical Society, Inc.)

Handsomely proportioned cherry turn-up, tip- or tilt-top table for the service of tea or breakfast; made with fluted and carved pedestal and base, claw-and-ball feet, molded rim, or dish top. (Courtesy, Connecticut Historical Society, Inc.)

Oval-top early-eighteenth-century painted tea table. (Courtesy, Antiquarian and Landmarks Society, Inc.)

Watson, *Annals of Philadelphia* (Philadelphia, 1830). Watson described what we are more apt to call a bird-cage table (see in Chapter 5) and what often was called a turn-up table at the time. Earlier, tea tables in the seventeenth century and the first part of the eighteenth century, were often delicately proportioned, small, rectangular designs. (See advertisement quoted under HAND BOARD. See also BREAKFAST TABLE; TURN-UP TABLE.)

TEA TONGS
Small tongs of silver or silver-plated metal used to lift tea from the caddy to the pot; similar to tongs used in the twentieth century to transport sugar cubes. "When seeing me one day crack one of the Philada. Biscuits into my Tea with the Nutcrackers, [the child] took another and try'd to do the same with the Tea-Tongs." (Benjamin Franklin from London, February 2, 1773, to his wife in Philadelphia.) *Writings of Benjamin Franklin,* ed., A. H. Smyth (New York, 1907).

TEA TRAY
The tray, at least large enough to hold the teapot, cream jug, and sugar basin, and often broad enough to carry the entire equipage needed by the hostess, made of wood, silver, silver-plated metal. "An assortment of very elegant Tea Trays, just imported on the *Kitty* from London; Amongst the devices on them are, the Death of Wolf, The Battle of the Boyne, Old Robin Gray, Landscapes, Ec. For sale at William Poyntell's store." *Federal Gazette* (Philadelphia), March 24, 1791. "James Jacks . . . has imported from London . . . [silver] Tea Trays from 10 to 50 inches, oval and round . . ." Ibid., April 15, 1797. (See also BUTLER'S TRAY, TEA-BOARD.)

TEA URN
The silver or silver-plated vessel with spigot used to hold the hot water needed for brewing tea; usually made in the classic urn or vase form, hence the name. Hot water was drawn off from the urn for use in the Teapot, *q.v.* Tea was not brewed in the tea urn. "At the head of the table there was an old silver tea-urn, into which, at the moment of our sitting down, a serious-visaged waiting-maid dropped a red-hot weight, and forthwith the noise of a violent boiling arose." Harriet Beecher Stowe, *Old Town Folks* (Boston, 1868). "I shall send you a Tea-Urn by the first ship. Your ever affectionate Father." (Benjamin Franklin from London to his son, William, December 2, 1772.) *The Writings of Benjamin Franklin,* ed., A. H. Smyth (New York, 1907).

TEA-URN STAND
(See URN STAND.)

TELEGRAPHIC DICTIONARY
Telegraph is a combination of two Greek words meaning to write at a distance; the term first was applied to a series of movable signposts, some of which also used lanterns. "The most simple contrivance consists of an upright post with two movable arms fixed on a common pivot, each of which may be [moved] to various positions, each position indicating a word or sentence." *Encyclopedia Americana* (Philadelphia, 1831). To simplify the telegrapher's work, and to guarantee understanding, several small books, now rare, were published, called Telegraphic Dictionaries, showing various combinations of positions of the telegraph's arms, each of which indicated a common word or combination of words. One of these, *Telegraph Vocabulary,* was published at Boston in 1832.

TELESCOPE
Then as now a name for "a long glass by which distant objects are viewed." (J) "The telescope discovers to us distant wonders in the heavens, and shows the milky way, and the bright cloudy spots, in a very dark sky, to be a collection of little stars."

Isaac Watts, *Logick* (London, 1725). "I beg the favour of you to send me a telescope. For a good one I would go as far as eight or ten guineas. I would have a light stand to keep it steady upon." (Order, September 8, 1772, from George Wythe, Williamsburg, Virginia, to London.) Frances Mason, *John Norton and Sons, Merchants of London and Virginia* (Richmond, 1935). (See also SPY-GLASS.)

TELESCOPE DINING TABLE
The contemporary name for the extension table developed in the nineteenth century; a design that allowed insertion of extra boards, slides, or leaves into the top surface, thus extending the table's length. "They . . . received their name from the slide action by which their length is varied. The compactness of their minimum size, capability of speedy extension, and the facility with which they may be adjusted to various measures, are their chief recommendations . . . [so that] they contrast favourably with the other varieties of dining tables, which they have in a great measure superseded . . . A space is formed for holding the loose top securely within the table itself . . . when the boards [do not] exeed four in number." Blackie and Son, *The Cabinet-Maker's Assistant* (London, 1853). (See also DRAW TABLE.)

TEMSE
A sifter or strainer, a fine "hair-sieve." (J) Thus, temsed bread was that made of flour sifted finer than usual.

TENT BED
Similar to the Field Bed, *q.v.,* and sometimes called a camp bed. The tent bed was made with four posts, a curved fabric-covered canopy and valances, and curtains so disposed that none of the framework could be seen. Popular throughout the eighteenth century and well into the nineteenth when J. C. Loudon declared they "are in universal use and scarcely require description." *An Encyclopedia of Cottage, Farm and*

Villa Architecture and Furniture (London, 1833). In his *A Collection of Designs for Household Furniture* (London, 1808), George Smith suggested "the furniture [be] calico, and trimmed with worsted or cotton fringe at pleasure."

TERMS for BUSTS
Term was a contemporary synonym for those stands or pedestals "generally made of mahogany, with the ornaments carved; their height regulated by the subject they are intended to support. The height, for a Bust as large as life, is between 3 and 4 feet." A. Hepplewhite, *Cabinet-Maker and Upholsterer's Guide* (London, 1788). Earlier, Chippendale illustrated four designs for what he called "Terms for Bustos etc." *The Gentleman and Cabinet-Maker's Director* (London, 1762). Term is an abbreviation of terminus, the architect's word for any pedestal with a sculptured figure at its top.

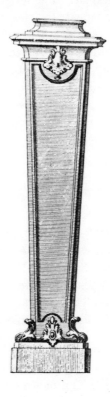

Term, shown in Thomas Chippendale's *Director* (London, 1762).

TERRESTRIAL GLOBE
(See GLOBES.)

TERRY CLOCK

The name often given by collectors to the New England pillar-and-scroll shelf-clock case because the design was first [1815–20] used extensively by Eli Terry, Plymouth, Connecticut, clockmaker.

TERSE

A small wooden keg or cask; "a firkin or rundlet containing nine gallons." (H)

TESTER BED

Collector's term for any bedstead with four high posts that support a flat frame or tester for a canopy. (See also BEDSTEAD, TENT BED.)

TÊTE-À-TÊTE SEAT

The term to describe a turn of the nineteenth-century small sofa or oversized chair, just large enough for two, of the type late-Victorians would call a loveseat. According to one contemporary designer, the tête-à-tête was "an article adapted to elegant apartments; the frames [should be] of rich wood, or [with] gold and bronze finishes; the covering of fine cloth, velvet, or calico; in dimension calculated for two persons to sit on." George Smith, *A Collection of Designs for Household Furniture* (London, 1808).

TEXTILES

(See separate listing at back of this section.)

THEODOLITE

The surveyor's instrument for measuring horizontal and vertical angles, and thus also the circumference. "For Sale by James Jacks . . . Ship and Pocket Spy Glasses, Surveyor's Compasses and Theodolites . . . *Gazette of the United States* (Philadelphia), August 2, 1798.

THEORBO

"A large lute for playing a thorough bass." (J)   The seventeenth- and eighteenth-century stringed instrument, made with a double neck and two sets of tuning pegs, the lower supporting the melody strings, the upper the bass.

THEOREM

The name given a type of popular early-nineteenth-century painting, produced with stencil patterns on cloth (velvet being especially favored), on close-grained hardwood plaques, on sheets of marble, tin, or pasteboard. (See also STENCIL PAINTING.)

THEW

An Old Saxon word for manners or quality, and an early synonym for a cucking stool. According to Webster in 1806, it simply meant "a stool" perhaps by then having become a colloquialism.

THIBBLE, THIBLE

An old term for "Slice, a Scummer, a Spatula," (J)   *qq.v.* (See also PEEL.)

THIMBLE

One of the seamstress' accessories; the "cap used on the needle finger" (W)   "by which women secure their fingers from the needle when they sew." (J)   Thimbles were made of steel, often silver-plated or gilt-washed; sometimes of ivory; and were sold by cutlers and jewelers. They were favored as gifts to girls upon completion of a satisfactory Sampler, *q.v.*, and to brides. "Charles Shipman . . . lately from England [offers] pounce boxes and ivory thimbles, ivory netting and knotting needles . . ." *The New York Journal or The General Advertiser,* August 6, 1767.

THIRDENDEALE, THRIDDENDEL,

A measure or "pewter flagon containing three pints," (H)   originally one of 84 gallons.

THREAD BOX

The box or case with a lid, intended for worktable use; made to hold spools, quills, or hanks of thread for use in sewing and embroidery; made of bone, metal, wood, leather-covered wood; often painted, monogrammed, or otherwise decorated. "James R. Woodbridge & Co. Have This Day Received an extensive assortment of Seasonable Goods, viz. . . . elegant . . . Shell Combs, Thread Boxes, Superfine Needles, Pins, Tapes, Threads, Sewing Silks, Twists . . . large assortment of Clothes and Cassimeres." *American Mercury* (Hartford, Connecticut), March 16, 1818. (See also THREAD CASE.)

THREAD CASE
A small case or leather folder for the pocket in which sewing needles, pins, and twists of thread were carried. "James Jacks . . . has imported from London . . . a large assortment of goods [including] Ladies and Gentlemen's morocco pocketbooks . . . morocco thread cases and memorandum books . . ." *Federal Gazette* (Philadelphia), November 27, 1797.

THRESHER
An early term for a feather duster commonly made of a turkey or goose wing.
> Save wing for a thresher when gander doth die,
> Save feathers of all things, the softer to lie.
> Thomas Tusser, *Five Hundreth Points of Good Husbandry* (London, 1597).

THRIFT BOX
A contemporary term for a pottery penny bank: "An earthen box for saving money in, so contrived that the coin cannot be got out without breaking it." (H)

THROWN CHAIR
An early synonym for turned chair, especially one with many spindles or turnings, such as the Carver or Brewster-type chairs. Throwing was an old word for turning, derived from throve, "the name of the turner's lathe." (H)

THUMSTAL(L)
Another contemporary term for the "thimble." (W)

THURINDALE
A synonym for "a pewter Flagon, *q.v.,* holding about three pints." (H)

TIDY
A colloquialism for "a workbag," (H) or Work Pocket, *q.v.*

TIFF GLASS, TIFF MUG
Any drinking vessel of good size used in serving tiff. Tiff, "a low word for liquor or drink," (J) probably was a form of syllabub, since it was described as having a certain acidity:
> with . . . small acid tiff,
> Wretched repast! my meagre corps sustain.
> John Philips, *The Splendid Shilling.*

(See also DRINKING VESSEL, SYLLABUB GLASS.)

TIGER TABLE
The collector's name, first used in the Late-Victorian era, for a table with a top veneered in striped woods, such as tulipwood or zebrawood, arranged to resemble the markings of tiger skin.

TILES
Decorative porcelain or delft squares set in parlor or chamber fireplace surrounds. A diversion for children was to "read the tiles," i.e., make up bedtime stories the themes of which were suggested by the tile decorations. "To be sold by Capt. Stephen Richards on Queen Street, Boston. All sorts of Dutch *Tyles,* viz. Scripture, Landskips of divers sorts, sea monsters, horsemen, soldiers, diamonds, et c. Also sets of brushes; London quart bottles, and a chest of Delph ware." *Boston Gazette,* February 6, 1738.

TILL
"A money box." (J) The colonial name for any small compartment, container, box, or drawer in which money was kept safe. The small boxes built into the interior of some chests also were called tills.

TILLER

Another form of "till, a small drawer," (J) jewel box or container for other valuables.

Search her cabinet, and thou shalt find
Each tiller there with love epistles lin'd.

John Dryden, *Juvenal.*

TILT-TOP TABLE

The collector's term for what originally was called a snap-table, as English collectors still do today, or a Turn-up Table, *q.v.* It was a tripod-base table with hinged top, made to fold back to a vertical position when not in use. Other names used for these today are tip table; tip-top table. (See also BIRD-CAGE, Chapter 5.)

TIMBAL, TYMBAL

The proper name of the Kettledrum, *q.v.;* sometimes spelled timbrel, as it was by Webster in 1806.

TIMBER DISH

A colloquialism for a "trencher" (H) or any dish or plate made from wood. (See also PLANCHER, TREEN.)

TIMEKEEPER, TIMEPIECE

The correct terms, and so used by our early manufacturers, for any device to measure time on a dial, but which did not have a bell to strike the hour. Thus, Aaron Willard (1757–1844) who made clocks in Grafton and Roxbury, Massachusetts, until 1823, differentiated in his label: "Common House Clocks, Table/Spring Clocks, and Time Pieces of different constructions, made by Aaron Willard, Boston." Another famous maker, Eli Terry (1772–1852), of New Windsor and Plymouth, Connecticut, noted the difference also in his application for a patent in 1797 for an "improvement in clocks, timekeepers and watches."

TINDERBOX

Tinder was another name for Match, *q.v.,* or any easily ignited material, such as shavings or bits of paper. The tinderbox held the tinder and usually the steel and flint needed to produce the spark which lit the tinder.

Tin tinderbox with candleholder top.

TIN KITCHEN

A popular nineteenth-century term for the Reflector Oven, *q.v.* "Several newly invented improvements for housekeeping were displayed [in the kitchen], amongst which was a tin roaster. Heretofore our meat and poultry had been baked in a brick oven, or roasted on a spit, resting on brackets for that purpose to the high iron andirons, common to every kitchen. Sometimes a turkey or goose was depended before the fire by a strong string hitched to a nail in the ceiling . . . This new 'tin kitchen' Aunt Betsey displayed as a rare implement of great value to the culinary art." (Description of a Newburyport home c. 1790.) Sarah Anna Emery, *Reminiscences of a Nonagenarian* (Newburyport, Massachusetts, 1879). The tin kitchen was developed late in the eighteenth century and remained in use for so long as cooking was done at the hearth—until cooking stoves or ranges became common between 1830 and 1850 along the Atlantic Coast, and much later in frontier settlements.

TIN OVEN

Another name for the open-faced Reflector Oven, *q.v.,* but more often applied to those examples not fitted with spits. "To make an English Rabbit, toast a slice of Bread brown on both sides, lay it on a Plate before the Fire, pour a glass of red wine over it, and let it soak the wine up; then cut some Cheese very thin, and lay it very thick over the Bread and put it in a Tin Oven before the Fire and it will be toasted and browned presently." Hannah Glasse, *Art of Cookery,* (London, 1747).

TIN ROASTER
(See REFLECTOR OVEN, TIN KITCHEN, TIN OVEN.)

TINSED BALL
"A child's ball wrought with worsted of various colors." (H)

TOASTER
A rectangular wire grid or clamp attached to a long handle, and which held bread before the fire; the clamp usually was set on a footed swivel bar or base that could be turned or reversed in order to brown both sides of the bread. The toasting utensil used at the kitchen hearth.

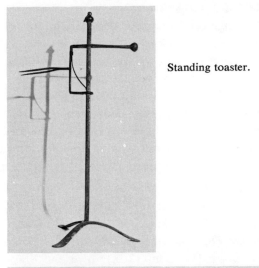

Standing toaster.

American eighteenth-century down-hearth-style toaster.

TOASTING FORK
A two-tined fork attached to a long handle,

Toasting fork.

used for toasting a slice of bread or other food at the parlor or chamber hearth.

TOASTING GLASS
Generally the same as the Firing Glass, *q.v.,* with the exception of the mid-Georgian type made with an especially slender and delicate stem so that it could be snapped or broken between finger and thumb at the appropriate moment. Needless to say, few of these survive.

TOASTING IRON
Another name for the Salamander, *q.v.*

TOAST RACK
The small tray for the service at table of toasted bread; divided by vertical risers or hoops of heavy silver or silver-plated wire into several sections, each just wide enough to hold one slice upright. "James Musgrave, No. 44, south Second Street, has just received from London, and is now opening an elegant and extensive assortment of Plated Goods, of the latest fashions, and warranted of the very best quality, manufactured in England, viz. Tea and coffee urns, plated and Japanned bread baskets of various patterns round and oval . . . sauce tureens, salts, toast racks . . ." *Pennsylvania Packet* (Philadelphia), November 6, 1800.

TOAST TRAY
A contemporary synonym for the Toast Rack, *q.v.* "James Jacks, Jeweller and Watchmaker . . . his elegant stock of goods [includes] best plated snuffers and stands, Silver edge fish knives and toast trays . . ." *Federal Gazette* (Philadelphia), November 27, 1797.

TOBACCO CAN, TOBACCO CANISTER
Covered containers or humidors especially made to keep tobacco moist and fresh. Although some were made of handsomely grained hardwoods, cork-lined, the majority were fashioned of lead, silver, brass, or silver-plated copper, often richly engraved or chased. Others were of varnished leather

or japanned tin and had painted decorations. "Thomas Russell, Brazier, near the Draw-Bridge in Boston . . . makes all sorts of Lead Work for Ships, Tobacco Cannisters, Ink Stands, Ec." *Boston News-Letter,* October 30, 1740.

TOBY JUG

The basic Toby was a pottery jug or pitcher made in the shape of a seated man holding a mug and a clay pipe; a design perhaps first made by Ralph Wood, the famous Staffordshire potter, shortly after 1760. There were numerous variations. The original inspiration is said to have been the character Toby Philpot, from the popular song, *The Brown Jug,* published in 1761. "Notice. At the Emes farm-house, Yorkshire, aged 76, Mr. Paul Parnell, farmer, grazier, and maltster, who during his lifetime drank out of one silver pint cup upwards of £200 sterling worth of Yorkshire Stingo, being remarkably attached to Stingo tipple of the home-brewed best quality. The calculation is taken at 2d. per cupful. He was the bon-vivant of whom O'Keefe celebrated in more than one of his Bacchanalian songs under the appellation of Toby Philpott." *Gentleman's Magazine,* London, 1810.

Eighteenth-century Toby jug. (*Newtown Bee,* photo by R. Scudder Smith.)

TODDY STICKS

A common term for the turned wooden muddlers used to break up sugar lumps in a drink.

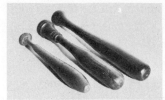

Toddy sticks.

TODDY TABLE

The small Mixing Table, *q.v.,* or wine stand with a top just large enough to hold a tray on which stood the necessary hot water container, spirits bottle, sugar basin, toddy spoon, and mugs.

TOILET(TE)

The contemporary 1750 to 1800 name for what later was called a Toilet Table, *q.v.*

TOILET GLASS

An eighteenth-century designation for a free-standing looking glass, a small form of the Cheval, *q.v.,* or horse looking glass made to swing between two standards. This was set on a dressing table or a chest of drawers. Such a glass made with a drawer or drawers in the base was called a box toilet glass. The same type of looking glass later was called a dressing glass.

TOILETTA

A term sometimes used to describe the toilette or Toilet Table, *q.v.* In their design book, *The Universal System of Household Furniture* (London, 1762), Ince and Mayhew illustrated three "Lady's Toilettas." Two lacked the adjustable looking glass and the fitted drawers. The third, was "a Ladies Toilet, with Drawers under the Glass; intended either for Japan or burnish'd Gold." The illustration showed a framed looking glass fixed above a double row of five small drawers each.

TOILET TABLE

A piece of fine furniture, a fitted dressing table, for a lady's chamber. According to Thomas Chippendale, one version of the "Toilet, or Dressing Table for a Lady [has] the glass, made to come forward into folding Hinges; [the glass] is in a carved Frame, and stands . . . upon a Plinth, between which are small Drawers. The drapery is supported by Cupids, and the Petticoat goes behind the feet of the table, which looks better." *The Gentleman and Cabinet-Maker's Director* (London, 1762).

The small drawers had compartments for the storage of bottles, boxes, combs, and "other necessaries." Similarly draped and canopied tables soon were popular in English homes: "The blue damask bed chamber is elegant . . . The toilette is in a bow window, all blue and white." Arthur Young, *A Six Month's Tour Through the North of England* (London, 1770).

After the Revolution, Americans continued to follow, and sometimes to simplify fashions in decorations first set in England: "The best chamber was elegant with gay patch hangings to the high square post bedstead, and curtains of the same draped the windows. A toilet table tastily covered with white muslin, and ornamented by blue ribbon bows, stood between the front windows. (Description of a Newburyport home, c. 1790.) Sarah Anna Emery, *Reminiscences of a Nonagenarian* (Newburyport, Massachusetts, 1879).

Toilet tables made by country joiners lacked the divided top, and the hinged looking glass; in place of the tiers of small drawers, one long drawer usually was set below the table top. By 1800 a backboard, similar to the splash board used on washstands, often was added. Many such simple tables were painted in light colors with painted stencil decorations.

TÔLE, TÔLE PEINTE
The French term for painted or lacquered metalware, corresponding to the Anglo-American japanned ware or Pontypool, *q.v.* The term tôle often is used by collectors today to designate any painted tin or tinned sheet-ironwares.

C. 1820 tôle or painted tin so-called document box. (Courtesy, Antiquarian and Landmarks Society, Inc.)

TOM
A cant term for "the close-stool." (H)

TOMAHAWK
One of the many Indian relics and tools collected today. This was a term, derived from the Algonquin Indian word, to describe the light ax used as a hand weapon and also as a hurling weapon by North American tribes. It was also a symbol of intent to make war. "The die is cast. We have at last solemnly offered the Tomahawk to the Indians, and they have accepted it. At a grand council held at Dayton in the State of Ohio on the 6th ult. propositions were made by Mr. Johnson to the chiefs of seven Indian Tribes, which have been eagerly acceded to. The weapon of death is placed in their hands—our enemies are to be their enemies . . . We say to the world and to posterity—what else could we do? . . . War was declared [with Great Britain] . . . If the Indians must engage in the present war, it is better for us to have them with us than against us." *The Richmond Enquirer* (Virginia), March 22, 1814.

TOM-TOM
(See INDIAN DRUM.)

569

TONGS

The iron hearth tool, resembling large pliers, "an instrument to hold fire, Ec with." (W) (See also EMBER TONGS; PIPE TONGS.)

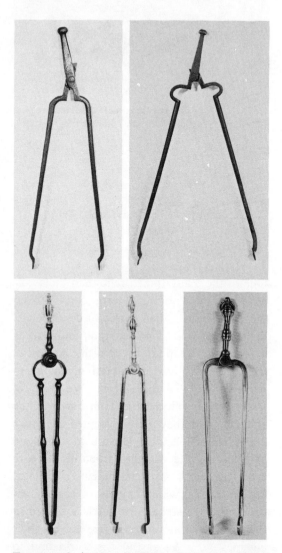

Tongs made in New England, shown in order of age from top left to lower right, from early-eighteenth-century iron through late-eighteenth-century brass types. (Courtesy, Antiquarian and Landmarks Society, Inc.)

TONMELE, TONNE

A large barrel or tub; a corruption or variation of tun.

TOOL(S)

"Any instrument of manual operation." (J) Tools listed in the House of Parliament Rates, 1660, for Imports and Exports—*Statutes of the Realm* (London, 1819), included: "Aule blades; Anvils; Anglers for carpenters; Axes, hatchets; Bodkins; Chizells for Joyners; Compasses of Iron for Carpenters; Files; Gimlets; Hammers with and without wooden handles; Horsemen's hammers; Melting Ladles; Pincers and plyers; Punsons and Gravers for goldsmiths; Hand Saws, whipsaws; Sheares for glovers, seamesters, taylers; Carving tools; Hand vices; Adzes."

TOOTHPICK CASE

A small, slim two-part pocket case of leather, gold, silver, ivory, or wood, usually just large enough to hold one ivory, silver, or gold pick. "James Jacks . . . has imported in the ship *William Penn,* and Brig *Fly* from London . . . Tortoise shell and ivory snuff boxes and tooth pick cases, with gold mounting and handsome devices, from 3 to 40 dollars." *Federal Gazette* (Philadelphia), November 27, 1797.

TORCHÈRE

A French term sometimes used as a synonym for Candlestand, *q.v.*

TOT

Usually thought of today as a small cordial glass or Taster, *q.v.;* during the seventeenth and eighteenth centuries, it signified a "small drinking cup holding about half a pint." (H)

TOWEL HORSE, TOWEL RACK, TOWEL RAIL

Alternative names for a narrow frame or rack set on a trestle base and with two or three horizontal bars to hold towels.

TOY

The common seventeenth- through the early-nineteenth-century term for any "trifle; a thing of no value; a plaything, a Bauble, *q.v.;* fans, silks, ribbands, laces, and Gew-gaws." *q.v.* (J) "An odd fancy." (W)

Nineteenth-century child's toy wagon. (Courtesy, Connecticut Historical Society, Inc.)

Painted c. 1800 toy cradle. (Courtesy, Antiquarian and Landmarks Society, Inc.)

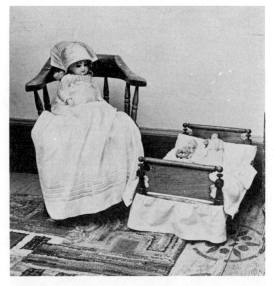

Mid-nineteenth-century dolls, doll bed, and child's armchair. (Courtesy, Antiquarian and Landmarks Society, Inc.)

TOY BOOK

A popular term for a child's story book. "Bookstore & Bindery. The following articles are offered as cheap as can be purchased in this city. Bibles, Testaments, Psalm Books and Dictionaries, Geographies, Spelling Books, Columbian Orators, Websters Elements, Primmers, Toy Books, Ec." *American Mercury* (Hartford, Connecticut), November 11, 1812.

TOY CHINA

Small sets made for children or toy-sized copies of the pottery or porcelain services used by their elders. "Am glad to hear my neice grows so finely. Have sent her a sett of small China for her amusement." (Letter from Benjamin Franklin at London, September 6, 1774 to Yorktown, Virginia.) *Writings of Benjamin Franklin,* ed., A. H. Smyth (New York, 1907).

Child's toy china or tea set of soft paste.

TOY IRON

(See under SAD IRON.)

TRADE GOODS

The all-inclusive term for baubles, trinkets, textiles, and the other more substantial wares with which the settlers bartered for furs for export; a trade that continued to the beginning of the twentieth century. "The Common Method of carrying on this Indian commerce is as follows: Gentlemen send for Goods proper for such a Trade from England, and then either Venture them out at their own risk to the Indian

Towns, or else credit some Traders with them of Substance and Reputation to be paid in skins at a certain Price agreed betwixt them. The Goods for the Indian Trade consist chiefly in Guns, Powder, Shot, Hatchets (which the Indians call Tomahawkes) Kettles, red & blue Planes, Duffields, Stroudwater Blankets, and some Cutlary Wares, Brass Rings and other Trinkets." William Byrd, *History of the Dividing Line* [1729] (Richmond, 1866).

TRAFALGAR CHAIR
Another name for the Nelson Chair, *q.v.,* as designed by Sheraton, and for various other chairs manufactured during the same period, so named for the publicity value.

TRAFFING DISH
A perforated wood or metal skimmer dish; "a bowl through which milk is strained into the tray in which it is set to raise cream." (H)

TRAMMEL
"An iron hook by which kettles are hung over a fire;" (H) an adjustable rack or rachet suspended from the lug pole or crane in the kitchen chimney.

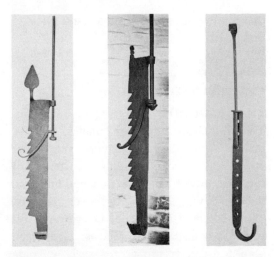

Three early-eighteenth-century New England height-adjustable iron trammels. (Courtesy, Antiquarian and Landmarks Society, Inc.)

TRANSOM
Specifically, the term for (1) "The vane of an instrument called a cross staff, being a piece of wood fixed across with a square socket upon which it slides," (B) but used also as a synonym (2) for the Weather Vane, *q.v.,* and by 1800, for (3) "a lintel over a doorcase." (W)

TRAP, TRAPPINGS, TRAPS
Cant terms for household goods or furnishings.

TRAPE
A pan, "platter or dish." (H)

TRAVEL CASE, TRAVELING CASE
The leather, leather- or cloth-covered wood or pasteboard fitted case of the type today called a shaving kit. " . . . a great variety of . . . Pocket and memorandum books, Gentlemen's travelling cases, complete with razors, Ec." [Joseph Anthony, Jr., Silversmith] *Pennsylvania Packet* (Philadelphia), December 7, 1790. (See also BANDBOX, DRESSING CASES, HATBOX, HAT CASE.)

TRAVEL DESK
(See PORTABLE DESK.)

TRAVELS
The contemporary term for any book or "account of occurrences and observations of a journey into foreign parts." (J) "Histories engage the soul by sensible occurrences; as also voyages, travels, and accounts of countries." Isaac Watts, *Logick* (London, 1725).

TRAY
According to Thomas Sheraton, trays are "boards with rims round them, on which to place glasses, plates and tea equipage." *Cabinet Dictionary* (London, 1803). The term signified any trencher, large plate, or dish made in the form of "a hollow trough of wood." (W) (See also BUTLER'S TABLE, SALVER, SERVER, TEA-

BOARD, TEA TRAY, VOIDER, WAITER.)

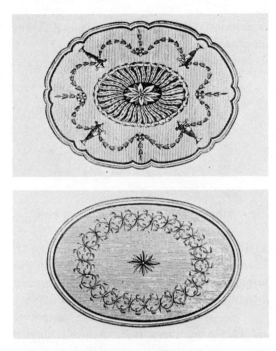

Two designs for inlaid wood tea trays, illustrated in Hepplewhite's *Guide* (London, 1794).

Plain painted c. 1810 New England tin tray with so-called lacy edge.

TRAYDRILL TABLE

Tray or trey, from the Middle-English adaptation of the Old-French *trei,* or Latin *tres,* words for three, signified the three at dice or cards; hence, this name was given to a three-sided card table—probably intended for use by devotees of the popular contemporary game ombre—by Ince and Mayhew, in *The Universal System of Household Furniture* (London, 1762). (See also OMBRE TABLE.)

TREBLE

An early term for a kind of pipe or Flute, *q.v.,* used throughout the seventeenth and eighteenth centuries. "I found them . . . in a poor condition . . . and took them to our inn, and there, after long stay, and hearing of Frank, their son, the miller, play upon his treble as he calls it, with which he earns part of his living, and singing of a country song, we sat down to supper." Samuel Pepys, *Diary,* September 17, 1663.

TREEN

The ancient Anglo-Saxon plural of tree, and so defined by Dr. Johnson in 1755 when he called it "an obsolete word." Webster in 1806 also regarded treen as obsolete. Since the 1930s, however, treen has been used by American collectors to dignify early wooden utensils and containers. The colonial manufacturer or purchaser referred to each artifact by a name signifying its use, and often collectively simply as cooper's ware. "John Henry Dyer, Cooper, lately arriv'd from London, living on Mr. Henshawe's Wharffe, near the South Market House in Boston, makes all sorts of Cooper's Ware, after the best manner, as Rum Hogsheads, Barrels, Caggs, Little tubs and Trays [platters or trenchers], as cheap and good as any in the Town." *Boston Gazette,* July 30, 1751.

Or, as we do today for woodenware: " . . . tho' their Country be over-run with Wood, yet they have all their Wooden Ware from England: their Cabinets, Chairs, Tables, Stools, Chests, Boxes, Cart-Wheels, and all other things, even so much as their Bowls and Birchen Rooms." Robert Beverley, *The History and Present State of Virginia* (London, 1721), describing the homes of wealthy planters.

TRENCHER

In the seventeenth and eighteenth centuries, trencher was the common term for any wooden plate from which an individual ate. "It being Lord Mayor's Day . . . I went to Guild Hall and to dinner. [There were] ten good dishes to a messe [table], with plenty of wine of all sorts; but it was very unpleasing that we had no napkins nor change of trenchers, and drunk out of earthen pitchers, and wooden dishes." Samuel Pepys, *Diary,* October 29, 1663. "Common White Trenchers, and red or painted trenchers" were listed in the House of Parliament Rates, 1660, for Imports and Exports—*Statutes of the Realm* (London, 1819). The large trencher or platter also was used in the kitchen as a mixing or cutting board. "When you use flour and butter, mix it together on the back of a trencher or a clean board, with a knife till it is smooth." Richard Briggs, *The New Art of Cookery* (Philadelphia, 1792). Although used until late in the nineteenth century for an individual service plate, after 1800 the word also described a serving platter, "a plate to cut meat on." (W) After pottery and porcelain came into general use, plain plates of these wares also were called trenchers.

TRESTLE
Correctly, the term for "the frame of a table; a movable [folding] form by which anything is supported." (J) Hence, trestle table, the collector's term for the table board and separate frame or trestle.

TRESTLE TABLE
The term is applied to any table board either loose or fixed on a frame or standard of trestle form. The supports are under either end of the board, set on a broad

Early-eighteenth-century trestle-foot table with removable board. (Courtesy, Antiquarian and Landmarks Society, Inc.)

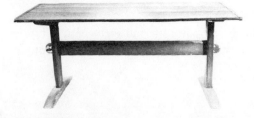

base, and connected with one or more stretcher rails.

TREVET, TRIVET
A descriptive term for "anything that stands on three legs [such as] a stool." (J) "A stool with three legs." (W)

Eighteenth-century American iron hearth trivet.

TRIANGLE
The musical instrument of percussion; in form, a rod of steel bent into the shape of a triangle, open at one angle. "This day my tryangle, which was put in tune yesterday, did please me very well. Ashwell playing upon it pretty well." Samuel Pepys, *Diary,* March 18, 1663.

TRI CROOKS, TWI CROOKS
At the kitchen hearth, the "little crooks bent contrary ways in order to lengthen out the trammels on which the pot-hooks are hung." (H)

TRIC-TRAC BOARD
The decorative game board used for trictrac, a variation of Backgammon, *q.v.,* played since the seventeenth century.

TRI-DDARN, TRI-DARN
The Welsh name for the Welsh press or cupboard; a cupboard base with three open shelves set above it to hold pewter.

TRIFLE DISH
Trifle was a popular, light dessert of eggs and cornstarch; the silver, porcelain, or glass trifle dish was the bowl in which it was served. "James and Arthur Jarvis . . . Have just open'd a Variety of glass, viz. . . . elegant cut sallad bowls and trifle dishes . . ." *The New-York Gazette and The Weekly Mercury,* December 6, 1771.

TRIMMEL

A colloquialism for the large wooden "salting tub" (H) for meat.

TRIO TABLES

The term used by Thomas Sheraton to describe what now is usually called a set or nest of three small occasional tables. "A sort of small work table, made in three parts, to shut up into each other, and which may be used either jointly or separately." *The Cabinet Dictionary* (London, 1803). (See also QUARTETTO TABLE.)

TRIPTYCH

Properly, the term for the altar piece composed of three painted leaves hinged together so they stand upright. Triptych also is used for a similarly hinged set of three looking-glass panels.

TROWCAN

A term for a "little dish," (H) perhaps a form of trow, a synonym for trough.

TRUCKLE BED

"A bed that runs on wheels under a higher bed." (J) Truckle was the Middle English word for a small, solid wheel or castor. A truckle bed was a low bedstead with shallow sides, set on castors so that when not in use it could be pushed beneath the standing high bedstead.

There's his chamber, his house, his castle, his standing-bed and trucklebed.

Shakespeare, *Merry Wives of Windsor*, IV, v.

Originally designed for use by a page or maid as Shakespeare indicates, truckle beds were brought out at night for children or guests, and were used also, because of their low height, as attic beds. (See also TRUNDLE BED.)

TRUG

A term in use from the sixteenth century well into the nineteenth century for any kind of simple wooden container, with or without a handle. "A wooden basket for carrying chips or vegetables" or "a tray for milk or the like." (H) The word itself may have been a variation of trough. (See also ASH TRUG.)

TRUNDLE BED

From the Saxon for any round, rolling object. Trundle, trendle, or trindle was the sixteenth-century term for a small wheel or roller, especially the wheel of a castor. To trundle an object was to make it roll; so, trundle bed. (See also TRUCKLE BED.)

TRUNK

An ancient name for a kind of chest, reminiscent of those ancient times when a lidded container was made of a hollowed-out section of tree trunk. In Colonial and Early-Federal frontier communities, this simple device also was employed when nec-

C. 1700 paneled truckle bed. (Courtesy, Antiquarian and Landmarks Society, Inc.)

C. 1750 round trunk. (Courtesy, Antiquarian and Landmarks Society, Inc.)

C. 1775 trunk. (Courtesy, Antiquarian and Landmarks Society, Inc.)

essary to create a so-called dug-out chest or trunk. Early chests or trunks with dome-shaped tops thus echo an older style as well as name. "Joseph Adam Fleming . . . to the Gentry and Public in General . . . carries on . . . Trunk work in all its branches, viz. Camp, Coach and portmantua trunks, ladies gilt ditto, fiddles and guitar cases, Plate and china ditto, hat and cap ditto, canteens and valeeses, furr cap and band boxes." *New York Independent Journal, or The General Advertiser* (February 2, 1785.)

TRUNNEL
A contemporary variation of tree nail, the term for a "long wooden pin to fasten a ship's planks." (W)

TUB
The term for a wide, shallow "wooden vessel of various sizes and uses." (W) (See also BASIN, KEELER.)

TUB CHAIR
A name applied to an upholstered easy armchair made with a high, semicircular back and specifically intended for sick persons. "Being both easy and warm, for the side wings coming quite forward keep out the cold air, which may be totally excluded from the person asleep, by laying some kind of covering over the whole chair." Thomas Sheraton, *The Cabinet Dictionary* (London, 1803).

TUMBLER
The name originally was given to a conical or tapered drinking vessel, somewhat resembling a horn in shape and which, once filled, had to be emptied before it could be put down without spilling the contents. Much later, the rounded base was squared off and the vessel no longer tumbled when set down. Tumblers were made of horn, waxed leather, hardwood, silver, and eventually, of glass. "Took five silver tumblers home, which I have bought." Samuel Pepys, *Diary,* October 20, 1664. "American Flint Glass Store. Removed from the store kept by

Engraved tumbler made at New Bremen Glass Manufactory of John Frederick Amelung (one of two dozen known pieces of Amelung), 8 inches high, smoky-greenish glass, made about 1790. (Courtesy, Connecticut Historical Society, Inc.)

Mr. Henry William Stiegel, near the Exchange, to the store of James and Arthur Jarvis between Burling and Beckman's Slips, in the Fly; who have for sale of the American manufacture, quart, pint and half pint decanters; pint, half pint, gill, and half gill, flint and common tumblers . . ." *New-York Gazette and Weekly Mercury,* February 8, 1773.

TUN DISH, TUNNING DISH
The "wooden funnel through which liquor is poured into casks." (H) Sometimes also called a tunnel or tunnle.

TUNE CLOCK
A contemporary term for the clock works that chimed the quarters and played a musical tune to denote the passing of an hour: "Simon Willard Begs leave to inform the publick that he has opened a shop in Roxbury Street, nearly opposite the road that runs off to Plymouth, where he carries on the business of Clock-Making in all its branches. Gentlemen may be supplied at said shop on the most reasonable terms, with clocks of different constructions, to run either a day, eight days, one month or a year, with once winding up; common eight-day repeating Clocks, Spring Clocks of all sorts, among which are, common spring table, spring chime, and spring tune Clocks, which will play different tunes every hour; also large [long-case] tune clocks which run with weights, will play every hour, repeat the quarters, Ec." *Massachusetts Spy, or Worcester Gazette,* March 11, 1784.

TUNNEGAR
A funnel. (See also TUN DISH.)

TURBOT KETTLE
In kitchenware, the iron or copper, fairly shallow kettle in which the turbot, or any large fish could be cooked whole. Turbot properly was the name for the European flatfish, but the term was used here for any similar flounder. "The most convenient utensil to boil fish in, is a turbot-kettle. This should be 24 inches long, 22 wide, and 9 deep. It is [also] an excellent vessel to boil a ham in, Ec., Ec." William Kitchiner, *The Cook's Oracle, and Housekeeper's Manual* (New York, 1830). Turbot kettles sometimes are confused with similar copper vessels in which confectioners boiled sugar.

TURNED CHAIR
The descriptive term for a chair, all posts and spindles of which are turned, such as the so-called Brewster or Carver chairs; earlier called a Thrown Chair, *q.v.*

TURNER
(See SPATULA.)

Early-eighteenth-century iron turner.

Eighteenth-century maple turner. (Courtesy, Antiquarian and Landmarks Society, Inc.)

TURN-UP BEDSTEAD
One of the important pieces of folding, space-saving furniture, this was a rope bed the side rails of which were hinged in the middle so that the lower half of the bedstead could be folded up and back against the head. "John Taylor, Upholsterer and House-Broker from London sells . . . Four Post, bureau, table, tent, field and turnup bedsteads, with silk and worsted damask, morine, harateen, china, printed cotton for check furnitures . . ." *The New-York Journal or General Advertiser,* March 24, 1768. (See also SLAW BED.)

577

TURN-UP STAND, TURN-UP TABLE

A contemporary description for the space-saving tea or breakfast table, usually called a tilt-top table today, the top so hinged to the pedestal that the board could be turned up when not in use. "1 kitchen table .50, 1 turn-up stand, 1.50 . . ." were listed in the Joseph Arnold estate inventory, Haddam, Connecticut, May 14, 1823. (See also TEA TABLE.)

(Courtesy, Connecticut Historical Society, Inc.)

TURNSCREW

The cabinetmaker's "chief tools are saws, axes, planes, chisels, files, gimlets, turnscrews, hammers and other tools which are used in common [with] the carpenter; but they are much finer than the tools required by the house-carpenter." *The Book of Trades* (London, 1805).

TURPIN

A cant term for "a kettle." (H)

TWIBEL, TWYBLE

"An iron tool used by paviers; a hulbert." (W) Two tools were given this name: A mattock or ax similar to a pickax, but, having instead of points, flat terminations, one of which was horizontal, the other perpen-dicular; and the tool used by carpenters and joiners for making mortises.

TWILL

A colloquialism for a quill or reed, and thus by extension, "a spool to wind yarn on." (H)

TYPE ORNAMENTS

The small decorations or printers' flowers used to ornament the printed page; separate blocks of copy, create borders on title pages, etc. The ornaments were cut individually by the white smith, and often made to order from the customer's design. "Brooks & Warrock, Jewelers . . . make and sell . . . cut and Ornaments for the Type-Press, with every other species of engraving." *Norfolk Herald* (Virginia), May 26, 1796. Similar type punches or sets of letters, rules and flowers were ordered by individuals with which to stamp Book Tags, *q.v.*

U

UMBRELLA

"Doctor Chancellor and the Rev. Mr. Duché were the first men in Philadelphia who were ever seen to wear umbrellas to keep off the rain. [During the eighteenth century] they were of oiled linen, very coarse and clumsy, with ratan sticks. Before, some doctors and ministers used an oiled linen cape hooked round their shoulders called a roquelane [but] only for severe storms." John F. Watson *Annals of Philadelphia* (Philadelphia, 1830). (See also KITTISOL, PARASOL.)

UNION SET

A contemporary description of the framed toilet looking glass set between two uprights and attached to a base of one or more small drawers. Many collectors today call these shaving mirrors.

UNIVERSAL TABLE

A late-eighteenth-century synonym for Pembroke Table, *q.v.*

URN

The general description of "a kind of vase of a roundish form, but biggest in the middle, like the common pitchers, now seldom used but in the way of ornaments over chimney pieces, Ec." (M) (See also COFFEE URN, KNIFE BOX, PEDESTAL, TEA URN, VASE.)

URN STAND

The small, handsome parlor stand to hold the tea urn; with a round, hexagonal, rectangular, or shaped top made with a shallow rim or gallery. The frieze usually served as a frame for a small slide or tray board on which the teapot sat, to be filled from the urn. Hepplewhite showed six designs for

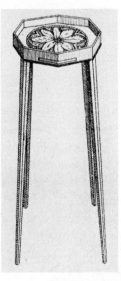

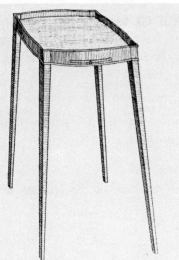

Two urn stands with slides as illustrated in Hepplewhite's *Guide* (London, 1794).

tea urn stands, "with their proper enrichments [decorative designs] which may be inlaid of various coloured woods, or painted and varnished. The slide draws out to set the tea-pot on; their height may be about 26 inches." A. Hepplewhite, *The Cabinet-Maker and Upholsterer's Guide* (London, 1794). (See also TEA URN.)

UTENSIL

The name for any "little domestick moveable, belonging principally to the kitchen; such are pots, pans, Ec." (M)

V

VALANCE, VALLANCE

The term for the drapery that "hangs around the tester of a bed." (W) Valances concealed the framework of the tester or top of the high four-post bed, adding a decorative finishing touch above the curtains. Valance also was the term for the short, gathered, or pleated hanging similarly used to hide the tops of window curtains.

VALICE, VALISE

A leather case in which to carry clothing while traveling. "Each dragoon [is to] furnish himself with a serviceable horse . . . a good saddle, bridle, mail-pillion and valice, holsters, and a breast-plate and crupper, a pair of boots and spurs, a pair of pistols, a sabre, and a cartouch-box, to contain twelve cartridges for pistols." *Connecticut Statutes* (Hartford), 1835.

VALLIONS

A common variation of the word, Valance, *q.v.*

VALLOW

A colloquialism for "a press for cheese." (H) (See also CHEESE PRESS.)

VANE

The term for "a plate that turns with the wind." (W) The Weather Vane, *q.v.,* or weathercock.

VASE

The name of "ornaments of sculpture placed on pedestals, representing the vessels of the ancients, as incense-pots, flower-pots, Ec. and occasionally enriched with basso relievo's." (M) "A vessel with a foot to it; a pot or ornament." (W) As such, the vase served two uses; it was a room decoration and sometimes also the outer case or container of the cistern, wine cooler, or knife-and-spoon cases. "The vases may be used [set atop pedestals or at the ends of sideboards] to hold water for the use of the butler, or iced water for drinking, which is inclosed in an inner partition, the ice surrounding it; or may be used as knife-cases in which case they are made of wood, carved, or inlaid; if used for water they may be made of wood or of copper japanned. The height of the vase is about 2 feet 3 inches." A. Hepplewhite, *The Cabinet-Maker and Upholsterer's Guide* (London, 1794). (See also KNIFE BOX, PEDESTAL, URN, and advertisement quoted under STONE CUTTER, Chapter 3.)

VASE-BACK CHAIR

A popular eighteenth-century term for the chair with a back splat in the shape of the classic vase. "Three designs [are shown] for hall chairs which are made all of wood . . . the designs with vase backs are new, and have been much approved." A. Hepplewhite, *The Cabinet-Maker and Upholsterer's Guide* (London, 1794).

VASE KNIFE CASE

The popular term for a Knife Case, *q.v.,* made in the classic vase shape. "They are usually made of satin or other light coloured wood and they may be placed at each end on the sideboards, or on a pedestal; the knives, Ec. fall into the body of the base, the top of which is kept up by a small spring which is fixed to the stem which supports the top; [they] may be made of copper, painted or japanned." A. Hepple-

white, *The Cabinet-Maker and Upholsterer's Guide* (London, 1794). "James Jacks, Jewellers . . . has for sale . . . an Assortment of elegant Vauze Knife Cases, with a variety of other Jewellery." *City Gazette and Daily Advertiser,* Charleston, South Carolina, October 5, 1795. (See also PEDESTAL, URN, VASE.)

VAT

The term, often spelled fat, for "a kind of vessel, used to hold wine, ale, beer, cyder, or any other liquor in the time of its preparation." (M) "A brewer's working tub." (W)

VELOM, VELLUM

"A finer sort of Parchment, [*q.v.*], prepared [in the same manner] from the skins of suckling-calves." *The Domestic Encyclopedia* (Philadelphia, 1821). "Finer, evener, and whiter than the common sort" of parchment. (M)

VENETIAN STOVE

Another name or variation of the "iron fireplace" designed by Benjamin Franklin and noted by Ince and Mayhew who provided, "Two Designs of Venetian or Philadelphia Stoves, which have been work'd . . . the bright work engraved is laid on black Japan'd Plates; they are very useful in preventing Smoak." *The Universal System of Household Furniture* (London, 1762). (See also FRANKLIN STOVE.)

VENICE GLASS

An old description signifying a "cup, goblet, or looking-glass made of fine crystal glass." (H)

VENTOSE

A synonym from the Anglo-Norman for Cupping Glass, *q.v.*

VERDEKYN

An old variation of the spelling of Firkin, *q.v.*

VERTICAL DIAL

The term for a kind of "sun-dial drawn on the plane of a vertical circle, or perpendicular to the horizon." (M) (See also SUNDIAL.)

VIAL

Anciently, any small vessel to hold liquids; later, a small stoppered bottle. "Send . . . 4 groce 8 oz. white glass Vials—2 groce 10 oz. Do." (Order, January 10, 1771, from James Carter, Williamsburg, Virginia, to London.) Frances Mason, *John Norton and Sons, Merchants of London and Virginia* (Richmond, 1935). (See also PHIAL.)

VICE

A tool; a clamp used by the smith and carpenter. "In smithery and other arts employed in metals, [this is] the instrument serving to hold fast anything they are at work upon, whether it be to be filed, bent, rivetted Ec." (M)

VINAIGRETTE

The term from the French *vinaigre,* vinegar, for the small, usually ornate hinged box of gold or silver in which an aromatic sponge was carried. These pocket boxes were used throughout the eighteenth and early nineteenth centuries until the use of vinegar and spices was superseded by smelling salts. (See also SMELLING BOTTLE.)

VINEYARD CAN

A contemporary synonym for the garden or watering can, made then as now with a handle and spout, of tin, copper, or sheet iron. "October 25, 1713. I was startled because I had spilt a whole Vineyard Can of water . . . and made the Reflection that our lives would shortly be spilt." Samuel Sewall, *Diary.*

VIOL, VIOLA

The common term for "a musical instrument of the same form with a violin, and struck like that with a bow." (M)

VIOL-DE-GAMBO

One of the early musical instruments, a six-stringed violin.

VIOLIN

The *"violino* or fiddle, a musical instrument mounted with four strings and struck or played with a bow." (M) "At night to my viollin in my dining-room, and afterwards to my lute there, and I took much pleasure to have the neighbours come forth into the yard to hear me." Samuel Pepys, *Diary,* November 21, 1660.

Violin as illustrated in Bonanni's *Cabinetto Armonica* (Rome, 1723).

VIRGIN

The popular eighteenth-century and early-nineteenth-century term for a stone hot-water bottle; considered by many, including a future Vice-President of the United States, a great improvement over the warming pan method of heating beds. "If I am cold in the night and an additional quantity of bed clothes will not answer the purpose of warming me, I will take a virgin to bed with me. What? Oh! Awful! What do I read? Do you know what a virgin is? It is a stone bottle, such as you buy with spruce beer and spa water, filled with boiling water, covered over or wrapped up in flannel and laid at a man's feet in bed . . . An old man, you see, may comfort himself . . . and not give the least jealousy to his wife, the smallest grief to his children, or any scandal to the world." (John Adams, from London December 27, 1786, to his wife, Abigail, at Cambridge.) *Letters of John Adams* (Boston, 1841).

VIRGINAL

"An old stringed musical instrument" (W) perhaps so called because it was popular with young ladies. In form, it was a small rectangular spinet, without legs, which might be set on a stand, table, or across one's knees. The plural often was used, written almost invariably as a "pair of virginals." "The wind carried the fire into the City . . . The [Thames] River [is] full of lighters and boats taking in goods, hardly one in three that had the goods of a house in, but that there was a pair of Virginalls in it." (Recording the Great Fire in London) Samuel Pepys, *Diary*. (See CLARI-CHORD.)

VITRINE

The term adopted from the French for a medal case or other small display cabinet with glass sides and door.

VIZARD

"A mask to disguise the face." (W) Carried and used in the manner of a lorgnette, these were satin, silk, or velvet masks on wire frames, attached to a holder, and often decorated with embroidery, seed pearls, or small gems. They came into fashion after the Restoration when many women attended the theater, no matter how licentious the dialogue. However, to disguise their features —and their enjoyment of the drama— many wore vizards or face masks, as Alexander Pope noted:

The fair sat panting at a courtier's play
And not a Mask went unimproved away;
The modest fan was lifted up no more,

And virgins smiled at what they blushed before.

"When the [Royal Theater] house began to fill, Lady Mary Cromwell put on her vizard, and so kept it on all the play; which of late is become a great fashion among the ladies, which hides their whole face. So to the Exchange to buy things with my wife; among others, a vizard for herself." Samuel Pepys, *Diary*, June 12, 1663. "Maskes, of velvett & sattin, Vizards, and Leather for Maskes" were listed in House of Parliament Rates, 1660, for Imports and Exports—*Statutes of the Realm* (London, 1819).

VOIDER

The contemporary term for "a vessel to carry table furniture in"; (W) that is, a large tray with a rim or basket for plates, dishes, and flatware and also the container in which leftover foods were removed.

VOLUME

The term for "a book, or writing, of a just bulk to be bound by itself." (M) (See also BOOK.)

W

WAFER BOX

". . . and 200 Wafers in a little Box." Samuel Sewall, *Diary,* January 19, 1722. The wafer was a small thin disc, about the size of a dime, used to seal letters, to attach papers such as a notary's statement to an affidavit, or to receive the impression of a

C. 1800 covered lignum vitae wafer box.

seal on any document such as a deed. To protect them from breaking, wafers were kept in a small box at the desk. These round, oval, or rectangular containers sometimes were footed, usually were finely made and, when of silver or pewter, engraved with a coat of arms or a cypher. Covers were removable by a top pull, or were hinged top-opening lids. One of the small receptacles or covered reservoirs in the large Standish, *q.v.,* was meant to hold wafers.

"Invoice of sundries to be shipt for Acct. of Ro[bert] C. Nicholas—1 Ream best Quarto writing Paper, 200 Dutch quills, 1 box best Wafers. Williamsburg, Virginia, October 27, 1773." Frances Mason, *John Norton and Sons, Merchants of London and Virginia* (Richmond, 1935).

Or wafers could be made at home in the kitchen: "Take very fine flour, mix it with the glair of eggs, isinglass, and a little yeast; mingle the materials; beat them well together, spread the batter, being made thin with gum water, on even tin plates, and dry them in an oven; then cut them for use. Make them what colour you please, by tingeing the paste with Brazil wood or vermilion for red; indigo or verditer, Ec., for blue; saffron and tumeric, or gamboge, Ec., for yellow." *The Domestic Encyclopedia* (Philadelphia, 1821). ". . . Best Philadelphia Glue, wrapping paper; Wafers, and wafer boxes . . . Charles Sigourney." *American Mercury* (Hartford, Connecticut), February 7, 1811.

WAFER IRONS

Two small, round or rectangular, iron griddles, hinged together, and attached to a long handle by which they were held over the fire to bake wafers or waffles. "To make Rose Wafers, Put the yolks of four eggs and three spoonfuls of Rose-water to a quart of flower, mingle them well, make them into a Batter with Cream and double-re-

fined Sugar, pour it on very thin, and bake it on Irons." John Nott, *Recipe Book* (London, 1723).

Early-eighteenth-century wafer irons, shown open and closed.

Heart-shaped wafer irons, perhaps made as a gift to an early-eighteenth-century bride. (Courtesy, Antiquarian and Landmarks Society, Inc.)

WAFER PRINT
A mold for wafers. (See also WAFER IRONS.)

WAFER TONGS
An alternative term for Wafer Irons, *q.v.*

WAFTER
A sword that had "the flat part placed in the usual direction of the edge, blunted for exercises." (H)   (See also BLUNT.)

583

WAGGONER
A kind of traveler's guide, this was a "routier, or book of charts, describing the seas, their coasts, Ec." (M)

WAG-ON-THE-WALL CLOCK
The collector's term for the inexpensive wooden-works wall clock, the weights or pendulum of which were not enclosed.

WAIN, WANE, WEYNE
All common terms for a wagon.

WAINSCOT CHAIR
Wainscot was used to describe large wall panels of deal and also the dado, or as Thomas Sheraton called it, "The wooden work which lines the walls of a room as high up as the surbase." *The Cabinet Dictionary* (London, 1803). The term also was used to denote any piece of furniture of solid wood construction, and is still used by collectors to mean any of the paneled or carved chairs of the early seventeenth century.

WAIT
A cant term for the "hautboy" (H) or oboe.

WAITER
A contemporary synonym for a Salver, *q.v.* "James Jacks, Jeweller and Watchmaker, next door below the President's, has Imported in the ship *Active,* Capt. Rinker, from London, and by other late arrivals from England, via Charleston . . . castors, waiters and decanters stands . . . castors with 4, 5, 8, and 10 cruets, plated waiters from 10 to 30 inches . . ." *Federal Gazette* (Philadelphia), January 7, 1800.

WAIT-TREBLE
A musical instrument, "a sort of Bagpipe," *q.v.* (H)

WALKER COLT
(See REVOLVER.)

WALKING STICK
A cane or staff, often nicely carved of handsomely grained hardwoods, with ornamental caps or heads of gold, silver, or ivory. "My fine crab-tree walking-stick, with a gold cap curiously wrought in the form of the Cap of Liberty, I give to my friend, and the friend of mankind, General Washington. If it were a sceptre, he has merited it, and would become it." Codicil, will of Benjamin Franklin, *Life and Essays* (Boston, 1845).

WALL BOX
Any small box, with or without a lid, made to be hung from a peg or nail, to hold articles in daily use, and thus, a general term for one type of candle box; spill box; pipe box; and less often, a salt box, each of which see.

C. 1800 painted wood wall boxes for candles or small utensils. (Courtesy, Antiquarian and Landmarks Society, Inc.)

WALL CLOCK
The common designation for any mural, or bracket, or shelf-clock case. "[They] are designated wall clocks as they are supported on a bracket, or hang on the wall, instead of resting on the floor. Besides being [often]

Popular mid-nineteenth-century wall clock had mahogany veneer case with ogee molding and thirty-hour movement by Chauncey Jerome of New Haven. Label with directions for setting and keeping the clock in order is inside of case which has landscape mezzotint behind glass panel.

Label in Jerome clock. (Courtesy, Connecticut Historical Society, Inc.)

an article of hall furniture, they are of frequent use in public offices, places of resort, Ec. They are usually of oak, frequently of mahogany, and sometimes of satinwood, or deal painted in flat tints . . . hatched with gilding." Blackie and Son, *The Cabinet-Maker's Assistant* (London, 1853). (See also LANTERN CLOCK.)

WALLER
An early colonial term for what today is more easily identified as a wall candle sconce: "Candle plates or Wallers of Brasse or Lattin" were listed in the House of Parliament Rates, 1660, for Imports and Exports—*Statutes of the Realm* (London, 1819). (See also SCONCE.)

Early-eighteenth-century brass waller or sconce. (Courtesy, Antiquarian and Landmarks Society, Inc.)

WALLET
Well into the nineteenth century this was the term for "a kind of bag, knapsack, double pouch." (W) Eighteenth-century references generally were to a kind of leather knapsack strapped to one's own or one's horse's back. "Before we marcht this Morning, every man took care to pack up some Buffalo Steaks in his wallet . . ." William Byrd, *History of the Dividing Line* [1729] (Richmond, 1866).

WALL GLASS, WALL MIRROR
(See MURAL LOOKING GLASS, PIER GLASS, LOOKING GLASS.)

WALL LIGHT
(See CANDLE PLATE, GIRANDOLE,

LOOKING GLASS ARMS, SCONCE, WALLER.)

WALLPAPER

Some papers, called painted papers or paper hangings, were imported from England shortly before 1700 to decorate the "forerooms" and best chambers in the homes of a few well-to-do merchants and officials. These early papers, usually 22-×32-inch sheets, had hand-colored stenciled designs; the stencils often were cut to order. Later, designs were printed from wooden blocks similar to those used in calico or linen printing, and the paper "squares" glued together in 6-, 9-, and 12-yard lengths, sometimes described as rolls. Paper was not manufactured in continuous rolls until about 1800.

The original French wallpapers were called dominoes or domino paper. These sheets, usually no more than 11×14 inches, were made by *dominotiers,* hence the name. Early dominoes were printed from blocks in one color, with other colors applied by hand to achieve polychrome effects.

The use of paper, even in one room, however, was too expensive a luxury for most. In New York in 1750, "The walls were whitewashed within and I did not anywhere see wallpaper with which the people of this country seem to be but little acquainted." Peter Kalm, *Travels in North America* (London, 1782).

In Boston eighteen years later, one paper hanger offered to trade his services to pay for purchases of other goods: "George Killcup, jun. Informs the Gentlemen and Ladies in Town and Country that he Paints Carpets and Other Articles, and papers rooms in the neatest manner. Said Killcup is ready to pay those he is indebted to in Painting or Papering Rooms." *Boston News-Letter,* March 17, 1768.

Although many ordered wallpapers to be painted in a variety of designs, landscape and marine scenes, others preferred monotones: "I suppose the Blue Room is too blue, the wood being of the same colour with the Paper, and so looks too dark. I would have you finish it as soon as you can, thus. Paint the Wainscot a dead white: Paper the Walls blue, Ec. tack the gilt Border round just above the Surbase and under the Cornish: If the Paper is not equal Coloured when pasted on, let it be brushed over again with the same Colour: —and let the Papier Machee musical figures be tack'd to the middle of the Ceiling;—when this is done, I think it will look very well." (Benjamin Franklin from London, June 22, 1767, to his wife at Philadelphia.) *Writings of Benjamin Franklin,* ed., A. H. Smyth (New York, 1907).

WALL-PLAT

"A mantel-shelf; a shelf fixed to the wall." (H) (See also SCONCE.)

WAMPUM

The word is from *wampi* or *wompi,* signifying *white* in the Massachusetts Indian language, and thus a description of the shells used in "wampum" belts. The term is used to designate shells, or "strings of shells used by the American Indians, as money. These, when united, form a broad belt, worn as an ornament or girdle, sometimes called *wampumpagne, wampeague,* or *wampumeague." Encyclopedia Americana* (Philadelphia, 1831). (See also PEAK.)

WARDROBE

Anciently this was the term for any room specifically set aside for chests, cupboards, lockers, or presses in which clothing was stored. During the late seventeenth century and throughout the eighteenth century the term signified a Clothes Press, *q.v.* However, as shown in Hepplewhite's design book, wardrobes eventually became "an article of considerable consequence, as the conveniences experienced in their use make them a necessary piece of furniture; they are usually made plain, but of the best mahogany. [One design] has three drawers [and] sliding shelves. The dimensions may be 4 feet long, 22 inches deep, 5 feet 6 inches high or more." *The Cabinet-Maker and Upholsterer's Guide* (London, 1794).

Wardrobe illustrated in Hepplewhite's *Guide* (London, 1794).

WARMING PAN

"A pan to warm a bed with." (W) This was the more common colonial term for what usually are called bed warmers by collectors today. "Ward & Bartholomew have just received additions to their stock of Goods, and are daily manufacturing many articles. Furniture, Brass Kettles, Warming pans, silver and other spoons, sugar tongs, snuffers and trays, tea trays and wine waiters, plated tea sets, castors . . ." *American Mercury* (Hartford, Connecticut), May 6, 1812.

"In taking the coals into the warming pan, remove therefrom any black coals in a burning state, and scatter upon those in the pan a little common salt; this will correct the unhealthy sulphurous vapour of the coals, and prevent their suffocating smell." Thomas Tegg, *Book of Utility* (London, 1828). (See also VIRGIN.)

Eighteenth-century brass warming pan with iron handle. (Courtesy, Antiquarian and Landmarks Society, Inc.)

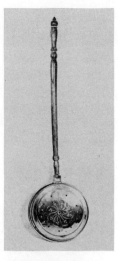

Eighteenth-century brass warming pan with turned wood handle. (Courtesy, Antiquarian and Landmarks Society, Inc.)

WARP
(See WEAVER'S LOOM.)

WASHBALL BOX

Washball was the common term for a ball or cake of hard soap. Handsomely turned hardwood, ivory, pottery, porcelain, pewter, silver, and brass boxes with covers were made to hold the usually scented washballs. They were kept on the dressing table or basin stand. (See also SOAP BOX.)

WASH BASIN

The basin specifically reserved for washing one's hands; made of pewter, silver, plated metal, pottery, or porcelain; one of the furnishings of the bed chamber or dressing room, and earlier of the dining parlor. "New Goods, Ward & Bartholomew Have lately received an assortment of Goods in their line [including] Brass Kettles; Brass Andirons; Shovel and Tongs; brass Warming Pans; do. Wash Basons . . ." *American Mercury* (Hartford, Connecticut), October

1, 1816. (See also EWER and BASIN, ROSE-WATER DISH.)

Redware wash basin.

Wash basin made at Bennington, Vermont.

WASH BOWL AND PITCHER

The common nineteenth-century term for what earlier had been known as a Ewer and Basin, *q.v.* Many were made in soft paste, stoneware, decorated ironstone, and usually kept on the wash stand in the kitchen or chamber.

Staffordshire wash bowl and pitcher. (Courtesy, Antiquarian and Landmarks Society, Inc.)

WASH HAND BASIN

The self-explanatory term for a chamber wash bowl, usually of pottery. ". . . be pleased to send A crate of Wash hand basons and Chamber Potts . . ." Order, February 6, 1773, from Thomas Everard, York County, Virginia, to London. Frances Mason, *John*

Norton and Sons, Merchants of London and Virginia (Richmond, 1935).

WASH HAND STAND

A more explicit contemporary term for the Basin or Wash Stand, *qq.v.* (See also quotation under STAND.)

WASH STAND

(See BASIN STAND.)

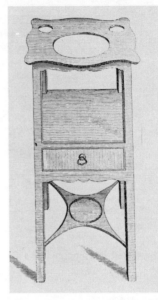

Basin stand illustrated in Hepplewhite's *Guide* (London, 1794).

Early-nineteenth-century wash stand by Isaac Wright & Co., Hartford, Connecticut. (Courtesy, Connecticut Historical Society, Inc.)

Wash tub.

WASH TUB
The later term for what first was called a Buck or Whirl-buck, *qq.v.*

WASK
Another name for a large wooden Beetle, *q.v.*

WATCH
"A pocket time-piece" (W) set in a silver, gold, steel, pinchback, brass, or copper-covered case and wound with a key. "To the Change after office, and received my watch from the watch-maker, and a very fine one it is, given me by Briggs, the scrivener. But, Lord, to see how much of my old folly and childishness hangs upon me still, that I cannot forbear carrying my watch in my hand, in the coach, all this afternoon, and seeing what o'clock it is one hundred times, and am apt to think with myself, how could I be so long without one." Samuel Pepys, *Diary,* May 13, 1665. (See also COMPASS DIAL, WATCH KEY.)

"A small portable movement or machine for the measuring of time, having its motion regulated by a spiral spring. Watches, strictly taken, are all such movements as shew the parts of time. As clocks are such as publish it, by striking on a bell, Ec. But commonly, the name watch is appropriated to such as are carried in the pocket, and clock to the large movement whether they strike or not." (M)

WATCH CALENDAR
An item of gentlemen's jewelry; a silver, gold, or pewter seal or fob attached to the watch by a link, or to the watch chain, fitted with a dial and movable plate to find any day in any month or year. "Samuel Brooks, Goldsmith, Jeweler, Ec., Philadelphia, executes every article . . . in the most elegant manner, of the best materials . . . His new improved Perpetual Calender Seals are calculated to point out the days of every month, as correct and easy as any Almanack and is a proper appendage to a watch . . ." *Federal Gazette* (Philadelphia), June 10, 1793.

WATCH FOB
(See FOB, WATCH SEAL.)

WATCH GLASS
Another name for the Half-hour Glass, *q.v.*

WATCH KEY
Keys to wind pocket watches were made by the silversmith and sold separately. Regarded as an article of jewelry and often worn on a chain, many had inset seals, ciphers, semiprecious stones. "London jewelry just received by Heydorn and Imlay. An exclusive assortment of Pearl, Topaz & Filigree Breast-Pins, Necklaces, Bracelets, ear and finger Rings—plain and Cornelian set Watch Keys of the newest fashion." *American Mercury* (Hartford, Connecticut), October 25, 1810.

WATCH PAPER
Now a separate collector's item, this was

Jacob Sargent watch paper. (Courtesy, Connecticut Historical Society, Inc.)

the tissue-thin paper label inserted in the back of a watch by the maker. (See also CLOCK PAPERS.)

WATCH SEAL

The term given the separate seal, later more commonly known as a watch fob, made of silver or gold by the smith who engraved it with cypher or crest; or by the lapidary who cut and carved seals from semiprecious stones. Some were made of gold or silver bands or circlets enclosing carved cornelian or other stones. The seal was attached to the watch by a series of links or fine chain, a plaited leather or silk thong or cord. "Dan Carrell . . . at the Sign of the Silver Coffee Pot . . . makes and sells watch-seals, coats of arms, and all manner of engraving on gold, silver, steel, etc. executed in the best manner . . ." *Charleston* (South Carolina) *City Gazette and Advertiser,* April 20, 1790. (See also CIPHER, SEAL, WATCH KEY.)

WATER CLOCK
(See HYDROSCOPE.)

WATER CROFT
A contemporary variation in spelling of water Carafe, *q.v.,* for "a glass jug to hold water." (H)

WATER CUP
A contemporary term for what today is called a water glass. "James and Arthur Jarvis . . . have just opened a Variety of Glass, viz. . . . elegant cut sweetmeat glasses, glass water cups . . ." *The New-York Gazette and The Weekly Mercury,* December 6, 1771.

WATER DIPPER
The long-handled tin or wood ladle, or long-handled cup, used at the cistern or well or other common water-supply source. "Many a traveller came out of his way to see me and the inside of my house, and, as an excuse for calling, asked for a glass of water. I told them that I drank at the pond, and pointed thither, offering to lend

them a dipper." Henry David Thoreau, *Walden* (Boston, 1854).

WATER GAGE
(See HYDROMETER.)

WATER GLASS
(See CLEPSYDRA, HOURGLASS.)

WATER ORGAN
(See HYDRAULICON.)

WATER PIPE
(See HOOKAH.)

WATER POT
A water pitcher, or watering can. (See also AIGUIERE, CARAFE, VINEYARD CAN.)

Watering pot; c. 1790 popular print.

WAX FIGURES, SCULPTURE
Small works of art formed of melted wax, colored and hardened. The still-life fruits and miniature portraits, usually set in cases or frames and sometimes protected by glass covers, are prized particularly today. "At present, wax is used for imitations of anatomical preparations, or of fruits; it also serves the sculptor for his models and studies; also for little portrait figures in *basso relievo.* The latter can be executed with delicacy and beauty." *Encyclopedia Americana* (Philadelphia, 1831).

WAX JACK
Another name for the Taper Jack, *q.v.,* or sealing-wax dispenser for the desk.

WAXLIGHT

"A wax candle." (W) (See also BOU-GIE.)

WAX PAN

The proper term for the removable nozzle or insert with a slight projecting rim set into the top of fine candlesticks for ease in removing candle ends. The separately made and sold Save-all, *q.v.*, was an inexpensive form of wax pan. Candleholders made with a projecting rim around the socket to catch drippings are said to have fixed nozzles or pans.

WAYWISER

The contemporary colloquialism for "an instrument to measure distances on a road, a Pedometer or Perambulator," *qq.v.* (W)

WEATHERCOCK

(See WEATHER VANE.)

WEATHERGLASS

The contemporary synonym for "a glass to show the weather by" (W) or "a barometer" and less often, "a thermometer." (J) "Walked to Greatorex's and have bespoke a weather-glasse of him." Samuel Pepys, *Diary,* September 22, 1662. "This day Greatorex brought me a very pretty weather-glasse for heat and cold." Ibid., March 23, 1663. (See also BAROMETER.)

WEATHER VANE

Both weather vane and weathercock are old terms to describe the plate, usually of metal, set on a vertical spindle so that it can turn with the wind and show the direction from which it is blowing. Vane is a corruption in conversation of fane, a Middle English word for the ornamental plate of tin, iron, copper, or brass. The more specific weathercock was and is applied to the vane in the form of a cock or rooster which turns with its head to the wind, or as Chaucer reported,

> *a Wedrcok that turneth his face*
> *With every wind.*

(See also FANE, FLY.)

New England weathervane. (*Newtown Bee,* photo by R. Scudder Smith.)

WEAVER'S LOOM

"The art of producing cloth, by the combination of fibres, is performed on a frame called a loom . . . On inspecting a piece of cloth, it is found to consist of two distinct sets of threads running perpendicularly to each other. The longitudinal threads constitute the warp, while the transverse threads are called the woof, weft, or filling . . . the warp is wound upon a cylindrical beam or roller. From this the thread passes through a harness, composed of moveable parts, called the heddles, consisting of a series of vertical strings, connecting to frames, and having loops through which the warp passes. . . . when they are moved reciprocally up and down, the relative position of the alternate threads of the warp is reversed. Each time that the warp is opened by the separating of its alternate threads, a shuttle, containing the woof, is thrown across it, and the thread or woof is immediately driven into place by a frame called a lay, furnished with thin reeds or wire placed among the warp like the teeth of a comb. The woven piece, as fast as it is completed, is wound up on a second beam opposite to the first." *Encyclopedia Americana* (Philadelphia, 1831).

WEIGH-BALK

A colloquialism for scales; properly the beam of the scales. (See also BALK.)

WELCH HOOK, WELSH HOOK

The name of a gardener's tool; "a kind of bill or axe having two edges." (H)

WELL-WINDER

Earlier called a Jack-roll, this was a long circular, wrought-iron spike similar in shape to the spit rod. It was inserted in a rounded block or shaved-off log of hardwood with 3 to 5 inches of the rod extending at one end, the iron handle section from the other. Set in rests or locks above the well-curb, the winder was used to let down and bring up the water bucket on a rope or chain.

Well-winder or Jack-roll in use at well; c. 1790 print.

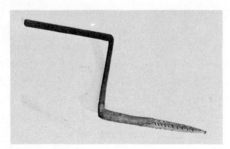

Well-winder.

WELSH CUPBOARD
(See WELSH DRESSER.)

WELSH DRESSER

A piece of kitchen furniture that combined the functions of cupboard and dresser or sideboard. This is the collector's term for a set of shallow open shelves so set above a deeper, closed cupboard that the top of the cupboard projects slightly and thus forms a table or dresser board.

WESTRIL

A term for the "short, underhand cudgel." (H)

WHATNOT

A cant term, apparently a contraction of what-does-it-not-hold? for an open cabinet or set of shelves for the display of ornaments, figurines, or small collections. Some were free-standing and rectangular; others were made to fit into a corner. "The whatnot serves occasional or incidental use, and belongs, indifferently, to the dining-room, drawing-room, or parlours; it should coincide with the proper character . . . of the apartment." Blackie and Son, *The Cabinet-Maker's Assistant* (London, 1853). "A very useful piece of furniture for the cottage parlor is one made in a great variety of forms, called a what-not by the English, and an etagere by the French. It usually stands in the corner of the room, and is employed as a stand for little articles, curiosities, books, or whatever trifles of useful and ornamental character may accumulate with no other special place devoted to them." A. J. Downing, *The Architecture of Country Houses* (New York, 1850). (See also ETAGERE, OMNIUM.)

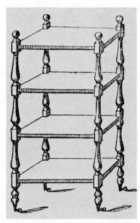

Whatnot as illustrated by A. J. Downing in *The Architecture of Country Houses* (New York, 1850).

WHEEL CHAIR
(See MACHINE CHAIR.)

WHEEL LOCK

The type of gunlock in which the powder was fired by the friction of a small wheel against a piece of iron pyrites or flint; the term used to distinguish a type of Musket, *q.v.,* so fitted from those with other types of gunlocks. (See also FIRELOCK, FLINTLOCK, MATCHLOCK.)

WHERRY CUP

A large cup or glass used for drinking wherry, a liquor made from the pulp of crab apples after the juice is pressed out.

WHETSTONE

"A stone to sharpen edge tools." (W) Whetstone, *noraculite,* hone, or whetstone slate, a kind of sandstone "dug up chiefly in northern counties of England, and near Easton and Oby, near Reading, Pennsylvania. It is a dusky yellow colour . . . and affords a useful article of trade . . . employed for sharpening knives, scythes, bills and other implements of rural and domestic economy." *The Domestic Encyclopedia* (Philadelphia, 1821). This was the stone used in the grinding wheel, and a synonym for that tool.

WHIFFING CUP

"A little cup," (H) perhaps a brandy snifter.

WHINGER, WHINYARD

In weaponry, "A large crooked sword, a cimeter." (W)

WHIP

Part of a lady's or gentleman's riding costume as well as a coachman's working accessory, whips were made in a variety of lengths of plaited leather or catgut. (Catgut or catling was the contemporary term for any string or thong made of sheep intestine.) Handles were made by jewelers and by turners of small wares from hardwood, ivory, whalebone, or waxed leather; were carved, inlaid with silver, gold, or brass; often bound with fine silver or gold wire. "Philadelphia made whips. Imported and sold at 129 Broad Street by Daniel Carrell; They are of whale bone and cat-gut, strongly mounted with silver, and sold cheaper than can be imported from England of the same quality. Any persons that would choose to send for whips of a particular description, by leaving their orders, shall be punctually complied with." *Charleston* (South Carolina) *City Gazette and Advertiser,* January 6, 1790. Whips had other uses in private disputes and public discipline: "September 10, 1707. Midweek, sentenced a woman that whipt a man, to be whipt; said a woman that had lost her Modesty was like Salt that had lost its Savor; good for nothing but to be cast on the Dung-hill." Samuel Sewall, *Diary.*

WHIPPING POST

The town or public "post to whip vagrants at." (W)

WHIPSAW

One of the tools, "a large saw for two persons." (W)

WHIRL-BOUK, WHIRL-BUCK

The colloquialism for a churn or bucket, "which is worked by whirling or turning it around," (H) as a small butter churn might be twirled between the hands, or a washtub moved to agitate artcles being laundered. (See also BUCK.)

WHIRLIGIG

Earlier the name of a type of fast carriage; later the name for a child's toy, "a whirling plaything for children." (W) (See also GIG.)

WHISHINS

A colloquialism for cushions. (See also QUISSIN.)

WHISK, WHISK BROOM

"A small besom," (W) a broom or brush for dusting cloth. Whisk (broom corn): "I enclose you some whisk seeds, it is a kind of corn, good for creatures; it must be planted in hills like Indian corn. The tops make the best thatch in the world, and of the same are made the whisks you use for velvet. I brought it from Virginia." (February 21, 1757.) *Writings of Benjamin Franklin,* ed., A. H. Smyth (New York, 1907).

WHISKET, WISKET

"A basket, a kind of scuttle," (W) made of straw or broom. (See also SCUTTLE.)

WHISKIN

The early colonial synonym for a shallow brown or wooden drinking bowl. "And we will have a whiskin at every rushbearing; a wassel cup at yule; a seed-cake at fastens [Lent]." *The Two Lancashire Lovers* (1640). (See also BROWN BOWL.)

WHISTLE

A small wind instrument, producing a shrill tone; basically a wood, metal, or ceramic tube, made either with four or six holes and thus played as one would a pipe, or with one opening into which the user blows. (See also BIRDCALL, STONE BIRD, QUAIL PIPE.)

Pewter whistle.

WHISTLING TANKARD

A product of the collector's wishful imagination, for it never existed. Metalsmiths usually pierced a small hole in any hollow casting or any seamed hollow part such as a finial or handle. This was done so that air, expanded by heat, could escape when the part to be added was soldered on. Not understanding the simple working necessity, amateur collectors have enjoyed the legend that the hole was provided so that ye olde tavern habitués could whistle for another drink.

WHITE CHAIRS, WHITE FURNITURE

The general term for furniture delivered unfinished; that is, not stained or painted. Thus Kemble Thomas of Philadelphia was billed for

"5 mo 24th 1745   To 6 white
                     Chairs   0. 18. 0.

10 mo 5   "   To 6 arch
              head Chairs
              & Couch   4. 4. 4."

Solomon Fussell Account Book, 1748–51, Stephen Collins papers, Mss. Division, Library of Congress. (See also note under TABLE CHAIR.)

WHITTLE

A colloquialism for (1) a blanket, (2) a fringed mantle of coarse shaggy cloth, "almost invariably worn by country women out of doors," (H) or (3) a knife.

WHORLBAT

Another name for the hurlbat, "a kind of gauntlet or leathern strap loaden with plummets," (M) whirled above the thrower's head to add momentum, then flung at a foe.

WICKER CHAIR
(See BASKET CHAIR.)

WIG CURLER
(See CRISPING IRON.)

WIG STAND

A small wood table standard with a mushroom-shaped or globe top to hold the wig not being worn.

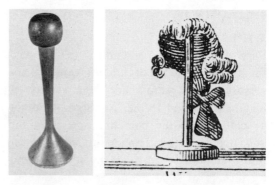

Turned maple wig stand. (Courtesy, Antiquarian and Landmarks Society, Inc.)

Wig on wig stand; c. 1790 popular print.

WILLOW-PATTERN CHINA
(See CANTON CHINA.)

WIMBLE

The name, from the Middle English term, for several tools used to bore holes, as a gimlet or an auger. Also a kind of long narrow sharp-pointed hollow rod or scoop with which to clean out the bored hole. "There is also gathered of the Larch tree a liquid Rosin very like in colour and in substance to the whiter hony [which] runneth out of the stocke of the tree when it has been gored even to the heart with a great and long auger and wimble." John Gerard, *The Herball or Generall Historie of Plantes* (London, 1636).

WIND GLASS
Another name for the hurricane shade. (See also HURRICANE GLASS.)

WIND GUN
A gun discharged by compressed air. (W) (See also AIR GUN.)

WINDLE
Something that is round, and therefore a "machine or wheel on which yarn is wound . . . [or a] bushel basket." (H)

WINDOW STOOL
The more common term late in the eighteenth century for the small upholstered seat earlier called a French Stool, *q.v.* These seats, usually wide enough to seat two, were designed for use in window recesses. Of those shown in his design book, Hepplewhite suggested some as "proper for mahog-

Window stool made by Lemuel Adams, 1796, Hartford, Connecticut. (Courtesy, Connecticut Historical Society, Inc.)

any or japan, covered with linen or cotton to match the chairs, [and others] peculiarly adapted for an elegant drawing-room of japanned furniture; the covering should be of taberray or morine, of a pea-green, or other light colour. The size of window stools must be regulated by the size of the place where they are to stand; their heights should not exceed the seats of the chairs [in the room]." *The Cabinet-Maker and Upholsterer's Guide* (London, 1794).

WINDSOR CHAIR
A number of imaginative histories have written to explain the origin of the Windsor chair. Among those most often repeated is that these stick chairs were so styled because George III once stopped at a subject's cottage near Windsor, and found the chair he was given so comfortable he ordered copies made for the palace. However, since George did not ascend the throne until 1760, that version is easily discounted. The version preferred by many American collectors is that such chairs first were manufactured in the mid-eighteenth century at Windsor, Connecticut. This also must be discounted since this chair style, called Windsor, was being made just after 1700 in England. That the term had for some time signified a specific type of chair is im-

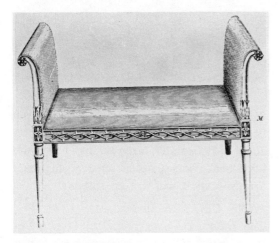

Window stool illustrated in Hepplewhite's *Guide* (London, 1794).

plied in the inventory of the estate of Samuel Powell, of Philadelphia, March 5, 1749, where "3 old wooden chears & 1 Winzer ditto" were listed among the parlor furniture and valued at 10 shillings. *Will Book I,* p. 231. Windsor chairs thus might have been found in any part of the house, including the hallways, as, for example, on February 15, 1770, Virginian Mann Page ordered "1 Dozn. Windsor Chairs for a Passage" from London. Frances Mason, *John Norton and Sons, Merchants of London and Virginia* (Richmond, 1935); hence disposing of a third popular theory that Windsors were used only as garden seats. The last version apparently has been based on the fact that many of the eighteenth-century Windsor chairs were originally painted green, black, red, blue or in whatever other color the first owner preferred. It is difficult for the novice collector to believe that the paint should not be removed. Terms generally used today to describe

Windsor writing-arm chair. (Courtesy, Antiquarian and Landmarks Society, Inc.)

Windsor writing-arm chair with candle and desk drawer.

Continuous-arm Windsor chair. (Courtesy, Antiquarian and Landmarks Society, Inc.)

variations in Windsor-chair styles include bow-back, captain's chair, chicken-coop, comb-back, cupid's bow, double bow-back, hoop-back, horseshoe, stepped or step-back Windsor, stick, and writing-arm chair.

WINE CISTERN
The round, oval, or rectangular open vessel in which wine bottles were cooled, usually set on a stand or made with attached

legs. Seventeenth-century wine cisterns were of silver, copper, brass, or pewter. The lead-lined wooden cistern, made of mahogany or other handsome wood with brass hoops and mounts, probably was made first in the early eighteenth century. (See also CELLARET, CISTERN, WINE COOLER, for variations in size and name.)

American c. 1840 pewter wine cooler. (*Newtown Bee*, photo by R. Scudder Smith.)

WINE COOLER

The term applied generally to the handsome silver vessel used on the sideboard to keep a single bottle cool.

WINE GOGGLER

A contemporary cant term for the decanter stand designed to hold two bottles side by side, the circular or hoop holders resembling the round spectacle frames commonly called goggles. "James Jacks . . . Has imported in the ship *William Penn,* and *Brig Fly* from London . . . a large assortment of goods [including] Wine goglers and knife trays silver edge . . . Large plated tea trays, from 6 inches to 30 inches . . ." *Federal Gazette* (Philadelphia), November 27, 1797.

WINE KEEPER

This was a contemporary synonym for the Cellaret, *q.v.* or *garde du vin.* "R. Green,

No. 81 Broad-way . . . has for sale . . . neat mahogany wine-keepers with Brass Hoops and Handles." *Independent Journal, or the General Advertiser* (New York), November 9, 1785.

WINE TABLE

Any of the late eighteenth-century small tables specifically designed to serve after-dinner drinkers were called wine tables. Specific designs often were given specific names, such as the Social Table, *q.v.*

WING BOOKCASE

A late-nineteenth-century term sometimes used to describe the three-part or break-front bookcase. (See BREAKFRONT, Chapter 5.)

WING CHAIR

The modern name for the upholstered easy chair with high back and wings; *i.e.,* the side projections called cheeks in the eighteenth century, and with turnover or scroll arms. (See also EASY CHAIR, SADDLE CHEEK CHAIR.)

WINTER

A kitchen hearth utensil, a kind of iron plate or trivet to hang on the grate for "warming anything on." (H)

WINTERPIECE

The common description of a painting of the winter landscape. "Let the work imitate the season it is intended to represent; as if you intend it for a winter-piece, represent felling of woods, sliding upon the ice, fowling by night, hunting of bears or foxes in the snow, making the trees everywhere naked, or laden with snow or a hoar-frost; the earth bare, without greenness, flowers, or cattle; the air thick or heavy; the water frozen; with carts passing over it, and boys playing upon it." (M)

WITHDRAWT

A colloquial term for a "Chest of Drawers," *q.v.* (H)

WOODCUTS

Engravings or prints made by cutting in wood "are much used by booksellers, Ec. to save the higher expense of engraving on copper, (also in calico printing). The cutters in wood begin by preparing a block of wood, usually of box or pear-tree; on this, when made very smooth, they draw their design with a pen or pencil, exactly as they would have it printed; or they fasten the design drawn on paper upon the block with paste, and a little vinegar, the drawing being turned towards the wood. When the paper is dry, they wash it gently off with a sponge dipped in water, till nothing is left on the block but the strokes of ink that form the design, which mark out what part of the block is to be cut off very carefully with the points of knives, chisels, or gravers, according to the delicacy of the work." *The Domestic Encyclopedia* (Philadelphia, 1821.)

WOOD DOOR FITTINGS

Strap hinges and latches carved from wood in the same shapes as those commonly made of iron. "Usually a good deal of whittling was expended on the latch, which was made of wood, in the form of an iron one." Henry David Thoreau, *The Maine Woods* (Boston, 1864). (See also HACKADAY, LOCK, STRAP HINGE.)

WOODEN NUTMEG

The nutmeg, one of the most popular imported spices, was so expensive as to be accounted a luxury. Some housewives wanted wooden nutmegs for "show." Others purchased the imitations unknowingly and so were cheated. "The whole race of Yankee Peddlers in particular are proverbial for dishonesty. They go forth annually in the thousands to lie, con, cheat, swindle, in short to get possession of their neighbors property in any manner it can be done with impunity. Their ingenuity in deception is confessedly great. They warrant broken watches to be the best timekeepers in the world; sell pinchbeck trinkets for gold; and always have a large assortment of wooden nutmegs and stagnant barometers." Thomas Hamilton, *Men and Manners in America* (Philadelphia, 1833). (See also NUTMEG GRATER.)

WOODENWARE

(See TREEN.)

WOOF

(See WEAVER'S LOOM.)

WOOLPACK

Another name for "A soft seat," (W) or cushion.

Eighteenth-century woolwinders with clock or measuring device. (Courtesy, Antiquarian and Landmarks Society, Inc.)

WOOLWINDER

Usually an X-shaped device, or two crossed bars, attached to a spindle so that they might be turned, and the spindle set into a simple pedestal standard. Yarn or wool, after being spun into threads, was wound into skeins on the X-frame to keep it smooth and free from tangles. (See also NIDDY-NODDY; SWIFT.)

WORK LIGHTS

A general term for those candleholders or lamps kept in one particular place or room because they were regularly needed there;

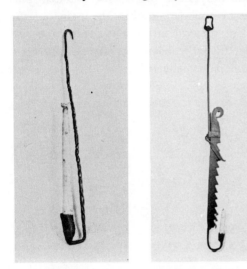

Early-eighteenth-century hanging work light.

Hanging work light with ratchet to adjust height.

Mid-eighteenth-century adjustable height work light to hang from beam or be set on table.

Mid-eighteenth-century hanging or standing work light. Courtesy, Antiquarian and Landmarks Society, Inc.

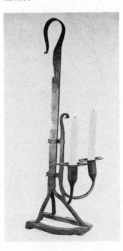

as, for example, the light usually suspended from a beam above a loom, or a light similarly suspended near the hearth so that the cook could check the progress of food cooking over the embers.

WORK POCKET

The contemporary term for a woman's large cloth handbag or wallet with a fold-over flap cover usually worn suspended by a ribbon or plaited cord from the sash, or pinned to the girdle or apron, thus becoming the extra "pocket" to hold sewing accessories and other small possessions. Many were embroidered in a flame stitch or crewel work pattern. The use, and the contents of one were described thusly:

"Lost in the 10th inst. between Wells's Tavern in East-Hartford & Scantic Meeting-House, Windsor, a Green silk Work Pocket, containing 1 buff colored shawl, 1 white cambrick pocket Handkerchief, 1 morroco Money-Purse containing $5 in Bills of this State and between 2 and 3 dollars in change, 1 Thread-case, 1 Thimble, and part of a paper of Pins. Whoever has found the same and will leave it at this office, or at Wells's Tavern, or give information where it may be found, shall be generously rewarded." *American Mercury* (Hartford, Connecticut), May 30, 1811.

Early-eighteenth-century flame-stitch work pocket. (Courtesy, Antiquarian and Landmarks Society, Inc.)

WORKTABLE

A contemporary term for the fitted sewing table or stand with a square or rectangular

599

top, under which a work pocket or bag was suspended from a light frame on runners. These were made from the late eighteenth century through the nineteenth in the prevailing furniture design. "Ladies work tables are popular English furniture for the sitting room and are usually made of mahogany or walnut and fitted up with a silk bag, attached to a frame that draws out. This bag is a very convenient receptacle of various articles of needlework, which otherwise would perhaps lie about upon chairs or sofas, to the discomfort of all parties, and the detriment of the work itself." A. J. Downing, *The Architecture of Country Houses* (New York, 1850).

WORK TABLES
Thomas Sheraton's term for a Nest of Tables, *q.v.*

WORM
A "long spirally winding pewter Pipe placed in a tub of water to cool and thicken the vapors in distilling of Spirits." (B) (See also STILL.)

WOVEN CLOTHS
(See TEXTILES and LEATHER, APPAREL at the back of this section.)

WRAST
A term for "a kind of Cittern," *q.v.* (H)

WRITING FIRE SCREEN
A combination high-backed writing table, or shallow desk, and fire screen popularized late in the eighteenth century. The reading flap or fall front of the desk covered shallow shelves or pigeonholes seldom of more than four-inch depth, in the top section. Space below the desk area was left open. The case, the back of which served as a screen, was set above high legs. Thus, the writer could stretch his feet to be warmed by the fire.

X

XYLOGRAPHY
The term, derived from the Greek words for wood and I write, sometimes applied to wood engraving.

XYLOPHONE
From the Greek words for wooden plus tone or sound, and thus the name of the ancient musical instrument made of a row of graduated wooden bars, struck with small hammers or mallets.

Y

YARD-OF-ALE
(See ALE-YARD.)

YARDWAND
A measure, the "stick to measure a yard by; a yard." (W) (See also METE-ROD; METEWAND.)

YARN WINDER
Another name for the Woolwinder, *q.v.*

YARRINGLES, YARRINGLE BLADES
Two old names for "a kind of reel or instrument with which hanks of yarn are wound on to clues, or balls." (M). (See SWIFT; WOOLWINDER; YARN WINDER.)

YETLING
At the kitchen hearth, "A small iron pan

with a bow [bale] handle and three feet;"
(H)   the stew pot.

YOKE-BACK CHAIR
A term used to describe a simple or country type of eighteenth-century chair because the top rail of the back suggested the double curve of the yoke used for carrying water or milk pails.

YO-YO
Trade-mark for a child's play toy. (See also JOUJOU.)

Z

ZILTER
Synonym for the powdering or "salting tub." (H)

ZITHER
The Austrian version of the ancient cithern, made with 30 to 40 wire strings above a shallow sounding box, and played by striking the strings with the thumb and fingers.

APPAREL

A general term including any "clothing, raiment, or dress" (W)   worn by men, women, or children to "dress, deck, adorn or to set off" their appearance. (W)

Items of apparel listed in the House of Parliament Rates, 1660, for Imports and Exports—*Statutes of the Realm* (London, 1819) included: "Bast or straw hats knotted and plain; Buskins of leather; Capps; children's capps; Night caps of Sattin, Velvet, silke knit, woollen, linnen; cawles of linnen for women; clokes of felt; French silk garters; cruell, lether, silk, velvet, woollen counterfiete gold and silver girdles; gantletts; Hatts of beaver, wool, felt, silk, straw, worsted; Hose of cruel; Mittens; Neckerchirs; Petticoates of Silk; Stockings; Monmouth plain and trimmed capps; cloke baggs; Doublets of leather; plaine gloves of Sheepe, kidd or Lambs leather, fringed and stitched with silke, furred with long wool, Bucksleather; cruel hatbands; leather, silk, woollen, kersey stockings; Wast Coates of Wadmoll, Cotton, Kerseys, Flannel, Worsted knit and woollen knit."

Terms for individual items of apparel most often encountered by the collector include the following:

ACKETOUN, ACTON
The name given the leather jacket, or tunic "sometimes worn under a coat of mail." (H)

ALEXANDRES
The popular name given to fashionable kid gloves imported from Paris in the 1820–40 period.

APRON
"A part of dress worn before" (W)   or over the gown. (See quotation under TUCKER. See also APRON-MAN, Chapter 3.)

BALDRICK
A contemporary name for "a girdle [or sash]. By some it is explained a bracelet; but I have not found it in that sense." (J)

BAND
An early term for a kind of man's cravat or neckcloth; also called a falling band because the two long ends of the cravat "fell" or hung down over the upper part of the gown.

BARBE
A kind of scarf, hood, or muffler which "covered the lower part of the face." (H)

BARMCLOTH, BARMSKIN, BARNSKYN

Variations of a colloquial term for the workman's "leather apron," (H) especially for those made of sheepskin.

BARVEL

"A short leathern apron; a bib." (H)

BASNET, BASSENET

Terms originally applied to a "type of light helmet . . . often very magnificently adorned," (H) and a cant term for a close-fitting cap.

BAXTER

A warm-weather "snowshoe"; a wide board strapped to the boot for ease in walking over sand or mud.

BEARING CLOTH

The embroidered cloth, often richly figured in gold or silver thread, in which children were wrapped at their christening.

> *Here's a sight for thee;*
> *Look thee, a bearing-cloth for a squire's*
>   *child!*

Shakespeare, *The Winter's Tale,* III, iii.

BELT

Made of leather, silk, or other textile, this was the uniform "girdle from which a sword, or some weapon is commonly hung." (J)

BONNET

Bonet. (Courtesy, Antiquarian and Landmarks Society, Inc.)

BOOT-HOSE

"Stockings to serve for boots; or spatter-dashes." (J)

BOOTS

Generally, "a shoe; specifically, a covering for the leg, used by horsemen." (J) ". . . Ladies Prunella Boots and Shoes, thick or thin soles, with or without heels. Morocco, Seal Skin and Leather, do. French Morocco and Bronze do. Misses Prunella Boots and shoes, thick or thin, with or without heels. Morocco do. Children's 500 pair Boots & Shoes, assorted. Gentlemen's Dress Boots, Bootees, Shoes and Pumps. Common do. Also a good supply of very stout Coarse Boots, Bootees, and Shoes for Men and Boys. All rips either sew'd, pegged or nailed, repaired free of charge to the purchaser. John Hutchins." *Columbian Register* (New Haven, Connecticut), December 12, 1829.

Half jack boots. (Courtesy, Antiquarian and Landmarks Society, Inc.)

Boy's leather boots. (Courtesy, Antiquarian and Landmarks Society, Inc.)

BROGUES

A general term for coarse, heavy shoes; "a sort of shoe made of the rough hide of any beast, commonly used by the wilder Irish." (H)

BUFF-JERKIN

"A leathern waistcoat, made of buff." (H)

BUSK

The term derived from the French *bois* or *bosco,* for wood, to describe a strip of wood, steel or whalebone "worn by women to strengthen their stays." (J) (See also SCRIMSHAW, STAYS.)

BUSKIN

"A kind of [leather or felt] shoe or half boot adapted to either foot, and worn by either sex." (M) The word is derived from the Dutch *broseken* for a "shoe which comes to the midleg." (J)

CABRIOLE, CAPRIOLE

"A lady's head-dress." (H)

CALSONS

"Close [fitting] linen trousers for men." (H)

CAMIS, CAMISADO, CAMISOLE

"A light, loose dress or robe, of silk or other material, [sometimes] a white shirt." (H)

CAP, Men's and Boys'

The term for "the garment that covers the head." (J)

> *Here is the cap your worship did be-*
>   *speak—*
> *Why this was molded on a porringer,*
> *A velvet dish.*
>
>   Shakespeare, *Taming of the Shrew*

"Charles Iankowith has constantly on hand a general assortment of all kinds of Russian and American Furs . . . Gentlemen's Grecian, Swiss, Bolivar, London and American Foraging, Sporting, Fishing, Travelling, and Fatigue Caps—also children's Fancy Caps, of every description, made to order." *Columbian Register* (New Haven, Connecticut), September 26, 1829. "Caps at wholesale and retail . . . an extensive assortment of Men's and Boy's Sea Otter, Hair and Fur Seal Caps, Also Patent Leather and Otter Caps . . . as low as can be found in the city. J. Atwater & Son. No. 52 State St." *Columbian Register* (New Haven,

Columbian Sentinel (New Haven, Connecticut), November 7, 1829.

Connecticut), November 7, 1829. "The skin of the Otter is very Soft and the Swedes make Caps and Socks of it . . ." William Byrd, *History of the Dividing Line* [1729] (Richmond, 1866).

CAPE

"The neck-piece of a cloak." (J)

CAPOUCH

"A monk's hood." (J)

CAPUCHIN

"A female garment, consisting of a cloak and hood, made in imitation of the dress of capuchin monks." (J)

CASSAQUE, CASSOCK

The term from the French *casaque,* for a "close garment, now generally that which clergymen wear under their gowns." (J) "A loose outward coat, particularly a military one." (H)

CASTOR

A name for the beaver, and thus "a fine hat made of the fur of a beaver." (J)

CAUL

"The net in which women enclose their hair." (J)

CHIOPPINE

"A high shoe, worn by ladies." (J)

CLOAK

From the Saxon word *lach,* the term for "the outer garment with which the rest are covered." (J)

CLOG

"A kind of additional shoe, worn by women to keep them from wet; a wooden shoe." (J) (See also PATTEN.)

COAT

"The upper garment." (J)

COIF, COIFFURE

Any headdress but specifically, "a lady's cap; a serjeant's cap." (J)

CRAVAT

"A neckcloth; anything worn about the neck." (J)

CREEPER

A popular name for "a kind of patten or clog worn by women." (J)

DICKEY

"A woman's under-petticoat; also a leathern apron." (H)

DOMINIE, DOMINO

The term for a "kind of hood; a kind of long dress." (W) "30th November 1771.

Gentleman's fashions from Paris, 1824, a time when knee breeches gradually were going out of style, replaced by fully cut trousers.

Dear Mamma, you don't know the fation here—I beg to look like other folk. You don't know what a stir would be made in Sudbury Street, were I to make my appearance there in my red Dominie and black Hatt. But the old cloak and bonnett together will make me a decent bonnett for common ocation aunt says." *Diary of Anna Green Winslow* (Boston, 1894).

DOUBLET
"The inner garment of a man; the waist coat; so-called from being double for warmth, or because it makes the dress double." (J)

DRAWERS
"The lower part of a man's dress." (J)

FARTHINGALE
"A hoop; circles of whalebone used to spread the petticoat to a wide circumference." (J)

FAVOR
"Anything worn openly as a token." (J) "A knot of ribands upon a hat." (W)

FONTANGE
"A knot of ribands worn on the head." (W) ". . . on the top of the head-dress." (J)

FROCK
The name commonly given any "dress; coat; a kind of close coat for men." (J) A long, loose garment; "a kind of loose coat." (H)

FROSTS
Clogs with spiked soles to enable the wearer to walk on ice more easily; "January 19, 1717. Great rain and very slippery; was fain to wear Frosts." Samuel Sewall, *Diary*.

FUR
"Skin with soft hair with which garments are lined for warmth; or covered for ornament." (J) Furs listed in the House of Parliament Rates, 1660, for Imports and Exports—*Statutes of the Realm* (London, 1819) included "Armins, Badger, Bare skin; Beaver; Budge, Calaben; Catts, Tim-ber Fitches; Foxes; Grays; Jennets; Leopard; Martrones; Miniver; Minkes, Mole skins; Otter; Ounce; Sables; Weazell; Wolfe; Wolverings."

GAITERS
"Coverings for the legs." (W) "Ladies Gaiter Boots. The subscriber is manufacturing a beautiful article of this description, which will be made to measure or supplied ready made as low as can be purchased in this city. Ladies are requested to call and examine his assortment, C. Butler." *The Columbian Register* (New Haven, Connecticut), July 21, 1829.

GALAGE, GALOCHE, GOLOSHES
"A shepherd's clog." (J)

GALLIGASKINS
"Large open hose in ludicrous language." (J)

GAMASHES
Gaiters; the term was applied to "a kind of loose drawers worn outside the legs over the other clothing, and much used by travellers. Also called gamogins or gambagoes, cases of leather to protect the shoes and stockings from the dirt when on horseback." (H)

GAMBAIDE, GAMBADO
From the Italian *gamba,* a leg, these were "boots worn upon the legs above the shoe." (J) "Spatterdashes used for riding." (W)

GARTER
"A band to tie up the stockings, a riband," (W) "by which the stocking is held upon the leg." (J)

GASKINS
"Very wide hose or breeches." (W)

GIAMBEUX
"Armor for the legs; greaves." (J)

GIRDLE
"A [sash] tied round the waist," (W) "or buckled." (J)

GLOVE

"A cover of the hands." (J)

GORGET

"Armor for the throat; a part of dress." (W) A term also used for a type of neckerchief or cravat.

GOWN

"A long upper garment; loose habit; dress."

GREAVES

"Armor used for the legs." (W)

HAT

A covering for the head said to have been first seen about the year 1400, at which time it became of use for country wear, riding, etc., taking the place of chaperoons or hoods.

HAUSTMENT

"A stiff undergarment to keep the body erect." (H)

HEADBAND

"A fillet or topknot." (W)

HERLOTS

Garters; "White latchets formerly used to tie the hose with." (H)

JACK BOOTS

The term for "very large [high] boots, serving for armor" (W) or protection against brush and mud. "As a Help to bear Fatigue I us'd to chew a Root of Ginsing as I Walk't along. This kept up my Spirits, and made me trip away as nimbly in my half Jack-Boots as younger men could in their shoes." William Byrd, *History of the Dividing Line* [1729] (Richmond, 1866).

JACKET

"A doublet; sometimes, the upper tunic; any kind of outer coat." (H)

JERKIN

The term for a kind of jacket or upper doublet, the skirt of which is divided into four sections.

JUMP, JUMPER

The workman's leather frock or overblouse; also, "a half-gown or sort of jacket; a sort of bodice used instead of stays." (H)

KERCHIEF

"A head-dress, a cloth used in dressing the head." (W)

KIRTLE

"An upper garment or gown." (W) A word used in the seventeenth century for a man's tunic or coat, as well as a woman's dress.

KITTISOL

A type of umbrella. (See previous listing, this chapter.)

LATCHET

The name of any silk, leather, gold, or silver cord, braided ribbon, or the like used as a clothe's "fastening [or] a shoestring." (W) "A handsome assortment of gentlemen's shoe and knee buckles and latchets, new patterns . . . [James Jacks]" *Federal Gazette* (Philadelphia), November 27, 1797.

MANTELET

"A kind of woman's short cloak." (W)

MANTLE

"A cloak." (W)

MANTUA

A term describing "a woman's gown, [of] a kind of silk." (W) (See also TEXTILES, quotation under NEGLiGEE.)

MILITARY UNIFORM ACCESSORIES

". . . Received an additional supply of Goods, by the Ship *Star,* from London— Guns, pistols, and swords, silver gilt and worsted Epaulets, gold and silver Laces, naval and military buttons, spangles, Cords, and Threads, Morocco and silk sword Belts and Hooks . . . Gold, silver, and gilt military hat bands . . . [James Jacks]." *Federal Gazette* (Philadelphia), November 21, 1798; January 7, 1800.

MILITARY UNIFORMS (OFFICERS)

"The American army at present have not been uniformly clothed, but both officers and soldiers wore their own clothes; nor did I see any colors to their regiments on the day of action . . . Doctor [Joseph] Warren's dress was a light-coloured coat, with a white satin waistcoat laced with silver, and white breeches, with silver loops . . . he was supposed to be the commander of the American army that day for General Putnam was about three miles distant . . ." (Report of John Clarke, First Lieutenant of [British] Marines, June 17, 1775.) *Bunker Hill* (Boston, 1875).

"R. Bacon offers for sale a complete Horseman's Uniform (as worn by the 1st regiment of Cavalry; viz. Coat (very elegant) Epaulett, Pantaloons, Vest and Cap. Also an Infantry Officers Coat. The whole very little worn and will be sold very low." *American Mercury* (Hartford, Connecticut), August 3, 1815.

MILITARY UNIFORMS (TROOPS)

". . . Wore or took away a grey roundabout jacket, one pair of white and one pair of blue woollen pantaloons, one pair fatigue trousers, one fatigue frock, two flannel shirts, and an uniform infantry cap . . ." E. Boardman, Cantonment, Pittsfield, Massachusetts. *American Mercury* (Hartford, Connecticut), May 20, 1817.

MILLINERY

"New Fashions. Miss M. S. Bradley has just returned from New York with the latest fashions in Millinery, consisting of colour'd Silk Hats, Bonnets, and Hoods— an elegant assortment of Ribbons, Fringes, and Trimmings for Habits and Pelisses, consisting of gilt frogs and Buttons, Silk do., Silk Braid and Cords . . . a good and cheap assortment of Gloves and Mitts— Corsets, Curls, Baskets, Ec." *Columbian Register* (New Haven, Connecticut), November 12, 1829.

MOB, MOBCAP

"A woman's cap," (W) usually completely covering the hair and tied beneath the chin.

MOCCASON, MOCCASIN, MOGGASON

"A shoe of soft lether without a sole, ornamented round the ankle." (W)   A word of Algonquin Indian origin; both the name and shoe style were adopted by the settlers.

MODESTY PIECE

"Lace, Ec. worn over the bosom." (W)

MORNING GOWN

"A loose gown for the morning," (W) worn at home.

MUFF

"A warm cover for the hands," (W)   worn by men and women. "Any man that took up a Man's Muff dropt on the Lord's Day between the Old Meeting House and the South Meeting House are desired to bring it to the Printer's Office and shall be rewarded. *Boston News-Letter,* March 5, 1715.

MUFFLER

"A kind of cover for the face or chin." (W)

NECKCLOTH

"A thing worn about men's necks." (W) (See also BAND, CRAVAT, STOCK.)

NEGLIGEE

From the French, négligé, for a dressing gown: "Mary Wallace and Clementia Ferguson, Just arrived from the kingdom of Ireland, intend to follow the business of mantua-making, and have . . . patterns of the following kind of wear. [for] Sacks, negligees, negligee-night-gowns, plain nightgowns, pattanlears, shepherdesses, romancloaks, cardinals, capuchins, dauphnesses, shades, lorrains, bonnets and hives." *The New York Mercury,* January 3, 1757.

NIGHTCAP

"A cap worn in bed or in an undress." (W) (See also QUEEN'S NIGHTCAP.)

NIGHTGOWN

The contemporary term for a woman's afternoon tea or at-home gown; "A very loose wide gown; an undress." (W) "Aug. 18, 1772. The 6 instant Mr. Saml. Jarvis was married to Miss Sukey Peirce, on the 13th I made her a visit in company with mamma and many others. The bride was dress'd in a white, satin night-gown." *Diary of Anna Green Winslow* (Boston, 1894).

NIGHT RAIL

"A linen covering for the shoulders," (W) a type of shawl.

PANTALOON

"A man's garment," (W) "in which the breeches and stockings are all of a piece." (J)

PANTHOSE

"A kind of loose, easy shoe; a slipper." (W)

PARTLET

"A ruff for the neck; loose collar." (W)

PATTEN(S)

The name used from the seventeenth century well into the nineteenth century for a type of shoe, "a clog shod with iron," (W) worn to protect one's good pumps of silk, velvet, or thin leather, from mire, water, or snow. The patten was a shaped sole and heel set above a ring of iron and was held to the foot by a wide band or strap of leather fitting over the instep. "I took my wife to Mr. Pierce's, she in her way being exceedingly troubled with a new pair of pattens, and I vexed to go so slow." Samuel Pepys, *Diary,* January 24, 1659/60.

Pair of pattens, 1790 penny print.

PELLESE, PELISSE

A cloak with slits or arm holes. "Elizabeth Brace, having taken a Store a few rods north of the Brick Meeting House, offers for sale a variety of Goods in the millinery line, consisting of Fine and low priced Straw Hats, Silk and velvet do., Caps and Turbans, Ostrich Plumes . . . merino handks. Mantua making, Dresses and Pelleses made from the latest New York fashions." *American Mercury* (Hartford, Connecticut), October 30, 1820.

PETTICOAT

"The lower part of a woman's dress; the habit of a boy in his infancy." (J) "An undergarment worn by women." (W)

QUEEN'S NIGHTCAP

The name given a woman's at-home or undress head covering of the style familiar to us from the portrait of Martha Washington. "March 28, [1772]. This minute I have received my queen's Night-cap—we like it. Aunt says that if the materials it is made of were more substantial than gauze, it might serve occasionally to hold anything measured by an ½ peck, but it is just as it should be, & very decent . . . But I got into one of my frolicks, upon sight of the Cap." *Diary of Anna Green Winslow* (Boston, 1894).

REDCOAT

One of the contemporary synonyms for the king's soldiers. The name referring to the scarlet uniform coat. "December 24, 1686. About 60 Red-Coats were brought to Town, landed at Mr. Pool's wharf, where drew up and so marched." Samuel Sewall, *Diary.*

SACK, SACQUE

"A woman's loose robe," (J) or negligee; that is, a loose gown open in front, worn over a pretty petticoat for full dress or formal evening wear.

SANDAL

"A loose shoe." (J)

SASH

"A belt worn by way of distinction; a silken band worn by officers in the army." (J)

SCARF

"Anything that hangs loose upon the shoulders or dress." (J)

SCATCHES

A contemporary cant term for a type of short "stilts to put the feet in to walk in dirty places." (B) (See also BAXTER, CLOG, PATTEN.)

SHIFT

"A woman's linen," (J) or undergarment.

SHIRT

"The under linen garment of a man." (J)

SHOE

"The cover of the foot." (J)

SHOE-TYE

"The ribband with which women tie their shoes." (J)

SILK HAT

The term for a man's high, narrow-brimmed hat of the early nineteenth century. "Silk Hats, Wholesale and Retail, the Subscriber has on hand and is constantly manufacturing Silk Hats of every variety . . . Particular hats made to order at short notice. Also —Fur hats of all descriptions, with an assortment of furs, Buffalo Robes, Seal caps, Ec. Ec. C. J. Allen." *The Columbian Register* (New Haven, Connecticut), November 17, 1829.

SIMAR

"A woman's robe." (J)

SKIRT

A term for the lower portion of a coat as well as for the more familiar article of woman's apparel.

Quilted red eighteenth-century skirt. (Courtesy, Antiquarian and Landmarks Society, Inc.)

Hat case or box. (Courtesy, Antiquarian and Landmarks Society, Inc.)

SKULLCAP

"A head piece." (J)

SLIPPER

"A kind of loose shoe, a morning shoe." (W)

SLOP(S)

A contemporary cant term, from the Dutch *sloove*, for covering; for "trowsers; open breeches." (J)

SMICKET, SMOCKET

A diminutive for smock, "the undergarment of a woman." (J)

SMOCK

"A shift." (J)

SOCK

"Something put between the foot and shoe. (J)   "A high theatrical shoe, a false stocking." (W)

SPATTERDASHES, SPATS

"Coverings for the legs by which the wet is kept off." (J)   (See also GARTERS.)

STAYS

"Bodice; a kind of stiff waistcoat made of whalebone, worn by ladies." (J)

STOCK

"Something made of linen; a cravat; a close neckcloth; anciently, a cover for the legs." (J)

STOCKINGS

"The covering of the leg. Stock in the old language made the plural stocken. Stocken was in time taken for a singular, and pronounced stocking." (J)   "Modern stockings, whether woven or knit, are formed of an indefinite number of little knots, called stitches, loops, or meshes. Woven stockings are manufactured on a machine of finely polished iron or steel." *The Book of Trades* (London, 1805).

STOLE

"A long vest." (J)

STOMACHER

"An ornamental covering worn by women on the breast." (J)

SUNDAY CLOTHES

"You should always keep some clothes to wear to church, or on particular occasions, which should not be worn everyday . . . Whenever it is necessary to get new clothes, those which have been kept for particular occasions will then come in as every-day

ones." (Letter from George Washington to his nephew, George, March 23, 1789.) *Collected Writings of George Washington,* ed., John G. Fitzpatrick (1876).

SURCOAT

"A short coat worn over the rest of the dress." (J)

SURTOUT

"A large coat worn over all the rest." (J)

TABERD

"A long gown." (J)

TARTAN

"A kind of soft woolen stuff." (W)

TIPPET

"Something worn about the neck." (J)

TUCKER

The term for a "slip of linen, Ec. about the breast." (W)   "I was dressed in my yellow coat, black bib and apron, my paste comb & all my past garnet & jet pins, together with my silver plume—my loket . . . striped tucker and ruffels & my silk shoes." [January 4, 1772], *Diary of Anna Green Winslow* (Boston, 1894).

UMBRELLA

(See previous listing, this chapter.)

WANTY

"A broad, lethern girth; a surcingle." (W)

WHALEBONE

The term signifying "a commodity procured from the whale, and used in stiffening in stays, fans, bulks, skreens, Ec. What we call whale-bone, or fins, is a horny labinal in the upper jaw of the balaena, which supply the place of teeth, but there are none such in the lower jaw. These laminae are commonly called whiskers, which, split and fashioned, are the whale-bone. The pizzle, or genital member of the animal, serves likewise for the same purpose." (M) So common was the use of whalebone or fin for women's stays that it was for years a synonym for a kind of corset. (See also SCRIMSHAW.) "Elias Pelletreau takes this method to inform the Merchants and the Public in general, that he has set up at his House on Golden-Hill, at the Sign of the Dish of Fry'd Oysters, a place for cutting of Whale Bone . . . He has also for Sale a parcle of Silver Smith's Tools, which he will sell cheap for cash." *The New-York Gazette and The Weekly Mercury,* May 24, 1773.

WRAPPER

A loose, enveloping outer garment; a type of cape. "Hull, Tounsend, Knevals & Co., Merchant-Tailors, Have just received from New York a splendid assortment of . . . the most fashionable Colours [including] Heavy blue and brown camblets for gentlemen's Cloaks and Wrappers . . ." *Columbian Register* (New Haven, Connecticut), December 12, 1829.

Mid-eighteenth-century man's costume; portrait of Ephraim Starr. (Courtesy, Wadsworth Atheneum, Hartford, Connecticut.)

Undress for August 1799.

Fashionable riding habits for July 1799.

Morning dress for October 1799.

Afternoon dress for October 1799.

Carriage dress.

ARMORIAL BEARINGS

The all-inclusive term for the coat of arms, shield, and/or crest that identifies membership or descent in an eminent family; often used as a decoration.

COATS OF ARMS

The combined shield, helmet, and crest. The term commemorates the early-twelfth-century practice of painting one's shield on a linen surcoat which was worn over the mail Armor, *q.v.*, for identification in battle. As an additional means of identification, a device from the shield was painted on the helmet. This developed into the crest, later affixed to the top of the coat of arms. Coats of arms, or the combination of shield, crest, and motto, were used also as an indication of rank and were set in windows in stained glass, carved or painted above doorways, engraved on seals, carved on tombs, and painted on carriage doors. Eventually they were used also on silver and porcelain, letter paper, and book plates, etc.

When American rebels banished the king's arms from display in the colonies by vanquishing his armies, individual citizens of the new nation technically gave up

Royal Arms used as decoration for engraved portrait of King James II, published in 1704.

Walker coat of arms used by both the English and American families.

any erstwhile claims to the privileges or appurtenances of British aristocracy. However, even as allegiance was sworn to a new national creed of equality, Americans set about proving, as Mark Twain is said to have declared later, that some were more equal than others. We chose to be republicans, "who think a commonwealth without monarchy the best government" (*cf.* the pledge of allegiance to the flag). preferring Dr. Johnson's short definition of a republic to his explanation of a complete democracy "in which the sovereign power is neither lodged in one man, nor in the nobles, but in the collective body of the people." Nevertheless, many yearned, not at all secretly, for the establishment of an aristocracy "which places the supreme power in the nobles, without a king and exclusively of the people"—a desire predicated, of course, on the belief they could be counted among the nobility. Many continued to think of themselves as English men and women, somehow simply freer-born here than they might have been on the other side of the Atlantic. Pride in an old family name and its history—however distant the connection—was inbred; so also was a belief that economic gain and concomitant social status were best proved and maintained by solid, material, outward symbols of their existence. The latter was supplied in the form of better built and more handsomely furnished houses, fine carriages, matched pairs of horses, and elegant costumes. The former was satisfied by the display of those ensigns armorial first borne by distant English ancestors. When such proper shields were lacking, it was easy enough to adopt and adapt old devices and to create their own new coats of arms. After all, one of the synonyms for the shield and crest was Achievement:

"The eschutcheon, or ensigns armorial, granted to any man for the performance of great actions." (J) (See HATCHMENT.)

Certainly victory in battle and the courage to create a new nation always historically have been considered great actions worthy of achievement.

"Thomas Reynolds, Seal Cutter, at Mr. Joseph Cooke's in Second Street, at the corner of Black Horse Alley, Cuts Coats of Arms, Crests and Cyphers . . . Any person wanting a drawing of his arms, may be furnished with one for two dollars."

Lack of extensive knowledge of one's family history never was necessarily a deterrent to any American's assumption of these trappings of privilege. Reynolds realistically offered assistance to the uncertain: "N.B. As several gentlemen are unacquainted with the Coats of Arms appertaining to their families, Reynolds informs his friends and the public, that Edmondson's Heraldry, which is now in the city Library, contains all the Coats of Arms ever used in Great Britain or Ireland." *Pennsylvania Herald* (Philadelphia), December 15, 1787. Thus, the Philadelphia seal cutter and his counterparts in other urban centers offered the same type of services that are advertised today by numerous heraldic artists and geneological research organizations. (See also CIPHER, SEAL.)

A complete list of all the terms used in describing coats of arms and their proper applications would require a separate volume. Space permits inclusion here only of those terms most frequently encountered by the collector.

ARGENT
The term designating use of the color silver or white.

ARMED
The term for birds or animals whose beaks, claws, horns, or teeth are given a specific color.

AUGMENTATION
The additional Charge, *q.v.,* given to, or made part of, a Coat of Arms, *q.v.,* as a mark of honor or recognition of special achievement. "There be now, for martial encouragement, some degrees and orders of chivalry, and some remembrances perhaps upon the eschutcheon." Francis Bacon, *Essays*.

BADGE
The mark of the owner, such as a dolphin, horse, knot, mermaid, or other symbol, "a token by which one is known." (J)

BAR
The horizontal band that is narrower than a Fess, *q.v.,* the part "laid across another." (J)

Bar.　　　　　　　　　　　Barry.

BARRY
The Field, *q.v.,* divided into equal numbers of horizontal bars, alternating in two colors. Thus, if there are three black bars, three white bars must also be used. (See BAR.)

BASTON

The narrow Bend, *q.v.*

Baston.

BEAVER

A general term for the Helmet, *q.v.,* but specifically for that "part of the helmet which is moved up and down to enable the wearer to drink; the shade over the eyes." (H)

BEND

The diagonal bend from the Dexter Chief, *q.v.,* to the Sinister, *q.v.,* base.

Bend.

BENDLET

A narrow Bend, *q.v.*

BENDY

The Shield, *q.v.,* divided into a series of Bends, *q.v.*

BILLETY

The Shield, *q.v.,* powdered or dotted with a series of tiny oblongs or billets, similar to short sections of logs.

BLASON, BLAZON

A Coat of Arms, *q.v.;* that is "an account of ensigns armorial in proper terms." (J) The term for the dress or surcoat "worn over the armor, on which the armorial bearings were blazoned." (H)

CADENCY, MARK OF

The variation in the Coat of Arms, *q.v.,* to indicate descent from a later branch of the family. This was done by changes of color or charges; additions of borders, Labels, and Charges, *qq.v.*

CANTON

A rectangular corner in the top right-hand part or Dexter Chief of a Shield, *qq.v.*

CHARGE

The animal or other object shown on a Shield, *q.v.,* "that which is born upon the colour." Henry Peacham, *The Compleat Gentleman* (London, 1661).

CHEVRON

The inverted V motif.

CHIEF

The upper or top portion of the Shield, *q.v.,* "so-called of the French word *chef,* the head or upper part; this possesses the upper third part of the escutcheon." Henry Peacham, *The Compleat Gentleman* (London, 1661).

COAT, COAT ARMOR

"That on which the ensigns armorial are portrayed." (J)   (See ARMOR.)

COUCHANT

The term is "understood of a lion or other beast, when lying down, but with his head raised, which distinguishes the posture of couchant from dormant, wherein he is supposed quite stretched out and asleep." (M)

COUPÉ, COUPED

The term to express "the head, or any limb of an animal, cut smooth off from the trunk." (M)

CREST

"The ornament of the helmet." (J) Originally, this was the fan-shaped piece of metal set on the top of the Helmet, *q.v.,* and painted with some device copied from the Coat of Arms, *q.v.* By the fourteenth century this commonly had been replaced by a piece of painted leather or wood showing a stylized beast, bird, or mythological monster. The Crest, *q.v.,* is used above the Shield, *q.v.,* and helmet in any pictorial representation of the arms; as a symbol of eminence of family; right to leadership, and blood descent:

"It was a crest ere thou wast born;
Thy father's father wore it."
Shakespeare, *As You Like It,* IV, ii.

CROSSLET
A little cross.

CRUSILLY
A description of the Shield, *q.v.,* powdered with Crosslets, *q.v.*

DEXTER
In descriptions of the Shield, *q.v.,* Dexter is the user's right side, and thus it is the left side presented to the viewer.

DORMANT
(See COUCHANT.)

ENGRAILED
An edge scalloped in a series of continuous concave curves. "A word used now only in heraldry, for to indent in curve lines." (J)

Engrailing.

ENSIGN
"The flag or standard." (J)

ERMINE
The white ground of a Shield, *q.v.,* powdered with black spots to simulate ermine fur.

ESCHUTCHEON, ESCUTCHEON
The Shield, *q.v.,* displaying the Armorial Bearings, *q.v.* "The shield of the family, the picture of the ensign armorial. *Eschutcheon* is a French word, from the Latin, *scutum,* leather; hence our English word buckler

signifying leather and buck of whose skins the ancient Britons made their shields." (J)

ESCROL
"The scroll, or long slip of parchment, as it were, on which a motto is placed." (M)

FESS, FESSE
The wide horizontal band crossing the middle of the field. "The fesse is so-called of the Latin word *fascia,* a bar or girdle, possessing one third part of the escutcheon over the middle." Henry Peacham, *The Compleat Gentleman* (London, 1661).

FIELD
The background or ground of a Charge or Shield, *qq.v.* "The surface of a shield." (J)

FITCHY
The designation for a Cross, *q.v.,* made with a sharp point or stake at the base.

Fitchy.

FLEUR-DE-LIS
The stylized lily.

FLORETTY
The cross with Fleur-de-lis, *q.v.,* terminals.

FLORY
The description of the Field, *q.v.,* that is powdered with Fleur-de-lis, *q.v.*

FRETTY
The description of a Field, *q.v.,* or ground covered by interlaced, diagonal bands or frets.

FUSIL
A diamond shape.

GORGED
Having a collar or other ornament about the neck.

GRIFFIN
One of the heraldic beasts with an eagle's head and lion's body.

GUARDANT
Facing the viewer.

GULE
The color red.

GYRON
A triangle-shaped section within a Shield, *q.v.*

GYRONNY
The description of a shield divided into a series of Gyrons, *q.v.*

Gyronny.

HATCHMENT
A painted display honoring a person after death. Hatchment is an old corruption of the word Achievement, *q.v.,* and is the general term for the Coat of Arms, *q.v.,* with all its ornaments; that is, the Shield, Crest, *qq.v.,* and motto of the deceased. In form, it was a rectangle, set at an angle and so was lozenge-shaped in appearance; usually painted on canvas stretched over a frame, on a board or leather panel, or worked as a tapestry, about 4 feet square. Originally, during the sixteenth century, hatchments were displayed for a six-to-twelve-month period from a balcony or

Hatchment hangs in left rear of portrait of the Duchess of Richmond, 1624.

The portraiture of the illustreous Princesse Frances Duchess of Richmond and Lenox daughter of Thomas V. Howard of Bindon sonne of Thomas Duke of Norfo: whose mother was Elisabeth daughter of Edward Duke of Buckingham Anno 1624 insculptum a Guilh. Passeo Londinum.

second-floor window of the owner's house. Hatchments memorializing prominent personages sometimes then were kept on display in his church (in Anglican parishes) or in the main hall of the manor house. The English custom was followed, albeit rarely, in some southern colonial communities and seldom in New England, save on the occasion of a monarch's or royal governor's death when the hatchment was displayed on the facade of the appropriate public building.

IMPALED
The term to describe a Shield, *q.v.*, bisected vertically in order to combine two Coats of Arms, *q.v.*, such as those of husband and wife, into one.

INDENTED
A zigzag edge.

LABEL
The narrow Bar, *q.v.*, across the upper portion of the Shield, *q.v.*, with three or five pendants signifying the Mark of Cadency, *q.v.*, for the eldest son.

LUCE
The heraldic term for a pike.

MANTLING
The stylized, conventional drapery shown hanging around the Shield and behind the Helmet, *qq.v.*

MARTLET, MERLOT
Two names for a small conventional bird without feet. "Used as a mark of distinction for younger brothers to put them in mind that they are to trust to the wings of virtue and merit in order to raise themselves, and not to their feet, they having little land to set their feet on." (M)

MAUNCH
A sleeve.

OR
The color gold or yellow.

ORDINARY
A term referring to any one of the common geometrical parts such as the Bend, Fesse, or Chevron, *qq.v.*

PALE
The vertical Band, *q.v.*, usually dividing the Shield, *q.v.*, down the center.

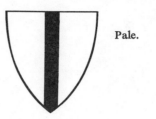

Pale.

PALY
A Shield divided into Pales, *qq.v.*

PASSANT
The representation of a heraldic beast as it walks and faces toward the dexter side, with the dexter foreleg raised. (See DEXTER.)

PASSANT GUARDANT
The beast walking with its head turned to the viewer.

PASSANT REGUARDANT
The beast looking back.

PILE
A narrow wedge shape pointing down the center of the Shield, *q.v.*

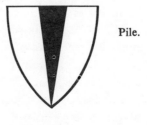

Pile.

RAMPANT
The term to describe the heraldic beast standing on its sinister back leg, with forepaws in the air. (See SINISTER.)

ROUNDEL
A decorative round panel, plate, or medallion.

ST. ANDREW'S CROSS
A cross formed on the shield by a bend and a bend sinister. (See also BEND, SHIELD, SINISTER.)

St. Andrew's Cross.

SALTIRE
The same as St. Andrew's Cross.

SHIELD
Generally a piece of Armor, *q.v.*, and here used as the symbol of protection, security, or defense; hence the symbol of a family or leader capable of offering such security. (See also ESCUTCHEON.)

SINISTER
The Latin word for left, used to designate the portion of the Shield, *q.v.*, on the user's left, the viewer's right.

TORSE
The twisted Band, *q.v.*, shown between Helmet and Crest, *qq.v.*

TORTEAU
A Roundel, *q.v.*

UNDY
The term for an undulating or wavy horizontal Bar, *q.v.*

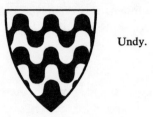

Undy.

VAIR
A stylized, counterchanged pattern of blue and white shapes on a Shield, *q.v.*

Vair.

VERT
The color green.

JEWELRY

The term jewel was used for a single precious stone, but also a word commonly used in early writings for any piece of jeweler's work, as a "ring or a brooch." (H)

". . . Peter Lorin, a jeweller from London, sets after the neatest & newest Fashions all sorts of Jewels, Rings, Ear-Rings, Solitairs, Lockets, Aigrettes, Stay-Hooks, Seals, as also Diamonds, Rubies, Emeralds, Saphires, or any other kind of stone to the best advantage, at very reasonable Rates." *The New York Weekly Post-Boy,* November 10, 1746.

The jewelry listed by Evelyn during the late seventeenth century continued in use through the eighteenth:

Firstly the chatelaine
To which a bunch of onyxes,

And many a golden seal there dangles,
Mysterious cyphers, and new fangles.
Diamond buckles too,
For garters and as rich for shoe.
A manteau girdle, ruby buckle,
A brilliant diamond ring for knuckle.
A sapphire bodkin for the hair,
Or sparkling diamond facets there;
Then turquoise, ruby, emerauld rings
For fingers, and such pretty things;
As diamond pendants for the ears
Must needs be had, and two pearl pears,
Pearl necklace, large and oriental,
And diamond, and of amber pale.

John Evelyn, *Mundus Muliebris* or *Voyage to Marryland* (London, 1690). (See also in forepart of this section, ABECEDARY, ABRACADABRA, AMULET, ANODYNE NECKLACE, BATTERSEA ENAMELED WARE, BEADS, BUCKLES, CHATELAINE, CONCHSHELL WORK, EAR-RINGS, GIMBAL, MOURNING LOCKET, MOURNING RING, PENDANT, POSY RING, WATCH SEAL.)

GEMSTONES

ADAMANT

"A stone imagined of impenetrable hardness." Hence, a synonym for "the diamond," but it also "is taken for the loadstone." (J)

ADAMANTINE

The name of an extremely hard gesso used in the decorative panels of looking glasses and clock cases, but rarely on furniture.

AGATES

"Semitransparent stones of the quartz family, capable of receiving a high polish, chiefly used for ornamental work, and particularly for necklaces and seals. They are occasionally made into cups, the handles of knives and forks, hilts of swords and hangers, and the top and bottoms of snuffboxes. The less ornamental kinds are made into small mortars, employed by enamellers and others, for pounding such substances as are too hard to be reduced in any other way. They are also made into instruments for pounding, colours, and into polishers for glazing of linen." *The Domestic Encyclopedia* (Philadelphia, 1821). "After that we went to Mr. Cade's to choose some pictures for our house. I to Pope's Head and bought me an aggate-hafted knife which cost me 5s." Samuel Pepys, *Diary*, November 21, 1660.

ALMANDINE

A type of ruby "coarser and lighter than the oriental, and nearer the colour of the granate." (J)

AMETHYST

"A precious stone of a violet colour bordering on purple. The oriental amethyst is the hardest, scarcest and most valuable; it is generally of a dove colour, though some are purple, and others white like the diamond. The German is of a violet colour and the Spanish are of three sorts. The best are the blackest or deepest violet; others are almost quite white, and some few tinctured with yellow . . . is easy to be engraved upon, and is next in value to the emerald." (J)

AQUA MARINA

"A name by which jewelers call the beryl on account of its sea green colour." (M)

ASTERIA

This is the proper name for "a beautiful pellucid gem of variable colours when viewed in different lights . . . known among jewelers by the name of cat's eye." (M)

BERYL

A pellucid gem, "called by our lapidaries *aqua marina,* of a bluish green colour, found in the East Indies and about the gold mines of Peru . . . It never receives any admixture of colour into it, nor loses the blue and green, but has its genuine tinge in the degree from a very deep and dusky to the palest imaginable of the hue of sea water." (M)

BERYL CRYSTAL

A species of imperfect crystal, "of an extreme pure, clear, and equal texture, and scarce ever subject to the slightest films or blemishes . . . of a very fine transparence and naturally of a pale brown." (M)

CAT'S-EYE

It "is a kind of opal of brownish grey colour tinged with green, yellow, white, or red. They are set in rings." *The Domestic Encyclopedia* (Philadelphia, 1821).

CHLORITE

"A species of jasper, of a green colour." (M)

CHRYSOLITE

The proper name of "a beautiful gem of a glittering splendor like gold, much valued, and called topaz by the moderns." (M)

"A precious stone of dusky green with a cast of yellow." (J)

CHRYSOPRASUS

"A precious stone of a yellow colour approaching to green." (J)

CORAL *Corallium*

"A hard, brittle, branched substance, both externally and internally of a deep bright red colour . . . found adhering to rocks and other bodies in the sea." (W)

To Make Artificial Coral: Take "cinnabar well beaten, a layer whereof is applied on a piece of wood well dried and polished, being first moistened with size; the whole is then again polished and for varnish, rub it over with the white of an egg." (W)

CORNELIAN, CARNELIAN

"So-called from its frequent flesh colour [this] is another kind of agate, usually red, though sometimes white, orange, or yellow. The kinds principally in request are pure white or bright red; and jewelers have the art of changing the colour of the yellow varieties to red, by heat. No stone is so much in request for seals as the cornelian; it is likewise cut into beads for necklaces, and stones for ear-rings; into crosses, bracelets, and other trinkets [many made in India]. The amount of different kinds of cornelian goods vended by the East India Company in 1807 was £11,187." *The Domestic Encyclopedia* (Philadelphia, 1821).

CORNISH DIAMOND

The name given to a "kind of crystal from their being found in Cornwall." (M)

DIAMOND

A precious stone of a "fine pellucid substance, of great hardness, susceptible of elegant tinges from metalline particles . . . of a vivid splendour, the most valuable of all gems." (M)

DOUBLET

The term among lapidaries for "a counterfeit stone composed of two pieces of crystal

or glass fastened together with paper colours between them, so as to appear the same to the eye as if the whole substance of the crystal had been tinged with these colours." (M)

EMERALD

The precious stone next in hardness to the ruby. "Our jewellers distinguish two kinds, the oriental and occidental. The emerald of the East Indies are evidently finer than those of any other part of the world. The genuine emerald is perhaps the most beautiful of all the gems; second only to the diamond in lustre and brightness." (M)

GEMS

Precious stones or jewels. "The chief of these are the diamond, ruby, sapphire, emerald, turquoise, opal, agate, pearl, crystal, Ec." (M) "Daniel Fueter, Silver Smith and Jeweller . . . has lately imported A Beautiful Assortment of Jewellry which for Elegance and Taste is greatly superior to anything hitherto brought to this Place; Consisting of a Great Variety of Rings, set knot Fashion, Entourage, Cluster, Ec. viz. Brilliant Diamonds and Rose Diamonds of all Sizes, Rubies, Topazes, Emerals, Saphirs, and all kinds of Precious Stones, warranted . . ." *The New-York Gazette and The Weekly Post-Boy,* March 10, 1763.

HYACINTH

A genus of pellucid gems "whose colour is red with an admixture of yellow." (M)

JET

The name of "a solid, dry opake substance . . . of a fine deep black colour, very glossy, and shining," (M) used for buttons, beads, and other small ornaments.

MOTHER OF PEARL

The *Aurus marina,* the shell of a "little sea-fish of the oyster kind, not of the pearl oyster. It is very smooth withinside, and of the whiteness and water of pearl itself, and it has the same lustre on the outside, after the first laminae have been cleared off with aqua fortis and the lapidaries drill. It is used in inlaid works, and in several toys, as snuff boxes, Ec." (M)

ONYX

"A kind of agate marked alternately with white and black, or white and brown, the colors arranged concentrically or confusedly. Both onyx, and sardonyx [whose colors are] in regular stripes and bands, one highly esteemed by lapidaries for vases, snuffboxes, and trinkets of various kinds. The ancients made those beautiful cameos [of sardonyx] which still ornament our cabinets." *The Domestic Encyclopedia* (Philadelphia, 1821).

OUNCE PEARL

The term given the smallest, or seed pearls, "from their being sold by the ounce." (M)

PASTE

This term, among jewelers, implies "an imitation of the different gems, made with a hard species of glass." (M)

PASTE EMERALD

"To counterfeit Emeralds. Take of natural crystal, four ounces; of red-lead, four ounces; verdigrease, 48 grains; crocus martis, prepared with vinegar, eight grains; let the whole be finely pulverized and sifted; put this into a crucible, leaving one inch empty; lute it well, and put it into a potter's furnace, and let it stand there as long as they do their pots. When cold, break the crucible, and you will find a matter of a fine emerald colour, which, after it is cut and set in gold, will surpass in beauty an oriental emerald." (M)

PEARL

The *Margarita* is a "hard, white shining body usually of a roundish figure, found in a testaceous fish resembling an oyster; in the common oyster, the muscle, the pinna marina, and several others. The pearls of which are often very good; but those of the true Indian berberi, or pearl-oyster, are in general superior to all." (M)

PERIDOT

This is "another name for the chrysolite." (W)

RUBY

"A precious stone of a red colour, next in hardness and value to a diamond." (J)

ZIRCON

The name given "a rare mineral, which is sometimes a gem [and which] occurs in crystals. All the varieties of zircon which possess transparency are cut and polished by the lapidary, but, in general, are not greatly esteemed. The exposure of some colors to heat deprives them of their hues, in which condition they have been sold for diamonds." *Encyclopedia Americana* (Philadelphia, 1831).

TEXTILES AND LEATHER

At the beginning of the second generation of our Colonial period, those woven cloths available for export and those favored as imports for use at home and for re-export to colonies, listed in the House of Parliament Rates, 1660, for Imports and Exports—*Statutes of the Realm* (London, 1819) included: "Flanders Bands of Bone lace; cut work of Flaunders; Barbers Aprons of Checks; Bayes of Florence; Botatocs or Bumbazines, narrow, broad, or of Silke; Buckrams, of Germany; of French making; Buffins, Mocadoes and Lille Grograms, narrow and broad; Burgasines or Callico Buckrams; Caddus or Cruel Ribbon; Caddice; Calicoes, fine or coarse; Linnen Cloth; Cambrides, fine or course; Callicoes, fine or course; Canvas; Damask; Diaper; Lawnes; Holland cloth; Drilling and duck; Silesia; Lockrums; Ozenbrigs; Twill and Ticking; Dornix; Satin, Velvet, Silke knitt; Canvas; Cahmblett, unwatered; Mohaire, watered, halfe silke, halfe haire; Felt; Dimitty; Durance or Suretty with thred or silk; Flax undrest and wrought; Flockes; Fustians, Holland or Dutch; Gadza with gold or silver; Grogrames; Hankirchers; Sackcloth; Says; Serges; Wadmol; Stuff; Worsted; Wool; Linsey Woolsey; Shag; Kersey; Velure." Leathers listed in 1660 included: "Buffe, cow hides of Barbary and Muscovia, Cow or Horsehides, India hides; Cony, Kid, Lambe, Otter, Sheep, Rabbit, Hare, Cats, Fox, Dogs, Elke, Wolfe, Badgers, Squirrel skins."

ADATAIS, ADATIS, ADATYS

"A muslin or cotton cloth, very clear, of which the piece is ten French ells long and three quarters broad. It comes from the E. Indies, and the finest is made at Bengal." (M)

ADENOS

"A kind of cotton called marine cotton. It comes from Aleppo by way of Marseilles." (M)

ALAMODE

The name of "a very thin, glossy black silk, chiefly used for hoods, scarfs, etc." (M) "A thin, black silk," (W) sometimes written *mode*. "Amos Bull, near the South Church in Hartford has for sale A quantity of low price Irish Linens, Callicoes, Muslins, Shawls, Handkerchiefs, Cambricks, Lawns, Gauzes, Ec. Sattins, Modes, Sarsenets, Diapers, Drawboys, Dimities, Merseilles Quilting; Cotton Denims, Royal Ribs, Velvets, Ec. Superfine Florentine; Sattinets, Lastings, Durants, Calamancaes, Moreens, Tabbyretts, Rattinets, Shalloons, Camlets, Corduretts, Flannels . . . Leghorn and Felt Hats, Ladies Stuff shoes . . . Green and Mahogany Oilcloths, Ribbands, Tasles,

American Mercury (Hartford, Connecticut), April 19, 1810.

Tapes, Laces, Cap and Ribban wire, Silk-Twist, Thread . . ." *Hartford* (Connecticut) *Courant,* December 28, 1789.

ANAPES

The name for a type of Fustian, *q.v.*

ANNIESTES

"Cotton cloths which come from the East Indies." (M)

ARIDAS

"A kind of taffety manufactured in the E.

Indies from a shining thread; drawn from certain plants, and hence they are stiled aridas, or herbs." (M)

ARMOISIN

"A silk stuff or kind of taffety manufactured in the E. Indies, at Lyons in France, and Lucca in Italy. That of the Indies is slighter than those made in Europe." (M)

Armesin. "A kind of taffeta." (H)

ARRAS

"Hangings of tapestry." (W) The name is taken from that of the early French mill center and served from the sixteenth through the nineteenth centuries as the generic term for handsomely woven wall hangings or tapestries:

> *In cypress cheste my arras counterpoints,*
> *Costly apparel, tents and canopies,*
> *Fine linen, Turkey cushions boss'd with*
> *   pearl,*
> *Valance of Venice gold in needle work,*
> *Pewter and brass and all things that*
> *   belong*
> *To house or housekeeping.*
>
> Shakespeare, *The Taming of the Shrew,*
> II, i.

ASBESTOS

"A fossile stone which may be split into threads and filaments . . . with a wonderful property of remaining unconsumed in the fire which only whitens it. Paper as well as cloth has been made of it." (M)

BAFTAS

"Plain India muslins from 7 8ths to 9 8ths wide." (W) (Fabrics were sold in measures of quarters and eighths; see under WEIGHTS and MEASURES.)

BAIZE

Used to describe a woolen fabric with a long nap, the name was derived originally from its color, hence the mention in many early inventories of bays or bayes. However, the fabric also was dyed: "This morning my brother's man brought me a new black baize waiste-coate, faced with silk."

Samuel Pepys, *Diary,* November ‚1, 1663. By 1800, baize meant simply "a sort of rough or nappy woolen cloth." (W)

BALZARINE

A type of fabric woven with narrow stripes alternating with broad stripes up to one inch wide.

BANDANNA

"For sale by Caleb Goodwin, a handsome assortment of Fall and Winter Goods, selected from late importations in New York [including] India cottons & checks, Oriental Cotton Shawls, Loom wisk or lambs wool Tippets. Madras, Silk, Cotton, Bandanno and Flag Handk'rs . . ." *American Mercury* (Hartford, Connecticut), October 14, 1812.

New Summer Goods.
May 20th 1811.
WILLIAM WATSON,

HAS this day received from Boston an additional supply of GOODS, which were bought with Cash, and will be sold at a very small advance, at RETAIL or WHOLESALE, VIZ.

ELEGANT light green Long Shawls, twill'd and plain.

do. do. do. 6-8 and 8-4 do.

do do. do. twill'd and plain Calicoes.

Best light printed Cambrics.

Coloured twill'd cambric Muslins.

Pink and buff striped cambric Ginghams.

Twill'd and plain white Lustring.

Pink, white, green, and blue Sarsenet.

Plain and figured lace Muslin.

Plain and figured lenau do.

Lenau half Handkerchiefs.

Long Lawns and Linens.

Muslin Robes, lace seeded Muslins.

Silk Chambray Muslins.

Bandanna, flag, and check'd silk Hkfs.

A great variety of figured Vestings.

Cambric Muslins from 1s. 10d. to 7s. 6d.

Calicoes from 1s. 2d. to 3s.

Ginghams from 1s. 4d. to 3s.

Cotton Shirting from 1s. 4d. to 3s. 9d.

Men's dark mixed and white cotton Hose.

Ladies' white and slate   do   do

Dimity from 2s. to 3s ; cambric do.

Light and dark Velvet Cords.

Gilt and plated coat and vest Buttons.

White stick Wire, Tapes.

India and English Checks.

Low priced Fans. Superfine bl'k & blue Cloths.

Hartford, Main-street, fronting Morgans's Bridge—3—3m

American Mercury (Hartford, Connecticut), May 30, 1811.

BARRACAN

"A sort of stuff, not diapered, something like camblet but of a coarser grain, used to make cloaks‚ surtouts, and such other garments to keep off the rain." (M)

BASTAS

Another spelling of Baftas, *q.v.,* or *baffetas.* "A cloth made of coarse white cotton thread, which comes from the East Indies, that of Surat is the best." (M)

BATISTE

"A sheer linen." (W)

BAUDKIN

The term for a "rich and precious species of stuff" introduced as early as the thirteenth century and said to have been "composed of silk, interwoven with threads of gold in a most sumptuous manner . . . a tissue of gold." (H)

BEAVER FUR CLOTH

"This is very valuable, especially in the more Northern Countries, where it is longer and finer. This the Dutch have lately contriv'd to mix with their Wool, and Weave into a Sort of Drugget, that is not only warm, but wonderfully light and soft. They also make Gloves and Stockings of it that keep out the cold almost as well as the Fur itself . . ." William Byrd, *History of the Dividing Line* [1729] (Richmond, 1866).

BENGAL

"A slight, Indian cotton-stuff" (W) made in fine stripes and plain weaves.

BERGAMOT

"The name of a coarse tapestry, manufactured with flocks of silk, wool, cotton, hemp, ox, cow, or goat's hair and supposed to be invented by the people of Bergamo." (M)

BEZANS

"Cotton cloths which come from Bengal; some are white and others striped with several colours." (M)

BIRD'S EYE

"To church, it being Whit-Sunday; my wife very fine in a new yellow bird's-eye hood, as the fashion is now." Samuel Pepys, *Diary,* May 14, 1665.

BOCASIN(E)

"Fine buckram or cotton." (W) "A sort of linen cloth." (J)

BOLZAS

"A kind of ticking imported from the East Indies." (M)

BOMBASE, BOMBASINE

A twilled fabric of silk and worsted, or cotton and worsted, or sometimes a fine worsted, often used for mourning clothes. Sometimes spelled bombazeen or bombazine, and usually dyed black. "A slight, black stuff mixed with silk." (W)

BOMBAZET

A twilled, unglazed cotton; this spelling apparently was a variation or substitute for Bombasine, *q.v.*

BONE LACE

"A coarse kind of lace, a flaxen lace." (W) The linen thread-lace knit on bone bobbins:

> *The spinsters and knitters in the sun,*
> *and the free maids that weave their thread*
> *with bones.*

> Shakespeare, *Twelfth Night,* II, iv.

BONTEN

"A narrow woolen stuff." (W)

BOREL, BUREL

"A coarse, brown woolen cloth." (W)

BOTANO

"A kind of blue linen." (H)

BOUCLE

A looped yarn which being woven produced attractive irregularities in the surface of the cloth.

BRAULS

"A species of cloth imported from the East Indies, composed of blue and white stripes." (M)

BRIDE-LACE

The name given the strip or band or ribbon of fine lace used to bind the sprigs of rosemary or other flowers worn at weddings.

BROADCLOTH

"A very fine kind of woolen cloth." (W) "I am desired by my Acquaintance the Revd. M. Gwatkin to send for the following Articles for him. I beg the favor of you to let me have them as soon as possible & that they may be the best in kind—5 yds. best superfine black brd. Cloth; 6 yds. fine Shalloon for Lining; Basket Coat & Waist coat Buttons & other necessary Trimmings." (Order from Robert C. Nicholas, September 7, 1771, Williamsburg, Virginia.) Frances Mason, *John Norton and Sons, Merchants of London and Virginia* (Richmond, 1935).

BROCADE

The term from the French *brocher,* to stitch, for a fabric woven with raised figures or patterns; originally cloth of gold and silver from India. Sometimes spelled brocado or brocard. "A kind of fine, flowered silk." (W) Brocade weaving gradually was superseded after 1820 by Jacquard patterns. "A stuff of gold, silver, or silk raised and enriched with flowers, foliages, and other ornaments according to the fancy of the manufacturers." (M) A fabric ornamented with a design in relief made by using extra weft threads.

BROCATELLE

The fabric woven of silk and wool, or linen and wool, in imitation of brocade; used for upholstery and draperies.

BRUSSELS LACE

The linen lace made at Brussels and used especially for pillowcases.

BUCKRAM, BUCK

Originally linen or wool stiffened with glue or gum, buckram commonly was used for soldiers' or servants' clothing, and for the covers of books; later it was "any sort of coarse cloth, dyed of several colors and afterwards gummed and calendered." (M) "Any person that has occasion to have any Linnen Cloth made into Buckram, or to buy Buckram readymade, or calendering any silk . . . they may apply themselves to Samuel Hall, lately from London . . . near the New North Brick Meeting House." *Boston News-Letter,* June 25, 1722.

BUFF

The colloquialism for a soldier's coat was derived from buffalo and meant the yellow-white leather made from buffalo or wild ox hide. "In buff and bandoleer for King Charles." Sir Walter Scott. "Philip Freeman, lately from London, makes and sells Buff and Cloth Colour after the neatest Manner; also makes all sorts of Gloves by whole-sale and retale . . . in Prison Lane, near the Town House in Boston." *Boston Gazette,* June 21, 1743.

BUFFALO CLOTH

"Buffalo hair is long and shagged, and so soft it will spin into thread not unlike Mohair, which may be wove into a Sort of Camlet. Some people have stockings knit of it." William Byrd, *History of the Dividing Line* [1729] (Richmond, 1866).

BUFFIN

"A coarse cloth." (W)

BUNTING

"A thin linen cloth." (W)

BURLAP

Originally a kind of Holland, later a coarse mixture of jute and hemp.

BURNET

A fine wool dyed dark brown, hence the name.

CADDIS

"A woolen fabric; a kind of tape or stuff." (W)

CAFFA

"Painted cotton cloths manufactured in the East Indies." (M)

CALAMANCO, CALIMANCO, CALLIMANCOE

"The name of a species of woolen stuff manufactured both in England and Brabant." (M) "Run away from Capt. Langden of the City of New York, a Servant-Maid, had on when She went away, a home-spun striped waistcoat and Petticoat, blew Stockings and new Shoes, and with her a Calico Wraper, and a striped Calamanco Wrapper besides other Cloaths . . . *"The New York Weekly Journal,* January 22, 1739. "A glossy wool woven in Flanders with a satin twill, checkered in the warp so that the checks appear only on one side; used for fine clothing, curtains, bed coverlets: A kind of woolen stuff." (W) "In the great Case . . . is contained two large fine Flanders Bedticks, and two pair large superfine Blankets . . ." (Benjamin Franklin from London, February 19, 1758 to his wife at Philadelphia.) *Writings of Benjamin Franklin,* ed., A. H. Smyth (New York, 1907).

CALICO, CALLICO

Originally the name for any cotton cloth imported from Callicut, India, or any Near Eastern city, hence the name. Callico were first printed in England in 1676. "A kind of linen [weave] made of cotton some of which are painted with various flowers of different colours; and others that are never dyed, having a stripe of gold and silver quite through the piece." (M) "A kind of printed cotton cloth." (W) "Francis Gray, Callicoe Printer, from Holland; Prints all sorts of Callicoes of several Colours to hold washing, at his House in Roxbury near the Meeting-House." *Boston Gazette,* June 16, 1735.

CAMACA

"A kind of silk or rich cloth [of which] curtains were often made." (H)

CAMBRIC(K)

"A species of very fine and beautiful linen made at Cambray in the French Nether-lands." (M) "A kind of fine linen from Flanders." (W) "Send 1 doz. red and white cambrick pocket handkerchfs; 1 ps. cambrick @ 40/." (Order from Nathaniel Burwell, September 3, 1770, James City County, Virginia.) Frances Mason, *John Norton and Sons, Merchants of London and Virginia* (Richmond, 1935). "Some small rements of cambrick for ruffles." (Order from James Minzies, June 12, 1773, Williamsburg.) Ibid.

CAMLET, CAMBLET, CHAMBLETT

Originally a mixture of silk and camel's hair, hence the name. "A sort of stuff of which the warp is of hair, and the woof half hair and half silk." (M) "This morning came home my fine camlet cloak, with gold buttons, and a silk suit, which cost me much money, and I pray God to make me able to pay for it." Samuel Pepys, *Diary,* July 1, 1660. "A stuff made of wool and silk." (W) Thomas Rogers of the Plymouth Colony had been a camlet merchant in England.

CAMLETEEN, CAMBLETEEN

A fine worsted made in imitation of camlet.

CANNEQUINS

"A species of cotton-linens, imported from the East Indies." (M)

CANQUE

"A kind of cotton cloth made in China." (M)

CANVAS

"A very clear unbleached cloth of hemp or flax wove regularly in little squares. It is used for making tapestry with the needle by passing the thread of gold, silver, silk or wool through the intervals or squares. Also a very coarse cloth of unbleached hemp used principally for making sails." (M)

CAPHA

"A kind of damask cloth." (H)

CARPMEAL, CARPNEL

"A kind of coarse cloth made in the north of England," (J) "in the reign of James I; a kind of white cotton cloth." (H)

CASHMERE

The fine soft cloth woven from the wool of Kashmir goats.

CASSIMERE

"George Corning has received New Goods. Superfine West of England Broadcloths and Cassimeres . . . selected from the late arrivals at Boston . . . will be sold as cheap as at any Store in this City. Among which are Blue, Black, Brown, Light Mixed, Dark Mixed, Bottle Green, Light Green and Drab Superfine, double and single Milled Cassimers. A good assortment of Fine and Common Cassimeres. Fine Drab Spanish Cassimere." *American Mercury* (Hartford, Connecticut), January 27, 1813.

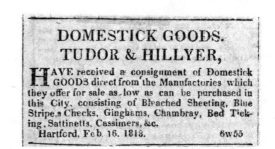

American Mercury (Hartford, Connecticut), February 16, 1818.

CHALLIS

An extremely fine, soft silk and wool fabric, printed or hand-blocked.

CHALONS

The term from Chalons-sur-Marne in France for a woolen coverlet first produced there. Shalloon is the anglicized form of *chalons.*

CHEVERIL

"Leather made of a kid's skin." (W)

CHINTS, CHINTZ

"Cloth of cotton made in India, and printed with colours." (J) "As coolness and airiness are the most desirable things from May to November, curtains are little used or to be desired in Summer . . . The coldness of the air and bright sun of winter render curtains grateful for protection from currents of air and from glare of light. For the plainest cottages, one would use chintz, which may be had for a few cents a yard." A. J. Downing, *The Architecture of Country Houses* (New York, 1850). "India cottons; fine printed calico." (W)

CLOTH

"In commerce [the word] implies all kinds of stuff woven in a loom, whether composed of wool, hemp, flax, Ec., but it is generally used to imply woolen cloth." (M) "To Sire W. Turner's and there bought my cloth, coloured, for a suit and cloak, to line with plush. I find that I must go handsomely, whatever it cost me." Samuel Pepys, *Diary,* October 22, 1664.

Costly thou thy habit as thy purse can
buy . . .
For the apparel oft proclaims the man.
Shakespeare, *Hamlet,* I, iii.

COATING

Any fabric, but especially wool, used for surtouts, overcoats, and cloaks. "James Christie has just opened and is now selling on the most reasonable terms for ready pay An Assortment of Goods suitable for the present season Among which are the following Articles, fiz.: Broadcloths, Coatings, Baizin of different colors and qualities with a variety of Hard Ware and Groceries." Norwich, Connecticut, *Packet,* November 21, 1788.

COLBERTINE

"A kind of lace for women." (W)

COPPER-PLATE-PRINTED COTTON

Pictorial representations, landscapes, flowers, and birds in stylized settings were printed on closely woven cotton cloth from engraved copper plates after about 1750: "There is also 56 yards of cotton printed curiously from Copper Plates, a new Invention, to make Bed and Window Curtains; and 7 yards Chair Bottoms, printed in the same way, very neat. These were my Fancy; but Mrs. Stevenson tells me I did wrong not to buy both of the same Colour. Also 7 yards of printed Cotton Blue Ground, to make you a Gown. I bought it by Candlelight, and liked it then, but not so well afterwards. If you do not fancy it, send it as a Present from me to sister Jenny." (Benjamin Franklin from London, February 19, 1758 to his wife at Philadelphia.) *Writings of Benjamin Franklin,* ed., A. H. Smyth (New York, 1907).

CORDUROY

From the French, *corde du roi,* signifying a corded silk fabric used by the king's tailor to sew his hunting costume; and expensive throughout the Colonial period. "I am in want of a few Articles for my own wear . . . a fashionable plain Hatt, a suit of Sky Blue Corderoy (with a new fashion Embroider'd button I mean a silver sprig on a button of the same Colour) The Coat to be faced with wt Silk but not lined through, a small Cape and a tight Cuff with buttons on them and pocket flaps. Let the Cloath be full and loose as I think myself rather lustier than when I left London." (Order from William Reynolds, York, Virginia, May 23, 1772.) *John Norton and Sons, Merchants of London and Virginia* (Richmond, 1935).

COTTON

"A soft downy substance of the plant of the same name. It is distinguished into two kinds, cotton in the wool, and spun cotton. The first is used in quilts, bed-gowns, Ec. The latter is more generally used, furnishing various cloths, muslins, callicoes, dimities and hangings; it is frequently joined with silk and flax in the composition of other stuffs." (M) "Benedict Arnold wants to buy a number of large Genteel fat Horses, Oats and Hay—And has to sell choice Cotton and Salt, by quantity or retail and other goods as usual." *Connecticut Gazette* (New Haven), January 24, 1766.

CRAPE, CREPE
"A light transparent stuff made with raw silk gummed and twisted in a mill" (M) and "used in mourning." (W) "A Thin stuff, loosely woven, of which the dress of the clergy is sometimes made." (J)

CREWEL
A kind of open embroidery stitch. "Hose of Cruel made in Mantua; Girdles, of cruell.: House of Parliament Rates, 1660, for Imports and Exports—*Statutes of the Realm* (London, 1819).

DAMASK
"Silk, woolen, Ec. woven into flowers." (W)

DARNEX, DARNIX, DORNICK, DORNEP, DARNAK
These were all contemporary variations of the name for a coarse sort of damask used for curtains; made of worsted, silk, wool, or thread. The name was derived from that of the town of Deornick in Flanders where this "species of linen cloth used in Scotland for the table" (J) was first produced.

DIAPER
"A sort of fine, flowered linen, a napkin." (W)

DIMITY
"White Dimity, plain or corded, is peculiarly applicable for [bed] furniture, which, with a fringe with a gimp head, produces an effect of elegance and neatness truly agreeable." A Hepplewhite, *The Cabinet-Maker and Upholsterer's Guide* (London, 1794).

DOWLAS
"Coarse linen imported from Brittany and chiefly worn by the lower classes." (H)

DRUGGET
"A slight kind of woollen stuff." (W) "A closely woven fabric of wool, wool mixed with silk, or wool mixed with linen, in use from the sixteenth through the eighteenth century: Please remember fashionable trimming to [use with] the duroys and druggetss for the people here will have everything the newst and best of their kind." (Peter Baynton to Thomas Randall, 15 May, 1725.) *Baynton Letterbook,* Historical Society of Pennsylvania. "A slight kind of woolen stuff." (J)

DUCAPE
"A kind of silk worn by women." (W) "Naphtaly Hart Meyers . . . in Hanover Square, continues to sell . . . Mechlin and Brussels Lace, Dresden Work, 12 yd., 16 yd. and 18 yd. Calicoes, English Chints, Ducape, white Satten, pink Persia, Silk Romals, spotted Bandanoes, Muslins, Clear ditto, Lawn Handkerchiefs, 7–8, 3–4 linnen, Recosin dito, Scotch Ozenbrigs, Ravens Duck, Broad Cloths, and Shalloons, Barragons, corded Druggets, Sagathies, brown Fustrans and Dimettes, Bombazeens, Women's crape Hatbands, ditto Love for Hoods . . ." *The New York Gazette and the Weekly Post-Boy,* May 5, 1755.

DUCK
"A species of fine canvas." (W) "American Duck equal to Russia, from Maynards Manufactory, Pittsfield, Mass. is for sale by Thomas K. Brace." *American Mercury* (Hartford, Connecticut), July 28, 1816.

DUNGAREE, DUNGRI
A coarsely woven fabric from Hindustan used for sails, work cloths.

DURANT
"A glazed woollen stuff." (W)

DUROY
A fine-wale corduroy.

EMERTIS
"Plain India muslins, thin and of inferior quality, about 7 8ths in width." (W)

FALDING
"A kind of coarse cloth." (J)

FELT

"A kind of stuff made by fulling wool, or wool and fur." (W)

FLANNEL

A kind of soft woolen cloth. "I am much more tender than I used to be, and sleep in a short Callico Bedgown with close sleeves, and Flannel Close-footed Trousers, for without them I get no warmth at all all Night. So it seems I grow older apace." (Benjamin Franklin from London, February 19, 1758, to his wife at Philadelphia.) *Writings of Benjamin Franklin,* ed., A. H. Smyth (New York, 1907). "A cotton cloth." (W)

FLORENTINE

"A species of silk cloth" (W) woven at Florence, Italy. "The European silk I understand is all yellow, and most of the India silk. What comes from China is white. The lustre of it, being the very finest [is from] Italy." (Benjamin Franklin from London, July 18, 1771, to Cadwallader Evans, Philadelphia.) *Writings of Benjamin Franklin,* ed., A. H. Smyth (New York, 1907). "A species of silk cloth." (W)

FRIEZE

"A coarse, warm cloth made first perhaps in Friesland." (J)

FUSTIAN

A fabric of mixed cotton and flax used for all types of clothing and blankets. "On the 11th of Nov. last, was stolen out of the yard of Mr. Joseph Coit, Joiner in Boston, living in Cross Street, a Woman's Fustian Petticoat, with a large work'd Embroider'd Border, being Deer, Sheep, Houses, Forrest, Ec., so worked. Whoever has taken the said Petticoat, and will return it to the owner thereof, or to the Printer, shall have 40s old Tenor Reward and no Questions ask'd." *Boston Gazette,* December 19, 1749. Governor William Bradford (1589–1657) of the Plymouth Colony had been a fustian maker in Yorkshire and a silk worker in Amsterdam.

GABARDINE

"A coarse frock, any mean dress." (J)

GALLOON

"A kind of lace, a kind of riband or binding" (W) "made of gold or silver, or of silk alone." (J)

GAUZE

"A very thin silk or linen." (W)

GHENT, GHENTING

The name for a type of Holland or linen, made at Ghent. "I am sending the . . . two fine Damask Tablecloths and Napkins, and 43 Ells of Ghentish Sheeting Holland [that] you ordered." (Benjamin Franklin from London, February 19, 1758, to his wife at Philadelphia.) *Writings of Benjamin Franklin,* ed., A. H. Smyth (New York, 1907).

GIMP

A word derived from gim, the Old English term for neat or spruce, "a silk twist or lace; edging." (W)

GINGHAM

"A cloth of cotton and linen, striped and glazed." (W)

GROGRAIN, GROGRAM

"A thick stuff made of silk and hair." (W)

GURRAHS

"India muslins, plain and coarse, from a yard to 9 8ths in width." (W)

Beerboom Gurrahs: "White cotton sheeting from Calcutta." (W)

HAGABAG, HUCKABACK

"A linen with raised figures on it." (W) "Be pleased to send me a piece of irish linen 2/6 per yard, two large damask table cloths, and four small huckaback." (Order from G. Wythe, Williamsburg, Virginia, May 9, 1768.) Frances Mason, *John Norton and Sons, Merchants of London and Virginia* (Richmond, 1935). "1 ps. Huckabeck Towelling." (Order from Martha Jacquelin, August 14, 1769, York, Virginia.) Ibid.

HANDKERCHIEF

"A piece of linen or silk." (W) " . . .
Bersalona Hankerchiefs & best of silk stocking a few pieces of good cambricks & the Remainder in What you Judge best Do not forget some good Clarett." (Thomas Riche to John Kidd, 3 October, 1754.) *Kidd Letterbook,* Historical Society of Pennsylvania.

HOLLAND

"A kind of fine strong linen." (W)

HUMHUM

"A plain coarse India cotton cloth." (W)

HUNTER

"A double milled forest cloth." (W)

JACONET

"A kind of coarse muslin." (W)

JEAN(S), JANES

A coarse cotton weave. "Run away . . . had on a dark brown cloth coat, with pinchbeck buttons, Jacket of a lighter color with wooden buttons . . . a white shirt, white Jane Breeches . . . and is very subject to drink. Thirty shillings Reward." *The New York Journal or The General Advertiser,* June 25, 1772.

JERSEY

"A combed wool; woolen yard." (W)

KENDAL-GREEN

"A kind of forester's green cloth, so-called from Kendall in Westmoreland, which was famous for its manufacture." (H)

KERSEY

"A coarse woolen stuff woven in ribs." (W)

In russet yeas and honest kersey noes.

Shakespeare, *Love's Labour Lost,* V, ii.
"The Subscriber continues to purchase plain Blue Cloth, white Woolen Kersey, Cotton do., brown Tow-Cloth, brown and white Linen thread, short Woolen Stockings and home-made woolen Flannels. Elisha Tracy, U. S. Army Deputy Commissary, Norwich." *American Mercury* (Hartford, Connecticut), January 6, 1812.

LAWN

"A fine linen." (W) "Amos Bull has just received for sale, an additional supply of Goods, among which are Nankeens, Leno, Thread Net, Muslin and Lawn Aprons and Handkerchiefs, Muslins and Muslinets, Black Calamancoe and Lustrings, Silk and Thread Stockings, Gloves, Ribbands, Fans . . ." *Hartford* (Connecticut) *Courant,* May 31, 1790.

LEATHER

The House of Parliament Rates, 1660, for Imports and Exports—*Statutes of the Realm* (London, 1819) included: "Bazill; Spanish or Cordivant; Spruce or Dansk Leather, Turkey & East India Cordivant."

LINE, LIND, LINEN, LINING, LINNEN, LINNING

A variety of spellings, all signifying linen; a cloth of hemp or flax. "I must get the favour of you to send in the spring the few articles mentioned and to take notice that the table cloths are to be Irish Linnen and I should be glad you'd be particularly careful to do everything that is possible that is requisite to shew they are of that Manufacture, as no other sort can be received: twelve fine table cloths, 10 quarters wide, Irish linnen; twelve Coarse ditto 10 quarters square, Irish linnen." (Order from Peyton Randolph, September 23, 1770, Williamsburg, Virginia.) Frances Mason, *John Norton and Sons, Merchants of London and Virginia.* (Richmond, 1935).

"After the ladies were gone from the table, we talked of the Highlanders not having sheets; and this led us to consider the advantage of linen. *Johnson:* 'All animal substances are less cleanly than vegetable. Wool, of which flannel is made, is animal substance; flannel therefore is not so cleanly as linen. I have often thought that if I kept a seraglio the ladies should all wear linen gowns or cotton. I mean stuffs made of vegetable substances, I would have no silk; you cannot tell when it is clean.

Linen detects its own dirtiness.'" James Boswell, *Journal of a Tour* [1773] *to the Hebrides* (London, 1785).

Flax: "The plant from which linen is made." (W)

LINSEY-WOOLSEY

The name for the fabric "made of linen and wool." (W)

LOCKRAM

"A sort of very coarse linen." (W) "A kind of cheap linen, worn chiefly by the lower classes. There was a fine sort of which shirt-bands, etc. were made." (H)

LUKES

"A kind of velvet." (H)

LUSTRING, LUTESTRING

A glossy silk. "A kind of silk cloth." (W) "Enclosed is a list of things for Mrs. Scott . . . 10 yds pink & white shot lustring, 10 yds each white ditto & 10 ditto Garnet, a blooming Colour, apron ruffles." (Order from James Munzies, merchant, Williamsburg, Virginia, June 12, 1773.) Frances Mason, *John Norton and Sons, Merchants of London and Virginia* (Richmond, 1935).

MAMODIS

"Coarse plain India muslins from 7 to 9 8ths in width." (W)

MANTUA

"A kind of silk [for women's gowns]." (W) Mantua was so synonymous with women's clothing that another name for a dressmaker or seamstress was mantua-maker: "Mary Morcomb, Mantua-Maker, from London . . . makes all sorts of negligees, Brunswick dresses, gowns, and every other sort of lady's apparel . . ." *The New-York Gazette and The Weekly Mercury,* May 7, 1770.

MARIGONGIS

"A very low-priced India muslin 3 4ths in width." (W)

MOHAIR

"A thread or stuff made of goat's hair." (W) "The blue Mohair Stuff is for the Curtains of the Blue Chamber. The Fashion [here] is to make one Curtain only for each Window. Hooks are sent to fix the Rails by at top, so that they might be taken down on Occasion. I almost wish I had left Directions not to paint the House till my Return." (Benjamin Franklin from London, February 14, 1765, to his wife at Philadelphia.) *Writings of Benjamin Franklin,* ed., A. H. Smyth (New York, 1907).

MOIRE

"I send you also . . . a piece of Crimson Morir for Curtains with Tassels, Line and Binding." (Benjamin Franklin, from London to his wife in Philadelphia, April 6, 1766.) *Writings of Benjamin Franklin,* ed., A. H. Smyth (New York, 1907).

MOREEN

"For a better kind of curtain, moreens of single colors, browns, drabs, crimsons, or blues, may be used, which though more expensive are more durable than cotton." A. J. Downing, *The Architecture of Country Houses* (New York, 1850).

MUSLIN

"A fine kind of cloth made of cotton." (W) "Consumption came in with silk stockings and muslin dresses; and can only be banished by woollen cloathing. A cold is the forerunner of cough, and these of consumption." *The Domestic Encyclopedia* (Philadelphia, 1821).

MUSLINET

"A coarse cotton cloth." (W)

NANKEEN

"The cloth made of a kind of yellow cotton, woven at Nankin, China; later manufactured at Manchester, England, and other mills and dyed yellow to resemble the Chinese prototype: A species of cotton cloth from China." (W) "May 31, 1790. Brig. William T. Henry, from Canton. Tea, coffee, silks, spices and nankeens for Gray & Orne, Benj. Hodges, George Dodge, Jno. Appleton, Samuel Hewes, Jr., Simon Elliott,

Robt. Wyer, Mark Haskell 9,783." Salem, Massachusetts' Customs House Records of goods imported.

ORGANZINE

A kind of "silk manufactured in Italy . . . the silk is wound from the skein upon bobbins; it is then sorted; it is twisted on a mill in the single thread; two threads thus spun are doubled, or drawn together through the fingers of a woman, who at the same time cleans them; it is then again drawn by a mill, that is, the two threads are twisted together and at the same time wound in skeins upon a reel. Formerly nothing but Italian silk was thrown into Organzine, but now the finer sorts of silk from the East Indies may be converted into it." *The Domestic Encyclopedia* (Philadelphia, 1821).

ORRIS

"Gold and silver lace." (W)

OSNABRUCK, OSSEMBRIKE, OSSENBRUDGE, OZNABRIG, OZNABURG

A variety of spellings for what today is known as oznaburg; a coarse linen used for toweling, upholstery, and servants' and children's clothing; so called for Osnabrück, Germany, where the cloth first was manufactured.

PENISTON(E)

A coarse woolen manufactured in Yorkshire. "I desire be Sent . . . good Lockerum, dowles, Canvice, Carsey, Searge and peniston . . ." (Order from Newport, Rhode Island, to London, December 7, 1666.) *The Letter Book of Peleg Sanford* (Providence, 1928). "Pomistones, Ordinary Pennistons, or Forrest Whites; single sorting Pennistons" were listed in the House of Parliament Rates, 1660, for Imports and Exports—*Statutes of the Realm* (London, 1819).

PLUSH

"Among manufacturers [is] a kind of stuff, having a sort of velvet knap on one side, composed regularly of a woof of a single woolen thread and a double warp, the one wool, and the other goat's or camel's hair. There are also other kinds of plush, some composed wholly of hair, others of worsted, and others of silk." *The Domestic Encyclopedia* (Philadelphia, 1821).

PRUCE

"A kind of lether; Prussian lether." (W)

PULLICAT(E)

"A sort of silk handkerchief," (W) from Calcutta.

PURL

"A sort of lace or border." (W)

RATTEEN

"A thick woollen stuff, twilled." (W)

RATTINET

"A twisted stuff thinner than ratteen." (W) "George Corning, Merchant tailor . . . Military Goods. Superfine and fine Scarlet Broadcloths; Superfine Scarlet, White and Buff Cassimeres; Red and White Rattinet; Red Silks and Twists. Military Buttons. Military and Dress Cloths made as usual in the Newest Style." *American Mercury* (Hartford, Connecticut), November 16, 1812.

RAVENSDUCK

"A species of thin duck." (W)

ROMAL

"A species of silk handkerchief." (W)

SACKCLOTH

"The cloth of which sacks are made; coarse cloth sometimes worn in mortification; [it is] stuff made of goat's hair, of a dark colour, worn by soldiers and mariners." (J)

SAGRI

Another name for Shagreen, *q.v.*

SAILCLOTH

A contemporary synonym for any canvas or duck so used. "We have here waistcoats for swimming, which are made of double sail-cloth, with small pieces of cork quilted in between them." (Benjamin Franklin, letter to Barbere Duborg [month unknown], 1773.) *The Writings of Benjamin Franklin,* ed., A. H. Smyth (New York, 1907). "Yarn for sailcloth is made of dressed hemp, and spun in the same manner that rope-yarn is spun. The spinners of this may make a good living; women are chiefly employed in it." *The Book of Trades* (London, 1805).

SAMITE
"A very rich silk, sometimes interwoven with gold or silver thread." (H)

SAMMARON CLOTH
"A cloth between flaxen and hempen, finer than one and coarser than the other." (H)

SANNAHS
"India muslins of various qualities." (W)

SARSENET, SARSNET
"A thin slight kind of silk." (H)

SATIN
"A kind of very soft, close and shining silk." (W) "In State-rooms, where a high degree of elegance and grandeur are wanted, bed (furnishings) are frequently made of silk or satin, figured or plain . . ." A. Hepplewhite, *The Cabinet-Maker and Upholsterer's Guide* (London, 1794).

SATINET, SATINETTE(E)
"A thin satin." (W) "One Cent Reward —Runaway from the service of the subscriber on the 7th ult. an indented apprentice to the potting business [who] had on when he went away a blue surtout coat, a blue undercoat, blue mixt satinett pantaloons, and is supposed to have had some other clothes with him . . . Abraham Day." *Norwalk* (Connecticut) *Gazette,* March 10, 1824.

SAX
"A delicate serge or woollen cloth." (W)

SAY
". . . please to send . . . green say, yard wide Cottens, duffles and Stript blan [kets] . . ." (Order from Newport, Rhode Island, January 10, 1667.) *The Letter Book of Peleg Sanford* (Providence, 1928). "Double Sayes or Flaunders Serges; Double Say' Mild Sayes; Honncot Say" were listed in the House of Parliament Rates, 1660, for Imports and Exports—*Statutes of the Realm* (London, 1819). Master Samuel Fuller (c. 1658–63) the Pilgrims' "Physition & Chururgeon" originally was a say maker in Sandwich, England.

SERGE
"A thin woolen cloth or stuff." (W)

SHAG
A worsted or silk fabric with a soft, velvet-like nap. "He brought me also my new gown of purple shagg; also, as a gift from my brother, a velvet hat, very fine to ride in, and the fashion, which pleases me." Samuel Pepys, *Diary,* November 1, 1663.

SHAGREEN
"A kind of very rough fish skin" (W) used as a thin covering in lieu of leather, for binding books, decorating small boxes or trunks, etc. Often dyed green, red, yellow.

SHALLOON
"A slight woolen stuff used for linings." (W)

SHAMMYLETHER
"The skin of a chamois [a wild goat], tanned." (W)

SHEEPSKIN
"The skins of sheep, after tanning and currying, are manufactured into a thin, and coarse, but useful kind of leather, which is much in request by saddlers, bookbinders, and others. These skins, are [also] converted into parchment, which is used for writing deeds on. The leather is particularly estimable for aprons, and is purchased by mechanicks for this purpose." *The Domestic Encyclopedia* (Philadelphia, 1821).

SILESIA

"A species of thin, coarse linen," (W) from Silesia, and from which we retain the adjective sleazy.

SILK

"The produce of worms, the soft smooth stuff made of it." (W)   "Then if you please to Send in Bone Lace to the Value of Five Pounds & in Taffety & other Silk to the value of 10 [pounds] as allsoe Some good Silke Buttons for Brest and Coate with Some Stitching & Soeing Silke." (Order from Newport, Rhode Island, to London, January 10, 1667.) *The Letter Book of Peleg Sanford* (Providence, 1928). "Bridges silke, Ferret or Floret silke, Fillozell or Paris silke; Granado; Naples Silke, black & colours; Orgazine; Pole & Spanish; Raw China; Raw Silke, short and long; Raw Morea; Satin Silke; Sleave Silke; Silke Nubbs or Husks; Throwne Silke" were listed in the House of Parliament Rates, 1660, for Imports and Exports—*Statutes of the Realm* (London, 1819).

SINDON

"Fine linen, a wrapper of fine linen." (W)

SPRUCELEATHER

A corruption of Prussian leather.

STUFF

"Anything, a texture." (W)   "Put on the stuff suit that I [had] made the last year, which is now repaired, and so did go to the office in it." Samuel Pepys, *Diary,* May 11, 1669. "Cloth or texture of any kind," but usually, "textures of wool thinner and slighter than cloth." (J)

SWANSDOWN

"A fine soft thick woolen cloth." (W)

SWANSKIN

"A fine and very soft kind of flannel." (W) "A parcel of Swanskin Blankets, 9–4, and 2–4 wide, of the first Quality, to be sold at P. M. Danett's Store, near the Fly-Market. Also yellow and red Flannels, embossed Serges; Men's and Women's worsted Hose, with a few pieces of superfine Cloths." *The New York Journal or The General Advertiser,* December 20, 1770.

TABBY

Originally a term for silk taffeta woven at Bagdad in a striped pattern; later, any watered silk. "Up betimes. Called by my tailor, and there first put on a summer suit this year; but it was not my fine one of flowered tabby vest, and coloured camelott tunique, because it was too fine with the gold lace at the bands that I was afraid to be seen in it." Samuel Pepys, *Diary,* May 11, 1669. "A kind of waved silk." (W)

TAFFETA, TAFFETY

"A sort of thin silk." (W)   "June 10, 1646. The trained band [militia] accompanied the body to the grave and the captain gave every one of them an eln of black taffeta for a mourning robe." John Winthrop, *Journal, History of New England* (Boston, 1825).

TAMMY

"A thin kind of woolen stuff." (W)

THREEPILE

"A very strong kind of velvet." (W)   "An old name for good velvet." (J)

THRUM

The name given "any coarse yarn." (J)

TICKEN, TICKING

"A strong cloth for bedcases." (W)   "Domestick Goods. Tudor & Hillyer have received a consignment of Domestick Goods direct from the Manufactories which they offer for sale as low as can be purchased in this city, consisting of Bleached Sheeting, Blue Stripes, Checks, Ginghams, Chambray, Bed Ticking, Sattinetts, Cassimers, Ec." *American Mercury* (Hartford, Connecticut), February 16, 1818.

TIFFANY

"A very thin kind of silk." (W)

Eighteenth-century toile in blue and white.

Red-and-white toile. (Courtesy, Antiquarian and Landmarks Society, Inc.)

TINSEL

"Lace resembling a false luster." (W)

TISSUE

"A cloth or silk wrought with gold or silver." (W) "There is a better Gown for you, of flower'd Tissue, 16 yards, of Mrs. Stevenson's Fancy, cost 9 Guineas; and I think it a great Beauty. There was no more of the Sort, or you should have had enough for a Negligee or Suit." (Benjamin Franklin from London, February 19, 1758, to his wife at Philadelphia.) *Writings of Benjamin Franklin,* ed., A. H. Smyth (New York, 1907).

TOILE

Monochromatic, usually floral designs, printed on unglazed cream-colored chintz, first imported by Portuguese traders from India in the seventeenth century, but the best were made by Oberkampf at Jouy, France, c. 1760.

TOW

Uncleansed or unbleached flax or linen. "Run away . . . a lusty lad . . . had on when he went away a Cinnamon colour'd plain course Kersey Coat, with large flat metal Buttons, a pair of Tow Trowsers, thick Shoes, an old Felt Hat." *The New-York Weekly Journal,* December 31, 1733.

VELVET, VELURE

"A silk with a thick pile upon it." (W) "[my spending] hath chiefly arisen from my layings-out in clothes for myself and wife; viz., for her about 12 £ and for myself 55 £, or thereabouts; having myself a velvet cloak, two new cloth shirts, black, plain both; a new shag goun, trimmed with gold buttons and twist, a new hat and silk tops for my legs, and many other things." Samuel Pepys, *Diary,* October 31, 1663.

VELVETEEN

"Cloth made of cotton and linen." (W)

VESSES

"A kind of worsted." (H)

WARD

"A sort of coarse cloth." (H)

WASHER

"A sort of Kersey cloth." (H)

WHEELSPUN

A general term for "strong coarse yarn" (H) from the spinning wheel.

WHITLETHER

"A lether dressed with alum." (W)

WOOL

"The fleece of a sheep woven into cloth." (J)

Blue-and-white homespun wool curtains. (Courtesy, Antiquarian and Landmarks Society, Inc.)

Woollen: "Cloth made of wool." (J) "August 6, 1642. Mr. Welde, Mr. Peter, and Mr. Hibbins who were sent the last year into England, had procured £500 which they sent over in linen, woolen, and other useful commodities for the country." John Winthrop, *Journal, History of New England* (Boston, 1852). Robert Cushman (1578–1625) of Plymouth Colony originally was a wool comber in Canterbury, England.

WORSTED
"A woolen yarn; yarn spun from combed wool." (W)

YARN
"Spun wool or flax, coarse woolen thred." (W)

WITHDRAWAL